Scheme
and
The Art of Programming

George Springer
Daniel P. Friedman

Foreword by Guy L. Steele Jr.

Scheme
and
The Art of Programming

The MIT Press
Cambridge, Massachusetts London, England

McGraw-Hill Book Company
New York St. Louis San Francisco Montreal Toronto

Third printing, 1991

This book was printed and bound in the United States of America

Library of Congress Cataloging-in-Publication Data
Springer, George, 1924–
    Scheme and the art of programming / George Springer, Daniel P.
Friedman.
      p. cm. — (The MIT electrical engineering and computer
science series)
   Includes bibliographical references.
   ISBN 0-262-19288-8 (MIT Press)   ISBN 0-07-060522-X (McGraw-Hill)
1. Electronic digital computers—Programming. 2. Object-oriented
programming. I. Friedman, Daniel P. II. Title. III. Series.
QA76.6.S686   1990
005.1—dc20   89-12949
                                                     CIP

To our families and our students.

Contents

Chapter 3 Data Abstraction and Numbers *73*

3.1 Overview *73*

3.2 Operations on Numbers *73*

3.3 Exact Arithmetic and Data Abstraction *84*

Chapter 4 Data Driven Recursion *95*

4.1 Overview *95*

4.2 Flat Recursion *95*

4.3 Deep Recursion *101*

4.4 Tree Representation of Lists *108*

4.5 Numerical Recursion and Iteration *115*

4.6 Analyzing the Fibonacci Algorithm *120*

Chapter 5 Locally Defined Procedures *129*

5.1 Overview *129*

5.2 Let and Letrec *129*

skip 5.3 Symbolic Manipulation of Polynomials *142*

5.4 Binary Numbers *155*

Chapter 6 Interactive Programming *163*

6.1 Overview *163*

6.2 Strings *163*

6.3 Implicit begin *166*

6.4 Input and Output *168*

6.5 Two Famous Problems *178*

Part 2 Procedures as Values *193*

Chapter 7 Abstracting Procedures *195*

7.1 Overview *195*

7.2 Procedures as Arguments and Values *195*

Part 4   Extending the Language   *447*

Part 5   Control   *513*

Foreword

I'm not going to spend much space talking about how great this book is, or how much I enjoyed reading the manuscript. Dan and George are good friends of mine, and they asked me to talk about Scheme. The book is about Scheme and about important ideas in programming, and they wanted a foreword to match. So I'm going to tell you what I think about Scheme.

*   *   *   *   *

Small is beautiful.
Small is powerful.
Small is easy to understand.
I like the Scheme programming language because it is small. It packs a large number of ideas into a small number of features.
How small is it?
It is the business of programming language standards committees to set on paper careful, accurate descriptions of programming languages. It is a difficult process; a standard must be both complete and concise. While not all committees achieve the same level of detail or brevity, nevertheless I think we may usefully compare the approximate number of pages in the defining standard or draft standard for several programming languages:

Common Lisp	1000 or more
COBOL	810
ATLAS	790
Fortran 77	430
PL/I	420
BASIC	360
ADA	340
Fortran 8x	300
C	220
Pascal	120
DIBOL	~90
Scheme	~50

Curious, is it not, that the spectrum should be bracketed—or perhaps I should say parenthesized—by two dialects of Lisp?

Far be it from me to suggest that size of a language description should be the primary measure of a language's merit, whether one thinks that larger or smaller is better. The uncertainty of this measure aside—thanks purely to typesetting issues the figures shown above may be off by a factor of two from a fair comparison—there is more to a language than the size of its library or the number of syntactic forms. One must inquire what the features accomplish for the user, how completely or how redundantly they cover the application space, and how smoothly they interact.

Carpentry is one of my hobbies. I make wooden toys—doll houses and trucks and blocks and jigsaw puzzles—for my children, and I rebuild the back stairs when necessary. My shop is not particularly complete, but it contains five hammers, six saws, thirty screwdrivers (one of them electric, with forty interchangeable tips), and hundreds of drill bits. Each has a specific purpose, and for precision work most cannot be replaced by any combination of the others. (On the other hand, I have to admit that if I break a bit I can usually come near enough in a pinch with the next closest size.) In some cases the business ends of several tools are the same, but they have different handles. I have a set of screwdrivers with wooden handles that I favor for long tasks, because they are less likely to cause blisters; another set with more deeply grooved plastic handles affords a tighter grip for greater torque.

Let me tell you, it is a joy to stand in the middle of a well-equipped shop and, when a particular task comes to hand, to reach out to the shelf or pegboard and grab precisely the tool needed for the job. That is what Common Lisp, or COBOL, or Fortran is like. But it takes years of experience to appreciate the fine distinctions.

I also carry a Swiss army knife, the Victorinox "Craftsman" model. It is a carpenter's shop in miniature. It has only one or two of each thing: two knives (large and small), two flat screwdrivers (large and small) and one Phillips screwdriver, a file, a saw, an excellent pair of scissors, a ruler (3 in/7.5 cm), an awl, bottle opener, can opener, tweezers, and of course the traditional plastic toothpick. It weighs five ounces (142 gm).

Now, I wouldn't want to rebuild my back stairs using only a Swiss army knife. But let me tell you, it is a joy to wander about in my life feeling virtually unburdened and yet, when some minor repair task comes to hand, to reach into my pocket and have such a variety of tools at my disposal. (The saw is only three inches long, but extremely sharp. I have used it to modify office furniture to accommodate Ethernet cables.) And my pocket tool set is perfectly adequate for illustrating the essence of saw-ness or screwdriver-ness to the interested novice, such as my six-year-old.

The original Scheme, which Gerald Jay Sussman and I defined—or rather, it seemed to me, *discovered*—in 1975, was a Swiss army knife. Hewing close to the spirit of Alonzo Church's lambda calculus, it had just one of anything if it had one at all.

The most important concept in all of computer science is abstraction. Computer science deals with information and with complexity. We make complexity manageable by judiciously reducing it when and where possible.

I regret that I cannot recall who remarked that computation is the art of carefully throwing away information: given an overwhelming collection of data, you reduce it to a useable result by discarding most of its content. (However, I clearly recall my father telling me that life is the art of carefully throwing away opportunities, an interesting coincidental parallel.)

Abstraction consists in treating something complex as if it were simpler, throwing away detail. In the extreme case, one treats the complex quantity as atomic, unanalyzed, primitive. The lambda calculus carries this to a pure, unadulterated extreme. It provides exactly three operations, plus a principle of startling generality. The operations are:

- Abstraction: give something a *name*.
- Reference: mention something by name.
- Synthesis: combine two things to make a complex.

Naming is perhaps the most powerful abstracting notion we have, in any language, for it allows any complex to be reduced for linguistic purposes to a primitive atom.

The inverse of abstraction is synthesis: the building up of complexity from lesser pieces. Industrial-strength programming languages provide dozens or hundreds of synthesizing features, such as arithmetic operations and control structures, that construct entities from varying numbers and kinds of others. Part of the ingenuity of the lambda calculus is to provide a single means of synthesis, one that combines the smallest useful number of pieces: two.

What are the things that may be combined? Again, programming languages that are truly macho (or macha, if you prefer) provide many choices: numbers of various kinds, characters, strings, arrays, functions, records, pointers. You can spend a semester or two just studying data structures. But in the lambda calculus there is only one kind of thing that may be combined. Here lies the rest of the ingenuity, the startling generalizing principle: the objects to be combined are instances of the abstraction mechanism itself! Abstraction is all there is to talk about: it is both the object and the means of discussion. Synthesis in the lambda calculus consists solely of taking a possibly already compound abstraction mechanism and subjecting it to abstraction, giving it a name so that it may be discussed later. That's it. But because the named thing can then be mentioned more than once, the lambda calculus is as powerful as any other means of computation.

For everyday purposes the lambda calculus is a bit spare. One can write the Bible, or all the works of Shakespeare, Tolstoy, Hemingway, or Ann Landers using only a few dozen letters and punctuation marks, but only a few of us—regarded as rather queer ducks by the rest of society—wish to sit around all day discussing letter forms, spelling, and rules of punctuation. More to the point, these great works are not best understood at the level of spelling and punctuation. We form words, we publish dictionaries. From words we establish cultures of shared stock phrases, clichés, proverbs, and fairy tales— complex concepts that we can then treat as primitive for the purposes of everyday discourse.

The original Scheme consisted of little more than the lambda calculus, a single means of producing side effects, some redundant control structures for convenience, and all the data structures and operations of MacLisp that one cared to use, such as numbers and lists, though we regarded these as secondary.

Scheme has grown a bit in the last fourteen years, but in a very conservative and judicious manner. I might add that I have had very little to do with the process. I have applied most of my efforts to Common Lisp, though cheering also for the good people who have been remolding Scheme, so I am in little danger of straining my shoulder when praising the results of their efforts.

Scheme today is more than a Swiss army knife, but rather less than a full workshop with hundreds or thousands of tools. I would call it a toolbox, a large one, filled with a careful selection of tools that will cover most jobs well, and a few tools whose primary purpose is to make it easy to make more tools. It's heavy-duty, but portable. It is easily comprehended, but every tool in it is "real," not a three-inch miniature.

Scheme is perfect for the classroom. It is small enough that the student can grasp it all within a semester, but large enough that it addresses the most important topics in programming language design. An important exception is static type checking. Scheme requires no type declarations, relying instead on run-time type discrimination. In this, Scheme certainly points up an area on which there is little agreement and in which it may be usefully contrasted with C, Fortran, or Pascal. Nearly everyone agrees that "+" should stand for addition. But type checking—hoo, boy!

Scheme focuses particular attention on the concepts of abstraction and generality to an extreme unmatched by any other programming language on my list. All objects in the language may be named, by a single uniform naming mechanism. All objects are first class.

- In Common Lisp, why are there many namespaces (variables, functions, go tags, block names, catch tags, ...)?
- In Pascal, why can't you return a procedure as the value of another procedure?
- In Fortran 77, why can't a procedure return an array?
- In C, why can't a procedure definition occur within another procedure?

Besides being useful in its own right, Scheme provides a simple, sound, and complete design with which to compare other languages and thus shed light on these questions.

Guy L. Steele Jr.
Cambridge, Massachusetts
July 1989

Preface

Programming should be from the beginning a creative and literate endeavor. Our goal is to expose the reader to the exhilaration of reading and creating beautiful programs. These programs should be concise in their expression, general in their application, and easily understood. These goals are achieved through creative use of abstraction techniques that capture recurrent patterns of computation and allow them to be simply used.

We believe the programming language Scheme is superior for use in an introductory programming course because it is both *simple* and *powerful*. It is simple enough that program design can be learned with a minimum of distraction by syntactic rules that govern the form programs must take. In a typical introductory course the complex syntax of programming languages such as C or Pascal must be mastered at the same time that elementary program design techniques are being learned. Invariably syntactic concerns take precedence over design issues, for nothing works if there are syntactic errors in a program. As a result, students often get the impression that programming, and computer science in general, is primarily concerned with memorizing details and unimaginatively adhering to intricate rules. Subsequent exposure to assembly language programming reinforces this view. Hopefully at a later time, typically in a software engineering or algorithm design course, programming will be experienced as a creative activity that rewards the elegant use of abstraction techniques and a good sense of style. But an unfortunate first impression of programming may persist, or it may even discourage further study of computer science altogether.

Using Scheme, we are able to focus primarily on issues of program design. This makes programming fun, and gives a more accurate impression of where the joys and challenges of programming lie. We also believe early attention to design issues helps to develop a program design aesthetic. This in turn provides a foundation for superior work and more creative fulfillment through the student's career as a programmer. There should be plenty of time in subsequent courses to learn the syntactic details of other languages, at which time these details will be easier to master.

Scheme's simplicity does not come at the expense of expressive power. Indeed, Scheme may be used to express a broader range of programming styles than its more complex brethren. The most popular styles are imperative, functional, and object-oriented. Scheme is flexible enough to support programming in all of these styles. Traditional programming languages support the imperative style, which makes frequent use of assignment statements to change the state of the computation.

In the last decade the functional style has gained prominence. It is characterized by the absence of assignment statements, and is closer in spirit to mathematics. In many cases the functional style yields more elegant and comprehensible programs. We feel it is important for students to learn basic functional programming techniques, such as recursion and functional composition, so that the benefits of this style may be enjoyed when solving problems for which it is well suited. Traditional programming languages impose restrictions that seriously restrict the use of functional programming techniques. Most functional programming languages, on the other hand, do not support assignment. This prohibits the use of the imperative programming style when it is most appropriate. Because Scheme supports both functional and imperative programming styles, we are able to teach both along with an understanding of when each is appropriate.

A recent advance in programming languages has been appreciation for the object-oriented style of programming. This style is particularly suitable for simulating objects in the "real world" and for structuring large systems in ways that allow recurrent patterns of computation to be shared by similar objects. Using Scheme, we are able to illustrate the principles of object-oriented programming in terms of more basic functional and imperative mechanisms.

This book is composed of five parts. The first two are concerned with functional programming. In the first part, both recursive and iterative programming techniques are developed. The second part deals with procedures whose values are procedures—so called *higher-order* procedures. The third part is about imperative programming. In the last two chapters of the third part, we take advantage of assignment and higher order procedures to develop an approach to object-oriented programming. In the fourth part, we show how we can extend the syntax of Scheme by adding new forms of expression. We use this ability to support unbounded objects, called streams. In the fifth part, we demonstrate a unique and powerful feature of Scheme: *first class escape procedures*, also called *continuations*. These make it possible to control program execution in ways that are difficult or impossible in other languages.

The exercises are an integral part of the presentation, making up one-fifth of this book. Exercises come in two varieties. As in most textbooks, there are exercises that reinforce the reader's understanding of the text. However, we have also included optional exercises that present extensions of the material in the text. These exercises are grouped in sequences and are designated as such before the first exercise in the sequence. They should be done in order, since each relies on the results of previous ones. A deeper understanding will be achieved by doing these exercises.

The dependency relationships between chapters is given in the following table. The underlined number $\underline{5}$ means that Chapter 5 has some information that is required but a full understanding of the material in Chapter 5 is not necessary. The italic number *5* means that some of the procedures defined in Chapter 5 are used, but it is enough to know what they do rather than how they are defined. The symbol ← may be read "depends on."

Ch										
2	←	1								
3	←	1	2							
4	←	1	2	3						
5	←	1	2	3	4					
6	←	1	2	3	4	5				
7	←	*1*	*2*	*3*	*4*	5				
8	←	*1*	*2*	*3*	*4*	5	$\underline{6}$	7		
9	←	*1*	*2*	*3*	*4*	5	$\underline{6}$	7		
10	←	*1*	*2*	*3*	*4*	5	$\underline{6}$	7	$\underline{8}$	9
11	←	*1*	*2*	*3*	*4*	5	$\underline{6}$	7	$\underline{9}$	
12	←	*1*	*2*	*3*	*4*	5	$\underline{6}$	7	$\underline{9}$	11
13	←	*1*	*2*	*3*	*4*	5	$\underline{6}$	7	11	12
14	←	*1*	*2*	*3*	*4*	5	$\underline{6}$	7	11	
15	←	*1*	*2*	*3*	*4*	5	$\underline{6}$	7	*14*	
16	←	*1*	*2*	*3*	*4*	5	$\underline{6}$	7	11	
17	←	*1*	*2*	*3*	*4*	5	$\underline{6}$	7	11	16

This book requires no previous knowledge of programming and high school algebra is its only mathematical prerequisite. The material has been class-tested for three years. We do not intend that the entire book be taught in any single semester. The first eleven chapters represent a one semester course. From the dependency table it follows that getting through Chapter 7 with or without Chapter 6 is essential. After that point the instructor has many choices for finishing the course. One sequence that represents an ambitious course for those on a semester system is to skip Chapter 6, and include Chapters 9, 11, 12, and 15. For those on a quarter system, we recommend as a similarly ambitious course dropping Chapters 9 and 15, and the last section of Chapter 12. This book may be used in a two semester sequence by covering the first eight chapters (Parts 1 and 2) in the first semester and finishing the book in the second semester. The book can be used in a self-teaching manner as long as the reader has access to Scheme. The book can also be used by experienced programmers who want an introduction to Scheme and functional programming. For them, we recommend cursory reading of the first five chapters, followed by Chapters 7, 12, and 14–17.

You are about to embark on a most exciting and rewarding experience. Programming, especially in Scheme, is fun!

Tigger on Scheme

The wonderful thing about Scheme is:
Scheme is a wonderful thing.
Complex procedural ideas
Are expressed via simple strings.
Its clear semantics, and lack of pedantics,
Help make programs run, run, RUN!
But the most wonderful thing about Scheme is:
Programming in it is fun,
Programming in it is FUN!

John Ramsdell, based on *Walt Disney's*
Winnie the Pooh and Tigger Too,
Random House, New York, 1975,
based on books written by A. A. Milne.

Acknowledgments

Many people contributed in various ways to the completion of this book. We want to thank those who generously contributed ideas for organization, content, and exercises. We are grateful to our friends who served as consultants when we needed advice. Our thanks also go to the many people who read the manuscript in its various stages of development and offered constructive suggestions. We are also indebted to those who worked the exercises in the text to check for clarity and correctness. Our appreciation is likewise extended to those teachers who taught from our manuscript and to their students who gave us helpful criticisms. The input from each class testing improved the book for the next class that used it. We also want to express our deep gratitude to those who offered us encouragement. So we thank

Hal Abelson, David Bartley, Andrea Berger, Bhaskar Bose, José Blakeley, David Boyer, Carl Bruggeman, Tom Butler, Venkatesh Choppella, Will Clinger, Olivier Danvy, Bruce Duba, Kent Dybvig, Sue Dybvig, Matthias Felleisen, Bob Filman, Elena Fraboschi, John Franco, Mary Friedman, Dennis Gannon, Nancy Garrett, John Gateley, Mayer Goldberg, Peter Harlan, Anne Hartheimer, Brian Harvey, Chris Haynes, Caleb Hess, Bob Hieb, Stan Jefferson, Steve Johnson, Rhys Price Jones, Simon Kaplan, Roger Kirchner, Eugene Kohlbecker, Julia Lawall, Shinnder Lee, Kevin Likes, Jim Marshall, Devin McAuley, Beverly Miller, Jim Miller, John Nienart, Eric Ost, Donald Oxley, Michael Pearlman, Frank Prosser, John Ramsdell, Ed Robertson, Richard Salter, Bruce Shei, John Simmons, Annemarie Springer, Todd Starr, Guy Steele, Gerry Sussman, Dirk Van Gucht, Mitch Wand, Mike White, John Winnie, and David Wise.

Our colleagues in the Computer Science Department at Indiana University also have our heartfelt appreciation. They provided a congenial atmosphere for research and writing, which made it a pleasure to be in Bloomington. We feel fortunate to belong to a department which provided an ideal environment for the development and use of Scheme and the writing of this book. We also want to thank the National Science Foundation for support of research that led to ideas used in this book. We want to acknowledge our appreciation to those in the Scheme Community who have worked hard on informal and formal standards for the language from its inception in 1975. Our special thanks go to the three vendors who made available to us their Scheme systems: Chez Scheme, MacScheme®, and PC Scheme. We found these very helpful in developing and testing our programs.

This book was set using the TeX typesetting system with much appreciated macros provided by Amy Hendrickson. We finally want to express our gratitude to Terry Ehling at the MIT Press and David Shapiro at the McGraw-Hill Book Co. for their expert guidance through the publication maze. It was a pleasure working with them.

Part 1

Data

Data are either individual units of information or collections of data. Before the book really begins in earnest, we are introduced to a *recursive* characterization of data. In Chapter 1, we study the way Scheme treats symbolic, numerical, and logical data.

In Chapter 2, we build procedures for processing symbolic data. We can think of the act of dining out as a procedure. We generally enter a restaurant, read a menu, order some food, eat that food, pay a bill, and exit. We do not think about the procedure for a particular restaurant, but we abstract over all restaurants. A primary goal of Part 1 is to present you with enough examples of how to abstract over data so that your procedures will be general. While developing your intuition for handling symbolic data, we introduce recursive procedures. Recursion is at the heart of Part 1. Not only are the data described recursively, but also the procedures, which process the data, are recursive.

In Chapter 3, we study numbers and operations over numbers. We introduce *iterative* processes as a special case of *recursive* processes. We conclude this chapter with the development of a rational number (fraction) abstract data type. Much of the theme of this book is the understanding of programming with abstract types and this is the first such example.

In Chapter 4, we continue building your intuition about recursion and iteration. Here we combine the various data types into different structures and characterize the procedures that process them.

We introduce local variables in Chapter 5. In order to package privately computational objects that work together, we introduce lexical scope.

Finally, in Chapter 6, we show some of the advantages of displaying information and entering data while a computation proceeds.

1   Data and Operators

... it is not the thing done or made which is beautiful, but the doing. If we appreciate the thing, it is because we relive the heady freedom of making it. Beauty is the by-product of interest and pleasure in the choice of action.

Jacob Bronowski,
The Visionary Eye

Computing is an art form. Some programs are elegant, some are exquisite, some are sparkling. My claim is that it is possible to write grand programs, noble programs, truly magnificent programs.

Donald E. Knuth,
from an article by William Marling
in *Case Alumnus*

1.1   Introduction

Computer programming is many faceted.

It is engineering. Computer programs must be carefully designed. They should be reliable and inexpensive to maintain. Like any other engineering discipline, computer programming has special challenges. The foremost challenge is managing complexity. As programs grow larger, the number of possible interactions between their pieces tends to grow much faster than the volume of code. Abstraction is the primary technique for managing complexity. An abstraction hides unnecessary detail and allows recurring patterns to be expressed concisely. In this book we emphasize several powerful techniques for building abstractions.

It is a craft. A program made with craftsmanship is both more serviceable and more satisfying. Programming requires proficiency born of practice (hence the many exercises in this book!). It requires great dexterity, though of a mental rather than a manual sort. As woodworkers enjoy working with their hands and fine tools, so programmers enjoy exercising their minds and working with a fine programming language.

It is an art. Fine programs are the result of more than routine engineering. They require a refined intuition, based on a sense of style and aesthetics that is both personal and practical. As an artistic medium, programming is highly plastic, unconstrained by physical reality. In programming, perhaps more than in other arts, less is more. Simplicity is nowhere more practical than in programming, where the bane is complexity. When just the right abstraction for a problem has been found, it may be a thing of beauty. We hope you take pleasure in the programs of this book.

It is not a science, but it is based on one: computer science. Though our primary concern in this book is with the techniques of programming, we will have occasion to introduce a number of important scientific results. We hope you find the language and style of this book to be vehicles for deeper understanding and appreciation throughout your study of computer science.

It is a literary endeavor. Of course, programs must be understood by computers, which requires mastery of a programming language. But that is not enough! Programs must be analyzed to understand their behavior, and most programs must be modified periodically to accommodate changing needs. Thus it is essential that programs be intelligible by humans as well as by computers. The challenge is to convey the necessary details without losing sight of the overall structure. This in turn requires creative use of abstractions and a good sense of style—habits we attempt to instill by example in this book.

But this book is ultimately about more than the craft of engineering artistic and literate programs. Programming teaches an algorithmic (step by well-specified step) approach to problem solving, which in turn encourages an algorithmic approach to gaining knowledge. This view of the world is providing numerous fresh insights in fields as diverse as mathematics, biology, and sociology, as well as providing tools that assist and extend our minds in almost every field of study. Thus programming ability, like mathematical and writing ability, is an asset of universal value.

Programming ability and literary ability have another thing in common. An essay or short story can be correct grammatically and can convey the information that the author intended and still not be a literary work of art. Computer programming has its own aesthetic, and good programmers strive to produce programs that evoke appreciative responses in their readers. Writing such programs requires both inspiration and the application of craftsmanship that employs a thorough command of the programming language and the metaphors it can support.

There are many languages from which to choose when designing a course to teach the principles of programming. Scheme was selected because it is an expressive language that provides powerful abstraction mechanisms for expressing the solutions to computational problems. This facilitates the writing of clear and satisfying programs. It is especially good as a vehicle for teaching programming because the student is not required to learn unnecessary rules and prohibitions before being able to write meaningful programs.

The programming language LISP (which stands for List Processing) was developed around 1960 by John McCarthy. (See McCarthy, 1960.) Scheme was derived from LISP by Gerald Jay Sussman and Guy Lewis Steele Jr. around 1975. (See Sussman and Steele, 1975.) A number of people have been involved in the evolution of Scheme since its inception and these developers of the language have published a series of reports describing the current state of the language. For the first such report, see Steele and Sussman, 1978. The third revised report appeared in 1986. (See Rees and Clinger, 1986.) The fourth revision is expected in 1989. There is also a working group preparing for an IEEE Standard for Scheme. A number of books about Scheme have appeared since then, including:

- *Structure and Interpretation of Computer Programs* by Abelson and Sussman with Sussman, MIT Press and McGraw-Hill Book Company, 1985.
- *The Little LISPer* by Friedman and Felleisen, MIT Press, 1987 and SRA Pergamon, 1989.
- *The Scheme Programming Language*, by Dybvig, Prentice-Hall, 1987.
- *Programming in Scheme* by Eisenberg, Scientific Press, 1988.
- *An Introduction to Scheme* by Smith, Prentice-Hall, 1988.

The following two publications are manuals for Scheme that accompany the implementations of Scheme on microcomputers:

- *MacScheme+Toolsmith*^{TM}, Semantic Microsystems, 1987.
- *PC Scheme*, by Texas Instruments, Scientific Press, 1988.

We encourage you to read them because each presents its own programming philosophy. We are all using the same language, but we have somewhat different stories to tell.

As you read these pages, remember that you should care how elegant your programs are. The task that confronts you is not only to learn a programming language but to learn to think as a computer scientist and develop an aesthetic about computer programs. Enjoy this as an opportunity to understand the creative process better. Solve problems not only for their solutions but also for an understanding of how the solutions were obtained.

1.2 The Computer

We begin by briefly describing the components of a computer. At this stage, it suffices to think of the computer as being composed of four components:

1. The *input device*, in this case the keyboard with the standard typewriter keys and some additional ones. Each key can perform several functions. On both the typewriter and the computer keyboard, we choose between lower and upper case by depressing the Shift key. On the computer, we can also hold down the Control (CTRL) key while pressing another key to get another behavior, and on some computers, we can similarly hold down the Alternate (ALT) key while pressing another key to get yet another behavior. Finally, pressing and releasing the Escape (ESC) key before pressing another key gives still another behavior. When a key is pressed, the result is usually shown on the screen.

2. The *processor*, in which the computing is done. This contains the internal memory of the computer, the arithmetic logic unit, and the registers where the computations take place.

3. The *output devices*: the video monitor on which the interactive computing is viewed, which we refer to as the screen, and the printer where printed copy of the output is produced.

4. The *external storage device*. In microcomputers, this often consists of two floppy disk drives. The user places diskettes into these drives and either reads files from a diskette into the computer's internal memory or writes from the internal memory to a file on a diskette. Many microcomputers and all larger computers have an internal disk on which files can be stored and accessed.

Implementations of Scheme are available on a wide variety of computers ranging from larger mainframe computers that support many users to individual workstations or personal computers.

1.3 Numbers and Symbols

In order to make a computer do something for us, we must communicate with the computer in a language that it "understands." The English language, which we are using for our communication in this paragraph, makes use of words and certain grammatical rules that enable us to combine words into sentences. The words themselves consist of certain strings of characters, that is, characters written one after the other with no blank spaces between them. The computer languages also have their analogs of words, which we call *symbols*. The characters used to make up the symbols are the same characters on a standard typewriter keyboard, with a few additions and deletions. We shall generally use the letters of the alphabet, the digits from 0 through 9, and some of the other characters on the keyboard. A few of the other characters on the keyboard have special meaning, just as certain characters like the period and comma have special meaning in English. In Scheme, the characters

```
( ) [ ] { } ; , " ' ` # \
```

have special meaning and cannot appear in symbols. Similarly, the characters

```
+ - .
```

are used in numbers and may occur anywhere in a symbol except as the first character. The following list contains examples of symbols in Scheme:

```
abcd r cdr p2q4 bugs? one-two *now&
```

Numbers are not considered to be symbols in Scheme; they form a separate category. Thus, as you would expect, `10`, `-753`, and `31.5` are Scheme numbers. In the English language, not every combination of letters gives us a meaningful word. We keep words that are meaningful in our minds or in a dictionary, and when we see or hear a word, we retrieve its meaning in order to use it. In much the same way, symbols may be assigned some meaning in Scheme. A symbol used to represent some value is called a *variable*. The computer must determine the meaning of each variable or number it is given. It recognizes that the numbers have their usual meaning. Scheme also keeps the meaning of certain variables that have been assigned values, and when it is given a symbol, it checks to see if it is one of those that has been kept. If so, it can use that meaning. Otherwise it tells us that the symbol has not yet been given a meaning.

To carry the analogy with the English language a step further, words are put together in sentences to express the thoughts you want to convey. The Scheme analog of a sentence is an *expression*. An expression may consist of a single symbol or number (or certain other items to be defined later), or a *list*, which is defined to consist of a left parenthesis, followed by expressions separated by blank spaces, and ending with a right parenthesis. We first discuss the use of expressions involving symbols or numbers, and return to discussing other types of data in Section 1.4.

When you turn on the computer and call up Scheme, you usually get a message telling what implementation of Scheme you are using. Then a *prompt* appears on the screen, prompting you to enter something. The nature of the prompt depends on the implementation you are using. The prompt we use in this book to simulate the output on the screen is a pair of square brackets surrounding a number. Thus the first prompt will be

```
[1]
```

If you type a number after the prompt and then press the <RETURN> key (sometimes referred to as the <ENTER> key),

```
[1] 7 <RETURN>
```

Scheme recognizes that the meaning of the character that you typed is the number 7. We say that the *value* of the character you typed is the number 7 or that what you type has been *evaluated* to give the number 7. Scheme then writes the value of what you type at the beginning of the next line and moves down one more line and prints the next prompt:

```
[1] 7 <RETURN>
7
[2]
```

Let us review what we have just seen. At the first prompt, you enter 7 and press <RETURN>. In general, an expression (or a collection of such expressions) you enter in response to the prompt and before pressing <RETURN> is called a *program*. In this example, Scheme reads your program, evaluates it to the number 7, prints the value 7 on the screen at the beginning of the next line, and then prints the next prompt one line lower. Thus Scheme does three things in succession: it reads, it evaluates, and it prints. We refer to this sequence of events performed by Scheme as its *read-eval-print loop*. After printing the prompt, Scheme waits for you to type the next program. In the example, when you press <RETURN>, Scheme completes one cycle of the loop and begins another.

What happens when a symbol is typed after the prompt? Suppose first that you type the symbol ten and press <RETURN>. If Scheme has not previously been given a meaning for the symbol ten, we say that ten has not been *bound* to a value. In the evaluate phase of the read-eval-print loop, no value is found for `ten`, and a message is printed informing you that an error was made and describing the nature of the error. For example,

```
[2] ten <RETURN>
Error: variable ten not bound.
```

(The actual message printed depends on the implementation of Scheme you are using.) How then do we assign a meaning or value to a symbol? Suppose we want to assign the value 10 to the symbol `ten`. For this purpose we use a *define expression*. (A define expression is an example of a *special form*: a form of expression identified by a special symbol called a *keyword*, which in this case is `define`.) The define expression is entered after the next prompt as follows:

```
[3] (define ten 10) <RETURN>
```

In this example, Scheme evaluates the third subexpression, which has the value 10, assigns that value to the symbol `ten`, and finally, in our implementation of Scheme, prints the next prompt. Since the value returned by a define expression is never used, that value is not prescribed in the specification of the language. For convenience in writing this book, we opt to suppress the value returned by a define expression.

Now let's see what happens when we enter the symbol `ten`:

```
[4] ten <RETURN>
10
```

This time, Scheme successfully evaluates the variable `ten`, so it prints the value 10.

We have seen that a variable is a symbol to which a meaning (i.e., a value) can be given. When a value is given to a variable, we say that the variable is *bound* to that value. In our previous example, the symbol `ten` is a variable bound to the value 10. In general, if *var* represents a variable and *expr* represents an expression whose value we would like to *bind* or assign to *var*, we accomplish the assignment by writing

$$(\text{define } \textit{var } \textit{expr})$$

The define expression is made up of a keyword, a variable name *var*, and an expression *expr*.

Now let's suppose that `ten` is bound to 10 and we want Scheme to print not the value 10 but instead to print the symbol `ten`. We want to have some way of telling Scheme not to evaluate **ten** but to print its *literal value* **ten**. The mechanism that Scheme provides for doing this is called *quoting* the symbol. We quote a symbol by enclosing in parentheses the word **quote** followed by the symbol:

$$(\texttt{quote } symbol)$$

For example, you quote the symbol **ten** by writing (**quote ten**). If you type (**quote ten**) and then **<RETURN>** in response to a Scheme prompt, you see

```
[5] (quote ten) <RETURN>
ten
```

From now on, we shall omit the **<RETURN>** notation. It is understood that each line that we type must be followed by **<RETURN>**. We use the word *enter* when we want to indicate that something is to be typed in response to the Scheme prompt. The value that Scheme prints in response to what we enter is said to be the value that the expression "evaluates to" or that is "returned." For example, we could have said, "If the symbol **ten** is bound to **10**, and you enter (**quote ten**), then Scheme evaluates it to **ten**, while if you enter **ten**, Scheme evaluates it to **10**."

In all cases, whether a symbol is bound to some value or not, when a quoted symbol is entered, the literal symbol is returned. Thus if we enter (**quote abc3**), Scheme returns **abc3**. It is not necessary to quote numbers, for the value of a number as an expression is the number itself.

```
[6] (quote abc3)
abc3
[7] (quote 12)
12
```

An object whose value is the same as the object itself is called a *constant*. At this point, the only constants we have seen are numbers.

It is somewhat inconvenient to have to type so much each time we want to quote a symbol, so an abbreviation for the quoting process is also available in Scheme. In order to quote a symbol, we need only place an apostrophe immediately before the symbol. Thus to quote the symbol **ten**, we simply write **'ten**. The apostrophe is referred to as "quote," and the expression **'ten** is verbalized as "quote ten." Thus the responses to the prompts **[6]** and **[7]** can also be made as follows:

```
[6] 'abc3
abc3
[7] '12
12
```

We can also assign to a variable a value that is the literal value of a symbol. For example, if we enter the following:[1]

```
[8] (define Robert 'Bob)
```

we bind the variable Robert to the symbol Bob. When we next enter Robert, we get

```
[9] Robert
Bob
```

so that Scheme has evaluated Robert and returned the value Bob.

We have two types of data so far, numbers and symbols. How are they used? The use of numbers should be no surprise, since we usually think of doing arithmetic operations on numbers to get answers to problems. We shall take a brief look at how we do arithmetic in Scheme in this section and then return for a more complete look at using numbers in Chapter 3. To perform the arithmetic operations on numbers, Scheme uses *prefix notation*; the arithmetic operator is placed to the left of the numbers it operates on. The numbers on which it operates are called the *operands* of the operator. Furthermore, the operator and its operands are enclosed in a pair of parentheses. Thus to add the two numbers 3 and 4, we enter (+ 3 4) and Scheme evaluates it and returns the answer 7. On the computer screen it looks like this:

```
[10] (+ 3 4)
7
```

---

[1] We are mixing lower and uppercase letters in our symbols and showing that Scheme returns the same mix of lower and uppercase letters as their literal values. Thus, if we enter 'Bob, Scheme returns Bob. An implementation of Scheme that preserves the case of letters is called *case preserving*, and in this book, we are assuming that the implementation is case preserving. There are some implementations that are not case preserving, which means that the case is changed to either all lowercase or all uppercase letters. Thus, in some implementations, all letters are returned in lowercase, and when we enter 'Bob, Scheme evaluates it to bob. Other implementations that are not case preserving return all uppercase letters, so that if we enter 'Bob, Scheme evaluates it to BOB.

Multiplication is performed with the operator *, subtraction with −, and division with /. How do we compute the arithmetical expression $3 \times (12 - 5)$? In prefix notation, we place the multiplication operator * first followed by the first number 3. The second operand to the operator * is the difference between 12 and 5, which itself is written as (- 12 5). Thus the whole arithmetic expression is entered as

```
[11] (* 3 (- 12 5))
21
[12] (+ 2 (/ 30 15))
4
```

In general, Scheme uses this prefix notation whenever it applies any kind of operator to its operands. We shall return to a more complete discussion of numerical computations in Chapter 3. A number of experiments with numerical operations are included in the exercises at the end of this section.

In summary, a symbol can be bound to a value using a special form that begins with the keyword define. When a variable that has been bound to a value is entered in response to a Scheme prompt, its value is returned. If we want Scheme to return the literal value of the symbol instead of the value to which it is bound, we quote the variable. The value of a quoted symbol is just the literal value of the symbol.

It is possible to keep a record of the session you have in Scheme. The particular mechanism for doing so depends on the implementation of Scheme you are using. If you are using a version of Scheme that uses the windowing capability of the computer, you may be able to send what is in the window to a file. In some implementations, it is possible to run Scheme in an editor and use the saving capability of the editor to preserve what you want from the session in a file. Some versions offer a transcript facility that you turn on at the beginning of the session and give it a filename, and then turn off at the end of the session. The session is then preserved in the named file. The manual for the Scheme you are using should identify the facility you have available to save your Scheme sessions.

We strongly recommend that you try each of the things discussed in this book at the computer to see how they work. Feel free to experiment with variations on these ideas or anything else that occurs to you. You get a much better feeling for computers and for Scheme if you "play around" at the keyboard.

Exercises

Exercise 1.1

Find out what method your implementation of Scheme has for recording your Scheme session in a file. Bring up Scheme on the computer and record this session in a file called "session1.rec." Enter each of the following to successive prompts: `15`, `-200`, `12345678901234`, `(quote alphabet-soup)`, `'alphabet-soup`, `''alphabet-soup`. (Note: Experiment with entering even larger positive and negative whole numbers and decimals and see what is returned.)

Exercise 1.2

Assume that the following definitions have been made in the given order:

```
(define big-number 10500900)
(define small-number 0.00000025)
(define cheshire 'cat)
(define number1 big-number)
(define number2 'big-number)
```

What values are returned when the following are entered in response to the prompt?

a. `big-number`
c. `'big-number`
e. `'cheshire`
g. `number2`

b. `small-number`
d. `cheshire`
f. `number1`
h. `'number1`

Conduct the experiment on the computer in order to verify your answers.

Exercise 1.3

What is the result of entering each of the following expressions in response to the Scheme prompt? Verify your answer by performing these experiments on the computer.

a. `(- 10 (- 8 (- 6 4)))`

b. `(/ 40 (* 5 20))`

c. `(/ 2 3)`

d. `(+ (* 0.1 20) (/ 4 -3))`

Exercise 1.4

Write the Scheme expressions that denote the same calculation as the following arithmetic expressions. Verify your answers by conducting the appropriate experiment on the computer.

a. $(4 \times 7) - (13 + 5)$

b. $(3 \times (4 + (-5 - -3)))$

c. $(2.5 \div (5 \times (1 \div 10)))$

d. $5 \times ((537 \times (98.3 + (375 - (2.5 \times 153)))) + 255)$

Exercise 1.5

If α, β, and γ are any three numbers, translate each of the following Scheme expressions into the usual arithmetical expressions. For example:

$$(+\ \alpha\ (+\ \beta\ \gamma))\quad \text{translates into}\quad \alpha + (\beta + \gamma)$$

a. `(+ `α` (- (+ `β` `γ`) `α`))`

b. `(+ (* `α` `β`) (* `γ` `β`))`

c. `(/ (- `α` `β`) (- `α` `γ`))`

1.4 Constructing Lists

So far, we have seen two data types, symbols and numbers. Another important data type in Scheme is *lists*. We all use lists in our daily lives—shopping lists, laundry lists, address lists, menus, schedules, and so forth. In computing, it is also convenient to keep information in lists and to be able to manipulate that information. This section shows how to build lists and how to perform simple operations on lists. In Scheme, a list is denoted by a collection of items enclosed by parentheses. For example, (1 2 3 4) is a list containing the four numbers 1, 2, 3, and 4. A special list that we make frequent use of is the empty list, which contains no items. We denote the empty list by ( ).

Scheme provides a procedure to build lists one element at a time. This procedure is called **cons**, a shortening of "constructor." We refer to **cons** as a *constructor* of lists. We now look at how **cons** works. We shall first perform a number of experiments and then describe its general behavior. Suppose we want to build a list that contains only the number 1. We enter the following:

```
[1] (cons 1 '())
(1)
```

We see from this example that we enclosed three things in parentheses: the variable **cons**, the number 1, and the *empty list* '( ). The first entry tells us the name of the procedure we are applying, and the remaining two entries tell what the procedure **cons** is operating on. The entries following the name of the procedure are called the *operands* of the procedure. The values of the operands are called the *arguments* of the procedure. In our case, the first argument is the first item in the list we are constructing, and the second argument is a list that contains the rest of the items in the list we are building. Scheme first reads what we enter. In its evaluation phase, the operands are evaluated, and the desired list is built. It then prints the list (1). (Note the parallel between the application of **cons** and the application of the arithmetic operations such as (+ 3 4). We again see that the operator is placed to the left of the operands, using prefix notation.) Let us bind the variable **ls1** to the list containing the number **1** by writing

```
[2] (define ls1 (cons 1 '()))
[3] ls1
(1)
```

The **define** expression we entered at the prompt [2] binds the variable **ls1** to the value obtained by evaluating the subexpression (**cons** 1 '()). That subexpression evaluates to the list (1). Thus **ls1** is bound to the list (1). Thus when the variable **ls1** is entered at the prompt [3], its value (1) is returned.

We now create a list with **2** as its first element and the elements of **ls1** as the rest of its elements. To accomplish this we write

```
[4] (cons 2 ls1)
(2 1)
[5] ls1
(1)
```

Once again, the two operands are evaluated—2 evaluates to itself and **ls1** to the list (1). Then a new list is formed having **2** as its first item and the items of **ls1** as the rest of its items, giving us (2 1). This is the value that is returned. At prompt [5], we verify that **ls1** is unchanged. Let us next bind the variable **ls2** to a list like the one in [4].

```
[6] (define ls2 (cons 2 ls1))
[7] ls2
(2 1)
[8] ls1
(1)
```

The expression entered at the prompt [9] binds the variable c to the literal value of the symbol **three**. We can now create a list containing **three** as its first element and the elements of ls2 as the rest of its elements by writing

```
[9] (define c 'three)
[10] (cons c ls2)
(three 2 1)
```

When we apply cons to its two operands, the operands are both evaluated. The first operand, c, evaluates to **three**, and the second operand, ls2, evaluates to the list (2 1). Then a new list is built with **three** as its first item and the elements of the list (2 1) as the rest of its elements. The value (**three** 2 1) is returned.

Continuing our experiment, we bind the variable ls3 to the value of (cons c ls2) using a define expression:

```
[11] (define ls3 (cons c ls2))
```

We now perform another experiment with cons. Let us build a list that has as its first item the list ls2 and as the rest of its items the same items as those in ls3. This is done by making ls2 the first operand and ls3 the second operand of cons:

```
[12] (cons ls2 ls3)
((2 1) three 2 1)
[13] ls3
(three 2 1)
[14] (define ls4 (cons ls2 ls3))
```

The first operand of cons evaluates to the list (2 1), and the second operand of cons evaluates to (**three** 2 1). Thus the procedure cons produces a new list that has as its first item the list (2 1), followed by the elements in ls3. This gives us the value that was returned by Scheme: ((2 1) **three** 2 1). Notice that when ls3 was entered in response to the prompt [13], (**three** 2 1), the original value of ls3, was returned, so cons did build a new list and did not affect the list ls3.

We are now in a position to summarize the facts that we observed in the experiments. The procedure cons takes two operands. We apply the procedure cons to these operands by enclosing the procedure name cons followed by its two operands in parentheses. In general, a procedure name followed by its operands, all enclosed in a pair of parentheses, is called an *application*, and we say that the operator is *applied* to its operands. When an application is evaluated by Scheme, all of the expressions in the list are evaluated in some unspecified order. The value of the first expression (the operator) informs Scheme of the kind of computation that is to be made (in our case, **cons** informs Scheme that a list is to be constructed). Then the computation defined by the procedure (the value of the operator) is performed on the arguments, which are the values of the operands. We assume for now that the second operand of **cons** evaluates to a list (which may be the empty list). Then a new list is created containing the value of the first operand as its first item followed by all of the items in the list to which the second operand evaluated. It is this new list that is returned as the value of the application. Since **cons** first evaluates its operands, the lists contain only values. So far, these values may be numbers, the literal value of symbols, and lists of these items. As we progress through the chapters of this book, we shall encounter other data types, all of which can be included in lists.

We have assumed in the discussion that the second operand of the cons application evaluates to a list. This is the usual situation that we shall encounter, but it is also possible for the second argument to **cons** not to be a list. We shall discuss this case in the next section. Furthermore, we see in **ls4** that a list may contain in it other lists. We say that the inner list is *nested* within the outer list. The nesting may be several levels deep, for a nested list may itself contain nested lists. Suppose we have a given list. Items that are not nested within lists contained in the given list are called the *top-level* items of the given list. Thus, if the given list is ((a b (c d)) e (f g) h), the top-level items are the list (a b (c d)), the symbol e, the list (f g), and the symbol h.

We can also build the list (2 1) in one step by applying **cons** twice as the next experiment illustrates:

```
[15] (cons 2 (cons 1 '()))
(2 1)
```

To construct the list ((2 1) three 2 1), we could write

```
[16] (cons (cons 2 (cons 1 '())) (cons 'three (cons 2 (cons 1 '()))))
((2 1) three 2 1)
```

The second and third **cons**'s build the list (2 1), and the fourth, fifth, and sixth build the list (three 2 1). Then the first **cons** constructs the desired list.

We have used parentheses in writing several types of expressions—in the application of a procedure to its arguments, in the special form with keyword **define**, and in a list of values. When Scheme sees an expression enclosed in parentheses, it assumes that the first item following the left parenthesis evaluates to a procedure such as **cons** or is a keyword such as **define**.[2] It then evaluates the expression according to what the first item tells it to do. What happens when we enter an expression such as **(2 1)** in response to a Scheme prompt?

```
[17] (2 1)
Error: bad procedure 2
```

This experiment shows that Scheme expected to see an application or special form, and when the first item in the list is not an operator or a keyword, it returned a message saying it detected an error. In this case it tried to treat the list as an application but discovered as its first item the number **2**, which is not a procedure.

Is there some way to enter a list of items that is to be taken literally? The answer is yes. Suppose we want to enter a list containing the following items: **three**, **2**, **1**. We use the quote symbol (apostrophe) and place it in front of the left parenthesis. This indicates that each of the items included in the parentheses is to be taken with its literal value. Thus to get a list containing the desired three items, we would enter **'(three 2 1)**. The symbol **three** should not be quoted within the parentheses since the outer quote already indicates that it should be taken with its literal value. Let's look at some more examples:

```
[18] '((2 1) three 2 1)
((2 1) three 2 1)
[19] '(a b (c (d e)))
(a b (c (d e)))
[20] (cons '(a b) '(c (d e)))
((a b) c (d e))
```

We now have a way of indicating whether a list we enter consists of literal values. If the expression beginning with a parenthesis is not quoted, Scheme

---

[2] We shall use several special forms in the coming chapters and then study their properties more fully in Chapter 14. They are called *special* because their operands are not evaluated as in procedure applications. If **(define ten 10)** were evaluated as a procedure application, the operands **ten** and **10** would first be evaluated, but since **ten** has not yet been bound, an error would result. In this special form, the symbol **ten** is not evaluated.

assumes that the expression is not a quoted list, and the first item in the list is examined to determine the nature of the expression and the computation that should follow. If the expression in parentheses is quoted, Scheme assumes that each item is to be taken literally.

We have now seen several procedures: the arithmetic operators +, *, -, and /, and the list-manipulating operator cons. Procedures form another type of data in Scheme. We have now encountered four types of data: numbers, symbols, lists, and procedures.

Exercises

Exercise 1.6
Using the symbols **one** and **two** and the procedure **cons**, we can construct the list (one two) by typing (cons 'one (cons 'two '())). Using the symbols **one**, **two**, **three**, and **four** and the procedure **cons**, construct the following lists without using quoted lists (you may use quoted symbols and the empty list):

a. (one two three four)

b. (one (two three four))

c. (one (two three) four)

d. ((one two) (three four))

e. (((one)))

Exercise 1.7
Consider a list **ls** containing n values. If α evaluates to any value, how many values does the list obtained by evaluating (cons α ls) contain?

Exercise 1.8
What is the result of evaluating '(a 'b)? (Try it!) Explain this result.

1.5 Taking Lists Apart

We have seen how to build lists using the constructor **cons**. We now consider how to take a list apart so that we can manipulate the pieces separately and build new lists from old. We accomplish this decomposition of lists using two *selector* procedures, `car` and `cdr`.[3] If *ls* represents a nonempty list of items, `car` applied to *ls* gives the first item in *ls*, while `cdr` applied to *ls* gives the list consisting of all items in *ls* with the exception of its first item. Both `car` and `cdr` take one operand that must evaluate to a nonempty list. Both `car` and `cdr` are not defined on an empty list, and applying them to an empty list produces an error.

Let's look at the behavior of the selector `car`. When its argument is a nonempty list, it returns the first top-level item in the list. Thus we have

```
[1] (car '(1 2 3 4))
1
```

It is rather space consuming to indicate what a procedure returns by reproducing what is seen on the computer screen. We shall adopt a more efficient notation in which we express the above by

```
(car '(1 2 3 4)) ⟹ 1
```

The double arrow "⟹" is read as "evaluates to" or "returns." Here are some other examples of applying the procedure `car` (As in the previous section, `ls4` is bound to the list `((2 1) three 2 1)`.)

```
(car '(a b c d)) ⟹ a
(car ls4) ⟹ (2 1)
(car '((1) (2) (3) (4))) ⟹ (1)
(car '(ab (cd ef) gh)) ⟹ ab
(car '(((hen cow pig)))) ⟹ ((hen cow pig))
(car '(())) ⟹ ()
```

When the selector `cdr` is applied to an argument that is a nonempty list, the list returned is obtained when the first item (the `car`) of the argument list is removed. Thus

```
(cdr '(1 2 3 4)) ⟹ (2 3 4)
(cdr ls4) ⟹ (three 2 1)
```

---

[3] The symbol `cdr` is pronounced "could-er." The names *car* and *cdr* had their origin in the way the list-processing language LISP was originally implemented on the IBM 704, where one could reference the "address" and "decrement" parts of a memory location. Thus *car* is an acronym for "contents of address register," and *cdr* is an acronym for "contents of decrement register."

```
(cdr '(a (b c) (d e f))) ⟹ ((b c) (d e f))
(cdr '((ant hill) (bee hive) (wasp nest)))
                          ⟹ ((bee hive) (wasp nest))
(cdr '(1)) ⟹ ()
(cdr '((1 2))) ⟹ ()
(cdr '(())) ⟹ ()
```

We now have three list-manipulating procedures: the constructor **cons** and the two selectors **car** and **cdr**. By applying these in succession, we can do almost anything we want with lists. For example, if we want to get the second item in the list (a b c d), we first apply **cdr** to get (b c d) and then apply **car** to the result to get **b**. We combine these applications of **cdr** and **car** into one expression by writing

```
(car (cdr '(a b c d))) ⟹ b
```

For the next example, let **list-of-names** be bound to the list ((Jane Doe) (John Jones)). We look at how we retrieve Jane Doe's last name from this list. If we first apply **car** to **list-of-names**, we get the list (Jane Doe). We now get the list (Doe) by applying **cdr**, and finally, we get **Doe** by applying **car**. We want to emphasize the distinction between the list (Doe) containing one item and the item **Doe** itself. All of these steps are combined in the following expression:

```
(car (cdr (car list-of-names))) ⟹ Doe
```

In this example, we see that the procedures **car** and **cdr** are applied in succession a number of times. The successive applications of **car**'s and **cdr**'s is facilitated by the use of the procedures **caar**, **cadr**, **caddr**, ..., **cddddr**. The number of a's and d's between the **c** and **r** tells us how many times we apply **car** or **cdr**, respectively, in order from right to left. For example, (cadr '(a b c)) is equivalent to (car (cdr '(a b c))) and is b. Similarly, (caddr '(a b c)) is equivalent to (car (cdr (cdr '(a b c)))) and is c. We can put up to four letters (a's or d's) between the **c** and **r**. We make use of these procedures in the next example.

Consider the following situation. We ask our helper to prepare a menu that has on it the two items: chicken soup and ice cream. He prepares the menu by using a define expression to bind the variable **menu** to the list (chicken soup ice cream):

```
(define menu '(chicken soup ice cream))
```

We find this unsatisfactory and want to use the items in the list **menu** to produce the list `((chicken soup) (ice cream))`, which groups together the related items. We build the new list one step at a time:

```
(car menu) ⟹ chicken
(cadr menu) ⟹ soup
(cons (cadr menu) '()) ⟹ (soup)
(cons (car menu) (cons (cadr menu) '())) ⟹ (chicken soup)
(cddr menu) ⟹ (ice cream)
```

We now have the two items that will make up our final list. We use **cons** to build the final answer. We first use **cons** to build a list around the list `(ice cream)` to get `((ice cream))` and then use **cons** again to build a list that has `(chicken soup)` as its first item and `(ice cream)` as its second item.

```
(cons (cddr menu) '()) ⟹ ((ice cream))
(cons (cons (car menu) (cons (cadr menu) '())) (cons (cddr menu) '()))
            ⟹ ((chicken soup) (ice cream))
```

The process shown here can be used to build and manipulate lists in just about any way we want. As we learn more about Scheme, we shall discover shortcuts that facilitate the manipulation of lists.

Up to now, we have assumed that the second argument to **cons** is a list. If it is not a list, we can still apply **cons**; the result, however, is not a list but rather a *dotted pair*. A dotted pair is written as a pair of objects, separated by a dot (or period) and enclosed by parentheses. The first object in the dotted pair is the car of the dotted pair, and the second object in the dotted pair is the cdr of the dotted pair. Thus `(cons 'a 'b) ⟹ (a . b)`, and `(car '(a . b)) ⟹ a`, while `(cdr '(a . b)) ⟹ b`. Much of the work in this book involves lists, which are built out of dotted pairs. For example, `'(a . ()) ⟹ (a)`, and `'(a . (b c)) ⟹ (a b c)`. Thus any item built with the constructor **cons** is referred to as a *pair*.

Exercise

Exercise 1.9
If α and β evaluate to any values, what is

a. `(car (cons α β))`

b. `(cdr (cons α β))`

The procedures **cons**, **car**, and **cdr** do not alter their operands. Let us demonstrate this with an experiment.

```
[1] (define a 10)
[2] (define ls-b '(20 30 40))
[3] (car ls-b)
20
[4] (cdr ls-b)
(30 40)
[5] (cons a ls-b)
(10 20 30 40)
[6] a
10
[7] ls-b
(20 30 40)
```

After all of these operations involving **car**, **cdr**, and **cons**, the values of the operands **a** and **ls-b** stayed the same when they were entered in [6] and [7] as they were when they were defined in the beginning.

So far, we have encountered three procedures—**car**, **cdr**, and **cons**—that help us manipulate lists and four procedures—+, *, -, and /—that allow us to operate on numbers. Another group of procedures, called *predicates*, applies a test to their arguments and returns true or false depending on whether the test is passed. Scheme uses **#t** to denote true and **#f** to denote false. The value of **#t** is **#t** and the value of **#f** is **#f**, so both of these are constants.[4] **#t** and **#f**, representing true and false, are known as *boolean* (or *logical*) values. They form a separate type of data to give us five distinct types: numbers, symbols, booleans, pairs (including lists), and procedures. More data types will be introduced in later chapters. We now look at several predicates that apply to these five data types.

The first predicate tests whether its argument is a number, and its name is **number?**. Like most other predicates, the name ends with a question mark, signaling that the procedure is a predicate. Thus if we apply the predicate **number?** to some object, **#t** is returned if the object is a number, and otherwise **#f** is returned. If we make the following definitions,

```
(define num 35.4)
(define twelve 'dozen)
```

---

[4] In some implementations of Scheme, the empty list () is returned instead of **#f** to indicate false.

we get the following results:

```
(number? -45.67) ⟹ #t
(number? '3) ⟹ #t
(number? num) ⟹ #t
(number? twelve) ⟹ #f
(number? 'twelve) ⟹ #f
(number? (+ 2 3)) ⟹ #t
(number? #t) ⟹ #f
(number? (car '(15.3 -31.7))) ⟹ #t
(number? (cdr '(15.3 -31.7))) ⟹ #f
```

In the last example, the operand evaluates to (-31.7), which is a list, not a number.

The predicate **symbol?** tests whether its argument is a symbol. With the definitions of **num** and **twelve** given above, we get the following results:

```
(symbol? 15) ⟹ #f
(symbol? num) ⟹ #f
(symbol? 'num) ⟹ #t
(symbol? twelve) ⟹ #t
(symbol? 'twelve) ⟹ #t
(symbol? #f) ⟹ #f
(symbol? (car '(banana cream))) ⟹ #t
(symbol? (cdr '(banana cream))) ⟹ #f
```

In the last example, (cdr '(banana cream)) evaluates to a list, not a symbol.

There is also a predicate **boolean?** to test whether its argument is one of the boolean values #t or #f.

```
(boolean? #t) ⟹ #t
(boolean? (number? 'a)) ⟹ #t
(boolean? (cons 'a '())) ⟹ #f
```

A *pair* is an object built by the constructor **cons**, and the predicate **pair?** tests whether its argument is a pair. For example, nonempty lists are constructed by **cons**, so they are pairs. We have

```
(pair? '(Ann Ben Carl)) ⟹ #t
(pair? '(1)) ⟹ #t
(pair? '()) ⟹ #f
(pair? '(())) ⟹ #t
```

```
(pair? '(a (b c) d)) ⟹ #t
(pair? (cons 'a '())) ⟹ #t
(pair? (cons 3 4)) ⟹ #t
(pair? 'pair) ⟹ #f
```

There is also a predicate **null?** which tests whether its argument is the empty list.

```
(null? '()) ⟹ #t
(null? (cdr '(cat))) ⟹ #t
(null? (car '((a b)))) ⟹ #f
```

Exercises

Exercise 1.10
If the operands α and β evaluate to any values, what is

a. (**symbol?** (**cons** α β))

b. (**pair?** (**cons** α β))

c. (**null?** (**cons** α β))

d. (**null?** (**cdr** (**cons** α '())))

Exercise 1.11
If a list **ls** contains only one item, what is (**null?** (**cdr ls**))?

We have given tests to determine whether an object is a number, a symbol, a boolean, or a list, but we have not given a test to determine whether it is a procedure. There is also a predicate **procedure?** which tests whether its argument is a procedure.

```
(procedure? cons) ⟹ #t
(procedure? +) ⟹ #t
(procedure? 'cons) ⟹ #f
(procedure? 100) ⟹ #f
```

At this point, we have introduced five data types: numbers, symbols, booleans, pairs, and procedures. As we progress through the book, we shall meet other data types, such as strings, characters, vectors, and streams. A question that we often ask is whether two objects are the same. Scheme offers several different predicates to test for the sameness of its arguments. Which predicate you use depends upon the information you seek and the data type of the objects. We list a number of these sameness predicates below and introduce others as the need arises. When both objects are numbers, we use the predicate = to test whether its arguments represent the same number. The predicate = is used only to test the sameness of numbers. It is safe to use it only on integers, since the representation of nonintegers in the computer can lead to undesirable results.

```
(= 3 (/ 6 2)) ⟹ #t
(= (/ 12 2) (* 2 3)) ⟹ #t
(= (car '(-1 ten 543)) (/ -20 (* 4 5))) ⟹ #t
(= (* 2 100) 20) ⟹ #f
```

There is also a predicate **eq?** to test the sameness of symbols. If its operands evaluate to the same symbol, **#t** is returned. For this example, assume that **Garfield** has been bound to **'cat**.

```
(eq? 'cat 'cat) ⟹ #t
(eq? Garfield 'cat) ⟹ #t
(eq? Garfield Garfield) ⟹ #t
(eq? 'Garfield 'cat) ⟹ #f
(eq? (car '(Garfield cat)) 'cat) ⟹ #f
(eq? (car '(Garfield cat)) 'Garfield) ⟹ #t
```

The predicate **eq?** returns **#t** if its two arguments are identical in all respects; otherwise it returns **#f**. Symbols have the property that they are identical if they are written with the same characters in the same order. Thus we use **eq?** to test for the sameness of symbols. On the other hand, each application of **cons** constructs a new and distinct pair. Two pairs constructed with separate applications of **cons** will always test **#f** using **eq?** even if the pairs they produce look alike. For example, let us make the following definitions:

```
[1] (define ls-a (cons 1 '(2 3)))
[2] (define ls-b (cons 1 '(2 3)))
[3] (define ls-c ls-a)
```

Then we have

```
[4] (eq? (cons 1 '(2 3)) (cons 1 '(2 3)))
#f
[5] (eq? ls-a '(cons 1 '(2 3)))
#f
[6] (eq? ls-a ls-b)
#f
[7] (eq? ls-a ls-c)
#t
```

In [4], cons is applied twice to build two distinct pairs, so #f is returned
even though both of the pairs look alike as lists (1 2 3). In [5], the variable
ls-a refers to the pair defined in [1], which is distinct from the pair defined
by the cons in [5], so #f is returned. In [6], ls-b refers to the pair built
by the cons in [2], which is distinct from that built in [1], so eq? again
evaluates to #f. Finally, ls-c is defined to be the value of ls-a, which is the
pair built by the cons in [1], so both ls-a and ls-c refer to the same pair,
and eq? evaluates to #t.

When we want to include numbers, symbols, and booleans in the types of
objects the predicate tests for sameness, we use the predicate eqv?. We shall
later see that eqv? also tests vectors, strings, and characters for sameness.

```
(eqv? (+ 2 3) (- 10 5)) ⟹ #t
(eqv? 5 6) ⟹ #f
(eqv? 5 'five) ⟹ #f
(eqv? 'cat 'cat) ⟹ #t
(eqv? 'cat 'kitten) ⟹ #f
(eqv? (car '(a a a)) (car (cdr '(a a a)))) ⟹ #t
```

We have not included lists among the data types we can test for sameness
using the predicates discussed. If we want a universal sameness predicate
that can be applied to test numbers, symbols, booleans, procedures, and lists
(and strings, characters, and vectors), we use the predicate equal?. In the
case of pairs constructed using separate applications of cons, equal? tests the
corresponding entries, and if they are the same, #t is returned. Thus equal?
tells us that the two lists (cons 'a '(b c d)) and (cons 'a '(b c d)) are
the same, whereas eq? and eqv? claim that they are different.

```
(equal? 3 (/ 6 2)) ⟹ #t
(equal? 'cat 'cat) ⟹ #t
(equal? '(a b c) (cons 'a '(b c))) ⟹ #t
(equal? (cons 1 '(2 3)) (cons 1 '(2 3))) ⟹ #t
(equal? '(a (b c) d) '(a (b c) d)) ⟹ #t
```

```
(equal? '(a (b c)) '(a (c b))) ⟹ #f
(equal? (cdr '(a c d)) (cdr '(b c d))) ⟹ #t
```

Now for the obvious question: How do we know which one to use? When a predicate must first test to determine the type of its arguments, it is less efficient than one designed specifically for the type of its arguments. Thus for numbers, = is the most efficient sameness predicate. Similarly, for symbols, **eq?** is the most efficient predicate. For testing only numbers or symbols, **eqv?** is more efficient than **equal?**. When we know that we shall be using numbers or symbols, then **eqv?** is the sameness predicate we use. When the discussion is limited to numbers, we use =.

When we respond to a prompt with a number or a quoted symbol, we have seen that the number or symbol is returned. If we enter a symbol that has been bound to a value, that value is returned. If we apply a procedure such as **car** to a list (1 2 3) by entering (**car** '(1 2 3)), the expression is evaluated and the value 1 is returned and printed on the screen. On the other hand, not every Scheme object is printable. If we enter only the name of a procedure, such as **car**, the procedure, which is the value of **car**, is returned, but not printed; instead a message is displayed, which indicates a procedure. In this book, we indicate a procedure by printing angle brackets surrounding the name of the procedure in italics. Thus, when we enter **car**, *<car>* is displayed. In general, when we use *<some-symbol>*, it denotes a procedure.

We now summarize our discussion of **cons**, **car**, **cdr**, and predicates by writing some facts that apply to their use. The list is certainly not all inclusive, and we recommend that you add your own entries to it to reinforce your understanding of the use of predicates. Let α and β be operands such that α evaluates to any value and β evaluates to any nonempty list. We then have:

- The number of items in (**cons** α β) is one greater than the number of items in β.
- (eq? α β) ⟹ #t
  implies
     (eqv? α β) ⟹ #t
       implies
          (equal? α β) ⟹ #t
- (eq? (cons α β) (cons α β)) ⟹ #f
- (eqv? (cons α β) (cons α β)) ⟹ #f
- (equal? (cons α β) (cons α β)) ⟹ #t
- (boolean? (eqv? α β)) ⟹ #t

- (null? (cdr (cons α '()))) $\Longrightarrow$ #t
- (equal? (cons (car β) (cdr β)) β) $\Longrightarrow$ #t
- (equal? (car (cons α β)) α) $\Longrightarrow$ #t
- (equal? (cdr (cons α β)) β) $\Longrightarrow$ #t
- (null? β) $\Longrightarrow$ #f
- (pair? β) $\Longrightarrow$ #t
- (pair? (cons α β)) $\Longrightarrow$ #t
- (pair? (cons α_1 α_2)) $\Longrightarrow$ #t

We have been introduced to five basic data types (numbers, symbols, booleans, pairs, and procedures), and we have seen a number of procedures to manipulate and test the data. In Chapter 2 we shall develop the tools to compute with lists, and in Chapter 3 we shall do the same for numbers.

Exercises

Exercise 1.12
Evaluate each of the following.

a. (cdr '((a (b c) d)))

b. (car (cdr (cdr '(a (b c) (d e)))))

c. (car (cdr '((1 2) (3 4) (5 6))))

d. (cdr (car '((1 2) (3 4) (5 6))))

e. (car (cdr (car '((cat dog hen)))))

f. (cadr '(a b c d))

g. (cadar '((a b) (c d) (e f)))

Exercise 1.13
We can extract the symbol a from the list (b (a c) d) using car and cdr by going through the following steps:

$$(cdr \ '(b \ (a \ c) \ d)) \Longrightarrow ((a \ c) \ d)$$
$$(car \ (cdr \ '(b \ (a \ c) \ d))) \Longrightarrow (a \ c)$$
$$(car \ (car \ (cdr \ '(b \ (a \ c) \ d)))) \Longrightarrow a$$

For each of the following lists, write the expression using car and cdr that extracts the symbol a:

a. (b c a d)

b. ((b a) (c d))

c. ((d c) (a) b)

d. (((a)))

Exercise 1.14

Decide whether the following expressions are true or false:

a. (symbol? (car '(cat mouse)))

b. (symbol? (cdr '((cat mouse))))

c. (symbol? (cdr '(cat mouse)))

d. (pair? (cons 'hound '(dog)))

e. (pair? (car '(cheshire cat)))

f. (pair? (cons '() '()))

Exercise 1.15

Decide whether the following expressions are true or false:

a. (eqv? (car '(a b)) (car (cdr '(b a))))

b. (eqv? 'flea (car (cdr '(dog flea))))

c. (eq? (cons 'a '(b c)) (cons 'a '(b c)))

d. (eqv? (cons 'a '(b c)) (cons 'a '(b c)))

e. (equal? (cons 'a '(b c)) (cons 'a '(b c)))

f. (null? (cdr (cdr '((a b c) d))))

g. (null? (car '(())))

h. (null? (car '((()))))

2   Procedures and Recursion

2.1 Overview

In Chapter 1 we used several Scheme procedures such as those bound to the numerical operators +, *, -, and /, the list-manipulating procedures bound to cons, car, and cdr, and the predicates that test their arguments and return #t or #f. One of the advantages of using the programming language Scheme is that the number of procedures provided by the language is relatively small, so we do not have to learn to use many procedures in order to write Scheme programs. Instead, Scheme makes it easy for us to define our own procedures as we need them. In this chapter, we discuss how to define procedures to manipulate lists. In Chapter 3, we shall see how to define procedures to do numerical computations. In this chapter, we also discuss how a procedure can call itself within its definition, a process called recursion. Finally, we introduce an elementary tracing tool to help us in debugging programs.

2.2 Procedures

The notation $f(x, y)$ is used in mathematics to denote a function; it has the name f and has two variables, x and y. We call the values that are given to the variables the *arguments* of the function. To each pair of arguments, the function associates a corresponding value. In computing, we are concerned with how that value is produced, and we speak about the sequence of computational steps that we perform to get the value returned by the function as an *algorithm* for computing the function's value. The way we implement the algorithm on the computer to get the desired value is called a *procedure* for computing the desired value. If **f** is the name of the procedure with variables **x** and **y**, we use a list version, (**f x y**), of the *prefix* notation $f(x, y)$ used in mathematics. In general, prefix notation places the procedure or function name in front of the variables. In the list version of prefix notation, the whole expression is surrounded by parentheses, and within the parentheses, the name of the procedure comes first, followed by the variables separated by spaces. Although we used a procedure taking two arguments in this illustration, the number of arguments depends on the procedure being used. For example, we have already seen the procedure **cons** takes two arguments, and the procedure **car** takes one.

Procedures such as those bound to the values of **+**, **cons**, **car**, **cdr**, **null?**, **eqv?**, and **symbol?** are provided by the system as standard routines. It is impossible for the system to provide all procedures needed. Therefore, it is important to be able to define procedures as they are needed. Scheme provides an elegant way of defining procedures based upon the lambda calculus introduced by the logician Alonzo Church. (See Church, 1941.) We illustrate this method with an example.

When we write (**cons 19 '()**), we get a list with one number in it, (**19**). If we write (**cons 'bit '()**), we get a list with one symbol in it, namely (**bit**). Now let's write a procedure of one variable that returns a list containing the value given to that variable as its only element. We do it with a *lambda* expression,

```
(lambda (item) (cons item '()))
```

A lambda expression is an example of a *special form*: a form of expression identified by a special symbol called a *keyword*, in this case **lambda**.[1]

If the procedure defined by this lambda expression is applied to **19**, the *parameter* **item**, which is in the list following the keyword **lambda**, is assigned (bound to) the value **19**. Then the following subexpression (known as the *body* of the lambda expression) is evaluated with the parameter **item** bound to **19**. The value of the body so obtained is returned as the value of the application. In this case, it returns the value of (**cons item '()**), which is (**19**). In summary, when a procedure that is the value of a lambda expression is applied to some value, the parameter is bound to that value, and the body

---

[1] Special forms look like applications but are not, and in order to recognize them, we have to memorize the keywords, such as **lambda** and **define**. We shall see other keywords later, but the list of keywords we have to memorize is small.

of the lambda expression is evaluated with this parameter binding. The value of the body is returned as the value of the application of the procedure.

The lambda expression has the syntax

$$(\texttt{lambda}\ (parameter\ \dots)\ body)$$

The keyword **lambda** is followed by a list that contains the parameters. The *ellipsis* (three dots) following *parameter* indicates that the list contains zero or more parameters. The next subexpression is the *body* of the lambda expression. The value of a lambda expression is the procedure, which can be applied to values appropriate for the evaluation of the body. These values must agree in number with the number of parameters in the lambda expression's parameter list. When the procedure is applied, the parameters are bound to the corresponding values, and the body is evaluated. The value of the body is then the value of the application.

In general, when a procedure is applied, the syntax is

$$(operator\ operand\ \dots)$$

where *operator* is a subexpression that evaluates to the procedure being applied, and the *operands* are subexpressions that evaluate to the *arguments* to which the procedure is applied. We stress that the arguments are the values of the operands. For example, in the application (* (+ 2 3) (- 7 1)), the operator * evaluates to the multiplication procedure, the two operands are (+ 2 3) and (- 7 1), and the two arguments are 5 and 6. The value of the application is then 30, the product of 5 and 6.

Thus to apply the procedure we defined above to build a list containing the symbol **bit**, we enter

```
((lambda (item) (cons item '())) 'bit)
```

and we get as the result (**bit**). Similarly,

```
((lambda (item) (cons item '())) (* 5 6)) ⟹ (30)
```

It is awkward to write the whole expression

```
(lambda (item) (cons item '()))
```

each time we want to apply the procedure. We can avoid this by giving the procedure a name and using that name in the procedure applications. This is done by choosing a name, say `make-list-of-one`, for this procedure and then defining `make-list-of-one` to have the desired procedure as its value. We write

```
(define make-list-of-one (lambda (item) (cons item '())))
```

This is easier to read if we display the parts more clearly on separate lines as follows:

```
(define make-list-of-one
  (lambda (item)
    (cons item '())))
```

Scheme ignores any spaces in excess of the one space needed to separate expressions. Scheme also treats `<RETURN>`'s as spaces until the one following the last right parenthesis that is entered to close the first left parenthesis in the expression. Thus Scheme reads the two ways of writing this definition of `make-list-of-one` as the same Scheme expression. The indentation sets off subexpressions, making the structure of the program easier to understand at a glance.[2]   To apply the procedure `make-list-of-one`, we enter the application

```
(make-list-of-one 'bit)
```

and `(bit)` is returned.

We have now written a program that builds a list containing one item. *Computer programs to perform various tasks are written by defining the appropriate procedure to accomplish the desired tasks.* As the tasks become more complicated, there are usually different ways of defining the procedures to achieve the desired results. It is the aim of this book to lead you through a series of learning experiences that will prepare you not only to be able to write such programs but to do so in a way that is efficient, elegant, and clear to read.

A word is in order about the choice of names for procedures and parameters. Since a symbol can have as many characters in it as we wish, programs will be easier to read if we choose names that describe the procedure or parameter.

---

[2] To make entering expressions easier, some implementations of Scheme provide automatic indenting and parenthesis matching. The automatic indenting places the cursor in the proper position for the start of the next line, and the parenthesis matching indicates the left parenthesis that a right parenthesis is closing.

Thus we used the name `make-list-of-one` for the procedure that converted a value into a list containing the value. In the lambda expression in the definition of the procedure `make-list-of-one`, we selected the name `item` for the parameter to indicate that it is expecting to be bound to the item that is to be included in the list.

Now let's write a procedure called `make-list-of-two` that takes two arguments and returns a list whose elements are those two arguments. The definition is:

```
(define make-list-of-two       ; This procedure creates
  (lambda (item1 item2)        ; a list of two items.
    (cons item1 (make-list-of-one item2))))
```

The parameter list following the keyword `lambda` consists of two parameters, `item1` and `item2`. You may be wondering about the semicolons in the first and second lines of the program and the statements following them. When Scheme reads an expression, it ignores all semicolons and whatever follows them on a line. This allows us to make remarks about the program so that the reader looking at it will know the intent of the programmer. Such remarks are called *documentation* and can make understanding programs easier. By choosing the names of variables carefully, you can reduce the amount of documentation necessary to understand a program. The documentation can also precede or follow the program if each line is preceded by a semicolon. In the programs in this book, we try to select variable names that make such documentation unnecessary. When we wish to make points of clarification, we shall state them in the accompanying discussion.

We apply the procedure `make-list-of-two` to the two symbols `one` and `two` by writing

```
(make-list-of-two 'one 'two) ⟹ (one two)
```

When we defined the procedure `make-list-of-two`, we used the parameters `item1` and `item2`. When we applied the procedure `make-list-of-two`, its two arguments were the values of the operands `'one` and `'two`.

In Section 1.5, we saw how to take a list containing four items (`menu` was bound to the list (`chicken soup ice cream`)) and build a new list containing the same items but grouped into two lists, each containing two items. We can use the procedure `make-list-of-two` to give us another way of doing that grouping. We define a procedure called `regroup` that has as its parameter `list-of-4`, which will be bound to a list of four items. It returns a list with the items in `list-of-4` regrouped into two lists of two items each. In the course of writing the definition of **regroup**, we shall find it clearer to make use of certain other procedures, which express what we want to appear in the list of the two items we create. We use these procedures in the definition of **regroup** and then define them afterward. The order in which the definitions are written does not matter, and it is often more convenient to use a procedure in a definition where it is needed, and then to define it later. In the definition that follows, we make use of two such *helping procedures*, **first-group** and **second-group**.

```
(define regroup
  (lambda (list-of-4)
    (make-list-of-two
      (first-group list-of-4)
      (second-group list-of-4))))
```

The procedure **make-list-of-two** is used to create a list of two items, the first item being a list consisting of the first two items in **list-of-4** and the second consisting of the last two items in **list-of-4**. To construct the first grouping, we use a helping procedure **first-group** that we define as:

```
(define first-group
  (lambda (ls)
    (make-list-of-two (car ls) (cadr ls))))
```

We define the helping procedure **second-group** as:

```
(define second-group
  (lambda (ls)
    (cddr ls)))
```

When **first-group** is applied to **list-of-4**, the parameter **ls** is bound to the list of four items and the helping procedure **make-list-of-two** is applied to build the desired list consisting of the first two items in the list of four items. Similarly, the helping procedure **second-group** produces the rest of the list of four items following the first two, that is, the list consisting of the last two items.

Now to get the new menu, we simply apply the procedure **regroup** to **menu**, and we get the desired list:

```
(regroup menu) ⟹ ((chicken soup) (ice cream))
```

What is gained by using these procedures over the method used in Chapter 1 in which everything was expressed in terms of **cons**, **car**, **cdr**, and so forth? The version in Chapter 1 is hard to understand when it is scanned, for we have to pause to work out what the constructors and selectors are doing. In the new version, you can look at the code for **regroup** and see immediately that it is making a list of two items; the first group is again a list of two items, the first two items in the list of four items, and the second group is a list consisting of the remaining two items in the list of four items. By carefully choosing the names of the procedures and parameters, we can make the programs easy to read and understand. In our case, the use of the three helping procedures, **make-list-of-two**, **first-group**, and **second-group**, make the program easier to understand. Often the helping procedures can be used in many programs. In reality, helping procedures are ordinary procedures that we happen to want to make use of in writing some program. Any procedure can be used as a helping procedure.

We have defined procedures to build lists containing one item and two items. Scheme provides a procedure **list**, which takes any number of arguments and constructs a list containing those arguments. For example,

```
(list 'a 'b 'c 'd) ⟹ (a b c d)
(list '(1 2) '(3 4)) ⟹ ((1 2) (3 4))
(list) ⟹ ()
```

We shall see how **list** is defined in Chapter 7.

There are two styles of writing programs, *top-down* and *bottom-up* programming. In both, we are looking for the solution of some problem and want to write a procedure that returns the desired solution as its value. For now, we refer to this as the main procedure. In top-down style, we first write the definition of the main procedure. The main procedure often uses certain helping procedures, so we write the definitions of the helping procedures next. These in turn may require other helping procedures, so we write those, and so on. In bottom-up style, we first write the definitions of the helping procedures that we anticipate using, and at the end, we write the main procedure. We shall use both styles of programming in this book.

We summarize this discussion by observing that the value of a lambda expression with the syntax

$$\text{(lambda }(\textit{parameter } \dots) \textit{ body)}$$

is a procedure. The *ellipsis* after *parameter* means that this is a list of zero or more parameters. When the procedure is applied, the parameters are bound to the arguments (i.e., the values of the operands), and the body is evaluated.

We can give the procedure a name by using a define expression with the structure

$$\text{(define } \textit{procedure-name lambda-expression}\text{)}$$

where *procedure-name* is the variable used as the name of the procedure.[3] We *apply* (*call* or *invoke*) such a named procedure by writing the application

$$(\textit{procedure-name operand} \ldots)$$

where the number of operands matches the number of parameters in the definition of the procedure. In general, when an application of the form

$$(\textit{operator operand} \ldots)$$

is evaluated, the *operands* and the *operator* are all evaluated in some unspecified order. The *operator* must evaluate to a procedure. The values of the *operands* are the arguments. The procedure binds the parameters to the arguments and evaluates the body, the value of which is the value of the application. Because the operands are first evaluated and it is their values, the arguments, that the procedure receives, we say the operands are *passed by value* to the procedure.

We have also encountered two expressions that are called *special forms*: those with the keywords `define` and `lambda`. These expressions are not applications because not all the items in the expressions are evaluated initially. For example, in a lambda expression, the parameter list is never evaluated and its body is not evaluated initially. Most computer languages have some keywords that have special meaning and cannot be used for other purposes. In Scheme the number of such keywords for special forms is relatively small. In Chapter 14, we shall see how we can add to Scheme our own special forms.

---

[3] Scheme also supports

$$\text{(define } (\textit{procedure-name parameter} \ldots)\ \textit{body}\text{)}$$

as a syntax for a define expression.

Exercises

When doing these exercises, you may find it convenient to save the definitions of the procedures in a file. These procedures can then be used again. They can be entered into Scheme from a file in which they were saved either by using a transfer mechanism or by invoking a loading procedure. In some implementations of Scheme, this is done with (load *"filename"*).

Exercise 2.1: second
Define a procedure called second that takes as its argument a list and that returns the second item in the list. Assume that the list contains at least two items.

Exercise 2.2: third
Define a procedure called third that takes as its argument a list and that returns the third item in the list. Assume that the list contains at least three items.

Exercise 2.3: firsts-of-both
The procedure firsts-of-both is defined as follows:

```
(define firsts-of-both
  (lambda (list-1 list-2)
    (make-list-of-two (car list-1) (car list-2))))
```

Determine the value of the following expressions:

a. (firsts-of-both '(1 3 5 7) '(2 4 6))

b. (firsts-of-both '((a b) (c d)) '((e f) (g h)))

Exercise 2.4: juggle
Define a procedure juggle that rotates a three-element list. The procedure juggle returns a list that is a rearrangement of the input list so that the first element of this list becomes the second, the second element becomes the third, and the third element becomes the first. Test your procedure on:

```
(juggle '(jump quick spot)) ⟹ (spot jump quick)
(juggle '(dog bites man)) ⟹ (man dog bites)
```

Exercise 2.5: `switch`

Define a procedure `switch` that interchanges the first and third elements of a three-element list. Test your procedure on the examples given in the previous exercise.

2.3 Conditional Expressions

Suppose we want to define a predicate that tests whether a value is a number, a symbol, an empty list, or a pair, and returns a symbol indicating its type. The structure of the test can be written in natural language as:

> If the value is a pair, return the symbol `pair`.
> If the value is an empty list, return the symbol `empty-list`.
> If the value is a number, return the symbol `number`.
> If the value is a symbol, return the symbol `symbol`.
> Otherwise, return the symbol `some-other-type`.

This description of the procedure using English gives a sequence of steps that we follow to carry out the computation. Such a sequence of steps describing a computation is called an *algorithm*. We implement the kind of "case analysis" given in the's algorithm using a *cond expression* (the *special form with keyword* `cond`). The keyword `cond` is derived from the word *conditional*. Using `cond`, we write a procedure called `type-of` that tests its argument and returns the type of the item as described above:

```
(define type-of
  (lambda (item)
    (cond
      ((pair? item) 'pair)
      ((null? item) 'empty-list)
      ((number? item) 'number)
      ((symbol? item) 'symbol)
      (else 'some-other-type))))
```

Let us analyze the cond expression. In this case, the cond expression has five *clauses*, each represented by two expressions enclosed in parentheses. The first clause, `((pair? item) 'pair)`, has as its first expression `(pair? item)`, which is a boolean or logical expression with the value `#t` or `#f` depending on whether the value bound to `item` is or is not a pair. We shall also refer to the boolean expression as the *condition*. If the condition evaluates to true, then the second expression in the clause (the *consequent*), `'pair`, is evaluated and `pair` is returned. If the condition in the first clause evaluates to false, the condition in the second clause ((null? item) 'empty-list) is evaluated. If one of the subsequent conditions is true, then its consequent is evaluated and that value is returned. The last clause has the keyword else as its first expression, and if all of the preceding conditions are false, the expression following else is evaluated, and its value is returned. The expression following else is referred to as the *alternative*.

In general, the syntax of a cond expression is

```
(cond
  (condition₁  consequent₁)
  (condition₂  consequent₂)
           .              .
           .              .
           .              .
  (conditionₙ  consequentₙ)
  (else alternative))
```

where for each $k = 1, \ldots, n$, the expressions ($condition_k$ $consequent_k$) and (else *alternative*) are called *clauses*. The $condition_k$ and $consequent_k$, for $k = 1, \ldots, n$, and the *alternative* are expressions, and else is a keyword. Each of the conditional parts of the clauses is evaluated in succession until one is true, in which case the corresponding consequent is evaluated, and the value of the cond expression is the same as the value of the consequent corresponding to the true condition. If none of the conditions is true, the cond expression has the same value as the alternative, which is in the last cond clause, known as the else clause.[4]

Scheme has another way of handling conditional expressions that have only two cases. We can also use the special form with keyword if. Suppose we want to write a procedure car-if-pair that does the following:

If its argument is a pair, return the car of the pair.
Otherwise, return the argument.

Here is the procedure car-if-pair using cond:

```
(define car-if-pair
  (lambda (item)
    (cond
      ((pair? item) (car item))
      (else item))))
```

---

[4] The else clause is optional. If it is omitted and all of the conditions are false, then Scheme does not specify the value that is returned as the value of the cond expression. We shall avoid using cond expressions that return unspecified values.

or using an if expression, it can be written as:

```
(define car-if-pair
  (lambda (item)
    (if (pair? item)
        (car item)
        item)))
```

In general, the syntax of an if expression is

$$(\text{if } condition \ consequent \ alternative)$$

or

$$(\text{if } condition \ consequent)$$

In the first case, if *condition* is true, the value of *consequent* is returned as the value of the if expression; if *condition* is false, the value of *alternative* is returned as the value of the if expression. In the second case, the alternative is not present. In this "one-armed if," if *condition* is true, the value of *consequent* is returned as the value of the if expression. If it is false, an unspecified value is returned.

If expressions can be nested, enabling us to write the procedure **type-of** given above as follows:

```
(define type-of
  (lambda (item)
    (if (pair? item)
        'pair
        (if (null? item)
            'empty-list
            (if (number? item)
                'number
                (if (symbol? item)
                    'symbol
                    'some-other-type))))))
```

Any cond expression can be written as nested if expressions, but as the number of cases increases, the nesting of the if expressions gets deeper, and the meaning of the whole conditional expression is obscured. Thus, using a cond expression is often advantageous when there are several cases.

The use of conditional expressions with either **if** or **cond** depends upon first evaluating a condition. The condition may be simple, such as (null? ls), or it may involve something like testing whether **ls** is a pair *and* whether its **car** is some symbol such as **cat**. A condition that involves a combination of two or more simple conditions is called a *compound* condition. We build compound conditions by combining simple conditions with the logical composition operators **and**, **or**, and **not**. The compound condition mentioned above can be written using **and** as follows:

```
(and (pair? ls) (eq? (car ls) 'cat))
```

The syntax of each of these logical operators is given below:

$$(\text{and } expr_1 \ expr_2 \ \dots \ expr_n)$$
$$(\text{or } expr_1 \ expr_2 \ \dots \ expr_n)$$
$$(\text{not } expr)$$

The and expression evaluates each of the subexpressions $expr_1$, $expr_2$, ..., $expr_n$ in succession. If any one of them is false, it stops evaluating the rest of the subexpressions, and the value of the and expression is **#f**. If all of the subexpressions have true values, the value of the last subexpression is returned as the value of the and expression.[5]

The or expression evaluates each of the subexpressions $expr_1$, $expr_2$, ..., $expr_n$ in succession. If any one of them is true, it stops evaluating the rest of the subexpressions, and the value of the or expression is the value of that first true subexpression. If all of the subexpressions are false, the value of the or expression is **#f**.

The value of the not expression is **#f** when *expr* has a true value, and it is **#t** when *expr* is false.

We illustrate the use of **and** and **or** in the following examples:

```
(define s-and-n-list?
  (lambda (ls)
    (and (pair? ls)
         (symbol? (car ls))
         (pair? (cdr ls))
         (number? (cadr ls)))))
```

---

[5] Scheme has a convention of treating any value that is not false as true. Thus (if 'cat 'kitten 'puppy) ⟹ kitten, since the condition 'cat evaluates to cat, which is not false. It is good programming style, however, for the conditions to be boolean expressions that evaluate to either #t or #f.

The predicate s-and-n-list? takes a list as its argument. The value of the expression (s-and-n-list? some-list) is #t if:

some-list is a pair,
and the first item in some-list is a symbol,
and the cdr of some-list is a pair,
and the second item in some-list is a number.

Otherwise, the value of (s-and-n-list? some-list) is #f. For example,

$$(\text{s-and-n-list? '(a 1 b))} \Longrightarrow \text{\#t}$$

while

$$(\text{s-and-n-list? '(a b 1))} \Longrightarrow \text{\#f}$$

The test to determine whether the list is a pair is necessary since we can only take the car of a pair. If the list is empty, the evaluation of the car of the list never takes place. The evaluation terminates on the first false value.

```
(define s-or-n-list?
  (lambda (ls)
    (and (pair? ls)
         (or (symbol? (car ls))
             (number? (car ls))))))
```

The predicate s-or-n-list? takes a list as its argument. The expression (s-or-n-list? some-list) $\Longrightarrow$ #t if:

some-list is a pair,
and either the first item in some-list is a symbol or it is a number.

Otherwise (s-or-n-list? some-list) $\Longrightarrow$ #f.

There are occasions when we want to test whether a list contains precisely one item, that is, whether the list is a *singleton* list. It is easy to define a predicate singleton-list? that tests whether its argument is a pair and whether it contains just one element. To test whether a pair contains just one element, it is enough to test whether its cdr is empty. Thus we can write

Program 2.1 singleton-list?

```
(define singleton-list?
  (lambda (ls)
    (and (pair? ls) (null? (cdr ls)))))
```

This definition makes use of the fact that the empty list is not a pair. Thus the nonempty list whose `cdr` is empty must contain just one item and is thus a singleton list.

Exercises

Exercise 2.6

Assume that a, b, and c are expressions that evaluate to #t and that e and f are expressions that evaluate to #f. Decide whether the following expressions are true or false.

a. `(and a (or b e))`

b. `(or e (and (not f) a c))`

c. `(not (or (not a) (not b)))`

d. `(and (or a f) (not (or b e)))`

Exercise 2.7

Decide whether the following expressions are true or false if **expr** is some boolean expression.

a. `(or (symbol? expr) (not (symbol? expr)))`

b. `(and (null? expr) (not (null? expr)))`

c. `(not (and (or expr #f) (not expr)))`

d. `(not (or expr #t))`

Exercise 2.8

Decide whether the following expressions are true or false using **s-and-n-list?** as defined in this section.

a. `(s-and-n-list? '(2 pair 12 dozen))`

b. `(s-and-n-list? '(b 4 u c a j))`

c. `(s-and-n-list? '(a ten))`

d. `(s-and-n-list? '(a))`

Exercise 2.9

Decide whether the following expressions are true or false using **s-or-n-list?** as defined in this section.

a. `(s-or-n-list? '(b))`

b. (s-or-n-list? '(c 2 m))

c. (s-or-n-list? '(10 10 10 10))

d. (s-or-n-list? '())

2.4 Recursion

We saw in Section 2.2 that certain procedures use other procedures as helping procedures. In this section, we define procedures that use themselves as helping procedures. When a procedure calls itself within the body of the lambda expression defining it, we say that the procedure is *recursive*. To introduce the idea of a recursive procedure, we set as our goal the definition of a procedure `last-item`, that, when applied to a nonempty list, returns the last top-level item in the list. Here are some examples of applications of `last-item`:

```
(last-item '(1 2 3 4 5))  ⟹  5
(last-item '(a b (c d)))  ⟹  (c d)
(last-item '(cat)) ⟹   cat
(last-item '((cat))) ⟹ (cat)
```

It is a good idea to begin with the simplest cases of the arguments to which the procedure is applied. In this case, the simplest nonempty list is a list containing only one item. For example, if the list is (a), then the last item is also the first item, and applying `car` to this list produces the last item. This would work with any list containing only one top-level item, for the car of the list is both its first and its last top-level item. Let us use the variable `ls` as the parameter in the definition of `last-item`. How can we test whether `ls` contains only one top-level item? When `ls` contains only one top-level item, its cdr is the empty list. Thus the boolean expression (null? (cdr ls)) returns #t when—and indeed only when—the nonempty list `ls` contains only one top-level item. Thus, we may use a cond expression to test whether we have the case of a one-item list and return the car of the list if that is the case. We can then begin our program as follows:

```
(define last-item
  (lambda (ls)
    (cond
      ((null? (cdr ls)) (car ls))
      ... )))
```

If we now consider a list `ls` containing more than one top-level item, the cdr of that list contains one fewer top-level items, but still includes the last item of the original list. Each successive application of `cdr` reduces the number of top-level items by one, until we finally have a list containing only one top-level item, for which we have a solution. In this sense, application of `cdr` to the list reduces the problem to a simpler case. This leads us to consider the list obtained by evaluating (`cdr ls`),[6] which contains all of the items of `ls` except its first item. The last item in (`cdr ls`) is the same as the last item in `ls`. For example, the list (`a b c`) and the list (`b c`), which is its cdr, have the same last item, `c`. Thus if we call the procedure `last-item` as a helping procedure to be applied to (`cdr ls`), we get the desired last item of the original list, and that solves our problem. Thus to complete the definition of `last-item`, we add the else clause to handle the case where the list contains more than one item:

Program 2.2 `last-item`

```
(define last-item
  (lambda (ls)
    (cond
      ((null? (cdr ls)) (car ls))
      (else (last-item (cdr ls))))))
```

To see that this does define the procedure `last-item` so that it returns the correct result for any nonempty list `ls`, we consider first a list (`a`) containing only one item. Then the condition in the first cond clause is true, and (`car ls`) does give us the last (which is also the first) item, `a`, in the list. Thus `last-item` works on any list containing only one item. Now let's consider the case in which `ls` is a list (`a b`) containing two items. Then its cdr, (`b`), contains one item, so the procedure `last-item` does work on (`cdr ls`), allowing us to use it as a helping procedure in the else clause to get the correct result. Thus `last-item` solves the problem for any list of two items. Now we use the fact that `last-item` works on the cdr of any three-item list to conclude that it

---

[6] It is common practice, when the context is clear, not to include the phrase *obtained by evaluating*. We say, "the list (cdr ls)" instead of "the list obtained by evaluating (cdr ls)" whenever the context makes it clear that we want the value of (cdr ls) rather than the literal list whose first item is cdr and whose second item is ls. When we want the literal list, and the context is not clear, we indicate so by quoting it.

works on the three-item list itself. We can continue this process of increasing by one the number of items in the list indefinitely, showing that `last-item` solves the problem for any list.

Since the procedure `last-item` called itself as a helping procedure, `last-item` is a recursive procedure. Our strategy in general in designing a recursive procedure on a list is first to identify the "simplest case" and write the expression that solves the problem for that case as the consequent in the first cond clause. We call this simplest case the *base case* or *terminating condition*. We then identify a simplifying operation, which on repeated application to the list produces the base case. Then in each of the other cases, we solve the problem with some expression that calls the recursive procedure as a helping procedure applied to the simplified list. In our example, the base case is the list consisting of only one item. The simplifying operation is `cdr`, and in the other cases, we see that the expression that solves the problem applies `last-item` to the simplified list (`cdr ls`).

To give us a better intuition about how `last-item` works, we shall apply `last-item` to the list (a b c). What is (`last-item` '(a b c))? We shall walk through the evaluation of this expression. The parameter `ls` is bound to the argument (a b c), and the cond expression is evaluated. In this case, (`cdr ls`) is not empty, so the alternative in the else clause is evaluated. This tells us to apply `last-item` to (`cdr ls`). Since (`cdr ls`) is (b c), we must evaluate (`last-item` '(b c)). We thus bind the parameter `ls` to the argument (b c) and enter the cond expression. Once again, (`cdr ls`) is not empty, so we evaluate the alternative in the else clause. This tells us to apply `last-item` to (`cdr ls`), which now is (c). Thus we must evaluate (`last-item` '(c)). We now bind the parameter `ls` to the argument (c) and enter the cond expression. This time (`cdr` '(c)) is the empty list. Thus the consequent is evaluated to give (`car` '(c))—c as the value of the expression.

The recursion in the illustration stops when the list is simplified to the base case. In that case, the condition in the first cond clause is true. We call the condition used to stop the recursion the *terminating condition*. In our example, the terminating condition is (`null?` (`cdr ls`)). Generally, whenever a recursive procedure is defined, a terminating condition must be included so that the recursion will eventually stop. (In Chapter 15 on streams, we shall see examples in which a terminating condition is not needed.) We usually begin the definition of a recursive procedure by writing the terminating condition as the first cond clause. We then proceed with the rest of the definition.

In the preceding discussion we introduced the *substitution model*. Using the substitution model, we can determine the value of an expression by substituting values for parameters. Through the first eight chapters, the substitution model suffices. From Chapter 9 on, however, there will be times when the substitution model does not work. From time to time, we use it to clarify a computation; most of the time, however, we use the general approach: the *environment model*. In that approach we just remember the bindings of variables and avoid any substitutions.

Let us next define a procedure `member?` that decides for us whether its first argument is `equal?` to one of the top-level items in the list that is its second argument. For example,

1. `(member? 'cat '(dog hen cat pig))` $\implies$ `#t`
2. `(member? 'fox '(dog hen cat pig))` $\implies$ `#f`
3. `(member? 2 '(1 (2 3) 4))` $\implies$ `#f`
4. `(member? '(2 3) '(1 (2 3) 4))` $\implies$ `#t`
5. `(member? 'cat '())` $\implies$ `#f`

In Example 3, `2` is not a top-level item in the list `(1 (2 3) 4)`, so `#f` is returned. We begin the definition of `member?` by determining the base case. Regardless of what `item` is, if `ls` is the empty list, `#f` is returned. This is the simplest case and will be taken as our base case. To test for the base case, we use the predicate `null?` so the terminating condition is `(null? ls)`. The consequent for the terminating condition is `#f`. We can therefore begin the definition of `member?` as a procedure having two parameters, `item` and `ls`:

```
(define member?
  (lambda (item ls)
    (cond
      ((null? ls) #f)
      ... )))
```

Now given any list, what is the simplifying operation that simplifies `ls` to the empty list? It is again the procedure `cdr`. Assume that `ls` is not empty. If we know the value of `(member? item (cdr ls))`, how do we get the value for `(member? item ls)`? Well, when is the latter statement true? It is true if either the first item in `ls` is the same as `item` or if `item` is a member of the rest of the list following the first item. This can be written as the `or` expression:

```
(or (equal? (car ls) item) (member? item (cdr ls)))
```

Thus in the case when `ls` is not empty, the above expression is true exactly

when the expression (member? item ls) is true. We then complete the definition of member? with

Program 2.3   member?

```
(define member?
  (lambda (item ls)
    (cond
      ((null? ls) #f)
      (else (or (equal? (car ls) item)
                (member? item (cdr ls)))))))
```

The procedure member? is recursive since it calls itself. Let us review the
reasoning used in the program for member?. If the terminating condition
(null? ls) is true, then item is not in ls, and the consequent is false. Otherwise we look at the alternative, which is true if either item is the first item
in ls or if item is in (cdr ls) and is otherwise false.

When member? calls itself with argument (cdr ls), its parameter is bound
to the value of (cdr ls), which is a shorter list than the parameter's previous
binding to ls. In each successive recursive procedure call, the list is shorter,
and the process is guaranteed to stop because of the terminating condition
(null? ls).

In order to use a list as the first argument to member? (as in Example 4),
we used the predicate equal? to make the sameness test in the else clause. If
we know that the items to which item is bound will always be symbols, we
can use eq? in place of equal?. The procedure so defined using eq? is named
memq? to distinguish it from member?, which is defined using equal? for the
sameness test. Similarly, if we know that the items to which item is bound
will always be either symbols or numbers, we can use eqv? for the sameness
test and call the procedure so defined memv?.[7]

We have now defined the procedure last-item, which picks the last top-
level item out of a list, and the procedure member?, which tests whether an
item is a top-level element in a given list. We continue illustrating how to
define recursive procedures with the definition of another useful procedure

---

[7] Scheme provides the three procedures member, memq, and memv, written without the question mark. These behave somewhat differently from the ones we defined with the question
mark in that if item is not found, false is returned, but if item is found in ls, the sublist
whose car is item is returned. For example, (memq 'b '(a b c)) $\Longrightarrow$ (b c).

for manipulating lists. The procedure **remove-1st** removes the first top-level occurrence of a given item from a list of items. For example,

1. `(remove-1st 'fox '(hen fox chick cock))`
   $\Longrightarrow$ `(hen chick cock)`

2. `(remove-1st 'fox '(hen fox chick fox cock))`
   $\Longrightarrow$ `(hen chick fox cock)`

3. `(remove-1st 'fox '(hen (fox chick) cock))`
   $\Longrightarrow$ `(hen (fox chick) cock)`

4. `(remove-1st 'fox '())` $\Longrightarrow$ `()`

5. `(remove-1st '(1 2) '(1 2 (1 2) ((1 2))))`
   $\Longrightarrow$ `(1 2 ((1 2)))`

In general, the procedure **remove-1st** takes two arguments, an element **item** and a list **ls**. It builds a new list from **ls** with the first top-level occurrence of **item** removed from it. We again begin looking at the simplest case, in which **ls** is the empty list. Since **item** does not occur at all in the empty list, the list we build is still the empty list. The test for the base case is then (**null? ls**), and the value returned in its consequent is (). Thus the definition of the procedure **remove-1st** begins with

```
(define remove-1st
  (lambda (item ls)
    (cond
      ((null? ls) '())
      ... )))
```

If **ls** is not empty, the procedure that simplifies it to the base case is again **cdr**. If we already know (**remove-1st item (cdr ls)**), that is, if we have a list consisting of the first top-level occurrence of **item** removed from (**cdr ls**), how do we build up a list that is obtained by removing the first top-level occurrence of **item** in **ls**? There are two cases to consider. Let's first consider the example in which we remove the first occurrence of **a** from the list (**a b c d**). Since **a** is the first item in the list, we get the desired result by merely taking the **cdr** of the original list. This is the first case we consider. If the first top-level item in **ls** is the same as **item**, then we get the desired list by simply using (**cdr ls**). This case can be added to the definition of **remove-1st** by writing

```
(define remove-1st
  (lambda (item ls)
    (cond
      ((null? ls) '())
      ((equal? (car ls) item) (cdr ls))
      ... )))
```

The only case left to be considered is when `ls` is not empty, and its first top-level item is not the same as `item`. Consider the example in which we apply `remove-1st` to remove the letter `c` from the list `(a b c d)`. The list is not empty and its first item is not `c`. Thus the list we build begins with `a` and continues with the items in `(b d)`. But `(b d)` is just the list obtained by removing `c` from `(b c d)`. The final result is then `(a b d)`, which was obtained by building the list

```
(cons (car '(a b c d)) (remove-1st 'c (cdr '(a b c d))))
```

In general, the list we are building now begins with the first element of `ls` and has in it the elements of `(cdr ls)` with the first top-level occurrence of `item` removed. But this is obtained when we cons[8] `(car ls)` onto `(remove-1st item (cdr ls))`, so the final case is disposed of by adding the else clause to the definition, which is given in Program 2.4.

Program 2.4 `remove-1st`

```
(define remove-1st
  (lambda (item ls)
    (cond
      ((null? ls) '())
      ((equal? (car ls) item) (cdr ls))
      (else (cons (car ls) (remove-1st item (cdr ls)))))))
```

To get a better understanding of how recursion works, let's walk through the evaluation of an application of the procedure `remove-1st`; for example

```
(remove-1st 'c '(a b c d))
```

---

[8] Scheme programmers use the verb *cons*, which has an infinitive "to cons", tenses "cons, cons'd, has cons'd", participle "consing", and conjugation "I cons, he conses, etc." We shall make frequent use of these words.

Since the list (a b c d) is not empty and the first entry is not c, the alternative in the else clause is evaluated. This gives us

$$\text{(cons 'a (remove-1st 'c '(b c d)))}$$

To get the value of this expression, we must evaluate the remove-1st subexpression. Once again, the list (b c d) is not empty, and the first item in the list is not the same as c. Thus the alternative in the else clause is evaluated. This gives us as the value of the whole expression above:

$$\text{(cons 'a (cons 'b (remove-1st 'c '(c d))))}$$

Once again, to get the value of this expression, we must evaluate the remove-1st subexpression. Now the list (c d) is not empty, but its first item *is* the same as c. Thus the condition in the second cond clause in the definition of remove-1st is true and the value of its consequent is (d). Thus the above expression has the value

$$\text{(cons 'a (cons 'b '(d)))}$$

which can be simplified to give the value

$$\text{(a b d)}$$

This is the value returned by the procedure call. In the next section, we shall see how the computer can help us walk through a procedure application.

In order to be able to remove a sublist from a given list, as in Example 5, the predicate equal? was used to test for sameness in the second cond clause. If we know that all of the arguments to which item will be bound are symbols, we can use eq? to test for sameness. The procedure defined using eq? instead of equal? is named remq-1st. Similarly, if we restrict the arguments to which item will be bound to symbols or numbers, we can use eqv? to test for sameness in the second cond clause, and we name the procedure so defined remv-1st.

Exercises

Exercise 2.10
Rewrite the definitions of the three procedures last-item, member? and remove-1st with the cond expression replaced by if expressions.

Exercise 2.11

The definition of **member?** given in this section uses an or expression in the else clause. Rewrite the definition of **member?** so that each of the two subexpressions of the or expression is handled in a separate cond clause. Compare the resulting definition with the definition of **remove-1st**.

Exercise 2.12

The following procedure, named **mystery**, takes as its argument a list that contains at least two top-level items.

```
(define mystery
  (lambda (ls)
    (if (null? (cddr ls))
        (cons (car ls) '())
        (cons (car ls) (mystery (cdr ls))))))
```

What is the value of **(mystery '(1 2 3 4 5))**? Describe the general behavior of **mystery**. Suggest a good name for the procedure **mystery**.

Exercise 2.13: **subst-1st**

Define a procedure **subst-1st** that takes three parameters: an item **new**, an item **old**, and a list of items **ls**. The procedure **subst-1st** looks for the first top-level occurrence of the item **old** in **ls** and replaces it with the item **new**. Test your procedure on:

```
(subst-1st 'dog 'cat '(my cat is clever))
                      ⟹ (my dog is clever)
(subst-1st 'b 'a '(c a b a c))
                      ⟹ (c b b a c)

(subst-1st '(0) '(*) '((*) (1) (*) (2)))
                      ⟹ ((0) (1) (*) (2))
(subst-1st 'two 'one '()) ⟹  ()
```

In order to be able to include lists as possible arguments to which the parameters **new** and **old** are bound, use **equal?** to test for sameness. Also define procedures **substq-1st** and **substv-1st** that use **eq?** and **eqv?** respectively, instead of **equal?** to test for sameness.

Exercise 2.14: `insert-right-1st`

The procedure `insert-right-1st` is like `remove-1st` except that instead of removing the item that it is searching for, it inserts a new item to its right. For example,

```
(insert-right-1st 'not 'does '(my dog does have fleas))
                         ⟹ (my dog does not have fleas)
```

The definition of `insert-right-1st` is

```
(define insert-right-1st
  (lambda (new old ls)
    (cond
      ((null? ls) '())
      ((equal? (car ls) old)
       (cons old (cons new (cdr ls))))
      (else (cons (car ls)
                  (insert-right-1st new old (cdr ls)))))))
```

Define a procedure `insert-left-1st` that is like `insert-right-1st` except that instead of inserting a new item to the right of the item it is searching for, it inserts it to its left. Test your procedure on

```
(insert-left-1st 'hot 'dogs '(I eat dogs))
                         ⟹ (I eat hot dogs)
(insert-left-1st 'fun 'games '(some fun))
                         ⟹ (some fun)
(insert-left-1st 'a 'b '(a b c a b c))
                         ⟹ (a a b c a b c)
(insert-left-1st 'a 'b '()) ⟹ ()
```

Exercise 2.15: `list-of-first-items`

Define a procedure `list-of-first-items` that takes as its argument a list composed of nonempty lists of items. Its value is a list composed of the first top-level item in each of the sublists. Test your procedure on:

```
(list-of-first-items '((a) (b c d) (e f))) ⟹ (a b e)
(list-of-first-items '((1 2 3) (4 5 6))) ⟹ (1 4)
(list-of-first-items '((one))) ⟹ (one)
(list-of-first-items '()) ⟹ ()
```

Exercise 2.16: `replace`

Define a procedure `replace` that replaces each top-level item in a list of items `ls` by a given item `new-item`. Test your procedure on:

```
(replace 'no '(will you do me a favor))
                    ⟹ (no no no no no no)
(replace 'yes '(do you like ice cream))
                    ⟹ (yes yes yes yes yes)
(replace 'why '(not)) ⟹ (why)
(replace 'maybe '()) ⟹ ()
```

Exercise 2.17: `remove-2nd`

Define a procedure `remove-2nd` that removes the second occurrence of a given item a from a list of items `ls`. You may use the procedure `remove-1st` in defining `remove-2nd`. Test your procedure on:

```
(remove-2nd 'cat '(my cat loves cat food))
                    ⟹ (my cat loves food)
(remove-2nd 'cat '(my cat loves food))
                    ⟹ (my cat loves food)
(remove-2nd 'cat '(my cat and your cat love cat food))
                    ⟹ (my cat and your love cat food)
(remove-2nd 'cat '()) ⟹ ()
```

Exercise 2.18: `remove-last`

Define a procedure `remove-last` that removes the last top-level occurrence of a given element `item` in a list `ls`. Test your procedure on:

```
(remove-last 'a '(b a n a n a s)) ⟹ (b a n a n s)
(remove-last 'a '(b a n a n a)) ⟹ (b a n a n)
(remove-last 'a '()) ⟹ ()
```

Exercise 2.19: `sandwich-1st`

Define a procedure `sandwich-1st` that takes two items, a and b, and a list `ls` as its arguments. It replaces the first occurrence of two successive b's in `ls` with b a b. Test your procedure on:

```
(sandwich-1st 'meat 'bread '(bread cheese bread bread))
                              ⟹ (bread cheese bread meat bread)
(sandwich-1st 'meat 'bread '(bread jam bread cheese bread))
                              ⟹ (bread jam bread cheese bread)
(sandwich-1st 'meat 'bread '()) ⟹ ()
```

Exercise 2.20: `list-of-symbols?`

Define a procedure `list-of-symbols?` that tests whether the top-level items in a given list `ls` are symbols. Write your definitions in three ways, first using `cond`, then `if`, and finally `and` and `or`. Test your procedures with:

```
(list-of-symbols? '(one two three four five)) ⟹ #t
(list-of-symbols? '(cat dog (hen pig) cow)) ⟹ #f
(list-of-symbols? '(a b 3 4 d)) ⟹ #f
(list-of-symbols? '()) ⟹ #t
```

Exercise 2.21: `all-same?`

Define a procedure `all-same?` that takes a list `ls` as its argument and tests whether all top-level elements of `ls` are the same. Test your procedure with:

```
(all-same? '(a a a a a)) ⟹ #t
(all-same? '(a b a b a b)) ⟹ #f
(all-same? '((a b) (a b) (a b))) ⟹ #t
(all-same? '(a)) ⟹ #t
(all-same? '()) ⟹ #t
```

2.5 Tracing and Debugging

We have now walked through several programs to understand their behavior. We had to evaluate expressions ourselves and make decisions as to which branches of conditional expressions to follow. The computer is able to do both of these, so we can take advantage of its power to relieve us of this kind of work. The tool we develop here enables us to walk through or, as it is technically known, *trace* our programs. We can also use this tool to find and correct errors in our programs, a process called *debugging*.

The computer can help us walk through or trace our programs if we make use of a procedure `writeln` (read as "write-line") that prints its arguments directly to the computer screen. Some Scheme implementations provide the procedure `writeln`, and if the one you are using does not make it available, you can enter its simple definition.[9] The procedure `writeln` takes any number of arguments. When we evaluate

---

[9] A more complete discussion of `writeln` and related procedures that write to the screen is presented in Chapter 7. You may enter the definition of `writeln` given in Program 7.5 if your implementation of Scheme does not provide it.

$$(\texttt{writeln } expr_1 \; expr_2 \; \ldots \; expr_n)$$

the expressions $expr_1 \; expr_2 \; \ldots \; expr_n$ are all evaluated; then their values are printed on the screen in order from left to right with no blank spaces between them. When the last value is printed, the cursor moves to the beginning of the next line. Like every other procedure, writeln must return a value, but we are not concerned with this value. In fact, different implementations of Scheme may return different values. Since it is *unspecified* in Scheme what value writeln returns, we shall assume in our implementation that the value returned is not printed on the screen.

For example, if the variable Jack is bound to the value Jill and the variable Punch is bound to the value Judy, the evaluation of (writeln Punch Jack) will print

JudyJill

on the screen with no space between the words. If we evaluate the expression (writeln 'Punch 'Jack), then the screen shows

PunchJack

We can control the spacing and print sentences on the screen if we use another type of data called *strings*. A string is any sequence of keyboard characters. In Scheme, a string is written as a sequence of characters enclosed with double quotes: ". Thus "This is a string." is an example of a string. If we want to include a double quote or a backslash in a string, we must precede it by a backslash.[10] Thus, we can write the string "He said \"Hello\".", which has "Hello" within double quotes. If we evaluate the expression

(writeln "This is a string.")

then

This is a string.

appears on the screen. Note that the double quotes are not printed with the string. Thus the evaluation of the expression

---

[10] A character, such as a backslash, which is used to change the normal meaning of what follows it is referred to as an *escape character*.

```
(writeln "He said \"Hello\".")
```

prints

```
He said "Hello".
```

A string is another example of a constant in Scheme. Thus if we enter a string in response to a prompt, the string is returned, including the double quotes.

```
[1] "This is a string."
"This is a string."
```

If we evaluate

```
(writeln "My friends Jack and " Jack ".")
```

we see on the screen:

```
My friends Jack and Jill.
```

The first occurrence of **Jack** is in the string, so it is printed literally as **Jack**. The second occurrence of **Jack** is not in a string, so it is evaluated, and its value **Jill** is printed. This time we have a space between the words **and** and **Jill**, since the blank space is included after the word **and** in the string. The last string in the writeln expression contains only the period.

The procedure **writeln** is usually evaluated as one of a sequence of expressions that are evaluated consecutively. This is accomplished by using the special form with keyword **begin**. A begin expression has any number of subexpressions following the keyword **begin**. Each of these subexpressions is evaluated consecutively in the order that it appears and the value of the last subexpression is returned as the value of the begin expression. For example,

```
[2] (begin
      (writeln "The remove-1st expression")
      (writeln "is applied to the list (1 2 3 4)")
      (writeln "to build a new list without the number 2.")
      (remove-1st 2 '(1 2 3 4)))
The remove-1st expression
is applied to the list (1 2 3 4)
to build a new list without the number 2.
(1 3 4)
```

When the preceding begin expression is evaluated, the four subexpressions are evaluated consecutively. The first three are writeln expressions, which print their arguments on the screen, with a new line starting after each writeln expression is evaluated. The values returned by the writeln expressions are ignored. The value of the last expression is the only value returned—that is the (1 3 4) that appears on the last line.

We want to stress that what is printed on the screen is not the value of the writeln expressions. Instead, what is printed on the screen is done as a *side effect*. A side effect causes some change to take place (in this case, the change was printing on the screen), but it is not a value that is returned. When using a begin expression, all of the subexpressions before the last one are included for their side effects and not for the values that they return. The value of the last subexpression is the only one returned. Here is another example to illustrate that only the value of the last subexpression is returned.

```
[3] (begin
     (+ 3 4)
     (- 5 11)
     (* 10 10))
100
```

The values of the first two subexpressions are ignored. In this case, the first two subexpressions did not produce any side effects, so although they were evaluated, we do not see any evidence of it and there really was no point in putting them there!

The syntax of the begin expression is

$$(\textbf{begin } expr_1 \; expr_2 \; \ldots \; expr_n)$$

where the expressions $expr_1$, $expr_2$, $\ldots$ $expr_n$ are evaluated in their given order, and the value of the last one, $expr_n$, is returned.

We now have all the tools we need to use writeln to help us walk through an application of remove-1st to remove the letter c from the list (a b c d). We "wrap" a helping procedure entering around the condition of each cond clause as we enter it and wrap a helping procedure leaving around the consequent (or alternative) as we leave the cond clause. The definitions of these helping procedures are given after the main program. The procedure entering takes three arguments: the value of the condition, the value of ls, and the identifying number of the cond clause: 1 for the first, 2 for the second, and 3 for the last. It tells us, using a writeln statement, which cond clause we are entering and the value of ls. The procedure leaving takes two arguments:

the value of the consequent (or alternative) and the identifying number of the cond clause. It tells us which cond clause we are leaving and the value of the consequent. When we run the program, we thus get a written record each time we enter or leave a cond clause. Inserting such writeln expressions into the definition of a procedure to study the evaluation of the procedure is one way of *tracing* the procedure. Program 2.5 contains the code for the procedure that traces remove-1st. The definition of the helping procedure entering is in Program 2.6, and of the helping procedure leaving is in Program 2.7.

When we enter a cond clause, the condition is the entering expression whose parameter test is bound to the value of the original condition of remove-1st. If test is true, it writes the fact that we are entering the cond clause with the appropriate identifying number and the current value of the variable 1s. In any event, test is returned as the value of the condition. If test is false, the next cond clause is entered. If test is true, the consequent of that cond clause is evaluated. If the else clause is entered, we use the quoted symbol else as the first argument of entering. Scheme treats the symbol else as true (since it is not false) so the alternative is evaluated.

The consequent (or alternative) in each cond clause of remove-1st-trace is a leaving expression. It has the value of the original consequent (or alternative) of the cond clause of remove-1st as the binding of its first parameter, result. When the leaving expression is evaluated, it tells us the identifying number of the cond clause and the value to which result is bound. It then returns result.

Now let's apply remove-1st-trace to see how this tracing information helps us see what is happening during the evaluation.

```
[1] (remove-1st-trace 'c '(a b c d))
    Entering cond-clause-3 with ls = (a b c d)
    Entering cond-clause-3 with ls = (b c d)
    Entering cond-clause-2 with ls = (c d)
Leaving cond-clause-2 with result = (d)
Leaving cond-clause-3 with result = (b d)
Leaving cond-clause-3 with result = (a b d)
(a b d)
```

This output tells us that we first entered the third cond clause with 1s bound to (a b c d). With this binding, the leaving expression in the alternative is evaluated, so that its first operand

$$(\text{cons 'a (remove-1st-trace 'c '(b c d)))} \qquad (1)$$

Program 2.5 `remove-1st-trace`

```
(define remove-1st-trace
  (lambda (item ls)
    (cond
      ((entering (null? ls) ls 1)
       (leaving '() 1))
      ((entering (equal? (car ls) item) ls 2)
       (leaving (cdr ls) 2))
      ((entering 'else ls 3)
       (leaving
         (cons (car ls) (remove-1st-trace item (cdr ls)))
         3)))))
```

Program 2.6 `entering`

```
(define entering
  (lambda (test input cond-clause-number)
    (begin
      (if test (writeln "   Entering cond-clause-"
                  cond-clause-number " with ls = " input))
      test)))
```

Program 2.7 `leaving`

```
(define leaving
  (lambda (result cond-clause-number)
    (begin
      (writeln "Leaving cond-clause-"
        cond-clause-number " with result = " result)
      result)))
```

is evaluated. Thus `remove-1st-trace` is called again, and a is waiting to be consed onto the value obtained before we can leave cond clause 3. The next message on the screen tells us that we are entering the third cond expression again with argument (b c d). This time, the alternative

$$\text{(cons 'b (remove-1st-trace 'c '(c d)))} \qquad (2)$$

is evaluated, and b is waiting to be consed onto its value before we can leave cond clause 3. As before, `remove-1st-trace` is called again before the leaving writeln expression is evaluated. This time, the first item in (c d) is the same as c, and we are told that we entered the second cond clause with `ls` bound to (c d). When we enter the consequent, the first operand in the leaving expression evaluates to (d). Then the writeln expression prints on the screen that we are leaving the second cond clause with the `result` bound to (d), and the value (d) is returned.

Cons expression (2) is waiting for the value of the `remove-1st-trace` call, and now that value is (d). With this value, the cons expression in (2) evaluates to (b d). We can now complete the evaluation of the leaving expression, which tells us that we are leaving cond clause 3 with `result` bound to (b d). But this is just the value that cons expression (1) is waiting for as the value of its `remove-1st-trace` invocation. Using the value (b d) as its last argument, cons expression (1) evaluates to (a b d). It was the first operand in the application of `leaving` in the third cond clause. Now that it has been evaluated, the writeln expression writes its message, which says that we are leaving cond clause 3 with `result` bound to (a b d). The `leaving` invocation now returns the value to which `result` is bound, (a b d), and that becomes the value of the original procedure call. The trace we made here illustrates well the order in which we enter and leave the cond clauses. We see that we do not leave the cond clause until a value is found for the recursive invocation of `remove-1st-trace`, and the evaluation of the cons expression can be completed.

In the previous example, we entered only the second and third cond clauses. If we invoke `remove-1st-trace` to remove an item from a list that does not contain it, we enter only the first and third cond clauses, as the following trace illustrates:

```
[2] (remove-1st-trace 'e '(a b c d))
   Entering cond-clause-3 with ls = (a b c d)
   Entering cond-clause-3 with ls = (b c d)
   Entering cond-clause-3 with ls = (c d)
   Entering cond-clause-3 with ls = (d)
   Entering cond-clause-1 with ls = ()
Leaving cond-clause-1 with result = ()
Leaving cond-clause-3 with result = (d)
Leaving cond-clause-3 with result = (c d)
Leaving cond-clause-3 with result = (b c d)
Leaving cond-clause-3 with result = (a b c d)
(a b c d)
```

Analyze the trace to be sure you can explain it in a manner similar to that used in the previous example.

We have used writeln expressions to trace a program by printing certain information about places in the program where the evaluation is being made and the values of certain variables at that place. This helps us understand how programs work. It is also an excellent tool for finding errors in programs. If a program is not doing what you expect it to do, you can put a writeln expression at certain places in the program where you think the error may be and look at the values of variables to compare them with what you expect at that place. By studying these values, you can frequently pinpoint the source of the error and make the appropriate changes to cause the program to work correctly. When the program is corrected and runs as you want, the writeln expressions used to locate the errors should be removed. Tracing a program with the writeln expressions placed at strategic points is a helpful and often used debugging tool.

Exercise

Exercise 2.22
In the first trace, the second and third cond clauses were entered. In the second trace, the first and third cond clauses were entered. Can you give a **remove-1st-trace** invocation that enters only the first and second cond clauses? Explain.

The last example of recursion in this chapter is the procedure **swapper**, which takes three arguments: an item **x**, an item **y**, and a list **ls**. It builds a new list in which each top-level occurrence of **x** in **ls** is replaced by **y**, and each top-level occurrence of **y** in **ls** is replaced by **x**. We are "swapping" **x** and **y** in **ls**. For example,

```
(swapper 'cat 'dog '(my cat eats dog food))
                                    ⟹ (my dog eats cat food)
(swapper 'john 'mary '(john loves mary)) ⟹ (mary loves john)
(swapper 'a 'n '(b n a n a n)) ⟹ (b a n a n a)
(swapper 'a 'b '(c (a b) d)) ⟹ (c (a b) d)
(swapper 'a 'b '()) ⟹ ()
```

In the fourth example, the **a** and **b** in the list are not at top level, so they are not swapped.

In order to define **swapper**, we begin with an analysis of the base case. What is the simplest case for this problem? If **ls** is empty, there is nothing to swap and the empty list is returned. Thus we take as the base case for **ls** the empty list, and we begin the definition as follows:

```
(define swapper
  (lambda (x y ls)
    (cond
      ((null? ls) '())
      ... )))
```

A nonempty list is simplified to the base case using the simplifying operation **cdr**. What is returned if we invoke (**swapper x y (cdr ls)**)? The result will be (**cdr ls**) with the items **x** and **y** interchanged. But this differs from (**swapper x y ls**) only in that the first item in (**swapper x y ls**) is missing. We will get (**swapper x y ls**) from (**swapper x y (cdr ls)**) by consing the correct first item onto (**swapper x y (cdr ls)**). There are three possibilities for this first item: it can be **x**, **y**, or neither. First, if (**car ls**) is **x**, we should cons **y** onto (**swapper x y (cdr ls)**), so the next cond clause in our definition can be added:

```
(define swapper
  (lambda (x y ls)
    (cond
      ((null? ls) '())
      ((equal? (car ls) x)
       (cons y (swapper x y (cdr ls))))
      ... )))
```

Program 2.8 `swapper`

```
(define swapper
  (lambda (x y ls)
    (cond
      ((null? ls) '())
      ((equal? (car ls) x)
       (cons y (swapper x y (cdr ls))))
      ((equal? (car ls) y)
       (cons x (swapper x y (cdr ls))))
      (else
       (cons (car ls) (swapper x y (cdr ls)))))))
```

Second, if `(car ls)` is `y`, we should cons `x` onto `(swapper x y (cdr ls))`, so the next cond clause can be added:

```
(define swapper
  (lambda (x y ls)
    (cond
      ((null? ls) '())
      ((equal? (car ls) x)
       (cons y (swapper x y (cdr ls))))
      ((equal? (car ls) y)
       (cons x (swapper x y (cdr ls))))
      ... )))
```

Finally, if `(car ls)` is neither `x` nor `y`, then we just cons `(car ls)` itself onto `(swapper x y (cdr ls))`, giving us the else clause and completing the definition given in Program 2.8.

If we invoke the procedure `swapper` with the arguments `'b`, `'d`, and `'(a b c d b)`, it should return the list `(a d c b d)` in which `b` and `d` have been interchanged. Let's walk through the program to see how it constructs this answer. In the first procedure call, `ls` is bound to `(a b c d b)`. This list is not empty, and its car is neither `b` nor `d`, so the else clause is evaluated and gives as the answer the cons expression:

$$(cons\ 'a\ (swapper\ 'b\ 'd\ '(b\ c\ d\ b)))$$

Let's refer to the value of this cons expression as *answer-1*, and that is the value that we are looking for to solve the problem. At this point, however, we have not yet evaluated the recursive invocation of **swapper**, so let's give its value the name *answer-2*. We can now rewrite *answer-1* as

answer-1 is:	(cons 'a *answer-2*)
answer-2 is:	(swapper 'b 'd '(b c d b))

We see that *answer-1* is waiting for the value of *answer-2*, so we move on to evaluating *answer-2* and we shall return to get the value of *answer-1* when *answer-2* is known.

To evaluate *answer-2*, we observe that the list (b c d b) begins with b, so the second cond clause is the one with the true condition, and evaluating its consequent gives us

answer-1 is:	(cons 'a *answer-2*)
answer-2 is:	(cons 'd *answer-3*)
answer-3 is:	(swapper 'b 'd '(c d b))

We still do not have a value for *answer-3*, so we once again set aside *answer-2* until we have a value for *answer-3*. Note that we are making a table of these various answers, with each successive entry placed below the preceding one. We shall often refer to this table, so we give it the name *return table*.

To evaluate *answer-3*, we see that (c d b) is not empty, and does not begin with b or d, so the alternative in the else clause is evaluated. We get for *answer-3*

```
(cons 'c (swapper 'b 'd '(d b)))
```

and we give the invocation of **swapper** within *answer-3* the name *answer-4*. This gives us the return table:

answer-1 is:	(cons 'a *answer-2*)
answer-2 is:	(cons 'd *answer-3*)
answer-3 is:	(cons 'c *answer-4*)
answer-4 is:	(swapper 'b 'd '(d b))

We have added *answer-3* to our return table to wait until we have the value of *answer-4*.

For the invocation of **swapper** in *answer-4*, the condition in the third cond clause is true, so our return table now becomes

answer-1 is:	(cons 'a *answer-2*)
answer-2 is:	(cons 'd *answer-3*)
answer-3 is:	(cons 'c *answer-4*)
answer-4 is:	(cons 'b *answer-5*)
answer-5 is:	(swapper 'b 'c '(b))

We have added *answer-4* to our return table to wait for a value for *answer-5*.

For the invocation of **swapper** in *answer-5*, the condition in the second cond clause is true, so the return table now becomes

answer-1 is:	(cons 'a *answer-2*)
answer-2 is:	(cons 'd *answer-3*)
answer-3 is:	(cons 'c *answer-4*)
answer-4 is:	(cons 'b *answer-5*)
answer-5 is:	(cons 'd *answer-6*)
answer-6 is:	(swapper 'b 'd '())

Once again we have added *answer-5* to the return table to wait until we have a value for *answer-6*. In the invocation of **swapper** in *answer-6*, the terminating condition in the first cond clause is true, and the value () is returned for *answer-6*.

What effect does this termination have on the return table? Although we have a value for *answer-6*, the computation does not stop, for we have to get the values of each of the waiting variables in our return table. Until now, on each recursive invocation of **swapper**, a new row was added to the return table waiting for a value. This time we got a value for *answer-6*, so we do not have to add a row to the return table. Instead we replace the **swapper** expression in the last row by its value (). We can now work our way back up the table one row at a time, replacing each variable on the right side by the value it has on the next row below. We shall write these replacements in a new table, starting with the value for *answer-6*.

answer-6 is:	()
answer-5 is:	(d)
answer-4 is:	(b d)
answer-3 is:	(c b d)
answer-2 is:	(d c b d)
answer-1 is:	(a d c b d)

The last row gives us the anticipated value for our invocation of **swapper**.

Let's take another look at the definition of the procedure **swapper**. In the last three cond clauses, something is consed onto

```
(swapper x y (cdr ls))
```

What that something should be is determined by testing the value of (car ls). We can write a helping procedure **swap-tester** that makes the test and returns the correct value to be consed onto

```
(swapper x y (cdr ls))
```

Assuming that we have such a test procedure, we can rewrite the definition of **swapper** as follows:

```
(define swapper
  (lambda (x y ls)
    (cond
      ((null? ls) '())
      (else (cons (swap-tester x y (car ls))
                  (swapper x y (cdr ls))))))))
```

We now define the helping procedure **swap-tester** to distinguish the three cases for us:

```
(define swap-tester
  (lambda (x y a)
    (cond
      ((equal? a x) y)
      ((equal? a y) x)
      (else a))))
```

When **swap-tester** is called within **swapper**, the arguments **x**, **y**, and (**car ls**) are substituted for the parameters **x**, **y** and **a**, respectively, and **swap-tester** returns the correct value to be consed onto

```
(swapper x y (cdr ls))
```

The use of such helping procedures often simplifies the writing and reading of programs. We shall make frequent use of this technique.

We could also have achieved the same effect without using the helping procedure **swap-tester** by using in **swapper** the cond expression of **swap-tester** in place of calling **swap-tester**. This leads to another version of **swapper**:

```
(define swapper
  (lambda (x y ls)
    (cond
      ((null? ls) '())
      (else (cons (cond
                    ((equal? (car ls) x) y)
                    ((equal? (car ls) y) x)
                    (else (car ls)))
                  (swapper x y (cdr ls))))))))
```

In this section, we have seen how to use writeln expressions to trace or debug a program. We have also seen how a return table is created when a recursive procedure is evaluated.

Exercises

Exercise 2.23
Identify what is printed on the screen and what is returned in each of the following:

```
a. (begin
     (writeln "(* 3 4) = " (* 3 4))
     (= (* 3 4) 12))

b. (begin
     (writeln "(cons 'a '(b c)) has the value " (cons 'a '(b c)))
     (writeln "(cons 'a '(b c)) has the value " '(a.b c))
     (writeln "(cons 'a '(b c)) has the value (a b c)")
     (cons 'a '(b c)))

c. (begin
     (writeln "Hello, how are you?")
     (writeln "Fine, thank you.  How are you? " 'Jack)
     (writeln "Just great!  It is good to see you again, " 'Jill)
     "Good-bye.  Have a nice day.")
```

Exercise 2.24: `describe`
With `describe` defined as

```
(define describe
  (lambda (s)
    (cond
      ((null? s) (quote '()))
      ((number? s) s)
      ((symbol? s) (list 'quote s))
      ((pair? s) (list 'cons (describe (car s)) (describe (cdr s))))
      (else s))))
```

evaluate each of the following expressions:

a. `(describe 347)`

b. `(describe 'hello)`

c. (describe '(1 2 button my shoe))

d. (describe '(a (b c (d e) f g) h))

Describe what describe does in general.

Exercise 2.25
Write a trace similar to the one used in `remove-1st-trace` to trace the procedure `swapper`, showing the binding of the parameter `ls` each time the cond expression is entered and whenever a cond clause is exited. Invoke the traced procedure `swapper-trace` on the arguments b, d, and (a b c d b) used in the example in this section.

Exercise 2.26
In the return table built for the invocation of `swapper` in this section, the computation did not stop when the terminating condition was true and the first cond clause returned (). Instead, the variables in the table were evaluated one by one until the value of the first was obtained to provide the value of the original invocation. This program behaved in this way because after each invocation of `swapper`, a `cons` still had to be completed. There was still an operation to perform after `swapper` was invoked. Do a similar analysis, building the return tables, on the two procedures `last-item` in Program 2.2 and `member?` in Program 2.3. In the first case, consider (`last-item` '(a b c)), and in the second case, consider (`member?` 'c '(a b c d)). In these two examples, there is no procedure waiting to be done after the recursive invocations of the procedure. Such programs are called *iterative*. We shall discuss the behavior of iterative programs more thoroughly in the chapter on numerical recursion.

Exercise 2.27
Does the answer change if cond clause 2 and cond clause 3 are interchanged in the definition of `swapper`? Does the same thing hold if cond clauses 1 and 2 are interchanged in `swap-tester`?

Exercise 2.28: tracing, test-tracing
A more generally applicable tracing tool than the procedure `leaving` given in Program 2.7 is the procedure `tracing` defined by

```
(define tracing
  (lambda (message result)
    (begin
      (writeln message result)
      result)))
```

Similarly, the procedure `test-tracing` defined by

```
(define test-tracing
  (lambda (test message input)
    (begin
      (if test (tracing message input))
      test)))
```

is useful for tracing the test part of a conditional expression. Rewrite the definition of `remove-1st-trace` using `test-tracing` and `tracing` instead of `entering` and `leaving` in such a way as to produce *exactly* the same output as that generated using `entering` and `leaving`.

---

3   Data Abstraction and Numbers

3.1 Overview

Many of the procedures we studied in Chapters 1 and 2 operated on lists and symbols. Another interesting area of applications deals with numerical computations. In this chapter, we study procedures that perform arithmetic operations on numbers. We also develop a program to do exact arithmetic using fractions instead of decimals, which are usually associated with computers. This will provide our first illustration of data abstraction.

3.2 Operations on Numbers

We shall discuss two types of numbers, *integers* and *real numbers*. The integers are the usual positive and negative counting numbers and zero:

$$\ldots, -4, -3, -2, -1, 0, 1, 2, 3, 4, \ldots$$

where, in this case, the ellipsis means that the list continues indefinitely in both directions.

The set of real numbers includes both positive and negative decimal numbers and zero. For example, 34.56, -3.456, 0.00034, and 17.0 are all real numbers. The integers are also considered to be real numbers, so we may also refer to the real number 5 or 5.0. We write real numbers with up to fifteen significant figures,[1] so $\frac{1}{3}$ will be written as 0.333333333333333 and $\frac{1}{3}$ multiplied by 10000 is written as 3333.33333333333. When the decimal point moves

---

[1] The number of significant figures represented is system dependent.

beyond the fifteenth digit, Scheme may switch over to scientific notation. For example, 0.333333333333333e45 represents the number one-third multiplied by 10 raised to the forty-fifth power—that is, by a one followed by forty-five zeros. Let's look at some simpler examples of scientific notation. The number 2.735e2 is the same as 273.5, since the e2 means that 2.735 is multiplied by a one followed by two zeros—that is, by 100. Another way of saying this is that the e2 means that the decimal point is moved two places to the right. Another example is 2.735e-2, which is the same as 0.02735, since e-2 means that 2.735 is multiplied by .01, or that the decimal point is moved two places to the left.

We use two predicates, `integer?` and `real?`, to test the type of a number. The expression (`integer? num`) is true if `num` is an integer and false otherwise. The expression (`real? num`) is true if `num` is any real number, including integers, and is otherwise false. Three other useful predicates are `zero?`, `positive?`, and `negative?`, which make the obvious tests to see whether their arguments are zero, positive, or negative, respectively.

The four basic arithmetic operations are given by the procedures associated with the variables + for addition, - for subtraction, * for multiplication, and / for division. These are applied to numbers with applications, as were the list operations in Chapter 2. For example, to add the two numbers 5 and 7, we enter the expression (+ 5 7), and the answer 12 is returned. Similarly[2]

```
(- 4 32) ⟹ -28
(* -15 -3) ⟹ 45
(/ -15 -3) ⟹ 5
(/ -16 -3) ⟹ 5.33333333333333
```

We recommend that you play around with these arithmetic operations on various kinds of numbers and see what results appear.

In many programs, the successor of a given integer n is desired, and rather than entering (+ n 1), we can use the successor procedure `add1` and write (`add1 n`). Thus

```
(add1 7) ⟹ 8
(add1 -37) ⟹ -36
```

---

[2] When division is performed with two integers, some implementations of Scheme return a fraction instead of a decimal. For example, (/ 2 3) is either displayed as 2/3 or as 0.66666666666666.

Program 3.1   add1

```
(define add1
  (lambda (n)
    (+ n 1)))
```

Program 3.2   sub1

```
(define sub1
  (lambda (n)
    (- n 1)))
```

Not all implementations of Scheme provide the procedure **add1**, so we include its definition in Program 3.1.

Similarly the predecessor procedure **sub1** can be used to get the integer that precedes a given integer. For example, instead of writing (- n 1), we can write (**sub1** n). Thus

```
(sub1 7) ⟹ 6
(sub1 -37) ⟹ -38
```

The definition of **sub1** is included in Program 3.2 in case the implementation of Scheme you are using does not provide it.

There are many more Scheme procedures defined on numbers. We present a brief list of these procedures in Figure 3.3 and make some short remarks about each. When the objects to be tested for sameness may or may not be numbers, **eqv?** and **equal?** both determine the type and apply the appropriate sameness test. When it is known that the objects to be tested for sameness are numbers, it is better to use =, which is specifically designed to apply to numbers and should be used only to compare numbers. When testing for 0, you should use **zero?**.

The computer's decimal representation 0.333333333333333 for the quotient (/ 1 3) is not the same as the fraction 1/3 but is, rather, an approximation to it, the use of which is made necessary by the way real numbers are represented in the computer. Thus we would not expect = to return true if we test (/ 1 3) and 0.333333333333333. In general, because the internal representation of certain numbers in the computer is only an approximation to the actual number, we refer to such numbers as *inexact* numbers. We consider numbers written with explicit use of a decimal point as being inexact,

Expression	Remarks
(= m n)	Tests whether the exact numbers m and n are equal.
(< m n)	Tests whether m is less than n.
(<= m n)	Tests whether m is less than or equal to n.
(> m n)	Tests whether m is greater than n.
(>= m n)	Tests whether m is greater than or equal to n.
(abs n)	Gives the absolute value of n. (abs 5) $\Longrightarrow$ 5 and (abs -5) $\Longrightarrow$ 5.
(ceiling n)	Gives the smallest integer (inexact) which is $\geq n$. (ceiling 5.3) $\Longrightarrow$ 6. (ceiling -5.3) $\Longrightarrow$ -5.
(floor n)	Gives the largest integer (inexact) which is $\leq n$. (floor 5.3) $\Longrightarrow$ 5. (floor -5.3) $\Longrightarrow$ -6.
(round n)	Rounds n to the nearest integer (inexact). If n is exactly halfway between two integers, it rounds it to the nearest even integer.
(truncate n)	Gives the integer (inexact) obtained by chopping off the decimal part of n.
(expt n k)	Raises n to the power k.
(sqrt n)	The square root of n, $n \geq 0$.
(max n...), (min n...)	The maximum and minimum of n..., respectively.
(exp n), (log n)	The exponential of n and logarithm of n to the base e, respectively.
(sin n), (cos n)	The trigonometric sine and cosine, respectively, of n (n in radians).
(asin n), (acos n)	The arc sine and arc cosine of n, respectively.
(tan n)	The tangent of n (n in radians).
(atan n)	The arc tangent of n.
(quotient n k)	The quotient of n divided by k.
(remainder n k)	The remainder of n divided by k with the sign of the dividend.
(modulo n k)	The remainder of n divided by k with the sign of the divisor.

Figure 3.3 Some of Scheme's mathematical operators

for example, 3.25, −0.05. Integers, written without decimal points, are *exact* numbers, and certain operations, such as + and *, preserve the exactness of numbers. One should use only the predicate = to test for the sameness of exact numbers.

We close this section with the definitions of several procedures that illustrate the use of arithmetic operations in recursive programs. The first procedure harmonic-sum sums the first n terms of the harmonic series, that is, it sums the series of the form

$$1 + \frac{1}{2} + \frac{1}{3} + \cdots + \frac{1}{n}$$

Our strategy again is to simplify the problem by reducing the number of terms n that are being summed. If n is zero, no terms are summed, and the sum is zero. This will serve as the terminating condition for our recursion.

```
(define harmonic-sum
  (lambda (n)
    (cond
      ((zero? n) 0)
      ... )))
```

To make the recursive step, we observe that we get (harmonic-sum n) from (harmonic-sum (sub1 n)) by adding the *n*th term. For any positive n, (harmonic-sum n) is the same as

```
(+ (/ 1 n) (harmonic-sum (sub1 n)))
```

so we complete the definition with

Program 3.4 harmonic-sum

```
(define harmonic-sum
  (lambda (n)
    (cond
      ((zero? n) 0)
      (else (+ (/ 1 n) (harmonic-sum (sub1 n)))))))
```

In programs dealing with numbers, it is often the case that the recursion is accomplished by reducing the numerical argument each time the procedure calls itself, and the smallest value of the numerical argument (in this case, n is zero) provides the terminating condition. Another simple illustration of this idea is the construction of a list containing a specified number of zeros. We define `list-of-zeros` which has parameter **n** and builds a list containing **n** zeros. Its code is given in Program 3.5.

Program 3.5   `list-of-zeros`

```
(define list-of-zeros
  (lambda (n)
    (cond
      ((zero? n) '())
      (else (cons 0 (list-of-zeros (sub1 n)))))))))
```

The procedure `length` takes as its argument a list of items `ls` and then tells how many top-level items are in the list. For example,

```
(length '(a b c d e)) ⟹ 5
(length '(1 (2 3) (4 5 6))) ⟹ 3
(length '(one)) ⟹ 1
(length '()) ⟹ 0
```

The procedure `length` is provided in all implementations of Scheme. We shall show the definitions of many of the procedures provided by Scheme because you will learn programming better by knowing how these basic procedures are defined. When you test our definitions of these procedures, it is good practice to use a different name for the procedure you define so that you do not override the definition of the procedure provided by Scheme. Thus for the procedure `length`, you can use the name `=length=` when you enter your definition.

To define `length`, we use recursion. The base case is the empty list whose length is zero, and the operation `cdr` is used to simplify longer lists. We begin the definition with the terminating condition:

```
(define length
  (lambda (ls)
    (if (null? ls)
        0
        ... )))
```

Suppose we know `(length (cdr ls))`; then we get `(length ls)` by simply adding one to `(length (cdr ls))`. This recursive step completes the last line of the definition:

Program 3.6 `length`

```scheme
(define length
  (lambda (ls)
    (if (null? ls)
        0
        (add1 (length (cdr ls))))))
```

The next procedure we define is `list-ref`, which takes as arguments a list of items `ls` and a (nonnegative) integer `n` and gives us the $(n+1)$st top-level item in `ls`. For example

```scheme
(list-ref '(a b c d e f) 3) ⟹ d
(list-ref '(a b c d e f) 0) ⟹ a
(list-ref '(a b c) 3)
           ⟹ Error: list-ref: Index 3 out of range for list (a b c)
(list-ref '((1 2) (3 4) (5 6)) 1) ⟹ (3 4)
(list-ref '() 0)
           ⟹ Error: list-ref: Index 0 out of range for list ()
```

The number n is called the *index* of the item extracted from the list `ls` by (`list-ref ls n`). If the index is greater than or equal to the length of the list of items `ls`, an error is announced. Since the first item in the list `ls` has index 0, we say that the indexing is *zero based*.

The strategy we use in this recursion is based on the observation that if we are looking for the nth item in the list, that item becomes the $(n-1)$st item in the `cdr` of the list. Thus we shall successively remove the first item from the list and simultaneously reduce the index of the desired item by one. If the index reaches zero and the list is not empty, the first item in the list is the item returned. We can determine whether the list will not become empty before or when the index becomes zero by testing whether the length of the list is larger than the index. If that is not the case, we signal an error. This enables us to write the first version of the definition of the Scheme procedure `list-ref` as follows:

```scheme
(define list-ref
  (lambda (ls n)
    (cond
      ((<= (length ls) n)
       (error "list-ref: Index" n "out of range for list" ls))
      ((zero? n) (car ls))
      (else (list-ref (cdr ls) (sub1 n))))))
```

The procedure `error` employed here to signal an error uses a procedure similar to `writeln` to print its arguments on the screen and then returns to the Scheme prompt. Most Scheme systems provide an `error` procedure. A definition of the procedure `error` is given in Chapter 7.

In the program for `list-ref`, the test for whether the length of `ls` is less than or equal to n is made on each recursive call. However, if the test is false on the first call, it will remain false in each successive recursive call, since both the length of the list and the index are reduced by one in each successive call. It would be a much better program if the test were made only once, and if it were false, then a helping procedure would be called that produces the desired item. We give such a definition next.

```
(define list-ref
  (lambda (ls n)
    (cond
      ((<= (length ls) n)
       (error "list-ref: Index" n "out of range for list" ls))
      (else (list-ref-helper ls n)))))
```

with the helping procedure defined as

```
(define list-ref-helper
  (lambda (ls n)
    (if (zero? n)
        (car ls)
        (list-ref-helper (cdr ls) (sub1 n)))))
```

In general, it is good practice to avoid redundant computations when recursive calls are made. The use of a helping procedure, as illustrated in this definition of `list-ref`, is a way of avoiding this kind of inefficiency. Once it is established that the length of the list is greater than the index, the helping procedure does the rest of the computation to find the item without calling the procedure `list-ref` again and determining the length of each `ls` repeatedly.

Another approach to defining `list-ref` derives from observing that if, during the recursive calls, the list `ls` becomes empty while the index n is nonnegative, the index must have been too large for the list. Thus the program can be written as:

Program 3.7 `list-ref`

```
(define list-ref
  (lambda (ls n)
    (cond
      ((null? ls)
       (error "list-ref: Index" n "out of range for list" ls))
      ((zero? n) (car ls))
      (else (list-ref (cdr ls) (sub1 n))))))
```

Exercises

We refer to a list of numbers as an *n-tuple*. Thus (1 3 5 7), (-1.3 2.5), (3), and () are examples of n-tuples. The numbers in an n-tuple are called *components*. In Exercises 3.1–3.4, you are asked to define several procedures on n-tuples. In all of the exercises in this section, you may use procedures you have already defined as helping procedures.

Exercise 3.1: `sum`
Define a procedure `sum` that finds the sum of the components of an n-tuple. Test your procedure on:

```
(sum '(1 2 3 4 5)) ⟹ 15
(sum '(6)) ⟹ 6
(sum '()) ⟹ 0
```

Exercise 3.2: `pairwise-sum`
Define a procedure `pairwise-sum` that takes two n-tuples of the same length, `ntpl-1` and `ntpl-2`, as arguments and produces a new n-tuple whose components are the sum of the corresponding components of `ntpl-1` and `ntpl-2`. Test your procedure on:

```
(pairwise-sum '(1 3 2) '(4 -1 2)) ⟹ (5 2 4)
(pairwise-sum '(3.2 1.5) '(6.0 -2.5)) ⟹ (9.2 -1.0)
(pairwise-sum '(7) '(11)) ⟹ (18)
(pairwise-sum '() '()) ⟹ ()
```

In an analogous way, define a procedure `pairwise-product` that produces an n-tuple whose components are the products of the corresponding components of `ntpl-1` and `ntpl-2`.

Exercise 3.3: `dot-product`

Define a procedure `dot-product` that takes two n-tuples of the same length, multiplies the corresponding components, and adds the resulting products. This exercise can be done either directly or by using the procedures defined in Exercises 3.1 and 3.2. Consider the advantages and disadvantages of each approach. Test your procedure on:

```
(dot-product '(3 4 -1) '(1 -2 -3)) ⟹ -2
(dot-product '(0.003 0.035) '(8 2)) ⟹ 0.094
(dot-product '(5.3e4) '(2.0e-3)) ⟹ 106.0
(dot-product '() '()) ⟹ 0
```

Exercise 3.4: `mult-by-n`

Define a procedure `mult-by-n` that takes a number `num` and an n-tuple `ntpl` as arguments and multiplies each component of `ntpl` by `num`. Test your procedure on:

```
(mult-by-n 3 '(1 2 3 4 5)) ⟹ (3 6 9 12 15)
(mult-by-n 0 '(1 3 5 7 9 11)) ⟹ (0 0 0 0 0 0)
(mult-by-n -7 '()) ⟹ ()
```

Exercise 3.5: `index`

Define a procedure `index` that has two arguments, an item `a` and a list of items `ls`, and returns the index of `a` in `ls`, that is, the zero-based location of `a` in `ls`. If the item is not in the list, the procedure returns -1. Test your procedure on:

```
(index 3 '(1 2 3 4 5 6)) ⟹ 2
(index 'so '(do re me fa so la ti do)) ⟹ 4
(index 'a '(b c d e)) ⟹ -1
(index 'cat '()) ⟹ -1
```

Exercise 3.6: `make-list`

Define a procedure `make-list` that takes as arguments a nonnegative integer `num` and an item `a` and returns a list of `num` elements, each of which is `a`. Test your procedure on:

```
(make-list 5 'no) ⟹ (no no no no no)
(make-list 1 'maybe) ⟹ (maybe)
(make-list 0 'yes) ⟹ ()
(length (make-list 7 'any)) ⟹ 7
(all-same? (make-list 100 'any)) ⟹ #t
```

Exercise 3.7: `count-background`

Define a procedure `count-background` that takes an item `a` and a list of items `ls` as arguments and returns the number of items in `ls` that are not `equal?` to `a`. Test your procedure on:

```
(count-background 'blue '(red white blue yellow blue red)) ⟹ 4
(count-background 'red '(white blue green)) ⟹ 3
(count-background 'white '()) ⟹ 0
```

Exercise 3.8: `list-front`

Define a procedure `list-front` that takes as arguments a list of items `ls` and a nonnegative integer `num` and returns the first `num` top-level items in `ls`. If `num` is larger than the number of top-level items in `ls`, an error is signaled. Test your procedure on:

```
(list-front '(a b c d e f g) 4) ⟹ (a b c d)
(list-front '(a b c) 4) ⟹ Error: length of (a b c) is less than 4.
(list-front '(a b c d e f g) 0) ⟹ ()
(list-front '() 3) ⟹ Error: length of () is less than 3.
```

Exercise 3.9: `wrapa`

Define a procedure `wrapa` that takes as arguments an item `a` and a nonnegative integer `num` and wraps `num` sets of parentheses around the item `a`. Test your procedure on:

```
(wrapa 'gift 1) ⟹ (gift)
(wrapa 'sandwich 2) ⟹ ((sandwich))
(wrapa 'prisoner 5) ⟹ (((((prisoner)))))
(wrapa 'moon 0) ⟹ moon
```

Exercise 3.10: `multiple?`

Define a predicate `multiple?` that takes as arguments two integers `m` and `n` and returns #t if `m` is an integer multiple of `n`. (Hint: Use `remainder`.) Test your procedure on:

```
(multiple? 7 2) ⟹ #f
(multiple? 9 3) ⟹ #t
(multiple? 5 0) ⟹ #f
(multiple? 0 20) ⟹ #t
(multiple? 17 1) ⟹ #t
(multiple? 0 0) ⟹ #t
```

Exercise 3.11: `sum-of-odds`

It can be shown[3] that the sum of the first n odd numbers is equal to n^2. For example,

$$1 + 3 + 5 + 7 = 16 = 4^2$$

Write a procedure `sum-of-odds` that sums the first n odd integers. Test your procedure by evaluating it for all values of n from 1 to 10 to see that each is the perfect square of the number of terms.

Exercise 3.12: `n-tuple->integer`

Define a procedure `n-tuple->integer` that converts a nonempty n-tuple of digits into the number having those digits. Test your program on the following:

```
(n-tuple->integer '(3 1 4 6)) ⟹ 3146
(n-tuple->integer '(0)) ⟹ 0
(n-tuple->integer '()) ⟹ Error: bad argument () to n-tuple->integer
(+ (n-tuple->integer '(1 2 3)) (n-tuple->integer '(3 2 1))) ⟹ 444
```

Exercise 3.13

If `ls` is a list of length 1000, how much "cdring" in `ls` is necessary in each of the three programs for `list-ref` presented in this section in order to find `(list-ref ls 4)`? Which of the three programs is most efficient?

3.3 Exact Arithmetic and Data Abstraction

The numbers discussed above were either integers for which the arithmetic operations of +, -, and * give exact results or are inexact numbers, which may be rounded decimal representations and for which the arithmetic operations give approximations. For division, even if the numerator and denominator are exact integers, the result may be an approximation; for example, (/ 1 3) might return the inexact number 0.33333333333333, which is not $\frac{1}{3}$. It is possible to do arithmetic with fractions (rational numbers) and get answers as exact fractions when arithmetic operations are performed. In this section, we shall develop such an exact arithmetic.

---

[3] Let $S = 1 + 3 + 5 + \cdots + (2n - 1)$. We get the same sum if we add the numbers in reverse order, so $S = (2n - 1) + (2n - 3) + \cdots + 3 + 1$. Adding the first terms of each sum, we get $2n$. Adding the second terms of each sum, we get $2n$ and in general adding corresponding terms in the two sums, we get the same sum, $2n$. There are n such corresponding pairs of terms, so $2S = n(2n)$ and $S = n^2$.

Data Abstraction and Numbers

Recall that a fraction (or rational number) $\frac{a}{b}$ is composed of two integers: a is its numerator, and b, which must be different from zero, is its denominator. For the moment, we do not concern ourselves with how the rational number or fraction is represented. We shall come back to that later in this section. For the time being, we use the fact that a rational number has a numerator and a denominator and assume that we have access to these two parts by means of two procedures numr and denr. Thus if rtl represents a rational number, then (numr rtl) is its numerator and (denr rtl) its denominator. These are called the two selector procedures for rational numbers, just as car and cdr were the two selector procedures for lists. We shall also assume that we have a constructor procedure that reassembles the rational number from its numerator and denominator. We call this constructor procedure make-ratl because it builds (or makes) a rational number from its parts. Thus for a rational number rtl, the expression

```
(make-ratl (numr rtl) (denr rtl))
```

is just the rational number rtl again. For example, (make-ratl 3 5) is the rational number with numerator 3 and denominator 5.

With these selector and constructor procedures, we proceed to build up the arithmetic of rational numbers without concerning ourselves with the representation of the rational numbers. We begin with the definition of a predicate rzero?, which tests whether a rational number rtl is equal to zero. We use the fact that a rational number is equal to zero only when its numerator is equal to zero. Thus we have:

Program 3.8   rzero?

```
(define rzero?
  (lambda (rtl)
    (zero? (numr rtl))))
```

Now we recall how two fractions are combined by the various arithmetic operations. For example, the sum of the fractions $\frac{a}{b}$ and $\frac{c}{d}$ has the numerator $(a*d) + (b*c)$ and the denominator $b*d$. Thus if x and y are two rational numbers, we define the sum procedure, say r+, in Program 3.9. The first argument to make-ratl is the numerator of the sum, and the second argument to make-ratl is the denominator of the sum.

Program 3.9 r+

```
(define r+
  (lambda (x y)
    (make-ratl
      (+ (* (numr x) (denr y)) (* (numr y) (denr x)))
      (* (denr x) (denr y)))))
```

Since the product of two fractions $\frac{a}{b}$ and $\frac{c}{d}$ is the fraction having numerator $a*c$ and denominator $b*d$, we can define the product procedure **r*** for rational numbers as follows:

Program 3.10 r*

```
(define r*
  (lambda (x y)
    (make-ratl
      (* (numr x) (numr y))
      (* (denr x) (denr y)))))
```

Similarly, the difference procedure **r-** is defined by

Program 3.11 r-

```
(define r-
  (lambda (x y)
    (make-ratl
      (- (* (numr x) (denr y)) (* (numr y) (denr x)))
      (* (denr x) (denr y)))))
```

If we invert a nonzero rational number $\frac{a}{b}$, we get $\frac{b}{a}$. The procedure **rinvert** in Program 3.12 carries out this operation . We now define the division operator **r/** in Program 3.13. The definition of **r/** reflects the familiar rule, "invert the divisor and multiply."

Another useful procedure is the predicate **r=** that tests whether two rational numbers are equal. Two rational numbers $\frac{a}{b}$ and $\frac{c}{d}$ are equal if $ad = bc$. Thus we can write the definition of **r=** given in Program 3.14.

Program 3.12 `rinvert`

```
(define rinvert
  (lambda (rtl)
    (if (rzero? rtl)
        (error "rinvert: Cannot invert " rtl)
        (make-ratl (denr rtl) (numr rtl)))))
```

Program 3.13 `r/`

```
(define r/
  (lambda (x y)
    (r* x (rinvert y))))
```

Program 3.14 `r=`

```
(define r=
  (lambda (x y)
    (= (* (numr x) (denr y)) (* (numr y) (denr x)))))
```

Program 3.15 `rpositive?`

```
(define rpositive?
  (lambda (rtl)
    (or (and (positive? (numr rtl)) (positive? (denr rtl)))
        (and (negative? (numr rtl)) (negative? (denr rtl))))))
```

We can similarly define a predicate **rpositive?** by using the fact that a rational number $\frac{a}{b}$ is positive if a and b are both positive or both negative. Thus we get Program 3.15.

The predicate **r>** tests whether a rational number **x** is greater than a rational number **y** by testing whether their difference is positive. This leads to Program 3.16. The definition of the predicate **r<**, which tests whether **x** is less than **y** is obtained by interchanging **x** and **y** in the last line of the definition of **r>**.

Many other familiar procedures can be built up in terms of these, and we can go on to develop an extensive arithmetic for rational numbers using

Program 3.16   r>

```
(define r>
  (lambda (x y)
    (rpositive? (r- x y))))
```

Program 3.17   max

```
(define max
  (lambda (x y)
    (if (> x y)
        x
        y)))
```

Program 3.18   rmax

```
(define rmax
  (lambda (x y)
    (if (r> x y)
        x
        y)))
```

what we have constructed up to this point. For example, we can define the procedure **rmax**, which selects the larger of its two arguments, or its second argument if they are equal. Before defining **rmax**, we show in Program 3.17 how the Scheme procedure **max** for two numbers can be defined. Similarly, we can define **rmax** as shown in Program 3.18.

The definition of the procedure **rmin**, which returns the smaller of its two arguments or the second if they are equal, is obtained from the definition of **rmax** by changing the **r>** to **r<**. We are now in a position to make an important observation. When two procedure definitions are as similar as **rmax** and **rmin**, we could have written one definition from which both could be obtained by passing the predicate **r>** or **r<** as an argument to the procedure. To demonstrate how this is done, let us use the parameter **pred** to stand for either of these predicates. Then we define the procedure **extreme-value** in Program 3.19.

Program 3.19   `extreme-value`

```
(define extreme-value
  (lambda (pred x y)
    (if (pred x y)
        x
        y)))
```

Now we can simply write

```
(define rmax
  (lambda (x y)
    (extreme-value r> x y)))
```

and

```
(define rmin
  (lambda (x y)
    (extreme-value r< x y)))
```

We get as a bonus the fact that **max** and **min** can also be obtained from **extreme-value**, for if **x** and **y** are real numbers, we can write

```
(define max
  (lambda (x y)
    (extreme-value > x y)))
```

and for **min** we have

```
(define min
  (lambda (x y)
    (extreme-value < x y)))
```

The predicates that were passed as arguments to the procedure **extreme-value** are procedures themselves. The ability to pass procedures as arguments to other procedures is a powerful tool in Scheme, and we shall make use of it many times. In Chapter 7, when we talk about procedures that return other procedures, we shall see a better way of writing these definitions.

We can also define a procedure **rprint** that prints the results of our calculations in the familiar form as a fraction by using the procedure **writeln**.

Program 3.20   `rprint`

```
(define rprint
  (lambda (rtl)
    (writeln (numr rtl) "/" (denr rtl))))
```

Thus if `rtl` represents the fraction $\frac{2}{3}$, (`rprint rtl`) displays 2/3.

We have gone a long way in our exact arithmetic using the selector procedures `numr` and `denr` and the constructor procedure `make-ratl` without ever saying what they are. Using the arithmetic operations for the rationals `r+`, `r*`, `r-`, and `r/` and the other procedures that we have defined, we can write many complicated programs using exact arithmetic on rational numbers. If someone were to give us the three procedures `numr`, `denr`, and `make-ratl`, we would not have to know how they are defined in order to use them, and other procedures depending on them, in programs we write.

If, in the course of writing a program, we need a rational number with numerator 2 and denominator 3, we simply write (`make-ratl 2 3`) for that number. Thus if we were writing a rational number package for someone else to use, all we would have to provide the user with are the procedures `numr`, `denr`, `make-ratl`, and the other procedures defined in terms of these and the user can compute with the package without ever being concerned about how the procedures `numr`, `denr`, and `make-ratl` themselves are defined. We have treated the rational numbers as *abstract data*. We are now free to choose any representation of the rational numbers we wish and to define the selectors and constructor procedures appropriately for the data representation we choose. What is especially nice about this approach is that we are free to change the data representation any time we wish, and when we only redefine the three procedures `numr`, `denr`, and `make-ratl`, the rest of the procedures we have written still work and do not have to be changed in any way. That is the power of abstraction.

So far, we have been able to write all of our procedures, but we have not been able to test them because we have not been given the constructor and the selectors. We have reached the point where we choose a representation of the rational numbers and define the selector and constructor procedures. For the first method of defining them, let us take the representation of the rational number with numerator `a` and denominator `b` to be (`list a b`), where `b` is never to be zero. We can then define the selectors `numr` and `denr` for the rational number `rtl` and the constructor `make-ratl` for the integers `int1` and `int2` as shown in Program 3.21. With these definitions, all of the

```
(define numr
  (lambda (rtl)
    (car rtl)))

(define denr
  (lambda (rtl)
    (cadr rtl)))

(define make-ratl
  (lambda (int1 int2)
    (if (zero? int2)
        (error "make-ratl: The denominator cannot be zero.")
        (list int1 int2))))
```

procedures we previously defined can be used with no modifications to make up our package for rational arithmetic.

To find the denominator of a rational number using the given list representation, we have to take the **car** of the **cdr** of the list representing the number. It is possible to have a representation that makes the denominator operation more efficient and uses less storage space if we use a dotted pair to represent the rational number. Thus the rational number that has numerator **a** and denominator **b** is represented by the dotted pair (a . b). Then the selectors are

```
(define numr
  (lambda (rtl)
    (car rtl)))

(define denr
  (lambda (rtl)
    (cdr rtl)))
```

and the constructor is

```
(define make-ratl
  (lambda (int1 int2)
    (if (zero? int2)
        (error "make-ratl: The denominator cannot be zero.")
        (cons int1 int2))))
```

3.3 Exact Arithmetic and Data Abstraction   *91*

Another natural representation to consider for the rational number with numerator **3** and denominator **4** is the symbol **3/4**. We do not have the tools to define the selectors and the constructor for this representation yet. A knowledge of how to operate with string and character data types is necessary to do so. However, each of the possibilities for representing the rational numbers gives rise to different definitions of the procedures **numr**, **denr**, and **make-ratl**, but none of the other procedures defined in our rational arithmetic package has to be changed in any way. They are all *representation independent*. If you want to change representations, only the constructor and selector procedures would have to be changed; the rest of the procedures would still be valid with no alterations. We defined only the three procedures **numr**, **denr**, and **make-ratl** in terms of the data objects (lists or dotted pairs in the examples) used by the computer; the rest of the procedures were defined in terms of these selector and constructor procedures with no reference to the data objects. Since the data objects were not specified in advance, we treat the data abstractly and develop the rest of the procedures using the abstract data. We can then specify concrete realizations of the data objects (or *data structures*) to run the procedures. This is data abstraction.

Exercises

Use the procedures defined in this chapter for rational arithmetic in defining the following procedures.

Exercise 3.14: **rminus**
Define a procedure **rminus** that takes a rational number as its argument and returns the negative of that number.

Exercise 3.15: **same-sign?**
Consider this definition of **rpositive?**:

```
(define rpositive?
  (lambda (rtl)
    (same-sign? (numr rtl) (denr rtl))))
```

Define **same-sign?** so that **rpositive?** is correct.

Exercise 3.16: **rabs**
Define a procedure **rabs** that takes a rational number and returns its absolute value.

Exercise 3.17: `make-ratl`

Scheme has a procedure **gcd** that takes as arguments two integers and returns their greatest common divisor, that is, the largest positive integer, which divides into the two given integers. For example,

```
(gcd 8 12)   ⟹  4
(gcd 8 -12)  ⟹  4
(gcd 0 5)    ⟹  5
```

Write the definition of the procedure **make-ratl** so that (**make-ratl a b**) is a list (**p q**) in which $p/q = a/b$ and p/q is reduced to lowest terms (so that 1 is the greatest common divisor of p and q) and in which q is positive. Test your procedure with:

```
(make-ratl 24 30)  ⟹   (4 5)
(make-ratl -10 15) ⟹   (-2 3)
(make-ratl 8 -10)  ⟹   (-4 5)
(make-ratl -6 -9)  ⟹   (2 3)
(make-ratl 0 8)    ⟹   (0 1)
```

Using this version of **make-ratl** ensures that the internal representation of each rational number is unique.

4   Data Driven Recursion

4.1 Overview

In this chapter, we continue our study of recursion over the top-level items in lists. Then we make the extension to recursion over the items in the nested sublists as well, giving us tree recursion. In certain of our computations, a return table is built while operations that have yet to be performed wait for recursive procedure calls to return values. We discuss another way of doing the computations, called iteration, in which there are no operations waiting for procedure calls to return values, and hence no return table need be constructed. The factorial procedure and Fibonacci sequences are introduced. To compare the efficiency of various methods for computing them, we investigate the growth of execution time as the argument grows, demonstrating linear and exponential growth rates.

4.2 Flat Recursion

We begin with three more examples of recursive procedures, with the recursion being done over the top-level items in lists. In our examples of recursion involving lists, we made the recursive step by applying the procedure to the **cdr** of the list. The **car** of the list was then treated as a unit, which is why the recursion was over the top-level items in the list. We refer to a recursion over the top-level items of a list as a *flat recursion*, and we say that the procedure so defined is *flatly recursive* or simply a *flat procedure*.

The first procedure we define is the two-argument version of the Scheme procedure **append**, which has as parameters two lists, **ls1** and **ls2** and builds a list that consists of the top-level items in `ls1` followed by the top-level items in `ls2`. We say that we are appending `ls2` to (the end of) `ls1`. For example,

```
(append '(a b c) '(c d)) ⟹ (a b c c d)
(append '() '(a b c)) ⟹ (a b c)
```

We define **append** using recursion on the first list, `ls1`. Cdring on `ls1` ultimately produces the base case in which `ls1` is empty. In the base case, when `ls1` is empty, `ls2` is returned. Thus we can begin the definition with the base case:

```
(define append
  (lambda (ls1 ls2)
    (if (null? ls1)
        ls2
        ... )))
```

To express (`append ls1 ls2`) in terms of (`append (cdr ls1) ls2`), observe that (`append (cdr ls1) ls2`) differs from (`append ls1 ls2`) only in the absence of the first top-level item in `ls1`. For example, if `ls1` is (a b c) and `ls2` is (d e), then (`append (cdr ls1) ls2`) gives us (b c d e), and only (`car ls1`) remains to be included. Thus when `ls1` is not empty, (`append ls1 ls2`) is the same as (`cons (car ls1) (append (cdr ls1) ls2)`). We can therefore complete the definition of **append**.

Program 4.1   append

```
(define append
  (lambda (ls1 ls2)
    (if (null? ls1)
        ls2
        (cons (car ls1) (append (cdr ls1) ls2)))))
```

Another procedure often used is the Scheme procedure **reverse**, which takes a list as its argument and builds a list consisting of the top-level items in its argument list taken in reverse order. For example,

```
(reverse '(1 2 3 4 5)) ⟹ (5 4 3 2 1)
(reverse '((1 2) (3 4) (5 6))) ⟹ ((5 6) (3 4) (1 2))
```

We again use recursion and look at what **reverse** does to the cdr of the list **ls**. In the first example above,

(reverse '(2 3 4 5)) $\Longrightarrow$ (5 4 3 2)

To get **reverse** of (1 2 3 4 5) from (5 4 3 2), we must put the 1 into the last position in the list. We can do this with the procedure **append** if we make the 1 into a list (1) and then append (1) to the end of (5 4 3 2). This is the key to writing the definition of the procedure **reverse**.

We take the empty list as the base case and note that if we reverse the items in the empty list, we still have the empty list. Thus we can begin the definition with the terminating condition, which says that if the list is empty, the empty list is returned.

```
(define reverse
  (lambda (ls)
    (if (null? ls)
        '()
        ... )))
```

To get (**reverse ls**) from (**reverse (cdr ls)**), we must append the list that is the value of (**reverse (cdr ls)**) to the front of the list that is the value of (**list (car ls)**). We then complete the definition with

Program 4.2 **reverse**

```
(define reverse
  (lambda (ls)
    (if (null? ls)
        '()
        (append (reverse (cdr ls)) (list (car ls))))))
```

A list of numbers (or n-tuple) is said to be sorted in increasing order if each number in the list is less than or equal to the number following it in the list. For example, (2.3 4.7 5 8.1) is sorted in increasing order. If we have two lists, each sorted in increasing order, we can merge them into a single list in increasing order. For example, if the list given above is merged with the list (1.7 4.7), we get the list (1.7 2.3 4.7 4.7 5 8.1).

Let us now write a procedure **merge**, which takes two n-tuples, **sorted-ntpl1** and **sorted-ntpl2**, which have already been sorted in increasing order, and builds the list obtained by merging them into one sorted n-tuple. If either list is empty, **merge** returns the other list. Otherwise we compare the car of the lists and cons the smaller one onto the list obtained by merging the rest of the two lists. This analysis leads to the following definition:

Program 4.3   merge

```
(define merge
  (lambda (sorted-ntpl1 sorted-ntpl2)
    (cond
      ((null? sorted-ntpl1) sorted-ntpl2)
      ((null? sorted-ntpl2) sorted-ntpl1)
      ((< (car sorted-ntpl1) (car sorted-ntpl2))
       (cons (car sorted-ntpl1)
             (merge (cdr sorted-ntpl1) sorted-ntpl2)))
      (else (cons (car sorted-ntpl2)
                  (merge sorted-ntpl1 (cdr sorted-ntpl2)))))))
```

We shall use **merge** in Chapter 10 when we discuss the sorting of lists.

The definition of **reverse** used the procedure **append**, which was defined earlier. It does not matter which was defined first, as long as both are defined when the procedure **reverse** is invoked.

The test of whether a nonnegative integer is even or odd gives us another good example of one procedure using another in its definition. There are many more direct ways of defining the predicates **even?** and **odd?**, but the one we present now was chosen because it illustrates how each of two procedures invokes the other in its definition. We use the fact that an integer is even if its predecessor is odd and odd if its predecessor is even. Starting with any nonnegative integer, reducing it successively by 1 will eventually bring it to 0, which is even. This analysis leads us to the following definitions:

Program 4.4   even?

```
(define even?
  (lambda (int)
    (if (zero? int)
        #t
        (odd? (sub1 int)))))
```

and

Program 4.5   odd?

```
(define odd?
  (lambda (int)
    (if (zero? int)
        #f
        (even? (sub1 int)))))
```

In the definition of the procedure **even?**, the procedure **odd?** is called, and in the definition of **odd?**, the procedure **even?** is called. This is an example of *mutual recursion* in which each procedure calls the other. The two procedures are said to be *mutually recursive*.

The procedure **remove-1st** defined in Chapter 2 removed the first top-level occurrence of an item from a list of items. Let us now define a procedure **remove** that removes *all* top-level occurrences of **item** from a list **ls**. As before, the recursion will be flat, but now we continue the recursion until all top-level occurrences of **item** have been removed from **ls**. The base condition is (**null? ls**), and when it is true, the empty list is returned. Thus we begin our definition with:

```
(define remove
  (lambda (item ls)
    (cond
      ((null? ls) '())
      ... )))
```

Next, if **ls** is not empty, (**remove item (cdr ls)**) is exactly the same as (**remove item ls**) when the first item in **ls** is **item**, for that item is removed. On the other hand, when the first item in **ls** is not **item**, then we must cons it onto (**remove item (cdr ls)**) in order to get (**remove item ls**). Thus we complete the definition, which is presented in Program 4.6.

The definition of **remove** differs from that of **remove-1st** in the middle clause of the cond expression. In **remove-1st** the recursion stopped when the first occurrence of **item** was found, whereas in **remove** the recursion continues. This difference is typical of what we see if we compare the definitions of procedures that stop after the first occurrence of an item to those that continue to the end of the list. The procedure **remove** uses **equal?** to test for sameness. You could write a version named **remq** that uses **eq?** to test for sameness and

Program 4.6 `remove`

```
(define remove
  (lambda (item ls)
    (cond
      ((null? ls) '())
      ((equal? (car ls) item) (remove item (cdr ls)))
      (else (cons (car ls) (remove item (cdr ls)))))))
```

a version named `remv` that uses `eqv?` to test for sameness. The exercises contain other procedures involving flat recursion that go to the end of the lists instead of stopping after the first occurrence of a given item.

Exercises

Exercise 4.1: `insert-left`
Define a procedure `insert-left` with parameters `new`, `old`, and `ls` that builds a list obtained by inserting the item `new` to the left of each top-level occurrence of the item `old` in the list `ls`. Test your procedure on:

```
(insert-left 'z 'a '(a b a c a)) ⟹ (z a b z a c z a)
(insert-left 0 1 '(0 1 0 1))  ⟹ (0 0 1 0 0 1)
(insert-left 'dog 'cat '(my dog is fun)) ⟹ (my dog is fun)
(insert-left 'two 'one '()) ⟹ ()
```

Exercise 4.2: `insert-right`
Define a procedure `insert-right` with parameters `new`, `old`, and `ls` that builds a list obtained by inserting the item `new` to the right of each top-level occurrence of the item `old` in the list `ls`. Test your procedure on:

```
(insert-right 'z 'a '(a b a c a)) ⟹ (a z b a z c a z)
(insert-right 0 1 '(0 1 0 1))  ⟹ (0 1 0 0 1 0)
(insert-right 'dog 'cat '(my dog is fun)) ⟹ (my dog is fun)
(insert-right 'two 'one '()) ⟹ ()
```

Exercise 4.3: `subst`
Define a procedure `subst` with parameters `new`, `old`, and `ls` that builds a list obtained by replacing each top-level occurrence of the item `old` in the list `ls` by the item `new`. Test your procedure on:

```
(subst 'z 'a '(a b a c a))  ⟹  (z b z c z)
(subst 0 1 '(0 1 0 1))  ⟹  (0 0 0 0)
(subst 'dog 'cat '(my dog is fun))  ⟹  (my dog is fun)
(subst 'two 'one '())  ⟹  ()
```

Exercise 4.4: `deepen-1`
Define a procedure `deepen-1` with parameter `ls` that wraps a pair of parentheses around each top-level item in `ls`. Test your procedure on:

```
(deepen-1 '(a b c d))  ⟹  ((a) (b) (c) (d))
(deepen-1 '((a b) (c (d e)) f))  ⟹  (((a b)) ((c (d e))) (f))
(deepen-1 '())  ⟹  ()
```

4.3 Deep Recursion

In this section, we consider recursion over all the sublists of a list. We say that the sublist (b c) is *nested* in the list (a (b c)). It is convenient to have some way of describing how deep the nesting is. If an item is not enclosed by parentheses, that item has *nesting level* 0. For example, the item `bird` has nesting level 0. The elements of a list such as (a b c) have nesting level 1. Thus b has nesting level 1 while the whole list (a b c) has nesting level 0. Then each additional layer of parentheses adds 1 to the nesting level, so that the nesting level of the item c in (a (b (c d))) is 3. The objects in the list that have nesting level 1 are the *top-level* objects of the list. The top-level objects in the list (a (b c) (d (e f))) are a, (b c), and (d (e f)).

We define a procedure `count-all` with parameter `ls` that counts those items in the list `ls` that are not pairs. For example

1. (count-all '((a b) c () ((d (e))))) ⟹ 6
2. (count-all '(() () ())) ⟹ 3
3. (count-all '(((())))) ⟹ 1
4. (count-all '()) ⟹ 0

To simplify our discussion, we use the adjective *atomic* to describe an item that is not a pair. In this case, all of the atomic items in the list were counted, not just the top-level items. Since the empty list is not a pair, the empty lists that are included as items within the lists of Examples 1, 2, and 3 are counted as atomic items in the lists.

The base case for the recursion is the empty list, for in that case, `count-all` returns zero. Thus the definition begins with:

```
(define count-all
  (lambda (ls)
    (cond
      ((null? ls) 0)
      ... )))
```

If `ls` is not empty, we proceed as we did in our previous examples and consider how we can get (`count-all ls`) from (`count-all (cdr ls)`). The two differ by the number of atomic items in (`car ls`). If (`car ls`) is atomic, then (`count-all ls`) has a value that is just one greater than the value of (`count-all (cdr ls)`). Thus we can continue the definition with:

```
(define count-all
  (lambda (ls)
    (cond
      ((null? ls) 0)
      ((not (pair? (car ls))) (add1 (count-all (cdr ls))))
      ... )))
```

When (`car ls`) is a pair (as is the case in Examples 1 and 3), we must count the atomic items in (`car ls`) and add that amount to the value of (`count-all (cdr ls)`) to get the value of (`count-all ls`). Thus we complete the definition with:

Program 4.7 `count-all`

```
(define count-all
  (lambda (ls)
    (cond
      ((null? ls) 0)
      ((not (pair? (car ls))) (add1 (count-all (cdr ls))))
      (else (+ (count-all (car ls)) (count-all (cdr ls)))))))
```

In fact, we can combine the last two cond clauses if we write the definition as follows:

```
(define count-all
  (lambda (ls)
    (cond
      ((null? ls) 0)
      (else (+ (if (pair? (car ls))
                   (count-all (car ls))
                   1)
               (count-all (cdr ls)))))))
```

The recursion described differs from flat recursion in that when the car of the list is a pair, we apply the procedure being defined both to the car and to the cdr of the list. In flat recursion, the procedure being defined was applied only to the cdr of the list. When the recursion is over all of the atomic items of a list, so that in the recursive step the procedure is applied to the car of the list and to the cdr of the list, we call it a *deep recursion*. A procedure defined using a deep recursion will be referred to as a *deeply recursive* procedure or simply a *deep procedure* to distinguish it from a flat procedure. Deep recursion is also called *tree recursion*.

Before leaving the definition of count-all, we should observe that we could have avoided the use of the not in the second cond clause by changing the order in which we considered the last two cases. That would give us the definition:

```
(define count-all
  (lambda (ls)
    (cond
      ((null? ls) 0)
      ((pair? (car ls))
       (+ (count-all (car ls)) (count-all (cdr ls))))
      (else (+ 1 (count-all (cdr ls)))))))
```

Many of the flat procedures defined earlier have analogs that are deep procedures. To illustrate this, we consider the procedure remove-all, which is analogous to remove. The procedure remove-all removes all occurrences of an item item from a list ls. For example,

```
(remove-all 'a '((a b (c a)) (b (a c) a)))  ⟹  ((b (c)) (b (c)))
```

The base case is the empty list, and when ls is empty, the empty list is returned. Thus we begin the definition of remove-all with:

```
(define remove-all
  (lambda (item ls)
    (cond
      ((null? ls) '())
      ... )))
```

We next express (remove-all item ls) in terms of (remove-all item (cdr ls)). If (equal? (car ls) item) returns true, then (remove-all item ls) is the same as (remove-all item (cdr ls)), and we have:

```
(define remove-all
  (lambda (item ls)
    (cond
      ((null? ls) '())
      ((equal? (car ls) item) (remove-all item (cdr ls)))
      ... )))
```

If (car ls) is a pair that is not the same as item, then we remove all occurrences of item from (car ls) and cons the result onto (remove-all item (cdr ls)). Thus,

```
(define remove-all
  (lambda (item ls)
    (cond
      ((null? ls) '())
      ((equal? (car ls) item) (remove-all item (cdr ls)))
      ((pair? (car ls))
       (cons (remove-all item (car ls)) (remove-all item (cdr ls))))
      ... )))
```

Finally, if (car ls) is atomic and is not the same as item, we must cons it back onto (remove-all item (cdr ls)) in order to get (remove-all item ls). We wrap up the definition in Program 4.8. We can combine the last two cond clauses if we rewrite the definition as follows:

```
(define remove-all
  (lambda (item ls)
    (cond
      ((null? ls) '())
      ((equal? (car ls) item) (remove-all item (cdr ls)))
      (else (cons (if (pair? (car ls))
                      (remove-all item (car ls))
                      (car ls))
                  (remove-all item (cdr ls)))))))
```

Program 4.8   `remove-all`

```
(define remove-all
  (lambda (item ls)
    (cond
      ((null? ls) '())
      ((equal? (car ls) item) (remove-all item (cdr ls)))
      ((pair? (car ls))
       (cons (remove-all item (car ls)) (remove-all item (cdr ls))))
      (else (cons (car ls) (remove-all item (cdr ls)))))))
```

In this example, we again see that when (`car ls`) is a pair not equal to `item`, the procedure `remove-all` is applied recursively to both the `car` and the `cdr` of `ls`. Thus `remove-all` displays this characteristic behavior of deeply recursive procedures.

We used `equal?` to test for sameness in the definition of `remove-all`. If the arguments to which `item` is bound are always symbols, we can use `eq?` to test for sameness. In this case, we know that the item that is the same as the symbol we are removing is never a pair, so it is expedient to test for `pair?` first. We can write the definition of `remq-all` as shown in Program 4.9. We can similarly define `remv-all`, which uses `eqv?` in place of `eq?`.

Program 4.9   `remq-all`

```
(define remq-all
  (lambda (symbl ls)
    (cond
      ((null? ls) '())
      ((pair? (car ls))
       (cons (remq-all symbl (car ls)) (remq-all symbl (cdr ls))))
      ((eq? (car ls) symbl) (remq-all symbl (cdr ls)))
      (else (cons (car ls) (remq-all symbl (cdr ls)))))))
```

When the flat procedure `reverse` is applied to a list, we get a new list with the top-level objects in reverse order. Thus,

(`reverse '(a (b c) (d (e f))))` $\Longrightarrow$ `((d (e f)) (b c) a)`

We can also define a procedure `reverse-all` that not only reverses the order of the top-level objects in the list but also reverses the order of the objects at each nesting level with the sublists. We would then have:

(reverse-all '(a (b c) (d (e f)))) $\Longrightarrow$ (((f e) d) (c b) a)

For the base case, the list is empty, and (reverse-all '()) returns the empty list. Thus the definition begins with:

```
(define reverse-all
  (lambda (ls)
    (cond
      ((null? ls) '())
      ... )))
```

To carry out the recursion, we build (reverse-all ls) from (reverse-all (cdr ls)). In the latter, all of the elements of (reverse-all (cdr ls)) are already in the correct order. We have to see how to include the items of (car ls). If (car ls) is a pair, we have to reverse its elements and place them at the end of (reverse-all (cdr ls)) with the procedure append. Thus we have:

```
(define reverse-all
  (lambda (ls)
    (cond
      ((null? ls) '())
      ((pair? (car ls))
       (append (reverse-all (cdr ls))
               (list (reverse-all (car ls)))))
      ... )))
```

In the remaining case, (car ls) is not a pair, so we merely place it at the end of (reverse-all (cdr ls)).

```
(define reverse-all
  (lambda (ls)
    (cond
      ((null? ls) '())
      ((pair? (car ls))
       (append (reverse-all (cdr ls))
               (list (reverse-all (car ls)))))
      (else
       (append (reverse-all (cdr ls))
               (list (car ls)))))))
```

Once again, in this recursion we see the typical form of a deep recursion. We applied `reverse-all` to both the car and the cdr of the list in the second cond clause.

It is instructive to look back at this definition of `reverse-all` and observe the similarity between the two alternatives that begin with `append` in the last two cond clauses. They differ only in the application of `reverse-all` to `(car ls)` in the last line. Because of this similarity, we can combine the two append expressions into one expression by putting the conditional branch after `(reverse-all (cdr ls))`. We get the following version of the definition of `reverse-all`:

Program 4.10 `reverse-all`

```
(define reverse-all
  (lambda (ls)
    (if (null? ls)
        '()
        (append (reverse-all (cdr ls))
                (list (if (pair? (car ls))
                          (reverse-all (car ls))
                          (car ls)))))))
```

In this section, we have seen how to write deeply recursive procedures. These have the characteristic property that a recursive step applies the procedure being defined to both the car and the cdr of the list.

Exercises

Exercise 4.5: `subst-all, substq-all`
Define a procedure `subst-all` with call structure `(subst-all new old ls)` that replaces each occurrence of the item `old` in a list `ls` with the item `new`. Test your procedure on:

```
(subst-all 'z 'a '(a (b (a c)) (a (d a))))
                        ⟹ (z (b (z c)) (z (d z)))
(subst-all 0 '(1) '(((1) (0)))) ⟹ ((0 (0)))
(subst-all 'one 'two '()) ⟹ ()
```

Also define a procedure `substq-all` in which the parameters `new` and `old` are only bound to symbols, so that `eq?` can be used for the sameness test.

Exercise 4.6: `insert-left-all`

Define a procedure `insert-left-all` with call structure `(insert-left-all new old ls)` that inserts the item `new` to the left of each occurrence of the item `old` in the list `ls`. Test your procedure on:

```
(insert-left-all 'z 'a '(a ((b a) ((a (c)))))))
                            ⟹ (z a ((b z a) ((z a (c)))))
(insert-left-all 'z 'a '(((a)))) ⟹ (((z a)))
(insert-left-all 'z 'a '()) ⟹ ()
```

Exercise 4.7: `sum-all`

Define a procedure `sum-all` that finds the sum of the numbers in a list that may contain nested sublists of numbers. Test your procedure on:

```
(sum-all '((1 3) (5 7) (9 11))) ⟹ 36
(sum-all '(1 (3 (5 (7 (9)))))) ⟹ 25
(sum-all '()) ⟹ 0
```

4.4 Tree Representation of Lists

There is a convenient way of thinking of a list graphically as a *tree* that has its root at the top and grows by branching downward. The original list is a *node* that is located at the *root*. Each top-level object in the list forms a new node connected to the root node by a *branch*. Each sublist itself then becomes the root of a *subtree*, and the tree grows downward. For example, the tree representing the list (a (b c d) ((e f) g)) is given in Figure 4.11. Each item or sublist of the original list is a node of this tree. Each sublist is itself the root of a subtree of the original tree. Thus ((e f) g) corresponds to the subtree given in Figure 4.12.

An item at the lower end of a branch that is not the top end of another branch is called a *leaf* of the tree. We can readily see how deeply an item is nested in the list by looking at its nesting level in the tree. For example, in Figure 4.11, the leaf a is at nesting level 1 and the leaf e at nesting level 3. We say that the *depth* of a list is the maximum of the nesting levels of all of its items. The list (a (b c d) ((e f) g)) has depth 3. With the tree growing downward, we can say that the depth of a list is the nesting level of its lowest leaves.

To *traverse* a tree, that is, to move down the tree from one node to another, we use the procedures `car` and `cdr`. Taking the `car` of a list corresponds to

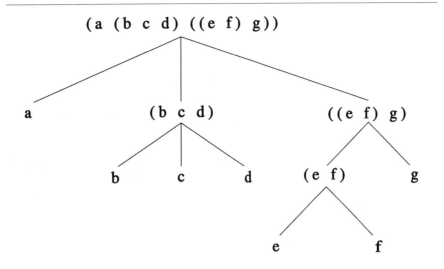

Figure 4.11 Tree representation of the list (a (b c d) ((e f) g))

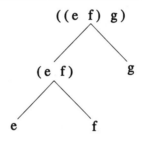

Figure 4.12 The subtree ((e f) g)

moving down one node on the leftmost branch of the tree. Taking the cdr of a list corresponds to considering the tree that is left when the leftmost branch is omitted. Thus when taking the car, we move down one level on the tree. When taking the cdr, we stay at the same level of the tree. With an appropriate sequence of car and cdr applications, we can reach any node of a tree. For example, in the tree in Figure 4.11, the node (e f) is reached using caaddr.

We define a procedure depth that takes item as its argument and returns its depth. The item may be either atomic or a list. If item is atomic, we

Program 4.13   depth

```
(define depth
  (lambda (item)
    (if (not (pair? item))
        0
        (max (add1 (depth (car item))) (depth (cdr item))))))
```

assign it depth 0. Since the empty list is atomic, it also has depth 0. We take
as the base case for the recursive definition the test (not (pair? item)), for
that corresponds to being at a leaf of the tree. We begin the definition of
depth with:

```
(define depth
  (lambda (item)
    (if (not (pair? item))
        0
        ... )))
```

The depth of the whole tree is the larger of the depth of its leftmost branch
and the depth of the rest of its branches. Taking the car of the list moves
down one node on the leftmost branch, so that the depth of the whole leftmost
branch is one greater than the depth of (car item). The depth of the rest
of the branches is just the depth of (cdr item). This gives us the definition
displayed in Program 4.13.

The procedure depth gives us the maximum number of levels in a tree
representing its argument. We next define a procedure that gives us a list of
the leaves on the tree as a list of atomic items, where each leaf is raised out
of its sublist to be at top level. We call this procedure flatten. When we
apply it to the list (a (b c d) ((e f) g)), we get (a b c d e f g). The
parameter of the procedure flatten will be ls. The base case is the empty
list, which flattens into itself. Thus we begin the definition of flatten with:

```
(define flatten
  (lambda (ls)
    (cond
      ((null? ls) '())
      ... )))
```

When ls is not empty, we build (flatten ls) from (flatten (cdr ls))
by first determining whether (car ls) is a pair. If it is, we flatten (car ls)

and append the already flattened `(flatten (cdr ls))` to it to get `(flatten ls)`. This gives us

```
(define flatten
  (lambda (ls)
    (cond
      ((null? ls) '())
      ((pair? (car ls))
       (append (flatten (car ls)) (flatten (cdr ls))))
      ... )))
```

In the remaining case, `(car ls)` is atomic, so we cons it onto `(flatten (cdr ls))`, and we complete the definition with

Program 4.14   flatten

```
(define flatten
  (lambda (ls)
    (cond
      ((null? ls) '())
      ((pair? (car ls))
       (append (flatten (car ls)) (flatten (cdr ls))))
      (else (cons (car ls) (flatten (cdr ls)))))))
```

We have discussed flat and deep recursion. A flat recursion is over the top-level items of a list. This is equivalent to a recursion over the nodes of the corresponding tree, which are one level below the root. A deep recursion is over all of the items in the list. This is equivalent to a recursion over the leaves of the corresponding tree. That is why deep recursion is also referred to as *tree recursion*.

We conclude this section with an example of a procedure that removes an item from a list but only the first (leftmost) occurrence of that item in the list. Let us name the procedure `remove-leftmost` and look at a couple of examples.

1. `(remove-leftmost 'b '(a (b c) (c (b a))))`
$$\implies \text{(a (c) (c (b a)))}$$
2. `(remove-leftmost '(c d) '((a (b c)) ((c d) e)))`
$$\implies \text{((a (b c)) (e))}$$

In Example 1, the first b that occurs in (b c) is removed, but the second b that occurs in (c (b a)) is not removed. We denote the item to be removed by item and the list by ls. The base case is again the empty list. When ls is empty, the empty list is returned. Thus we begin the definition with the terminating condition:

```
(define remove-leftmost
  (lambda (item ls)
    (cond
      ((null? ls) '())
      ... )))
```

In order to take care of arguments like that in Example 2, we use equal? as the sameness predicate. If (car ls) is the same as item, the answer is (cdr ls), so we continue the definition with:

```
(define remove-leftmost
  (lambda (item ls)
    (cond
      ((null? ls) '())
      ((equal? (car ls) item) (cdr ls))
      ... )))
```

If (car ls) is atomic and is not the same as item, the answer is obtained by consing (car ls) to the list obtained by removing the leftmost item from (cdr ls). Thus we get:

```
(define remove-leftmost
  (lambda (item ls)
    (cond
      ((null? ls) '())
      ((equal? (car ls) item) (cdr ls))
      ((not (pair? ls))
       (cons (car ls) (remove-leftmost item (cdr ls))))
      ... )))
```

We still have the case in which (car ls) is a nonempty list not equal to item. If we analyze the recursion by looking at

```
(remove-leftmost item (cdr ls))
```

we see that we get a list with the first occurrence of item removed; but we do not know whether this was the first occurrence of item in ls. We want to

Program 4.15 `remove-leftmost`

```
(define remove-leftmost
  (lambda (item ls)
    (cond
      ((null? ls) '())
      ((equal? (car ls) item) (cdr ls))
      ((not (pair? (car ls)))
       (cons (car ls) (remove-leftmost item (cdr ls))))
      ((member-all? item (car ls))
       (cons (remove-leftmost item (car ls)) (cdr ls)))
      (else (cons (car ls) (remove-leftmost item (cdr ls)))))))
```

Program 4.16 `member-all?`

```
(define member-all?
  (lambda (item ls)
    (if (null? ls)
        #f
        (or (equal? (car ls) item)
            (and (not (pair? (car ls)))
                 (member-all? item (cdr ls)))
            (and (pair? (car ls))
                 (or (member-all? item (car ls))
                     (member-all? item (cdr ls))))))))
```

remove only the first occurrence of item in ls, and its first occurrence may
not be in (cdr ls). In order to use this kind of argument, we must first
check to see whether the first occurrence of item in ls is in (car ls). We
do that with the helping procedure member-all?, a deeply recursive version
of member?, that we define after this definition. If item is in (car ls), we
cons (remove-leftmost item (car ls)) onto (cdr ls) to get the answer.
Otherwise, we cons (car ls) onto (remove-leftmost item (cdr ls)) to
get the answer. Thus we complete the definition as shown in Program 4.15.
The definition of member-all? is presented in Program 4.16.

A look at the definition of remove-leftmost reveals that the consequent in
the third cond clause and the alternative in the else clause are the same. We
can eliminate the repetition by interchanging the order of the tests we make.
The new version is given in Program 4.17.

Program 4.17 `remove-leftmost`

```
(define remove-leftmost
  (lambda (item ls)
    (cond
      ((null? ls) '())
      ((equal? (car ls) item) (cdr ls))
      ((and (pair? (car ls)) (member-all? item (car ls)))
       (cons (remove-leftmost item (car ls)) (cdr ls)))
      (else (cons (car ls) (remove-leftmost item (cdr ls)))))))
```

The recursion in the procedure `remove-leftmost` differs from the list recursions done earlier in that we have to test whether `item` is in the car of the list before proceeding to build the answer. This means cdring through the car of the list twice in some cases. We shall return to the consideration of `remove-leftmost` in Chapter 5, where a definition is presented that avoids this double cdring. We have now seen various examples of both flat and deep (tree) recursions.

Exercises

Exercise 4.8: `count-parens-all`
Write the definition of a procedure `count-parens-all` that takes a list as its argument and counts the number of opening and closing parentheses in the list. Test your procedure on:

```
(count-parens-all '()) ⟹ 2
(count-parens-all '((a b) c)) ⟹ 4
(count-parens-all '(((a ()) b) c) () ((d) e))) ⟹ 14
```

Exercise 4.9: `count-background-all`
Define a procedure `count-background-all` that takes as its arguments `item` and a list `ls` and returns the number of items in `ls` that are not the same as `item`. Use the appropriate sameness predicate for the data shown in the examples. Test your procedure on:

```
(count-background-all 'a '((a) b (c a) d)) ⟹ 3
(count-background-all 'a '((((b (((a)) c)))))) ⟹ 2
(count-background-all 'b '()) ⟹ 0
```

Program 4.18 `fact`

```
(define fact
  (lambda (n)
    (if (zero? n)
        1
        (* n (fact (sub1 n)))))))
```

Exercise 4.10: `leftmost`

Define a procedure `leftmost` that takes a nonempty list as its argument and returns the leftmost atomic item in the list. Test your procedure on:

```
(leftmost '((a b) (c (d e)))) ⟹ a
(leftmost '((((c ((e f) g) h))))) ⟹ c
(leftmost '(() a)) ⟹ ()
```

Exercise 4.11: `rightmost`

Define a procedure `rightmost` that takes a nonempty list as its argument and returns the rightmost atomic item in the list. Test your procedure on:

```
(rightmost '((a b) (d (c d (f (g h) i) m n) u) v)) ⟹ v
(rightmost '((((((b (c))))))))) ⟹ c
(rightmost '(a ())) ⟹ ()
```

4.5 Numerical Recursion and Iteration

Recursion can also be used in numerical calculations. We consider several examples in this section. We begin with the procedure `fact`, which takes a nonnegative integer n as its parameter and returns its factorial—that is, the number multiplied successively by all the positive integers less than that number. For example, `(fact 5)` has the value $5 \times 4 \times 3 \times 2 \times 1 = 120$. We derive this procedure using much the same kind of reasoning as we used with lists, but instead of using `cdr` to reduce the size of the argument, we use `sub1`. Eventually the successive applications of `sub1` to the argument will reduce it to 0. We use the convention that the factorial of 0 is 1, so that `(fact 0)` is 1. The recursive step in this case is done by considering `(fact (sub1 n))`, which gives us the successive products of all of the positive integers less than n. To get `(fact n)` from `(fact (sub1 n))`, all we have to do is multiply it by n. From this, we get the definition for `fact` in Program 4.18.

When the procedure `fact` is applied to a number, say 3, a return table is built much the same as the one that was built for the procedure `swapper` in Chapter 2. The value of (`fact` 3) is denoted by *answer-1*. It is 3 times (`fact` 2), so the evaluation of *answer-1* must wait until *answer-2* is evaluated, where *answer-2* is (`fact` 2). Thus the first two rows of the return table are:

$$\begin{array}{ll} \textit{answer-1 is} & (* \ 3 \quad \textit{answer-2}) \\ \textit{answer-2 is} & (\texttt{fact} \ 2) \end{array}$$

When we evaluate (`fact` 2), the return table becomes

$$\begin{array}{ll} \textit{answer-1 is} & (* \ 3 \quad \textit{answer-2}) \\ \textit{answer-2 is} & (* \ 2 \quad \textit{answer-3}) \\ \textit{answer-3 is} & (\texttt{fact} \ 1) \end{array}$$

When we evaluate (`fact` 1), the return table becomes

$$\begin{array}{ll} \textit{answer-1 is} & (* \ 3 \quad \textit{answer-2}) \\ \textit{answer-2 is} & (* \ 2 \quad \textit{answer-3}) \\ \textit{answer-3 is} & (* \ 1 \quad \textit{answer-4}) \\ \textit{answer-4 is} & (\texttt{fact} \ 0) \end{array}$$

where (`fact` 0) is 1. Now that we have found that *answer-4* is 1, we work our way up the table, replacing each answer on the right side by the value obtained for it in the row below. This process is known as *backward substitution*. This gives us:

$$\begin{array}{ll} \textit{answer-4 is} & 1 \\ \textit{answer-3 is} & 1 \\ \textit{answer-2 is} & 2 \\ \textit{answer-1 is} & 6 \end{array}$$

so (`fact` 3) is 6. In finding (`fact` 3), the return table has four rows. In the last row, the value of the variable on the left was obtained directly from the terminating condition of the program. Then each of the other three variables on the right was computed with a multiplication, so there were three multiplications required to complete the computation of (`fact` 3). The building up of the return table and the subsequent backward substitution may be summarized in the following:

```
(fact 3)
(* 3 (fact 2))
(* 3 (* 2 (fact 1)))
(* 3 (* 2 (* 1 (fact 0))))
(* 3 (* 2 (* 1 1)))
(* 3 (* 2 1))
(* 3 2)
6
```

In general, to find the factorial of the number n, there would be $n + 1$ invocations of procedure fact. Thus the return table has $n + 1$ rows. In the last row, the value on the right is found to be 1—the value returned when the terminating condition is true. In each of the other n rows of the return table, a multiplication is performed to find the value on the right, making a total of n multiplications to complete the computation.

We observed that a return table is constructed when we compute the factorial using the recursive procedure fact. When the terminating condition becomes true, the backward substitution must be performed on the return table to get the answer. When the computation requires the construction of a return table and backward substitution to get the answer, we say that the computation is using a *recursive process*. We now look at another way of defining a procedure to compute the factorial of a number that does not build a return table. Instead, at each recursive invocation of the procedure, the computations are performed without having to wait for other needed values, and when the terminating condition is true, the answer is already computed and is returned. In general, when the computer carries out a computation without building a return table, so that backward substitution is not necessary, the computational process is called an *iterative process*.

We have seen that in programs like the one written for fact, there is an operation waiting for the value returned by the recursive procedure call. The computational process so defined is not implemented as an iterative process. On the other hand, we saw several iterative procedures, such as member?, in which no operations waited for values returned by the recursive procedure calls. In some programming language implementations, when an iterative procedure is executed, it is still possible that a return table is built up and later reduced by backward substitution. However, in Scheme, when a procedure is intended to be iterative, the computation is always implemented in such a way that no return table is needed.

To implement the computation of the factorial procedure as an iterative process, we define a procedure named fact-it that has two parameters: n, which is the integer whose factorial we are computing, and acc, another integer, called an *accumulator*, which stores the answer at each step. Here is how it works in computing the factorial of 3. Initially, n is bound to 3 and acc is bound to 1. On each recursive invocation of fact-it, n is reduced by 1, and acc is replaced by its old value multiplied by the previous value of n. When the base case (zero? n) is true, acc is equal to the answer 6. This is illustrated in the following table. The initial values of n and acc are in the first row. The entries in the first column decrease by 1 while each entry in the second column is computed by multiplying the two entries in the preceding row.

n	acc
3	1
2	3
1	6
0	6

To define fact-it, we begin with the base case for which n is zero. When (zero? n) is true, the accumulator has the answer, so acc is returned. Thus we begin the definition with:

```
(define fact-it
  (lambda (n acc)
    (if (zero? n)
        acc
        ... )))
```

If n is not zero, we call fact-it with n reduced by one and the accumulator multiplied by n, so the definition is completed with:

Program 4.19   fact-it

```
(define fact-it
  (lambda (n acc)
    (if (zero? n)
        acc
        (fact-it (sub1 n) (* acc n)))))
```

Let's walk through an invocation (fact-it 3 1), writing the successive recursive invocations of fact-it, and finally writing the value 6 that is returned:

```
(fact-it 3 1)
(fact-it 2 3)
(fact-it 1 6)
(fact-it 0 6)
6
```

In this computation, no return table is built up waiting for uncomputed values to be returned. The accumulator is bound to the answer when the terminating condition is true, and the answer is returned without any backward substitution. The fact that there is no waiting operation on each recursive invocation of fact-it is seen when we look at the last line of the definition. After the procedure call, there is no further operation to be done. Compare this last line with the last line,

$$(* \; n \; (fact \; (sub1 \; n)))$$

in the definition of fact. We see that after the procedure fact is called, the result must still be multiplied by n. When fact-it is called, no additional operations are performed on the result. Thus fact-it runs as an iterative process, but fact does not. When we trace this iterative procedure, we see that the computation does not build up a return table of operations waiting for values to be returned.

If we count the number of times we call the procedure fact-it and the number of multiplications, we see that the total number of multiplications is the same for the procedures fact-it and fact. However, the backward substitution in the return table, which is built up when evaluating fact, requires more memory space than is needed when evaluating the iterative fact-it, which needs no return table. In the next section, we look at another example, the computation of the Fibonacci numbers, where the difference is more dramatic.

To compute the factorial of 3, we invoke (fact-it 3 1). If we do not like to write the extra argument for the accumulator, we can define an iterative version of fact that takes only one argument by writing

```
(define fact
  (lambda (n)
    (fact-it n 1)))
```

Exercises

Exercise 4.12
Enter the procedure **fact** into the computer and compute (**fact n**) for n = 10, 20, 30, 40, 50 and 100. You will have an opportunity to observe how the implementation of Scheme you are using displays large numbers.

Exercise 4.13
What happens when you invoke (**fact 3.5**)?

Exercise 4.14: **harmonic-sum-it**
Define an iterative procedure **harmonic-sum-it** that sums the first n terms of the harmonic series

$$1 + \frac{1}{2} + \frac{1}{3} + \frac{1}{4} + \frac{1}{5} + \cdots$$

Test your procedure by summing the harmonic series for 10 terms, 100 terms, 1000 terms, and 10,000 terms. It can be shown that

$$\frac{1}{2} + \frac{1}{3} + \cdots + \frac{1}{n} \leq \log n \leq 1 + \frac{1}{2} + \frac{1}{3} + \cdots + \frac{1}{n-1}$$

where $\log n$ is the natural logarithm of n. Using the Scheme procedure **log**, verify this inequality for the values of the sums computed above.

4.6 Analyzing the Fibonacci Algorithm

The following problem appeared in a textbook written in 1202 by the Italian mathematician Leonardo of Pisa, who was the son of Bonacci, so his nickname, taken from "filius Bonacci," became Fibonacci. How many pairs of rabbits are born of one pair in a year? It was assumed that every month a pair of rabbits produces another pair and that rabbits begin to bear young two months after their own birth.

The sequence of numbers that give the number of pairs of rabbits each month is 1, 2, 3, 5, 8, 13, 21, 34, 55, 89, 144, 233, 377. This tells us that at the end of one month, the first pair had a pair of offsprings, so we have two pairs. At the end of two months, only one pair is old enough to have offsprings, so we have three pairs. At the end of three months, the first pair of offsprings is old enough to bear young, so this time we get two new pairs, and we have five pairs altogether. If we continue in this way, we generate the sequence given above. Observe that each number in the sequence is the sum of the two numbers preceding it. It has become customary to begin the sequence with 0, 1, and use the algorithm that says that the next number is always the sum of the preceding two numbers. The nth number in this sequence is called the nth Fibonacci number.

We now define a procedure fib that takes a nonnegative integer n as its parameter and returns the Fibonacci number corresponding to n. We have (fib 0) is 0, (fib 1) is 1, (fib 2) is 1, (fib 3) is 2, and in general, for $n > 1$, (fib n) is the sum of (fib (- n 1)) and (fib (- n 2)). We now use this last recursive condition to define the procedure fib in Program 4.20.

Program 4.20 fib

```
(define fib
  (lambda (n)
    (if (< n 2)
        n
        (+ (fib (- n 1)) (fib (- n 2)))))))
```

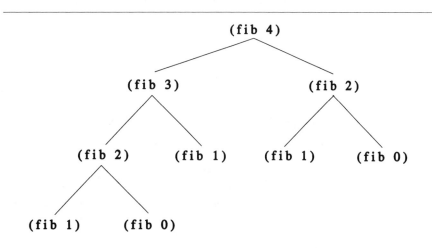

Figure 4.21   Recursion tree for (fib 4)

To trace how (fib 4) is evaluated, we make a tree (Figure 4.21) in which the root is labeled (fib 4). This is evaluated by adding (fib 3) and (fib 2), so our tree will have two branches, one going to a node (fib 3) and the other to a node (fib 2). Each of these gives rise to two branches, (fib 3) giving rise to branches to the nodes (fib 2) and (fib 1), and (fib 2) giving rise to branches to the nodes (fib 1) and (fib 0). This continues until all of the leaves are either (fib 1) or (fib 0), which are known to be 1 and 0, respectively. This tree is an example of a *binary tree* because each node that is not a leaf has at most two branches going down from it.

From Figure 4.21, we see that each node corresponds to a procedure call that is made in evaluating (fib 4). In this case, there are nine procedure calls. Each *branch point* (a node from which two branches originate) corresponds to an addition, so there are four additions. In a similar way, we can build a recursion tree for (fib 5), and we will have fifteen nodes and seven branch points, hence fifteen procedure calls and seven additions. We suggest that you draw the recursion trees for (fib 5) and for (fib 6) to see how large they are and count the number of procedure calls and additions. It is not difficult to see from the trees that if (calls-fib n) tells how many procedure calls there are in computing (fib n) and (adds-fib n) tells how many additions there are in computing (fib n), then these procedures satisfy the relations

```
(calls-fib 0)  is 1
(calls-fib 1)  is 1
(calls-fib n)  is (add1 (+ (calls-fib (- n 1)) (calls-fib (- n 2))))
```

and

```
(adds-fib 0)  is 0
(adds-fib 1)  is 0
(adds-fib n)  is (add1 (+ (adds-fib (- n 1)) (adds-fib (- n 2))))
```

We get Table 4.22 for these quantities.

n	0	1	2	3	4	5	6	7	8	9	10
(fib n)	0	1	1	2	3	5	8	13	21	34	55
(calls-fib n)	1	1	3	5	9	15	25	41	67	109	177
(adds-fib n)	0	0	1	2	4	7	12	20	33	54	88

Table 4.22 Count of procedure calls and additions

The number of procedure calls and the number of additions increase so rapidly because in each procedure call, fib calls itself twice. This leads to

acc1	acc2
0	1
1	1
1	2
2	3
3	5
5	8
8	13

Table 4.23   Accumulator values for the iterative Fibonacci procedure

inefficiency since the same `fib` is called with the same arguments a number of times, so that the different recursive calls repeat each other's work. In the tree shown in Figure 4.21, (`fib 2`) is invoked twice and (`fib 1`) is invoked three times. We next look at an iterative method for computing the Fibonacci numbers.

A clue to how to set up an iterative process for computing the Fibonacci numbers is found by observing that it takes the previous two numbers to compute the next number in the sequence. Thus we have to store two numbers at each step. We begin by storing the first two Fibonacci numbers, 0 and 1 in accumulators, which we call `acc1` and `acc2`. Thus at the start,

acc1	acc2
0	1

At each step, `acc1` holds the current Fibonacci number and `acc2` holds the next one. Thus we can describe the algorithm that takes us from one step to the next as follows:

1. The new value of `acc1` is the same as the previous value of `acc2`.

2. The new value for `acc2` is the sum of previous values of `acc1` and `acc2`.

We apply these rules to extend the table to show the next six steps, as displayed in Table 4.23.

We are now ready to define a procedure `fib-it` that takes three arguments, a nonnegative integer n, and the two accumulators, `acc1` and `acc2`, and returns the Fibonacci number corresponding to n. There are two ways that we can use the algorithm given to write the code. In the first method, we can use the value stored in `acc1` (initially 0) to give us the answer. In that case, one iteration of the algorithm gives us (`fib 1`), two iterations give us (`fib 2`), and in general n iterations give us (`fib` n) for any positive n. In the

Program 4.24 `fib-it`

```
(define fib-it
  (lambda (n acc1 acc2)
    (if (= n 1)
        acc2
        (fib-it (sub1 n) acc2 (+ acc1 acc2)))))
```

second method, we can use the value stored in `acc2` (initially 1) to give us the answer. In this case, one iteration of the algorithm gives us (`fib 2`), two iterations give us (`fib 3`), and in general, $(n-1)$ iterations give us (`fib` n). The second method is more efficient for getting the value of (`fib` n). We opt to implement the second method.

Our iterative procedure `fib-it` takes three parameters: the positive integer n and the two accumulators `acc1` and `acc2`. To implement the algorithm stated above, we successively replace `acc2` by the sum of `acc1` and `acc2`, and replace `acc1` by the previous value of `acc2`. Then to compute the nth Fibonacci number, we must repeat the process $(n-1)$ times. We use the variable n as a counter and reduce it by one on each pass. When n reaches 1, the accumulator `acc2` contains the answer. This leads to the definition given in Program 4.24.

Let's walk through (`fib-it 6 0 1`) to see how this works. On successive passes through the program, the following procedure calls are made:

```
(fib-it 6 0 1)
(fib-it 5 1 1)
(fib-it 4 1 2)
(fib-it 3 2 3)
(fib-it 2 3 5)
(fib-it 1 5 8)
8
```

and the answer is the final value of `acc2`, which is 8. To compute the sixth Fibonacci number, we only make six procedure calls and 5 additions. In general, to compute the nth Fibonacci number, we make n procedure calls and do $n-1$ additions. This is a noticeable improvement over the number of procedure calls and additions when `fib` is invoked. The iterative version, `fib-it`, is certainly more efficient and saves a considerable amount of time in computing the Fibonacci numbers. The ordinary recursive version, `fib`, is less efficient but it does have the advantage of being easier to define directly in terms of the rule that defines the Fibonacci numbers.

Again, if we do not want to include the initial values of the accumulators in each procedure call, we can define the iterative version of `fib` as

```
(define fib
  (lambda (n)
    (if (zero? n)
        0
        (fib-it n 0 1)))))
```

We have seen that some methods of evaluating a given expression may take more resources than other methods. The study of the efficiency of various algorithms is called the *analysis of algorithms*. Let us denote the total resources used in computing an expression that depends on an argument n to be (`res` n). In our discussion, `fib` depended on the argument n, and we can define as the resources used the sum of (`calls-fib` n) and (`adds-fib` n). Inspection of the table for (`calls-fib` n) shows that the following relation exists between (`calls-fib` n) and (`fib` n):

$$\text{(calls-fib } n) = \text{(add1 (* 2 (sub1 (fib (add1 } n))))))$$

Similarly, (`adds-fib` n) and (`fib` n) are related by

$$\text{(adds-fib } n) = \text{(sub1 (fib (add1 } n)))$$

so that

$$\text{(res } n) = \text{(add1 (* 3 (sub1 (fib (add1 } n))))))$$

We now derive an estimate for (`fib` n). If you prefer, you can skip to the formula for (`fib` n) given at the end of the derivation. We use the fact that if a procedure satisfies the Fibonacci *recurrence relation* $F(n) = F(n-1) + F(n-2)$ and the *initial conditions* $F(0) = 0$ and $F(1) = 1$, then $F(n) = $ (`fib` n) for all n. We begin by making a rather arbitrary assumption: that $F(n)$ gets large like some number a raised to the nth power. We then look for restrictions that can be placed on the number a in order for the function a^n to satisfy the Fibonacci recurrence relation. If we are lucky enough to find such conditions that determine a, we have solved the problem of finding a formula for $F(n)$. Substitution of a^n into the recurrence relation gives us

$$a^n = a^{n-1} + a^{n-2}$$

and dividing through by a^{n-2} gives us the simple relation

$$a^2 = a + 1$$

This quadratic equation has the positive root

$$a = \frac{(1 + \sqrt{5})}{2}$$

and the negative root

$$b = \frac{(1 - \sqrt{5})}{2}$$

which are approximately 1.618 and -0.618, respectively.

It is easily verified that since both a^n and b^n satisfy the Fibonacci recurrence relation, then for any pair of numbers A and B, the sum $F(n) = Aa^n + Bb^n$ also satisfies the same recurrence relation. We thus try to find values of A and B so that $F(0) = 0$ and $F(1) = 1$. The constants A and B will now be evaluated from the fact that

$$F(0) = 0 = A + B$$
$$F(1) = 1 = Aa + Bb$$

We find that $A = -B = 1/\sqrt{5}$ and that with these values of A and B, $F(n)$ and (**fib** n) are the same for $n = 0$ and $n = 1$, and that they both satisfy the Fibonacci recurrence relation for all n. This means that they are the same for all n, and we have

$$(\textbf{fib } n) = F(n) = \frac{1}{\sqrt{5}}(a^n - b^n) = \frac{1}{\sqrt{5}}\left[\left(\frac{1 + \sqrt{5}}{2}\right)^n - \left(\frac{1 - \sqrt{5}}{2}\right)^n\right]$$

Thus (**fib** n) is somewhat less than 1.7^n, and (**res** n) is somewhat less than $3(1.7^n)$.

In general, we say that the procedure (**res** n) is of order $O(f(n))$ for some function f of n if there is a constant K such that (**res** n) $\leq Kf(n)$ when n is sufficiently large. In our case, we can say (**res** n) $= O(1.7^n)$ and since it grows like the nth power of a number greater than 1, we say that (**res** n) has *exponential order* when computing (**fib** n).

On the other hand, the operation count (**res** n) for computing (**fib-it** n **0 1**) is $2n - 1$, which is simply $O(n)$. Here the n does not appear in an exponent, but rather (**res** n) is simply a constant times n. We say that in this case, (**res** n) has *linear order*. Thus the time required to compute (**fib** n) grows exponentially with n, while the time required to compute (**fib-it** n

Program 4.25 `reverse-it`

```
(define reverse-it
  (lambda (ls acc)
    (if (null? ls)
        acc
        (reverse-it (cdr ls) (cons (car ls) acc)))))
```

0 1) grows linearly with n. We have seen what a dramatic difference this makes.

In our two examples of iterative programs, we used procedures defined on numbers. It is also possible to use similar methods to write iterative versions of some of the list-processing procedures we considered earlier. For example, consider the procedure `reverse`, which takes a list of items `ls` and returns a list with the items in reverse order. We can write an iterative version `reverse-it` that takes two arguments, a list of items `ls` and an accumulator `acc`, which is initialized to be the empty list. The code for `reverse-it` is given in Program 4.25. We now can obtain the procedure `reverse` by writing

```
(define reverse
  (lambda (ls)
    (reverse-it ls '())))
```

We leave it as an exercise to compare this iterative version with the earlier recursive version of `reverse`. If we actually walk through each version with a simple example, we see that the accumulator already is the answer when `ls` is empty, whereas in the recursive version, we still have to use backward substitution in a return table to get the answer. Furthermore the iterative version does not use the helping procedure `append`. Generally, iterative versions tend to require more arguments.

Exercises

Exercise 4.15
Rewrite the recursive version of the procedure `fib` with the line

```
(writeln "n = " n)
```

inserted just below the line `(lambda (n)`. Then compute `(fib 4)` and compare the results with the tree in Figure 4.21. Also compute `(fib 5)` and `(fib 6)` and observe how the number of recursive calls to `fib` increases.

Exercise 4.16
Rewrite the iterative version of the procedure `fib-it` with the line

```
(writeln "n = " n ", acc1 = " acc1 ", acc2 = " acc2)
```

inserted just below the line

```
(lambda (n acc1 acc2)
```

Compute (`fib-it` 4 0 1) and compare the output with the output for (`fib` 4) in the preceding exercise. Do the same for (`fib-it` 5 0 1) and (`fib-it` 6 0 1).

Exercise 4.17: `calls-fib, adds-fib`
Write the definitions of the procedures `calls-fib` and `adds-fib` discussed in this section. Test your procedures on the values given in Table 4.22. Also evaluate each of these procedures for larger values of n to get an idea of their rates of growth.

Exercise 4.18: `length-it`
Write an iterative version `length-it` of the procedure `length` that computes the length of a list.

Exercise 4.19: `mk-asc-list-of-ints, mk-desc-list-of-ints`
Write an iterative procedure `mk-asc-list-of-ints` that, for any integer n, produces a list of the integers from 1 to n in ascending order. Then write an iterative procedure `mk-desc-list-of-ints` that, for any integer n, produces a list of integers from n to 1 in descending order.

Exercise 4.20: `occurs, occurs-it`
Define both recursive and iterative versions of a procedure `occurs` that counts the number of times an item occurs at the top level in a list. Call the iterative version `occurs-it`. Test your procedures by counting how many times the item a occurs at top level in each of the following lists:

```
(a b a c a d)
(b c a (b a) c a)
(b (c d))
```

5   Locally Defined Procedures

5.1 Overview

When we bind a variable to some value using **define**, we are able to use that variable to represent the value to which it is bound either directly in response to a Scheme prompt or within a program that we are writing. Does this mean that we have to think of new names for every variable we use when we write many programs? No. Scheme gives us a mechanism for limiting where bindings are in effect. In this chapter, we look at ways of binding variables so that the binding holds only within a program or part of a program. The main tools for doing this are two special forms with keywords **let** and **letrec**. After introducing them, we use them to implement polynomials as a data type in Scheme. We then apply the polynomial methods we develop to a discussion of binary numbers, which form the basis of machine computation.

5.2 Let and Letrec

You may have wondered how Scheme knows what value to associate with various occurrences of a variable. When some value is assigned to a variable, we may think of that information being stored in a table with two columns: the left one for variable names and the right one for the associated values. Such a table is called an *environment*. A number of variables (such as those bound to procedures) like **+**, *****, **car**, and **cons** are predefined. These definitions are kept in a table which we call the *initial global environment*. This initial global environment is in place whenever you start up Scheme. When a given variable is encountered in an expression, Scheme looks through its environment to see if the variable has been bound to a value. Naturally, the variable + is bound to the arithmetic operation we usually associate with the addition procedure, and so on.

In addition to having the predefined Scheme variables, we have seen how to use **define** to bind a variable to a desired value. The expression (**define** *var val*) binds the variable *var* to the value *val*. We can again think of the variables we define ourselves as being placed in a table which we call the *user global environment* and when a variable is encountered in an expression, the *global environment* (which includes both the user and initial global environments) is scanned to see if that variable is bound to a value. If a binding cannot be found, a message is written saying that the variable is unbound in the current environment. The user global environment remains in effect until the user exits from Scheme.

Variables are also used as parameters to procedures that are defined by a lambda expression. For example, in the lambda expression

```
(lambda (x y) (+ x y))
```

the variables **x** and **y** occurring in the body (+ **x y**) of the lambda expression are *locally bound* (or *lambda bound*) in the expression (+ **x y**) since the **x** and **y** occur in the list of parameters of that lambda expression. If we apply the procedure, which is the value of this lambda expression, to the arguments 2 and 3, as in

```
((lambda (x y) (+ x y)) 2 3)
```

we can think of a new table being made, called a *local environment*, which is associated with this procedure call. In this local environment, **x** is locally bound to 2 and **y** is locally bound to 3. Then substituting 2 for **x** and 3 for **y** gives (+ **x y**) the value 5, and

```
((lambda (x y) (+ x y)) 2 3)
```

returns the value 5.

A variable occurring in a lambda expression that is not lambda bound by that expression is called *free* in that expression. If we consider the expression

```
(lambda (f y) (f a (f y z)))
```

the variables **f** and **y** are lambda bound in the expression, and the variables **a** and **z** are free in the expression. When the application

```
((lambda (f y) (f a (f y z))) cons 3)
```

is evaluated, the operator (which is the lambda expression) and its two operands are first evaluated. When the lambda expression is evaluated, bindings are found for the free variables in a nonlocal environment. Then, with these bindings for the free variables, the body of the lambda expression is evaluated with **f** bound to the procedure, which is the value of **cons**, and **y** bound to 3. If either of the free variables is not bound in a nonlocal environment, a message to that effect appears when the application is made. On the other hand, if **a** is bound to 1 and **z** is bound to (**4**) in a nonlocal environment, then this application evaluates to (**1 3 4**).

We used the term *nonlocal* environment in the previous paragraph when we referred to the bindings of the free variables in the body of a lambda expression. Those bindings may be found in the global environment or in a local environment for another lambda expression. This is illustrated by the following example:

```
((lambda (x)
   ((lambda (y)
      (- x y))
    15))
 20)
```

The variable **x** is free in the body of the inner lambda expression, but its binding is found in the local environment for the outer lambda expression. The value of the expression is 5.

In the example

```
(lambda (x y) (+ x y))
```

the local bindings hold only in the body (+ **x y**) of the lambda expression, and when we leave the body, we can for the moment think of the local environment as being discarded. The expression (+ **x y**) is said to be in the scope of the variable **x** (and also of **y**). In general, an expression is said to be in the *scope* of a variable **x** if that expression is in the body of a lambda expression in which **x** occurs in the list of parameters.

By looking at a Scheme program, one can tell whether a given expression is in the body of some lambda expression and determine whether the variables in that expression are lambda bound. A language in which the scope of the variables can be determined by looking only at the programs is called *lexically scoped*. Scheme is such a language.

Scheme provides several other ways of making these local bindings for variables, although we shall later see that these are all ultimately related to lambda bindings. The two that we discuss here are let expressions and letrec expressions. To bind the variable *var* to the value of an expression *val* in the expression *body*, we use a let expression (which is a special form with keyword **let**) with the syntax:

$$(\text{let } ((var\ val))\ body)$$

To make several such local bindings in the expression *body*, say var_1 is to be bound to val_1, var_2 to val_2, ..., var_n to val_n, we write

$$(\text{let } ((var_1\ val_1)\ (var_2\ val_2)\ ...(var_n\ val_n))\ body)$$

The scope of each of the variables var_1, var_2, ..., var_n is only *body* within the let expression. For example, the expression

```
(let ((a 2) (b 3))
  (+ a b))
```

returns 5. Here **a** is bound to 2 and **b** is bound to 3 when the body (+ **a** **b**) is evaluated. Another example is

```
(let ((a +) (b 3))
  (a 2 b))
```

returns 5, since **a** is bound to the procedure associated with + and **b** is bound to 3. Similarly, in the expression

```
(let ((add2 (lambda (x) (+ x 2)))
      (b (* 3 (/ 2 12))))
  (/ b (add2 b)))
```

the variable **add2** is bound to the procedure to which (**lambda** (**x**) (+ **x** 2)) evaluates, which increases its argument by 2, and **b** is bound to 0.5, and the whole expression returns 0.2.

The local binding always takes precedence over the global or other nonlocal bindings, as illustrated by the following sample computation:

```
[1] (define a 5)          [5] (let ((a 5))
[2] (add1 a)                      (begin
6                                   (writeln (add1 a))
[3] (let ((a 3))                    (let ((a 3))
      (add1 a))                       (writeln (add1 a)))
4                                   (add1 a)))
[4] (add1 a)              6
6                         4
                          6
```

The **define** expression makes a binding of **a** to 5. When **a** is encountered in (**add1 a**) in **[2]**, its value is found in the global environment and 6 is returned. In **[3]**, **a** is locally bound to 3, and the expression (**add1 a**) is evaluated with this local binding to give the value 4. The scope of the variable **a** in the let expression is only the body of the let expression. Thus in **[4]**, the value of the variable **a** in (**add1 a**) is again found in the global environment, where **a** is bound to 5, so the value returned for (**add1 a**) is 6. In **[5]**, we see a version of the same computation in which no global bindings of **a** are made, but here the local binding takes precedence over the nonlocal bindings.

We get a better understanding of the meaning of the let expression

```
(let ((a 2) (b 3))
  (+ a b))
```

when we realize that it is equivalent to an application of a lambda expression:

```
((lambda (a b) (+ a b)) 2 3)
```

To evaluate this application, we first bind **a** to 2 and **b** to 3 in a local environment and then evaluate (**+ a b**) in this local environment to get 5.

In general, the let expression

$$(\text{let } ((var_1 \ val_1) \ (var_2 \ val_2) \ \dots \ (var_n \ val_n)) \ body)$$

is equivalent to the following application of a lambda expression:

$$((\text{lambda } (var_1 \ var_2 \ \dots \ var_n) \ body) \ val_1 \ val_2 \ \dots \ val_n)$$

From this representation, we see that any free variable appearing in the operands $val_1, val_2, \dots, val_n$ is looked up in a nonlocal environment. For example, let's consider

```
[1] (define a 10)           [4] (let ((a 10) (b 2))
[2] (define b 2)                  (let ((a (+ a 5)))
[3] (let ((a (+ a 5)))             (* a b)))
       (* a b))             30
   30
```

In this example, a is bound globally to 10 in [1], and b is bound globally to 2 in [2]. Then in [3], the expression (+ a 5) is first evaluated.[1]   The variable a is free in the expression (+ a 5), so the value to which a is bound must be looked up in the nonlocal (here global) environment. There we find that a is bound to 10, so (+ a 5) is 15. The next step is to make a local environment where a is bound to 15. We are now ready to evaluate the body of the let expression (* a b). We first try to look up the values of a and b in the local environment. We find that a is locally bound to 15, but b is not found there. We must then look in the nonlocal (here global) environment, and there we find that b is bound to 2. With these values, (* a b) is 30, so the let expression has the value 30. In [4], we see a similar program in which the free variables are looked up in a nonlocal but not global environment. Looking back at the let expressions, we see how the lexical scoping helps us decide which environment (local or nonlocal) to use to look up each variable.

It is important to keep track of which environment to use in evaluating an expression, for if we do not do so, we might be surprised by the results. Here is an interesting example:

```
[1] (define addb
       (let ((b 100))
         (lambda (x)
           (+ x b))))
[2] (let ((b 10))
       (addb 25))
   125
```

Because b is bound to 10 in [2] and (addb 25) is the body of the let expression with this local environment, one might be tempted to say that the answer in [2] should have been 35 instead of 125. In [1], however, the lambda expression falls within the scope of the let expression in which b is bound to

---

[1] The symbol + is also free in (+ a 5), and its value is found in the initial global environment to be the addition operator. The number 5 evaluates to itself. Similarly, the symbol * is free in the body, and its value is found in the initial global environment to be the multiplication operator.

100. This is the binding that is "remembered" by the lambda expression, and when it is later applied to the argument 25, the binding of 100 to b is used and the answer is 125.

Let's look at [1] again. The variable addb is bound to the value of the lambda expression, thereby defining addb to be a procedure. The value of this lambda expression must keep track of three things as it "waits" to be applied: (1) the list of parameters, which is (x), (2) the body of the lambda expression, which is (+ x b), and (3) the nonlocal environment in which the free variable b is bound, which is the environment created by the let expression in which b is bound to 100. The value of a lambda expression is a procedure (also called a *closure*), which consists of the three parts just described. In general, the value of any lambda expression is a procedure (or closure) that consists of (1) the list of parameters (which follows the keyword lambda), (2) the body of the lambda expression, and (3) the environment in which the free variables in the body are bound at the time the lambda expression is evaluated. When the procedure is applied, its parameters are bound to its arguments, and the body is evaluated, with the free variables looked up in the environment stored in the closure. Thus in [2], (addb 25) produces the value 125 because the addb is bound to the procedure in which b is bound to 100.

Consider the following nested let expressions:

```
(let ((b 2))
  (let ((add2 (lambda (x) (+ x b)))
        (b 0.5))
    (/ b (add2 b))))
```

The first let expression sets up a local environment that we call Environment 1 (Figure 5.1).

b ⟶ 2

Figure 5.1   Environment 1

The inner let expression sets up another local environment, which we call Environment 2. The first entry in this environment is add2, which is bound to the value of (lambda (x) (+ x b)). The x in (+ x b) is lambda bound in that lambda expression, and the value of b can be found in Environment 1.

But the inner let expression is in the body of the first let expression, so Environment 1 is in effect and we find that the value associated with b in Environment 1 is 2. Thus we have Environment 2 (Figure 5.2).

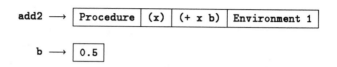

Figure 5.2   Environment 2

All of the variables in the expression to which add2 is bound are either bound in that expression itself (as was x) or are bound outside of the let expression (as was b). We are now ready to evaluate the expression (/ b (add2 b)). In which environment do we look up b? We always search the environments from the innermost let or lambda expression's environment outward, so we search Environment 2 first, finding that b is bound to 0.5. Thus the whole expression is (/ 0.5 2.5), which evaluates to 0.2.

As an example of how let is used in the definitions of procedures, we reconsider the definition of the procedure remove-leftmost, which was given in Program 4.15. Recall that our objective is to produce a list the same as the list ls except that it has removed from it the leftmost occurrence of item. In the base case, when ls is empty, the answer is the empty list. If (car ls) is equal to item, (car ls) is the leftmost occurrence of item and the answer is (cdr ls). If neither of the cases is true, there are two possibilities: either (car ls) is a pair, or it is not a pair. If it is a pair, we want to determine whether it contains item. In Program 4.15, we used member-all? to determine this. Another way is to check whether (car ls) changes when we remove the leftmost occurrence of item from it. If so, then item must belong to (car ls), in which case the answer is

```
(cons (remove-leftmost item (car ls)) (cdr ls))
```

But if we use this approach, we have to evaluate

```
(remove-leftmost item (car ls))
```

twice, once when making the test and again when doing the consing. To avoid the repeated evaluations of the same thing, we use a let expression to bind a variable, say rem-list, to the value of

```
                    (remove-leftmost item (car ls))
```

and use `rem-list` each time the value of this expression is needed. Here is
the new code for `remove-leftmost`:

Program 5.3   `remove-leftmost`

```
(define remove-leftmost
  (lambda (item ls)
    (cond
      ((null? ls) '())
      ((equal? (car ls) item) (cdr ls))
      ((pair? (car ls))
       (let ((rem-list (remove-leftmost item (car ls))))
         (cons rem-list (cond
                          ((equal? (car ls) rem-list)
                           (remove-leftmost item (cdr ls)))
                          (else (cdr ls))))))
      (else (cons (car ls) (remove-leftmost item (cdr ls)))))))
```

In a let expression

$$\text{(let ((}var\ val\text{))}\ body\text{)}$$

any variables that occur in *val* and are not bound in the expression *val* itself
must be bound outside the let expression (i.e., in a nonlocal environment), for
in evaluating *val*, Scheme looks outside the let expression to find the bindings
of any free variables occurring in *val*. Thus

```
(let ((fact (lambda (n)
              (if (zero? n)
                  1
                  (* n (fact (sub1 n)))))))
  (fact 4))
```

will return a message that `fact` is unbound. You should try entering this code
to become familiar with the messages that your system returns. This message
refers to the `fact` occurring in the lambda expression (written here in italics),

which is not bound outside of the let expression.[2]   Thus if we want to use a recursive definition in the "*val*" part of a let-like expression, we have to avoid the problem of unbound variables that we encountered in the above example. We can avoid this difficulty by using a letrec expression (a special form with keyword letrec) instead of a let expression to make the local binding when recursion is desired.

The syntax for letrec is the same as that for let:

$$(\texttt{letrec } ((var_1 \ val_1) \ (var_2 \ val_2) \ \ldots \ (var_n \ val_n)) \ body)$$

but now any of the variables var_1, var_2, ..., var_n can appear in any of the expressions val_1, val_2, ..., val_n, and refer to the locally defined variables var_1, var_2, ..., var_n, so that recursion is possible in the definitions of these variables. The scope of the variables var_1, var_2, ..., var_n now includes val_1, val_2, ..., val_n, as well as *body*. Thus,

```
(letrec ((fact (lambda (n)
                 (if (zero? n)
                     1
                     (* n (fact (sub1 n)))))))
  (fact 4))
```

has the value 24.

We can also have mutual recursion in a letrec expression, as the next example illustrates:

```
(letrec ((even? (lambda (x)
                  (or (zero? x) (odd? (sub1 x)))))
         (odd? (lambda (x)
                 (and (not (zero? x)) (even? (sub1 x))))))
  (odd? 17))
```

has the value #t.

In Program 5.4 we take another look at the iterative version of the factorial procedure discussed in Program 4.19, this time written with letrec. Here we are able to define the procedure fact with parameter n and define the iterative helping procedure fact-it within the letrec expression. This enables us to

---

[2] If we call (fact 0), the value 1 is returned, since the consequent of the if expression is true and the alternative, in which the call to fact is made, is not evaluated. In this case no error message would result.

Program 5.4 fact

```
(define fact
  (lambda (n)
    (letrec ((fact-it
               (lambda (k acc)
                 (if (zero? k)
                     acc
                     (fact-it (sub1 k) (* k acc))))))
      (fact-it n 1))))
```

Program 5.5 swapper

```
(define swapper
  (lambda (x y ls)
    (letrec
      ((swap
         (lambda (ls*)
           (cond
             ((null? ls*) '())
             ((equal? (car ls*) x) (cons y (swap (cdr ls*))))
             ((equal? (car ls*) y) (cons x (swap (cdr ls*))))
             (else (cons (car ls*) (swap (cdr ls*))))))))
      (swap ls))))
```

define an iterative version of **fact** without having to use a globally defined helping procedure. There is an advantage to keeping the number of globally defined procedures small to avoid name clashes. Otherwise you might forget that you used a name for something else earlier and assign that name again.

The letrec expression provides a more convenient way of writing code for procedures that take several arguments, many of which stay the same throughout the program. For example, consider the procedure **swapper** defined in Program 2.8, which has three parameters, **x**, **y**, and **ls**, where **x** and **y** are items and **ls** is a list. Then (**swapper x y ls**) produces a new list in which **x**'s and **y**'s are interchanged. Note that in Program 2.8 each time we invoked **swapper** recursively, we had to rewrite the variables **x** and **y**. We can avoid this rewriting if we use **letrec** to define a local procedure, say **swap**, which takes only one formal argument, say **ls***, and rewrite the definition of the procedure **swapper** as shown in Program 5.5.

The parameter to swap is ls*, and when the locally defined procedure swap is called in the last line of the code, its argument is ls, which is lambda bound in the outer lambda expression. We could just as well use the variable ls instead of ls* as the parameter in swap since the lexical scoping specifies which binding is in effect. When we call swapper recursively in the old code, we write all three arguments, whereas when we call swap recursively in the new code, we must write only one argument. This makes the writing of the program more convenient and may make the code itself more readable.

In this section, we have seen how to bind variables locally to procedures using the special forms with keywords let and letrec. We use these important tools extensively in writing programs that are more efficient and easier to understand.

Exercises

Exercise 5.1
Find the value of each of the following expressions, writing the local environments for each of the nested let expressions. Draw arrows from each variable to the parameter to which it is bound in a lambda or let expression. Also draw an arrow from the parameter to the value to which it is bound.

a. (let ((a 5))
     (let ((fun (lambda (x) (max x a))))
       (let ((a 10)
             (x 20))
         (fun 1))))   5

b. (let ((a 1) (b 2))
     (let ((b 3) (c (+ a b)))
       (let ((b 5))
         (cons a (cons b (cons c '()))))))   1 5 3

Exercise 5.2
Find the value of each of the following letrec expressions:

a. (letrec
     ((loop
        (lambda (n k)
          (cond
            ((zero? k) n)
            ((< n k) (loop k n))
            (else (loop k (remainder n k)))))))
     (loop 9 12))   3

b. (letrec
     ((loop
        (lambda (n)
          (if (zero? n)
              0
              (+ (remainder n 10) (loop (quotient n 10)))))))
     (loop 1234))

Exercise 5.3
Write the two expressions in Parts a and b of Exercise 5.1 as nested lambda
expressions without using any let expressions.

Exercise 5.4
Find the value of the following letrec expression.

```
(letrec ((mystery
           (lambda (tuple odds evens)
             (if (null? tuple)
                 (append odds evens)
                 (let ((next-int (car tuple)))
                   (if (odd? next-int)
                       (mystery (cdr tuple)
                                (cons next-int odds) evens)
                       (mystery (cdr tuple)
                                odds (cons next-int evens))))))))
  (mystery '(3 16 4 7 9 12 24) '() '()))
```

Exercise 5.5
We define a procedure **mystery** as follows:

```
(define mystery
  (lambda (n)
    (letrec
      ((mystery-helper
         (lambda (n s)
           (cond
             ((zero? n) (list s))
             (else
               (append
                 (mystery-helper (sub1 n) (cons 0 s))
                 (mystery-helper (sub1 n) (cons 1 s))))))))
      (mystery-helper n '()))))
```

What is returned when **(mystery 4)** is invoked? Describe what is returned
when **mystery** is invoked with an arbitrary positive integer.

Exercise 5.6: `insert-left-all`

Rewrite the definition of the procedure `insert-left-all` (See Exercise 4.6.) using a locally defined procedure that takes the list `ls` as its only argument.

Exercise 5.7: `fib`

As in Program 5.4 for `fact`, write an iterative definition of `fib` using `fib-it` (See Program 4.24.) as a local procedure.

Exercise 5.8: `list-ref`

Program 3.7 is a good definition of `list-ref`. Unfortunately, the information displayed upon encountering a reference out of range is not as complete as we might expect. In the definitions of `list-ref`, which precede it, however, adequate information is displayed. Rewrite Program 3.7, using a letrec expression, so that adequate information is displayed.

5.3 Symbolic Manipulation of Polynomials

One of the advantages of a list-processing language like Scheme is its convenience for manipulating symbols in addition to doing the usual numerical calculations. We illustrate this feature by showing how to develop a symbolic algebra of polynomials. By a *symbolic algebra* we mean a program that represents the items under discussion as certain combinations of symbols and then performs operations on these items as symbols rather than as numerical values.

We begin by reviewing what is meant by a polynomial. An expression $5x^4$ is referred to as a *term* in which 5 is the *coefficient* and the exponent 4 is the *degree*. In general, a term is an expression of the form $a_k x^k$, where the coefficient a_k is a real number and the degree k is a nonnegative integer. The symbol x is treated algebraically as if it were a real number. Thus we may add two terms of the same degree, as illustrated by $5x^4 + 3x^4 = 8x^4$. In general, the sum of two terms of like degree is a term of the same degree with coefficient that is the sum of the coefficients of the two terms. This rule is expressed in symbols by

$$a_k x^k + b_k x^k = (a_k + b_k)x^k$$

A term can also be multiplied by a real number, as illustrated by $7(5x^4) = 35x^4$. In general, when we multiply the term $a_k x^k$ by the real number c, the product is a term that has coefficient ca_k and the same degree; thus

$$c(a_k x^k) = (ca_k)x^k$$

We may also multiply two terms using the following rule: the product of two terms is a term with degree equal to the sum of the degrees of the two terms and with coefficient equal to the product of the coefficients of the two terms. This is expressed symbolically by

$$(a_j x^j)(b_k x^k) = (a_j b_k)x^{j+k}$$

Here is how it looks in a numerical example: $(3x^4)(7x^5) = 21x^9$. It is customary to write a term of degree 0 by writing only its coefficient. The term $a_1 x^1$ of degree 1 is usually written as $a_1 x$, omitting the exponent 1 on x. Thus $3x^0$ is written as 3, and $5x^1$ is written as $5x$. Terms of positive degree with coefficients 0 are generally omitted.

Two terms of like degree can be added to produce a term of the same degree, but two terms of different degrees do not produce a term when added. Instead, we can only indicate the addition by placing a plus sign between the two terms. A *polynomial* is a sum of a finite number of terms, usually arranged in order of decreasing degree. The *degree* of the polynomial is the maximum of the degrees of its terms. Thus the polynomial $3x^4 + 5x^2 + 12$ has degree 4, and the terms of degree 3 and 1 have coefficient 0 and are not written. In general, a polynomial of degree n is of the form

$$a_n x^n + a_{n-1} x^{n-1} + \cdots + a_2 x^2 + a_1 x + a_0$$

where the coefficients a_k, for $k = 0, \ldots, n$ denote real numbers. The sum of two polynomials is the polynomial obtained by adding all of the terms of both polynomials, using the rule given above for adding terms of like degree. Thus the sum of

$$3x^4 + 5x^2 + 12 \quad \text{and} \quad 7x^5 + 6x^4 - x^2 + 11x - 15$$

is the polynomial

$$7x^5 + 9x^4 + 4x^2 + 11x - 3$$

The term of highest degree in a polynomial is known as its *leading term*, and the coefficient of the leading term is known as its *leading coefficient*. The leading term of $3x^4 + 5x^2 + 12$ is $3x^4$, and its leading coefficient is 3.

Our goal is to write programs that produce the sum and product of polynomials. We saw the definition of the sum in the discussion above, and later we shall define the product. As in our development of exact arithmetic in Chapter 3, we again assume that certain constructor and selector procedures for polynomials have been predefined and return to their definition later in this section when we consider the actual representation of the polynomials in the computer. We proceed to describe what these selector and constructor procedures do when applied to a polynomial.

There are three selector procedures: `degree`, `leading-coef`, and `rest-of-poly`. If `poly` is a polynomial, then (`degree poly`) is the degree of `poly` and (`leading-coef poly`) is the leading coefficient of `poly`. There is a zero polynomial, `the-zero-poly`, which has degree zero and leading coefficient zero. Finally, (`rest-of-poly poly`) is the polynomial obtained from a polynomial of positive degree, `poly`, when its leading term is removed. If `poly` is of degree zero, (`rest-of-poly poly`) is `the-zero-poly`.

The constructor procedure is called `poly-cons`. If n is a nonnegative integer, a is a real number, and p is `the-zero-poly` or a polynomial of degree less than n, then (`poly-cons n a p`) is the polynomial obtained by adding the leading term ax^n to the polynomial p. In particular, for any polynomial `poly`, the value of

```
(poly-cons (degree poly)
           (leading-coef poly)
           (rest-of-poly poly))
```

is `poly`. We shall adopt another convention, which says that a polynomial of positive degree cannot have zero as its leading coefficient. Thus if `poly` has degree less than n for some positive n, then (`poly-cons n 0 poly`) evaluates to `poly`.

Using these procedures, we proceed to develop our symbolic algebra of polynomials. We begin by devising a test to see if a polynomial is `the-zero-poly`. All we have to ask is whether both its degree and leading coefficient are zero. Thus we define `zero-poly?` in Program 5.6.

Program 5.6 `zero-poly?`

```
(define zero-poly?
  (lambda (poly)
    (and (zero? (degree poly)) (zero? (leading-coef poly)))))
```

Program 5.7 shows how we build a term having degree `deg` and coefficient `coef`. The term so defined is itself a polynomial of degree `deg` consisting of only one term. A polynomial consisting of one term is also referred to as a *monomial*. If we are given a polynomial `poly`, we get its leading term by applying the procedure `leading-term`, which we define in Program 5.8 using `make-term`.

Locally Defined Procedures

Program 5.7 `make-term`

```
(define make-term
  (lambda (deg coef)
    (poly-cons deg coef the-zero-poly)))
```

Program 5.8 `leading-term`

```
(define leading-term
  (lambda (poly)
    (make-term (degree poly) (leading-coef poly))))
```

We next define the procedure `p+` such that if `poly1` and `poly2` are two polynomials, then `(p+ poly1 poly2)` is the sum of `poly1` and `poly2`. Let us recall that the sum of two terms bx^k and cx^k of the same degree k is a term $(b+c)x^k$ also of degree k. The sum of two polynomials is then the polynomial obtained by adding the terms of like degree in the two polynomials. Our algorithm for adding the two polynomials `poly1` and `poly2` is:

- If `poly1` is `the-zero-poly`, their sum is `poly2`; if `poly2` is `the-zero-poly`, their sum is `poly1`.
- If the degree of `poly1` is greater than the degree of `poly2`, their sum is a polynomial that has the same leading term as `poly1`, and the rest of their sum is the sum of `(rest-of-poly poly1)` and `poly2`.
- If the degree of `poly2` is greater than the degree of `poly1`, their sum is a polynomial that has the same leading term as `poly2` and the rest of their sum is the sum of `(rest-of-poly poly2)` and `poly1`.
- If `poly1` and `poly2` have the same degree n, the degree of their sum is n, and the leading coefficient of their sum is the sum of the leading coefficients of `poly1` and `poly2`, and the rest of their sum is the sum of `(rest-of-poly poly1)` and `(rest-of-poly poly2)`.

This algorithm for the sum, `p+`, of `poly1` and `poly2` leads to Program 5.9.

In this program, the use of the let expression enabled us to write each of the cond clauses more concisely and more clearly. For example, had we not used the let expression, the first cond clause would have looked like

Program 5.9   p+

```
(define p+
  (lambda (poly1 poly2)
    (cond
      ((zero-poly? poly1) poly2)
      ((zero-poly? poly2) poly1)
      (else (let ((n1 (degree poly1))
                  (n2 (degree poly2))
                  (a1 (leading-coef poly1))
                  (a2 (leading-coef poly2))
                  (rest1 (rest-of-poly poly1))
                  (rest2 (rest-of-poly poly2)))
              (cond
                ((> n1 n2) (poly-cons n1 a1 (p+ rest1 poly2)))
                ((< n1 n2) (poly-cons n2 a2 (p+ poly1 rest2)))
                (else
                  (poly-cons n1 (+ a1 a2) (p+ rest1 rest2)))))))))
```

```
((> (degree poly1) (degree poly2))
 (poly-cons (degree poly1)
            (leading-coef poly1)
            (p+ (rest-of-poly poly1) poly2)))
```

Such use of let expressions often makes programs more readable.

We next define the product **p*** of two polynomials **poly1** and **poly2**. The product of the terms $a_k x^k$ and $a_m x^m$ is the term $(a_k \times a_m)x^{k+m}$. To multiply a term $4x^2$ times a polynomial $3x^5 + 2x^3 + 4x + 5$, we multiply each of the terms of the polynomial by $4x^2$ and add the resulting terms to get

$$12x^7 + 8x^5 + 16x^3 + 20x^2$$

Now to multiply two polynomials,

$$4x^2 + 3x + 2 \quad \text{and} \quad 3x^5 + 2x^3 + 4x + 5$$

we first multiply each term of the first by the entire second polynomial to get the three polynomials

$$12x^7 + 8x^5 + 16x^3 + 20x^2$$
$$9x^6 + 6x^4 + 12x^2 + 15x$$
$$6x^5 + 4x^3 + 8x + 10$$

and then we add these three polynomials to get the desired product:

$$12x^7 + 9x^6 + 14x^5 + 6x^4 + 20x^3 + 32x^2 + 23x + 10$$

We now translate the above example into an algorithm for multiplying any two polynomials poly1 and poly2. It will be convenient to define locally the product t* of a term trm and a polynomial poly. The algorithm for this is:

- If poly is the-zero-poly, then (t* trm poly) is just the-zero-poly.
- Otherwise the degree of their product is the sum of the degrees of trm and poly. The leading coefficient of their product is the product of the coefficient of trm and the leading coefficient of poly. The rest of their product is just the product of trm and the rest of poly.

Once t* has been defined, the product p* of poly1 and poly2 can be defined using the following algorithm:

- If poly1 is the-zero-poly, then (p* poly1 poly2) is just the-zero-poly.
- Otherwise, we multiply the leading term of poly1 by poly2, and add that to the product of the rest of poly1 and poly2.

This leads us to Program 5.10 for p*. In this program, t* is defined locally using a letrec expression since it is a recursive definition. The lambda expression for the procedure p* is placed within the body of the letrec expression for t* so that the local procedure it defines is available for use in p*-helper. The letrec expression that defines p*-helper is used because the variable poly2 is not changed in the recursive invocations of the procedure being defined. Thus it is better programming style not to carry it along as a parameter. We define the local procedure p*-helper that has as its only parameter the polynomial p1 that is bound to poly1 when it is later invoked.

Program 5.11 defines a unary operation negative-poly such that when poly is a polynomial, (negative-poly poly) is its negative: the polynomial with the signs of all of its coefficients changed. We compute it by multiplying poly by the polynomial that is a term of degree 0 and leading coefficient -1.

Now that we have the negative of a polynomial, we can define the difference p- between poly1 and poly2 as shown in Program 5.12.

We now consider how to find the value of a polynomial poly when a number is substituted for the variable x. To evaluate the polynomial $4x^3 + 8x^2 - 7x + 6$ for $x = 5$, we substitute 5 for x and get $4(5^3) + 8(5^2) - 7(5) + 6$. The polynomial can be evaluated at a given value of x by computing each term $a_k x^k$ separately

Program 5.10   p*

```
(define p*
  (letrec
    ((t* (lambda (trm poly)
           (if (zero-poly? poly)
               the-zero-poly
               (poly-cons
                 (+ (degree trm) (degree poly))
                 (* (leading-coef trm) (leading-coef poly))
                 (t* trm (rest-of-poly poly)))))))
    (lambda (poly1 poly2)
      (letrec
        ((p*-helper (lambda (p1)
                      (if (zero-poly? p1)
                          the-zero-poly
                          (p+ (t* (leading-term p1) poly2)
                              (p*-helper (rest-of-poly p1)))))))
        (p*-helper poly1)))))
```

Program 5.11   negative-poly

```
(define negative-poly
  (lambda (poly)
    (let ((poly-negative-one (make-term 0 -1)))
      (p* poly-negative-one poly))))
```

Program 5.12   p-

```
(define p-
  (lambda (poly1 poly2)
    (p+ poly1 (negative-poly poly2))))
```

and then adding the results. For example, we have

$$4(5^3) + 8(5^2) - 7(5) + 6 = 4 \times (5 \times 5 \times 5) + 8 \times (5 \times 5) - 7 \times (5) + 6$$

but this is very inefficient. If we evaluate this by computing each x^k by multiplying x by itself $k - 1$ times and then multiplying the result by a_k, we would be using k multiplications. For a polynomial of degree n, we must add the number of multiplications for each term, which is $1 + 2 + 3 + \cdots + n = n(n+1)/2$ multiplications, to which we add the n additions needed to add up the terms, and we get a grand total of $n(n+1)/2 + n$ operations. We can reduce this number of operations significantly by using the method of nested multiplication, also known as *Horner's rule*, or *synthetic division*.

Before we derive the method of nested multiplication, we consider as an example the polynomial $P(x) = 4x^3 + 8x^2 - 7x + 6$. If we write the constant term first and factor an x out of the rest of the terms, we get $P(x) = 6 + x(-7 + 8x + 4x^2)$. We next factor an x out of the terms after the -7 in the parentheses, to get $P(x) = 6 + x(-7 + x(8 + x(4)))$. For $x = 5$, this becomes $6 + 5(-7 + 5(8 + 5(4)))$. Whereas evaluating the polynomial $P(x)$ in its original form required nine operations, in this last form only six operations are required—three multiplications and three additions.

In the general case of a polynomial of degree n, we note that all terms of degree 1 or more contain a factor of x, so we can factor it out to get our polynomial in the following form:

$$a_0 + x(a_1 + a_2x + a_3x^2 + \cdots + a_nx^{n-1})$$

We repeat this process, starting with the term a_1, to represent our polynomial as:

$$a_0 + x(a_1 + x(a_2 + a_3x + \cdots + a_nx^{n-2}))$$

By continuing to factor out an x from the terms after the constant term, we finally arrive at the result:

$$a_0 + x(a_1 + x(a_2 + x(a_3 + \cdots + x(a_{n-1} + xa_n)\ldots)))$$

In this method of evaluating the polynomial, we have n multiplications and n additions, so there are altogether $2n$ operations. In this way, the number of operations grows linearly with n (that is, like n to the first power, or using the notation of Chapter 3, $O(n)$) while in the previous way, it grew quadratically (that is, like n to the second power, or $O(n^2)$).

We next define a procedure poly-value such that (poly-value poly num) is the value of the polynomial poly when num is substituted for x. A clue for defining this procedure recursively (in fact, iteratively) comes from observing that if we think of the last expression $a_{n-1} + xa_n$ as a coefficient b, then the expression is just a polynomial of degree $n - 1$ having leading coefficient b and all terms of degree less than $n - 1$ the same as those in poly. In implementing this, we obtain a_{n-1} by taking the leading coefficient of (rest-of-poly poly). But this works only if (rest-of-poly poly) has degree

Program 5.13   poly-value

```
(define poly-value
  (lambda (poly num)
    (letrec
      ((pvalue (lambda (p)
                 (let ((n (degree p)))
                   (if (zero? n)
                       (leading-coef p)
                       (let ((rest (rest-of-poly p)))
                         (if (< (degree rest) (sub1 n))
                             (pvalue (poly-cons
                                       (sub1 n)
                                       (* num (leading-coef p))
                                       rest))
                             (pvalue (poly-cons
                                       (sub1 n)
                                       (+ (* num (leading-coef p))
                                          (leading-coef rest))
                                       (rest-of-poly rest)))))))))) 
      (pvalue poly))))
```

$n - 1$, that is, when $a_{n-1} \neq 0$. Thus, if (rest-of-poly poly) has degree less than $n - 1$, we use $x a_n$ for b. Thus the code for **poly-value** in Program 5.13 treats two cases depending upon the degree of **rest**.

This program is iterative since when **pvalue** is called in the if clauses, no further operation is performed after the application of **pvalue**. Moreover, because the procedure of one argument **pvalue** appears first in both the consequent and the alternative of the last if expression, it can be pulled out of the if expression so that the body of the last let expression reads

```
(pvalue (if (< (degree rest) (sub1 n))
            (poly-cons
             ...)
            (poly-cons
             ...)))
```

The last thing we illustrate before thinking about the representation of the polynomial is how to build a given polynomial. For example, if we want to define **p1** to be the polynomial

$$5x^3 - 3x^2 + x - 17$$

Program 5.14   The five basic definitions (Version I)

```
(define the-zero-poly '(0))

(define degree
  (lambda (poly)
    (sub1 (length poly))))

(define leading-coef
  (lambda (poly)
    (car poly)))

(define rest-of-poly
  (lambda (poly)
    (cond
      ((zero? (degree poly)) the-zero-poly)
      ((zero? (leading-coef (cdr poly)))
       (rest-of-poly (cdr poly)))
      (else (cdr poly)))))

(define poly-cons
  (lambda (deg coef poly)
    (let ((deg-p (degree poly)))
      (cond
        ((and (zero? deg) (equal? poly the-zero-poly)) (list coef))
        ((>= deg-p deg)
         (error "poly-cons: Degree too high in" poly))
        ((zero? coef) poly)
        (else
          (cons coef
                (append (list-of-zeros (sub1 (- deg deg-p)))
                        poly)))))))
```

we simply write

```
(define p1 (poly-cons 3 5
             (poly-cons 2 -3
               (poly-cons 1 1
                 (poly-cons 0 -17 the-zero-poly)))))
```

Using the concept of data abstraction again, we have been able to develop a symbolic algebra of polynomials without knowing how the polynomials are represented. We did this by assuming that we had the selector and constructor procedures and the zero polynomial. We shall now see several ways in which these can be defined.

A polynomial is completely determined if we give a list of its coefficients, where we enter a zero when a term of a given degree is missing. The degree of the polynomial is then one less than the length of the list of coefficients. Thus the polynomial

$$a_n x^n + a_{n-1} x^{n-1} + \cdots + a_1 x + a_0, \qquad a_n \neq 0$$

can be represented by the list $(a_n \; a_{n-1} \; \cdots \; a_1 \; a_0)$. For example, the polynomial $5x^3 - 7x^2 + 21$ is represented by the list $(5 \; -7 \; 0 \; 21)$, where the zero corresponds to the term $0x^1$ that is suppressed in $5x^3 - 7x^2 + 21$.

If this representation of a polynomial as a list of its coefficients is adopted, we can make the five basic definitions for the symbolic algebra of polynomials as shown in Program 5.14. Since we required that the leading coefficient of a polynomial be different from zero, we put a zero test in the second cond clause in the definition of `rest-of-poly` to skip over the missing zeros. In the definition of `poly-cons`, the third cond clause guards against a leading coefficient of zero, and the last line uses the procedure `list-of-zeros` defined in Program 3.5 to fill in missing zeros if `deg` differs from the degree of p by more than 1.

The above representation of a polynomial by its list of coefficients has an obvious disadvantage when we try to represent the polynomial $x^{1000} + 1$. We would have to construct a list of 1001 numbers, all zero except the first and last. The above representation is perfectly adequate when we are dealing with polynomials of low degree, but it becomes cumbersome when we have to write "sparse" polynomials of high degree. The following representation of polynomials is more convenient for such higher-degree polynomials; we represent the polynomial by a list of pairs of numbers. In each pair, the first element is the degree of a term, and the second element is the coefficient of that term. The pairs corresponding to terms with zero coefficients are not included, except for `the-zero-poly`, which is represented by `((0 0))`. The pairs are ordered so that the degrees decrease. Thus the polynomial

$$a_n x^n + a_{n-1} x^{n-1} + \cdots + a_1 x + a_0, \qquad a_n \neq 0$$

has the representation $((n \; a_n) \; (n\text{--}1 \; a_{n-1}) \; \cdots \; (1 \; a_1) \; (0 \; a_0))$, for those terms with $a_i \neq 0$. We then can write the five basic definitions for the algebra of polynomials as shown in Program 5.15.

There may be other representations of polynomials that are more convenient to use in special circumstances. The advantage of our approach using data abstraction is that we only need to define `the-zero-poly`, `degree`,

Program 5.15   The five basic definitions (Version II)

```
(define the-zero-poly '((0 0)))

(define degree
  (lambda (poly)
    (caar poly)))

(define leading-coef
  (lambda (poly)
    (cadar poly)))

(define rest-of-poly
  (lambda (poly)
    (if (null? (cdr poly))
        the-zero-poly
        (cdr poly))))

(define poly-cons
  (lambda (deg coef poly)
    (let ((deg-p (degree poly)))
      (cond
        ((and (zero? deg) (equal? poly the-zero-poly))
         (list (list 0 coef)))
        ((>= deg-p deg)
         (error "poly-cons: Degree too high in" poly))
        ((zero? coef) poly)
        (else
          (cons (list deg coef) poly))))))
```

leading-coef, rest-of-poly, and poly-cons, and the rest of our algebra of polynomials is still valid with no modifications.

Exercises

Exercise 5.9
Implement the algebra of polynomials in the two ways indicated in the text. For each implementation, test each of the procedures p+, p-, and p* with the polynomials

$$p_1(x) = 5x^4 - 7x^3 + 2x - 4$$

$$p_2(x) = x^3 + 6x^2 - 3x$$

and using poly-value, find $p_1(-1)$, $p_1(2)$, $p_2(0)$, and $p_2(-2)$.

Exercise 5.10
Look closely at the definition of p+ (see Program 5.9). When n1 is greater than n2, the variables a2 and rest2 are ignored. Similarly, when n1 is less than n2, the variables a1 and rest1 are ignored. Rewrite p+ so that this wasting of effort disappears. *Hint*: You will need to use let within the consequents of cond clauses.

Exercise 5.11: poly-quotient, poly-remainder
Define a procedure poly-quotient that finds the quotient polynomial when poly1 is divided by poly2 and a procedure poly-remainder that finds the remainder polynomial when poly1 is divided by poly2.

Exercise 5.12
Another representation of polynomials as lists that can be used is a list of coefficients in the order of increasing degree. The list of pairs representation given above can also be written in order of increasing degree. Consider the advantages and disadvantages of these representations compared to those given above.

Exercise 5.13
How would the constructors and selectors be defined if we use

(cons deg coef) instead of (list deg coef)

in our second representation using lists of pairs?

Exercise 5.14
The definition of t* in Program 5.10 is flawed. Each time t* is invoked recursively it evaluates both (degree trm) and (leading-coef trm), although these values never change. In addition, the variable trm does not need to be passed to t* because trm never changes. Explain how these two flaws are eliminated in the following definition of p*.

```
(define p*
  (let
    ((t* (lambda (trm poly)
           (let ((deg (degree trm))
                 (lc (leading-coef trm)))
             (letrec
               ((t*-helper
                  (lambda (poly)
                    (if (zero-poly? poly)
                        the-zero-poly
                        (poly-cons
                          (+ deg (degree poly))
                          (* lc (leading-coef poly))
                          (t*-helper (rest-of-poly poly)))))))
               (t*-helper poly))))))
    (lambda (poly1 poly2) ...)))
```

Exercise 5.15: `append-to-list-of-zeros`
In the first version of `poly-cons` presented in Program 5.14, poly is appended
to a list of zeros. The procedure `list-of-zeros` requires one recursion to
build the list of zeros and `append` requires another. Two recursions over the
list of zeros is inefficient. The program can be rewritten so as to require
only one recursion over the list of zeros. One suggestion for doing so is to
combine the construction of the list of zeros and the appending of poly into
one procedure `append-to-list-of-zeros`, which takes two parameters, n and
x and produces a list that contains x preceded by n zeros. This procedure can
be written either recursively or iteratively. Try your hand at both versions
and test them in `poly-cons`.

5.4 Binary Numbers

Information is stored in the computer in the form of binary numbers. One
may loosely think of the memory cells in which information is stored as a
row of switches, each having two positions: on and off. If a switch is on, it
represents the digit 1, and if it is off, it represents the digit 0. The information
contained in one such switch is called a *bit*, and eight bits of information
usually constitute a *byte* of information. Since there are 2^8 different settings
for eight switches, we can represent 256 different values by using one byte. In
this section, we shall discuss the representation of numbers in binary form,
and more generally, as numbers with an arbitrary base.

First recall that in the decimal system, each digit in a number is a place-holder representing the number of times a certain power of 10 is counted. Thus 4,723 is the same as

$$4 \times 10^3 + 7 \times 10^2 + 2 \times 10^1 + 3 \times 10^0$$

The 10 is called the *base* of the number system. We can think of any number represented in this way as a polynomial in which the variable x has been replaced by 10. In the same way, we can represent any number as a polynomial in which the variable x has been replaced by the base b and the coefficients are taken to be numbers between 0 and $b - 1$. It is customary to write a number in the base b system using the placeholder concept as a string of digits, each digit being the corresponding coefficient in the polynomial. For example, for base 2 (*binary numbers*), the digits are 0 and 1 and the polynomial

$$1 \times 2^6 + 1 \times 2^5 + 0 \times 2^4 + 0 \times 2^3 + 1 \times 2^2 + 0 \times 2^1 + 1 \times 2^0$$

can be represented as 1100101.

In general, for binary numbers, the number

$$a_n 2^n + a_{n-1} 2^{n-1} + \cdots + a_1 2 + a_0$$

is written in the form $a_n a_{n-1} \ldots a_1 a_0$. We first consider the problem of finding the decimal number when we are given its binary representation. This is precisely the problem of evaluating a polynomial when the variable x has the value 2. We can use the results of the last section if we represent our binary number as a polynomial of degree n that has the coefficient a_k for the term of degree k, for $k = 0, 1, \ldots, n$. We define a procedure `digits->poly` that takes a list of the digits of a binary number as its argument and returns a polynomial of degree one less than the number of digits and that has the given digits as its coefficients. The polynomial is constructed by the local procedure `make-poly`, which has as its parameters the degree `deg` of the polynomial, which is one less than the number of digits in the binary number, and `ls`, which is the list of digits of the binary number. If we already have the polynomial for the binary number obtained when the first digit is removed, that is, for parameters (`sub1 deg`) and (`cdr ls`), we get the polynomial for the parameters `deg` and `ls` by adding the term having degree `deg` and coefficient (`car ls`). This leads us to the definition given in Program 5.16.

Now to convert from the binary representation of a number to the decimal number, we use the procedure `binary->decimal` given in Program 5.17, which takes a list of the binary digits as its argument and returns the decimal

Program 5.16 `digits->poly`

```
(define digits->poly
  (lambda (digit-list)
    (if (null? digit-list)
        (error "digits->poly: Not defined for the empty list")
        (letrec
          ((make-poly
             (lambda (deg ls)
               (if (null? ls)
                   the-zero-poly
                   (poly-cons deg (car ls)
                     (make-poly (sub1 deg) (cdr ls)))))))
          (make-poly (sub1 (length digit-list)) digit-list)))))
```

Program 5.17 `binary->decimal`

```
(define binary->decimal
  (lambda (digit-list)
    (poly-value (digits->poly digit-list) 2)))
```

number. As an example, we find the decimal number for the representation of the binary number 11001101.

```
(binary->decimal '(1 1 0 0 1 1 0 1))  ⟹ 205
```

If we have a polynomial, say $1x^2 + 1$, which corresponds to the binary number 101, how do we recover the list of binary digits (1 0 1)? To do this, we define a procedure `poly->digits` that takes a polynomial `poly` corresponding to a binary number and returns a list of the digits of that binary number. For example,

```
(poly->digits (digits->poly '(1 1 0 1 0 1)))  ⟹ (1 1 0 1 0 1)
```

Consider `(rest-of-poly poly)`; if its degree is one less than the degree of `poly`, then `(poly->digits poly)` is just

```
(cons (leading-coef poly) (poly->digits (rest-of-poly poly)))
```

Program 5.18 `poly->digits`

```
(define poly->digits
  (lambda (poly)
    (letrec
      ((convert
         (lambda (p deg)
           (cond
             ((zero? deg) (list (leading-coef p)))
             ((= (degree p) deg)
              (cons (leading-coef p)
                    (convert (rest-of-poly p) (sub1 deg))))
             (else
              (cons 0 (convert p (sub1 deg))))))))
      (convert poly (degree poly)))))
```

Otherwise, we have to cons zeros onto the list to take into account the gap in the degrees between the leading term and the next term with nonzero coefficient. In order to do this, it is convenient to introduce a local procedure, which we call **convert**. It keeps track of the degree of the term being considered, even if the coefficient is zero. Thus **convert** has two parameters: p, which is a polynomial, and **deg**, which is an integer representing the degree of the term. We define **poly->digits** as shown in Program 5.18.

We also want to convert from the decimal number to its binary representation. We shall do this with the procedure **decimal->binary**, which takes a decimal number and returns a list of the digits in its binary representation. We can easily derive the algorithm if we recall that we want to find the coefficients $a_n, a_{n-1}, \ldots, a_0$ in the polynomial corresponding to the number q, which we now write using nested multiplication:

$$q = a_0 + 2(a_1 + \cdots + 2(a_{n-1} + 2a_n) \cdots)$$

Observe that a_0, which must be either 0 or 1, is just the remainder r_0 when q is divided by 2, since $q = a_0 + 2(somenumber)$. Recall that r_0 is 0 if q is even, and it is 1 if q is odd. If we let q_0 be the quotient when q is divided by 2, then we have

$$q_0 = a_1 + 2(a_2 + \cdots + 2(a_{n-1} + 2a_n) \cdots)$$

We now repeat this process to find that a_1 is the remainder r_1 when q_0 is divided by 2, and so forth. In general, if q_k is the quotient when q_{k-1} is

Quotient	Remainder
197	
98	1
49	0
24	1
12	0
6	0
3	0
1	1
0	1

Figure 5.19   Conversion of 197 to its binary representation

divided by 2 and if r_k is the remainder when q_{k-1} is divided by 2, then $a_k = r_k$.

For example, to convert the decimal number 197 to binary form, we do our work in two columns; the first gives the quotient, and the second gives the remainder when the successive numbers are divided by 2. Figure 5.19 shows this computation. Each line in the table represents the quotient and the remainder when the previous quotient is divided by 2. The binary representation of the number is found by reading the remainders from the bottom of the table to the top: 11000101. We will then have

```
(decimal->binary 197) ⟹ (1 1 0 0 0 1 0 1)
```

Implementing this algorithm is accomplished in Program 5.20 by building up the polynomial corresponding to the binary number term by term as the remainders are obtained. The first term we build has degree 0 and the degrees increase by one each time a new remainder is found. Thus we are able to define **decimal->binary** with the help of **dec->bin**, which has a second parameter **deg** that keeps track of the degree of the term, starting from zero and increasing by one in each recursive invocation.

We now have

```
(decimal->binary (binary->decimal '(1 0 1 1 0))) ⟹ (1 0 1 1 0)
(binary->decimal (decimal->binary 143)) ⟹ 143
```

Two other number systems that are commonly used in computing are the *octal* (base 8) and the *hexadecimal* (base 16) systems. For octal, the base b in the polynomial representation is replaced by 8, and in hexadecimal, the base b is

Program 5.20 `decimal->binary`

```
(define decimal->binary
  (lambda (num)
    (letrec
      ((dec->bin
         (lambda (n deg)
           (if (zero? n)
               the-zero-poly
               (p+ (make-term deg (remainder n 2))
                   (dec->bin (quotient n 2) (add1 deg)))))))
      (poly->digits (dec->bin num 0)))))
```

replaced by 16. The digits $0, 1, 2, 3, 4, 5, 6, 7$ are used for octal numbers and the digits $0, 1, 2, 3, 4, 5, 6, 7, 8, 9, A, B, C, D, E, F$ for hexadecimal numbers. Here A stands for 10, B for 11, ..., F for 15.

Exercises

Exercise 5.16
Convert each of the following decimal numbers to base 2.

   a. 53

   b. 404

Exercise 5.17
Convert each of the following base 2 numbers to decimals.

   a. 10101010

   b. 1101011

Exercise 5.18: `octal->decimal, hexadecimal->decimal`
Look over the programs for `binary->decimal` and `decimal->binary` and see what changes have to be made to get definitions for the four procedures:

```
octal->decimal
hexadecimal->decimal
decimal->octal
decimal->hexadecimal
```

Since we are representing our hexadecimal numbers as lists of digits, we can use the number 10 for A, 11 for B, and so on, so that `(12 5 10)` is the list representation of the hexadecimal number `C5A`. Define one pair of conversion procedures `base->decimal` and `decimal->base` that take two arguments, the number to be converted and the base, where the base can be any positive integer. Then define a procedure `change-base` that changes a number `num` from base `b1` to base `b2`, where `num` is a list of digits. Thus (`change-base num b1 b2`) is a list of digits that gives the base `b2` representation of `num`. Test your program on:

```
(change-base '(5 11) 16 8) ⟹ (1 3 3)
(change-base '(6 6 2) 8 2) ⟹ (1 1 0 1 1 0 0 1 0)
(change-base '(1 0 1 1 1 1 1 0 1) 2 16) ⟹ (1 7 13)
```

Exercise 5.19: `binary-sum, binary-product`

Define two procedures, `binary-sum` and `binary-product`, that take two binary numbers as arguments and return the sum and product of those numbers in binary form. This can be done in two ways. First, you could convert both numbers to decimal form, perform the arithmetic operation, and then convert to binary form. You could, on the other hand, treat the binary numbers as polynomials and perform the arithmetic operations on these polynomials, using the appropriate carrying rules for binary numbers. Write programs for `binary-sum` and `binary-product` using both approaches.

Exercise 5.20: `binary->decimal, decimal->binary`

We have presented the conversions from binary to decimal and from decimal to binary as applications of the algebra of polynomials developed in this chapter. Write the two procedures `binary->decimal` and `decimal->binary` directly from the definitions of binary and decimal numbers, using the list representation for binary numbers and not making use of the polynomial algebra.

6   Interactive Programming

In this chapter, we begin by taking a brief look at the string data type. We then illustrate some of the input and output features available in Scheme by developing a program to find the square root of numbers. After implementing the basic square root algorithm, we look at ways of viewing intermediate results and of providing data at run time. We close this chapter with a look at two famous problems: the Tower of Hanoi and the Eight Queens problem, both of which demonstrate ways of outputting data.

6.2 Strings

Strings form an important data type, and there are a number of operations that can be performed on strings. A brief introduction to strings was presented in Chapter 2. Recall that a string is written in Scheme as a sequence of keyboard characters enclosed within double quotes. We now look at a few of the procedures in Scheme for manipulating strings. For example, the predicate **string?** tests whether its argument is a string; **string-length** takes a string as its argument and returns the number of characters in the string, including blank spaces; and **string-append** takes any number of strings as arguments and forms a new string by appending (or *concatenating*) them. The procedure **substring** has the call structure

$$\text{(substring } string \ start \ end)$$

where *string* is a given string, and *start* and *end* are integers satisfying the inequalities $0 \leq start \leq end \leq L$ where L represents the length of *string*. It returns a string, which is a substring of *string* consisting of those characters beginning with the zero-based index *start* and including all of the characters up to but not including the one with index *end*. Thus the length of the substring is just the difference between *end* and *start*. It is also possible to convert a symbol, such as `'hello` into the string `"hello"` using the procedure `symbol->string`. Below are some examples illustrating string operations:

```
(string-length "This is a string") ⟹ 16
(string-length "") ⟹ 0
(string-append "This is" " a string") ⟹ "This is a string"
(string-append "12" "34" "56") ⟹ "123456"
(substring "This is a string" 0 4) ⟹ "This"
(substring "This is a string" 4 6) ⟹ " i"
(substring "This is a string" 5 13) ⟹ "is a str"
(symbol->string 'hello) ⟹ "hello"
(string=? "This is a string" "This is a string") ⟹ #t
(string=? "This is a string" "This is a STRING") ⟹ #f
(string-ci=? "This is a string" "This is a STRING") ⟹ #t
```

The predicate `string=?` tests whether two strings are the same and distinguishes between upper- and lowercase. The predicate `string-ci=?` treats upper- and lowercase as though they were the same character. (The "ci" stands for *case insensitive*.) Thus the next to the last example above is false, and the last example is true.

We illustrate the use of these string procedures by defining a procedure `string-insert` that inserts a string `insrt` into a string `strng` so that the first character in `insrt` has index `n` in the resulting string. For example,

```
(string-insert "45" "123678" 3) ⟹ "12345678"
```

The definition appends the substring of `strng` consisting of those characters with indices less than `n`, the string `insrt`, and the substring of `strng` consisting of those characters with indices `n` or greater. This gives us the definition in Program 6.1.

We shall introduce more string-handling procedures as they are needed in our discussions and see examples of how they are used.

Program 6.1   string-insert

```
(define string-insert
  (lambda (insrt strng n)
    (string-append
      (substring strng 0 n)
      insrt
      (substring strng n (string-length strng)))))
```

Exercises

Exercise 6.1: substring?
Define a predicate **substring?** with two parameters, **sstr** and **strng**, that
tests whether the string **sstr** is a substring of **strng**. *Hint*: This can be done
using **string-length**, **substring**, and **string=?**. Test your predicate on the
following:

```
(substring? "s a s" "This is a string.") ⟹ #t
(substring? "ringer" "This is a string.") ⟹ #f
(substring? "" "This is a string.") ⟹ #t
```

Exercise 6.2: string-reverse
Define a procedure **string-reverse** that takes a string as its argument and
returns a string that is the given string with its characters in reverse order.
Hint: You may find the following procedure useful:

```
(define substring-ref
  (lambda (strng n)
    (substring strng n (add1 n))))
```

Test your procedure on the following:

```
(string-reverse "Jack and Jill") ⟹ "lliJ dna kcaJ"
(string-reverse "mom n dad") ⟹ "dad n mom"
(string-reverse "") ⟹ ""
```

Exercise 6.3: palindrome?
A string is a palindrome if the reverse of the string is the same as the string.

For example, "mom" and "dad" are examples of palindromes. Define a predicate `palindrome?` that tests whether a given string is a palindrome. Test your predicate on the following:

```
(palindrome? "able was I ere I saw elba") ⟹ #t
(palindrome? "mom n dad") ⟹ #f
```

6.3 Implicit begin

The use of **begin** enables us to evaluate several expressions sequentially and return the value of the last expression. This is useful in an if expression that expects just one expression in each of its clauses. There are certain special forms in Scheme that have an *implicit begin* built into their definitions. These include the special forms with keywords **lambda**, **let**, **letrec**, and **cond**. For example, writing

```
(lambda (x y)
  (writeln x)
  (writeln y)
  (+ x y))
```

is the same as

```
(lambda (x y)
  (begin
    (writeln x)
    (writeln y)
    (+ x y)))
```

Similarly, in the case of **let** and **letrec**, the body may consist of several expressions so that

```
(let ((a 3) (b 4))
  (writeln a)
  (writeln b)
  (+ a b))
```

is the same as

```
(let ((a 3) (b 4))
  (begin
    (writeln a)
    (writeln b)
    (+ a b)))
```

In a cond expression, each of the clauses contains a condition and a consequent
that is evaluated if the condition is true. The consequent may consist of several
expressions, which are then evaluated in sequential order as if they were in a
begin expression.

Exercise

Exercise 6.4

An example of the use of implicit begins in cond clauses is given below:

```
(define mystery
  (lambda (pos-int)
    (letrec ((helper
                (lambda (n count)
                  (cond
                    ((= n 1)
                     (newline)
                     (writeln "It took " count " steps to get to 1."))
                    ((even? n)
                     (writeln count
                       ". We divide " n " by 2.")
                     (helper (/ n 2) (add1 count)))
                    (else
                     (writeln count
                       ". We multiply " n " by 3 and add 1.")
                     (helper (+ (* n 3) 1) (add1 count)))))))
      (helper pos-int 0))))
```

In this example, each cond clause uses an implicit begin. What is the output
of (mystery 9)? Invoke mystery with a few other positive integer arguments. Safe recursive programs contain a terminating condition which eventually halts the computation. No one has, as yet, been able to demonstrate
that mystery is safe. Nor has a positive integer argument been found for
which mystery is unsafe.

6.4 Input and Output

We have been using the keyboard to enter Scheme expressions, and we have seen Scheme send its output to the screen. The Scheme expressions we enter are evaluated after we press the <RETURN> key, and then the result is printed out. There are programs in which we would like to enter additional data while the evaluation is taking place or in which we would like to print out not only the final result but some intermediate results of the computation.

As an example illustrating the desire to see intermediate results, we look at a program to compute the square root of a number by the method of successive averaging known as Newton's method. If we have an estimate u for the square root of a positive number a, a better estimate is always given by the average of u and $\frac{a}{u}$, that is, by v where[1]

$$v = \frac{1}{2}\left(u + \frac{a}{u}\right) \tag{1}$$

Suppose we start with the estimate $u = 1$ and use formula (1) to compute v. We then substitute this value v for u in (1) to get the next value v. We continue this process until we are satisfied with the value we get; but what criterion should we apply to decide that we are satisfied? We decide how many decimal places we want in the answer, say five, and stop when we get two successive estimates that are the same to five decimal places. In particular, we shall stop the calculation when u and v differ by less than the agreed-upon tolerance, 0.000005. To test whether u and v are closer than the given tolerance, we shall use the predicate **close-enough?** defined by writing

```
(define tolerance 0.000005)

(define close-enough?
  (lambda (u v)
    (< (abs (- u v)) tolerance)))
```

We can describe the algorithm as follows:

1. Make an initial estimate $u = 1$ for the square root of a.

---

[1] To make this plausible, recall that we are looking for the number s having the property that $s \times s = a$. If the estimate u is too large, then $\frac{a}{u}$ is too small, and their average v is a better approximation to s. Similarly when the estimate u is too small, $\frac{a}{u}$ is too large, and their average v is a better approximation to s.

Program 6.2   `square-root`

```
(define square-root
  (lambda (a)
    (letrec
      ((next-estimate
         (lambda (u)
           (let ((v (/ (+ u (/ a u)) 2)))
             (if (close-enough? u v)
                 v
                 (next-estimate v))))))
      (next-estimate 1))))
```

2. If u is an estimate for the square root of a, then the next estimate is given by the v calculated in (1).

3. We continue applying Step 2 with the previously calculated value of v used as the new value of u to get the next value of v until u and v differ by less than `tolerance`.

Program 6.2 is a procedure that implements this algorithm.

We use this program to compute a few square roots:

```
[1] (square-root 100)
10.0
[2] (sqrt 100)
10.0
[3] (square-root 1000)
31.6227766016838
[4] (sqrt 1000)
31.6227766016838
[5] (square-root 2)
1.41421356237469
[6] (sqrt 2)
1.4142135623731
```

In [2], [4], and [6], we called the built-in square root procedure `sqrt` to compare its (presumably correct) results with our approximation. We see that we got more than just five-decimal-place accuracy. This averaging method is known to halve the error until the error is less than 1 in absolute value and then to double the number of decimal-place accuracy with each successive averaging. In order to see that this is actually happening, it would be interesting to be able to see each of the successive averages. We would like to send the value v to the screen each time it is computed.

Scheme provides several procedures that enable us to send output to the screen or, as we shall see in Chapter 15, to a file. We already have used the procedure writeln to write to the screen when we traced procedures. The one we now use is display, and later in this section we shall discuss others. The Scheme procedure display is called with only one argument, and it has the side effect of printing that argument on the screen. The value that it returns in not specified in Scheme, and we shall assume that our implementation does not print a value for display. For example:

```
[7] (begin
     (display "Is")
     (display " ")
     (display 1.4142)
     (display " the square root of 2?"))
Is 1.4142 the square root of 2?
```

To put a space between the items being printed with display, we have to print a space using (display " "). Strings are printed without the double quotes. If we want to print the string "the square root of 2?" on the next line, we use the Scheme procedure newline, which takes no arguments and has the effect of moving the cursor to the beginning of the next line. Scheme does not specify a value for newline, and we again assume that our implementation does not print a value for newline. We now use newline to print the string "the square root of 2?" on the next line instead of on the same line as the other items.

```
[8] (begin
     (display "Is")
     (display " ")
     (display 1.4142)
     (newline)
     (display "the square root of 2?")
     (newline))
Is 1.4142
the square root of 2?
```

Program 6.3 `square-root-display`

```
(define square-root-display
  (lambda (a)
    (letrec ((next-estimate (lambda (u)
                              (let ((v (/ (+ u (/ a u)) 2)))
                                (if (close-enough? u v)
                                    v
                                    (begin
                                      (display v)
                                      (newline)
                                      (next-estimate v)))))))
      (next-estimate 1))))
```

We now define the square root procedure using `display` to print the intermediate results on the screen (Program 6.3).[2] When we call `square-root-display`, we get the output shown in Figure 6.4. We can now observe that the convergence of the `square-root` algorithm does display the convergence behavior described.

Since we have only asked for five-decimal-place accuracy in the answer, it would be more appropriate to print the final answer to five places. This can be done using the Scheme procedure `round`, which rounds a number to the closest integer. If we have a number like the one obtained for (`square-root` 2), we round it to five places by first multiplying it by 1.0e+5 (i.e., 100000.0), to get 141421.356237469. This result is then rounded to the nearest integer using `round` to get 141421, and to get the final answer, we divide by 1.0e+5, yielding the result 1.41421, which is correct to five decimal places. In Program 6.5, we define a general procedure `round-n-places` that has as parameters an integer `n` and a decimal number `dec-num` and returns the number rounded off to n decimal places.

Then to get the answer to (`square-root` 2) rounded off to five decimal places, we write:

(`round-n-places` 5 (`square-root` 2)) $\implies$ 1.41421

If we are rounding many numbers off to five decimal places, it is convenient to define a procedure `round-5-places` as

---

[2] Although the invocation of the local procedure next-estimate is within the begin expression, this is still an iterative program, since the value of the recursive invocation of next-estimate is returned directly as the value of next-estimate.

```
[9] (square-root-display 100)
50.5
26.240099009901
15.0255301199868
10.8404346730269
10.0325785109606
10.0000528956427
10.0000000001399
10.
[10] (square-root-display 1000)
500.5
251.249000999001
127.614558163459
67.725327360826
41.2454260749912
32.7452493444886
31.6420158686508
31.622782450701
31.6227766016843
31.6227766016838
[11] (square-root-display 2)
1.5
1.41666666666667
1.41421568627451
1.41421356237469
```

Figure 6.4   Display of intermediate results

Program 6.5   round-n-places

```
(define round-n-places
  (lambda (n dec-num)
    (let ((scale-factor (expt 10 n)))
      (/ (round (* dec-num scale-factor)) scale-factor))))
```

```
(define round-5-places
  (lambda (dec-num)
    (round-n-places 5 dec-num)))
```

and then simply write

```
(round-5-places (square-root 2)) ⟹ 1.41421
```

In `square-root-display`, each successive value of **v** was printed out on a new line. Suppose we want to print out all of the successive values on one line. Then we would not follow each application of `display` with an application of `newline`. We would only use `newline` before returning the final answer to set it off from the intermediate values.

```
(if (close-enough? u v)
    (begin
      (newline)
      v)
    (begin
      (display v)
      (display " ")
      (next-estimate v)))
```

Here, (`display v`) prints the value of **v** to the screen; then (`display " "`) prints a blank space after the value of **v**. Thus the successive numbers will be separated by blank spaces. The final answer **v** will be on a new line. For example, with the procedure `square-root-display` redefined this way, we get:

```
[12] (square-root-display 2)
1.5 1.41666666666667 1.41421568627451
1.41421356237469
```

The procedure `display` prints the string `"the square root of 2?"` without double quotes. For the occasions when we do want the double quotes to be printed in addition to the string, we can use the Scheme procedure `write` instead of `display`. If we use `write` instead of `display` in [8], we get

```
[13] (begin
      (write "Is")
      (write " ")
      (write 1.4142)
      (newline)
      (write "the square root of 2?")
      (newline))
"Is"" "1.4142
"the square root of 2?"
```

Program 6.6   read-demo

```
(define read-demo
  (lambda ()
    (display "Enter data (enter done when finished): ")
    (let ((response (read)))
      (cond
        ((eq? response 'done) (display "Thank you. Good-bye."))
        (else (display "You entered: ")
              (write response)
              (newline)
              (read-demo)))))))
```

We also see that (**write** " ") prints a blank space with double quotes around it, whereas (**display** " ") prints just the blank space.

It is also possible to enter data interactively while a procedure is running by making use of the Scheme procedure **read**. When the procedure **read** is invoked with no arguments, the computer stops and waits for an expression to be entered from the keyboard. The value entered from the keyboard is returned by (read). In Chapter 15, we shall see how **read** may be called with one argument to read from a file instead of from the keyboard. In Program 6.6, we illustrate the use of **read** by writing a simple program that asks us to enter data, reads the data we enter, and then tells us what data we entered. A statement written to the screen asking us to do something is called a *prompt.* A statement that shows what we entered in response to the prompt is said to *echo* what we entered.

The first thing to notice about **read-demo** is that it is written as a procedure of no arguments; the parameter list in the lambda expression is the empty list (). A procedure of no arguments is called a *thunk*, and it is invoked by merely enclosing the name of the procedure in parentheses. For example, if we write

```
(define greeting
  (lambda ()
    (writeln "Hello. How are you?")))
```

then the procedure greeting is called as follows:

```
[14] (greeting)
Hello. How are you?
```

In the definition of **read-demo**, the first display expression prompts us for data. The let expression binds the variable **response** to the object that is produced by the read expression. During the evaluation, the computer pauses and waits for us to enter a datum from the keyboard, and it is that datum that is bound to **response**. We chose to use **write** instead of **display** to print the response in order to show it exactly as it was entered. Thus when a string is entered with double quotes, it is printed on the screen with the double quotes. Had we used **display** instead of **write**, a string would be printed without the double quotes. In order to stop the recursion, we enter **done**. The condition terminating the recursion tests **response** to see if it is the same as **done** using the predicate **eq?**. Here is a sample run using **read-demo** when a number, a symbol, and a string are entered in response to the prompt asking for a datum. The responses are presented in italics to distinguish them from the prompts.

```
[16] (read-demo)
Enter data (enter done when finished): 6.5432
You entered: 6.5432
Enter data (enter done when finished): Hello
You entered: Hello
Enter data (enter done when finished): "How are you?"
You entered: "How are you?"
Enter data (enter done when finished): done
Thank you. Good-bye.
```

We now define **interactive-square-root** in such a way that it prompts us for the numbers for which square roots are desired.

Program 6.7   `interactive-square-root`

```
(define interactive-square-root
  (lambda ()
    (writeln "Enter the number whose square root you want,"
             " or enter done to quit:")
    (let ((n (read)))
      (if (eq? n 'done)
          (writeln "That's all, folks.")
          (begin
            (writeln "The square root of " n " is " (square-root n))
            (newline)
            (interactive-square-root))))))
```

The first writeln expression provides a prompt for us to enter a number. Then the let expression binds the value given by (read) to n. When the expression (read) is evaluated, the computer pauses and waits for the user to enter a datum at the keyboard. In this case the datum is a number, which is bound to n. When n is not the symbol done, the writeln expression evaluates its operands, which includes the expression (square-root n) and echoes n while printing its square root. It is good practice to echo back the number n along with its square root to be sure that you did not make the mistake of entering a wrong number when you responded to the prompt. Next the procedure interactive-square-root is called, and the process is repeated until the symbol done is entered as a terminating condition. Below is an example of an interactive session after calling interactive-square-root:

```
[1] (interactive-square-root)
Enter the number whose square root you want, or enter done to quit:
100
The square root of 100 is 10

Enter the number whose square root you want, or enter done to quit:
1000
The square root of 1000 is 31.6227766016838

Enter the number whose square root you want, or enter done to quit:
done
That's all, folks.
```

The interactive-square-root example illustrates the use of prompts to ask the user to enter something at the terminal, and it illustrates the use of a read expression to bind a value to a variable interactively. It also shows the echoing of input data in the result to verify that the correct data were entered. Study this example to understand these concepts fully. In this section, we have seen that output from our programs can be sent to the screen using the four procedures display, write, newline, and writeln. Input from the keyboard can be entered during the evaluation of an expression using the procedure read.

Exercises

Exercise 6.5
Write an interactive program that prompts for a number and then prints the square and the square root of that number. It continues prompting for

numbers until *stop* is entered. The display should include the appropriate text to identify the input and output.

Exercise 6.6: *Making change*
Write a program that prompts for an amount of money; for example

```
For what amount do you want change? $
```

and the user enters a number like 23.45. The program then tells how this amount is made up of 100 dollar, 20 dollar, 10 dollar, 5 dollar and 1 dollar bills and of quarters, dimes, nickels, and pennies. The output should say something like:

```
Your change is:
1 twenty-dollar bill
3 one-dollar bills
1 quarter
2 dimes
```

The program should then ask if you want change for another amount and terminate if the answer is "no."

Exercise 6.7: *Weekday of a given date*
A Reverend Zeller developed a formula to compute the day of the week for any given day of the Gregorian calendar. The input to the algorithm is specified in the following manner:

- m is the month of the year, with March as $m = 1$. *January and February are months 11 and 12 of the previous year.*

- d is the day of the month.

- y is the year of the century.

- c is the *previous* century.

For example, for July 4, 1989, $m = 5$, $d = 4$, $y = 89$, and $c = 19$, while for January 25, 1989, $m = 11$, $d = 25$, $y = 88$, and $c = 19$. The algorithm to compute the day of the week is:

1. Take the integer part of $(13m - 1)/5$. Call this a.

2. Take the integer part of $y/4$. Call this b.

3. Take the integer part of $c/4$. Call this e.

4. Compute $f = a + b + e + d + y - 2c$.

5. Set r equal to f modulo 7.

6. r tells us the day of the week, with Sunday corresponding to $r = 0$, Monday to $r = 1$, etc.

Write a program that prompts for the month, the day, and the year. The month should be entered in the usual way with January as 1 and December as 12. The year should also be entered in the usual way (e.g., 1989). The program should then convert these data to what is needed by the algorithm and compute the day. The output should be a statement such as "1/13/1989 is a Friday." The program should ask whether another day is desired and terminate if the user responds with "no."

6.5 Two Famous Problems

These two problems, known by the names Tower of Hanoi and Eight Queens, are included in this chapter to illustrate how information is displayed while the program is running. The Tower of Hanoi[3] problem was apparently originated by the French mathematician Edouard Lucas in the nineteenth century. The following story is told in connection with the problem:

> In the great Temple of Brahma in Benares, on a brass plate beneath the dome that marks the Center of the World, there are 64 disks of pure gold which the priests carry one at a time between three diamond needles according to Brahma's immutable law: No disk may be placed on a smaller disk. In the Beginning of the World, all 64 disks formed the Tower of Brahma on one needle. Now, however, the process of transfer of the tower from one needle to another is in midcourse. When the last disk is finally in place, once again forming the Tower of Brahma but on a different needle, then will come the End of the World, and All will turn to dust.

We shall formulate the problem so as to have three posts, labeled L (for left), C (for center), and R (for right), and n disks of decreasing diameter (in going from bottom to top) all on the left post. Our goal is to move the n disks to the right post, so that at the end they will again be stacked in order of decreasing diameter in going from bottom to top. The two rules are that we can move only one disk at a time and we must never put a larger disk on

---

[3] For a fuller account of the Tower of Hanoi puzzle, see Hofstadter, 1985.

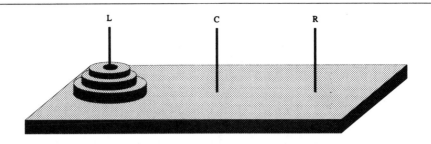

Figure 6.8 The Tower of Hanoi

top of a smaller one. Figure 6.8 illustrates the initial configuration for three disks.

This problem lends itself to a beautiful recursive solution. The idea is that if we have solved it for moving $n-1$ disks from a source post to a destination post (making use of the third post as a help post), we can immediately solve it for moving n disks from a source post (say L) to a destination post (say R) by making the following moves:

1. With n disks on the source post L, we use the fact that we know the solution for $n-1$ disks to move the top $n-1$ disks to the post C. (In these moves, the destination post R serves as the help post.)

2. Now the largest disk is the only one on the source post L and the destination post R is empty. We move the largest disk from the source post L to the destination post R.

3. Making use of the now-empty post L as a help post, we now move the $n-1$ disks from post C to the destination post R.

We have now solved the problem for n disks under the assumption that we knew the solution for $n-1$ disks. If we have only one disk $(n=1)$, the solution is easy: one merely carries that one disk from the source post to the destination post. This case serves as the base case for our recursion. To be able to write the solution to this problem, let us represent a single move that carries a disk from a post called **source** to a post called **destination** by a pair (**source destination**). For example, the move that carries a disk from L to C is denoted by the pair (L C). A list of these pairs gives a sequence of moves; for example, ((L C) (L R) (C R)) says that we first move the top disk from post L to post C, then the top disk on post L is moved to post R, and finally the top disk on post C is moved to post R.

The procedure to solve the Tower of Hanoi problem for **n** disks is called `tower-of-hanoi` and its definition begins with

```
(define tower-of-hanoi
  (lambda (n)
    ... ))
```

We now define a local recursive procedure `move` that moves n disks from the post denoted by `source` to the post denoted by `destination` making use of the post called `helper`. Thus `move` takes the four arguments n, `source`, `destination`, and `helper` and produces a list of pairs that is the solution of the problem of moving n disks from the post `source` to the post `destination`. Thus we continue the definition with

```
(define tower-of-hanoi
  (lambda (n)
    (letrec
      ((move
        (lambda (n source destination helper)
          ... ))))))
```

The terminating condition for the recursion on n is the case in which n is 1. Then we merely move the disk from the `source` to `destination`, and the solution is a list whose only member is the pair consisting of `source` and `destination`. Thus we have

```
(define tower-of-hanoi
  (lambda (n)
    (letrec
      ((move
        (lambda (n source destination helper)
          (if (= n 1)
              (list (list source destination))
              ... )))))))
```

Now for any $n > 1$, we make use of the three steps given above. Step 1 tells us to move $n - 1$ disks from `source` to `helper`, so we first invoke

```
(move (sub1 n) source helper destination)
```

which produces a list of pairs giving the moves that carry the first $n - 1$ disks from the source post to the helper post making use of the destination post. We append to that list the list containing the single move from the source

Program 6.9   `tower-of-hanoi`

```
(define tower-of-hanoi
  (lambda (n)
    (letrec
      ((move
         (lambda (n source destination helper)
           (if (= n 1)
               (list (list source destination))
               (append
                 (move (sub1 n) source helper destination)
                 (cons
                   (list source destination)
                   (move (sub1 n) helper destination source)))))))
      (move n 'L 'R 'C))))
```

post to the destination post. The resulting list is then consed onto the list of pairs produced by

```
(move (sub1 n) helper destination source)
```

which moves the $n - 1$ disks from the helper post to the destination post making use of the source post. These three steps enable us to complete the definition of the local procedure move:

```
(define tower-of-hanoi
  (lambda (n)
    (letrec
      ((move
         (lambda (n source destination helper)
           (if (= n 1)
               (list (list source destination))
               (append
                 (move (sub1 n) source helper destination)
                 (cons
                   (list source destination)
                   (move (sub1 n) helper destination source)))))))
      ... )))
```

Now that the local procedure move is defined, we call it for n disks located on the source L and with destination R with the help of the post C. Thus the complete solution is in Program 6.9.

Program 6.10   `display-tower-of-hanoi`

```
(define display-tower-of-hanoi
  (let ((show-move (lambda (s d)
                     (display s)
                     (display " --> ")
                     (display d))))
    (lambda (n)
      (letrec
        ((move
           (lambda (n source destination helper)
             (if (= n 1)
                 (begin
                   (show-move source destination)
                   (newline))
                 (begin
                   (move (sub1 n) source helper destination)
                   (show-move source destination)
                   (display ", ")
                   (move (sub1 n) helper destination source)))))
                 (move n 'L 'R 'C)))))
```

Now to solve the Tower of Hanoi problem for three disks moving them from the post L to the post R with the help of the post C, we enter

```
[1] (tower-of-hanoi 3)
((L R) (L C) (R C) (L R) (C L) (C R) (L R))
```

This shows the seven moves that solve the problem for $n = 3$.

A minor modification of this program will enable us to see the individual moves as they are being generated by the local procedure **move**. As written now, the local procedure **move** builds a list of the individual pairs (**list source destination**) and returns that as the answer. Now we ask it to send those pairs, without parentheses, to the screen instead of building a list of them. The code to do this is shown in Program 6.10. With this new definition, we get the following output:

```
[3] (display-tower-of-hanoi 3)
L --> R
L --> C, R --> C
L --> R, C --> L
C --> R, L --> R
```

It is good practice to walk through the program and explain how the output is obtained.

The second problem we discuss in this section is that of the Eight Queens. The challenge in this problem is to place eight chess queens on a chess board in such a way that no queen is attacking any other queen.[4] How many different solutions are there to this problem? One such is shown in Figure 6.11.

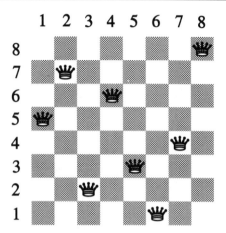

Figure 6.11   An Eight Queens Solution

Let us number the columns from 1 to 8 going from left to right and the rows from 1 to 8 going from the bottom to the top. The data structure we use to denote the positions of the 8 queens on the board is a list of integers of length 8 in which the kth integer in the list denotes the row of the queen in the kth column. This data structure is permissible since the nature of the problem rules out the possibility of two queens being on the same column. The queens illustrated in Figure 6.11 are represented by the position list

$$(5\ 7\ 2\ 6\ 3\ 1\ 4\ 8)$$

In general the last element in the position list denotes the row of the queen in the eighth column, so we denote the positions of the three rightmost queens on the board in Figure 6.11 by (1 4 8). We call a position list *legal* if none

---

[4] For those not familiar with the rules of chess, a queen attacks another piece if the queen and the other piece are on the same horizontal, vertical, or 45-degree diagonal line.

Program 6.12 `legal?`

```
(define legal?
  (lambda (try legal-pl)
    (letrec
      ((good?
         (lambda (new-pl up down)
           (cond
             ((null? new-pl) #t)
             (else (let ((next-pos (car new-pl)))
                     (and
                       (not (= next-pos try))
                       (not (= next-pos up))
                       (not (= next-pos down))
                       (good? (cdr new-pl)
                              (add1 up)
                              (sub1 down)))))))))
      (good? legal-pl (add1 try) (sub1 try)))))

(define solution?
  (lambda (legal-pl)
    (= (length legal-pl) 8)))

(define fresh-try 8)
```

of the queens in the list attacks any other queen in the list. The position list
(1 4 8) is legal, but the position lists (8 4 8) and (6 4 8) are not legal,
the first because two queens are on the same row and the second because two
queens are on the same diagonal. Naturally, a list containing just one element
is legal. Program 6.12 defines a predicate that tests whether adding a new
queen to a legal position list is legal.

When do we know that we have a solution? When we have a legal position
list that is of length **8**. For this problem, we will define a predicate **solution?**
that returns true if its argument, a legal position list, is of length **8**. We need
one other piece of information before we can start. We need a constant **fresh-
try**, which has the value 8.

The Eight Queens problem is interesting because it represents a simple
problem in backtracking. When you make guesses to find a solution, you
often make a wrong guess and follow that wrong guess with other guesses
until it becomes clear that the set of guesses you have made will lead to a
failure. The undoing of such guesses is referred to as *backtracking*.

Program 6.13   `build-solution`

```
(define build-solution
  (lambda (legal-pl)
    (cond
      ((solution? legal-pl) legal-pl)
      (else (forward fresh-try legal-pl)))))
```

— is it a full list

→ try placing an element to a partial list

Imagine that we have the position list (6 4 1 7 5 3 8) and are about to place the last queen on the chess board. The queen we placed most recently was the 6. Now we discover that we cannot place the last queen, so it must be that 6 was a bad choice. Because we try the positions in a column in decreasing order, the next possibility is 5. We try this list with 5, 4, 3, 2, and 1, and they all fail. When we decrease it one more time we get 0, so we backtrack. This time we use 3 and (1 7 5 3 8). Neither 3, 2, nor 1 can be used, so once again we backtrack. Once again we get 0. The 0 indicates that there are no queens that can be added, so we backtrack again. This time we use 6 and (5 3 8). We discover that although we cannot use 6, 5, 4, or 3, we can use 2. Once the 2 has been placed in the position list, we try to place another queen, starting in position 8. This means we look for a five-position list from the possibilities: (8 2 5 3 8), (7 2 5 3 8), (6 2 5 3 8), (5 2 5 3 8), (4 2 5 3 8), (3 2 5 3 8), (2 2 5 3 8), and (1 2 5 3 8). If one of these works, then we will be looking for a six-position list among eight possibilities. If none of these works, then we backtrack and try to find a four-position list from the single possibility 1 and (5 3 8). This process, which consists of moving forward toward a solution as far as possible and then backing up when we have hit a dead end, terminates with a solution if there is one and terminates with the empty list if there are no solutions.

To solve the Eight Queens problem, we use the three procedures: **build-solution**, **forward**, and **backtrack**. When **build-solution** (defined in Program 6.13) is called, we know that its argument is a legal position list, so that termination follows if it is the correct length. If it is not the correct length, we call **forward** with an attempt that may or may not be legal. This attempt will use **fresh-try** (i.e., 8) and a legal position list.

The procedure **forward** (see Program 6.14) is always called with a try and a position list. If the try is 0, then we know that we have tried all positions in this column, and none of them works, so we must backtrack. If the try is not a 0, then adding try might make a legal position list. If so, we invoke **build-solution** with the new legal position list. If not, we try again.

Program 6.14 `forward`

```
(define forward
  (lambda (try legal-pl)
    (cond
      ((zero? try) (backtrack legal-pl))
      ((legal? try legal-pl) (build-solution (cons try legal-pl)))
      (else (forward (sub1 try) legal-pl)))))
```

Program 6.15 `backtrack`

```
(define backtrack
  (lambda (legal-pl)
    (cond
      ((null? legal-pl) '())
      (else (forward (sub1 (car legal-pl)) (cdr legal-pl))))))
```

We next discuss `backtrack` (see Program 6.15). At the time `backtrack` is invoked, we know that its argument is either the empty list, or it is a legal position list that has shown no promise. If it is the empty list, that means we have backtracked as far as is possible and could not find a solution. This is the result when you solve the Three Queens problem on a 3 × 3 board. When this happens, we have no solution. It is more likely, however, that the legal position list has shown no promise. Hence, we sacrifice that position list and try the next one. This is accomplished by subtracting one from the car of the current position list.

With these three procedures, we can now produce a solution to the Eight Queens problem.

```
[1] (build-solution '())
(5 7 2 6 3 1 4 8)
```

Generalizing this program to get more solutions is not difficult if we notice that how we look at a solution is a matter of judgment. When we get a solution, we can add it to a list of solutions, but also we may imagine that that solution has shown no promise and backtrack over it. This way, we will be forced to search for another solution, since the one we have has shown, in a manner of speaking, no promise. This technique is called *failure-driven backtracking*. For example, if we want three solutions, we can write

```
[2] (let ((sol1 (build-solution '())))
     (let ((sol2 (backtrack sol1)))
      (let ((sol3 (backtrack sol2)))
       (list sol1 sol2 sol3))))
((5 7 2 6 3 1 4 8) (4 7 5 2 6 1 3 8) (6 4 7 1 3 5 2 8))
```

From here, it is an easy step to get all solutions. Each time we get a solution, we save it in a list and backtrack over it to get another solution, until there are no solutions left. In the experiment below, we are interested just in the number of solutions.

```
[3] (define build-all-solutions
     (lambda ()
      (letrec
        ((loop (lambda (sol)
                 (cond
                  ((null? sol) '())
                  (else (cons sol (loop (backtrack sol))))))))
        (loop (build-solution '())))))
[4] (length (build-all-solutions))
92
```

The procedures build-solution and forward rely on three global variables: legal?, solution?, and fresh-try. Program 6.16 is a procedure that frees us from concern about these three variables. By scoping these variables, we see how to make the not-so-general procedure for solving the Eight Queens problem work for a larger class of problems.

Just getting answers is not satisfying. Backtracking should be witnessed. As we have done earlier in this chapter, we are going to display selected information so that you can get a better idea of how these procedures work. The procedure forward is uninteresting because it is just monitoring the counting-down procedure; thus we shall not trace forward. However, we will display the position list on entrance to backtrack and build-solution. In the trace we reverse the lists to make the trace more readable. By placing

```
(writeln "Backtrack     : " (reverse legal-pl))
```

and

```
(writeln "Build-Solution : " (reverse legal-pl))
```

Program 6.16   searcher

```
(define searcher
  (lambda (legal? solution? fresh-try)
    (letrec
      ((build-solution
        (lambda (legal-pl)
          (cond
            ((solution? legal-pl) legal-pl)
            (else (forward fresh-try legal-pl)))))
       (forward
        (lambda (try legal-pl)
          (cond
            ((zero? try) (backtrack legal-pl))
            ((legal? try legal-pl)
             (build-solution (cons try legal-pl)))
            (else (forward (sub1 try) legal-pl)))))
       (backtrack
        (lambda (legal-pl)
          (cond
            ((null? legal-pl) '())
            (else
              (forward (sub1 (car legal-pl)) (cdr legal-pl))))))
       (build-all-solutions
        (lambda ()
          (letrec
            ((loop (lambda (sol)
                     (cond
                       ((null? sol) '())
                       (else (cons sol (loop (backtrack sol))))))))
            (loop (build-solution '()))))))
      (build-all-solutions))))
```

as the first expression in **backtrack** and **build-solution**, respectively, we get a trace. If we only want to trace until the first solution is found, as shown below, then we replace the *body* of the letrec by (**build-solution** '()). As you study the trace below, remember that the position list has been *reversed*, and hence the last item in each list is the one most recently entered.

```
[5] (searcher legal? (lambda (x) (= (length x) 7)) 7)
Build-Solution : ()
Build-Solution : (7)
Build-Solution : (7 5)
Build-Solution : (7 5 3)
Build-Solution : (7 5 3 6)
Build-Solution : (7 5 3 6 4)
Backtrack      : (7 5 3 6 4)
Backtrack      : (7 5 3 6)
Build-Solution : (7 5 3 1)
Build-Solution : (7 5 3 1 6)
Build-Solution : (7 5 3 1 6 4)
Build-Solution : (7 5 3 1 6 4 2)
(2 4 6 1 3 5 7)
```

Exercises

Exercise 6.8

An interesting question we can ask is how many moves M_n are needed to move a tower of n disks from the source post to the destination post. We can get a simple equation satisfied by M_n if we recall that we first used M_{n-1} moves to move the top $n - 1$ disks to the helper post, then we used one move to carry the largest one from the source disk to the destination disk, and finally we used M_{n-1} moves to take the $n - 1$ disks from the helper post to the destination post. This leads to the difference equation $M_n = 1 + 2M_{n-1}$. We also know that if we have only one disk on the source post, it takes only one move to take it to the destination post. Thus $M_1 = 1$. Then $M_2 = 1 + 2M_1 = 1 + 2$, and $M_3 = 1 + 2M_2 = 1 + 2 + 2^2$. Show by induction that $M_n = 1 + 2 + 2^2 + 2^3 + \cdots + 2^{n-1}$. Sum this geometric series for M_n by multiplying it termwise by 2 and then computing $2M_n - M_n$ to get the final result $M_n = 2^n - 1$. Estimate the number of digits in the number M_{64} to determine how many disks the priests of the Temple of Brahma must move before All turns to dust.

Exercise 6.9

Write a program that solves the Tower of Hanoi problem for n disks and k posts. All of the disks are initially on the first post. They should be moved to the kth post with a minimum number of moves, placing no disk on top of a smaller disk in the process.

Exercise 6.10: queens

The Eight Queens problem can be restated to apply to n queens placed on an

$n \times n$ board so that none attacks any of the others. Write a procedure **queens** that takes n as an argument and solves the problem for an arbitrary n. Test your solution for $n = 3$, 4, 5, and 6.

Exercise 6.11:   The Good Sequences

The Good Sequences problem may be stated as follows: a finite list of 1's, 2's, and 3's is called a good sequence if it does not contain two identical subsequences that are adjacent. Thus (1 2 3 2 3 1) is not good because (2 3) appears twice as adjacent subsequences. On the other hand, (1 2 3 2 1 3) is a good sequence. Methods similar to those used in solving the Eight Queens problem can be used to show that for any n, one can find a good sequence of length n. Generate all good sequences of length n.

Exercise 6.12

Change the definition of **build-all-solutions** so that instead of building a list of all the answers, it displays the answers, one per line. Redefine your solution so that it displays five solutions per line. Redefine the previous solution to display n per line.

Exercise 6.13

The backtrack trace represents the search for the first solution of the Seven Queens problem. Show what would be printed if we traced the second solution. You may solve this by hand or by modifying the program.

Exercise 6.14

A standard technique for improving the efficiency of programs is to remove invocations of **length**. In the procedures used to solve the Eight Queens problem, we did not integrate the **solution?** test into the program because we wanted to give you a relatively general program for doing backtracking. Given that all you are concerned about solving is the Eight Queens problem, rewrite the set of procedures so that there are no **length** invocations.

Exercise 6.15

Sets of procedures can sometimes be combined. For example, we do not need both the **backtrack** and **forward** procedures. If we combine these two procedures, we will be left with only two procedures: **build-solution** and the combined procedure. Test **build-solution** and the combined procedure. Furthermore, we can take the resultant procedure and combine it with **build-solution**. This would leave us with just one procedure, **build-solution**. Test this new **build-solution**.

Exercise 6.16: `blanks`

In the trace of `backtrack` and `build-solution`, we use strings with sequences of blank characters. As the number of characters in such strings increases, they become more and more difficult to read. A solution is to write a procedure `blanks` that generates a string of *n* blank characters. Run the trace by redefining `backtrack` and `build-solution` to use `blanks` as defined below.

```
(define blanks
  (lambda (n)
    (cond
      ((zero? n) "")
      (else (string-append " " (blanks (sub1 n)))))))
```

Part 2

Procedures as Values

Procedures that take numbers as arguments and have numbers as values are called simple arithmetic operations. Examples are addition and multiplication. Procedures that take procedures as arguments and have procedures as values are called higher-order operations. One use we will make of these higher-order procedures will be to show how we define a procedure that combines similar characteristics of several different procedures. The activity of combining properties of several procedures is also known as abstracting over procedures, a natural generalization of abstracting over data. Not only is the dining out procedure that we discussed in the introduction to Part 1 an abstraction of the dining activity, but it can be made to work for other external consuming activities. Instead of eating in a restaurant, we watch a movie in a theater, and instead of reading from a menu, we read a marquee. We still enter, pay, and exit, so we can abstract the procedures within the *dining out* procedure, and now we can refer to it as the *consuming* procedure. If we feed the *consuming* procedure the activities of reading the menu and eating, then we will once again have the *dining out* procedure, but if we feed it the activities of reading the marquee and watching a movie, we will have the *movie-going* procedure.

A predicate tests whether a value is true or false. Quantifiers tell us whether some or all objects satisfy a predicate. Set theory is about collections of elements and the properties of operations over such collections. In Chapter 8, we develop a set algebra with quantifiers using higher-order procedures. The essence of reasoning with higher-order procedures is the point of this part.

Procedures as Values

7   Abstracting Procedures

7.1 Overview

In this chapter, we first see how procedures can be passed as arguments to other procedures and how procedures may be the values of other procedures. We illustrate these ideas with a development of the Ackermann procedure. We then show how a procedure of two arguments may be rewritten as a procedure of one argument whose value is a procedure of one argument. This process is called currying. We next look at several programs that are similar in structure and we abstract these common features in a program that can be used easily to generate any other program with these features. This process is called *procedural abstraction.* Flat recursion on lists is often encountered in programming, so we have selected it as the first candidate for abstraction. That is followed by an abstraction of deep recursion.

7.2 Procedures as Arguments and Values

In this section, we shall study the use of procedures as arguments to other procedures and as values of procedures. In Chapter 1, we included procedures as a type of datum and have on occasion used procedures as arguments to other procedures. For example, in the definition of `max` in terms of `extreme-value` in Chapter 3, we passed the procedure `>` as an argument to the procedure `extreme-value`. In Scheme, all procedures may be used as arguments to other procedures and as values of procedures. This idea is illustrated by many examples in this section.

Suppose we have a list of numbers, such as (1 3 5 7 9), and we want to

Program 7.1   map

```
(define map
  (lambda (proc ls)
    (if (null? ls)
        '()
        (cons (proc (car ls)) (map proc (cdr ls))))))
```

produce a new list that is obtained from the old by adding 1 to each item in the list, so that in our example, we would get (2 4 6 8 10). We can define a procedure add1-to-each-item that takes a list ls and returns the new list with each number augmented by 1.

```
(define add1-to-each-item
  (lambda (ls)
    (if (null? ls)
        '()
        (cons (+ 1 (car ls)) (add1-to-each-item (cdr ls))))))
```

Now if we want to add 2 to each element, we have to write the definition again but with (+ 1 (car ls)) replaced by (+ 2 (car ls)). Since we may want to perform many different operations on the elements of the list, it would be more efficient if we had a procedure that takes as arguments both the procedure we wish to apply to each element and the list. There is a Scheme procedure map that has the parameters proc and ls and returns a list that contains those elements that are obtained when the procedure proc of one argument is applied to each element of ls. Thus

(map add1 '(1 3 5 7 9)) $\Longrightarrow$ (2 4 6 8 10)

A definition of map is given in Program 7.1. To add 2 to each element in the list, we pass the procedure of one argument, (lambda (num) (+ num 2)), as the first argument to map. Thus we have

(map (lambda (num) (+ num 2)) '(1 3 5 7 9)) $\Longrightarrow$ (3 5 7 9 11)

We can also apply map with a procedure that operates on lists as its first argument. For example:

(let ((proc (lambda (ls) (cons 'a ls))))
  (map proc '((b c) (d e) (f g h)))) $\Longrightarrow$ ((a b c) (a d e) (a f g h))

Program 7.2 `for-each`

```
(define for-each
  (lambda (proc ls)
    (if (not (null? ls))
        (begin
          (proc (car ls))
          (for-each proc (cdr ls))))))
```

```
(let ((x 'a))
  (let ((proc (lambda (ls) (member? x ls))))
    (map proc '((a b c) (b c d) (c d a))))) ⟹ (#t #f #t)
```

Observe that the elements of the list making up the second argument to `map` must be of the correct type for the procedure that is applied to them. In the first of these two examples, `proc` is a procedure that takes a list as its argument and conses the symbol `a` onto the list. Thus each element of the second argument to `map` is a list, and the list that is returned consists of sublists, each of which begins with the `a` that was consed onto it.

There are procedures, such as `display`, that produce side effects of interest to us rather than their returned values. If we apply such a procedure to each item in a list, the list that is returned is not what interests us but only the side effects produced by the procedure. In such cases, we use the Scheme procedure `for-each` instead of `map` to apply the side-effecting procedure to the elements of the list. When `for-each` is applied with a side-effecting procedure as its first argument and a list as its second argument, the procedure is applied to each item in the list, the desired side effects are produced, and the value that is returned is unspecified, that is, it depends upon the implementation of Scheme being used. A definition of `for-each` is given in Program 7.2. An example using `for-each` is:

```
[1] (for-each display '("Hello." " " "How are you?"))
Hello. How are you?
```

We shall see several more examples of the use of `for-each` below. But first we introduce the form of `lambda` that is used to define a procedure that takes an arbitrary number of arguments. We use this *unrestricted lambda* to define the procedures `writeln` and `error`, which we have been using.

In a lambda expression, the keyword `lambda` is followed by a list of parameters. Its syntax is

$$(\texttt{lambda} \; (\textit{parameter}_1 \; \ldots) \; \textit{expr}_1 \; \textit{expr}_2 \; \ldots)$$

where zero or more parameters are in the list of parameters and where the number of arguments passed to the procedure, which is the value of this lambda expression, must match the number of parameters. The body of the lambda expression consists of one or more expressions, which are evaluated in order and the value of the last one is returned. Suppose we want to define a procedure **add** that can be applied to arbitrarily many numbers and returns their sum. For example, we would like to have

```
(add 1 3 5 7 9) ⟹ 25
(add 1 3 5 7 9 11) ⟹ 36
(add 1 3 5 7 9 11 13) ⟹ 49
```

It is possible to define a procedure that can be applied to any number of arguments using the unrestricted **lambda**, whose syntax is

$$(\texttt{lambda} \; \textit{var} \; \textit{expr}_1 \; \textit{expr}_2 \; \ldots)$$

and it may be applied to any number of operands by invoking

$$((\texttt{lambda} \; \textit{var} \; \textit{expr}_1 \; \textit{expr}_2 \; \ldots) \; \textit{operand}_1 \; \ldots)$$

If the operands $\textit{operand}_1 \ldots$ have the values $\textit{arg}_1 \ldots$, then the variable $\textit{var}$ is bound to the *list* of arguments $(\textit{arg}_1 \; \ldots)$. The expressions $\textit{expr}_1 \; \textit{expr}_2 \ldots$ in the body are evaluated with this binding in effect.

Program 7.3   add

```
(define add
  (letrec ((list-add
             (lambda (ls)
               (if (null? ls)
                   0
                   (+ (car ls) (list-add (cdr ls)))))))
    (lambda args
      (list-add args))))
```

As an example, Program 7.3 shows the definition of a procedure **add** that produces the sum of its arguments. For example, (add 1 2 3 4 5) ⟹ 15.

Program 7.4 list

```
(define list (lambda args args))
```

Program 7.5 writeln

```
(define writeln
  (lambda args
    (for-each display args)
    (newline)))
```

Program 7.6   error

```
(define error
  (lambda args
    (display "Error:")
    (for-each (lambda (value) (display " ") (display value)) args)
    (newline)
    (reset)))
```

The general strategy for using this form of **lambda** is to remember that **args** is a list, so we define a local procedure **list-add** that takes a list as its argument and let it do what we want **add** to do. Then we call **list-add** with the list **args** as its argument.

Similarly, the procedure **list** is defined in Program 7.4 so that

(list 'a 'b 'c 'd) $\Longrightarrow$ (a b c d)

Two procedures, **writeln** and **error**, can also be defined using the unrestricted lambda. These are shown in Programs 7.5 and 7.6. The procedure of no arguments **reset** in Program 7.6 returns the user to the prompt. Many implementations of Scheme provide the procedure **reset**. A discussion of the concepts used to define **reset** is given in Chapter 16. (See Exercise 16.6.)

Suppose we now want to find the maximum of two numbers in a list **ls**. We cannot invoke (**max ls**), since the list **ls** is not the correct data type for an argument to **max**, which expects each of its arguments to be a number. If **ls** were, for example, (2 4), we would be looking at the expression (**max** '(2 4)), which has the wrong type of argument for **max**. We could write a recursive program that would compute the maximum of the values in **ls**.

Program 7.7   add

```
(define add
  (lambda args
    (if (null? args)
        0
        (+ (car args) (apply add (cdr args))))))
```

However, there is the Scheme procedure, **apply**, that allows us to apply a procedure of k arguments to a list of k items, and the results are the same as if the items in the list were passed as the k arguments. The procedure **apply** has the call structure

$$(\text{apply } proc \text{ } list\text{-}of\text{-}items)$$

where the procedure *proc* takes the same number of arguments as the number of items in the list *list-of-items*. It returns the value obtained when we invoke *proc* with the items in *list-of-items* as its arguments. For example, we can call

```
(apply max '(2 4)) ⟹ 4
(apply + '(4 11)) ⟹ 15
```

The use of **apply** gives us another way to define procedures using the unrestricted **lambda**. Program 7.7 illustrates it by redefining the procedure **add** given in Program 7.3, this time using **apply** in the recursive invocation of **add** on the list (**cdr args**). There **add** is defined to apply to an arbitrary number of numbers, so it cannot be applied directly to (**cdr args**), which is a list of numbers. Thus we use **apply** to invoke **add** on the items in the list (**cdr args**).

The Scheme procedures + and * are also defined to take an arbitrary number of arguments. Thus we have:

```
(+ 1 3 5 7 9) ⟹ 25
(+ 5) ⟹ 5
(+) ⟹ 0
(* 2 4 6) ⟹ 48
(* 5) ⟹ 5
(*) ⟹ 1
```

Similarly, the Scheme procedures `max` and `min` are defined to take one or more arguments. Thus we have

```
(max 5 -10 15 -20) ⟹ 15
(min 5 -10 15 -20) ⟹ -20
```

An object in Scheme is said to be a *first-class object* if it can be passed as an argument to procedures, can be returned by procedures, and variables may be bound to it. We have been using data objects such as numbers, symbols, or lists of numbers or symbols as arguments to procedures and as values of procedures, and we have bound them to variables using `define`, `lambda`, `let` and `letrec`. Procedures are also treated as first-class objects in Scheme. This is not the case in many other programming languages. We now explore further the implications of procedures as first-class objects.

To discuss the composition of two procedures, we first look at the composition of two functions from a mathematical point of view. Assume that f and g are functions that take one argument and that each value of the function g is a valid argument of the function f. We can then speak of the composition h of the two functions f and g to be the function of one argument defined by $h(x) = f(g(x))$; that is, to get the value of h at x, we first evaluate g at x, and then invoke f on the value $g(x)$. This idea can be interpreted for the procedures we use in our programs. We now define a procedure `compose` that takes two procedures `f` and `g` as parameters and returns another procedure that is the composition of `f` and `g`.

Program 7.8 `compose`

```
(define compose
  (lambda (f g)
    (lambda (x)
      (f (g x)))))
```

The body of the first lambda expression constructs the procedure

```
(lambda (x)
  (f (g x)))
```

with one parameter **x**. Thus (`compose f g`) is a procedure of one argument, and we invoke this new procedure on **8** by writing ((`compose f g`) **8**). As an example, let us take `add1` for `g` and `sqrt` for `f`. Then we can define the composition `h` by writing

```
(define h (compose sqrt add1))
```

The new procedure `h` is the procedure that adds 1 to `x` and then takes the square root of the result; expressed mathematically, $h(x) = \sqrt{x+1}$. If we invoke `h` with argument 8, we get (`h` 8) $\Longrightarrow$ 3. Observe that we have passed the procedures `sqrt` and `add1` as arguments to the procedure `compose`. Furthermore, the value of the procedure `compose` is itself a procedure of one argument. This illustrates both the fact that we can pass procedures, such as `sqrt` and `add1`, as arguments to a procedure and we can have the value of a procedure be a procedure.

If we reverse the order of the two procedures `add1` and `sqrt` as arguments of `compose` in our previous example, we get the procedure

```
(define k (compose add1 sqrt))
```

The procedure `k` so defined first takes the square root of its argument and then adds one to the result; that is, $k(x) = \sqrt{x}+1$. Thus `k` is quite a different function from h.

Exercise

Exercise 7.1
What operand do we pass to `k` to get the same value as (`h` 8)?

We next develop several basic arithmetic procedures that lead to an interesting example that illustrates the use of procedures as values. The procedure `plus` may be defined in terms of `add1` and `sub1` by making use of the fact that to add two nonnegative integers `x` and `y`, we can add 1 to `x` repeatedly `y` times. This leads to Program 7.9. Similarly, using the fact that multiplication of positive integers can be considered as repeated addition, `times` can be defined in terms of `plus` and `sub1` as shown in Program 7.10. This says that multiplication of positive integers `x` and `y` is the same as adding `x` to itself `y` times. In the same way, we can consider raising `x` to the exponent `y` as multiplying `x` by itself `y` times, so we can write the procedure `exponent` as shown in Program 7.11.

Program 7.9 plus

```
(define plus
  (lambda (x y)
    (if (zero? y)
        x
        (add1 (plus x (sub1 y))))))
```

Program 7.10 times

```
(define times
  (lambda (x y)
    (if (zero? y)
        0
        (plus x (times x (sub1 y))))))
```

Program 7.11 exponent

```
(define exponent
  (lambda (x y)
    (if (zero? y)
        1
        (times x (exponent x (sub1 y))))))
```

Program 7.12 super

```
(define super
  (lambda (x y)
    (if (zero? y)
        1
        (exponent x (super x (sub1 y))))))
```

The three procedures we have defined follow a simple pattern. Using this pattern, we can define another procedure, which we call **super**, that uses **exponent** and **sub1**, as shown in Program 7.12. What does **super** do? Let us evaluate (**super** 2 3).

Program 7.13   superduper

```
(define superduper
  (lambda (x y)
    (if (zero? y)
        1
        (super x (superduper x (sub1 y))))))
```

Program 7.14   super-order

```
(define super-order
  (lambda (n)
    (cond
      ((= n 1) plus)
      ((= n 2) times)
      (else (lambda (x y)
              (cond
                ((zero? y) 1)
                (else ((super-order (sub1 n))
                       x
                       ((super-order n) x (sub1 y)))))))))))
```

```
(super 2 3) ⟹ (exponent 2 (super 2 2))
            ⟹ (exponent 2 (exponent 2 (super 2 1)))
            ⟹ (exponent 2 (exponent 2 (exponent 2 (super 2 0))))
            ⟹ (exponent 2 (exponent 2 (exponent 2 1)))
            ⟹ (exponent 2 (exponent 2 2))
            ⟹ (exponent 2 4)
            ⟹ 16
```

Thus (super 2 3) is 2^{2^2}. In the same way we get that (super 2 4) is $2^{2^{2^2}}$ (a tower of 4 twos), which is 65,536. We see that super yields large numbers even with relatively small arguments like 2 and 4.

We now go to the next step and define superduper using super and sub1, as shown in Program 7.13. Then (superduper 2 3) is (super 2 4) or 65,536, and (superduper 2 4) is (super 2 65536), which is a tower of 65,536 twos. This is a very large number.

We can continue defining successive procedures by this process, but we must make up a new name for each one. It would be better to define a procedure super-order that depends upon a number n, so that (super-order 1) is the same procedure as plus, (super-order 2) is the same procedure as times, (super-order 3) is the same procedure as exponent, and so forth. The definition of super-order is given in Program 7.14. If n is 1, super-order is the same as plus, and if n is 2, then super-order is the same as times. For each value of n, (super-order n) is a procedure of two arguments; for example, ((super-order 4) 2 3) is the same as (super 2 3) or simply 16. We can now write any procedure in the sequence by selecting the appropriate value for the parameter n in (super-order n). For example, the procedure that comes after superduper is (super-order 6).

If all three of the arguments, n, x, and y, in super-order are the same, it is called the Ackermann procedure. Specifically, we can define

Program 7.15   ackermann

```
(define ackermann
  (lambda (n)
    ((super-order n) n n)))
```

Then

```
(ackermann 1) is the same as (plus 1 1)       which is 2.
(ackermann 2) is the same as (times 2 2)      which is 4.
(ackermann 3) is the same as (exponent 3 3)   which is 27.
(ackermann 4) is the same as (super 4 4)      which is 4^{4^{4^4}}
```

To get an estimate of how large (ackermann 4) is, we first note that 4^4 is 256. To estimate $4^{4^4} = 4^{256}$, we set $x = 4^{256}$ and take the logarithm to get $\log_{10} x = 256 \log_{10} 4 = 154.13$. Thus we get $4^{256} \approx 10^{154}$ as our estimate for 4^{4^4}. Finally we estimate

$$4^{4^{4^4}}$$

similarly. If we set $y = $ (ackermann 4), then $\log_{10} y \approx 10^{154} \log_{10} 4 \approx 10^{154} 0.602$. Then $y \approx 10^{10^{153}}$, which means that (ackermann 4) has approximately 10^{153} digits. Can you estimate the magnitude of (ackermann 5)? The Ackermann procedure played an important role as an example in the general theory of recursive functions. (See, for example, Minsky, 1967.) It certainly does grow fast as n increases.

We see in the definition of **super-order** that we have a procedure with parameter **n** whose value is itself a procedure with parameters **x** and **y**, illustrating again how procedures are first-class objects in Scheme. We shall explore these ideas further in the next section, which deals with procedural abstraction.

Exercises

Exercise 7.2: compose3
Use the procedure compose to define a procedure compose3 that takes as arguments three procedures, f, g, and h, and returns the composition k such that for each argument x, $k(x) = f(g(h(x)))$.

Exercise 7.3: compose-many
Use the unrestricted lambda to define a composition procedure compose-many that forms the composition of arbitrarily many procedures of one argument. Test your procedure on

```
((compose-many add1 add1 add1 add1) 3) ⟹ 7
((compose-many sqrt abs sub1 (lambda (n) (* n n))) 0.6) ⟹ 0.8
(let ((f (lambda (n) (if (even? n) (/ n 2) (add1 n)))))
  ((compose-many f f f f f f) 21))                    ⟹ 4
```

Exercise 7.4: subtract
Based on the technique used in this chapter to define plus, times, etc., define the procedure subtract that has as parameters two nonnegative integers x and y, with x ≥ y, and returns the difference between x and y.

Exercise 7.5
In the following experiment, fill the blanks with the values of the expressions.

```
[1] (let ((h (lambda (x) (cons x x))))
      (map h '((1 2) (3 4) (5 6))))
    ?_____
[2] (map (lambda (x) (cons x x)) '((1 2) (3 4) (5 6)))
    ?_____
[3] (map (lambda (x) (+ 5 x)) '(1 2 3 4))
    ?_____
[4] (let ((n 5))
      (let ((proc (lambda (x) (+ n x))))
        (map proc '(1 2 3 4))))
    ?_____
```

```
[5] (define iota
      (lambda (n)
        (letrec ((iota-helper
                    (lambda (k acc)
                      (cond
                        ((zero? k) (cons 0 acc))
                        (else (iota-helper (sub1 k) (cons k acc)))))))
          (iota-helper (sub1 n) '()))))
[6] (letrec ((fact
                (lambda (n)
                  (if (zero? n) 1 (* n (fact (sub1 n)))))))
      (map fact (iota 6)))
?_____
[7] (map (lambda (x) (+ x (add1 x))) (iota 5))
?_____
[8] (define mystery
      (lambda (len base)
        (letrec
          ((mystery-help
              (lambda (n s)
                (if (zero? n)
                    (list s)
                    (let ((h (lambda (x)
                               (mystery-help (sub1 n) (cons x s)))))
                      (apply append (map h (iota base)))))))
            (mystery-help len '())))))
[9] (mystery 4 3)
?_____
```

Exercise 7.6: `map-first-two`

Define a procedure, `map-first-two`, that works exactly like `map` except that
the procedure argument is always a procedure of two arguments instead of
just one argument. Use the first and second elements of the list as the first
pair of arguments to the procedure, then the second and third elements, then
the third and fourth elements, and so on, until the end of the list is reached.
If there are fewer than two elements in the list, the empty list is the value.
Test your procedure on:

```
(map-first-two + '(2 3 4 5 7)) ⟹ (5 7 9 12)
(map-first-two max '(2 4 3 5 4 1)) ⟹ (4 4 5 5 4)
```

Exercise 7.7: `reduce`

Define a procedure, `reduce`, that has two parameters, `proc` and `ls`. The
procedure `proc` takes two arguments. The procedure `reduce` reduces the list

ls by successively applying this operation: it builds a new list with the first two elements of the preceding list replaced by the value obtained when proc is applied to them. When the list is reduced to containing only two elements, the value returned is the value of proc applied to these two elements. If the original list ls contains fewer than two elements, an error is reported. Here is how the successive stages in the reduction look when proc is + and ls is (3 5 7 9):

$$(3\ 5\ 7\ 9) \rightarrow (8\ 7\ 9) \rightarrow (15\ 9) \rightarrow 24$$

Test your procedure on:

```
(reduce + '(1 3 5 7 9)) ⟹ 25
(reduce max '(2 -4 6 8 3 1)) ⟹ 8
(reduce (lambda (x y) (and x y)) '(#t #t #t #t)) ⟹ #t
```

The last example is not written as (reduce and '(#t #t #t #t)) because and is a keyword of a special form and not a procedure. Keywords only appear in the first position of a list.

Exercise 7.8: andmap

Define a predicate andmap that takes two arguments, a one-argument predicate pred and a list ls. The value returned by andmap is true when pred applied to each of the elements of ls is true. If pred applied to any one of the elements of ls is false, andmap returns false. The solution

```
(define andmap
  (lambda (pred ls)
    (reduce (lambda (x y) (and x y)) (map pred ls))))
```

is unacceptable because of the extra recursion. Test your predicate on:

```
(andmap positive? '(3 4 6 9)) ⟹ #t
(andmap positive? '(3 -1 4 8)) ⟹ #f
(let ((not-null? (compose not null?)))
  (andmap not-null? '((a b) (c) (c d e)))) ⟹ #t
```

Exercise 7.9: map2

Define map2, which is exactly like map except that its procedure argument is always a procedure that takes two arguments, and it takes an additional argument that is a list the same length as its second argument. The additional list is where it gets its second argument. Test your procedure on:

```
(map2 + '(1 2 3 4) '(5 7 9 11)) ⟹ (6 9 12 15)
```

```
(map2 (let ((n 5))
        (lambda (x y)
          (and (< x n) (< n y))))
      '(1 3 2 1 7)
      '(9 11 4 7 8)) ⟹ (#t #t #f #t #f)
```

Exercise 7.10: map, ormap

We now present a definition of map that accepts any number of arguments.

$$(\text{map } proc \; ls_1 \; ls_2 \; ... ls_n)$$

where *proc* is a procedure that takes n arguments and each of the n lists has the same length. This generalizes the procedures map and map2 given above.

```
(define map
  (lambda args
    (let ((proc (car args)))
      (letrec ((map-helper
                (lambda (a*)
                  (if (any-null? a*)
                      '()
                      (cons
                        (apply proc (map car a*))
                        (map-helper (map cdr a*)))))))
        (map-helper (cdr args))))))
```

This program, as written, is incorrect because the two invocations of *map* within the definition refer to the simple map we defined earlier in the chapter. Add a definition of the simple map to the letrec (in the same way that even? and odd? are in the same letrec) so that no names will be changed in the definition of map-helper, and write any-null? using the definition of ormap given below.

```
(define ormap
  (lambda (pred ls)
    (if (null? ls)
        #f
        (or (pred (car ls)) (ormap pred (cdr ls))))))
```

What does this version of map return when the n lists are not of equal length?

Exercise 7.11

To test your understanding of scope, determine the value of the expression

```
(letrec ((a (let ((a (lambda (b c)
                        (if (zero? b) c (a (sub1 b))))))
             (lambda (x) (a x x)))))
  (a 3))
```

7.3 Currying

The procedure + takes two numbers as arguments and returns their sum. The procedure add1 adds 1 to its argument. We can also define a procedure add5 that adds 5 to its argument by writing

```
(define add5
  (lambda (n)
    (+ 5 n)))
```

This can clearly be done for any number in place of 5. Another way of approaching this problem makes use of the fact that a procedure may return another procedure as its value. We can define a procedure curried+ that has only one parameter, m, and returns a procedure having one parameter n, that adds m and n:

```
(define curried+
  (lambda (m)
    (lambda (n)
      (+ m n))))
```

Thus (curried+ 5) returns a procedure defined by

```
(lambda (n) (+ m n))
```

where m is bound to 5. To add 5 and 7, we would then invoke

```
((curried+ 5) 7) ⟹ 12
```

We can now define add5 by writing

```
(define add5 (curried+ 5))
```

Moreover, we can define **add8** by writing

```
(define add8 (curried+ 8))
```

and we clearly can do the same for any other number in place of **8**. What underlies this method is the fact that we can take any procedure that has two parameters, say **x** and **y**, and rewrite it as a procedure with one parameter **x** that returns a procedure with one parameter **y**. The process of writing a procedure of two parameters as a procedure of one parameter that returns a procedure of one parameter is called *currying* the procedure.[1] It is often advantageous to use a curried procedure when you want to keep one argument fixed while the other varies, so in essence, you are using a procedure of one argument.

We next use currying to rewrite the definitions of four procedures in a way that demonstrates certain common structural features that they possess. In the next section, we shall abstract these common features and write a single procedure from which the original four and many others can be obtained. The four procedures are **member?**, **map**, **sum**, and **product**.

The procedure **member?** can be defined as follows:

```
(define member?
  (lambda (item ls)
    (if (null? ls)
        #f
        (or (equal? (car ls) item)
            (member? item (cdr ls))))))
```

It tests whether the object **item** is a top-level object in the list **ls**. We are going to apply the procedure **member?** with the same object **item** but different lists **ls**, so we define the curried procedure **member?-c**, which is a procedure with parameter **item** and returns a procedure that has the parameter **ls** and tests whether **item** is a top-level member of **ls**. We do that in Program 7.16. Observe the following points in the definition of **member?-c**:

1. **member?-c** is a procedure with one parameter **item**.

2. The procedure **member?-c** returns a procedure **helper** that has one parameter **ls**.

---

[1] Conceived by Moses Schönfinkel in 1924 (See Schönfinkel, 1924) and named after the logician Haskell B. Curry.

Program 7.16 member?-c

```
(define member?-c
  (lambda (item)
    (letrec
      ((helper
         (lambda (ls)
           (if (null? ls)
               #f
               (or (equal? (car ls) item) (helper (cdr ls)))))))
      helper)))
```

3. We introduced the letrec expression to avoid having to pass the argument item each time we make a recursive procedure call, since item does not change throughout the program.

We can now define the original procedure member? in terms of member?-c by writing

```
(define member?
  (lambda (a ls)
    ((member?-c a) ls)))
```

As another example of currying, we look at the definition of the procedure map, presented in Program 7.1, which has two parameters, a procedure proc, and a list ls. It applies the procedure proc elementwise to ls and returns a list of the results. For example,

```
(map add1 '(1 2 3 4)) ⟹ (2 3 4 5)
```

Its definition is:

```
(define map
  (lambda (proc ls)
    (if (null? ls)
        '()
        (cons (proc (car ls)) (map proc (cdr ls))))))
```

This can be written in curried form by using the procedure apply-to-all, which takes one argument proc and is itself a procedure of the argument ls. We give its definition in Program 7.17. We can write map in terms of apply-to-all by defining

Program 7.17 apply-to-all

```
(define apply-to-all
  (lambda (proc)
    (letrec
      ((helper
         (lambda (ls)
           (if (null? ls)
               '()
               (cons (proc (car ls)) (helper (cdr ls)))))))
      helper)))
```

Program 7.18   sum

```
(define sum
  (letrec
    ((helper
       (lambda (ls)
         (if (null? ls)
             0
             (+ (car ls) (helper (cdr ls)))))))
    helper))
```

Program 7.19   product

```
(define product
  (letrec
    ((helper
       (lambda (ls)
         (if (null? ls)
             1
             (* (car ls) (helper (cdr ls)))))))
    helper))
```

```
(define map
  (lambda (proc ls)
    ((apply-to-all proc) ls)))
```

We next look at two more procedures that take lists as arguments. The first,

Program 7.20 `swapper-m`

```
(define swapper-m
  (lambda (x y)
    (letrec
      ((helper
         (lambda (ls)
           (cond
             ((null? ls) '())
             ((equal? (car ls) x) (cons y (helper (cdr ls))))
             ((equal? (car ls) y) (cons x (helper (cdr ls))))
             (else (cons (car ls) (helper (cdr ls))))))))
      helper)))
```

sum, assumes that the objects in the list are numbers and returns the sum of the numbers in the list, and the second, **product**, assumes that the objects in the list are numbers and returns the product of the numbers in the list. We write their definitions in Programs 7.18 and 7.19 in such a way that they demonstrate the same structure as the preceding definitions of **member?-c** and **apply-to-all**. We could have written the procedures **sum** and **product** without the letrec expressions, but we have chosen to do it this way to be able to compare the structure of these two procedures with the structure of **member?-c** and **apply-to-all** when we abstract this structure in the next section.

We close this section with an example that is similar to currying, this time modifying a procedure with three parameters to get a procedure with two parameters that returns a procedure with one parameter. We look at the procedure **swapper** introduced in Program 2.8. Its definition is:

```
(define swapper
  (lambda (x y ls)
    (cond
      ((null? ls) '())
      ((equal? (car ls) x) (cons y (swapper x y (cdr ls))))
      ((equal? (car ls) y) (cons x (swapper x y (cdr ls))))
      (else (cons (car ls) (swapper x y (cdr ls)))))))
```

We modify it to get a procedure **swapper-m** (we use **-m** for "modified") that has the two parameters **x** and **y** and that returns a procedure of one parameter **ls**. Its definition is given in Program 7.20. To swap the numbers 0 and 1 in the list (0 1 2 0 1 2), we would invoke

```
((swapper-m 0 1) '(0 1 2 0 1 2)) ⟹ (1 0 2 1 0 2)
```

This example illustrates that a generalization of currying can be used to re-define a procedure with $n = m + k$ parameters to become a procedure with m parameters that returns a procedure with k parameters. The term currying refers to redefining a procedure with n parameters to be expressed as n procedures, each having only one parameter.

In this section, we have introduced the concept of currying a procedure of two arguments to get a procedure of one argument that returns a procedure of one argument. This technique is useful when we want to consider the behavior of the procedure as the second argument varies while the first argument is fixed. More generally, a procedure of $n = m + k$ arguments may be modified to get a procedure of m arguments that returns a procedure of k arguments.

Exercises

Exercise 7.12: `curried*`
Curry the procedure `*` to get a procedure `curried*` and use it to define the procedure `times10` that multiplies its argument by 10. Test your procedures on:

```
((curried* 25) 5) ⟹ 125
(times10 125) ⟹ 1250
```

Exercise 7.13: `swapper-c`
Curry the procedure `swapper-m` so that the curried procedure `swapper-c` has one parameter `x`. It returns a procedure with one parameter `y`, which in turn returns a procedure with one parameter `ls`. That procedure swaps `x` and `y` in `ls`.

Exercise 7.14: `round-n-places`
In Program 6.5, the procedure `round-n-places` was defined to take two parameters, `n` and `dec-num`, and returned the number `dec-num` rounded off to `n` decimal places. Rewrite the definition of `round-n-places` so that it takes one parameter, `n`, and returns a procedure with one parameter, `dec-num`, that rounds the number `dec-num` off to `n` decimal places. We can then write

```
(define round-5-places (round-n-places 5))
```

to get the procedure that rounds a given number off to five decimal places.

Exercise 7.15: `subst-all-m`
Modify the deeply recursive procedure `subst-all`, which has the parameters `new`, `old`, and `ls`, to get a procedure `subst-all-m` with the two parameters `new` and `old`, which returns a procedure with the parameter `ls`, which replaces each occurrence of `old` in `ls` by `new`. Test your procedure on:

```
((subst-all-m 1 0) '(0 1 2 0 1 2)) ⟹ (1 1 2 1 1 2)
((subst-all-m 1 0) '(0 1 2 ((0 1 2)))) ⟹ (1 1 2 ((1 1 2)))
```

Exercise 7.16: `extreme-value-c`
In Program 3.19, the procedure `extreme-value` was defined and then it was used to define the procedures `rmax` and `rmin` by passing it the appropriate predicate. Write the definition of the procedure `extreme-value-c`, which takes the predicate `pred` and returns a procedure that finds the maximum of its two arguments or the minimum of its two arguments, depending upon `pred`. Then express `rmax` and `rmin` in terms of `extreme-value-c`.

Exercise 7.17: `extreme-value-c`
In the previous exercise, the procedure `(extreme-value-c pred)` expects only two arguments. Rewrite the definition of `extreme-value-c` using the unrestricted lambda so that `(extreme-value-c pred)` is a procedure that takes arbitrarily many numbers as arguments and returns the extreme value (maximum or minimum) depending upon the predicate `pred`.

Exercise 7.18: `between?`, `between?-c`
Define a predicate `between?` that has three numbers x, y, and z, as parameters and returns true when y is strictly between x and z, that is, when x < y < z. Then define `between?-c`, a curried version of `between?`, where each of the procedures has only one parameter. That is, `between?-c` has the parameter x and returns a procedure that has the parameter y, which in turn returns a procedure with the parameter z, that tests whether y is strictly between x and z. Test your procedure on:

```
(((between?-c 5) 6) 7) ⟹ #t
(((between?-c 5) 5) 7) ⟹ #f
(((between?-c 5) 4) 7) ⟹ #f
```

Exercise 7.19: `andmap-c`, `ormap-c`
Consider this definition of `andmap-c`:

```
(define andmap-c
  (lambda (pred)
    (letrec
      ((and-help
         (lambda (ls)
           (cond
             ((null? ls) #t)
             (else (and (pred (car ls)) (and-help (cdr ls))))))))
      and-help)))
```

Fill in the blanks below.

```
[1] (define all-positive? (andmap-c positive?))
[2] (all-positive? '(3 4 8 9))
?_____
[3] (all-positive? '(3 -1 4 8))
?_____
[4] ((andmap-c (compose not null?)) '((a b) (c) (c d e)))
?_____
```

Now define the procedure ormap-c, which takes a predicate as an argument and returns a predicate that accepts a list as a value. We can define ormap (see Exercise 7.10) using ormap-c as follows:

```
(define ormap
  (lambda (pred ls)
    ((ormap-c pred) ls)))
```

Test ormap-c by filling in the blanks below.

```
[5] (define some-positive? (ormap-c positive?))
[6] (some-positive? '(3 4 8 9))
?_____
[7] (some-positive? '(3 -1 4 8))
?_____
[8] ((ormap-c (compose not null?)) '(() () (a b) (c) (c d e)))
?_____
```

Exercise 7.20: is-divisible-by?, prime?
Consider the definition

```
(define is-divisible-by?
  (lambda (n)
    (lambda (k)
      (zero? (remainder n k)))))
```

A *prime number* is a positive integer greater than 1 that is not divisible by any positive number other than 1 and itself. Using `is-divisible-by?`, write a definition of the procedure `prime?` that tests whether a positive integer $n > 2$ is prime by first testing whether it is odd and greater than 1 and then testing whether it is not divisible by any of the odd integers from 3 to the largest odd integer less than or equal to the square root of n. Why is it necessary only to try integers less than the square root of n?

Exercise 7.21
Justify the statement "If we restrict ourselves to using only lambda expressions having only one parameter in its list of parameters, we can still define any procedure, regardless of how many parameters it has." Note that the currying examples in this section show how to define procedures having two and three parameters using only lambda expressions with one parameter.

7.4 Procedural Abstraction of Flat Recursion

In this section, we show how to abstract the structure of flatly recursive procedures to obtain a general procedure in terms of which the various special cases can be defined. We illustrate this idea by looking for common structural features in the four procedures `member?-c`, `apply-to-all`, `sum`, and `product` defined in Section 7.3. A comparison of the code for these four procedures yields the fact that the four lines

```
(letrec
  ((helper
     (lambda (ls)
       (if (null? ls)
```

and the last line

```
helper
```

are identical in all four programs. Furthermore, in all four, we do something to `(car ls)` and make the recursive call to `helper` on `(cdr ls)`. We want to define a procedure `flat-recur` that abstracts the structure of these four programs; that is, it embodies the common features of these programs, and they can all be derived from it by using suitable parameters. Let us see how much of `flat-recur` we can write based on the above observations.

```
(define flat-recur
  (lambda ( _____ )
    (letrec
      ((helper
        (lambda (ls)
          (if (null? ls)
            _____
            _____ )))))
      helper)))
```

How do we fill in the blanks? Let us first look at the blank that is the consequent of the if expression. It is the action taken when **ls** is empty. We call this consequent of the test **(null? ls)** the *seed* and denote it by the variable **seed**. This will be the first parameter in the outer lambda expression. Table 7.21 shows the seed for each of the four cases.

Procedure	seed
member?-c	#f
apply-to-all	()
sum	0
product	1

Table 7.21   Seeds for the four procedures

The other blank in the if expression is in the action taken on (car ls) and (helper (cdr ls)) when (null? ls) is false. The action taken on (car ls) and (helper (cdr ls)) is a procedure that takes (car ls) and (helper (cdr ls)) as arguments, and we call this procedure list-proc. We write list-proc as a procedure with the parameters **x** and **y**. When list-proc is invoked, **x** will be bound to (car ls) and **y** will be bound to (helper (cdr ls)) to give us the alternative action when (null? ls) is false. For example, the alternative action in the case of **apply-to-all** is

```
(cons (proc (car ls)) (helper (cdr ls)))
```

If **list-proc** is the value of

```
(lambda (x y) (cons (proc x) y))
```

then

```
(list-proc (car ls) (helper (cdr ls)))
```

is the desired alternative action. We pass `list-proc` as the second parameter in the outer lambda expression. Table 7.22 gives `list-proc` for each of the four programs.[2]

Procedure	list-proc
member?-c	(lambda (x y) (or (equal? x item) y))
apply-to-all	(lambda (x y) (cons (proc x) y))
sum	+
product	*

Table 7.22   The four list procedures

We are now ready to define the procedure `flat-recur`, which takes `seed` and `list-proc` as arguments and produces precisely the procedure with parameter `ls` that abstracts the structure of the four procedures. (See Program 7.23.) We can then write each of the four procedures in terms of this new procedure. Furthermore, we can use it to write any procedure using recursion on a list of top-level items.

We can now write the four procedures using `flat-recur` as follows:

```
(define member?-c
  (lambda (item)
    (flat-recur #f (lambda (x y) (or (equal? x item) y)))))

(define apply-to-all
  (lambda (proc)
    (flat-recur '() (lambda (x y) (cons (proc x) y)))))

(define sum (flat-recur 0 +))

(define product (flat-recur 1 *))
```

---

[2] The procedure that we selected for `list-proc` in the case of `member?-c` does more processing than is necessary, for it loses the benefit of the behavior of `or`. Generally when the first argument to `or` is true, the value `#t` is returned without evaluating the second argument. However, when `list-proc` is called, both arguments are first evaluated, and then the `or` expression is evaluated, so the argument to which `y` is bound is always evaluated. Even though the resulting version of `member?-c` is less efficient, it illustrates the principle of procedural abstraction and a feature that one should be aware of when applying it.

Program 7.23   flat-recur

```
(define flat-recur
  (lambda (seed list-proc)
    (letrec
      ((helper
         (lambda (ls)
           (if (null? ls)
               seed
               (list-proc (car ls) (helper (cdr ls)))))))
      helper)))
```

You may be concerned that the procedure `list-proc` in these last two examples has a different structure from those in the first two examples. This is really not the case, since we could also have used `(lambda (x y) (+ x y))` in place of the variable `+`, and we could have used `(lambda (x y) (* x y))` in place of the variable `*`.

The process we have used here looks for common features in several programs and then produces a procedure that embodies the code that is similar in all of these programs. It enables us to express each of the original procedures more simply. This process is called *procedural abstraction*. This is a very powerful programming tool that should be exploited when it is applicable.

The procedure `flat-recur` can be used whenever a program does recursion on the top-level objects in a list. We now see an example of how we can use it to define the procedure `filter-in-c`. Let `ls` be a list and suppose that we have a predicate `pred` that we want to apply to each top-level object in the list. If the result of applying `pred` to an object in the list is false, then the object is to be dropped from the list. Thus the procedure `filter-in-c` returns a list consisting of those objects from `ls` that "pass" the test. This program involves recursion on the top-level objects in the list `ls`, and if `ls` is empty, `filter-in-c` returns the empty list, so `seed` is `()`. To get `list-proc` we shall again use `x` for the `(car ls)` and `y` for `(helper (cdr ls))`. Then if `pred` applied to `x` is true, we cons `x` to `y`; otherwise we just return `y`. Thus the `list-proc` of `flat-recur` can be written as

```
(lambda (x y)
  (if (pred x)
      (cons x y)
      y))
```

Program 7.24 `filter-in-c`

```
(define filter-in-c
  (lambda (pred)
    (flat-recur
     '()
     (lambda (x y)
       (if (pred x)
           (cons x y)
           y)))))
```

and we can define `filter-in-c` as shown in Program 7.24. If we do not want to use `filter-in-c` in curried form, we can define the procedure `filter-in` as:

```
(define filter-in
  (lambda (pred ls)
    ((filter-in-c pred) ls)))
```

Here are some examples using `filter-in`:

```
(filter-in odd? '(1 2 3 4 5 6 7 8 9)) ⟹ (1 3 5 7 9)
(filter-in positive? '(1 0 2 0 3 0 4)) ⟹ (1 2 3 4)
(filter-in (lambda (x) (< x 5)) '(1 2 3 4 5 6 7 8 9)) ⟹ (1 2 3 4)
```

In this section, we have illustrated the process of procedural abstraction of flat recursion. We defined a procedure `flat-recur` from which procedures that use flat recursion can be derived by passing `flat-recur` the appropriate arguments. This is a powerful tool that can often be used to make programs easier to write and to understand.

Exercises

Exercise 7.22: `mult-by-scalar`
In Exercise 3.1, we called a list of numbers an n-tuple. Using `flat-recur`, define a procedure `mult-by-scalar` that takes as its argument a number c and returns a procedure that takes as its argument an n-tuple ntpl and multiplies each component of ntpl by the number c. Test your procedure on:

```
((mult-by-scalar 3) '(1 -2 3 -4)) ⟹ (3 -6 9 -12)
((mult-by-scalar 5) '()) ⟹ ()
```

Exercise 7.23: `filter-out`
The procedure `filter-out` takes two arguments, a predicate `pred` and a list `ls`. It removes from the list `ls` all of its top-level elements that "pass" the test, that is, it removes those top-level objects `item` for which (`pred item`) is true. Write the definition of `filter-out` using a local procedure `filter-out-c` that is defined using `flat-recur`.

Exercise 7.24: `insert-left`
Starting with the procedure `insert-left` described in Exercise 4.1 and using `flat-recur`, define the modified version `insert-left-m` that takes as parameters the new and old values and returns a procedure with the list as its parameter. Then define `insert-left` using `insert-left-m`.

Exercise 7.25: `partial`
Let `proc` be a procedure of one numerical argument with numerical values.

a. Define a procedure `partial-sum` that computes the sum of the numbers (`proc` i) for i ranging from k to n, where $k \leq n$. For example,

```
(partial-sum (lambda (m) (* m m)) 3 7) ⟹ 135
```

b. Define a procedure `partial-product` that computes the product of the numbers (`proc` i) for i ranging from k to n, where $k \leq n$. For example

```
(partial-product (lambda (m) (* m m)) 3 7) ⟹ 6350400
```

c. Define an abstraction of `partial-sum` and `partial-product` named `partial` so that `partial-sum` and `partial-product` can be defined as

```
(define partial-sum (partial 0 +))
(define partial-product (partial 1 *))
```

7.5 Procedural Abstraction of Deep Recursion

The deeply recursive procedures defined in Chapter 4 use recursion on nested sublists rather than being limited to top-level objects of lists. They also display a common structure that can be abstracted in a procedure `deep-recur`. We now look at some deeply recursive procedures to find their common structure and then formulate the definition of `deep-recur`.

We start with `filter-in-all-c`, which takes a `pred` as its argument and returns a procedure that has a list `ls` as its parameter and, when applied to ls, drops from the list those items that do not "pass" the test. For example, if **pred** is **odd?** and **ls** is `((4 5) 2 (3 5 (8 7)))` we have

```
((filter-in-all-c odd?) ls) ⟹ ((5) (3 5 (7)))
```

The code for **filter-in-all-c** is given in Program 7.25. We define **filter-in-all** as the procedure of two arguments, **pred** and **ls**, in terms of **filter-in-all-c** as shown in Program 7.26.

In the same way, we define **sum-all** as a procedure of one argument **ls**, which is a list of numbers, such that `(sum-all ls)` is the sum of all of the numbers in **ls**. For example

```
(sum-all '(3 (1 4) (2 (-3 5)))) ⟹ 12
```

The code for **sum-all** is presented in Program 7.27. Both of these procedures, **sum-all** and **filter-in-all-c**, share the following lines:

```
(letrec
  ((helper
    (lambda (ls)
      (if (null? ls)
.....................
(let ((a (car ls)))
  (if (or (pair? a) (null? a))
............................
helper
```

We are going to define a procedure **deep-recur** to abstract the structure of these two procedures. Let us see how much of the code we can fill in from the above observations.

```
(define deep-recur
  (lambda ( _____ )
    (letrec
      ((helper
        (lambda (ls)
          (if (null? ls)

              _____
              (let ((a (car ls)))
                (if (or (pair? a) (null? a))

                    _____
                    _____ ))))))
      helper)))
```

Program 7.25 `filter-in-all-c`

```scheme
(define filter-in-all-c
  (lambda (pred)
    (letrec
      ((helper
         (lambda (ls)
           (if (null? ls)
               '()
               (let ((a (car ls)))
                 (if (or (pair? a) (null? a))
                     (cons (helper a) (helper (cdr ls)))
                     (if (pred a)
                         (cons a (helper (cdr ls)))
                         (helper (cdr ls)))))))))
      helper)))
```

Program 7.26 `filter-in-all`

```scheme
(define filter-in-all
  (lambda (pred ls)
    ((filter-in-all-c pred) ls)))
```

Program 7.27 `sum-all`

```scheme
(define sum-all
  (letrec ((helper
             (lambda (ls)
               (if (null? ls)
                   0
                   (let ((a (car ls)))
                     (if (or (pair? a) (null? a))
                         (+ (helper a) (helper (cdr ls)))
                         (+ a (helper (cdr ls)))))))))
    helper))
```

Once again, we use the variable **seed** to denote the consequent of the first if expression with test (null? ls). In the case of **sum-all**, **seed** is 0, and in the case of **filter-in-all-c**, **seed** is (). We take **seed** to be the first parameter for the outer lambda expression.

In the consequent of the second if expression with test (or (pair? a) (null? a)), the local procedure **helper** for **filter-in-all-c** invokes

```
(cons (helper a) (helper (cdr ls)))
```

and the local procedure **helper** for **sum-all** invokes

```
(+ (helper a) (helper (cdr ls)))
```

We refer to the procedure that is applied to (helper a) and (helper (cdr ls)) as **list-proc**. We fill the blank with the application

```
(list-proc (helper a) (helper (cdr ls)))
```

and to generate the expression needed for **filter-in-all-c**, we bind **list-proc** to **cons**, and to generate the expression needed for **sum-all**, we bind **list-proc** to **+**. We take **list-proc** as the third parameter to the outer lambda expression. We next consider what to use as the second parameter.

In both of our examples, the alternative of the second if expression with test (or (pair? a) (null? a)) is a procedure invocation that involves **a** and (helper (cdr ls)). For **filter-in-all-c**, we want to generate the expression

```
(if (pred a) (cons a (helper (cdr ls))) (helper (cdr ls)))
```

while for **sum-all**, we need

```
(+ a (helper (cdr ls)))
```

We can generate both of these using a procedure **item-proc** that has two parameters, **x** and **y**. If we fill the blank with

```
(item-proc a (helper (cdr ls)))
```

then to get what we need for **sum-all**, we bind **item-proc** to **+**. To get what we need for **filter-in-all-c**, we bind **item-proc** to

Program 7.28 `deep-recur`

```
(define deep-recur
  (lambda (seed item-proc list-proc)
    (letrec
      ((helper
        (lambda (ls)
          (if (null? ls)
              seed
              (let ((a (car ls)))
                (if (or (pair? a) (null? a))
                    (list-proc (helper a) (helper (cdr ls)))
                    (item-proc a (helper (cdr ls)))))))))
      helper)))
```

```
(lambda (x y)
  (if (pred x)
      (cons x y)
      y))
```

We are now in a position to write a procedure `deep-recur` that abstracts the structure of these procedures (and those in the exercises at the end of this section). The procedure `deep-recur` has three parameters: `seed`, `item-proc`, and `list-proc`. It returns `helper`, which is a procedure with only one parameter `ls`. Combining the observations made above, we get the definition presented in Program 7.28.

In particular, we can now write

```
(define sum-all (deep-recur 0 + +))
```

and

```
(define filter-in-all-c
  (lambda (pred)
    (deep-recur
      '()
      (lambda (x y)
        (if (pred x)
            (cons x y)
            y))
      cons)))
```

In this chapter, we looked at the definitions of the four procedures **sum**, **product**, **member?-c**, and **filter-in-c**, all of which performed flat recursion, and abstracted from them their common structural features. We then defined the procedure **flat-recur**, which incorporated those common features and took as arguments the things that produced the features of the four procedures that were not common to them all. This enabled us to recover the original four procedures and others that do flat recursion from **flat-recur** by passing to **flat-recur** the appropriate arguments. We then did a similar thing with procedures that performed deep recursions. We abstracted from the two procedures **filter-in-all-c** and **sum-all** their common features and defined the procedure **deep-recur**. We were able to recover the original two procedures by passing to **deep-recur** the appropriate arguments. This process of defining a procedure incorporating the common structural features of a class of procedures, and then obtaining the procedures in that class by passing the abstraction the appropriate arguments, is what we called procedural abstraction.

Exercises

Exercise 7.26: **remove-all-c**, **product-all**
Write the definitions of **remove-all-c** and **product-all** for arbitrary lists. The procedure **remove-all-c** takes an object **item** as its argument and returns a procedure of the list **ls**, which removes all occurrences of **item** in **ls**. The call (**product-all ls**) returns the product of all of the numbers in the list of numbers **ls**. In both procedures, preserve the structure displayed in the above definitions of **sum-all** and **filter-in-all-c** using **letrec**.

Exercise 7.27: **remove-all-c**, **product-all** *(continued)*
Define the two procedures **product-all** and **remove-all-c** described in the previous exercise using **deep-recur**.

Exercise 7.28: **filter-out-all**
In a manner analogous to that used in Exercise 7.23, use **deep-recur** to define the deeply recursive procedure **filter-out-all-c**, and then use it to define **filter-out-all**.

Exercise 7.29: **subst-all-m**
The procedure **subst-all-m** was described in Exercise 7.15. Define it using **deep-recur**.

Exercise 7.30: `reverse-all`

The procedure `reverse-all` was defined in Program 4.10. Define it using `deep-recur`.

Exercise 7.31: `flat-recur`

Define `flat-recur` using `deep-recur`.

Exercise 7.32: `deep-recur`

Define `deep-recur` using `flat-recur`. Hint: Use `letrec`.

8   Sets and Relations

8.1   Overview

Sets play a fundamental role in the development of mathematics and logic. In this chapter, we show how sets may be introduced as a data structure in Scheme. We first define various procedures that give information about how many elements satisfy certain given conditions. These procedures are called quantifiers. We then present an implementation of set theory; that is, we define sets as a data type and develop the usual set operations. In the last section, we apply sets to a discussion of functions and relations. Throughout the discussion, we make use of the fact that procedures are first-class objects. We use them as values and pass them as arguments.

8.2   Quantifiers

We study various procedures in this section that we shall use later in our discussion of sets. If we are given two items, these procedures are used to tell whether both, at least one, or neither of the items satisfy some condition. In a sense, they give an idea of how many of the items satisfy the condition; hence these procedures are called *quantifiers*. In this section, we introduce the quantifiers **both**, **at-least-one**, and **neither**; after sets have been introduced in the next section, we add to this list the quantifiers **for-all**, **there-exists**, and **none**.

    The first of these is a procedure **both** that has a predicate **pred** as its parameter and returns another predicate that has two parameters, **arg1** and **arg2**. It is true if and only if **pred** is true for both **arg1** and **arg2**. It is easy to write the definition of both:

Program 8.1   both

```
(define both
  (lambda (pred)
    (lambda (arg1 arg2)
      (and (pred arg1) (pred arg2)))))
```

For example, if we want to test whether two lists are both nonempty, we can invoke the predicate

$$(both\ (lambda\ (ls)\ (not\ (null?\ ls))))$$

on the two lists. Then

$$((both\ (lambda\ (ls)\ (not\ (null?\ ls))))\ '(a\ b\ c)\ '(d\ e)) \implies \#t$$

Incidentally, the predicate in this case can also be written as

$$(both\ (compose\ not\ null?))$$

Thus

$$((both\ (compose\ not\ null?))\ '(a\ b\ c)\ '(d\ e)) \implies \#t$$

We similarly define a procedure **neither** that has as parameter a predicate **pred**. It returns another predicate that has two parameters, **arg1** and **arg2**. Its value is true if and only if neither (**pred arg1**) nor (**pred arg2**) is true. Here is its definition:

Program 8.2   neither

```
(define neither
  (lambda (pred)
    (lambda (arg1 arg2)
      (not (or (pred arg1) (pred arg2))))))
```

Thus

```
((neither null?) '(a b c) '(d e))  ⟹  #t
```

Another useful procedure is **at-least-one**, which has as its parameter a predicate **pred**. It returns another predicate that has two parameters, **arg1** and **arg2**. Its value is true when either (**pred arg1**) or (**pred arg2**) is true. Below is its definition:

Program 8.3   at-least-one

```
(define at-least-one
  (lambda (pred)
    (lambda (arg1 arg2)
      (or (pred arg1) (pred arg2)))))
```

Here is how it works:

```
((at-least-one even?) 1 3)  ⟹   #f
((at-least-one even?) 1 2)  ⟹   #t
```

We can play with logic a little to show that we can take one of these three procedures as basic and express the other two in terms of it. For example, let us take **neither** as the basic one and try to express **both** and **at-least-one** in terms of **neither**. Given two lists, if we want to say that both lists are empty, we can also say that neither of the lists is not empty. In general, saying that both items satisfy a predicate is the same as saying that neither of them does not satisfy the predicate. Thus we can write

```
(define both
  (lambda (pred)
    (lambda (arg1 arg2)
      ((neither (lambda (arg) (not (pred arg)))) arg1 arg2))))
```

Suppose we have a procedure definition of the form

$$\text{(define } name \text{ (lambda } (arg1 \ ...) \ (proc \ arg1 \ ...)))$$

where corresponding arguments are exactly the same in both places. We can often simplify the definition to be

$$\text{(define } name \ proc)$$

since in both versions, (*name* *x* ...) is the same as (*proc* *x* ...). For example, this *simplification rule* tells us that the expression

```
(lambda (a ls) (cons a ls))
```

evaluates to a procedure that behaves the same as `cons`.

Observe next that we can rewrite the expression

```
(lambda (arg) (not (pred arg)))
```

which appears in the last line of the definition of **both**, to be

```
(lambda (arg) ((compose not pred) arg))
```

which, according to the above simplification rule, has the same value as

```
(compose not pred)
```

We can therefore rewrite the definition of **both** to be

```
(define both
  (lambda (pred)
    (lambda (arg1 arg2)
      ((neither (compose not pred)) arg1 arg2))))
```

We can apply the simplification rule again to see that

```
(lambda (arg1 arg2) ((neither (compose not pred)) arg1 arg2))
```

is the same as

```
(neither (compose not pred))
```

so we obtain the final version of **both** to be

```
(define both
  (lambda (pred)
    (neither (compose not pred)))))
```

This kind of simplification was possible because we curried out the parameter **pred** when we decided on the form of the definitions. This kind of simplification actually leads to a definition that reflects the way we verbalize it in

English. We said above that both satisfy the predicate when neither does not satisfy it. We see here another advantage of currying.

In a similar manner, we can show that `at-least-one` can be defined in terms of `neither` by

```
(define at-least-one
  (lambda (pred)
    (lambda (arg1 arg2)
      (not ((neither pred) arg1 arg2)))))
```

This says that at least one of the two satisfies the predicate when it is not true that neither satisfies the predicate.

Exercises

Exercise 8.1
Show that the procedure **both** can be taken as the basic quantifier and that the other two, **neither** and **at-least-one**, can be defined in terms of **both**.

Exercise 8.2
Start with **at-least-one** as the basic quantifier, and define **neither** and **both** in terms of **at-least-one**.

Exercise 8.3: `equal?`
Use the procedures of this section to write a definition of the Scheme predicate **equal?** that tests whether two expressions are the same. If neither of the expressions is a pair, it uses **eqv?** to test their equality. Otherwise it recursively tests the car and the cdr of the expressions until it can use **eqv?**. Test your predicate on

```
(equal? '(a (b c (d e) f)) '(a (b c (d e) f))) ⟹ #t
(equal? '(a ((b d) c) e) '(a (b d) c e)) ⟹ #f
(equal? '(a ((b d) c) e) '(a ((d b) c) e)) ⟹ #f
```

In this section, we develop a data type called *sets*. We treat sets as an abstract data type that has certain basic operators whose existence we first assume and later implement when we choose a representation of sets. An implementation of sets must begin with the specification of the kinds of objects that are allowed as the basic building blocks. The collection of all such base objects is called the *universe of discourse* or simply the *universe*.

The objects contained in a set are referred to as *elements* or *members* of the set. In talking about sets, we use the notation of the mathematical logicians and enclose the elements of sets in braces. Thus a set containing the elements a, b, and c is written as $\{a, b, c\}$. A set may contain other sets as elements, as illustrated by the set $\{\{a, b\}, \{b, c\}, \{d, e\}\}$, which contains the three elements $\{a, b\}$, $\{b, c\}$, and $\{d, e\}$. There is a set called the *empty set* that contains no elements. Logicians write it as $\emptyset$.

Either an element is in a set or it is not; it makes no sense to speak of multiple occurrences of an element in a set. This is an important distinction between lists and sets, since (a a) and (a) are two different lists, while we never write $\{a, a\}$, since $\{a\}$ is the set containing the element a, and repetition of the element a is superfluous. Furthermore, the order in which the elements of a set are written is immaterial. Thus $\{a, b, c\}$ and $\{b, c, a\}$ represent the same set, whereas (a b c) and (b c a) represent different lists.

We now consider how we implement sets. We denote the empty set by the-empty-set. There is a predicate to test whether a set is empty: empty-set?. We also use a predicate set? that tests whether an object is a set. The base elements of our sets belong to some universe for which there is a sameness predicate, which we assume is equal?.

We now introduce the selectors and a constructor for use with sets. There are two selectors, pick and residue. The selector pick takes a set as its argument and returns an element of that set. Since order of elements is not meaningful in sets, we cannot say that pick selects the first member of a set. If obj is an object and s is a set, then the invocation ((residue obj) s) returns a set that contains all of the elements of s except obj. If obj is not in the set s, then ((residue obj) s) returns the set s. The constructor is called adjoin. If obj is an object and s is a set, then (adjoin obj s) returns a set that contains obj and all of the members of s. With these basic operators, we now proceed to develop additional operations on sets.

We begin with the definition of a procedure **make-set** that takes any number of arguments and returns a set containing those arguments as elements. Thus the invocation (**make-set** 'a 'b 'c) returns the set {a, b, c}. We use the unrestricted **lambda** to define this procedure that takes an arbitrary number of arguments. If there are no arguments, **the-empty-set** is returned. Otherwise we apply **make-set** to all but the first of the arguments and then add the first to that set using the constructor **adjoin**. This is just our usual flat recursion when using the unrestricted **lambda**.

Program 8.4   make-set

```
(define make-set
  (lambda args
    (letrec
      ((list-make-set
         (lambda (args-list)
           (if (null? args-list)
               the-empty-set
               (adjoin
                 (car args-list)
                 (list-make-set (cdr args-list)))))))
      (list-make-set args))))
```

In Section 8.2, we introduced the three quantifiers **both**, **at-least-one**, and **neither**, each of which took two arguments. We now define analogs of these that take a set as their argument. The analog of **neither** is the quantifier **none**, the analog of **at-least-one** is the quantifier **there-exists**, and the analog of **both** is the quantifier **for-all**. We start with the procedure **none** that takes a predicate **pred** as its parameter. It returns a predicate that has a set **s** as its parameter and is true when **pred** is false for all elements in **s**. For example,

```
(let ((s (make-set 2 4 6 8 10 12)))
  ((none odd?) s))                      ⟹ #t
(let ((s (make-set 1 2 3 4 5 6)))
  ((none odd?) s))                      ⟹ #f
```

Here is the definition of **none**:

Program 8.5   `none`

```
(define none
  (lambda (pred)
    (letrec
      ((test
         (lambda (s)
           (or (empty-set? s)
               (let ((elem (pick s)))
                 (and (not (pred elem))
                      (test ((residue elem) s)))))))))
        test)))
```

Again, if **pred** is a predicate and **s** is a set, the expression

$$((there-exists \; pred) \; s)$$

is true when there is at least one element in **s** for which **pred** is true. We can define **there-exists** in terms of **none** using the fact that there is an element of **s** satisfying **pred** only when it is not the case that none of the elements of **s** satisfies the predicate.

```
(define there-exists
  (lambda (pred)
    (lambda (s)
      (not ((none pred) s)))))
```

The expression in the last line of this definition of **there-exists** can be written as

$$((compose \; not \; (none \; pred)) \; s)$$

Then the simplifying rule of Section 8.2 can be used to give us the following form of the definition:

Program 8.6   `there-exists`

```
(define there-exists
  (lambda (pred)
    (compose not (none pred))))
```

The procedure **for-all** is called with the call structure (**(for-all pred)**
s) and is true only when **pred** is true for all of the elements in **s**. We can
again express **for-all** in terms of **none** if we observe that **pred** is true for all
of the elements in **s** only when there are no elements in **s** for which **pred** is
not true. Thus we can write

```
(define for-all
  (lambda (pred)
    (lambda (s)
      ((none (lambda (x) (not (pred x)))) s))))
```

Once again, we can use **compose** in the expression in the last line and the
simplifying rule to give Program 8.7.

Program 8.7 for-all

```
(define for-all
  (lambda (pred)
    (none (compose not pred))))
```

We can test for the sameness of objects or sets with a sameness procedure
called **set-equal**. We define **set-equal** so that it can be used to test for the
equality of both elements of sets and sets themselves. We use **set-equal** in a
curried form, so that if **obj1** and **obj2** are objects, then (**(set-equal obj1)**
obj2) is true when **obj1** is the same as **obj2**. You may have expected the
name **set-equal?** instead of **set-equal**. We use **set-equal** because when it
is passed an operand, its value is a procedure and not a truth value. We can
define the predicate **set-equal?** in terms of **set-equal** by writing:

```
(define set-equal?
  (lambda (obj1 obj2)
    ((set-equal obj1) obj2)))
```

If **obj1** and **obj2** are base elements of a set, they belong to a universe, and
their sameness can be tested with the predicate **equal?**. On the other hand, if
the objects are sets, we use the criterion of sameness used in set theory. First,
it says that a set S is a *subset* of a set T if each element of S is also an element
of T. Then if S is a subset of T and T is a subset of S, the two sets must
contain exactly the same elements and hence are equal sets. The definition

Program 8.8   `set-equal`

```
(define set-equal
  (lambda (obj1)
    (lambda (obj2)
      (or (and ((neither set?) obj1 obj2)
               (equal? obj1 obj2))
          (and ((both set?) obj1 obj2)
               ((subset obj1) obj2)
               ((subset obj2) obj1)))))))
```

of `set-equal` makes mutually recursive use of the procedure `subset`, which is defined later. Program 8.8 shows the code for `set-equal`.

We now define a procedure `element` that tests whether an object is an element of a given set. If the object is denoted by `obj` and the set is denoted by `s`, then `((element obj) s)` is true when `obj` is an element of `s`. We have again chosen to curry the procedure because it simplifies some of the programs that make use of it. We want to see whether there is an element in the set `s` that is equal to `obj`. We thus want to use the quantifier `there-exists` with an argument that tests whether a given member of the set `s` is equal to `obj`. But `(set-equal obj)` is precisely that predicate, for it tests whether its argument is the same as `obj`. This is a good illustration of how currying can help us. If we had the ordinary predicate `set-equal?`, with two arguments, we wouldn't be able to create the `obj`-specific version so easily. We'd have to say `(lambda (s) (set-equal? s obj))` instead, and that's harder to read. We then have

```
(define element
  (lambda (obj)
    (lambda (s)
      ((there-exists (set-equal obj)) s))))
```

Using the simplifying rule of Section 8.2, we may rewrite the definition of `element` to be

```
(define element
  (lambda (obj)
    (there-exists (set-equal obj))))
```

We now see that the last line is merely the composition of the two procedures, there-exists and set-equal. We can then rewrite the definition of element to be

Program 8.9   element

```
(define element (compose there-exists set-equal))
```

These steps in rewriting the definition of element again show us how the use of currying can enable us to express our ideas in more compact and convenient form.

The invocation ((element obj) s) tests for the set-theoretic relation

$$obj \in s$$

which says that the object obj is a member of the set s. The set-theoretic relation

$$s \ni obj$$

which says that the set s contains the object obj as a member, is tested for by the predicate (contains s). For example, $b \in \{a, b, c\}$ and $\{a, b, c\} \ni b$. Program 8.10 shows the definition of contains.

Program 8.10   contains

```
(define contains
  (lambda (set)
    (lambda (obj)
      ((element obj) set))))
```

A set s1 is a subset of a set s2 if each member of s1 is also a member of s2. This subset relation is denoted by s1 $\subseteq$ s2. For example, $\{a, c\} \subseteq \{a, b, c, d\}$. We also say that a set s1 is a *superset* of s2 if s2 is a subset of s1. The superset relation is denoted by s1 $\supseteq$ s2. Thus $\{a, b, c, d\} \supseteq \{a, c\}$. We first define the procedure superset such that if s1 and s2 are sets, then ((superset s1) s2) tests whether s1 is a superset of s2. We want to determine whether all elements of s2 are contained in s1. The predicate (contains s1) tests whether its argument is a member of s1, so we can use it as the argument to for-all to test whether all of the elements of s2 are contained in s1. Thus we get Program 8.11. We define the procedure subset using superset, as shown in Program 8.12.

Program 8.11 superset

```
(define superset
  (lambda (s1)
    (lambda (s2)
      ((for-all (contains s1)) s2))))
```

Program 8.12 subset

```
(define subset
  (lambda (s1)
    (lambda (s2)
      ((superset s2) s1))))
```

The number of elements in a set is called the *cardinal number* of the set. For example, the cardinal number of the set $\{a, b, c, d\}$ is 4, and the cardinal number of the set $\{\{a, b\}, \{c, d\}, \{e, f\}\}$ is 3, while each of the elements of this set is itself a set with cardinal number 2. It is an easy matter to define the procedure **cardinal**, which determines the cardinal number of its argument set. To do so, we use recursion on the elements of the set. The cardinal number of **the-empty-set** is 0, which gives us our terminal condition. If the set **s** is not empty, we pick out one element and compute the cardinal number of the rest of the set. To get the cardinal number of **s**, we have to add 1 to the cardinal number of the rest of the set. Here is the definition:

Program 8.13 cardinal

```
(define cardinal
  (lambda (s)
    (if (empty-set? s)
        0
        (let ((elem (pick s)))
          (add1 (cardinal ((residue elem) s)))))))
```

The structure of this definition is typical of programs that perform recursion over the elements of a set **s**. We pick an element out of **s**, then apply the procedure to the rest of the set, and perform the appropriate operation on it to get the result of applying the procedure to **s**.

Program 8.14 `intersection`

```
(define intersection
  (lambda (s1 s2)
    (letrec
      ((helper
         (lambda (s1)
           (if (empty-set? s1)
               the-empty-set
               (let ((elem (pick s1)))
                 (if ((contains s2) elem)
                     (adjoin elem (helper ((residue elem) s1)))
                     (helper ((residue elem) s1))))))))
      (helper s1))))
```

The *intersection* of two sets s1 and s2 is the set consisting of those elements of s1 that are also elements of s2. The intersection of s1 and s2 is denoted by s1 ∩ s2. For example, $\{a, b, c, d\} \cap \{b, d, e\} = \{b, d\}$. We define a procedure intersection that returns the intersection of its two arguments. This definition uses recursion on the elements of s1. Since s2 is not affected in each recursive call, we define a local procedure helper that has only the one parameter s1. When s1 is empty, the intersection is the-empty-set. Otherwise, we select an element elem from s1 and take the intersection of the rest of the set s1 with s2. If elem is contained in s2, we adjoin it to the intersection of the rest with s1. Otherwise, we simply return the intersection of the rest with s1. The definition is given in Program 8.14.

The *union* of the sets s1 and s2 is the set consisting of all of the elements that are either in s1 or in s2. It is denoted by s1 ∪ s2. For example, $\{a, b, c, d\} \cup \{b, d, e\} = \{a, b, c, d, e\}$. We define a procedure union that takes two sets as arguments and returns their union. We again use recursion on the set s1. This time, when s1 is empty, the union is s2. This is our terminal condition. The recursion proceeds as in the case of intersection, but now we want to adjoin elem to the union of the rest of the set s1 with s2 when elem is *not* contained in s2. Thus we get the definition in Program 8.15.

The *difference* between the sets s1 and s2 is the set consisting of those elements of s1 that are not in s2. It is denoted by s1 \ s2. For example, $\{a, b, c, d\} \setminus \{b, d, e\} = \{a, c\}$. We define a procedure difference in a manner similar to that used to define intersection and union. This time, when s1 is empty, the-empty-set is returned. And when elem is *not* contained in s2, it is adjoined to the difference between the rest of s1 and s2. This leads us

Program 8.15   union

```
(define union
  (lambda (s1 s2)
    (letrec
      ((helper
        (lambda (s1)
          (if (empty-set? s1)
              s2
              (let ((elem (pick s1)))
                (if (not ((contains s2) elem))
                    (adjoin elem (helper ((residue elem) s1)))
                    (helper ((residue elem) s1)))))))))
      (helper s1))))
```

Program 8.16   difference

```
(define difference
  (lambda (s1 s2)
    (letrec
      ((helper
        (lambda (s1)
          (if (empty-set? s1)
              the-empty-set
              (let ((elem (pick s1)))
                (if (not ((contains s2) elem))
                    (adjoin elem (helper ((residue elem) s1)))
                    (helper ((residue elem) s1)))))))))
      (helper s1))))
```

to the definition of difference in Program 8.16.

The structural similarity of the definitions of intersection, union, and difference is striking. This common structure is an obvious candidate for procedural abstraction. The three programs differ in what set is returned when the terminal condition is true. We call that set the base-set. And they differ in the predicate that is applied to decide whether to adjoin the element elem picked from the set s1. We call that predicate pred. We use base-set and pred as parameters to the procedure set-builder, which abstracts the structure of the three preceding programs. (See Program 8.17.)

Program 8.17 `set-builder`

```
(define set-builder
  (lambda (pred base-set)
    (letrec
      ((helper
         (lambda (s)
           (if (empty-set? s)
               base-set
               (let ((elem (pick s)))
                 (if (pred elem)
                     (adjoin elem (helper ((residue elem) s)))
                     (helper ((residue elem) s))))))))
      helper)))
```

Procedure	base-set	pred
intersection	the-empty-set	(contains s2)
union	s2	(compose not (contains s2))
difference	the-empty-set	(compose not (contains s2))

Table 8.18 Base sets and predicates for abstraction

We can now rewrite the definitions of **intersection**, **union**, and **difference** using **set-builder**. Table 8.18 shows the values taken on by **base-set** and **pred** in the definitions of these three procedures. With these correspondences, we get

```
(define intersection
  (lambda (s1 s2)
    ((set-builder (contains s2) the-empty-set) s1)))

(define union
  (lambda (s1 s2)
    ((set-builder (compose not (contains s2)) s2) s1)))

(define difference
  (lambda (s1 s2)
    ((set-builder (compose not (contains s2)) the-empty-set) s1)))
```

Program 8.19 `family-union`

```
(define family-union
  (lambda (s)
    (if (empty-set? s)
        the-empty-set
        (let ((elem (pick s)))
          (union elem (family-union ((residue elem) s)))))))
```

Program 8.20 `family-intersection`

```
(define family-intersection
  (lambda (s)
    (if (empty-set? s)
        the-empty-set
        (letrec
          ((fam-int
             (lambda (s)
               (let ((elem (pick s)))
                 (let ((rest ((residue elem) s)))
                   (if (empty-set? rest)
                        elem
                        (intersection elem (fam-int rest))))))))
          (fam-int s)))))
```

If the set S has as its members other sets, we can ask for the union of the member sets. The union of the sets that are members of the set S is called the *family union* of S. We represent it symbolically by $\bigcup S$. For example, $\bigcup\{\{a,b\},\{b,c,d\},\{a,e\}\} = \{a,b,c,d,e\}$. We define (in Program 8.19) a procedure `family-union` that takes as its parameter a set **s** whose elements are sets and returns the union of all of the elements of **s**.

In a similar manner, the family intersection of a set S whose elements are sets is the intersection of all of the elements of S. It is denoted by $\bigcap S$ and is illustrated by $\bigcap\{\{a,b,c\},\{a,c,e\},\{a,b,c,f\}\} = \{a,c\}$. We define (in Program 8.20) the procedure `family-intersection` that takes the parameter **s**, which is a set whose elements are sets, and returns the intersection of all of the sets in **s**.

Why is `family-intersection` more complicated than `family-union`? In `family-union`, the use of `the-empty-set` acts as an identity for `union` in

Program 8.21   `set-map`

```
(define set-map
  (lambda (proc s)
    (if (empty-set? s)
        the-empty-set
        (let ((elem (pick s)))
          (adjoin (proc elem)
                  (set-map proc ((residue elem) s)))))))
```

the same way as 0 acts as an *identity* for plus (see Program 7.9) and 1 acts as an identity for times (see Program 7.10). For intersection, there is no computable identity. Moreover, the-empty-set acts as an *annihilator* for intersection in the same way that 0 acts as an annihilator for ×. We must avoid passing the-empty-set to intersection. This is accomplished by terminating the recursion when we reach a set that contains a single set.

The next procedure we define before looking into how we represent sets is set-map, which takes two parameters, a procedure proc and a set s. It returns the set consisting of those elements that are obtained when proc is applied to each of the elements of s. For example, if proc is the procedure cardinal and s is the set $\{\{a\}, \{b, c\}, \{d, e\}, \{a, c, f\}\}$, then (set-map proc s) evaluates to the set $\{3, 2, 1\}$. Similarly, if s is $\{-1, 0, 1\}$, then (set-map add1 s) evaluates to the set $\{0, 1, 2\}$. We define set-map in Program 8.21.

Suppose we have a list of objects and we want to convert it into a set containing the same objects. All we have to do is use the procedure apply to apply make-set to the list. Thus we define a procedure list->set as

Program 8.22   `list->set`

```
(define list->set
  (lambda (ls)
    (apply make-set ls)))
```

In a similar way, we can ask for a procedure that takes the elements of a set and builds a list containing those elements. This is done by picking elements out of the set and consing them onto a list. Program 8.23 shows how the procedure set->list can be defined.

We have now included enough of the procedures for manipulating sets for

Program 8.23 `set->list`

```
(define set->list
  (lambda (s)
    (if (empty-set? s)
        '()
        (let ((elem (pick s)))
          (cons elem (set->list ((residue elem) s)))))))
```

you to get an idea of how to define set operations. We are now ready to consider ways of representing sets. This is done in the next section.

Exercises

Exercise 8.4

In this section, we showed that **there-exists** and **for-all** can be defined in terms of **none**. Show that we could have taken **there-exists** as the basic one and defined the other two in terms of it. Similarly, show that we could have taken **for-all** as the basic one and defined the other two in terms of it.

Exercise 8.5: `for-one`

Consider the definition of the three-parameter procedure **for-one**, given below. Its first parameter is a predicate, **pred**. Its second parameter is a procedure of one argument, **found-proc**, and its third parameter is a procedure of zero arguments, **not-found-proc**. It returns a procedure that takes a set **s** as its parameter. If **s** is empty or if the predicate **pred** is false for all items in **s**, then the procedure **not-found-proc** is invoked. If **s** contains an element for which **pred** is true, then the procedure **found-proc** is invoked on that element.

```
(define for-one
  (lambda (pred found-proc not-found-proc)
    (letrec ((test
               (lambda (s)
                 (if (empty-set? s)
                     (not-found-proc)
                     (let ((v (pick s)))
                       (if (pred v)
                           (found-proc v)
                           (test ((residue v) s))))))))
      test)))
```

Here is an example of how it works:

```
((for-one
    (lambda (x) (> x 7))
    (lambda (v) (+ v 8))
    (lambda () "Not found"))
 (make-set 2 4 6 19 21 7))
```

returns the value 27 (or possibly 29, depending upon which element was selected first). Define **there-exists** and **for-all** using **for-one**.

Exercise 8.6
Show, using a discussion analogous to that used with **element** in this section, that we can also write the definition of **superset** as

```
(define superset (compose for-all contains))
```

8.4 Representing Sets

We have now defined the set procedures that enable us to manipulate sets as a data type. These definitions all depend upon the six basic representation-dependent terms: **the-empty-set**, **empty-set?**, **set?**, **pick**, **residue**, and **adjoin**. We now show how these can be defined.

We first specify that the universe contains only objects for which **equal?** is the sameness predicate. The first representation that we use for a set of elements is a *tagged list* of those elements. A *tag* is a unique string that is placed in the car position of a pair which enables us to distinguish tagged objects from other ones. We define the tag for sets to be:

```
(define set-tag "set")
```

We make this distinction in order to define the predicate **set?** which will determine whether its argument is a pair and its car is that unique tag. For example, we represent the set {a, b, c} as the tagged list ("set" a b c). In this first representation, we allow repeated elements in the lists. However, if an element occurs once in a list, that element belongs to the set represented by the list, and any other occurrences of that element in the list are ignored. Thus the lists ("set" a b c) and ("set" a b a c b b) represent the same set {a, b, c}. We divide the six basic definitions into two groups, the first of which is used in both of our representations. This shared group includes

Program 8.24   The shared basic definitions for sets

```
(define the-empty-set (cons set-tag '()))

(define empty-set?
  (lambda (s)
    (eq? s the-empty-set)))

(define set?
  (lambda (arg)
    (and (pair? arg) (eq? (car arg) set-tag))))

(define pick
  (lambda (s)
    (let ((ls (cdr s)))
      (if (null? ls)
          (error "pick: The set is empty.")
          (list-ref ls (random (length ls)))))))
```

the-empty-set, empty-set?, set?, and pick (see Program 8.24). We use the procedure **random** in defining **pick** in order to select *some* element from the list. The procedure **random** takes a positive integer n as an argument and returns some randomly selected integer k in the range $0 \leq k < n$. We chose to use a randomly selected element from the list rather than the car of the list or any other specific element of the list in order to convey the idea that the set is unordered. Random number generators are discussed in Footnote 1 of Section 10.2.5 and the procedure described there is defined in Exercise 13.3.

The definitions in Program 8.25 of the remaining two basic procedures, **adjoin** and **residue**, reflect the fact that we allow repetitions in the representation. We make use of the procedure **remove** (see Program 4.6).

Here are some examples of how the procedures behave using our representation that allows repetitions of items in the lists.

```
((set-equal (list->set '(a b a b)))
 (list->set '(b a a)))                          ⟹ #t
((element 'a) (make-set (list->set '(a))
                        (list->set '(a a))
                        (list->set '(a a a))))  ⟹ #f
((element 'a) (make-set (list->set '(a))
                        'a
                        (list->set '(a a))))    ⟹ #t
```

Program 8.25   `adjoin, residue` (Version I)

```
(define residue
  (lambda (elem)
    (lambda (s)
      (let ((ls (remove elem (cdr s))))
        (cond
          ((null? ls) the-empty-set)
          (else (cons set-tag ls)))))))

(define adjoin
  (lambda (elem s)
    (cons set-tag (cons elem (cdr s)))))
```

```
(union (make-set 1 1 2 3 4)
       (make-set 3 4 4 5 6 6)) ⟹ ("set" 1 2 3 4 4 5 6 6)
(intersection (make-set 1 2 3 3 4 5)
              (make-set 3 4 4 5 6 7)) ⟹ ("set" 3 4 5)
(difference (make-set 1 1 2 3 3 4 5)
            (make-set 3 4 4 5 6 7)) ⟹ ("set" 1 2)
(set-map cardinal (make-set (list->set '(a b c))
                            (list->set '(a b a))
                            (list->set '(a a a))
                            (list->set '()))) ⟹ ("set" 3 2 1 0)
(family-intersection (make-set (list->set '(a b c d d))
                               (list->set '(a c d e))
                               (list->set '(c d e f))))
                                        ⟹ ("set" c d)
```

Another representation for a set s is a list that contains the elements of s but does not allow repetition of elements. The selector `residue` now has to remove only the first occurrence of its first argument from the set since there are no repetitions. Thus it uses `remove-1st` (Program 2.4) instead of `remove`. The constructor `adjoin` must now test to determine whether its first argument, the object, is already an element of its second argument, the set. It adds the object to the set only if it is not already a member of the set. Program 8.26 shows the definitions of `adjoin` and `residue` for the representation with no repetitions.

Here are some examples of how some of the procedures defined in Section 8.3 look when using the second representation of sets:

Program 8.26   The basic definitions for sets (Version II)

```
(define residue
  (lambda (elem)
    (lambda (s)
      (let ((ls (remove-1st elem (cdr s))))
        (cond
          ((null? ls) the-empty-set)
          (else (cons set-tag ls)))))))

(define adjoin
  (lambda (elem s)
    (cond
      ((member? elem (cdr s)) s)
      (else (cons set-tag (cons elem (cdr s)))))))
```

(union (make-set 1 2 3) (make-set 2 3 4)) $\Longrightarrow$ ("set" 1 2 3 4)
(intersection (make-set 1 2 3) (make-set 2 3 4)) $\Longrightarrow$ ("set" 2 3)
(difference (make-set 1 2 3) (make-set 2 3 4)) $\Longrightarrow$ ("set" 1)

You now might ask, "Which representation is better?" Each has its advantages. For example, in the first representation, the selector **residue** does more work than its counterpart in the second representation since it has to remove all occurrences of the element that was picked, while in the second representation, it only has to remove the first occurrence. In the second representation, **adjoin** does more work since it has to check whether the element to be added is already in the tagged list. The lists involving no repetitions represent the sets more compactly. Thus there is a trade-off when choosing between these two representations.

We have built into our universe, not only symbols, numbers, and booleans, but any data for which **equal?** works, and that includes lists. Here are some examples using this tagged-list representation of sets where some elements are lists.

(union (make-set 1 '(1 2) '(2 3))
       (make-set 1 2 '(1 2) '(3 4)))
       $\Longrightarrow$ ("set" (2 3) 1 2 (1 2) (3 4))
(union (make-set 1 (make-set 1 2) (make-set 2 3))
       (make-set 1 2 (make-set 1 2) (make-set 3 4)))
       $\Longrightarrow$ ("set" ("set" 2 3) 1 2 ("set" 1 2) ("set" 3 4))

```
(family-union
  (make-set
    (make-set 1 2) (make-set 2 3) (make-set 3 4)))
        ⟹ ("set" 1 2 3 4)
```

We have now seen another application of data abstraction in this development of the set data type. We defined all of the set operations using six basic definitions, and only these six depend upon the specific representation of the sets that we use. We then showed how to define these six using two different representations of sets. The extensive use we made of currying in the definitions of many of the set operations made it possible to use composition of procedures to simplify several definitions. It also enabled us more easily to define new procedures in terms of others with certain arguments fixed. For example, if we want to remove the number 0 from sets of numbers, we can apply (residue 0) to any such set of numbers and get the desired result. We also saw another example of the abstraction of the structure of several procedures in **set-builder**. In the next section, we shall apply sets to a discussion of functions and relations.

Exercises

Exercise 8.7
Use this definition of **pick** to implement sets with lists having repetitions:

```
(define pick
  (lambda (s)
    (car (cdr s))))
```

In the following exercises, use only operations on sets. Do not use operations on sets that depend upon the representation of the sets.

Exercise 8.8
The procedures **union** and **intersection** defined in this section each took two sets as arguments. Rewrite these definitions using the unrestricted **lambda** so that both take an arbitrary number of sets as arguments. Test your procedures on the following examples:

```
(union
  (make-set 1 2 3 4)
  (make-set 1 3 4 5)
  (make-set 2 1)) ⟹ ("set" 1 2 3 4 5)
```

```
(intersection
  (make-set 1 2 3 4)
  (make-set 1 3 4 5)
  (make-set 1 5 6 3 7)) ⟹ ("set" 1 3)
```

Abstract the structure of these two definitions to get a procedure from which
union and **intersection** can both be obtained by passing the procedural
abstraction appropriate arguments.

Exercise 8.9: **symmetric-difference**
Define the set procedure **symmetric-difference** that has two sets **s1** and **s2**
as parameters and returns the set consisting of those elements that are either
in **s1** but not in **s2** or in **s2** but not in **s1**. For example,

```
(symmetric-difference
  (make-set 1 2 3 4 5)
  (make-set 3 4 5 6 7)) ⟹ ("set" 1 2 6 7)
```


Exercise 8.10: **power-set**
Define a set procedure **power-set** that has a set **s** as parameter and returns
the set consisting of all subsets of **s**. For example,

```
(power-set (make-set 'a 'b 'c))
    ⟹ ("set" ("set" a b c) ("set" a b) ("set" a c)
             ("set" a) ("set" b c) ("set" b) ("set" c) ("set"))
```

Hint: Assume that **power-set** is defined for the rest of the set when an element
is picked out.

Exercise 8.11: **select-by-cardinal**
Let **s** be a set whose elements are sets. Define a set procedure **select-by-
cardinal** that has an integer **int** as its parameter and returns a procedure
with parameter **s** that builds the set of all of those elements of **s** that have
cardinal **int**. For example,

```
((select-by-cardinal 2)
 (make-set (make-set 'a) (make-set 'a 'b) (make-set 'a 'b 'c)
           (make-set 'b 'c) (make-set 'b)))
                    ⟹ ("set" ("set" a b) ("set" b c))
```

8.5 Ordered Pairs, Functions, and Relations

As an application of sets, we show how ordered pairs and the Cartesian product of two sets are defined and use these ideas to develop the logical concepts of functions and relations. We present a development of ordered pairs based upon the development of sets presented in the preceding sections.

An *ordered pair* is a pair of elements in which the order is significant; that is, (x, y) and (y, x) represent different ordered pairs as long as x and y are not the same. We again treat ordered pairs as an abstract data type and introduce the basic operations that apply to ordered pairs and then look at possible representations of ordered pairs. Ordered pairs have two selectors and one constructor. There is a selector called `op-1st` that takes an ordered pair as its argument and returns the first element in the ordered pair. Similarly, there is a selector called `op-2nd` that returns the second element in the ordered pair. Finally, there is a constructor that is called `make-op` such that (`make-op x y`) is the ordered pair containing `x` as its first member and `y` as its second member. There is also a predicate `op?` that tests whether its argument is an ordered pair.

We now consider ways of representing ordered pairs. We present three different representations in this section: sets, two-element lists, and dotted pairs. Logicians usually start with sets and build other concepts from them. In our first representation, we show how this can be carried out in Scheme. Compared to the last two representations, the first is quite complicated. It shows the natural advantage the list or dotted-pair representations have for representing ordered pairs. If you are not interested in the set theory development of ordered pairs, you can skip over the next two paragraphs and go on to the list and dotted-pair representations.

We first represent ordered pairs as sets. A naive first attempt would represent the ordered pair (x, y) with the set $\{x, y\}$. However, there is a problem: if $x \neq y$, then $(x, y) \neq (y, x)$, but $\{x, y\} = \{y, x\}$ since order is immaterial in sets. We can get around this difficulty by representing the ordered pair (x, y) by the set $\{\{x\}, \{x, y\}\}$. Then the ordered pair (y, x) is represented by the set $\{\{y\}, \{y, x\}\}$, which is not the same set as that used to represent (x, y), as long as x is not the same as y. We identify the first element of the ordered pair represented by $\{\{x\}, \{x, y\}\}$ by noting that it is the only element in the intersection $\{x\} \cap \{x, y\}$ of the two member sets. Similarly, if x and y are not equal, the second element of the ordered pair is the only element in the set difference between $\bigcup\{\{x\}, \{x, y\}\}$ and $\bigcap\{\{x\}, \{x, y\}\}$. If x and y are equal, pick the first element of the ordered pair. It should be observed that the same

Program 8.27   Basic definitions for ordered pairs (Version I)

```
(define make-op
  (lambda (x y)
    (make-set (make-set x) (make-set x y))))

(define op?
  (lambda (set)
    (and (set? set)
         ((for-all set?) set)
         (= (cardinal (family-intersection set)) 1)
         (or (= (cardinal set) 1)
             ((both (lambda (x) (= (cardinal x) 2)))
              set
              (family-union set))))))

(define op-1st
  (lambda (op)
    (pick (family-intersection op))))

(define op-2nd
  (lambda (op)
    (let ((fam-int (family-intersection op)))
      (let ((diff (difference (family-union op) fam-int)))
        (pick (if (empty-set? diff) fam-int diff))))))
```

ordered pair is represented by $\{\{x\}, \{x, y\}\}$, $\{\{x\}, \{y, x\}\}$, and $\{\{y, x\}, \{x\}\}$.

Using this representation in terms of sets, the definitions of the four basic procedures for ordered pairs are given in Program 8.27. Given the first element x and the second element y of the ordered pair, the constructor **make-op** produces the ordered pair $\{\{x\}, \{x, y\}\}$. To understand the definition of op?, observe that it is possible for the cardinal number of an ordered pair to be equal to one. This is illustrated by $\{\{a\}, \{a, a\}\}$, which represents the ordered pair (a, a). We have $\{\{a\}, \{a, a\}\} = \{\{a\}, \{a\}\} = \{\{a\}\}$, so its cardinal number is one.

There are other ways of representing ordered pairs that we can also use. For example, we can let an ordered pair containing the elements x and y be represented by (list x y). This is using a representation by proper lists. Then we have the definitions given in Program 8.28.

Another representation that is also a reasonable one to use represents the pair containing x and y as a dotted pair containing those two elements, that

Program 8.28   Basic definitions for ordered pairs (Version II)

```
(define make-op
  (lambda (x y)
    (list x y)))

(define op?
  (lambda (ls)
    (and (pair? ls) (pair? (cdr ls)) (null? (cddr ls)))))

(define op-1st
  (lambda (op)
    (car op)))

(define op-2nd
  (lambda (op)
    (cadr op)))
```

Program 8.29   Basic definitions for ordered pairs (Version III)

```
(define make-op
  (lambda (x y)
    (cons x y)))

(define op?
  (lambda (pr)
    (pair? pr)))

(define op-1st
  (lambda (op)
    (car op)))

(define op-2nd
  (lambda (op)
    (cdr op)))
```

is, as (cons x y). We then have the definitions given in Program 8.29. The definitions in Programs 8.28 and 8.29 can be simplified using the simplification rule of Section 8.2. See Exercise 8.12.

The *Cartesian product* of the two sets S_1 and S_2 is the set of all ordered pairs

Program 8.30 `cartesian-product`

```
(define cartesian-product
  (lambda (s1 s2)
    (if (empty-set? s1)
        the-empty-set
        (let ((elem (pick s1)))
          (union (set-map (lambda (x) (make-op elem x)) s2)
                 (cartesian-product ((residue elem) s1) s2))))))
```

(x, y) with $x \in S_1$ and $y \in S_2$. The mathematical notation for the Cartesian product of S_1 and S_2 is $S_1 \times S_2$. For example, the Cartesian product of the two sets $\{a, b, c\}$ and $\{d, e\}$ is the set of pairs

$$\{(a, d), (a, e), (b, d), (b, e), (c, d), (c, e)\}$$

The set procedure that forms the Cartesian product of two sets is defined in Program 8.30.

A *relation* R from a set X to a set Y is defined to be a subset of the Cartesian product of the two sets X and Y. Thus the relation R is a set of ordered pairs in which the first element is in X and the second element is in Y. The empty set is also a relation having no elements. For example, if X is the set (**make-set a b c**) and Y is the set (**make-set 0 1**), then the following is a relation from X to Y:

(make-set (make-op 'a 0) (make-op 'a 1) (make-op 'c 1))

The *domain* of the relation R from X to Y is defined to be the subset of X consisting of all elements of X that appear as first elements of some ordered pair in R. In our example above, the domain of the relation is the set $\{a,c\}$. The *range* of the relation R is defined to be the subset of Y consisting of all elements of Y that appear as second elements of some ordered pair in R. Given a relation **rel**, we can define procedures **domain** and **range** that return the domain and the range of **rel**, respectively. (See Program 8.31.)

A **binary relation** on a set S is a subset of the Cartesian product of S with itself. For example, if **bob**, **tom**, and **jim** are members of the set **boys**, then a binary relation **is-older-than-relation** on the set **boys** is given by

Program 8.31   domain, range

```
(define domain
  (lambda (rel)
    (set-map op-1st rel)))

(define range
  (lambda (rel)
    (set-map op-2nd rel)))
```

```
(define is-older-than-relation
  (make-set (make-op 'tom 'bob)
            (make-op 'tom 'jim)
            (make-op 'bob 'jim)))
```

We can define a predicate **is-older-than?** that has as its two parameters two members **b1** and **b2** of the set **boys** and returns true if the ordered pair (**make-op b1 b2**) is an element of the binary relation **is-older-than-relation**. For example, we can write

```
(define is-older-than?
  (lambda (b1 b2)
    ((contains is-older-than-relation) (make-op b1 b2))))
```

Suppose we are given a relation **rel** from one set to another. We now write the definition of a procedure **subrelation/1st** that builds a new relation consisting of all pairs from the relation **rel** that have a given element as their first elements. Using our example above, when we enter

```
((subrelation/1st is-older-than-relation) 'tom)
```

the subrelation consisting of the two ordered pairs starting with **tom** is returned. See Program 8.32.

A *function* from a set X to a set Y is defined to be a relation from X to Y in which no two ordered pairs with the same first elements have different second elements. Since functions are relations, domain and range are already defined for functions. This definition of a function as a set of ordered pairs is equivalent to the definition we have been using throughout the book. If we have a function denoted by $y = f(x)$ with x in the domain X and y in the range Y, this is the relation consisting of the ordered pairs (x, y) satisfying $y = f(x)$. With this view of functions, the factorial function is the

Program 8.32   subrelation/1st

```
(define subrelation/1st
  (lambda (rel)
    (lambda (arg)
      ((set-builder
         (lambda (x) ((set-equal (op-1st x)) arg))
         the-empty-set)
       rel))))
```

Program 8.33   function?

```
(define function?
  (lambda (rel)
    (or (empty-set? rel)
        (let ((subrel ((subrelation/1st rel) (op-1st (pick rel)))))
          (and (= (cardinal subrel) 1)
               (function? (difference rel subrel)))))))
```

set $\{(0,1),(1,1),(2,2),(3,6),\ldots\}$. We now write the definition of a predicate function? that tests whether a relation is a function. (See Program 8.33.) If the given relation rel is nonempty, this procedure looks at the subset of all ordered pairs in rel that have the same first element as some ordered pair (pick rel) in rel. If the number of distinct second elements in this subset is greater than 1, false is returned. Otherwise the procedure is repeated on the relation obtained by removing that subset from rel. This process continues until no more ordered pairs are left to test, in which case true is returned.

The *value* of a function f at an element x in the domain of f is the second element in the ordered pair in f that has x as its first element. In Program 8.34, we define a procedure value that takes a function fun as its parameter and returns a procedure that takes as its parameter an element arg in the domain of fun and returns the value of fun at arg.

Let us summarize what we have accomplished. In Chapter 1, we introduced lists as a data type having the constructor cons and the two selectors car and cdr. Here we have developed sets as a data type having the constructor adjoin and the two selectors pick and residue. Using these, we defined many procedures that manipulate sets. We used lists in several representations of sets. We then proceeded to define ordered pairs using sets. Ordered pairs are another data type having the constructor make-op and the two selectors

Program 8.34 `value`

```
(define value
  (lambda (fun)
    (lambda (arg)
      (op-2nd (pick ((subrelation/1st fun) arg))))))
```

`op-1st` and `op-2nd`. These were used to define relations and functions on
sets. It is interesting to observe that if we start with sets as our basic data
type, we can use sets as we did to define ordered pairs, and then we can use
ordered pairs as a representation of lists. For any two elements, **x** and **y**, we
define (`cons x y`) to be (`make-op x y`). We then define `car` to be `op-1st`
and `cdr` to be `op-2nd`. The empty list () is represented by `the-empty-set`.
Using these definitions of `cons`, `car`, `cdr`, and (), we can proceed to define
all of the procedures on lists that were defined in the earlier chapters. Thus
we have come full circle. We can take sets as our basic data type and develop
lists in terms of sets, or we can take lists as our basic data type and develop
sets in terms of lists.

We leave it to the reader to develop more of the theory of functions and
relations in the exercises. The many examples in this chapter should make
it clear how powerful a tool it is to be able to pass procedures as arguments
to other procedures and to be able to have procedures whose values are procedures. We have seen how convenient it is to be able to curry procedures.
All of this is possible because procedures are treated as first-class objects in
Scheme.

Exercises

Exercise 8.12

In Programs 8.28 and 8.29, we can rewrite the definition of `op-1st` as (`de-
fine op-1st car`) using the simplifying rule of Section 8.2. Redefine all of
the procedures in Programs 8.28 and 8.29 for which the simplifying rule is
applicable.

In the following exercises, use the set operations developed in this chapter.
Make your programs independent of the representation of sets being used.
Many of the problems in this list use the results of previous problems, so do
them in order.

Exercise 8.13: `relation?`
Define a predicate `relation?` that tests whether a set is a relation.

Exercise 8.14: `inverse-relation`
The inverse of an ordered pair (a, b) is the ordered pair (b, a). The inverse of a relation R is the relation obtained when each ordered pair is replaced by its inverse. Define a procedure `inverse-relation` that takes as its argument a relation and returns its inverse relation.

Exercise 8.15: `one-to-one?`
A function is called *one-to-one* if its inverse relation is also a function. Write the definition of a predicate `one-to-one?` that tests whether a function is one-to-one. See the preceding exercise.

Exercise 8.16: `make-relation`
A convenient way of defining a relation `rel` is to give an arbitrary number of pairs (x y) that corresponds to the ordered pairs (make-op x y) in `rel`. Thus (make-relation '(1 2) '(1 3) '(2 3)) corresponds to the relation $\{(1, 2), (1, 3), (2, 3)\}$. Define the procedure `make-relation`.

Exercise 8.17: `reflexive?`
A binary relation R on a set S is called *reflexive* if for each x in S, the ordered pair (x, x) is an element of R. Define a predicate `reflexive?` that tests whether a given relation `rel` is reflexive.

Exercise 8.18: `symmetric?`
A binary relation R on a set S is called *symmetric* if it is equal as a set to its inverse relation. See Exercise 8.14. Define a predicate `symmetric?` that tests whether a given relation `rel` is symmetric.

Exercise 8.19: `function-compose`
Suppose that f and g are functions such that the range of g is a subset of the domain of f. The composition of f with g is the function consisting of all ordered pairs (x, y) with x in the domain of g and y in the range of f and for which there exists an element z such that $(x, z) \in g$ and $(z, y) \in f$. Define the procedure `function-compose` such that (function-compose f g) is the composition of f with g. Your procedure should first test whether the range of g is a subset of the domain of f.

Sets and Relations

Exercise 8.20: `relation-compose`

If Q and R are binary relations on a set S, then the composition of Q with R is the relation composed of all ordered pairs (x, y) such that for some $z \in S$, there exists an ordered pair $(x, z) \in R$ and an ordered pair $(z, y) \in Q$. Define the procedure `relation-compose` such that `(relation-compose q r)` is the composition of the relation q with the relation r.

Exercise 8.21: `transitive?`

A binary relation R on a set S is called *transitive* if the composition of R with R is a subset of R. Define a predicate `transitive?` that tests whether a relation `rel` is transitive. See the preceding exercise.

```
(transitive?
  (make-relation '(1 2) '(1 3) '(1 4) '(2 3) '(2 4) '(3 4))) ⟹ #t
(transitive?
  (make-relation '(0 0) '(1 1) '(2 2) '(3 3) '(4 4))) ⟹ #t
(transitive?
  (make-relation '(1 1) '(1 2) '(3 2) '(2 1))) ⟹ #f
```

Exercise 8.22: `equivalence-relation?`

A binary relation `rel` on a set S is called an *equivalence relation* if it is reflexive, symmetric, and transitive. Write the definition of the predicate `equivalence-relation?` that tests whether a given relation is an equivalence relation. See Exercises 8.17, 8.18, and 8.21.

```
(equivalence-relation?
  (make-relation '(0 0) '(1 1) '(2 2) '(3 3))) ⟹ #t
(equivalence-relation?
  (make-relation '(0 0) '(0 1) '(1 0) '(1 1))) ⟹ #t
(equivalence-relation?
  (make-relation '(0 0) '(0 1) '(1 1) '(2 2))) ⟹ #f
```

Part 3

Managing State

What is change? If we think further about the dining experience of Part 1's introduction, changes took place. Eating left you full, lessened the world's food supply, enriched the purse of the restaurant's proprietor, and depleted your buying power. All of these are changes. The state of the world after you left the restaurant changed. Managing state means that all the effects of a change must be taken into account.

Part 3 is about combining the management of state with the style of programming that we have so far developed. In Chapter 9, we introduce a new data structure, the vector. A vector is like a list, except that we access it with operations that use the elements' indices, which are nonnegative integers, instead of with operations that find the first element and the rest of the elements. In addition to the formal operations on vectors, we introduce an operation that permanently changes the contents of a portion of a vector. We use this operation to show the role of such state-changing operations in general in enhancing the efficiency of correct procedures.

In Chapter 10, we use changing of state to develop some efficient procedures for sorting and searching data stored in vectors. In Chapter 11, we strengthen your intuition about writing procedures that use state-changing operations by introducing such operations over lists and local variables. This leads to Chapter 12, where we build an object-oriented system by merging higher-order procedures with state-changing operations. In Chapter 13, we use object-oriented programming to build a gas station simulation.

9   Using Vectors

9.1 Overview

We have been using lists as our basic data type, and for most of the applications we have had so far, lists have been adequate. They do have one disadvantage that is apparent when we have a long list ls. Let's say it contains 1000 elements, and we want to know what the element with zero-based index 900 is. One way we can access that information is by applying cdr 900 times and then applying car. That seems like a lot of work, so we use the Scheme procedure list-ref defined in Program 3.7, which does the cdring for us, and we invoke (list-ref ls 900). But the computer is doing just as much work to access the 900th element of the list for us. It would be nice to have a data type in which we could store elements and look directly into the 900th (or any other) place and see what is there. Being able to access any element in a list using the same amount of computer resources is called *random access* into the list. What we now have available to us in lists is *sequential access*, in which we have to cdr from the beginning of the list to the desired element. In this chapter, we study a data type called vectors. Like lists, vectors are used to store data. We discuss several possible implementations of vectors, the last of which will provide data storage with random access.

9.2 Vectors

In mathematics, a vector is a function defined on a set of integers, say from 0 to $n - 1$, which assigns to each such integer a value that is said to be the element with that integer as its index. A mathematical representation of a vector with three elements, say *a* with index 0, *b* with index 1, and *c* with index 2, is ⟨*a*, *b*, *c*⟩. The word *vector* is also used as a data type in Scheme that associates an element with each integer from zero to some given number. The elements stored in a vector can be data of any type—for example, numbers, symbols, lists, or procedures. For the external representation of a vector with elements a, b, and c, Scheme uses #(a b c). In general Scheme's external representation of a vector is a sharp symbol, #, followed by the elements enclosed in parentheses.

As with the other data types we have studied, we begin with certain basic procedures in terms of which we define the rest of the procedures involving vectors. The actual representation of the vectors and the basic procedures will be defined in several ways after we develop the other procedures in a representation-independent fashion. The first of our four basic procedures is the predicate `vector?`, which tests whether its argument is a vector. The second one is the procedure `vector-length`, which takes a vector as its argument and returns the number of elements in the vector.

The selector for vectors is called `vector-ref`. It has the call structure (`vector-ref` *vec k*), where *vec* is a vector and *k* is a nonnegative integer less than the length of *vec*. It returns the element in *vec* that has index *k*. To illustrate the use of this selector, we define a procedure `view` (See Program 9.1 and Exercise 9.2.) that takes a vector and displays its external representation. If `vec` is the vector with the elements 1, 2, 3, and 4, we have

(view vec) *displays* #(1 2 3 4)

The indices of the elements of the vector `vec` go through the range from zero to one less than the length of the vector `vec`. Thus we locally define `highest-index` to be one less than (`vector-length` vec). The local procedure `loop` displays in order the elements of `vec`, each, except for the last one, followed by a space. Thus the desired output is obtained by first displaying "#(", then invoking (`loop` 0) to display the elements of `vec`, and finally displaying ")". In our implementation, we assume that the value returned by a display expression is suppressed, so the same is true of `view`.

The constructor `vector-generator`, which we use for vectors, is a curried procedure with the call structure

((vector-generator *gen-proc*) *size*)

The operand *size* is a nonnegative integer that is the length of the vector we are constructing. The generating procedure *gen-proc* is a procedure that takes an index as its argument and returns the value to be associated with

Program 9.1 view

```
(define view
  (lambda (vec)
    (let ((highest-index (sub1 (vector-length vec))))
      (letrec ((loop (lambda (i)
                       (display (vector-ref vec i))
                       (if (< i highest-index)
                           (begin
                             (display " ")
                             (loop (add1 i)))))))
        (display "#(")
        (loop 0)
        (display ")")))))
```

that index in the vector we are constructing. The index is any integer in the range from zero to one less than *size*. When passed a generating procedure, **vector-generator** returns a procedure. When that procedure is passed an integer specifying the vector's length, it returns a vector having the specified size and whose elements are determined by the generating procedure. As an example of the use of **vector-generator**, if we want to construct a vector of length 6 having 0 for each of its elements, we can write

```
[1] (view ((vector-generator (lambda (i) 0)) 6))
#(0 0 0 0 0 0)
```

Here are some additional examples:

```
[2] (view ((vector-generator add1) 6))
#(1 2 3 4 5 6)
[3] (view ((vector-generator (lambda (i) i)) 5))
#(0 1 2 3 4)
[4] (view ((vector-generator (lambda (i) '())) 4))
#(() () () ())
[5] (define squares (vector-generator (lambda (i) (* i i))))
[6] (view (squares 4))
#(0 1 4 9)
[7] (view (squares 6))
#(0 1 4 9 16 25)
```

Later we shall give ways of representing vectors and defining these basic procedures. We now show how to define the other procedures that we need, making use of the four basic procedures. The first one is the Scheme procedure **make-vector**, which builds a vector of a prescribed size and fills all of its elements with the same specified value. If a fill value is not given, all of the elements of the vector are filled with something, say (), although this fill value is not specified by Scheme. Thus we define the procedure **make-vector** that takes either one or two arguments. Its first argument is always the size of the vector we are building, and the optional second argument is the value we use to fill the elements of the vector. To accomplish the definition of a procedure with an optional second argument, we use the unrestricted **lambda** in its definition. Thus **make-vector** has as its parameter a symbol denoted by **args**. We distinguish between the two cases by testing whether (**cdr args**) is empty. If it is, we construct a vector of length (**car args**) and fill it with (). Never rely upon this fill value in your programs because the Scheme procedure **make-vector** does not specify the fill value if you do not include it as a second argument. Thus you may be surprised to find the implementation providing something other than (), and your program will not run correctly. If you want to use the fill value in your program, specify it as the second argument to **make-vector**, and that value is used to fill the vector that is constructed. Here is the code for **make-vector**:

Program 9.2   make-vector

```
(define make-vector
  (lambda args
    (let ((fill-value
            (if (singleton-list? args)
                '()
                (cadr args))))
      ((vector-generator (lambda (i) fill-value)) (car args)))))
```

A convenient way of building a vector with given elements is to start with a list containing those elements and converting the list into a vector using the Scheme procedure **list->vector** that takes a list **ls** as its parameter. The size of the vector being created is then the length of **ls**, and the generating procedure is simply (**lambda (i) (list-ref ls i)**). We then get Program 9.3. Because **list-ref** is doing a recursion from the beginning of the list for each index i, this is a very inefficient way of defining **list->vector**. We consider a more efficient definition later.

Program 9.3   `list->vector`

```
(define list->vector
  (lambda (ls)
    ((vector-generator (lambda (i) (list-ref ls i))) (length ls))))
```

Another convenient way of building a vector with given elements is provided by the Scheme procedure `vector`, which takes an arbitrary number of arguments and returns a vector having those arguments as its elements. The length of the vector returned is the same as the number of arguments. Since the number of arguments is arbitrary, we must use the unrestricted `lambda`. The definition of `vector` is:

Program 9.4   `vector`

```
(define vector
  (lambda args
    (list->vector args)))
```

Here are some experiments illustrating the use of these procedures:

```
[1] (view (make-vector 5))
#(() () () () ())
[2] (view (list->vector '(1 2 3 (4 5 6))))
#(1 2 3 (4 5 6))
[3] (view (vector 'a 'b '(a b c)))
#(a b (a b c))
[4] (view (vector 6 'symbol 5))
#(6 symbol 5)
```

The length of a vector is fixed when it is defined. Suppose we have defined a vector **vec** of length **k**, and we find that we need a longer vector, say one of length **n**, that has its first **k** elements the same as those of **vec**. We say that the new vector is an *extension* of **vec** of length **n**. We now use `vector-generator` to define the procedure `vector-stretch` that takes as its parameters a vector **vec** and a number **new-size** and returns an extension of **vec** of length **new-size**. Its code is in Program 9.5. Although we use the name `vector-stretch`, the new vector may also be the same length as or shorter than the original vector.

Program 9.5 `vector-stretch`

```
(define vector-stretch
  (lambda (vec new-size)
    (let ((size (vector-length vec)))
      (let ((gen-proc (lambda (i)
                        (if (< i size)
                            (vector-ref vec i)
                            '()))))
        ((vector-generator gen-proc) new-size)))))
```

If the extension of a vector **vec** is the same size as **vec**, the extension is a *copy* of **vec**. Thus we define the procedure **vector-copy** as shown in Program 9.6.

Program 9.6 `vector-copy`

```
(define vector-copy
  (lambda (vec)
    (vector-stretch vec (vector-length vec))))
```

The procedure **vector-copy** gives us a copy of its argument with none of its elements changed. Suppose we want a copy of the vector **vec** with the element with index **k** replaced by the value **val**. We can define a new copying procedure that has the **k**th element changed, as shown in Program 9.7.

Program 9.7 `vector-update`

```
(define vector-update
  (lambda (vec k val)
    (let ((gen-proc (lambda (i)
                      (if (= i k)
                          val
                          (vector-ref vec i)))))
      ((vector-generator gen-proc) (vector-length vec)))))
```

We can now give another version of the Scheme procedure `list->vector`, this time using **vector-update**. In this version, we first build a vector **vec**

Program 9.8   `list->vector`

```
(define list->vector
  (lambda (ls)
    (let ((vec (make-vector (length ls))))
      (letrec
        ((convert (lambda (ls* v i)
                    (if (null? ls*)
                        v
                        (let ((new-v (vector-update v i (car ls*))))
                          (convert (cdr ls*) new-v (add1 i)))))))
        (convert ls vec 0)))))
```

having the same length as the list `ls` that we are converting into a vector.
Then we form a loop using a letrec expression in which we start with the
vector `vec` and successively use `vector-update` to give us a new vector `new-v`
that has the appropriate element changed to the corresponding element in
the list. This new vector is passed to the local procedure `convert`, which
continues this process until all of the elements of `vec` have been updated. Its
definition is given in Program 9.8. We make an improvement in the procedure
`list->vector` later in this section. At that time, we shall eliminate the need
to pass the vector `new-v` as an argument to `convert` and shall produce an
$O(n)$ version instead of $O(n^2)$.

Suppose we have a vector `vec` and want to construct a new vector whose
elements are obtained by applying the procedure `proc` to the corresponding
elements of `vec`. To accomplish this, we use a vector analog of the list procedure `map`. We call the vector version `vector-map`, and we define it by:

Program 9.9   `vector-map`

```
(define vector-map
  (lambda (proc vec)
    ((vector-generator (lambda (i) (proc (vector-ref vec i))))
     (vector-length vec))))
```

For example,

```
[1] (view (vector-map add1 (vector 10 11 12 13)))
#(11 12 13 14)
[2] (view (vector-map even? (vector 10 11 12)))
#(#t #f #t)
[3] (view (vector-map
            (lambda (elem) (list 'a elem))
            (vector 10 11 12 13)))
#((a 10) (a 11) (a 12) (a 13))
```

In the language used with vectors, one usually refers to numbers as *scalars*. We call a vector a *numerical vector* if all of its elements are numbers. The product of a scalar c and a numerical vector $\langle a_1, a_2, \ldots, a_n \rangle$ is the vector $\langle ca_1, ca_2, \ldots, ca_n \rangle$. The procedure multiply-by-scalar takes as parameters a scalar c and a numerical vector vec and returns their product. It is defined by

Program 9.10   multiply-by-scalar

```
(define multiply-by-scalar
  (lambda (c vec)
    (vector-map (lambda (elem) (* c elem)) vec)))
```

We define an analog to vector-map, called vector-apply-elementwise-to-both, for a binary procedure proc and two vectors of the same length, which applies proc to the corresponding elements of the two vectors.

Program 9.11   vector-apply-elementwise-to-both

```
(define vector-apply-elementwise-to-both
  (lambda (proc)
    (lambda (vec1 vec2)
      (let ((gen-proc
              (lambda (i)
                (proc (vector-ref vec1 i) (vector-ref vec2 i)))))
        ((vector-generator gen-proc) (vector-length vec1))))))
```

The sum of two numerical vectors vec1 and vec2 of the same length is the vector whose elements are the sums of the corresponding elements of **vec1** and **vec2**. We define the vector operator **vec+** that adds two vectors by simply using **vector-apply-elementwise-to-both** with + as its operand. Similarly we define the vector operator **vec*** that multiplies two vectors elementwise by applying **vector-apply-elementwise-to-both** with * as its operand.

Program 9.12   vec+, vec*

```
(define vec+ (vector-apply-elementwise-to-both +))

(define vec* (vector-apply-elementwise-to-both *))
```

The use of **vec+** and **vec*** is illustrated by:

```
[1] (view (vec+ (vector 1 3 5 7 9) (vector 9 7 5 3 1)))
#(10 10 10 10 10)
[2] (view (vec* (vector 1 3 5 7 9) (vector 9 7 5 3 1)))
#(9 21 25 21 9)
```

We now look at the problem of adding all of the elements of a numerical vector. We first need the length of the vector, which we locally define to be **size**. Then we set up a local recursion on the index, starting with index 0. When the index reaches **size**, there are no more elements to add. We define **vector-sum** to be:

Program 9.13   vector-sum

```
(define vector-sum
  (lambda (vec)
    (let ((size (vector-length vec)))
      (letrec
        ((helper
           (lambda (i)
             (if (= i size)
                 0
                 (+ (vector-ref vec i) (helper (add1 i)))))))
        (helper 0)))))
```

In a similar way, we define **vector-product**, which takes the product of the elements of a numerical vector:

Program 9.14   `vector-product`

```
(define vector-product
  (lambda (vec)
    (let ((size (vector-length vec)))
      (letrec
        ((helper
           (lambda (i)
             (if (= i size)
                 1
                 (* (vector-ref vec i) (helper (add1 i)))))))
        (helper 0)))))
```

Here are some examples:

```
(vector-sum (vector 1 3 5 7 9)) ⟹ 25
(vector-product (vector 1 3 5 7 9)) ⟹ 945
```

It should occur to you when looking at the last two definitions that they are very similar in structure, and that they are ideal candidates for abstraction. Let's define a procedure `vector-accumulate` that abstracts the structure of those two procedures. There are just two essential differences: the value returned when the terminating condition is true, which we call the **seed**, and the operator applied in the alternative, which we call **proc**. Then the definition of `vector-accumulate` is given in Program 9.15. We can now rewrite the definitions of `vector-sum` and `vector-product` using `vector-accumulate`:

```
(define vector-sum (vector-accumulate + 0))
```

```
(define vector-product (vector-accumulate * 1))
```

We defined `list->vector`, but we have not yet defined the Scheme procedure `vector->list` that produces a list with the same elements as a given vector. But that is just a recursion on the index with the procedure **cons** and the seed (). We can then use `vector-accumulate` to define `vector->list` as shown in Program 9.16. Then

```
(vector->list (vector 1 2 3 4)) ⟹ (1 2 3 4)
(vector->list (vector 'abc 3 4)) ⟹ (abc 3 4)
```

Program 9.15   `vector-accumulate`

```
(define vector-accumulate
  (lambda (proc seed)
    (lambda (vec)
      (let ((size (vector-length vec)))
        (letrec
          ((helper
             (lambda (i)
               (if (= i size)
                   seed
                   (proc (vector-ref vec i) (helper (add1 i)))))))
          (helper 0))))))
```

Program 9.16   `vector->list`

```
(define vector->list (vector-accumulate cons '()))
```

Suppose that the elements of the vector $\langle 15.50,\ 8.95,\ 12.00 \rangle$ represent the price of items we want to buy and the elements of the vector $\langle 2,\ 5,\ 3 \rangle$ represent the number of each of those items we want. The total amount of money we spend on the purchases is $2 \times \$15.50 + 5 \times \$8.95 + 3 \times \$12.00 = \$111.75$. We found it by taking the products of the corresponding elements in the two vectors and then summing the products. This type of computation involving two vectors is used so often that it is given a name. It is called the *dot-product* of the two vectors. In general, if u is the numerical vector $\langle a_0,\ a_1,\ \ldots,\ a_{n-1} \rangle$ and v is the numerical vector $\langle b_0,\ b_1,\ \ldots,\ b_{n-1} \rangle$, the dot product $u \cdot v$ of u and v is the number $a_0 b_0 + a_1 b_1 + \ldots + a_{n-1} b_{n-1}$. We already have a procedure `vec*` that computes the vector whose elements are the products of the corresponding elements of two vectors of the same length. We also have a procedure `vector-sum` that sums the components of a vector. The composition of these two procedures gives us the dot product:

```
(define dot-product (compose vector-sum vec*))
```

where we use a more general version of `compose` that allows its second argument to be a procedure of arbitrarily many arguments. It is defined by

```
(define compose
  (lambda (f g)
    (lambda args
      (f (apply g args)))))
```

Although this is the dot product of two vectors, it is not an efficient way of
getting it. In the process of computing the dot product, the first procedure
applied, `vec*`, constructs a vector containing the products of corresponding
elements of the original two vectors. This is a rather costly and unnecessary
construction, since we can just make one pass down the elements of the two
vectors and accumulate the sum of the products as they are formed. The
definition of `dot-product` using this process is

```
(define dot-product
  (lambda (vec1 vec2)
    (let ((size (vector-length vec1)))
      (letrec ((loop (lambda (i)
                       (cond
                         ((= i size) 0)
                         (else (+ (* (vector-ref vec1 i)
                                     (vector-ref vec2 i))
                                  (loop (add1 i)))))))
        (loop 0)))))
```

An even more efficient way of computing the dot product of two vectors
uses an accumulator to store the intermediate sums. Its code is given in
Program 9.17.

9.3 Representing Vectors

We have gone a long way without discussing the actual representation of
vectors we use in the computations and the definitions of the basic procedures.
It is now time to address these questions. Since a vector is mathematically
characterized as a function from the index to the element with that index, we
can first look at a representation of a vector as a tagged pair. The car of the
pair is the tag `vector-tag` whose value is `"vector"`.

```
(define vector-tag "vector")
```

The cdr of the pair is another pair whose car is the vector's length, and
whose cdr is a procedure. That procedure takes an index as a parameter and

Program 9.17 dot-product

```
(define dot-product
  (lambda (vec1 vec2)
    (let ((size (vector-length vec1)))
      (letrec
        ((loop
          (lambda (i acc)
            (if (= i size)
                acc
                (loop (add1 i)
                      (+ acc (* (vector-ref vec1 i)
                                (vector-ref vec2 i)))))))
        (loop 0 0)))))
```

returns the element of the vector with that index. We make the convention
that the indices are zero based. With these conventions, we define vector?
and vector-length in Program 9.18.

Program 9.18 vector?, vector-length

```
(define vector?
  (lambda (arg)
    (and (pair? arg) (eq? (car arg) vector-tag))))

(define vector-length
  (lambda (vec)
    (car (cdr vec))))
```

The constructor vector-generator has the generating procedure gen-proc
as its parameter. It returns a procedure that has the vector's length size as
its parameter. That in turn returns the vector being constructed, which is a
tagged pair containing the size and the procedure gen-proc. The definitions
of vector-ref and vector-generator are given in Program 9.19.

A tagged pair containing a list in place of a procedure can also be considered
as a representation of a vector. This is the second representation of vectors
we develop. We only need to redefine vector-ref and vector-generator as
in Program 9.20. As we mentioned in the Overview, the elements in such lists
are accessed with list-ref. vector-generator contains a loop that invokes

Program 9.19 `vector-ref`, `vector-generator` Version I

```
(define vector-ref
  (lambda (vec i)
    ((cddr vec) i)))

(define vector-generator
  (lambda (gen-proc)
    (lambda (size)
      (cons vector-tag (cons size gen-proc)))))
```

Program 9.20 `vector-ref`, `vector-generator` Version II

```
(define vector-ref
  (lambda (vec i)
    (list-ref (cddr vec) i)))

(define vector-generator
  (lambda (gen-proc)
    (lambda (size)
      (cons vector-tag
            (cons size
                  (letrec
                    ((loop (lambda (i)
                             (cond
                               ((= i size) '())
                               (else (cons (gen-proc i)
                                           (loop (add1 i)))))))))
                    (loop 0)))))))
```

`gen-proc` on each pass and builds a list of the results. We now have

```
[1] (vector 100 200 300 400 500)
("vector" 5 100 200 300 400 500)
[2] (view (vector 100 200 300 400 500))
#(100 200 300 400 500)
```

With these two representations of vectors, we have implemented the properties of vectors specified in the mathematical definition; that is, we have associated an element with each index. However, we have not considered the other question raised in the Overview, random access. It is clear that the list representation does not provide random access to the elements, for we have to cdr down the list until we find the element with the desired index, and the computer resources used in this cdring increase with the index. It may appear as though the representation of the vector using a procedure that assigns an element to each index gives true random access to the elements, but consider the following situation where vectors are represented as procedures:

```
(let ((a (make-vector 4 5)))
  (let ((b (vector-update a 1 10)))
    (let ((c (vector-update b 2 20)))
      (let ((d (vector-update c 3 30)))
        (vector-ref d 0)))))              ⟹ 5
```

In order to compute (vector-ref d 0), we first invoke the procedure representing the vector d with argument 0 to find that it invokes the procedure representing the vector c with argument 0, which in turn invokes the procedure representing b with argument 0, which in turn invokes the procedure representing a with argument 0, which returns the value 5. If we had asked for (vector-ref d 3), the value 30 would have been returned with just the one procedure invocation. Thus, the resources needed to access the different elements of d depend upon the indices of the elements.

We do not have to give up on random access because Scheme has an implementation of vectors that does provide it. The third representation we discuss is that provided by Scheme. The external representation of a vector in Scheme as a list preceded by a sharp sign, #, is how we have been displaying vectors with the procedure view. Thus the vector with elements 20, 30, 40, and 50 is written as #(20 30 40 50). This is a representation, not an expression that evaluates to a vector. Like lists, vector constants must be quoted, so that when we enter a quoted vector, we get

```
[1] '#(10 u (+ 2 3) "Mary")
#(10 u (+ 2 3) "Mary")
[2] (writeln '#(10 20 (+ 10 20) 40 50))
#(10 20 (+ 10 20) 40 50)
[3] (vector 10 20 (+ 10 20) 40 50)
#(10 20 30 40 50)
```

The basic procedures vector?, vector-length, and vector-ref are provided by Scheme. Our fourth basic procedure, vector-generator, is not in Scheme, but we can use the two Scheme procedures make-vector and vector-set! to define it. We have already discussed make-vector, but vector-set!

is new. With the list and procedure representation of a vector, when we want to change an element with index k in a vector vec to the new value c, we invoke (vector-update vec k c), which makes a copy of the vector with a given element changed. The original vector vec still has its original elements, and only the copy has the element with index k changed to c. With the procedure vector-set!, we invoke (vector-set! vec k c), and we *do not* create a new vector, but instead we change the element with index k in vec to have the value c. Thus vector-set! is not a constructor, since it does not create a new vector. Instead, we call such procedures *mutators* or *mutation procedures* that cause a mutation or change in the original vector. Its call structure is (vector-set! *vec i obj*), where *vec* is a vector, *i* is an index, and *obj* is an object that becomes the element with index *i* in *vec*. The element that previously had index *i* in *vec* is replaced with *obj*. The value returned by an invocation of vector-set! is not specified, so do not use the returned value since it depends upon the implementation of Scheme. Programs that do use such values are not portable; that is, they cannot be used with other implementations of Scheme. The purpose of an invocation of vector-set! is to change a vector, which is a side effect. As such, it can be used in begin expressions where side effects are done. It is a convention in Scheme to place an exclamation mark, !, at the end of the names of mutation procedures. The exclamation mark is read as "bang," so we read vector-set! as "vector set bang." We follow our convention of not displaying whatever is returned by side-effecting procedures. As with define, writeln, and the others, we shall not display what a vector-set! expression returns.

As an example of the use of vector-set!, consider

```
[1] (define v1 (vector 0 2 4 6 8))
[2] v1
#(0 2 4 6 8)
[3] (vector-set! v1 2 5)
[4] v1
#(0 2 5 6 8)
```

Using vector-set!, we now present the definition of our basic constructor vector-generator. The program for vector-generator first constructs a vector vec of the desired length size (≥ 0), with unspecified elements. Then it enters a loop with index i going from 0 to size. For each i less than size, it changes the ith element of vec to be the generating procedure genproc applied to i. When the index i reaches its upper limit size, the vector vec has had all of its entries changed, and since the if expression has only a consequent, some value (unspecified in Scheme) is returned. But this value is ignored, since the letrec expression is the first expression in an implicit begin expression. The value returned by the whole begin expression is the vector vec. The structure of this program makes use of the fact that the vector vec is changed by side effects. The mutation is done in the loop within the letrec expression, and when its work is finished, the vector vec is returned. Program 9.21 contains the code for vector-generator.

Program 9.21 vector-generator

```
(define vector-generator
  (lambda (gen-proc)
    (lambda (size)
      (let ((vec (make-vector size)))
        (letrec
          ((loop (lambda (i)
                    (if (< i size)
                        (begin
                          (vector-set! vec i (gen-proc i))
                          (loop (add1 i)))))))
          (loop 0))
        vec)))))
```

When we use vector-set!, we are interested in its side effects, and we do not use the value that it returns. If we do want to use the updated vector that has been reset by an invocation of vector-set!, we can use a mutating version of vector-update, which we call vector-update!. It first uses vector-set! to set the element with the given index to a new value and then returns the vector. It is defined in Program 9.22.

Program 9.22 vector-update!

```
(define vector-update!
  (lambda (vec i c)
    (vector-set! vec i c)
    vec))
```

When we presented the second definition of list->vector, we mentioned that we would give another version in which it would not be necessary to pass the newly created vector as an argument to the local procedure convert. We can now do it using vector-set!. We first create a vector having the same length as the list using make-vector. Then we cdr down the list, changing the entry in the vector to be the corresponding entry in the list. The code is in Program 9.23.

Program 9.23   list->vector

```
(define list->vector
  (lambda (ls)
    (let ((vec (make-vector (length ls))))
      (letrec
        ((convert
           (lambda (ls i)
             (if (not (null? ls))
                 (begin
                   (vector-set! vec i (car ls))
                   (convert (cdr ls) (add1 i)))))))
        (convert ls 0))
      vec)))
```

In this program, we again see that vector-set! is used in a begin expression for its side effect of changing an element in a vector. The mutation of the vector is accomplished in the body of the local procedure convert. When the letrec expression is finished, the vector vec is returned.

When mutation is introduced, we must adopt a different point of view about computing than when we use functional programming. Programs that make use of mutation are referred to as *imperative-style programs*. In functional programming, an object is passed as an argument to a procedure and a new object is created, but the original one does not change. If we start with a vector a, which is (vector 2 4 6), and let b be (vector-update a 1 5), then the vector a has not been changed, and we have

```
[1] (let ((a (vector 2 4 6)))
      (let ((b (vector-update a 1 5)))
        (view a) (newline)
        (view b) (newline)))
#(2 4 6)
#(2 5 6)
```

On the other hand, if we use the mutator vector-update! instead of vector-update, we actually do change the vector a, and we have

```
[2] (let ((a (vector 2 4 6)))
      (let ((b (vector-update! a 1 5)))
        (writeln a)
        (writeln b)))
#(2 5 6)
#(2 5 6)
```

In the first let expression in [2], the vector a has a certain state that is
determined by its elements. When vector-update! is invoked in the second
let expression, the state of a is changed. When objects change over time, we
say that at any given time the object is in a certain *state* that is determined by
certain state variables (in our example, they are the elements of the vector).
If we know the state of an object, we know its behavior at that time. When
using mutators, one must be conscious of the fact that each object has a
certain state and that an invocation of a mutation procedure causes a change
in the state of the object. We shall introduce other mutators in Chapter 11
and discuss the changes in state they cause. At this point, we give another
illustration comparing programming in functional style using vector-update
with programming in imperative style using the mutator vector-update!.

We next look at the problem of reversing the elements of a vector. To do so,
we define a procedure vector-reverse that has a vector vec as its parameter
and returns a vector having the same elements as vec but in reverse order. We
first define a vector-reversing procedure in functional style without mutation.
We use either of the first two representations of vectors (either as tagged
procedures or as lists). The idea that we use in writing this definition is to
use two indices, i and j. The lower index i starts at 0, and the upper index
j starts at the index of the last element. The elements with indices i and
j are swapped, and then i is increased by 1 and j is decreased by 1. The
swapping and changing indices continue until either the two indices coincide
(this happens when the length of the vector is odd) or until i is greater than
j (this happens when the length of the vector is even). The resulting vector is
returned. The swapping is done with a helping procedure called swap-maker
that has a vector vec as its parameter and returns a procedure that has two
indices index1 and index2 as parameters and returns a copy of vec that has
its elements with indices, index1 and index2, interchanged. The code for
vector-reverse is in Program 9.24.

We now give the definition of swap-maker in Program 9.25. We first store
the element with index index1 in a local variable temp. Then vector-update
is invoked on vec and returns a new vector having its element with index

Program 9.24   `vector-reverse` (functional version)

```
(define vector-reverse
  (lambda (vec)
    (letrec
      ((switch
         (lambda (v i j)
           (if (>= i j)
               v
               (let ((swapv (swap-maker v)))
                 (switch (swapv i j) (add1 i) (sub1 j)))))))
      (switch vec 0 (sub1 (vector-length vec))))))
```

Program 9.25   `swap-maker` (functional version)

```
(define swap-maker
  (lambda (vec)
    (lambda (index1 index2)
      (let ((temp (vector-ref vec index1)))
        (vector-update
          (vector-update vec index1 (vector-ref vec index2))
          index2
          temp)))))
```

index1 changed to the element with index index2. Now `vector-update` is
again invoked, this time on the vector that was returned. It returns a new
vector that has its element with index index2 changed to `temp`, completing
the swap.

We illustrate the use of `vector-reverse` with the following experiment:

```
[1] (let ((a (vector 1 2 3 4 5)))
      (let ((b (vector-reverse a)))
        (view a) (newline)
        (view b) (newline)))
#(1 2 3 4 5)
#(5 4 3 2 1)
```

We now write the definitions of corresponding procedures with mutations.
Program 9.26 gives the code for `vector-reverse!`. We are able to make
a few optimizations in the program, taking advantage of the fact that the
vectors have state that changes with invocations of the mutators. Now we

do not have to pass the vector **vec** as an argument to the local procedure **switch** and **switch** does not have to return a value. We can also define the local procedure **swapv!** before the letrec expression defining **switch**. This time, the helping procedure (**swap-maker vec**) (see Program 9.27) returns a mutator that uses **vector-update!** actually to interchange the elements with indices **index1** and **index2** in the vector **vec** itself. When **switch** finishes its work, the vector **vec** has its elements in reverse order. After the invocation of **switch**, the altered vector **vec** is returned as the value of the procedure **vector-reverse!**. Thus using mutation reduces the need to pass vectors as arguments to procedures and for procedures to return vectors as values. In general, mutation provides for efficient communication between procedures and faster running, more efficient programs.

We repeat the experiment, this time using the mutating version:

```
[2] (let ((a (vector 1 2 3 4 5)))
      (let ((b (vector-reverse! a)))
        (writeln a)
        (writeln b)))
#(5 4 3 2 1)
#(5 4 3 2 1)
```

Notice that this time, the invocation of **vector-reverse!** on the vector **a** actually changed the vector **a** itself, whereas in the previous version not involving mutation, the vector **a** remained unchanged.

Program 9.26   vector-reverse! (imperative version)

```
(define vector-reverse!
  (lambda (vec)
    (let ((swapv! (swap-maker vec)))
      (letrec
        ((switch (lambda (i j)
                   (if (< i j)
                       (begin
                         (swapv! i j)
                         (switch (add1 i) (sub1 j)))))))
        (switch 0 (sub1 (vector-length vec))))
      vec)))
```

Program 9.27 `swap-maker` (imperative version)

```
(define swap-maker
  (lambda (vec)
    (lambda (index1 index2)
      (let ((temp (vector-ref vec index1)))
        (vector-update!
          (vector-update! vec index1 (vector-ref vec index2))
          index2
          temp)))))
```

Comparing these two versions of vector-reversing procedures, we see that when we are willing to abandon the original elements occupying various positions in a vector, we may use the same vector and update individual positions. The values associated with the indices are changing, but they are in the same vector, not a copy of the vector. Imagine a vector of length N to be a set of N transparent shoe boxes fastened together at the sides and as elements use billiard balls with values written on them. Then when we use **vector-update!**, we open the lid, take out the ball that is in the box, and replace that ball with a different ball. We always use the same shoe boxes. The vector itself is not changing, but its contents are. The shoe boxes did not change; only their contents did. By using **vector-update!** we have shown that the communication structure associated with vectors as arguments and values can be lessened. What makes mutation really important, however, has to do with random access and the way virtually all computers are designed. Random access provides *constant time*; that is, the time required to access any element in the vector is the same. Sequential access in lists provides *linear time* in which the time is proportional to the index of the element. Thus we see that using mutation considerably improves the running time of programs.

In summary, we have now seen three approaches to implementing vectors. In the first two representations, mutations are not used. When we want to change an element with a given index in a vector, we use **vector-update**, which constructs a new vector that has the new element, and the original vector is left unchanged. Such programming without mutations is called functional programming. In our third approach to vectors, we use the mutator **vector-set!** to change an element with a given index in a vector, and this actually makes the changes in the original vector itself so as to change the state. Such programming with mutations is called imperative programming. We gain using mutation because the way it is implemented in Scheme gives us random access to the elements in the vector. The price we pay is that we actually change elements in the original vector when we use `vector-set!`, so if we need it for some reason after the invocation of `vector-set!`, we must first make a copy of the original vector using `vector-copy` and apply the mutation procedures to the copy. The vector data type has analogs in other programming languages where they are often called one-dimensional arrays. In the rest of this book, unless we state otherwise, we use the Scheme implementation of vectors with the mutator `vector-set!`.

Exercises

Exercise 9.1: `successive-powers`
Define a procedure `successive-powers` that constructs a vector of length n whose entries are the successive powers of the number `base`. The element with index 0 is the 0th power of `base`. The procedure should be curried so that its first parameter is `base`, and the procedure that is returned has parameter n. Test your procedure on

```
((successive-powers 2) 8)  ⟹  #(1 2 4 8 16 32 64 128)
((successive-powers 3) 5)  ⟹  #(1 3 9 27 81)
```

Exercise 9.2
A vector of zero length can be displayed by #(). Rewrite the definition of `view` to support vectors of zero length.

Exercise 9.3: `vector-view`
We defined a procedure `view` when we used the procedural representation of a vector to display the vector in the notation using a sharp sign followed by a list of elements. Define a procedure `vector-view` that works like `view`, except that it displays the vector using angle bracket notation with commas as used in mathematics. Take into account the observation of Exercise 9.2. With all three representations of vectors given in this chapter, (`vector-view` (`vector` 10 20 30)) should display <10, 20, 30>. A similar program, `set-view` can be defined using braces instead of angle brackets.

Exercise 9.4
Let v1 be the vector (`vector` 1 2 3 4) and let v2 be (`vector-copy` v1). What does each of the following expressions return? Test them with each of the three representations of vectors.

   a. (eq? v1 v2), (eq? v1 v1)

b. `(eqv? v1 v2)`, `(eqv? v1 v1)`

c. `(equal? v1 v2)`, `(equal? v1 v1)`

What conclusions can be drawn about the use of these predicates?

Exercise 9.5: `vector-linear-search`
The vectors under consideration in this exercise contain elements that can be tested for sameness with the predicate `equal?`. Define a procedure `vector-linear-search` that has as its parameters a vector `vec` and an object `obj`. It returns the smallest index whose element is the same as `obj`. If the object is not in the vector, an appropriate message is returned. Test your program on:

```
(vector-linear-search '#(g n p r a d l b s) 'a) ⟹ 4
(vector-linear-search '#(29 13 96 -5 24 11 9 -15 0 2) 11) ⟹ 5
```

Exercise 9.6: `vector-append`, `vector-reverse`
Use `vector-generator` to define vector analogs of **append** and **reverse**.

9.4 Matrices

We have used lists and vectors to store data. In both of these, the elements are sequentially organized, so that we can index the elements starting with zero and increasing the index by one for each successive element. We often use this way of organizing information, but there are also occasions where such a sequential organization is not the best way of organizing the information. Many times a table is a more convenient way of presenting data. For example, in a telephone book, each person has several entries: a name, an address, and a phone number. The data are entered in rows, each row containing the information for one person. If we take the first entries in all of the rows, we get the first column; the second entries of all rows form the second column; and in general, the nth entries in all rows form the nth column. The table in Figure 9.28 contains four rows and three columns. Each entry in the table can be located if we are given two indices, the zero-based index of the row and the zero-based index of the column. Thus in our table, "3314 Valley Dr." is the item with row index 2 and column index 1.

A *matrix* is a table in which each of the entries has two indices, the first being the zero-based row index and the second being the zero-based column index. In our discussion, we refer to the element in the matrix A having row index i and column index j as the element a_{ij}. If the matrix has m rows and n

"Jones, John"	"2117 Plum St."	"412–8421"
"Jones, M. S."	"1392 First Ave."	"424–7773"
"Jose, Michael W."	"3314 Valley Dr."	"421–0035"
"Joslin, Joan P."	"2550 Western Blvd."	"412–5531"

Figure 9.28 A table with four rows and three columns

columns, we call it an "m by n matrix." This is sometimes written as "$m \times n$ matrix." For example, if A denotes the table given in Figure 9.28, then A is a 4×3 matrix, and "424–7773" is the value of element a_{12}.

Unlike vectors, matrices are not a Scheme data type, so we have to decide upon a representation for matrices, and we have to define the building blocks in terms of which the matrix procedures are defined. We begin with two procedures, **num-rows** and **num-cols**, that take a matrix as argument and return the number of rows and the number of columns, respectively. We also use a selector **matrix-ref** that has the call structure

$$((\text{matrix-ref } mat) \ row\text{-}index \ column\text{-}index)$$

where *mat* is a matrix and *row-index* and *column-index* are nonnegative integers. It returns the element of the matrix *mat* with indices *row-index* and *column-index*. Thus, if **A** represents the matrix in Figure 9.28, we can write

```
[1] (define A-ref (matrix-ref A))
[2] (A-ref 1 2)
"424-7773"
[3] (A-ref 2 1)
"3314 Valley Dr."
```

We also use a constructor that is an analog of **vector-generator**. We call it **matrix-generator**, and it has the call structure

$$((\text{matrix-generator } gen\text{-}proc) \ nrows \ ncols)$$

where *nrows* and *ncols* are the number of rows and columns, respectively, of the matrix we are constructing. The procedure *gen-proc* takes as its arguments two indices and produces the element with those indices in the matrix being constructed.

We now decide how to represent a matrix. Let us assume that we are defining an $m \times n$ matrix A. There are m rows and n columns in A, and altogether there are $m \times n$ elements in A. Each of the m rows contains n elements. One way of representing A is as a vector V that contains the $m \times n$ elements of the matrix. But we must have a way of knowing the correspondence between elements of V and elements of A. It will be clearer if we look at a concrete example first and then generalize the method we develop. Consider the matrix in Figure 9.29.

$$A = \begin{pmatrix} 5 & 2 & 3 & 7 \\ 1 & 4 & 0 & 5 \\ 8 & 3 & 1 & 2 \end{pmatrix}$$

Figure 9.29   A 3×4 matrix

We have followed the usual mathematical convention of writing such numerical matrices (or tables) enclosed by large parentheses. This matrix, A, has three rows and four columns. There are two ways of writing the elements of a matrix sequentially, both of which are used in practice. One is to write the rows one after the other, to get the sequence of elements

$$5 \ 2 \ 3 \ 7 \ 1 \ 4 \ 0 \ 5 \ 8 \ 3 \ 1 \ 2$$

This way is called *row major* order. The other way is to write the columns one after the other, to get the sequence of elements

$$5 \ 1 \ 8 \ 2 \ 4 \ 3 \ 3 \ 0 \ 1 \ 7 \ 5 \ 2$$

This way of writing the elements is called *column major* order. We arbitrarily choose to use the row major order in our representation of matrices.

Now that we are agreed on row major order, we must have a way of knowing where one row ends and the next begins. In our example, there are in all 12 elements in the matrix, as we can see by counting the number of elements in the sequence. Since we know that there are 4 elements in each row, we can divide 12 by 4 to get that there are 3 rows. We need someplace to store the number 4, which tells us the number of elements in each row. Let us agree to put it at the end of the sequence of numbers and store the whole sequence in a vector. Thus we represent the matrix A as the value of

(**vector** 5 2 3 7 1 4 0 5 8 3 1 2 4)

Program 9.30   `num-cols`

```
(define num-cols
  (lambda (mat)
    (let ((size (sub1 (vector-length mat))))
      (vector-ref mat size))))
```

Consider the element 0 in this vector. It has index 6 in the vector. What indices does it have in the matrix A? Here is how we can compute them using information we can extract from the vector A. The vector A has length 13, and the last element is a 4. We use this last element to conclude that the matrix has rows of length 4. Thus it has four columns. If we remove the last element, there are 12 elements left, so the matrix has $12/4 = 3$ rows. Now if we start at the beginning of the vector and collect the elements in groups of four, we see that 0 is in the second group and is the third element in that group. Thus 0 is in the second row and third column. Using zero-based indices, we see that 0 has row index 1 and column index 2. We can get these indices easily by noting that the row index is the quotient when the index 6 is divided by the row length 4, and the column index is the remainder when 6 is divided by 4.

Now let's reverse the process and start with the element in A having row index 1 and column index 2. We find its index in the vector representing A by multiplying the row index 1 by 4, which is the number of elements in each row of A, and then adding the column index 2. Thus the index of that element in the vector is $(1 \cdot 4) + 2 = 6$.

In general, we represent an $m \times n$ matrix, `mat`, by a vector containing $mn+1$ elements, the last of which is a number telling us the number of columns of `mat`, which is the same as the number of elements in each row of `mat`. The elements of the matrix are enumerated in row major order, making up the first mn elements. We can define the procedure `num-cols` for this representation as shown in Program 9.30, for all we have to do is access the last element in the vector representing the matrix.

To get the number of rows of the matrix, we merely divide one less than the length of the vector representing the matrix by the number of columns. Thus we get Program 9.31.

We now define `matrix-ref` that has the matrix `mat` as its parameter and returns a procedure that has as its parameters the row index `i` and the column index `j`, and it in turn returns the element of `mat` with those indices. To find the element in the vector representation of the matrix, we must multiply the

Program 9.31 num-rows

```
(define num-rows
  (lambda (mat)
    (let ((size (sub1 (vector-length mat))))
      (/ size (vector-ref mat size)))))
```

row index i by the number of columns in the matrix **mat** and add to that product the column index j. This gives us:

Program 9.32 matrix-ref

```
(define matrix-ref
  (lambda (mat)
    (let ((ncols (num-cols mat)))
      (lambda (i j)
        (vector-ref mat (+ (* i ncols) j))))))
```

Exercise

Exercise 9.7

The selector **matrix-ref** should contain in its definition a range test for the indices i and j and return an error if either is out of range. Rewrite the definition so that it contains such a test.

We now turn our attention to the constructor **matrix-generator**, which is defined using **vector-generator**. We first have to build the generating procedure of one argument that generates the vector representing the matrix. If we are given the index **k** of an element **e** in the vector representation, the corresponding row index is the quotient obtained when **k** is divided by **ncols**, and the corresponding column index is just the remainder obtained when **k** is divided by **ncols**. Recall that **ncols** is the number of elements in each row of the matrix. Then to get the row index, we can count the number of groups of **ncols** elements we can remove before including the element **e** with index **k**. The number of such groups is the zero-based row index of the element **e** in the matrix. But that number of groups is what we mean by the quotient obtained when **k** is divided by **ncols**. The next such group of **ncols** elements contains e, and its zero-based index in that group is the column index of e in the matrix. But that zero-based index is also the remainder when k is divided by ncols. Thus we can take as the vector-generating procedure of one argument

```
(lambda (k)
  (gen-proc (quotient k ncols) (remainder k ncols)))
```

The length of the vector representing the matrix is one more than the product of nrows and ncols. We can then write:

Program 9.33 `matrix-generator`

```
(define matrix-generator
  (lambda (gen-proc)
    (lambda (nrows ncols)
      (let ((size (* nrows ncols)))
        (let ((vec-gen-proc
                (lambda (k)
                  (if (< k size)
                      (gen-proc (quotient k ncols)
                                (remainder k ncols))
                      ncols))))
          ((vector-generator vec-gen-proc)
           (add1 size)))))))
```

As an example, we construct a 3 × 5 matrix having all of its elements zero by writing (make-zero-matrix 3 5) where

```
(define make-zero-matrix (matrix-generator (lambda (i j) 0)))
```

In mathematics, the rows and the columns of a matrix are considered to be vectors. We adopt this point of view and define the procedures row-of and column-of that are used to select a row or a column of a matrix. It is convenient to curry the procedures row-of and column-of. To get the row of the matrix mat with zero-based index i, we invoke ((row-of mat) i), and to get its column with zero-based index j, we invoke ((column-of mat) j). These two procedures are defined by:

Program 9.34   `row-of`

```
(define row-of
  (lambda (mat)
    (let ((mat-ref (matrix-ref mat))
          (number-of-columns (num-cols mat)))
      (lambda (i)
        (let ((gen-proc (lambda (j) (mat-ref i j))))
          ((vector-generator gen-proc) number-of-columns))))))
```

and

Program 9.35   `column-of`

```
(define column-of
  (lambda (mat)
    (let ((mat-ref (matrix-ref mat))
          (number-of-rows (num-rows mat)))
      (lambda (j)
        (let ((gen-proc (lambda (i) (mat-ref i j))))
          ((vector-generator gen-proc) number-of-rows))))))
```

$$\begin{pmatrix} 5 & 1 & 8 \\ 2 & 4 & 3 \\ 3 & 0 & 1 \\ 7 & 5 & 2 \end{pmatrix}$$

Figure 9.36   The transpose of the matrix in Figure 9.29

The *transpose* of an $m \times n$ matrix A is an $n \times m$ matrix whose rows are the columns of A. The transpose of the matrix in Figure 9.29 is the 4×3 matrix given in Figure 9.36. To find the transpose of a matrix, we use the procedure **matrix-transpose** (see Program 9.37) that takes as its argument a matrix and returns its transpose. The key to writing the program is the observation that the element with indices i, j in the transpose of A is the same as the element with indices j, i in A. It is easily defined using **matrix-generator**.

Program 9.37 `matrix-transpose`

```
(define matrix-transpose
  (lambda (mat)
    (let ((mat-ref (matrix-ref mat)))
      (let ((gen-proc (lambda (i j) (mat-ref j i))))
        ((matrix-generator gen-proc)
         (num-cols mat)
         (num-rows mat)))))))
```

The elements of matrices can be any of the data types we have been using in Scheme. For numerical matrices, that is, matrices whose elements are numbers, we can define useful arithmetic operations. For example, if A and B are two matrices of the same size (same number of rows and same number of columns), we can define the sum $A + B$ to be the matrix whose elements are the sums of the corresponding elements of A and B. Similarly, we can multiply the matrix A by a scalar (number) c, and the resulting product cA is the matrix whose elements are c times the corresponding elements of A. It is also possible to define a useful multiplication rule for certain pairs of matrices. It is not customary to define the product to be the matrix whose elements are the products of corresponding elements of the two matrices. The following example illustrates the multiplication rule normally used.

A factory produces four products, W, X, Y and Z, at each of two sites, R and S. Each product uses steel, plastic, and rubber. Product W uses 4 units of steel, 2 units of plastic, and 2 units of rubber. Product X uses 5 units of steel, 2 units of plastic, and 2 units of rubber. Product Y uses 4 units of steel, 3 units of plastic, and 1 unit of rubber. Product Z uses 3 units of steel, 5 units of plastic, and 2 units of rubber. The cost of the steel, plastic, and rubber at site R is \$8, \$4, and \$5 per unit, respectively, and at site S is \$7, \$5, and \$4 per unit, respectively. To find the material costs of making one unit of each product at each of the two sites, we set up the following matrices:

	Units Used				Cost Per Unit	
	Steel	*Plastic*	*Rubber*		*Site R*	*Site S*
W	4	2	2			
X	5	2	2	*Steel*	\$8	\$7
Y	4	3	1	*Plastic*	\$4	\$5
Z	3	5	2	*Rubber*	\$5	\$4

Let's consider the cost of making a unit of Product Y at Site R. We multiply the number of units of each material by the corresponding cost at that site and add these products. This is the dot product of the third row of the Units Used matrix and the first column of the Cost Per Unit matrix. The result is $4 \cdot \$8 + 3 \cdot \$4 + 1 \cdot \$5 = \$49$. We compute the cost of making a unit of each product at each of the sites by finding the dot product of the appropriate row of the Units Used matrix and the appropriate column of the Cost Per Unit matrix. This leads to the following tabulation of the results:

$$
\begin{array}{c}
& \textit{Site R} \quad \textit{Site S} \\
\begin{array}{c} W \\ X \\ Y \\ Z \end{array}
\left(\begin{array}{cc}
\$50 & \$46 \\
\$58 & \$53 \\
\$49 & \$47 \\
\$54 & \$54
\end{array} \right)
\end{array}
$$

From this example, we make the following observations about the way the product of two matrices is defined. In order to be able to find the product AB for two matrices, they must be *compatible*, which means that the number of columns of A must be the same as the number of rows of B. If two matrices A and B are compatible, then the rule for computing their product AB is: if A is an $m \times n$ matrix and B is an $n \times k$ matrix, then their product AB is an $m \times k$ matrix. The element with indices i, j in AB is the dot product of the ith row vector of A and the jth column vector of B.

We have developed the tools that enable us to translate this rule directly into the definition of the procedure `matrix-product` that takes two compatible matrices as arguments and returns their matrix product.

```
(define matrix-product
  (lambda (mat-a mat-b)
    (let ((a-row (row-of mat-a))
          (b-col (column-of mat-b)))
      (let ((gen-proc
              (lambda (i j) (dot-product (a-row i) (b-col j)))))
        ((matrix-generator gen-proc)
         (num-rows mat-a) (num-cols mat-b))))))
```

This way of defining `matrix-product` follows directly from the rule describing matrix multiplication, but it is not an efficient way of doing it. Before actually taking the dot product, the row and column vectors had to be constructed. However, the answer does not require having these vectors. We can take the product of two elements at a time and accumulate their sum directly from the matrices without building the row and column vectors. Each element in the ith row of A has first index i, and each element in the jth column of B has second index j. Thus the ith row of A has the elements $a_{i,0}, \ a_{i,1}, \ldots, a_{i,n-1},$

Program 9.38 `matrix-product`

```
(define matrix-product
  (lambda (mat-a mat-b)
    (let ((ncols-a (num-cols mat-a))
          (a-ref (matrix-ref mat-a))
          (b-ref (matrix-ref mat-b)))
      (if (not (= ncols-a (num-rows mat-b)))
          (error "matrix-product:"
            "The matrices are not compatible.")
          (let
            ((gen-proc
               (lambda (i j)
                 (letrec
                   ((loop
                      (lambda (r acc)
                        (if (= r ncols-a)
                            acc
                            (loop (add1 r)
                                  (+ acc (* (a-ref i r)
                                            (b-ref r j))))))))
                   (loop 0 0)))))
            ((matrix-generator gen-proc)
             (num-rows mat-a) (num-cols mat-b)))))))
```

and the jth column of B has the elements $b_{0,j}$, $b_{1,j}, \ldots, b_{n-1,j}$. Thus to form the dot product of the ith row and jth column, we must add all products of the form $a_{i,r} b_{r,j}$ where r takes all integer values from 0 to $n-1$. In Program 9.38, we redefine `matrix-product` to do this summation of products directly and include a test for compatibility.

So far this treatment of matrices has not involved mutation. If we use a purely functional representation of vectors and their procedures, all of the procedures defined for matrices are purely functional. We can introduce a mutator `matrix-set!` that is similar to `vector-set!`. When we do so, the matrix must be considered as having state with the state variables the elements in the matrix. `matrix-set!` performs a mutation on the elements of the matrix. It has the call structure

$$((\text{matrix-set!} \; mat) \; row\text{-}index \; column\text{-}index \; obj)$$

where *mat* is a matrix whose element with indices given by *row-index* and

Program 9.39   `matrix-set!`

```
(define matrix-set!
  (lambda (mat)
    (let ((ncols (num-cols mat)))
      (lambda (i j obj)
        (vector-set! mat (+ (* i ncols) j) obj)))))
```

column-index is changed to the value of *obj*. Continuing the previous example from Figure 9.28, we have

```
[4] (define A-set! (matrix-set! A))
[5] (A-set! 2 1 "1922 River St.")
[6] (A-ref 2 1)
"1922 River St."
```

The mutator `matrix-set!` is defined in terms of `vector-set!` in Program 9.39.

In this section, we saw how matrices can be implemented using vectors. In a vector, each element has one index, and we refer to a vector as being one-dimensional. In a matrix, each element has two indices, the row index and the column index. We refer to a matrix as being two-dimensional. In some languages, the analogs of vectors and matrices are called one- and two-dimensional arrays. In Exercise 9.14, three-dimensional arrays are implemented, and the extension to higher-dimensional arrays is carried out in a similar manner. We use vectors to provide random access to stored data in our next chapter, which is on sorting and searching.

Exercises

Exercise 9.8:   `matrix`

Define a procedure `matrix` that takes two arguments, m and n, and returns a procedure that takes as its $m \times n$ arguments the elements of the $m \times n$ matrix it creates. (Hint: Use an unrestricted `lambda`.) For example, to create the matrix in Figure 9.29, we write

```
((matrix 3 4) 5 2 3 7
              1 4 0 5
              8 3 1 2)
```

Exercise 9.9: `mat+`

Define a procedure `mat+` that takes matrices A and B as arguments and returns their sum $A + B$. A and B must have the same number of rows and the same number of columns. If a_{ij} is the element of A with indices i, j, and b_{ij} is the element of B with indices i, j, then the element of $A + B$ with indices i, j is $a_{ij} + b_{ij}$.

Exercise 9.10: `matrix-multiply-by-scalar`

Define a procedure `matrix-multiply-by-scalar` that takes as arguments a number c and a matrix A and returns the matrix cA, which has as elements c times the corresponding elements of A.

Exercise 9.11: `matrix-view`

Define a procedure `matrix-view` that takes an $m \times n$ matrix as its argument and prints the matrix in the format shown below. If m is the matrix given in Figure 9.29 an invocation of (`matrix-view m`) should print

```
5  2  3  7
1  4  0  5
8  3  1  2
```

Next, include a tag `matrix-tag` and generalize the procedure `view` to display a vector, set, or matrix depending on the type of its argument. (See Exercise 9.3)

Exercise 9.12: *Column major order*

Suppose we had used the column major order for listing the elements of a matrix in the vector representation. Write the definitions of the following procedures using column major order: `num-rows`, `num-cols`, `matrix-ref`, `matrix-set!`, and `matrix-generator`.

Exercise 9.13: *Vector of vectors*

An $m \times n$ matrix can also be represented as a vector of length m in which the element with index i is a vector of length n containing the elements in row i of the matrix. Thus the matrix

$$\begin{matrix} 2 & 1 & -3 \\ 4 & -2 & -1 \end{matrix}$$

is represented as the vector

```
(vector (vector 2 1 -3) (vector 4 -2 -1))
```

For this representation of matrices, define the procedures `num-rows`, `num-cols`, `matrix-ref`, `matrix-set!`, and `matrix-generator`.

Exercise 9.14

The method used in this chapter for representing an $m \times n$ matrix as a vector of length $mn + 1$ can be extended to higher-dimensional arrays. For example, an element a_{ijk}, in a three-dimensional array A is indexed with three indices, i, j, and k, where $i = 0, 1, \ldots, m_1 - 1$, $j = 0, 1, \ldots, m_2 - 1$, and $k = 0, 1, \ldots, m_3 - 1$. We would then represent A as a vector of length $m_1 \cdot m_2 \cdot m_3 + 2$. The integer m_n for $n = 1, 2, 3$ is the size of the matrix in dimension n and we say that A is an $m_1 \times m_2 \times m_3$ array. The last two entries in the vector representation can be taken to be m_2 and the product $m_2 m_3$. Using this information, describe the vector representation more completely, and define the procedures **size-dim-1**, **size-dim-2**, and **size-dim-3** that are the analogs of **num-rows** and **num-cols** and return the values m_1, m_2, and m_3, respectively. Also define the procedures **array-ref**, **array-set!** and **array-generator**, which are analogs of the corresponding matrix procedures. These considerations can be extended to give arrays of any dimension.

10   Sorting and Searching

10.1 Overview

The process of rearranging the data in a list to put them in some specified order, such as alphabetical order or increasing numerical order, is called *sorting* the list. The process of locating a given item in a list is called *searching* the list for the given item. In this chapter, we develop routines for sorting and searching both lists and vectors. We also develop a relational calculus for retrieving from a table those items that satisfy some specified conditions.

10.2 Sorting

We use tables to store many kinds of data, such as names, grades, or salaries. It is more convenient to access data in tables if the data are arranged in some increasing or decreasing order. For example, names are most conveniently arranged in alphabetical order, and test grades are often most conveniently arranged in decreasing order. There are many different methods for sorting a table into a desired order. We shall look at a few of them in this section.

10.2.1 Insertion Sort

Our first sorting technique is called an *insertion sort*. Suppose we are given a nonempty list **ls** of numbers that are not ordered and that we wish to rearrange to be in increasing order. We first think about the problem recursively. If the list of numbers contains only one number, the list is already sorted, and we are done. If the list contains at least two numbers, and if we recursively

Program 10.1   `insertsort`

```
(define insertsort
  (lambda (ls)
    (if (singleton-list? ls)
        ls
        (insert (car ls) (insertsort (cdr ls))))))
```

Program 10.2   `insert`

```
(define insert
  (lambda (a ls)
    (cond
      ((null? ls) (cons a '()))
      ((< a (car ls)) (cons a ls))
      (else (cons (car ls) (insert a (cdr ls)))))))
```

invoke `insertsort` on `(cdr ls)`, we get a correctly sorted list containing all but the first number. To get the completely sorted list, all we have to do is insert `(car ls)` into its correct position in the already sorted part `(insertsort (cdr ls))`. For this insertion, we afterward define a procedure `insert` that inserts a number a into the correct place in a sorted list `ls`. Program 10.1 contains the definition of `insert-sort`, and Program 10.2 contains that of `insert`.

While `(cdr ls)` is not empty, `insertsort` invokes `insert` to insert `(car ls)` into `(insertsort (cdr ls))`. Until `(cdr ls)` is empty, the value of `(insertsort (cdr ls))` is not known, so a return table is built. When `ls` is finally reduced to contain a single number, then `(insertsort (cdr ls))` is just the "sorted" list containing that single number. Then each of the insertions that has been waiting in the return table can be evaluated, and the final sorted list is built up. Figure 10.3 shows how the recursive insertion sort routine sorts a list of numbers. We start with the list (50 40 30 20 10). When we reach the invocation of `insertsort` on (10), the sorted sublist (10) is returned, and the invocations of `insert` that have been waiting in the return table are evaluated with sorted sublists as their second arguments.

We also write an iterative instead of recursive version of insertion sort. This version will be written using Scheme vectors to store the data. We define a mutation procedure called `vector-insertsort!` that takes as its argument a vector containing the numbers to be sorted into ascending order and changes

```
(insertsort '(50 40 30 20 10))
(insert 50 (insertsort '(40 30 20 10)))
(insert 50 (insert 40 (insertsort '(30 20 10))))
(insert 50 (insert 40 (insert 30 (insertsort '(20 10)))))
(insert 50 (insert 40 (insert 30 (insert 20 (insertsort '(10))))))
(insert 50 (insert 40 (insert 30 (insert 20 '(10)))))
(insert 50 (insert 40 (insert 30 '(10 20))))
(insert 50 (insert 40 '(10 20 30)))
(insert 50 '(10 20 30 40))
(10 20 30 40 50)
```

Figure 10.3   Return table for `insertsort`

that vector into one with the same elements sorted as desired. The value it returns is unspecified, as is the case with many mutators. It is more convenient to insert the numbers to the left instead of to the right when using vectors. Our sort of the vector #(60 50 30 40 10 20) proceeds as shown in Figure 10.4. At each stage, we can picture the process as removing the next item to be inserted and shifting those before it to the right until we come to the place where the item belongs.

The sort is accomplished by applying the following algorithm. We assume that all elements to the left of the element with index **k** have been sorted. We then save the element with index **k** in a variable **val**, freeing up the kth position so that we can shift into it. The element with index **k** is then inserted into the correct position by successively testing each element to its left and shifting it one place to the right until a smaller element is encountered. To do this, procedure `vector-insertsort!` uses a local procedure, `sortloop`, which is first invoked with the index 1, since that is the index of the first element to be inserted. The local procedure `sortloop` calls the procedure `vector-insert!` to do the insertion for each successive index. Each time it is called, say with index **k**, all of the elements with indices less than **k** have already been sorted, and `vector-insert!` inserts the element with index **k** in the correct place relative to the first **k** elements. Now the elements with indices less than **k** + 1 are in the correct order. This insertion process continues until the index **k** reaches the length of the original vector, by which time all of the elements have been inserted. When **k** is equal to **size**, the condition in the if expression is false, and the if expression returns some unspecified value. We assume in this book that the implementation of Scheme we are employing does not print the value returned on the screen. The code for `vector-insertsort!` is given in Program 10.5.

```
                                        #(60 50 30 40 10 20)
            Insert 50                   #(60       30 40 10 20)
                                        #(50 60 30 40 10 20)
            Insert 30                   #(50 60       40 10 20)
                                        #(50       60 40 10 20)
                                        #(    50 60 40 10 20)
                                        #(30 50 60 40 10 20)
            Insert 40                   #(30 50 60       10 20)
                                        #(30 50    60 10 20)
                                        #(30    50 60 10 20)
                                        #(30 40 50 60 10 20)
            Insert 10                   #(30 40 50 60       20)
                                        #(30 40 50    60 20)
                                        #(30 40    50 60 20)
                                        #(30    40 50 60 20)
                                        #(    30 40 50 60 20)
                                        #(10 30 40 50 60 20)
            Insert 20                   #(10 30 40 50 60    )
                                        #(10 30 40 50    60)
                                        #(10 30 40    50 60)
                                        #(10 30    40 50 60)
                                        #(10    30 40 50 60)
                                        #(10 20 30 40 50 60)
```

Figure 10.4   Steps in sorting with **vector-insertsort!**

Program 10.5   **vector-insertsort!**

```
(define vector-insertsort!
  (lambda (v)
    (let ((size (vector-length v)))
      (letrec ((sortloop (lambda (k)
                           (if (< k size)
                               (begin
                                 (vector-insert! k v)
                                 (sortloop (add1 k)))))))
        (sortloop 1)))))
```

We now consider the definition of vector-insert!. The procedure vector-insert! is applied with first argument k when those elements of the vector with indices less than k have already been sorted. It inserts the element with index k into the correct place in the sorted part, so that those elements with indices less than k + 1 are now sorted. Here is how vector-insert! works. If it is called with index k, it lets val be the element with index k. The local procedure insert-h is then called with index k. When insert-h is called with some index m as argument, it compares val with the element comp having index m − 1. If val is less than comp, we still have not found the correct place for val, so comp is moved up to have index m, and insert-h is called again with argument m − 1 to compare val with the element with index m − 2. On the other hand, if val is not less than comp, m is the correct index for val, and we assign it with (vector-set! vec m val). Each time insert-h is invoked, its argument is one less than on the previous invocation. If its argument is zero, then there are no more elements to the left to which to compare it, and val must be the first element in the vector. Thus (zero? m) is the terminating condition for the recursion. The code for vector-insert! is in Program 10.6.

Program 10.6 vector-insert!

```
(define vector-insert!
  (lambda (k vec)
    (let ((val (vector-ref vec k)))
      (letrec ((insert-h
                (lambda (m)
                  (if (zero? m)
                      (vector-set! vec 0 val)
                      (let ((comp (vector-ref vec (sub1 m))))
                        (if (< val comp)
                            (begin
                              (vector-set! vec m comp)
                              (insert-h (sub1 m)))
                            (vector-set! vec m val)))))))
        (insert-h k)))))
```

Throughout this definition, we used the fact that vector-set! is a mutation procedure that changes the vector v as a side effect. When a vector v is passed as an argument to vector-insertsort!, its elements are actually reordered within that vector, so when we look at v after the sorting, its elements are sorted. This is a different behavior from the procedure `insertsort`, which returns a sorted copy of the original list and the original list is not affected. If we want a procedure to apply insertion sort to a vector and return a sorted copy of that vector but leave the original vector unaffected, we can use the following procedure, `vector-insertsort`:

```
(define vector-insertsort
  (lambda (vec)
    (let ((v (vector-copy vec)))
      (vector-insertsort! v)
      v)))
```

Here is an example of how these sorting procedures work:

```
[1] (define numlist (list 60 50 40 30 20 10))
[2] (insertsort numlist)
(10 20 30 40 50 60)
[3] numlist
(60 50 40 30 20 10)
[4] (define numvec (vector 60 50 40 30 20 10))
[5] (vector-insertsort numvec)
#(10 20 30 40 50 60)
[6] numvec
#(60 50 40 30 20 10)
[7] (vector-insertsort! numvec)
[8] numvec
#(10 20 30 40 50 60)
```

We next perform an operation count on `insertsort` to study its efficiency in sorting a list of length n. The procedure `insert` successively inserts the kth number into the already sorted list of numbers with indices from $k + 1$ to $n - 1$. The process starts with k equal to $n - 2$ and decreases k by 1 after each insertion. When the sorted list to the right of the kth number has m members, inserting the kth number in the correct place can require up to m comparisons between the kth number and the numbers in the sorted list. In applying insertion sort to a list of n numbers, the first insertion is done on a list of one number, the second insertion is done on a list of two numbers, and so on, with the kth insertion done on a list of k numbers. There will be $n - 1$ such insertion loops, so the total number of comparisons needed will be *at most* $1 + 2 + 3 + \cdots + (n - 1) = n(n - 1)/2$. This formula represents the worst possible situation, in which one has to go to the end of the sorted list in each case to put the inserted number in the correct place. This was the case in the example above. But in general, we can say that on the average, we would have to search halfway through the list to find the correct place to insert the number, so the expected number of comparisons in insertion sort is $n(n-1)/4$. Because the expected number of comparisons is $O(n^2)$, we call this a method of order n^2 or simply a quadratic method. If the list is already sorted, the first comparison in each insertion determines the correct place, so for a list of n correctly sorted numbers, only n comparisons are required.

10.2.2 Mergesort

The insertion sort discussed in the previous section is a quadratic method requiring on the order of n^2 comparisons to sort a list or vector of n elements. We have seen that on the average it takes about 2,500 comparisons to sort a list of 100 items. There are several methods of order $n \log_2 n$ that reduce this number considerably, so that a list of 100 items can be sorted with fewer than 700 instead of the approximately 2,500 comparisons of the previous method. For a list of 1,000 numbers, insertion sort takes approximately 250,000 comparisons, while the $n \log_2 n$ method takes about 10,000 comparisons. This is a substantial improvement, and we now look at one such method, called *natural mergesort*. In Program 4.3, we defined the procedure **merge**, which takes two sorted lists and merges them into a single sorted list. The **nat-mergesort** procedure takes advantage of whatever order already exists in the list by grouping the original list into a list of sublists, each sublist consisting of those elements that are already correctly ordered. For example, if the original list is (2 3 4 1 2 3 2 1), the first step is to insert parentheses to group the members into the four sublists ((2 3 4) (1 2 3) (2) (1)). Then each of the successive pairs of sublists is merged to give half as many sublists, each of which is still correctly ordered. In our example, the next step produces ((1 2 2 3 3 4) (1 2)). This process of merging successive pairs of sublists is continued until there is only one correctly ordered list, at which point the sort is completed. In our example, the next merge operation yields ((1 1 2 2 2 3 3 4)), and the car of this list is the desired sorted list.

In the grouping phase of our sorting procedure, we made the sublists as large as possible so that each sublist is sorted. This grouping method is what adds the adjective *natural* to the name *mergesort*. Another grouping method, which leads to the procedure called *mergesort* without the adjective *natural* is the following. We group the elements of our original list so that there is one element in each sublist. Thus in the example above, our initial grouping yields ((2) (3) (4) (1) (2) (3) (2) (1)). Since each sublist of one element is sorted, we can merge successive pairs of sublists to get ((2 3) (1 4) (2 3)

Program 10.7 `make-groups`

```
(define make-groups
  (lambda (ls)
    (cond
      ((null? ls) '())
      ((null? (cdr ls)) (list ls))
      (else (let ((a (car ls))
                  (gps (make-groups (cdr ls))))
              (if (< (cadr ls) a)
                  (cons (list a) gps)
                  (cons (cons a (car gps)) (cdr gps))))))))
```

(1 2)). Then successive sorted lists are merged to give ((1 2 3 4) (1 2 2 3)) and then ((1 1 2 2 2 3 3 4)). The development of this version of the mergesort procedure is left as an exercise.

The first step in performing the natural mergesort is to group the data into sublists so that in each sublist, the data are correctly ordered. In order to carry out this grouping, we define a procedure `make-groups` that takes a list of numbers, `ls`, as its argument and returns a list with the numbers in the same order but arranged in largest possible sublists in which the numbers are nondecreasing. If `ls` is empty, then there are no sublists, and () is returned. This serves as the terminating condition for our recursion. Similarly, if (cdr ls) is empty, then `ls` consists of only one element, so there is only one group consisting of the `ls` itself. Thus the list of groups is simply (list ls). Now, if we let `gps` denote (make-groups (cdr ls)), there are two cases to consider in order to get (make-groups ls). If the first number in `ls` is greater than the second number in `ls`, then the first sublist in (make-groups ls) is a singleton list containing just that first number. Thus we have (cons (list (car ls)) gps) as the result. On the other hand, if the first number in `ls` in not greater than the second number in `ls`, then it must be added to the first group already in `gps`. Thus the result is (cons (cons (car ls) (car gps)) (cdr gps)). We can now complete the definition of `make-groups` in Program 10.7.

We next use `merge` in the procedure `pair-merge`, which merges successive pairs of sublists that resulted from applying `make-groups` to `ls`. By merging successive pairs, we mean that the first two sublists are merged, then the third and fourth sublists are merged, and so on until there are no pairs left to merge. If there were originally an odd number of sublists, one would be left over as

Program 10.8 `pair-merge`

```
(define pair-merge
  (lambda (sublists)
    (cond
      ((null? sublists) '())
      ((null? (cdr sublists)) sublists)
      (else (cons (merge (car sublists) (cadr sublists))
                  (pair-merge (cddr sublists)))))))
```

the last sublist of the list returned by **pair-merge**. Thus the procedure **pair-merge** has as its parameter **sublists**, which is a list of sublists, and in each sublist the numbers are in ascending order. It returns a list in which each successive pair of **sublists** has been merged. Its straightforward definition is given in Program 10.8.

To do the mergesort, we now need a procedure that applies **pair-merge** repeatedly until there is only one sublist. We test for whether the list contains only one sublist by checking whether the cdr of the list is empty. Thus we can define the procedure **nat-mergesort**, which has as its parameter **ls** a list of numbers and returns a list with those numbers sorted in ascending order. It performs a natural mergesort by first grouping the numbers in largest possible ascending sublists and then repeatedly merging successive pairs of sublists until the list contains only one sublist. Program 10.9 shows the definition of **nat-mergesort**.

Program 10.9 `nat-mergesort`

```
(define nat-mergesort
  (lambda (ls)
    (if (null? ls)
        '()
        (letrec ((sort (lambda (gps)
                         (if (null? (cdr gps))
                             (car gps)
                             (sort (pair-merge gps))))))
          (sort (make-groups ls))))))
```

To see that the **nat-mergesort** procedure is $O(n \log n)$, we consider a worst case in which we have n numbers arranged in descending order, and we sort them into ascending order. This is a worst case because the grouping forms a list of n lists, each containing only one number. On each pass through the list, the procedure sort halves the number of sublists by merging successive pairs. The question we must first answer is: "How many times can we divide a number n by 2, rounding up to the next higher integer each time, until we reach 1?" For example, if we start with seven numbers, the first pass of sort produces four sublists. This is obtained by dividing $\frac{7}{2} = 3.5$ and then rounding up to 4, corresponding to the list ((6 7) (4 5) (2 3) (1)). Next we divide 4 by 2 and get two sublists: ((4 5 6 7) (1 2 3)). Finally when we divide 2 by 2, we get one sublist, which is the sorted list.

What we have asked is: "What is the smallest power k for which $2^k \geq n$?" Again if $n = 7$, then $2^2 = 4$ and $2^3 = 8$, so the value of k is 3. But the statement $2^3 = 8$ means exactly the same thing as the statement $\log_2 8 = 3$, and in general, the statement $2^k = n$ means exactly the same thing as the statement $\log_2 n = k$. Thus the number of passes through the list to get to the sorted list is at most $\log_2 n$ rounded up to the next higher integer if it is not a whole number. We can use the *ceiling* procedure to do this rounding and use the usual notation $\lceil \log_2 n \rceil$. In merging two lists that together contain m numbers, at most $m - 1$ comparisons are needed, so if all of the sublists together contain n numbers, the number of comparisons needed in any one pass of sort through the list will never exceed n. Since we make at most $\lceil \log_2 n \rceil$ passes through the list and each pass needs at most n comparisons, we have a total of at most $n \lceil \log_2 n \rceil$ comparisons. Thus nat-mergesort is $O(n \log n)$.

There are also situations in which we want to sort a list of numbers into decreasing order. The sorting procedures given can easily be modified to do this; for example, in nat-mergesort, one only has to change the < to > in the two procedures merge and make-groups. It would be even more convenient to use procedural abstraction here and write one nat-mergesort procedure that takes an additional argument rel that will be either < or >, and replace the inequalities in merge and make-groups by rel.

An iterative vector version of mergesort can also be defined. Since we shall be sorting data stored in vectors, we look at such a version. A recursive vector version of mergesort is outlined in the exercises. The iterative sorting program has three parts. We first determine the group size, with initial value 1. From the group size, we determine the end points of the groups. Then we merge successive pairs of groups, with the usual proviso that if there is an odd number of groups, one is left over after the merging. After the merge phase, we double the group size and repeat the process. This continues until

Program 10.10 `vector-merge!`

```
(define vector-merge!
  (lambda (newvec vec)
    (lambda (left top-left right top-right)
      (letrec
        ((mergeloop
           (lambda (left right i)
             (cond
               ((and (< left top-left) (< right top-right))
                (if (< (vector-ref vec left) (vector-ref vec right))
                    (begin
                      (vector-set! newvec i (vector-ref vec left))
                      (mergeloop (add1 left) right (add1 i)))
                    (begin
                      (vector-set! newvec i (vector-ref vec right))
                      (mergeloop left (add1 right) (add1 i)))))
               ((< left top-left)
                (vector-set! newvec i (vector-ref vec left))
                (mergeloop (add1 left) right (add1 i)))
               ((< right top-right)
                (vector-set! newvec i (vector-ref vec right))
                (mergeloop left (add1 right) (add1 i)))))))
        (mergeloop left right left)))))
```

the group size is the same as the length of the vector, at which time the sort is completed. Since the initial group size is 1 for all groups, this is an ordinary rather than a natural mergesort.

The merging phase is done by the procedure `vector-merge!`, which merges two adjacent groups in a vector `vec`. Suppose that the group in `vec` with indices from `left` up to, but not including, `top-left` and the group with indices from `right` (usually the same as `top-left`) up to, but not including, `top-right` have already been sorted. The mutation procedure `vector-merge!` merges these two groups into the vector `newvec`. The steps are similar to those used in the procedure `merge`. The definition of `vector-merge!` is given in Program 10.10.

We now carry out the sort using the procedure `vector-mergesort!`, given in Program 10.11, which has a vector `vec1` to be sorted as its parameter. Since the mutator `vector-merge!` merges two adjacent groups of one vector into another vector, we must always have another vector into which to carry out

Program 10.11 `vector-mergesort!`

```scheme
(define vector-mergesort!
  (lambda (vec1)
    (let ((vec-size (vector-length vec1)))
      (let ((adjust (lambda (k) (min k vec-size)))
            (vec2 (make-vector vec-size))
            (max-index (sub1 vec-size)))
        (letrec
          ((merge-pass
             (lambda (group-size count)
               (if (> group-size max-index)
                   (if (even? count) (vector-change! vec1 0 max-index vec2))
                   (let ((newvec (if (odd? count) vec2 vec1))
                         (vec (if (odd? count) vec1 vec2)))
                     (let ((merge! (vector-merge! newvec vec)))
                       (letrec
                         ((group-ends
                            (lambda (left top-left right top-right)
                              (if (<= left max-index)
                                  (begin
                                    (merge! left top-left right top-right)
                                    (let ((new-right (+ top-right group-size)))
                                      (group-ends
                                        top-right
                                        (adjust new-right)
                                        new-right
                                        (adjust (+ new-right group-size)))))))))
                         (group-ends 0 (adjust group-size)
                           group-size (adjust (* 2 group-size)))))
                     (merge-pass (* group-size 2) (add1 count))))))))
          (merge-pass 1 1))))))
```

this merge. Rather than create a new vector on each merging pass through the vector, we make a second vector **vec2** and alternate merges from **vec1** into **vec2** and from **vec2** into **vec1** on successive merging passes.

On the first pass through the vector, we assume that each group contains only one item, so the parameter **group-size** to the local procedure **merge-pass** is given the initial value 1, and its second parameter **count** is set to 1. On each successive merging pass through the vector, two adjacent groups are

Program 10.12 `vector-change!`

```
(define vector-change!
  (lambda (vec1 j k vec2)
    (letrec ((loop (lambda (i)
                     (if (<= i k)
                         (begin
                           (vector-set! vec1 i (vector-ref vec2 i))
                           (loop (add1 i)))))))
      (loop j))))
```

merged so `group-size` is doubled. On each merging pass, `count` is increased by 1. When `count` is odd, the merging is done from `vec1` to `vec2`, and when `count` is even, the merging is done from `vec2` to `vec1`.

The end points of each pair of adjacent groups are the four parameters of the local procedure `group-ends`; these are `left`, `top-left`, `right`, and `top-right`. The parameter `left` is the left end point of the left group, and `right` is the left end point of the right group of an adjacent pair of groups. We get `top-left` by adding `group-size` to `left`, but with a large enough `group-size`, `top-left` can exceed the length of the vector. In order to avoid this, we use the local procedure `adjust`, which limits the size of its argument to be at most the length of the vector `vec1`. The value of `right` is obtained by adding `group-size` to `left`. And finally, we get `top-right` by adjusting the sum of `right` and `group-size`. The mutator `vector-merge!` is then invoked with these parameters to merge the two adjacent groups, and the pass through the vector is made by repeated invocations of `group-ends` to determine the successive pairs of groups. When a pass is completed, `merge-pass` is invoked with the next `group-size` and count. Finally, when `group-size` reaches the length of the vector, there is only one group and the vector is sorted. If it is `vec2` that happens to be storing the sorted items, the mutator `vector-change!` is invoked to copy `vec2` into `vec1`. The definitions of `vector-mergesort!` and `vector-change!` are given in Programs 10.11 and 10.12, respectively.

The mutator `vector-change!` copies the segment of `vec2` with indices between j and k into `vec1`, actually changing the items in `vec1`. This vector version of mergesort sorts a vector in just about the same time as the list version of mergesort sorts a list of the same size. It is somewhat slower than natural mergesort, but it has the advantage of not requiring a return table since it is iterative.

10.2.3 Quicksort

There is another popular method of sorting data stored in lists or in vectors, called *quicksort*. When the data are rather randomly distributed, quicksort is $O(nlogn)$ like mergesort, but in the worst cases, when the data are nearly sorted, it is of order $O(n^2)$ like insertion sort. An advantage of the vector version of quicksort over the vector version of mergesort is that the sorting is done by mutation within the original vector, and no temporary storage vector is necessary.

We first look at the algorithm for carrying out a quicksort of a list of n numbers into increasing order.

1. We first select an item in the list, which we call the pivot. For convenience, we shall select the first item in the list, although selecting other items as the pivot sometimes improves the performance of the method.

2. The rest of the items in the list are copied into one of two lists. Those less than the pivot are copied into the left list, and the rest are copied into the right list. The order of the items in these two lists is immaterial.

3. A new list is created in which the items in the left group are followed by the pivot, which is, in turn, followed by the items in the right group.

4. The quicksort algorithm is then repeated recursively starting again from Step 1 on the items in the left group and on the items in the right group. On each application of the algorithm, the groups decrease in size, and when all groups have been decreased so as to consist of a single element, the original list is sorted.

The program implementing this algorithm to sort a list of numbers into increasing order is called **quicksort**. It first checks to see whether the list is empty or if it consists of a single number. In these cases, it merely returns the original list. Otherwise, it calls the local helping procedure called **collect**, which carries out Steps 1 through 3 of the quicksort algorithm The procedure **collect** has the pivot as its first parameter, the rest of the list as its second parameter **ls**, and two accumulators, **lgroup** and **rgroup**, as its third and fourth parameters. The first of these accumulators, **lgroup**, stores those elements of the list that are less than the pivot to give us the left group, and the second of the accumulators, **rgroup**, stores those elements that are greater than or equal to the pivot to give us the right group. The procedure **collect** tests each element of the list **ls** to determine whether it is less than

Program 10.13 `quicksort`

```
(define quicksort
  (letrec
    ((collect
       (lambda (pivot ls lgroup rgroup)
         (if (null? ls)
             (append (quicksort lgroup) (cons pivot (quicksort rgroup)))
             (if (< (car ls) pivot)
                 (collect pivot (cdr ls) (cons (car ls) lgroup) rgroup)
                 (collect pivot (cdr ls) lgroup (cons (car ls) rgroup)))))))
     (lambda (ls)
       (if (or (null? ls) (null? (cdr ls)))
           ls
           (collect (car ls) (cdr ls) '() '())))))
```

the pivot. If it is, it conses it onto `lgroup`; otherwise it conses it onto `rgroup`. When `ls` is finally empty, the pivot is consed onto the quicksort of `rgroup`, which is then appended to quicksort of `lgroup`. The definition of `quicksort` is given in Program 10.13.

We also present the vector version of quicksort, which we call `vector-quicksort!`. It has the property that it sorts the data within the given vector without having to make a copy of it, as mergesort must do. This is an advantage if the amount of memory available is small and making a copy uses too much of the memory. Like `vector-mergesort!`, `vector-quicksort!` is a mutator that changes the order of the elements in the original vector.

To illustrate how `vector-quicksort!` implements the quicksort algorithm in place (that is, within the given vector), we shall walk through the sorting of the vector

$$\#(6\ 4\ 9\ 7\ 8\ 2\ 5\ 6\ 9)$$

To see how this version of quicksort works, we place our left index finger below the item to the right of the pivot (the item with index 1) and our right index finger below the last item in the vector (the item with index 8 in our example). This is illustrated by the arrows under the items:

$$\#(6\ 4\ 9\ 7\ 8\ 2\ 5\ 6\ 9)$$

We now go though a sequence of steps designed to move the pivot into its final position, so that all items to its left will be less than or equal to the pivot and all items to its right will be greater than or equal to the pivot.

1. *Searching Up.* We compare the item above our left index finger with the pivot and if it is not greater than the pivot, we move our left index finger one entry to the right and compare that item with the pivot. We continue moving to the right until we encounter an item that is greater than the pivot. We then hold our left index finger at that position. If we pass beyond the last item, we go back to it. In our case, we have moved to the item with index 2, and the positions are given by:

$$\#(6\ 4\ 9\ 7\ 8\ 2\ 5\ 6\ 9)$$

2. *Searching Down.* We next compare the item above our right index finger with the pivot and if it is not less than the pivot, we move our right index finger one entry to the left and compare that item with the pivot. We continue moving to the left until we encounter an item that is less than the pivot. We hold our right index finger at that position. If we come to the first item, we stop there. In our example, we move down until we encounter the item 5 with index 6.

$$\#(6\ 4\ 9\ 7\ 8\ 2\ 5\ 6\ 9)$$

3. *Swapping.* Swapping allows us to move both values from the wrong location to the right location. As long as our left index finger is to the left of our right index finger, we swap the items to which our index fingers are pointing, and we move our left index finger one item to the right and our right index finger one item to the left. This gives us:

$$\#(6\ 4\ 5\ 7\ 8\ 2\ 9\ 6\ 9)$$

We repeat steps 1, 2, and 3 starting with our index fingers pointing to the 7 and 2 and using the same pivot, 6. Since our left index finger is pointing to the item 7, which is greater than the pivot, and our right index finger is pointing to the item 2, which is less than the pivot, we swap those two items and move our index fingers to the next item, our left index finger moving right and our right index finger moving left. This gives:

$$\#(6\ 4\ 5\ 2\ 8\ 7\ 9\ 6\ 9)$$

We again repeat steps 1, 2, and 3 starting with our index fingers both pointing to 8 with index 4 and using the same pivot, 6. Since our left index finger is pointing to 8, which is greater than the pivot, it stays where it is. Our right index finger is pointing to 8, which is greater than the pivot, so it moves one to the left and comes to 2, which is less than the pivot, so it stays there. We now have:

$$\#(6\ 4\ 5\ \underset{\times}{2}\ 8\ 7\ 9\ 6\ 9)$$

4. *Partition.* After searching up and searching down, our left index finger is pointing to an item that is to the right of the item to which our right index finger is pointing. When this happens, we swap the pivot item with the item to which our right index finger is pointing. This gives us:

$$\#(2\ 4\ 5\ 6\ 8\ 7\ 9\ 6\ 9)$$

We next partition the vector into three parts: the left part consists of all items to the left of the pivot 6 (these items are all less than 6); the pivot itself makes up the middle part; and the right part consists of all items to the right of the pivot (these items are all greater than or equal to 6).

$$\#(2\ 4\ 5\ 6\ 8\ 7\ 9\ 6\ 9)$$

We now apply Steps 1 through 4 to the left and right parts, choosing the leftmost item in each part as the pivot. We continue doing this until each part contains only one point. When we reach that point, the vector is sorted.

In the definition of vector-quicksort! in Program 10.14, the sorting is done by the helping procedure qsort, which has as parameters the lowest and highest indices of the part of the vector to be sorted. As long as there is more than one item in that part—that is, the lowest index, low, is less than the highest index, high—the helping procedure partition (defined later) is called to carry out Steps 1 though 4, and the final position of the pivot is called middle. Then the qsort procedure is invoked on both the left part and the right part.

The procedure partition selects the pivot as the first item in the group to be partitioned and then calls the local procedure search, which in turn invokes the local procedures search-up and search-down to carry out Steps 1 and 2 given above. The indices of the items that search-up and search-down locate are named new-left and new-right, respectively. If new-left is

Program 10.14 `vector-quicksort!`

```
(define vector-quicksort!
  (lambda (v)
    (letrec
      ((qsort (lambda (low high)
                (if (< low high)
                    (let ((middle (partition v low high)))
                      (qsort low (sub1 middle))
                      (qsort (add1 middle) high))))))
      (qsort 0 (sub1 (vector-length v))))))
```

less than **new-right**, the items with these indices are swapped, using the procedure **vector-swap!** defined in Program 10.16, and the searching continues as described in Step 3. Otherwise, the pivot is swapped with the item with the index **new-right**, and **new-right** is returned as the value of **partition**. The definition of **partition** is given in Program 10.15.

To get an idea of why quicksort is $O(n \log_2 n)$ for some lists, let's assume that the items to be sorted are well mixed so that the correct location of the pivot is near the middle of the list each time a left group or a right group is sorted. Let's also assume that the list contains $n = 2^m$ items; then $m = \log_2 n$. On the first pass, there will be approximately n comparisons with the pivot (actually $n - 1$). If the correct location of the pivot item is near the middle of the list, the left group and the right group each contain approximately $\frac{n}{2}$ items. Thus to sort each of them will take approximately $\frac{n}{2}$ comparisons, and since there are two groups, the total is again approximately $2(\frac{n}{2}) = n$ comparisons. Again assuming that the correct location of each pivot is near the middle of the group, we have four groups each, containing approximately $\frac{n}{4}$ items, so again approximately n comparisons will be needed to sort them all. Since each partitioning is assumed to divide the group into two groups of essentially equal size, the length of the list is divided by 2 on each pass, so after m passes, each group will contain only one item. Thus there are m passes, and each pass makes n comparisons, so there are $nm = n \log_2 n$ comparisons in all. A similar but more involved analysis shows that if the list is well mixed, quicksort is $O(n \log_2 n)$.

On the other hand, when the original list is already sorted (or nearly sorted), then the first pass requires n comparisons, only to find that the left group is empty and the right group contains $n-1$ items. Thus it takes $n-1$ comparisons

Program 10.15 `partition`

```scheme
(define partition
  (lambda (v low high)
    (let ((pivot (vector-ref v low)))
      (letrec
        ((search
           (lambda (left right)
             (letrec
               ((search-up
                  (lambda (i)
                    (cond
                      ((= i (add1 right)) (sub1 i))
                      ((> (vector-ref v i) pivot) i)
                      (else (search-up (add1 i))))))
                (search-down
                  (lambda (i)
                    (cond
                      ((or (= i (sub1 left)) (< (vector-ref v i) pivot)) i)
                      (else (search-down (sub1 i)))))))
               (let ((new-left (search-up left))
                     (new-right (search-down right)))
                 (if (< new-left new-right)
                     (begin
                       (vector-swap! v new-left new-right)
                       (search (add1 new-left) (sub1 new-right)))
                     (begin
                       (vector-swap! v low new-right)
                       new-right)))))))
        (search (add1 low) high)))))
```

Program 10.16 `vector-swap!`

```scheme
(define vector-swap!
  (lambda (vec i j)
    (let ((temp (vector-ref vec i)))
      (vector-set! vec i (vector-ref vec j))
      (vector-set! vec j temp))))
```

to partition the right group and that partitioning again leads to an empty left group and a right group containing $n - 2$ items. Continuing this way, we see that it will take

$$n + (n - 1) + (n - 2) + \cdots + 2 = \frac{1}{2}(n^2 + n - 2)$$

comparisons, which is $O(n^2)$. Thus quicksort has the strange property that it is the most efficient method for sorting data that are completely unsorted and least efficient for data that are nearly sorted.

10.2.4 Sorting Alphabetically

Often the data to be sorted consist of names that one would like to have rearranged in alphabetical order. Scheme provides a convenient way to do alphabetical sorts. Strings can be compared to decide which precedes the other in alphabetical order. To decide whether one string precedes another string, Scheme provides a predicate **string<?** that takes two strings as arguments and is true if its first argument precedes its second argument lexicographically (i.e., in the order in which they would appear in a dictionary). The usual lexicographic order is modified to place the digits 0 through 9 first, then all of the capital letters, followed by all of the lowercase letters. A complete listing of the order of the characters, including the punctuation characters, is given in the ASCII Code Table, which is discussed in Appendix A. For example,

```
(string<? "Johnson, James" "Johnston, John") ⟹ #t
(string<? "Cleveland, Ohio" "Cincinnati, Ohio") ⟹ #f
```

There are also predicates **string>?**, **string<=?**, and **string>=?** that do the expected things. The predicates **string<?** and **string>?** can be used in place of **<** and **>** in the sorting programs to sort names into alphabetical order. If the sort routine had been abstracted to take an additional argument **rel**, then the alphabetical sort could have been accomplished by passing **rel** the value **string<?** or **string>?**.

The data being sorted are sometimes in a table that can be sorted in many different ways depending upon which column of the table we want in sorted order. For example, a table may contain personnel data for a company. Each row of the table contains the data for an individual employee. In the study of databases, each row of the table is referred to as a *record*. The first column contains the name, with last name first. The second column contains the employee's identification number; the third column, the employee's age; the

Name	Id	Age	Yr.Emp	Supervisor	Salary
(define table10-17					
'(("Smith, Harold W."	2324	43	1974	"Fox, Charles Q."	49325)
("Jones, Mary Ann"	1888	54	1965	"none"	65230)
("White, Thomas P."	3403	34	1982	"Smith, Harold W."	27300)
("Williams, John"	2451	46	1970	"Jones, John Paul"	41050)
("Brown, Susan E."	3620	28	1984	"Williams, John"	18500)
("August, Elizabeth"	2221	45	1971	"Jones, John Paul"	44100)
("Jones, John Paul"	1990	55	1965	"Jones, Mary Ann"	63700)
("Wilson, William W."	2455	46	1970	"August, Elizabeth"	41050)
("Black, Burton P."	3195	38	1978	"Smith, Harold W."	31420)
("Fox, Charles Q."	2400	41	1981	"Jones, John Paul"	52200)
("Blue, Benjamin J."	3630	26	1984	"Williams, John"	18500)))

Table 10.17 A table represented as a list

fourth column, the year when the employee joined the company; the fifth column, the employee's supervisor; and the sixth column, the employee's annual salary in dollars. Each of these columns is called a *field*, and each field has a *field name*. The third field has the field name "Age." To process the data in Scheme, one can represent it as a list (or in some cases, as a vector or a list of vectors depending on which data structure is easier to process). Table 10.17 shows such a table represented as a list.

To sort the data in this table, we must first decide which field we are going to sort on; that field is referred to as the *sort key* or simply the *key*. We can sort these data so that the names are in alphabetical order, in which case we are sorting on the first field, or we are sorting with the key "Name." One could also sort the data by any of the other fields, depending upon the use we are making of the data. The sorted data are then returned with the same records but reordered so that the sorted field is in the desired order. We must modify the less-than predicate (or **rel** in the abstracted version) of the sort routine so that it makes the comparison on the appropriate member of each row and then moves the *whole row* as a unit as the sorting is done.

10.2.5 Timing the Sorting Routines

Which of the sorting routines is best? We compare them by recording the time each takes to sort the same lists of numbers into increasing order. We use lists of randomly generated numbers as the test data. Many implementations of Scheme provide a procedure **random** (see Exercise 13.3) that takes a positive

integer argument n and returns a pseudo-random number in the range 0 to
n-1, including the end values.[1]   Program 10.18 defines `random-list`, which
has as its output a list of n such randomly generated integers, each of which
is between 0 and $n - 1$.

Program 10.18   `random-list`

```
(define random-list
  (lambda (n)
    (letrec ((build-list
               (lambda (k)
                 (if (zero? k)
                     '()
                     (cons (random n) (build-list (sub1 k)))))))
      (build-list n))))
```

We then define the test data as

```
(define rand100 (random-list 100))
(define rand200 (random-list 200))
(define rand400 (random-list 400))
(define v-rand100 (list->vector rand100))
(define v-rand200 (list->vector rand200))
(define v-rand400 (list->vector rand400))
```

We can measure the time that each of the three sorting procedures takes to
sort these lists (or vectors) using the procedure `timer`, which we now define.
When we pass `timer` a procedure `proc` and its argument `arg`, it tells us both
the time in seconds that it took to run `(proc arg)` and the answer returned
by `(proc arg)`. In order to do the timing, we assume that the Scheme we
are using has a way of getting the time of day accurate to hundredths of a
second. We assume that we can access the time of day by calling a procedure

---

[1] Such sequences $\{x_k\}$, $k = 0, 1, \ldots$ of pseudo-random numbers can be generated in the
following way. Consider a congruence relation of the form $f(x) = ax \bmod m$, where m is
a large prime integer and a is an integer in the range 2, 3, ..., $m - 1$. Good choices for
m and a are $m = 2^{31} - 1 = 2,147,483,647$ and $a = 7^5 = 16,807$. We choose an initial
seed s_1 and generate the sequence $s_{k+1} = f(s_k)$, $k = 1, 2, \ldots$. Then $u_k = s_k/m$ is a
pseudo-random number in the range $0 \le u_k < 1$, and a pseudo-random integer x_k in the
range $0 \le x_k \le n - 1$ is the integer part of nu_k. (See Park and Miller 1988.)

of no arguments called **time-of-day**.[2] In Program 10.19, we define a timing
procedure that uses **time-of-day**, which is assumed to be a thunk.

Program 10.19   timer

```
(define timer
  (lambda (proc arg)
    (let ((start (time-of-day)))
      (let ((val (proc arg)))
        (let ((finish (time-of-day)))
          (let ((elapsed-time (/ (- finish start) 100)))
            (writeln "Time = " elapsed-time ", Answer = " val)))))))
```

When a let expression, which contains several pair bindings, such as

$$(\text{let } ((var_1 \ val_1) \ (var_2 \ val_2) \ \ldots \ (var_n \ val_n))$$
$$body)$$

is evaluated, there is no guarantee in what order the pair bindings (var_k
val_k) are evaluated. In **timer**, we have to be sure that the order of the pair
binding is as shown in the code, so we had to nest the let expressions. In
addition, the last nesting was required because the *val*-part of the last let
expression contained the *var*-part of the previous let expression, which would
not be allowed if these two pair bindings were in the same let expression.
Scheme also has the special form **let***, which has syntax similar to **let**:

$$(\text{let*} \ ((var_1 \ val_1) \ (var_2 \ val_2) \ \ldots \ (var_n \ val_n))$$
$$body)$$

which is equivalent to a sequence of nested let expressions each containing one
of the pair bindings:

$$(\text{let } ((var_1 \ val_1))$$
$$(\text{let } ((var_2 \ val_2))$$
$$\ldots$$
$$(\text{let } ((var_n \ val_n))$$
$$body) \ \ldots \ ))$$

---

[2] Although the way of getting the time of day has not been standardized, all Schemes have
some way of either getting the time of day or of timing a procedure.

The pair bindings in a let* expression are evaluated from left to right, and any *val*-part may contain *var*'s from previous pair bindings. This enables us to define `timer` in the following way:

```
(define timer
  (lambda (proc arg)
    (let* ((start (time-of-day))
           (val (proc arg))
           (finish (time-of-day))
           (elapsed-time (/ (- finish start) 100)))
      (writeln "Time = " elapsed-time ", Answer = " val))))
```

Sort Time in Seconds			
Number of Items	100	200	400
insertsort	0.55	2.69	10.76
nat-mergesort	0.17	0.38	0.88
quicksort	0.11	0.22	0.60
vector-insertsort!	0.39	1.71	6.21
vector-mergesort!	0.33	0.65	1.48
vector-quicksort!	0.22	0.44	1.05

Table 10.20   Comparison on random data

The results of using `timer` on the various sort routines we have developed are given in Table 10.20.[3]   The three mutators `vector-insertsort!`, `vector-mergesort!`, and `vector-quicksort!` were called by first making a local copy of the vector to be sorted and then calling the timer on the invocation of the mutator. For example, for `vector-insertsort!` we have

```
(let ((v (vector-copy v-rand100)))
  (timer vector-insertsort! v))
```

The time for the two insert sorts increases approximately by a factor of four each time the length of the data is doubled, whereas mergesort's and quicksort's time increases by a factor between two and three.

---

[3] The test was conducted in PC-Scheme (Version 3.02) on a Zenith 386 microcomputer.

We have seen the behavior of the various sorting routines on a list of randomly distributed integers. It is also interesting to compare their behavior on lists that are nearly sorted. Suppose we have a list starting with 50 and followed by the integers from 1 to 100 in their natural order. We want to sort this list into increasing order. This is equivalent to saying we want to insert 50 into the sorted list of integers from 1 to 100. We shall test our six sorting routines on this problem of inserting 50 into the integers from 1 to 100, as well as the problems of inserting 100 into the integers from 1 to 200 and of inserting 200 into the integers from 1 to 400. The vector versions are tested on the vectors obtained by converting the lists to vectors. The results are shown in Table 10.21.

Sort Time in Seconds			
Number of Items	101	201	401
insertsort	0.05	0.11	0.17
nat-mergesort	0.06	0.11	0.16
quicksort	0.38	1.37	5.98
vector-insertsort!	0.05	0.11	0.17
vector-mergesort!	0.28	0.66	1.42
vector-quicksort!	0.44	1.59	5.93

Table 10.21   Comparison on nearly sorted data

In this kind of insertion into a sorted list, insertion sort and natural mergesort are about equally fast, and quicksort is much slower. We cannot recommend any one of these routines as being the best. We must choose the sorting routine that is best suited to do the job we have in mind for it. There are many other sorting routines that have their advantages for specific kinds of sorting jobs. However, we shall not explore this subject any further in this book. There is an extensive literature on this topic in which you can read about other ways of sorting data.

Exercises

Exercise 10.1: decr-ints
Define a procedure decr-ints that, given an integer n as its argument, pro-

duces a list of the integers in decreasing order from n to 1. Use this procedure to create test lists and vectors of length 25, 50, and 100, and use these to time the sorting routines developed in this section. Explain why these lists provide a "worst case" for all three.

Exercise 10.2: `nat-mergesort`
Rewrite the definition of `nat-mergesort` so that it is curried and takes as its first argument a binary relation `rel` and returns a procedure that takes a list as its argument. It returns the list sorted so that successive pairs of elements satisfy the binary relation. For example, if the list contains numbers, to sort the list in ascending order we use the procedure (`nat-mergesort <`), and to sort a list of names in lexicographic order we use the procedure (`nat-mergesort string<?`). Test your procedure on suitable lists of numerical data and lexicographic data.

Exercise 10.3
Modify the mergesort program so that it can sort Table 10.17 by any one of the six fields, and in the case of numerical fields, the sort can be in either increasing or decreasing order. Test your program by sorting the data into four separate tables, the first sorted alphabetically by Name, the second into increasing order by Id, the third by decreasing order of Salary, and the fourth by increasing Date of Employment.

Exercise 10.4: `mergesort`
We implemented the natural mergesort in which the original list is grouped into the largest possible ordered sublists. The ordinary mergesort routine groups the elements into sublists of one element each. Then the sublists are merged pairwise until there is only one sublist. Define a procedure `mergesort` that implements the ordinary mergesort. Compare the times for `mergesort` and `nat-mergesort` to sort random lists of length 100, 200, and 400 numbers and to do the insertions done in the second time tests. Write the definition of a recursive vector version of mergesort that uses the two procedures `vector-merge!` and `vector-change!` given in this section. The algorithm is outlined below.

a. Make a vector, `store`, that has the same length as the vector `vec` to be sorted.

b. Define a local procedure `sort` that takes as its parameters `first` and `last`, which are the indices of the first and last items, respectively, in the group within `vec` to be sorted in a given recursive pass. The initial values of `first` and `last` are 0 and one less than the length of `vec`, respectively.

c. As long as **first** is less than **last**, let **mid** be the index of the item that is halfway between **first** and **last**. Then in a **begin** expression (which may be implicit), do Steps d through g.

d. Invoke **sort** on the group from **first** to **mid**.

e. Invoke **sort** on the group from (**add1 mid**) to **last**.

f. Invoke **vector-merge**! on the appropriate arguments to merge the sorted groups in **vec** from **first** to **last** into the vector **store**.

g. Copy the part of **store** between **first** and **last** into **vec**.

Compare the times for this version of mergesort to sort the various test vectors with the times for the iterative vector version and with the times for natural mergesort and ordinary mergesort to sort the test lists.

10.3 Searching

Suppose we have a list containing many items and we want to determine whether a certain item is in the list and, in the case of a table, retrieve the information in the row containing the item. We can easily write a program that searches through the list from the beginning until the given item is found, and if it reaches the end of the list without finding it, the program indicates that the element is not in the list. A vector version of this procedure is in Exercise 9.5. If each of the entries in a list of n items is accessed equally frequently, we would on the average expect to have to go through half of the list to find an item, and this would take on the average $n/2$ comparisons. Such a method is called a *linear search* through the list for the given item.

If the list is already sorted into increasing (or decreasing) order, there is a more efficient method for searching for a given item, which we call the *target*. This more efficient method, called *binary search*, is described next. There is a well-known guessing game in which one player, A, challenges another, B, to guess the number A is thinking, knowing only that the number (or target) is between 1 and 100, including both 1 and 100. B may ask any question, but A can answer only "yes" or "no." The object is to determine the target by asking the least number of questions. The most efficient strategy for asking the questions is to divide the interval in which the target must lie into two equal parts and question whether the target lies in one of these parts. For example, the first question could be: "Is the number greater than 50?" If the answer is yes, the next question should be: "Is the number greater than 75?" By halving the length of the interval in which the target can lie with each question, it takes only seven questions to reduce the length of the interval to 1, at which point the number is determined.

The game described is an example of a binary search. This method requires random access of the items, so it will be more efficient to use vectors as the data structure to store the data. If the vector has length n, we start by looking at the item with index $n/2$. If it is equal to the target, we are finished. If it is less than the target, we know that the target lies in the right half of the vector, so we repeat the search procedure in the right half of the vector. If the item with index $n/2$ is greater than the target, we know that the target lies in the left half of the vector, and we repeat the search procedure in the left half of the vector. This procedure divides the length of the vector by two every time it is repeated, so it takes at most k steps to reach the point where the length is reduced to one and the item is found, where $2^k = n$; that is, $k = \log_2 n$. Thus a vector of 1,000 items that would take an average of 500 comparisons to find an item using linear search would take at most 10 comparisons to find the item using binary search.[4] This points out the advantage of using a method that is $O(\log n)$ instead of $O(n)$.

Since we shall want to use the binary search program to search for items in vectors that may either be sorted in increasing or in decreasing order, or in fact, in vectors of names that are sorted lexicographically, we shall write a general version of `binary-search` that takes as a parameter a relation `rel` and returns a binary search procedure that takes a vector and a target as its parameters. We can then pass `<`, `>`, or `string<?` to accomplish the three kinds of searches mentioned above. Program 10.22 shows the code for such a version of `binary-search`.

We apply this procedure to search a vector of names arranged alphabetically as follows:

```
[1] (let ((names (vector "Ann S" "Ben J" "Ed A" "Guy S" "Kay W")))
      ((binary-search string<?) names "Guy S"))
3
```

If we have many alphabetical searches to perform, it may be convenient to define a procedure `alpha-search` in terms of `binary-search` by writing

```
(define alpha-search (binary-search string<?))
```

---

[4] Actually, the procedure binary-search may involve two comparisons at each step in order to determine whether the target is less than, greater than, or equal to the test value, so the number of comparisons for a vector of 1,000 items could be as high as 20.

Program 10.22 `binary-search`

```
(define binary-search
  (lambda (rel)
    (lambda (vec target)
      (letrec
        ((search
           (lambda (left right)
             (if (< right left)
                 (writeln "The search failed.")
                 (let ((middle (floor (/ (+ left right) 2))))
                   (let ((mid-val (vector-ref vec middle)))
                     (cond
                       ((rel target mid-val)
                        (search left (sub1 middle)))
                       ((rel mid-val target)
                        (search (add1 middle) right))
                       (else middle)))))))))
        (search 0 (sub1 (vector-length vec)))))))
```

and then we can apply this procedure to a vector of strings as follows:

```
[2] (let ((names (vector "Ann S" "Ben J" "Ed A" "Guy S" "Kay W")))
      (alpha-search names "Ed A"))
  2
```

Exercises

Exercise 10.5: `list-linear-search`
Write a program `list-linear-search` that takes an arbitrary list of numbers and a number and searches through the given list linearly from the beginning until it finds the number. If it finds the number, it returns the zero-based index of that number in the list; if it does not find the number, it returns an appropriate message.

Exercise 10.6
Write the procedures that are used to sort the personnel data in Table 10.17 on the field of names, and then use binary search to locate a given name and return the personnel data for that individual. Use vectors to store the data and use the vector sort routine you wish.

10.4 Relational Calculus

We have seen how information is stored in tables. Table 10.17, which contains personnel data for a company, is an example of such a table. In accessing information stored in a table, we often want to get all items that satisfy certain conditions. For example, in Table 10.17 we can ask for the personnel data for all people who joined the company after 1980. Similarly, we can ask for all people over 40 years of age whose salaries are over $50,000. We now develop a *relational calculus* that will enable us to access data in this way using the quantifiers `for-all` and `there-exists` and the procedures `set-builder` and `set-map` defined in Chapter 8. We assume in this section that the data are stored in lists.

In order to use these predicates conveniently, we use the procedure `apply`, which enables us to apply a procedure of several arguments to a list that contains the same number of arguments. We define the procedure `unlist`, which is a curried version of `apply`, in Program 10.23. Here `proc` is a procedure that takes n arguments and `ls` is a list of n objects suitable to be the arguments of `proc`. Then

$$((\text{unlist } operator) \ (\text{list } operand_1 \ \ldots \ operand_n))$$

is equivalent to

$$(operator \ operand_1 \ \ldots \ operand_n)$$

For example, `((unlist +) '(2 3))` returns 5.

In the tables in which we store our data, we do not want to have two rows exactly the same. For that reason, we take, as the data structure to represent the table, a set whose elements are lists, each of which is one row of the table. We use the set procedures to manipulate the information stored in the table. For example, if we want to use the information in Table 10.17, we convert it to a set using

```
(define set10-17 (list->set table10-17))
```

To proceed with the development of our relational calculus, let us first assume that we have a predicate `pred`, which is a question that will be true or false on a given record in the set depending upon what values the items in the record have. We first look at an example of how `for-all` can be applied to `set10-17`. Suppose we want to see if *all* of the employees are over 25 years

Program 10.23 `unlist`

```
(define unlist
  (lambda (proc)
    (lambda (ls)
      (apply proc ls))))
```

of age. We write the predicate `age-test?`, which has as arguments the field names in our table and tests to see if the age entry is over 25. We shall, in general, find it convenient to invoke `unlist` on the predicates we define in this section so that the quantifiers can process them directly.

```
(define age-test?
  (unlist
    (lambda (name id age yr-emp supervisor salary)
      (> age 25))))
```

Then we apply the procedure `for-all` to `set10-17` with the predicate `age-test?` in the following way:

```
((for-all age-test?) set10-17) ⟹ #t
```

It returns true since all of the employees are over 25 years of age. Had we replaced the 25 by 35 in `age-test?`, `for-all` would have returned false, since some of the employees are not over 35.

In a similar way we can use the procedure `there-exists`. For example, if we want to know if anyone under 50 years of age receives a salary over $50,000, we write the predicate `age<50&salary>50000?` as follows:

```
(define age<50&salary>50000?
  (unlist
    (lambda (name id age yr-emp supervisor salary)
      (and (< age 50) (> salary 50000)))))
```

Then we apply the procedure `there-exists` and get

```
((there-exists age<50&salary>50000?) set10-17) ⟹ #t
```

since Mr. Fox is 41 years old and receives a salary of $52,200.

We now consider an example using both `for-all` and `there-exists`. We say that *name1 precedes name2* if *name1* comes before *name2* in the lexicographic ordering. Using `set10-17` again, we ask whether the following statement is true: "For all employees, either the employee's name precedes his/her supervisor's name, or there exists another employee whose name precedes that of the first employee and whose supervisor's name precedes the name of the first employee's supervisor." If the first employee's name is denoted by **n** and his/her supervisor's name is denoted by **s**, then we have asked that either **n** precedes **s**, or there is another person whose name is denoted by **n*** and whose supervisor's name is denoted by **s***, for which **n*** precedes **n** and **s*** precedes **s**. We can now express this statement in terms of **there-exists** and **for-all** as follows:

```
((for-all
   (unlist
     (lambda (n i a y s p)
       (or (string<? n s)
           ((there-exists
              (unlist
                (lambda (n* i* a* y* s* p*)
                  (and (string<? n* n) (string<? s* s)))))
            set10-17)))))
 set10-17)
```

The parameters for the inner lambda expression had to be chosen to be variables different from those of the first lambda, for if we had used **n** and **s** as the parameters in the inner lambda expression, we would have had

```
(and (string<? n n) (string<? s s))
```

This would always be false and is certainly not what we want. Although the names selected for parameters in a lambda expression are generally arbitrary, it is necessary to watch for name conflicts in combining such procedures as **for-all** and **there-exists**. (Incidentally, the expression above returns false since the conditions are not met by the employee Wilson whose supervisor is August.)

The two procedures **for-all** and **there-exists** return true or false depending on the predicate and the set constructed from the data table. We shall refer to that set as the table, even though it is a set. To obtain the names and ages of all persons in Table 10.17, we write

```
(define name&age
  (unlist
    (lambda (name id age yr-emp supervisor salary)
      (list name age))))
```

If we then call the procedure `set-map` as follows

```
(set-map name&age set10-17)
```

we get a table of all of the names in Table 10.17 followed by the field of ages. The other fields have not been included. We call this new table the *projection* of Table 10.17 onto the name and age fields. In a similar way, we can obtain projections of Table 10.17 onto any of its fields.

Sometimes we want to get the actual rows of the table for which some predicate is true. In particular, suppose we want to get the data from the table about all people who are over 45 years of age. The data we want for each one are the Id, the Age, the Year Employed, and the Salary. We write a predicate `over-45?` as follows:

```
(define over-45?
  (unlist
    (lambda (name id age yr-emp supervisor salary)
      (> age 45))))
```

We next invoke the procedure `set-builder` to get the subset `over-45-set` of `set10-17` consisting of all entries for which the age is greater than 45.

```
(define over45-set
  ((set-builder over-45? the-empty-set) set10-17))
```

To get the desired output, namely, the Id, Age, Year Employed, and Salary, for each of the selected employees, we project the set `over45-set` onto the four desired fields using `set-map` and then pass the resulting set to `set->list` to construct the new table.

```
(set->list
  (set-map
    (unlist
      (lambda (name id age yr-emp supervisor salary)
        (list id age yr-emp salary)))
    over45-set))
                    ⟹ ((1888 54 1965 65230)
                       (2451 46 1970 41050)
                       (1990 55 1965 63700)
                       (2455 46 1970 41050))
```

The procedure `set-map` builds a new set consisting of parts of the rows of the given table, then the list representation of the set contains no repetitions. In our previous example, had we asked for the retrieved data to be the age,

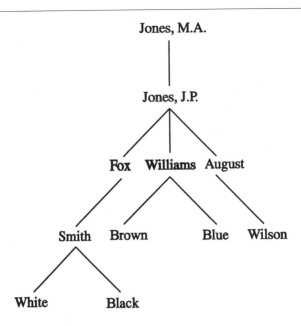

Figure 10.24 Organizational chart for Table 10.17

year employed, and the salary, we would have had two rows like (46 1970 41050), but set-map would have included only one of them in the set. To avoid such loss of information, at least one of the fields over which you project should identify each individual uniquely.

In Table 10.17, each person has an immediate supervisor. The organizational chart for the company is given in Figure 10.24. White is under immediate supervision of Smith but remotely under Fox, J. P. Jones, and M. A. Jones. Blue is under the immediate supervision of Williams, but remotely under J. P. Jones and M. A. Jones. We can ask the question: "Who is the closest common supervisor for both White and Blue?" Going up the tree from these two, we see that their closest common supervisor is J. P. Jones. We shall write a program to find the closest common supervisor of two members in a supervision tree determined by a table such as Table 10.17. We make the assumption that each person has at most one immediate supervisor and that the tree is connected so that there is one person at the very top.

The program will first start at one of the two members and build the path up the chart until it goes as high as it can. The path will be a list consisting of the names starting with one member, say, White, and containing (in order) all of the names on the path until the top, M. A. Jones. To build this path, we

Program 10.25 `find-supervisor`

```
(define find-supervisor
  (unlist
    (lambda (name id age yr-emp supervisor salary)
      (lambda (v) (if (string=? name v) supervisor #f)))))
```

need the procedure `build-path`, which takes a name like Smith in the table, determines his supervisor (Fox), and adds Smith to the path, then determines Fox's supervisor, and so on. When a person finally has no supervisor, that person is added to the path, and the path terminates. The procedure that determines a person's supervisor is called `find-supervisor`. For Table 10.17, its definition is given in Program 10.25. When given the entries in a row of the table, `find-supervisor` returns a procedure that takes the name of a person, and if that person's name is in the given line, it returns that person's supervisor; otherwise it returns false.

The strategy we use to find the closest common supervisor for two people, say x and y, once their two path-lists to the top have been found is to start at the rear of each path-list, where the two path-lists have the same person (in our case, M. A. Jones) and move simultaneously toward the front in both lists until the corresponding elements in the two lists differ. The preceding name (the last one for which the two lists agree) is the closest common supervisor. In Figure 10.24, the two paths to White and Blue split apart at J. P. Jones, so he is their closest common supervisor. It is easier to cdr down a list from the front to the back, so we reverse each of the two path-lists found for x and y, so that they now agree in their first elements. The procedure `find-ccs` then cdr's down the lists comparing their first elements. When these first disagree, the previous one is returned as the closest common supervisor. The code for the procedure `closest-common-supervisor` is given in Program 10.26. When reading the code for `closest-common-supervisor`, keep in mind that when `closest-common-supervisor` is applied below, the parameter `test-procedure` is bound to `find-supervisor`. Since the tables we use are sets of lists, we use the set operations `pick` and `residue` defined in Chapter 8 as the selectors for sets.

When the procedure `closest-common-supervisor` is called with the arguments White and Blue, we get

Program 10.26   `closest-common-supervisor`

```
(define closest-common-supervisor
  (letrec
    ((find-ccs
       (lambda (path1 path2)
         (let ((rest1 (cdr path1)) (rest2 (cdr path2)))
           (if (string=? (car rest1) (car rest2))
               (find-ccs rest1 rest2)
               (car path1))))))
    (lambda (test-procedure)
      (lambda (table)
        (letrec
          ((build-path
             (lambda (tbl u)
               (if (empty-set? tbl)
                   (list u)
                   (let ((next (pick tbl)))
                     (let ((v ((test-procedure next) u)))
                       (if (not v)
                           (build-path ((residue next) tbl) u)
                           (cons u (build-path table v)))))))))
          (lambda (x y)
            (find-ccs
              (reverse (build-path table x))
              (reverse (build-path table y)))))))))
```

[1] (((closest-common-supervisor find-supervisor)
       set10-17)
     "White, Thomas P." "Blue, Benjamin J.")
"Jones, John Paul"

In this chapter, we have demonstrated how data are handled using lists,
vectors, and sets. We chose the data structure for storing the data that was
most convenient for the application we had in mind. For a binary search, a
vector was used. For sorting, vectors or lists were used to store the data. For
using the relational calculus to search in a table, we found sets of lists to be
a convenient data structure. We have so far developed these important data
types to store data. In later chapters, we shall introduce several more useful
data types, such as the one called objects with which we shall implement
stacks and queues (Chapter 12) and the one called streams (Chapter 15).

Exercises

Exercise 10.7: `set-builder-map`

There is some redundancy in using both `set-builder` and `set-map` to find the projection of the set of those over 45 onto the fields Id, Age, Year Employed, and Salary. We used an invocation of the form

(set-map *proc* ((set-builder *pred base-set*) *some-set*))

Instead we can construct a procedure `set-builder-map`, which first determines if *pred* of an element returns true, and if so it then adjoins the *proc* of that element to the result. Its call structure is

((set-builder-map *pred proc base-set*) *some-set*)

For example, we can restate the earlier example using `set-builder-map`.

```
((set-builder-map
    over-45?
    (unlist
      (lambda (name id age yr-emp supervisor salary)
        (list id age yr-emp salary)))
    the-empty-set)
  set10-17)
```

Define the procedure `set-builder-map`.

Exercise 10.8

Write a procedure that accesses the data in Table 10.17 and returns the names and identification numbers of all employees who are over 40 years of age, were hired before 1975, and whose salaries are over $43,000.

Exercise 10.9

Table 10.27 contains the monthly sales for January and February for the employees listed according to their identification numbers, arranged in increasing order. These are the same employees whose personnel data are given in Table 10.17. The owner of the company wants a table that contains the employees' names in alphabetical order and their January sales. Modify the sorting, searching, and relational procedures given in this chapter to produce the desired table. You may find it convenient to add some additional arguments (predicates, test procedures, tables, etc.) to some of the procedures given above.

	Id	Jan-Sales	Feb-Sales
(define table10-27 '((1888		22300	33000)
	(1990	61080	49320)
	(2221	41000	52200)
	(2324	25550	31500)
	(2400	31010	25250)
	(2451	28800	16500)
	(2455	72050	50010)
	(3195	60500	40220)
	(3403	31100	22500)
	(3620	31100	22500)
	(3630	26300	19400)))

Table 10.27   Sales for January and February

Exercise 10.10
The procedure `closest-common-supervisor` defined in Program 10.26 computes the paths using the local procedure `build-path`, which recursively produces the path-list. This path-list is later reversed when it is used as an argument to `find-ccs`. Rewrite the definition of `closest-common-supervisor` so that `build-path` also has an accumulator as an argument and builds the list iteratively. The final value of the accumulator is then the desired list in the order from the top of the tree to the bottom, and reversing it is no longer necessary when it is used as an argument to `find-ccs`.

Exercise 10.11:   List of Vectors
This experiment assumes a *list* of *vectors* representation of `table10-17`.

```
[1] (define age (lambda (vec) (vector-ref vec 2)))
[2] (define age-test? (lambda (vec) (> (age vec) 25)))
[3] ((andmap-c age-test?) table10-17)
#t
```

Redo the examples of Section 10.4 using this representation. What are its advantages and disadvantages?

11   Mutation

11.1 Overview

In Chapter 9, we used the mutator `vector-set!` to change the entries in a
vector. The use of this and related mutators allowed us to write our programs
in a different style. With side effects on vectors, we showed in Chapter 10
that we can achieve better communication between the program parts and
we can define procedures that run more efficiently. In this chapter, we study
several other mutators. First, we look at a mutator that changes the binding
of a variable, and then we look at mutators that modify lists.

11.2 Assignment and State

A variable can be globally bound to a value using `define`. Furthermore, a
variable can be locally bound to a value using `lambda`, `let`, and `letrec`. Once
any of these bindings has been made, we may want to change the value to
which a variable is bound. Scheme provides a special form with keyword `set!`
for this purpose. If the variable *var* is already bound to some value (either
globally or locally) and we wish to change the value to which *var* is bound to
be the value of the expression *val*, all we have to write is

   (set! *var* *val*)

and Scheme evaluates *val* and binds that value to *var*. Scheme does not
specify what a set! expression returns, so the value returned is implementation
dependent. In this book, we suppress the value returned by the invocation of

a set! expression and write the next prompt. The use of **set!** is illustrated in the following:

```
[1] (define f (lambda (x) (+ x 10)))
[2] (f 5)
15
[3] (set! f (lambda (x) (* x 10)))
[4] (f 5)
50
[5] (let ((f (lambda (x) (+ x 100))))
    (writeln (f 5))
    (set! f (lambda (x) (* x 100)))
    (f 5))
105
500
[6] (f 5)
50
```

In this example, the define expression is used to bind **f** to the procedure that adds 10 to its argument. In [2], **f** applied to 5 returns 15. In [3], a set! expression is used to rebind **f** to the procedure that multiplies its argument by 10. We see the effect of this rebinding in [4] when the application of **f** to 5 now returns 50. The let expression in [5] locally binds **f** to a procedure that adds 100 to its argument. In the body of the let expression, (**f** 5) is written to the screen and produces 105. Then a set! expression is used to rebind **f** to the procedure that multiplies its argument by 100. Observe that this rebinding affects only the local binding of the variable **f**. Then the value of (**f** 5) is returned, producing the value 500. In [6], **f** is again applied to 5, and the global binding of **f** is used to give the value 50. The set! expression within the let expression affected only the local binding of **f**.

We may think of the set! expression looking up the variable *var* in the relevant environment (local or global, determined by the lexical scoping) and actually replacing the value to which *var* is bound with the value of *val*. Although implementations of Scheme generally allow us to change the binding of a globally defined variable by defining it again using **define**, we do not recommend doing so. Such changes in the bindings should be done with **set!**. However, before a variable can be rebound using **set!**, it must have been bound to some value either globally using **define** or locally using **lambda** or one of the other binding forms.

We can use **set!** in the following implementation of stacks. A *stack* is a data structure used to store objects. An object can be put into the stack with an operator called push! that takes the object as its argument. The last object put into the stack is removed by the operator pop!. It is characteristic of stacks that the last object that was entered is the first object removed. This property is described with the name *LIFO*, which stands for "last in, first out." Thus, if we push the numbers 10, 20, and 30 onto the stack in the given order, on the first pop, 30 is removed, on the second pop, 20 is removed, and on the third pop, 10 is removed.

We now look at one way of implementing stacks (we shall return to the subject again in Chapter 12 for a better implementation). For our present purposes, we implement a stack as a list of objects. The car of the list will be the top of the stack. We next describe several procedures that perform operations on a stack. The procedure empty? tests whether the stack is the empty list. The procedure top returns the top of the stack, that is, the car of the stack. The procedure push! adds its argument to the top of the stack. The procedure pop! removes the top of the stack. Finally, the procedure print-stack prints the whole stack. The definitions of these procedures are given in Program 11.1.

We have elected to print a stack with the word TOP: preceding it to show which end is the top of the stack. Thus the stack containing the numbers 1, 2, 3, and 4, with 1 on top will be printed as

```
TOP: 1 2 3 4
```

With the definitions given above, we perform the following experiment:

```
[1] (push! 'a)
[2] (push! 'b)
[3] (push! 'c)
[4] (top)
c
[5] (pop!)
[6] (print-stack)
TOP: b a
```

We next illustrate the use of set! in a discussion of *memoizing*. Let us suppose that we want to find the value of a procedure proc that on each invocation requires a long computation before it returns an answer. We also assume that we call this procedure often with various arguments. It would save time if we could store each new value that the procedure computes in a table, and each time the procedure is called, the table is first checked to see if the procedure has already been invoked with that argument. Then the already

Program 11.1   Procedures defining a stack

```scheme
(define stk '())

(define empty?
  (lambda ()
    (null? stk)))

(define top
  (lambda ()
    (if (empty?)
        (error "top: The stack is empty.")
        (car stk))))

(define print-stack
  (lambda ()
    (display "TOP: ")
    (for-each (lambda (x) (display x) (display " ")) stk)
    (newline)))

(define push!
  (lambda (a)
    (set! stk (cons a stk))))

(define pop!
  (lambda ()
    (if (empty?)
        (error "pop!: The stack is empty.")
        (set! stk (cdr stk)))))
```

computed value is returned rather than recomputing it. If it has not already been computed, then it is computed, and the new value is both returned and entered into the table. Since we are assuming that the computation of **proc** is a relatively long process, it is more efficient to look the value up in the table rather than recompute it. This process of making a table of values that have already been computed and searching through this table each time the procedure is called to see whether the value has already been computed for the current argument is referred to as memoizing the procedure.

The data structure that we use to serve as a table in which to store the already-computed values is a list, which we call **table**. Each entry in **table** is a dotted pair (**arg . val**), in which **val** is the value of (**proc arg**). Thus if the procedure is the Fibonacci procedure `fib` and we have already computed `fib` for arguments 2, 4, and 6, then `table` is `((2 . 1) (4 . 3) (6 . 8))`. We can also use proper lists as the entries in the table; in that case, `table` would look like `((2 1) (4 3) (6 8))`. The dotted-pair representation has the advantage of being more efficient, since in building the table, only one consing operation is necessary to build the dotted pair `(cons 2 1)`, whereas two consing operations are necessary to build the list `(cons 2 (cons 1 '()))`. Similarly, to obtain the second item in the dotted pair, we use `cdr`, whereas in the list case, we first have to take the `cdr` and then take the `car`. We use the procedure `1st` to access the first item and `2nd` to access the second item of a list. If we are using lists of two items, `1st` is then `car`, and `2nd` is `cadr`. If the list has three items, we also use `3rd` instead of `caddr`, and if the list has four items, we include `4th` for `cadddr`. These are easier to read than the multiple car/cdr chains.

To look up whether `fib` has already been computed for argument 4, the procedure `lookup` is used. The procedure `lookup` has four parameters, an object `obj`, a list of pairs `table`, and two procedures: `success-proc`, which takes one argument, and `failure-proc`, which takes no arguments. If there is a pair in `table` that has `obj` as its first element, then we say that the lookup succeeded, and we invoke `success-proc` on that pair. If there is no pair in `table` that has `obj` as its first element, our lookup failed, and we invoke `failure-proc`. These two procedures, `success-proc` and `failure-proc`, are known as the *success continuation* and the *failure continuation*, respectively, because they tell how to continue the computation when we either find `obj` in `table` or fail to find it. For example:

```
(lookup 4 '((1 1 1) (2 4 8) (4 16 64) (6 36 216))
  (lambda (pr) (2nd pr))
  (lambda () 0))                                        ⟹ 16
```

and

```
(lookup 3 '((1 1 1) (2 4 8) (4 16 64) (6 36 216))
  (lambda (pr) (2nd pr))
  (lambda () 0))                                        ⟹ 0
```

In these examples, `table` is a list of items, each item being a list of three numbers. The success continuation tells us to return the second element in the pair. The failure continuation tells us to return 0. In the first example, 4 is found to be the first element in the third pair, so 16 is returned. In the second example, 3 is not found as the first element of any of the pairs, so 0 is returned.

The definition of lookup is straightforward. The strategy used in this definition is to search the list of pairs until we either find a pair starting with obj or reach the end of the list. Since obj, success-proc, and failure-proc do not change in the recursion, we begin with a letrec expression to define a local procedure, lookup, which has only the one parameter table. Because of lexical scoping, we can use the same name lookup for both the local procedure and the global procedure. Program 11.2 shows the definition of lookup.

Program 11.2   lookup

```
(define lookup
  (lambda (obj table success-proc failure-proc)
    (letrec ((lookup (lambda (table)
                      (if (null? table)
                          (failure-proc)
                          (let ((pr (car table)))
                            (if (equal? (car pr) obj)
                                (success-proc pr)
                                (lookup (cdr table)))))))))
      (lookup table))))
```

We illustrate the use of lookup in the definition of the Scheme procedure assoc, which has two parameters, obj and a list of pairs table. If a pair in table has obj as its first element, that pair is returned; otherwise false is returned. For example:

```
(assoc 4 '((1) (2 1) (3 1 5) (4 3) (6 8))) ⟹ (4 3)

(assoc 5 '((1) (2 1) (3 1 5) (4 3) (6 8))) ⟹ #f
```

The code for assoc is easily written using lookup. We have only to take the identity procedure as the success continuation and the constant procedure that always returns false as the failure continuation. See Program 11.3.

We are now ready to write the procedure memoize, which takes a procedure proc as its parameter and returns another procedure that is the memoized

Program 11.3   assoc

```
(define assoc
  (lambda (obj table)
    (lookup obj table (lambda (pr) pr) (lambda () #f))))
```

Program 11.4   memoize

```
(define memoize
  (lambda (proc)
    (let ((table '()))
      (lambda (arg)
        (lookup arg table
          (lambda (pr) (cdr pr))
          (lambda ()
            (let ((val (proc arg)))
              (set! table (cons (cons arg val) table))
              val)))))))
```

version of proc. The definition of memoize is presented in Program 11.4.[1]

To memoize the Fibonacci procedure fib, we first define fib as before:

```
(define fib
  (lambda (n)
    (if (< n 2)
        n
        (+ (fib (- n 1))
           (fib (- n 2))))))
```

We now show two different ways of approaching the memoization of fib. The first way, which does not lead to the most efficient way of computing it, is to define fib-m as follows:

```
(define fib-m (memoize fib))
```

Evaluate (fib-m 6) first. Since (fib 6) has not yet been computed, fib is computed recursively to get its value 8. This value is added to the table in the

---

[1] The line (lambda (pr) (cdr pr)) in the definition of memoize can be replaced by cdr. Can you explain why?

Program 11.5 `memo-fib`

```
(define memo-fib
  (memoize (lambda (n)
             (if (< n 2)
                 n
                 (+ (memo-fib (- n 1))
                    (memo-fib (- n 2)))))))
```

set! line of code for `memoize`, and `table` is now bound to `((6 . 8))`. When `(fib-m 6)` is evaluated again, the new binding is in effect. In this way, `set!` changes the value of the lexical binding of the variable `table`.

If `(fib-m 6)` is called again, the lookup with argument 6 produces the pair `(6 . 8)` and by taking its cdr, we get the answer 8. If this is now repeated with `(fib-m 100)`, the first time it is called, the tree recursion will involve approximately $3(1.7^{100})$ operations, which is more than 10^{22}. If, however, `(fib-m 100)` is called a second time, the answer is found with just one lookup in the table, a significant improvement in efficiency since the table contains only two items at this point. If the table does get large after many procedure calls with different arguments, the iteration in `lookup` makes the search in the table take time, so there is a trade-off that must be weighed between the efficiency of the procedure evaluation and the table lookup. Later, we shall consider the use of vectors to represent the table of stored values. Random access into the table for our lookups makes the memoizing process more efficient than iteration through the table from its beginning.

A more practical use for the memoizing procedure can be made if we use it in the recursive invocations of `fib` that are made in the definition of the procedure `fib` itself. In computing `(fib 6)` recursively, one computes `fib` for arguments 5, 4, 3, 2, and 1. Suppose that the first time any one of these is found, its (*arg* . *val*)-pair is added to `table`. Then whenever `fib` is called with this same argument in the tree recursion, the value is already known from the table lookup and need not be recomputed. This will save time in the original computation of `(fib 6)`, and if we call `(fib 7)`, it is the sum of `(fib 6)` and `(fib 5)`, both of which are already in the table. This is a great saving in time. Program 11.5 shows how we write this memoized version of `fib`.

It is possible to get a feeling for how much memoizing improves the efficiency of a computation by using the "timer" defined in Program 10.19. Below is an experiment involving computations of the memoized procedures defined above:

```
[1] (timer fib 20)
Time = 7.69, Answer = 6765
[2] (timer fib 25)
Time = 85.19, Answer = 75025
[3] (timer fib-m 20)
Time = 7.69, Answer = 6765
[4] (timer fib-m 20)
Time = 0, Answer = 6765
[5] (timer fib-m 25)
Time = 85.25, Answer = 75025
[6] (timer fib-m 25)
Time = 0, Answer = 75025
[7] (timer memo-fib 20)
Time = 0, Answer = 6765
[8] (timer memo-fib 25)
Time = 0, Answer = 75025
[9] (timer memo-fib 100)
Time = 0.22, Answer = 354224848179261915075
[10] (timer memo-fib 100)
Time = 0, Answer = 354224848179261915075
```

Exercise

Exercise 11.1

To see how dramatically memoizing reduces the number of recursive invocations of **fib**, trace the procedures **fib** and **memo-fib** by placing **(display n)** **(display " ")** before the if expressions. Then invoke the traced procedures with arguments 6, 7, and 10. Be sure that you understand the results.

Because the elements of a vector can be accessed randomly with equal ease, vectors can be used effectively for making tables. When a list is used as the data structure for a table and the table lookup is done with **assoc** or with **lookup**, the iterative search tests each entry until the correct one is found. If we are looking for an entry that is not near the beginning of the list, the search is costly in time. In a vector, we can access any entry with equal facility. Let us rewrite **memoize** for a procedure that takes a nonnegative integer as its argument. This time **table** is a vector in which we store values. We must fix a largest value for the arguments that we store in the table, since we must specify the length of the vector in advance.[2]   Let us suppose that memoization will take place for arguments that are at most equal to some number **max-arg**, and then we can take (**add1 max-arg**) as the length of the vector. To find the value of the procedure **proc** for a given argument **arg**, we must first determine whether that value has already been entered into the table. We use **vector-ref** for the lookup and let **item-stored** be (**vector-ref table arg**). The test to determine whether a value has been stored for the argument **arg** is (**null? item-stored**). If the procedure we are memoizing takes on the value (), we would not be able to distinguish it from the ()'s used to fill the original table. To avoid having to put restrictions on the values assumed by the procedure, we enter (**list val**) instead of **val** into the table whenever a new procedure value is added. Then **item-stored** finds a list containing the value, and to get the value itself, we must take (**car item-stored**). The definition of **vector-memoize** is given in Program 11.6.

Program 11.6   `vector-memoize`

```
(define vector-memoize
  (lambda (max-arg)
    (lambda (proc)
      (let ((table (make-vector (add1 max-arg) '())))
        (lambda (arg)
          (if (> arg max-arg)
              (proc arg)
              (let ((item-stored (vector-ref table arg)))
                (if (pair? item-stored)
                    (car item-stored)
                    (let ((val (proc arg)))
                      (vector-set! table arg (list val))
                      val)))))))))
```

This memoizing procedure can be used in exactly the same way as the one we defined earlier for numerical procedures like **fib**. It is more efficient when many entries have been made into the table since the random access of the vector makes lookup faster.

We can use this memoizing procedure to compute fibonacci numbers by

---

[2] This is a disadvantage of using vectors instead of lists as the data structure for the table. We shall look at a way of removing this restriction when we discuss hashing in Chapter 12.

calling the procedure `memo-fib`, now defined by:

```
(define memo-fib
  ((vector-memoize 100)
   (lambda (n)
     (if (< n 2)
         n
         (+ (memo-fib (- n 1)) (memo-fib (- n 2)))))))
```

This allows table lookup up to argument 100.

Let us summarize what we have learned about `set!` in this extended example. A set! expression is a special form with the following syntax:

(**set!** *var val*)

First, Scheme evaluates the expression *val*. Then Scheme looks for the lexical binding of *var*, and the value of that binding is changed so that *var* is bound to the value of *val*. If *var* is not bound to some value, then in many implementations, the set! expression returns an error message, for `set!` changes only existing bindings; it does not create new bindings. It is important to realize that `set!` does this rebinding as a side effect, and in Scheme `set!` returns an unspecified value, so that different implementations of Scheme could return different things, and you should not rely on using the value returned in your programs. The fact that `set!` does its rebinding as a side effect means that you can use `set!` in a begin expression (implicit or explicit) before the last clause and accomplish the rebinding.

We next illustrate the use of `set!` by showing how we can simulate an imperative style of programming. Imperative-style programs consist of statements executed sequentially, each one of which performs a certain action on the variables or provides input or output. For example, an assignment statement that assigns a value 10 to a variable a is given by (set! a 10). An output statement that prints the value of the variable a on the screen is given by (writeln a). Branching is accomplished using a conditional statement, which we can do using either a cond or an if expression. If we want to execute a statement that is not the next one in the sequential order, we use a "goto"-type statement, which we accomplish by invoking a *thunk*, that is, a procedure of no arguments. This has the effect of making the next statement to be executed be the first statement in the body of the thunk. We show such a program by rewriting the definition of the procedure member? in this imperative style. Recall first an iterative version of member?:

```
(define member?
  (lambda (item ls)
    (cond
      ((null? ls) #f)
      ((equal? (car ls) item) #t)
      (else (member? item (cdr ls))))))
```

An imperative version of **member?** is given in Program 11.7.

Program 11.7   Imperative version of **member?**

```
(define member?
  (lambda (item ls)
    (let ((goto (lambda (label)
                  (label))))
      (letrec
        ((start
          (lambda ()
            (cond
              ((null? ls) #f)
              ((equal? (car ls) item) #t)
              (else (goto reduce)))))
         (reduce
          (lambda ()
            (set! ls (cdr ls))
            (goto start))))
        (goto start)))))
```

The variable that is assigned values by the statements in the program is
ls. The procedure goto invokes the thunk, which is its argument. The letrec
expression defines the thunks, which control the order in which the statements
are executed in the program. In the last line of the program, we see that the
first thunk invoked is start. The body of this thunk is a cond expression
that has three clauses. In the first of these, the condition tests whether the
list ls is empty. If so, #f is returned. The second condition in the thunk
start tests whether the first value in the list ls is item, in which case the
value #t is returned. The else clause in the thunk start moves control to the
body of reduce, where the list ls is assigned the value (cdr ls) and control
is moved back to start. It is important to realize that no variable is passed
to start when control is moved to start. Instead, the value assigned to the

Program 11.8 `while-proc`

```
(define while-proc
  (lambda (pred-th body-th)
    (letrec ((loop (lambda ()
                     (if (pred-th)
                         (begin
                           (body-th)
                           (loop))))))
      (loop))))
```

variable `ls` is changed by the `set!` statement, and that is the value of `ls` used on the next invocation of `start`. In functional programming, new values are passed as arguments to procedures, whereas in this imperative programming style, the new values of variables are given by assignment statements using mutation procedures such as `set!`.

An advantage of using a computer instead of hand calculation is the possibility of doing repetitive operations a large number of times with few instructions. This is done in a language like Scheme by repetitively invoking a procedure with different arguments until a termination condition is reached. One method of repeating certain operations in imperative-style programming uses a *while loop*. We can illustrate the use of *while* by introducing the procedure `while-proc`, which takes as parameters a predicate thunk `pred-th` and a body thunk `body-th`. As long as the invocation of `pred-th` returns true, `body-th` is invoked followed by an invocation of `loop`. It is assumed that in the body of `body-th`, mutations will occur that eventually will make the invocation of `pred-th` false. When that happens, the loop is completed. The while loop depends on side effects to produce the desired results. The code for the procedure `while-proc` is presented in Program 11.8. We have implemented `while-proc` here as a procedure that takes two thunks as arguments. In the exercises in Chapter 14, we shall implement a while expression as a special form that has the predicate and the body themselves as subexpressions rather than thunks made out of them.

We show an example of the use of `while-proc` by giving another definition of `member?`, this time in an imperative style using a while loop. Here, we introduce a local boolean variable `ans` that will be initialized to `#f`. In the loop, the predicate thunk `pred-th` tests whether the list `ls` is empty or the variable `ans` is true. As long as neither one is true, the body thunk `body-th` is invoked. This tests whether the first value in the list `ls` is `item`. If it is, then

ans is assigned the value true. Otherwise, the list ls is assigned the value
(cdr ls). The loop then repeats the invocation of the predicate thunk, and
if it is true, the body thunk is invoked again. If it is false, the loop returns
something, but since it was called within an implicit begin expression, the
value it returns is ignored and the value of ans is returned. This definition of
member? follows:

```
(define member?
  (lambda (item ls)
    (let ((ans #f))
      (while-proc
        (lambda () (not (or (null? ls) ans)))
        (lambda ()
          (if (equal? (car ls) item)
              (set! ans #t)
              (set! ls (cdr ls)))))
      ans)))
```

In this imperative style, recursion can be done only by explicitly building
the return table. Using set! in Scheme, we can simulate that behavior. In
Program 2.8, we defined the procedure swapper recursively. We first reproduce a recursive definition and then implement it in this imperative style,
replacing recursion with the explicit construction of the return table, which
we implement as a stack.

```
(define swapper
  (lambda (a b ls)
    (letrec ((loop (lambda (ls*)
                     (cond
                       ((null? ls*) '())
                       ((equal? (car ls*) a)
                        (cons b (loop (cdr ls*))))
                       ((equal? (car ls*) b)
                        (cons a (loop (cdr ls*))))
                       (else
                        (cons (car ls*) (loop (cdr ls*))))))))
      (loop ls))))
```

Most languages have a looping mechanism that repeats some operation until
a terminating condition is satisfied. We once again use the procedure while-
proc for that purpose. Notice that in the recursive program for swapper,
until ls* is empty, something is consed onto the recursive invocation of loop

with argument (cdr ls*). Thus, that something is added to a return table on each loop. We accomplish this in our imperative-style program by pushing that something onto a stack, and when ls* is finally empty, we repeatedly cons the top of the stack onto our answer and pop the stack until the stack is empty. Thus our code will have two loops; the first pushes the appropriate thing onto the stack until the list is empty, and the second pops the stack until it is empty. We assume here that the stack stk has been globally defined and is empty when the procedure swapper is called.

Program 11.9 swapper

```
(define swapper
  (lambda (a b ls)
    (let ((ls* ls) (ans '()))
      (while-proc
        (lambda () (not (null? ls*)))
        (lambda ()
          (cond
            ((equal? (car ls*) a) (push! b))
            ((equal? (car ls*) b) (push! a))
            (else (push! (car ls*))))
;         (print-stack)
          (set! ls* (cdr ls*))))
      (while-proc
        (lambda () (not (empty?)))
        (lambda ()
          (set! ans (cons (top) ans))
;         (writeln "Answer = " ans)
          (pop!)
;         (print-stack)
                    ))
      ans)))
```

Program 11.9 contains the imperative-style code for swapper. We have included some print-stack and writeln expressions to obtain a trace of the program. Semicolons have been placed in front of these output expressions to show that they are not part of the swapper program. To get the trace, remove the semicolons. An example of an application of swapper is given in

```
[1] (swapper 1 2 '(1 2 3 1 2 3))
TOP: 2
TOP: 1 2
TOP: 3 1 2
TOP: 2 3 1 2
TOP: 1 2 3 1 2
TOP: 3 1 2 3 1 2
Answer = (3)
TOP: 1 2 3 1 2
Answer = (1 3)
TOP: 2 3 1 2
Answer = (2 1 3)
TOP: 3 1 2
Answer = (3 2 1 3)
TOP: 1 2
Answer = (1 3 2 1 3)
TOP: 2
Answer = (2 1 3 2 1 3)
TOP:
(2 1 3 2 1 3)
```

Figure 11.10   Trace of the imperative-style `swapper`

Figure 11.10. The stack grows during the first loop, and the answer is being built before each pop of the stack during the second loop.

In this example, the stack was defined globally and given the name `stk`. Each of the stack operations referred to this stack in its definition. If we had needed two stacks, say `stk1` and `stk2`, we would have had to define two sets of stack operations and use the right ones with each of the two stacks. This is an inconvenient way of working with stacks, so we shall look further into this matter in Chapter 12 and develop a better way of implementing stacks using what is known as object-oriented programming.

The stack is an object that changes with each `push!` and `pop!`. An object that changes with time is said to be in a given state between changes. We say that such an object has *state*. Its state can be described by certain descriptors, called its *state variables*. In the case of the stack, we can consider its list representation as a state variable that completely describes the stack. The mutators such as `set!` and `vector-set!` and the procedures derived from them such as `push!` and `pop!` are used to change the state of objects. In most of our Scheme programs, we can use procedure applications and recursion and avoid the use of mutators altogether. There will be times, however, when we find it convenient to use mutators.

In mathematics and logic, a function is a rule that assigns to each of its arguments a certain value, and the presentation in Section 8.5 developed this point of view. We have been using the term *procedure* to describe the programs we have been writing in Scheme. It would have been appropriate to use the term *function* as long as we do not have side effects and the value returned by the function is completely determined by its arguments; that is, the function returns the same value every time it is invoked with the same arguments. This is no longer the case when side effects are present. It is more accurate to use the term *procedure* instead of *function* since side effects are allowed, and this is the custom in Scheme.

Exercises

Exercise 11.2: `pascal-triangle`
In the Pascal triangle, each number is the sum of the two numbers in the line above it and on each side of it. The first six lines of the triangle are shown below:

```
          1
        1   1
      1   2   1
    1   3   3   1
  1   4   6   4   1
1   5  10  10   5   1
```

Using a zero-based counting system and denoting the number in the *n*th row and the *k*th column by (pascal-triangle n k), (pascal-triangle 4 2) is 6, and (pascal-triangle 5 1) is 5. The algorithm that we use to build the triangle line by line says that (pascal-triangle n k) is the sum of (pascal-triangle (- n 1) (- k 1)) and (pascal-triangle (- n 1) k). We consider that each row of the triangle is continued with a zero at each end. Use this algorithm to define the procedure pascal-triangle, which we use in several exercises in this section. Analyze this algorithm to determine the number of additions performed when (pascal-triangle n k) is computed. Test your procedure on:

```
(pascal-triangle 10 5) ⟹    252
(pascal-triangle 12 6) ⟹    924
(pascal-triangle 14 7) ⟹   3432
(pascal-triangle 16 8) ⟹  12870
```

Exercise 11.3: `timer2`

Write the definition of a procedure `timer2` that finds the time elapsed from the time a procedure `proc` is called to the time when the value is returned, assuming that the procedure `proc` is a procedure of two arguments. Test your procedure on the procedure `pascal-triangle`, defined in the preceding exercise, when the following procedure calls are made: (`pascal-triangle 10 5`), (`pascal-triangle 12 6`), (`pascal-triangle 14 7`), and (`pascal-triangle 16 8`).

Exercise 11.4: `combinations`

It can be shown that (`pascal-triangle n k`) represents the number of different ways **k** objects can be selected from a list of **n** distinct objects. This number is often denoted by $\binom{n}{k}$. The notation $n!$ is used for the factorial of n, which we compute with the procedure `fact`. It can be shown that the number $\binom{n}{k}$ can be computed using the formula $\frac{n!}{k!(n-k)!}$. Write the definition of a procedure `combinations` that uses this formula instead of the algorithm given in Exercise 11.2. Compare it with `pascal-triangle` by timing it for the values of the arguments given in Exercise 11.2. Also compute (`combinations 100 50`).

Exercise 11.5: `lookup2`

Write the definition of a procedure `lookup2` that takes five arguments: two Scheme objects `obj1` and `obj2`, and a list of triples `trilist` and a success and a failure continuation. It searches through the list from beginning to end looking for a triple in which the first element is `obj1` and the second element is `obj2`. If such a triple is found, it passes that triple to the success continuation. Otherwise, the failure continuation is invoked. Test your procedure on:

```
(lookup2 'a 'c '((a b 5) (a c 7) (b c 9))
  (lambda (tr) tr) (lambda () '()))        ⟹ (a c 7)
(lookup2 'a 'c '((a b 5) (c a 7) (b c 9))
  (lambda (tr) tr) (lambda () '()))        ⟹ ()
```

Exercise 11.6: `memoize2`

Write the definition of the procedure `memoize2`, which memoizes a procedure `proc` of two arguments.

Exercise 11.7

Memoize the procedure `pascal-triangle` in Exercise 11.2 to define a procedure `memo-pascal-triangle` in a manner analogous to the definition of

Program 11.11   Mystery program for Exercise 11.10

```
(define mystery
  (lambda (a b ls)
    (let ((ls* ls) (ans '()) (goto (lambda (label) (label))))
      (letrec
        ((push
           (lambda ()
             (cond
               ((null? ls*) (goto pop))
               ((eq? (car ls*) a) (push! b) (goto reduce))
               ((eq? (car ls*) b) (push! a) (goto reduce))
               (else (push! (car ls*)) (goto reduce)))))
         (reduce
           (lambda ()
             (set! ls* (cdr ls*))
             (goto push)))
         (pop
           (lambda ()
             (cond
               ((empty?) ans)
               (else
                 (set! ans (cons (top) ans))
                 (pop!)
                 (goto pop))))))
        (goto push)))))
```

memo-fib in this section. Time both a call of pascal-triangle and a call of memo-pascal-triangle on each of the arguments used in Exercise 11.2.

Exercise 11.8: **timer***
Define a procedure **timer*** that times a procedure of an arbitrary number of arguments. For example, if **proc** is a procedure of four arguments and we want to time the application (**proc** 1 0 2 3), we would call (**timer*** **proc** 1 0 2 3). Use the unrestricted **lambda** and **apply**.

Exercise 11.9
In the imperative-style program for **swapper**, the stack and its operations were defined nonlocally. Rewrite this program with the stack and its operations defined locally within the definition of **swapper** and test your procedure on the example given in Figure 11.10.

Exercise 11.10

In the imperative-style program for **swapper**, we used while loops to repeat certain steps when a given condition is true. In some languages, while loops are not implemented so another device must be used. Such languages often use a "goto" statement as a means of returning control to a previous step in the program. As in the first imperative version of **member?** in Program 11.7, we can simulate a goto statement by invoking a procedure of no arguments (a thunk). Program 11.11 is a mystery program that is written in imperative style and invokes various thunks to move the control to the body of the thunks. Assume that a global stack **stk** is initially empty. What is returned when we invoke:

```
(mystery 'a 'z '(c r a z y))
```

11.3 Box-and-Pointer Representation of Cons Cells

The box-and-pointer representation gives us a convenient graphical way of visualizing the objects constructed using **cons**. An object that is not a pair, such as a number, a symbol, or a boolean, is denoted by enclosing the object in a box (i.e., we put a square or rectangle around the object). For example, we represent the number 5 by enclosing the numeral 5 in a box. The constructor **cons** produces a pair represented by a *cons cell*, which is a double box (a horizontal rectangle divided into two boxes by a vertical line) with a pointer (arrow) emerging from the center of each of the two boxes. The pointer emerging from the center of the box on the left points to the box containing the car of the pair represented by the cons cell. The pointer from the center of the box on the right points to the box containing the **cdr** of the pair represented by the cons cell. Figure 11.12(a) shows the box-and-pointer representation of the improper list (or dotted pair) (**cons 3 4**). The pointer from the left side points to the **car**, which is 3, and the pointer from the right side points to the **cdr**, which is **4**. When (**cons 3 4**) is entered into Scheme, the improper list (3 . 4) is returned. We call the pointer from the left side of a cons cell the *car pointer* and the pointer from the right side of a cons cell the *cdr pointer*.

The value of (**cons 3 (cons 4 5)**) is represented by two cons cells, one for each **cons**. Figure 11.12(b) shows the box-and-pointer configuration for this value. The car pointer of the first cons cell points to the number 3, and the cdr pointer of the first cons cell points to the second cons cell. The car pointer of the second cons cell points to the number **4**, and the cdr pointer of the second cons cell points to the number **5**. In this way, we can build up

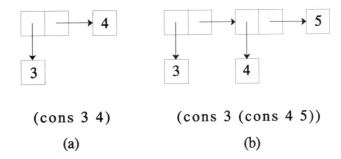

(cons 3 4)　　　　(cons 3 (cons 4 5))

(a)　　　　　　　(b)

Figure 11.12　Box-and-pointer diagrams

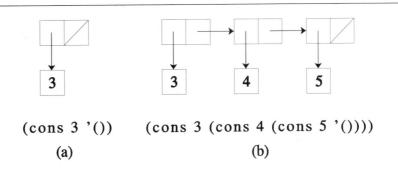

(cons 3 '())　　(cons 3 (cons 4 (cons 5 '())))

(a)　　　　　　　(b)

Figure 11.13　Box-and-pointer diagrams for proper lists

the box-and-pointer representations of the values of more complicated cons expressions.

We now look at the representation of a proper list. We begin with the list (cons 3 '()), for which Scheme displays (3). Once again a cons cell is created by cons, and this time the car pointer points to the number 3. But how shall we represent the fact that the cdr pointer points to ()? We indicate that the cdr is the empty list by drawing a diagonal line in the right half of the cons cell. This is illustrated in Figure 11.13(a).

The list (cons 3 (cons 4 (cons 5 '()))), which appears on the screen as (3 4 5), is represented as the linked cells in Figure 11.13(b). Another interesting list to consider is

(cons (cons 3 '()) (cons 4 (cons 5 '())))

which appears on the screen as ((3) 4 5). The box-and-pointer representation contains four cons cells as illustrated in Figure 11.14. The first **cons** creates a cell in which the car pointer points to the cons cell created by the second **cons**, in which the car pointer points to **3** and the cdr pointer indicates (). The cdr pointer of the first cons cell points to the cons cell created by the third **cons**. The car pointer in the third cons cell points to **4**, and its cdr pointer points to the cons cell created by the fourth **cons**. In this fourth cons cell, the car pointer points to **5**, and the cdr pointer indicates (). Thus each **cons** in an expression creates a new cons cell in which the car pointer points to the car part and the cdr pointer points to the cdr part of the cell.

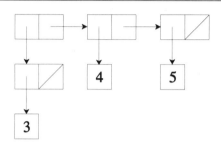

(cons (cons 3 '()) (cons 4 (cons 5 '())))

Figure 11.14 Box-and-pointer diagram

If we define a to be **(cons 3 '())** by writing

(define a (cons 3 '()))

we can indicate this binding by a pointer from the name a to the cons cell created by **cons**, as illustrated in Figure 11.15(a). If we now use **set!** to change this binding, say

(set! a (cons 4 (cons 5 '())))

we can think of this as disconnecting the pointer from a to the linked cells representing **(cons 3 '())** and connecting it to the linked cells representing **(cons 4 (cons 5 '()))**, as illustrated in Figure 11.15(b).

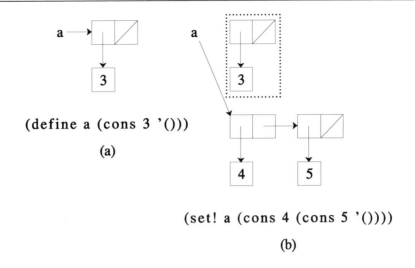

(define a (cons 3 '()))

(a)

(set! a (cons 4 (cons 5 '()))))

(b)

Figure 11.15   Representing define and set!

Now suppose that **a** and **b** are defined as:

```
(define a (cons 1 (cons 2 '())))
```

```
(define b (cons (cons 3 '()) (cons 4 (cons 5 '()))))
```

as illustrated in Figure 11.16(a,b). We next define **c** to be:

```
(define c (cons a (cdr b)))
```

The **cons** in the definition of **c** creates a cons cell (to which **c** points) in which the car pointer points to the same cell as does **a** and the cdr pointer points to the same cell as does the cdr pointer of the cons cell to which **b** points. This is illustrated in Figure 11.16(c). It is clear from this representation that **a** and **b** have not been changed when we defined **c**, and a $\Longrightarrow$ (1 2), b $\Longrightarrow$ ((3) 4 5), and c $\Longrightarrow$ ((1 2) 4 5).

The procedures **set-car!**, **set-cdr!**, and **append!**, which we discuss next, actually do change the objects to which they are applied. For example, when we use the same definitions of **a** and **b** given above and illustrated in Figure 11.16(a,b), and invoke

```
(set-car! b a)
```

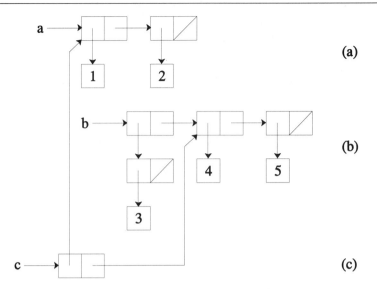

(a)

(b)

(c)

Figure 11.16 `(define c (cons a (cdr b)))`

then the car pointer of the cons cell to which b points is disconnected and is made to point to the same linked cell as does a. This is illustrated in Figure 11.17. Now:

```
b ⟹ ((1 2) 4 5)
a ⟹ (1 2)
```

Thus b has been changed by `set-car!` so that we can say that `set-car!` caused a mutation in the list structure of b. This enables us to use `set-car!` in begin expressions since this mutation is a side effect. Let us compare b and c. They are `equal?`, but not `eq?`. Also the application of `set-car!` had the effect of disconnecting the previous car of b (see the dotted box in Figure 11.17) which is now "garbage" to be recycled in the next "garbage collection." In general, cells are garbage if they are *not* pointed to by nongarbage.

The invocation (`set-cdr!` *pair value*) does the same kind of reconnecting of the cdr pointer of *pair* so that it points to *value*. The box-and-pointer diagrams in Figure 11.18 illustrate c and d defined by

```
(define c (cons 1 (cons 2 (cons 3 '()))))

(define d (cons 4 (cons 5 (cons 6 '()))))
```

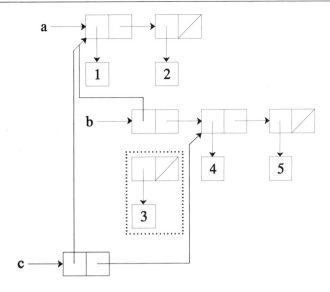

Figure 11.17 (set-car! b a) in Figure 11.16

Let us first define **w** to be

    (define w (cons c d))

so that **w** ⟹ ((1 2 3) 4 5 6). (See Figure 11.18.)

We pause to make an important observation about the predicate **eq?**. Two items are the same in the sense of **eq?** if they point to the same object. From Figure 11.18, we see that

    (eq? (car w) c) ⟹ #t

since they both point to the same chain of linked cells.

If we next call

    (set-cdr! c d)

the cdr pointer of **c** is changed to refer to **d** (Figure 11.19) and now **c** ⟹ (1 4 5 6). But the side effects of (**set-cdr! c d**) extend to all objects that have pointers to c; now **w** ⟹ ((1 4 5 6) 4 5 6). Thus care must be taken when using procedures like **set-car!** and **set-cdr!** that cause mutations in the list structure that unexpected or unwanted changes in other data objects do not

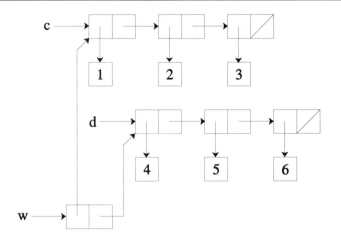

Figure 11.18 (eq? (car w) c) $\Longrightarrow$ #t

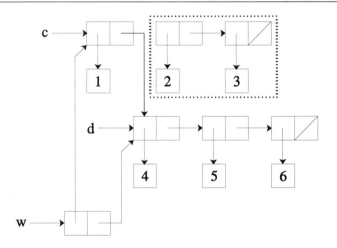

Figure 11.19 (set-cdr! c d) in Figure 11.18

occur. The two procedures **set-car!** and **set-cdr!** cause mutations in the list structure of data objects, but the values that they return are unspecified and may differ in different implementations of Scheme. Thus to write programs that are *portable* (run in various implementations of Scheme), it is necessary to avoid using the values returned by these procedures.

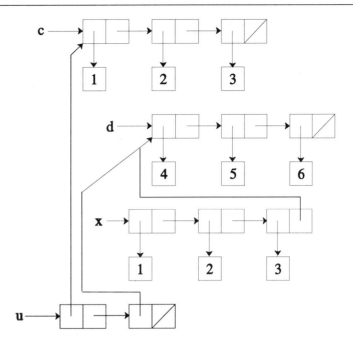

Figure 11.20 (define x (append c d))

The procedure **append** was defined in Program 4.1 as:

```
(define append
  (lambda (ls1 ls2)
    (if (null? ls1)
        ls2
        (cons (car ls1) (append (cdr ls1) ls2)))))
```

If **c** and **d** are again defined as in Figure 11.18, and we define

```
(define u (cons c (cons d '())))
```

and

```
(define x (append c d))
```

then **append** makes a copy of **c** and changes the cdr pointer of the last cons cell in this copy to point to **d**. (See Figure 11.20.) Then:

Program 11.21   last-pair

```
(define last-pair
  (lambda (x)
    (if (pair? (cdr x))
        (last-pair (cdr x))
        x)))
```

Program 11.22   append!

```
(define append!
  (lambda (ls1 ls2)
    (if (pair? ls1)
        (begin
          (set-cdr! (last-pair ls1) ls2)
          ls1)
        ls2)))
```

```
x ⟹ (1 2 3 4 5 6)
c ⟹ (1 2 3)
d ⟹ (4 5 6)
u ⟹ ((1 2 3) (4 5 6))
```

In making the copy of c, x had to create three cons cells.

The procedure append! offers a more efficient way of appending one list to another. However, it has side effects that must be considered, so it should not be used indiscriminately. Let us begin by defining the procedure last-pair (see Program 11.21), which takes as its argument a nonempty list and returns the list consisting of the last value in the list. For example:

```
(last-pair '(1 2 3)) ⟹ (3)
```

We then define append! in Program 11.22. Here last-pair cdr's down the list ls1 until it reaches the last pair in ls1. Then set-cdr! redirects the cdr pointer to ls2 instead of the empty list. The last line in the begin expression returns this mutated list ls1. For example, if we apply append! to the two lists c and d defined above by writing

```
(define y (append! c d))
```

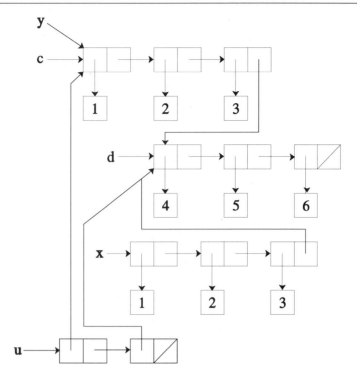

Figure 11.23 `(define y (append! c d))` in Figure 11.20

then **y** is obtained by connecting the cdr pointer of the last cons cell in **c** to **d**. (See Figure 11.23.) We now have

```
y ⟹ (1 2 3 4 5 6)
c ⟹ (1 2 3 4 5 6)
d ⟹ (4 5 6)
x ⟹ (1 2 3 4 5 6)
u ⟹ ((1 2 3 4 5 6) (4 5 6))
```

The last result is a side effect of using **append!** on **c**, for the **c**, which also appears in the definition of **u**, has been mutated. The value of **x** is not changed because it originally makes a copy of **c** and has no pointer to **c**. Thus each time we have a choice of using one of the procedures **set-car!**, **set-cdr!**, or **append!**, we must decide whether we want a copy of the original lists made by using suitable procedures of **cons**, **car**, **cdr**, and **append** or mutations of the original lists taking into account the possible side effects. We must be

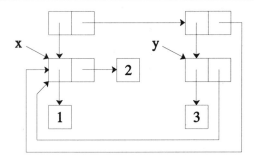

Figure 11.24 Box-and-pointer diagram for Exercise 11.12

careful that undesirable side effects do not occur when using **set-car!**, **set-cdr!**, and **append!**. In the next chapter, we shall see examples where these procedures can safely be used because the variables affected are local and the side effects can be controlled.

Exercises

Exercise 11.11
Draw a box-and-pointer diagram for the following:

```
(let ((x (list 1 2 3)))
  (let ((y (list 4 5 6)))
    (let ((z (cons x y)))
      (set-cdr! x y)
      z)))
```

Exercise 11.12
Write a let expression in the style of Exercise 11.11 that generates the entire structure shown in the box-and-pointer diagram in Figure 11.24.

Exercise 11.13

a. Draw a box-and-pointer diagram for the following:

```
(let ((x (cons 1 1)))
  (set-car! x x)
  (set-cdr! x x)
  x)
```

b. Define a procedure that recognizes such cons cells.

c. Define a procedure that takes a list as its argument and removes all occurrences of such cons cells.

Exercise 11.14
Conduct the following experiment, explaining the results:

```
[1] (define mystery
      (lambda(x)
        (let ((box (last-pair x)))
          (set-cdr! box x)
          x)))
[2] (define ans (mystery (list 'a 'b 'c 'd)))
[3] ans
?_____
```

Exercise 11.15
Let us consider only flat lists in this exercise. We know that we can write a procedure that determines the length of a list. We allow, however, that the cdr of the last cell of the list might point back to some portion of the list. For example,

```
(let ((x (list 'a 'b 'c 'd 'e)))
  (set-cdr! (last-pair x) (cdr (cdr x)))
  x)
```

We can print such lists by invoking (writeln x); however, the printing of the list will not terminate. Redefine writeln so that if it discovers one of these lists, it prints something appropriate. For example,

```
(writeln x) ⟹ (a b c d e c d e ...)
```

Hint: Define a predicate cycle? which determines if a list is a flat cycle. Also, reconstruct a list like (a b c d e c d e ...) that has the string "..." as the last of its nine elements.

Exercise 11.16: efface
Create the box-and-pointer diagrams for x, y, z, a, a*, b, b*, c, and c* before and after the invocation of efface in test-efface.

```
(define efface
  (lambda (x ls)
    (cond
      ((null? ls) '())
      ((equal? (car ls) x) (cdr ls))
      (else (let ((z (efface x (cdr ls))))
              (set-cdr! ls z)
              ls)))))

(define test-efface
  (lambda ()
    (let ((x (cons 1 '())))
      (let ((y (cons 2 x)))
        (let ((z (cons 3 y)))
          (let ((a (cons 4 z)) (a* (cons 40 z)))
            (let ((b (cons 5 a)) (b* (cons 50 a)))
              (let ((c (cons 6 b)) (c* (cons 60 b)))
                (writeln x y z a a* b b* c c*)
                (efface 3 c)
                (writeln x y z a a* b b* c c*)))))))))
```

Exercise 11.17

Using the definition of **efface** from Exercise 11.16, describe the behavior of
(test-efface2) and (test-efface3). Explain the difference.

```
(define test-efface2
  (lambda ()
    (let ((ls (list 5 4 3 2 1)))
      (writeln (efface 3 ls))
      ls)))

(define test-efface3
  (lambda ()
    (let ((ls (list 5 4 3 2 1)))
      (writeln (efface 5 ls))
      ls)))
```

Exercise 11.18: smudge

Create the box-and-pointer diagrams for **x, y, z, a, a*, b, b*, c,** and **c*** before
and after the invocation of **smudge** in **test-smudge**.

```
(define smudge
  (lambda (x ls)
    (letrec
      ((smudge/x
         (lambda (ls*)
           (cond
             ((null? (cdr ls*)) ls*)
             ((equal? (car ls*) x) (shift-down ls* (cdr ls*)))
             (else (smudge/x (cdr ls*)))))))
      (if (null? ls)
          ls
          (begin
            (smudge/x ls)
            ls)))))

(define shift-down
  (lambda (box1 box2)
    (set-car! box1 (car box2))
    (set-cdr! box1 (cdr box2))))

(define test-smudge
  (lambda ()
    (let ((x (cons 1 '())))
      (let ((y (cons 2 x)))
        (let ((z (cons 3 y)))
          (let ((a (cons 4 z)) (a* (cons 40 z)))
            (let ((b (cons 5 a)) (b* (cons 50 a)))
              (let ((c (cons 6 b)) (c* (cons 60 b)))
                (writeln x y z a a* b b* c c*)
                (smudge 3 c)
                (writeln x y z a a* b b* c c*)))))))))
```

Exercise 11.19: count-pairs

The procedure count-pairs counts the number of cons cells in a data structure. It is defined using the global variable *seen-pairs* and the helping predicate dont-count?.

```
(define *seen-pairs* '())
```

```
(define count-pairs
  (lambda (pr)
    (if (dont-count? pr)
        0
        (begin
          (set! *seen-pairs* (cons pr *seen-pairs*))
          (add1 (+ (count-pairs (car pr))
                   (count-pairs (cdr pr)))))))))

(define dont-count?
  (lambda (s)
    (or (not (pair? s)) (member? s *seen-pairs*))))
```

a. Create a box-and-pointer diagram for **y** just prior to the invocation of **count-pairs** in the procedure **test-count-pairs**.

```
(define test-count-pairs
  (lambda ()
    (let ((x (cons 'a (cons 'b (cons 'c '())))))
      (let ((y (cons x (cons x (cons x x)))))
        (set-cdr! (last-pair x) x)
        (writeln (count-pairs y))
        (count-pairs y)))))
```

b. Explain the behavior of **test-count-pairs**. Why are the answers different? Rewrite **count-pairs** functionally so that the two answers are the same. *Hint*: Look back at the definition of **vector-insertsort!** in Program 10.5.

c. Rewrite **count-pairs** using local state, which gets changed with **set!**. Here is a skeleton:

```
(define count-pairs
  (lambda (pr)
    (count-pairs/seen pr '())))

(define count-pairs/seen
  (lambda (pr seen-pairs)
    (letrec
      ((count (lambda (pr) ...)))
      (count pr))))
```

d. Rewrite `count-pairs` using private local state. *Hint*: Look at the skeleton below. We must set `seen-pairs` back to the empty list just prior to invoking `count`. Here is a skeleton:

```
(define count-pairs
  (let ((seen-pairs "any list of pairs"))
    (letrec
      ((count (lambda (pr) ...)))
      (lambda (pr)
        (set! seen-pairs '())
        (count pr)))))
```

e. Rewrite `count-pairs` using private local state, setting `seen-pairs` to the empty list after invoking `count` instead of before invoking `count`. This way we know that `seen-pairs` is always the empty list before and after invoking `count-pairs`.

The next seven problems are related. Work them in order and you will learn about what computers cannot do.

Exercise 11.20:   Turing Tapes
Consider a list that grows in both directions: `(... c b a x y ...)`. We call such a list an *unbounded tape*, or just **tape**. We use a positive number of 0's as left and right borders to indicate where the *interesting information* on the tape resides: `(... 0 c b a x y 0 ...)`. Any symbol would work as the border symbol; no border value can appear within the interesting information on the tape, for if it did then it would indicate a border. Included as part of the data abstraction of a tape is a location on the tape. Tapes can be read only a character at a time. For the purposes of this discussion, `x` is the character being read on the above tape.

There are four procedures defined over tapes. The first one is `at`, which takes a tape and returns the character being read. The second one is `over-write`, which takes a character, `c`, and a tape, and returns an equivalent tape except that the character being read is replaced by `c`. We can characterize the relation between `overwrite` and `at` with the following equation. Let `t` be a tape and let `c` be a character; then:

$$(\text{at } (\text{overwrite } c\ t)) \equiv c$$

The third and fourth procedures are `left` and `right`. These take a tape and return an equivalent tape except that the character being read is the one just to the left (or right) of the one that was previously being read. In our example, this would mean that the character being read is now **a** (or **y**). Since the tape is unbounded in both directions, there is no concern about falling off the tape. We have the identities:

$$(\text{left } (\text{right } tape)) \equiv tape \equiv (\text{right } (\text{left } tape))$$

In our use of tapes, we always do **overwrite** followed by either **left** or **right** but not both. We refer to this operation as *reconfiguring* the tape. In order to reconfigure a tape, we need a character to write and a direction in which to move:

```
(define reconfigure
  (lambda (tape character direction)
    (if (eq? direction 'left)
        (left (overwrite character tape))
        (right (overwrite character tape)))))
```

We now consider a possible representation of tapes. In this representation a tape is composed of two non-null, finite lists. We call these two lists *left part* and *right part*. The left part contains everything to the left of where we are reading until the left end of the tape, but it is *reversed*. In our example, that is (a b c 0). The right part contains everything from where we are reading until the right end of the tape. In our example above, that is (x y 0). Thus, the tape is represented by the list ((a b c 0) (x y 0)). We can now define **at** and **overwrite**:

```
(define at
  (lambda (tape)
    (let ((right-part (2nd tape)))
      (car right-part))))

(define overwrite
  (lambda (char tape)
    (let ((left-part (1st tape)) (right-part (2nd tape)))
      (let ((new-right-part (cons char (cdr right-part))))
        (list left-part new-right-part)))))
```

We have only to define the procedures **left** and **right**. Let us consider what is involved in moving to the right. In our example this would mean that we are looking at **y**. If that is so, then the right part would become (y 0). What would happen to the **x**? Since it is now to the left of where we are reading, it would be moved into the left part and would become the first item in the left part. Here is a first try at **right**:

```
(define right
  (lambda (tape)
    (let ((left-part (1st tape)) (right-part (2nd tape)))
      (let ((new-left-part (cons (car right-part) left-part))
            (new-right-part (cdr right-part)))
        (list new-left-part new-right-part)))))
```

This is very close to correct, but it might violate the restriction that the left part and the right part must be non-null. Consider invoking **right** on the tape **((y x a b c 0) (0))**. Using this incorrect version of **right**, the new tape would become **((0 y x a b c 0) ())**, and that violates the non-null condition that each part must satisfy. If **new-right-part** is the empty list, we must replace it by **(0)**, which represents the right end of the tape. Here is the improved version of **right**:

```
(define right
  (lambda (tape)
    (let ((left-part (1st tape)) (right-part (2nd tape)))
      (let ((new-left-part (cons (car right-part) left-part))
            (new-right-part (cdr right-part)))
        (list new-left-part (check-null new-right-part))))))

(define check-null
  (lambda (part)
    (if (null? part)
        (list 0)
        part)))
```

Write the procedure **left**, and test **reconfigure** with the procedure below:

```
(define test-reconfigure
  (lambda ()
    (let ((tape1 (list (list 'a 'b 'c 0) (list 'x 'y 0))))
      (let ((tape2 (reconfigure tape1 'u 'right))
            (tape3 (reconfigure tape1 'd 'left)))
        (let ((tape4 (reconfigure tape2 'v 'right))
              (tape5 (reconfigure tape3 'e 'left)))
          (let ((tape6 (reconfigure tape4 'w 'right))
                (tape7 (reconfigure tape5 'f 'left)))
            (let ((tape8 (reconfigure tape6 'x 'right))
                  (tape9 (reconfigure tape7 'g 'left)))
              (list tape8 tape9))))))))
```

Exercise 11.21: `list->tape, tape->list`

Define a pair of procedures that builds an interface for handling tapes. The first procedure, `list->tape`, takes a list, `ls`, of characters that contains no 0's and produces a tape, `t`, with the condition that `ls` is the same as `(right t)` minus trailing zeros. For example, if `ls` is `(x y)`, then `(list->tape ls)` returns `((0) (x y 0))`. The procedure `tape->list` takes a tape and returns a list. The resultant list does not keep track of where on the tape it is reading. Hence, it is *not* always the case that `(list->tape (tape->list t)) = t`; however, it is always the case that `(tape->list (list->tape ls)) = ls`. For example, if the tape, `t`, is `((a b c 0) (x y 0))`, then `(tape->list t)` is `(c b a x y)`, but `(list->tape '(c b a x y))` is `((0) (c b a x y 0))`, not `((a b c 0) (x y 0))`. Not only must the left part be reversed, but no 0's should appear in the resultant list. Rewrite `test-reconfigure` so that it uses `list->tape` and `tape->list`.

Exercise 11.22

In the procedure `test-reconfigure` from the previous exercise, we used `tape1` twice. Generally that does not happen. More frequently, a tape is used as an argument in an iterative program. Consider the following experiment:

```
[1] (define shifter
      (letrec
        ((shift-to-0
           (lambda (tape)
             (let ((c (at tape)))
               (cond
                 ((equal? c 0) tape)
                 (else (shift-to-0 (reconfigure tape c 'right)))))))))
        shift-to-0))
[2] (shifter (list (list 0) (list 'a 'b 'c 0)))
```

When the tape is used in this fashion, we no longer need to make a new copy each time we reconfigure the tape. For example, we can redefine `overwrite` to change the value that `at` returns just by using `set-car!`:

```
(define overwrite
  (lambda (char tape)
    (let ((right-part (2nd tape)))
      (set-car! right-part char)
      tape)))
```

In changing the definition of overwrite, we exchanged one invocation of set-car! for three uses of cons and one use of cdr, but test-reconfigure no longer produces the same result. Why? Redefine right and left to use as few invocations of cons as possible. Test shifter as in [2].

Exercise 11.23
We can write interesting procedures that begin with an empty tape (i.e, (list->tape '())). Test the procedures below using an empty tape and determine which ones do not halt:

```
(define busy-beaver
  (letrec
    ((loopright
       (lambda (tape)
         (let ((c (at tape)))
           (cond
             ((equal? c 'a)
              (loopright (reconfigure tape 'a 'right)))
             (else (maybe-done (reconfigure tape 'a 'right)))))))
     (maybe-done
       (lambda (tape)
         (let ((c (at tape)))
           (cond
             ((equal? c 'a) (reconfigure tape 'a 'right))
             (else (continue (reconfigure tape 'a 'left)))))))
     (continue
       (lambda (tape)
         (let ((c (at tape)))
           (cond
             ((equal? c 'a)
              (maybe-done (reconfigure tape 'a 'left)))
             (else (loopright (reconfigure tape 'a 'right))))))))
    loopright))

(define endless-growth
  (letrec
    ((loop
       (lambda (tape)
         (let ((c (at tape)))
           (cond
             ((equal? c 0)
              (loop (reconfigure tape 'a 'right))))))))
    loop))
```

```
(define perpetual-motion
  (letrec
    ((this-way
       (lambda (tape)
         (let ((c (at tape)))
           (cond
             ((equal? c 'a)
              (that-way (reconfigure tape 0 'right)))
             (else (that-way (reconfigure tape 'a 'right)))))))
     (that-way
       (lambda (tape)
         (let ((c (at tape)))
           (cond
             ((equal? c 'a)
              (this-way (reconfigure tape 0 'left)))
             (else (this-way (reconfigure tape 'a 'left))))))))
    this-way))

(define pendulum
  (letrec
    ((loopright
       (lambda (tape)
         (let ((c (at tape)))
           (cond
             ((equal? c 'a)
              (loopright (reconfigure tape 'a 'right)))
             (else (loopleft (reconfigure tape 'a 'left)))))))
     (loopleft
       (lambda (tape)
         (let ((c (at tape)))
           (cond
             ((equal? c 'a)
              (loopleft (reconfigure tape 'a 'left)))
             (else (loopright (reconfigure tape 'a 'right))))))))
    loopright))
```

Exercise 11.24

Each of the procedures in the previous exercise looks about the same. Each takes a tape as an argument. Then it reconfigures the tape according to the current character and either returns the reconfigured tape or passes it along to another procedure. We can think of each cond line as a list of five elements. For example, the first cond line of continue in busy-beaver could be represented by: (continue a a left maybe-done). We can interpret this line as follows: *From the state of* continue, *if there is an* a, *overwrite it with an* a, *move* left, *and consider only the lines that start with* maybe-done. The entire busy-beaver procedure could be represented by a list of all the transcribed cond lines:

```
(define busy-beaver-lines
  '((loopright a a right loopright)
    (loopright 0 a right maybe-done)
    (maybe-done a a right halt)
    (maybe-done 0 a left continue)
    (continue a a left maybe-done)
    (continue 0 a right loopright)))
```

We use the convention that we start the computation at (car (car busy-beaver-lines)). We also assume that halt is self-explanatory.

Using the representation of tapes that we have developed thus far, define a procedure run-lines that takes a set of lines, like the busy-beaver-lines, and a tape and returns the same result as (busy-beaver tape). The procedure below will get you started. You need only define the procedures called by run-lines.

```
(define run-lines
  (lambda (lines tape)
    (letrec
      ((driver
         (lambda (state tape)
           (if (eq? state 'halt)
               tape
               (let ((matching-line
                       (find-line state (at tape) lines)))
                 (driver
                   (next-state matching-line)
                   (reconfigure
                     tape
                     (next-char matching-line)
                     (next-direction matching-line))))))))
      (driver (current-state (car lines)) tape))))
```

Such a set of lines is called a *Turing machine*, named for Alan M. Turing. Turing claimed that with a small set of characters, including the 0, he could use his machines to compute whatever a computer could. Then he showed that no one can write a procedure test-lines, like run-lines, that takes an arbitrary machine and an arbitrary tape and determines whether (run-lines machine tape) halts. This result is so important that it has been given a name, the *halting problem*. All this was done in 1936!

Exercise 11.25
Often it is possible to remove a test by careful design. In the definition of re-configure, there is a superfluous test. Rewrite busy-beaver replacing 'left by left and 'right by right, so that a revised definition of reconfigure works.

Exercise 11.26:   New Representation
Consider a representation of tapes that keeps what it is reading separately. For example, we might choose a list of three elements

```
(at left-part right-part-less-at)
```

Then we could redefine overwrite and right as follows:

```
(define overwrite
  (lambda (char tape)
    (let ((left (2nd tape)) (right (3rd tape)))
      (list char left right))))

(define right
  (lambda (tape)
    (let ((char (1st tape))
          (left (2nd tape))
          (right (3rd tape)))
      (list (car right)
            (cons char left)
            (check-null (cdr right))))))
```

Use this representation of tapes and test busy-beaver. Then redefine all necessary procedures so that the use of cons is minimal.

12   Object-Oriented Programming

12.1 Overview

A different perspective on computing is provided by object-oriented programming. In this style of programming, certain objects are defined that respond to messages passed to them. Figuratively, we can think of an object as a computer dedicated to solving a particular type of problem. The input is the message passed to the object, the object does the computation, and the output is the value returned by the object. In this chapter, we see how such objects are defined, and we illustrate the use of objects to define such data structures as stacks and queues.

12.2 Boxes, Counters, Accumulators, and Gauges

In Chapters 3 and 5, the concept of data abstraction was discussed and illustrated. We saw there that we can write programs that are independent of the representation of the data and are based on certain predefined basic procedures, including the constructors and selectors used on the data type. The actual representation of the data was then used only in defining these basic procedures. We develop the idea of data abstraction further by defining certain objects that are combined with certain operations. It is not necessary for users to know how these objects and operators are implemented in order to use them. They only have to know the interface. An example of such an object is a stack that has associated with it such operations as **push!** and **pop!**. This offers a degree of security in the handling of data and makes it possible to change the internal representation of the object without the user's being aware of any changes. Before looking at stacks and queues, we introduce the case expression, which makes it easier for us to define the various objects we shall study.

12.2.1 The Case Expression

Scheme provides a special form with keyword **case** that selects one of a sequence of clauses to evaluate based upon the value of an argument (or message) that it is passed. To see how **case** is used, let us first look at a procedure that tells us whether a letter is a vowel or a consonant. We can define it as

```
(define vowel-or-consonant
  (lambda (letter)
    (cond
      ((or (eq? letter 'a)
           (eq? letter 'e)
           (eq? letter 'i)
           (eq? letter 'o)
           (eq? letter 'u))
       'vowel)
      (else 'consonant)))))
```

This procedure can also be defined using the special form **case** as follows:

```
(define vowel-or-consonant
  (lambda (letter)
    (case letter
      ((a e i o u) 'vowel)
      (else 'consonant)))))
```

The value of **letter** is matched with each of the items (keys) in the list in the first clause of the case expression. If there is a match, the expression following the list of keys is evaluated and returned as the value of the case expression. Thus if **letter** evaluates to one of a, e, i, o, or u, **vowel** is returned. Otherwise, the next clause is evaluated, and since in this case it is the else clause, **consonant** is returned. In case **letter** evaluates to one of the five vowels, it is more convenient to use the case expression, which matches it with the possible key values rather than the cond expression, which must list a separate test for each possibility.

The syntax of **case** is

```
(case target
   (keys expr₁ expr₂ ...)
   ...
   (else expr₁ expr₂ ...))
```

where *target* is an expression that is evaluated and its value is compared
with the keys. Each clause begins with *keys*, which is a list of items each of
which is matched (using eqv?) with the value of *target* to decide which of the
clauses will be selected for evaluation. When the first such match is found, the
expressions *expr* ... following the *keys* are evaluated in order and the value
of the last is returned (there is an implicit begin following each *keys*). If no
match is found and the optional else clause is present, then the expressions
expr ... in the else clause are evaluated. If no else clause is present, then
some unspecified value is returned. It is good programming style always to
include an else clause even if only for reporting an error.

Below are some additional simple examples demonstrating the use of case:

```
[1] (case 'b
      ((a) (display "a was selected: ") (cons 'a '()))
      ((b) (display "b was selected: ") (cons 'b '()))
      ((c) (display "c was selected: ") (cons 'c '()))
      (else (display "None were selected.")))
b was selected: (b)

[2] (case (remainder 35 10)
      ((2 4 6 8) "positive and even")
      ((1 3 5 7 9) "positive and odd")
      ((-2 -4 -6 -8) "negative and even")
      ((-1 -3 -5 -7 -9) "negative and odd")
      (else "zero"))
"positive and odd"
```

In the various objects we shall define in this chapter, we shall use internal
representations of the data, which are not supposed to be apparent to the user.
In order to secure the data structures used, we introduce, in Program 12.1,
the procedure for-effect-only, which evaluates its operand to perform the
side effects and then returns the string "unspecified value". Following our
usual convention, we will not display "unspecified value".

```
(define for-effect-only
  (lambda (item-ignored)
    "unspecified value"))
```

12.2.2 Boxes

A *box* is a place in which a value can be stored until it is needed later. A new box containing a given initial value is created by the procedure **box-maker**. There are five operations that we shall perform on a box. We use one of these operations to put a value into the box and another to show the value in the box. The operation that puts a value into the box is called **update!** and the operation that shows the value in the box is called **show**. Another useful operation, called **swap!**, puts a new value into the box and returns the old contents of the box. The operation called **reset!** resets the value stored in the box to its initial value. The ability to perform a reset operation is somewhat unusual. The operation **type**, specified for all objects, tells what kind of object is being sent a message. In this case the type is **"box"**. In general, the operations that are performed on an object are called *methods*. In the case of a box, there are five methods: **update!**, **show**, **swap!**, **reset!**, and **type**.

The objects, such as boxes, are themselves procedures. To apply one of the methods to an object, we invoke the object on the (quoted) name of the method followed by any additional arguments appropriate for that method. We then say that we send the name of the method and any additional arguments as a *message* to the object. We can use the call structure:

$$(object \ 'method\text{-}name \ operand \ \dots)$$

where *object* is sent the message consisting of the quoted method name and zero or more operands. On the other hand, we find it more suggestive and, in fact, more flexible to introduce the procedure **send**, which is used to send the message to the object. When we use **send**, we use the call structure

$$(send \ object \ 'method\text{-}name \ operand \ \dots)$$

The following shows a typical construction of a box **box-a** that is initialized with (+ 3 4) and a box `box-b` that is initialized with 5. We shall describe the actual mechanism for constructing boxes after looking at the example.

```
[1] (define box-a (box-maker (+ 3 4)))
[2] (define box-b (box-maker 5))
[3] (send box-a 'show)
7
[4] (send box-b 'show)
5
[5] (send box-a 'update! 3)
[6] (send box-a 'show)
3
[7] (send box-b 'update! (send box-a 'swap! (send box-b 'show)))
[8] (send box-a 'show)
5
[9] (send box-b 'show)
3
[10] (send box-a 'reset!)
[11] (send box-a 'show)
7
[12] (send box-a 'type)
"box"
[13] (send box-a 'update 27)
Error: Bad method name: update sent to object of box type.
```

In [3], in order to see what is stored in `box-a`, we send the message `show` to `box-a`, and in [5], in order to change the value stored in `box-a`, we send it the message `update!` and the new value 3. In [13], we forgot to include the exclamation mark on the word `update`, and an error was signaled. The sending of these quoted method names and arguments as messages to the objects leads to a style of programming referred to as *message-passing style*.

In Program 12.2, we define `box-maker`. It takes as its argument an initial value stored in the box. It returns a procedure that takes an arbitrary number of arguments and is hence defined using the unrestricted `lambda` whose parameter list is denoted by `msg`. Each invocation of `box-maker` returns an object that we refer to as a box. Thus, in our experiment presented above, `box-a` and `box-b` are examples (or *instances*) of boxes. Also, in [3], the message consists of the single item `'show`, whereas in [5], the message consists of two items, the method name `'update!` and the operand 3. In the code given below for `box-maker`, we use `1st` and `2nd` to denote `car` and `cadr`,

Program 12.2 `box-maker`

```
(define box-maker
  (lambda (init-value)
    (let ((contents init-value))
      (lambda msg
        (case (1st msg)
          ((type) "box")
          ((show) contents)
          ((update!) (for-effect-only (set! contents (2nd msg))))
          ((swap!) (let ((ans contents))
                     (set! contents (2nd msg))
                     ans))
          ((reset!) (for-effect-only (set! contents init-value)))
          (else (delegate base-object msg)))))))
```

Program 12.3 `delegate`

```
(define delegate
  (lambda (obj msg)
    (apply obj msg)))
```

respectively. We also use `msg` to denote the message. `delegate` is defined in Program 12.3.

In order to be able to reset the box to its initial value, `init-value`, it is necessary to preserve that value. Thus a local variable `contents` is introduced to hold the current value stored in the box. It is initialized with `init-value`. In the case clause that matches `swap!`, a let expression binds `ans` to the current contents of the box. Then `set!` puts the new value into the box, but the old value `ans` that was stored in the box is returned. Whenever the else clause is reached, no match was found for the method name, so the message is passed on (or *delegated*)[1] to another object, which attempts to respond to it. (We find that it is more suggestive to use the procedure name

---

[1] When an object cannot respond to a message, there are mechanisms other than delegation which have been developed. One common mechanism is *inheritance*. We have chosen to use delegation instead of inheritance; however, all programs expressible with inheritance are also expressible with delegation.

Program 12.4 `base-object`

```
(define base-object
  (lambda msg
    (case (1st msg)
      ((type) "base-object")
      (else invalid-method-name-indicator))))
```

Program 12.5 `send`

```
(define send
  (lambda args
    (let ((object (car args)) (message (cdr args)))
      (let ((try (apply object message)))
        (if (eq? invalid-method-name-indicator try)
            (error "Bad method name:" (car message)
                   "sent to object of"
                   (object 'type)
                   "type.")
            try)))))
```

delegate instead of *apply* to pass the message on to another object, although
the two procedures `delegate` and `apply` behave the same by our simplification
rule.) In this case, the object to which the message is delegated is the `base-
object`, which returns `invalid-method-name-indicator`, which is bound to
the string `"unknown"`.

```
(define invalid-method-name-indicator "unknown")
```

The procedure `send` then generates the appropriate invocation of `error`. The
definitions of `base-object` and `send` are contained in Programs 12.4 and 12.5.

We shall define many different types of objects in this chapter using object
makers similar to `box-maker`. These will each contain an else clause that
must handle method names for which there is no match. One of the major
advantages of using `send` is that all these else clauses will have exactly the
same call structure

```
(else (delegate object msg))
```

and `send` takes the appropriate action. When writing the definitions of the
object makers and when using the objects, we must remember that:

1. Every object should respond to the method name **type**.

2. When no match is found for a method name, the else clause should delegate the message to some object, which in some cases may be **base-object**.

3. Use **send** to pass messages to objects.

In this implementation of a box, the data structure used to store a value in the box is just a variable. The user is not concerned with this fact when using the box to store the value. We could have used a different data structure, such as a cons cell, in which to store the value. In the program below for **box-maker**, init-value is initially stored in the car position of a cons cell, which we denote by **cell**. The procedure **set-car!** is used to change the value stored in the box. This alternative version of **box-maker** is in Program 12.6.

Program 12.6   **box-maker** (Alternative)

```
(define box-maker
  (lambda (init-value)
    (let ((cell (cons init-value "any value")))
      (lambda msg
        (case (1st msg)
          ((type) "box")
          ((show) (car cell))
          ((update!) (for-effect-only (set-car! cell (2nd msg))))
          ((swap!) (let ((ans (car cell)))
                     (set-car! cell (2nd msg))
                     ans))
          ((reset!) (for-effect-only (set-car! cell init-value)))
          (else (delegate base-object msg))))))))
```

12.2.3 Counters

A *counter* is an object that stores an initial value and each time it is called, the stored value is changed according to some fixed rule. The counter has two arguments: the initial value stored and the procedure describing the action to be taken each time the counter is updated. For example, (**counter-maker** 10 sub1) is a counter with initial value 10 that decrements the counter by 1 when it is updated. The counter responds to the method names: **type**, **update!**, **show**, and **reset!**. The definition of **counter-maker** follows:

Program 12.7 `counter-maker` (Methods Disabled)

```
(define counter-maker
  (lambda (init-value unary-proc)
    (let ((total (box-maker init-value)))
      (lambda msg
        (case (1st msg)
          ((type) "counter")
          ((update!) (let ((result (unary-proc (send total 'show))))
                        (send total 'update! result)))
          ((swap!) (delegate base-object msg))
          (else (delegate total msg)))))))
```

The counter locally defines the box `total`, which contains the initial value stored in the counter. When the counter receives the message consisting of the method name `update!`, the unary update procedure `unary-proc` is applied to the value stored in the box `total` to obtain the new value which is then stored in `total`. For example, if we wanted the counter to count up by 1 each time it is updated, we can use `add1` as the unary update procedure. To create a counter with initial value 0 that increases the stored value by 5 each time it is updated, we write:

$$(\text{counter-maker } 0 \text{ (lambda } (x) \text{ } (+ \text{ } 5 \text{ } x)))$$

The counter is not supposed to respond to `swap!`. Thus if such messages are sent to a counter, they are delegated to `base-object` rather than to a box, which does respond to `swap!`. Since the counter responds to the messages `show` and `reset!` the same as the box `total`, the else clause merely passes these messages to `total`. Thus the message `show` displays the value currently stored in the counter, and `reset!` resets the counter to its initial value. The fact that the response of the counter to these messages can be found by passing them to the box is called *delegation*. The work of the counter is "delegated" to the behavior of the box.

The approach of catching the method names that are to be disabled, like `swap!`, is only one way of supporting the interface. Another alternative is to catch all the method names to be enabled. Thus, we can rewrite `counter-maker` using this view. As long as we delegate to the base object all the method names that are meaningless, we can use either approach. On one hand we are throwing the illegal method names out (i.e., *disabling* them), and on the other, we are delegating the legal ones (i.e., *enabling* them). In any

Program 12.8   `counter-maker` (Methods Enabled)

```
(define counter-maker
  (lambda (init-value unary-proc)
    (let ((total (box-maker init-value)))
      (lambda msg
        (case (1st msg)
          ((type) "counter")
          ((update!) (send total 'update!
                            (unary-proc (send total 'show))))
          ((show reset) (delegate total msg))
          (else (delegate base-object msg)))))))
```

event, both have the same effect, and each has aspects that recommend it. If we are delegating to an object with many legal method names, and only a few illegal ones, then we should disable illegal method names; otherwise we are free to choose to enable legal method names. A version of `counter-maker`, which enables legal method names, is presented in Program 12.8.

12.2.4 Accumulators

An *accumulator* is an object that has the initial value `init-value`. Each time it receives a message consisting of the method name `update!` and a value `v`, the binary update procedure `binary-proc` is applied to the value stored in the accumulator and `v`; the result is the new value stored in the accumulator. For example, if `acc` is an accumulator that initially stores the value 100 and has subtraction (`-`) as its binary update procedure, it is defined by

```
(define acc (accumulator-maker 100 -))
```

and

```
(send acc 'update! 10)
```

causes the number 90 to be stored in `acc`. If we then update `acc` with 25, we write

```
(send acc 'update! 25)
```

and the number 65 is stored in the accumulator.

Program 12.9 `accumulator-maker`

```
(define accumulator-maker
  (lambda (init-value binary-proc)
    (let ((total (box-maker init-value)))
      (lambda msg
        (case (1st msg)
          ((type) "accumulator")
          ((update!)
           (send total 'update!
             (binary-proc (send total 'show) (2nd msg))))
          ((swap!) (delegate base-object msg))
          (else (delegate total msg)))))))
```

The accumulator uses a box, called **total**, to store its values. In addition to responding to the message consisting of **update!** and a value, it uses delegation to pass such messages as **show** and **reset!** to the box **total**. Program 12.9 contains the code for **accumulator-maker**.

12.2.5 Gauges

A *gauge* is the last object to be defined in this section. A gauge is similar to a counter, but it has two unary update procedures, one to count up and the other to count down. The one to count up is called **unary-proc-up**, and the one to count down is called **unary-proc-down**. The gauge responds to two update messages **up!** and **down!**. It stores its values in a box called **total**. When the gauge receives the message **up!**, the update procedure **unary-proc-up** is invoked on the value stored in **total** to get the new value stored in **total**. Similarly, when the gauge receives the message **down!**, the update procedure **unary-proc-down** is invoked on the value stored in **total** to get the new value stored in **total**. The gauge also responds to the messages **show** and **reset!** by delegation from **total**. For example, to create a gauge **g** with initial value **10**, which either adds **1** or subtracts **1**, we write

```
(define g (gauge-maker 10 add1 sub1))
```

and

```
(send g 'up!)
```

causes the number **11** to be stored in **g**, while

Program 12.10   gauge-maker

```
(define gauge-maker
  (lambda (init-value unary-proc-up unary-proc-down)
    (let ((total (box-maker init-value)))
      (lambda msg
        (case (1st msg)
          ((type) "gauge")
          ((up!) (send total 'update!
                    (unary-proc-up (send total 'show))))
          ((down!) (send total 'update!
                     (unary-proc-down (send total 'show))))
          ((swap! update!) (delegate base-object msg))
          (else (delegate total msg)))))))
```

```
(send g 'down!)
```

returns the number stored in **g** to **10**. Program 12.10 contains the definition of **gauge-maker**.

Exercises

Exercise 12.1: `acc-max`
Define an accumulator **acc-max** that has initial value 0 and each time it is updated, it compares the value stored with a new value and stores the maximum of the two. Then test **acc-max** by updating it in succession with the numbers 3, 7, 2, 4, 10, 1, 5 and find the maximum by passing **acc-max** the **show** message.

Exercise 12.2: `double-box-maker`
Define a procedure **double-box-maker** that takes two arguments, **item1** and **item2**, and stores these values in two boxes, the **left** and **right**, respectively. An instance of **double-box-maker** responds to the following messages: **show-left**, **show-right**, **update-left!**, **update-right!**, and **reset!**.

Exercise 12.3: `accumulator-maker, gauge-maker`
In the definitions of **accumulator-maker** and **gauge-maker** method names that are illegal have been disabled. Rewrite the last two lines of each of these

procedures so that instead of disabling illegal method names, we enable legal method names and disable all others.

Exercise 12.4: `restricted-counter-maker`
Our implementation of `counter-maker` places no restrictions on the possible values that can be stored in the counter. Define `restricted-counter-maker` to take an additional argument, a predicate `pred`. No value is stored in a restricted counter unless it satisfies the predicate. If a value fails to satisfy the predicate, then a reset occurs. For example, if the predicate is `(lambda (n) (and (> n 0) (< n 100)))` and we try to bring the restricted counter up to 105, it will reset to its initial value.

Exercise 12.5
Define the hour hand of a 12-hour clock as a restricted counter. (See the preceding exercise.)

Exercise 12.6
Define a 12-hour clock that has both a minute and an hour hand. This clock is to be constructed from two objects. One of them will be the 12-hour clock, which displays only its hour hand, and the other, the minute hand, will be built using a modified restricted counter. Such a counter is created using `modified-restricted-counter-maker`, which includes an additional argument. This new argument is a reset procedure that is invoked in place of the built-in reset in the `restricted-counter-maker`. When the minute hand of the clock is about to pass to 60 minutes, the reset procedure is used not only to reset the minute hand to 0 but also to update the hour hand. Do not forget to initialize the clock. The new clock is itself to be an object created by the procedure of one argument, `clock-maker`, that responds to two messages: `show` and `update!`. (See the preceding exercise.)

Exercise 12.7
As was done in Chapters 8 and 9, tag the objects by adding `object-tag` as `"object"`. Then define the simple procedures `object?` and `make-object`. Wrap `make-object` around `(lambda msg ...)` and redefine `send`.

Exercise 12.8
Is it possible to implement an accumulator with a `counter-maker` instead of a `box-maker`? Is it possible to implement a counter with an `accumulator-maker` instead of a `box-maker`?

As we saw in Chapter 11, a stack is an ordered collection of items into which new items may be inserted at one end and from which items may be removed from the same end. The end at which items may be inserted or removed is called the *top* of the stack. The image that is often conjured up when thinking of a stack is the rack of trays in a cafeteria, in which one takes the top one, and trays are added from the top. As the stack builds up, the item that was put on first is buried deeper and deeper, and as things are removed from the stack, the one that was put on first is the last one to be removed. The item that was added to the stack last is the first one to be removed. Thus a stack is referred to as a *last-in-first-out* data structure, or a *LIFO*.

The stack has several methods associated with it;

- `empty?`, which tests whether the stack is empty.
- `push!`, which adds an item to the top of the stack.
- `top`, which returns the item at the top of the stack.
- `pop!`, which removes an item from the top of stack.
- `size`, which returns the number of items on the stack.
- `print`, which prints the items on the stack.

An experiment with stacks is given in Figure 12.11. The two stacks, r and s, are created in `[1]` and `[2]`. In the definitions of r and s, we see that **stack-maker** is a thunk, that is, a procedure of no arguments. Its definition is given in Program 12.12.

In the code for **stack-maker**, we used a list as the internal representation of the stack. The user need never know how it is represented, for if we change the representation, we can alter the definitions of the methods so that when their names are passed as messages to the stack, the results seen by the user are the same as those produced by the above code. Even when the stack is printed, it does not show the internal representation of the stack.

Exercise

Exercise 12.9

In arithmetic, parentheses are used to form groupings of numbers and operators. For example, one writes $3*(4+2)$. In more complicated expressions, three different kinds of separators are used to form groupings: parentheses '(', ')', brackets '[',']', and braces '{','}'. Here is an expression that uses all three

```
[1] (define r (stack-maker))
[2] (define s (stack-maker))
[3] (send s 'print)
TOP:
[4] (send r 'print)
TOP:
[5] (send s 'empty?)
#t
[6] (send s 'push! 'a)
[7] (send s 'push! 'b)
[8] (send s 'push! 'c)
[9] (send s 'top)
c
[10] (send s 'print)
TOP: c b a
[11] (send s 'empty?)
#f
[12] (send r 'empty?)
#t
[13] (send r 'push! 'd)
[14] (send s 'size)
3
[15] (send s 'pop!)
[16] (send s 'pop!)
[17] (send s 'print)
TOP: a
[18] (send r 'print)
TOP: d
```

Figure 12.11   Using stack operations

kinds of grouping symbols:

$$13 + 5*\{[14 - 3*(12 - 7)] - 15\}$$

Write a program that will scan a mathematical expression made up of the four basic operations $+,-,*,$ and $/$ and the three kinds of separators and test whether the separators are correctly nested. The examples $(3 - 4]$ and $(5 - [2 + 4) + 1]$ are not correctly nested. This is a natural problem for the use of a stack, for whenever a left-grouping symbol is encountered, it is pushed onto the stack, and whenever a right-grouping symbol is encountered, the stack is popped and the left symbol that comes off the stack is compared to the right symbol just encountered. If they are of different types, the nesting is not correct. You can model the arithmetic expression as a list of numbers,

Program 12.12   stack-maker

```scheme
(define stack-maker
  (lambda ()
    (let ((stk '()))
      (lambda msg
        (case (1st msg)
          ((type) "stack")
          ((empty?) (null? stk))
          ((push!) (for-effect-only
                     (set! stk (cons (2nd msg) stk))))
          ((top) (if (null? stk)
                     (error "top: The stack is empty.")
                     (car stk)))
          ((pop!) (for-effect-only
                    (if (null? stk)
                        (error "pop!: The stack is empty.")
                        (set! stk (cdr stk)))))
          ((size) (length stk))
          ((print) (display "TOP: ")
                   (for-each
                     (lambda (x)
                       (display x)
                       (display " "))
                     stk)
                   (newline))
          (else (delegate base-object msg)))))))
```

operators, and grouping symbols. Since Scheme uses these symbols as special characters, one cannot use them as grouping symbols in the list modeling the arithmetic expression. Thus use the strings "(", ")", "[", "]", "{", and "}" in place of the grouping symbols. The above arithmetic expression, in this representation, looks like

```
(13 + 5 * "{" "[" 14 - 3 * "(" 12 - 7 ")" "]" - 15 "}")
```

Test your program on the examples given here and on several additional tests you devise, some correctly and others incorrectly nested.

12.4 Queues

A *queue* is an ordered collection of items into which items are inserted at one end, called the *rear*, and from which items are removed at the other end, called the *front*. People waiting in line for service normally form a queue in which new people join the line at the rear and people are served from the front. Similarly, processes waiting to be run on a computer are put into a queue to await their turn. Stacks are called *LIFO* lists because the last one in is the first one out. Queues are called *FIFO* lists because the first one in is the first one out. Adding an item to the rear of the queue is called *enqueuing* the item, and removing an item from the front of the queue is called *dequeuing*. We implement a queue as an object with the following methods:

- `empty?`, which tests whether the queue is empty.
- `enqueue!`, which adds an item to the rear of the queue.
- `front`, which returns the item at the front of the queue.
- `dequeue!`, which removes the item from the front of the queue.
- `size`, which returns the number of items in the queue.
- `print`, which prints the items in the queue.

Our first implementation of a queue will imitate the way we implemented a stack. The data structure we choose for the queue is a list, with the first element of the list the front of the queue. To dequeue an element, we essentially take the cdr of the list. To enqueue an element, we must put it at the end of the list, so we can make a list of the element and append that onto the end of the queue. The code for such an implementation is presented in Program 12.13.

The implementation using lists as the data structure for the queue produces the results we want, but it does it inefficiently. The trouble is that when we enqueue an item, we use `append!`, which must cdr down q until the last pair and then we attach the cdr pointer to the list containing the new item. The longer the queue, the more "expensive" it is to cdr down q to get to the last pair. It would be better to have an implementation that could attach the new item to the end of the queue without having to cdr down the whole queue. We accomplish this by introducing a second pointer called `rear`, which points to the last cons cell in the queue. When the queue is empty, the pointer q points to a cell formed by (cons '() '()), and `rear` also points to that cell. Only the `cdr` of q is used.

Program 12.13   `queue-maker`

```
(define queue-maker
  (lambda ()
    (let ((q '()))
      (lambda msg
        (case (1st msg)
          ((type) "queue")
          ((empty?) (null? q))
          ((enqueue!) (for-effect-only
                        (let ((list-of-item (cons (2nd msg) '())))
                          (if (null? q)
                              (set! q list-of-item)
                              (append! q list-of-item)))))
          ((front) (if (null? q)
                       (error "front: The queue is empty.")
                       (car q)))
          ((dequeue!) (for-effect-only
                        (if (null? q)
                            (error "dequeue!: The queue is empty.")
                            (set! q (cdr q)))))
          ((size) (length q))
          ((print) (display "FRONT: ")
                   (for-each
                     (lambda (x) (display x) (display " "))
                     q)
                   (newline))
          (else (delegate base-object msg)))))))
```

Figure 12.14(a) shows a box-and-pointer representation of such a queue that has in it the numbers 1 and 2, with 1 at the front. Figure 12.14(b) shows how the new item 3 is added to the queue by setting the cdr of **rear** to be `(cons 3 '())` and then setting **rear** itself to point to the last cons cell in the list. Our new definition of `queue-maker` is given in Program 12.15. A sample session using a queue is given in Figure 12.16.

Exercises

Exercise 12.10

Add a message to the queue defined in Program 12.15 called `enqueue-list!`

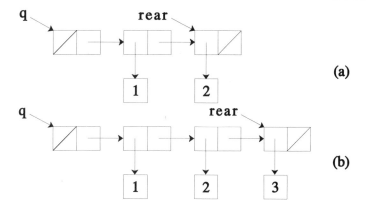

Figure 12.14   Box-and-pointer diagram for a queue

that takes as an argument a list `ls` and enqueues each of the elements of the list to the queue preserving their order. For example, if the queue `a` contains the elements 1, 2, 3, with 1 at the front, and if `ls` is `(list 4 5 6)`, then after invocation of `(send a 'enqueue-list! ls)`, the queue `a` contains the elements 1, 2, 3, 4, 5, 6 with 1 at the front. Do not use **append!**. Why?

Exercise 12.11
Revise the definition of **queue-maker** in Program 12.15 to include a message enqueue-many! that enqueues any number of items at one time. For example, `(send a 'enqueue-many! 'x 'y 'z)` has the same effect as

```
(begin
  (send a 'enqueue! 'x)
  (send a 'enqueue! 'y)
  (send a 'enqueue! 'z))
```

Exercise 12.12:   `queue->list`
Define a procedure `queue->list` that takes as its argument a queue `q`, with `size` disabled, and returns a list of the elements in `q` without destroying the queue. In order to do this, one can first enqueue a unique element such as `(list '())`. Then cons the front of the queue onto the list, and also enqueue the front onto the queue. Now dequeue the queue, so that what was at the front is now at the rear of the queue. Repeat this operation of consing the front of the queue to the list, enqueuing the front of the queue so that it is at the rear, and then dequeuing the queue, until the unique element you enqueued

Program 12.15 `queue-maker`

```
(define queue-maker
  (lambda ()
    (let ((q (cons '() '())))
      (let ((rear q))
        (lambda msg
          (case (1st msg)
            ((type) "queue")
            ((empty?) (eq? rear q))
            ((enqueue!) (for-effect-only
                          (let ((list-of-item (cons (2nd msg) '())))
                            (set-cdr! rear list-of-item)
                            (set! rear list-of-item))))
            ((front) (if (eq? rear q)
                         (error "front: The queue is empty.")
                         (car (cdr q))))
            ((dequeue!) (for-effect-only
                          (if (eq? rear q)
                              (error "dequeue!: The queue is empty.")
                              (let ((front-cell (cdr q)))
                                (set-cdr! q (cdr front-cell))
                                (if (eq? front-cell rear)
                                    (set! rear q))))))
            ((size) (length (cdr q)))
            ((print) (display "FRONT: ")
                     (for-each
                       (lambda (x)
                         (display x)
                         (display " "))
                       (cdr q))
                     (newline))
            (else (delegate base-object msg))))))))
```

reaches the front. When it is dequeued, you have a list of the elements that are in the queue, and the queue is intact.

Exercise 12.13
Rework the previous problem with the method name size enabled.

```
[1] (define q (queue-maker))
[2] (send q 'empty?)
#t
[3] (send q 'enqueue! 1)
[4] (send q 'enqueue! 2)
[5] (send q 'enqueue! 3)
[6] (send q 'size)
3
[7] (send q 'front)
1
[8] (send q 'print)
FRONT: 1 2 3
[9] (send q 'empty?)
#f
[10] (send q 'dequeue!)
[11] (send q 'print)
FRONT: 2 3
```

Figure 12.16   Using queue operations

Exercise 12.14

In the first version of a queue given in this section, the message `enqueue!` contains the code (`append! q list-of-item`). Discuss the correctness and the efficiency of the code for a queue if that line of code is replaced by (`append q list-of-item`) or by (`set! q (append q list-of-item)`).

12.5 Circular Lists

In the previous sections, we defined both the stack and the queue as objects. In the internal representation of these objects, we used lists. In the case of the queue, we used pointers to keep track of the front and the rear of the queue. There is another way of treating stacks and queues that is more elegant. It makes use of a data type known as a circular list. In this section, we first implement circular lists as objects and then use them to define both the stack and the queue, making use of delegation to take advantage of the properties of the circular list.

In an ordinary list, the cdr pointer of the last cons cell points to the empty list. This is denoted by placing a diagonal line in the right hand side of the last cons cell. If, instead, the cdr pointer of the last cons cell of the list points back to the first cons cell in the list, we say that the list is a *circular list*. The

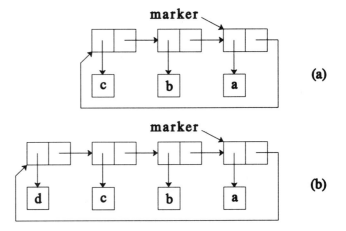

Figure 12.17 Box-and-pointer diagrams for a circular list

box and pointer diagram for a circular list containing the three items **c**, **b**, and **a** is shown in Figure 12.17a. Note that **marker** is a pointer to the cons cell whose **car** is **a**. Then to make the list circular, **(cdr marker)** points back to the cell whose **car** is **c**. To add an item **d** to this circular list, we cons **d** to **(cdr marker)** and then reset the **cdr** pointer of **marker** to point to the cons cell with **d** as its **car**. (See Figure 12.17b.) Thus inserting **d** into a nonempty circular list can be accomplished by invoking:

```
(set-cdr! marker (cons 'd (cdr marker)))
```

Similarly, to remove **d** from the resulting circular list, we note that **(cdr (cdr marker))** does not contain the item **d**, so we only have to write

```
(set-cdr! marker (cdr (cdr marker)))
```

to get back to the circular list in Figure 12.17a.

In general, we make an ordinary list circular by letting **marker** be a pointer to the end of the list. Then we set the cdr pointer of **marker** to point to the beginning of the list. The item to which the cdr pointer of **marker** points is referred to as the head of the circular list. As an object, a circular list responds to the following messages:

- **empty?**, which tests whether the circular list is empty.
- **insert!**, which adds an item to the circular list.

- **head**, which returns the head of the circular list, that is, the item that is just past the marker.
- **delete!**, which removes the head of the circular list.
- **move!**, which shifts the marker to point to the head of the circular list, thus making a new item the head.
- **size**, which returns the number of items in the circular list.
- **print**, which displays the circular list.

The code for **circular-list-maker** is given in Program 12.18. Initially, **marker** is locally defined to be the empty list, and when the method name **empty?** is received, it tests whether **marker** is the empty list. The message sent to insert an item into the circular list consists of two parts, the method name **insert!** and the item to be inserted. There are two cases to consider when inserting an item. If the list is empty, we first make a list consisting of the item to be inserted and then change **marker** to point to that list. Then we have to make the list circular, so we make the cdr pointer of **marker** point back to **marker** itself. We now have a circular list containing only the one item we inserted.

On the other hand, if the list is not empty, we use the fact that (**cdr marker**) points back to the head of the list when we cons the item to be inserted (that is, (**2nd msg**)) onto (**cdr marker**). Once we have added the new item to the head of the list, we reset the cdr pointer of **marker** to point to the cell containing the new item, which becomes the new head of the list. We use the word *head* in spite of the fact that a circular list does not have a head or a tail. However, we may think of the cdr pointer of the cons cell to which **marker** points as pointing back to the head of the list to make the list circular. And we may think of **marker** itself as pointing to the last cell in the list.

If the list is empty when a **delete!** message is received, an error is signaled. If the list contains only one item (that is, if (**cdr marker**) points back to **marker** itself), then **marker** is set equal to the empty list. Otherwise, we again refer to the "head" of the list as the cons cell to which (**cdr marker**) points. Then we reset the cdr pointer of **marker** to point to (**cdr (cdr marker)**).

When we found the size of such objects as stacks and queues, we used the procedure **length** on their internal list representations. This requires cdring down the list while counting. We have given a more efficient way of doing this by keeping the size in a gauge and incrementing or decrementing it appropriately when we insert or delete something from the circular list.

We have to be careful in writing the code for a circular list that we do not get into an infinite loop, going around the circle of pointers indefinitely.

Program 12.18 `circular-list-maker`

```
(define circular-list-maker
  (lambda ()
    (let ((marker '())
          (size-gauge (gauge-maker 0 add1 sub1)))
      (lambda msg
        (case (1st msg)
          ((type) "circular list")
          ((empty?) (null? marker))
          ((insert!) (send size-gauge 'up!)
                     (for-effect-only
                       (if (null? marker)
                           (begin
                             (set! marker (cons (2nd msg) '()))
                             (set-cdr! marker marker))
                           (set-cdr! marker (cons (2nd msg) (cdr marker))))))
          ((head) (if (null? marker)
                      (error "head: The list is empty.")
                      (car (cdr marker))))
          ((delete!) (for-effect-only
                       (if (null? marker)
                           (error "delete!: The circular list is empty.")
                           (begin
                             (send size-gauge 'down!)
                             (if (eq? marker (cdr marker))
                                 (set! marker '())
                                 (set-cdr! marker (cdr (cdr marker))))))))
          ((move!) (for-effect-only
                     (if (null? marker)
                         (error "move!: The circular list is empty.")
                         (set! marker (cdr marker)))))
          ((size) (send size-gauge 'show))
          ((print) (if (not (null? marker))
                       (let ((next (cdr marker)))
                         (set-cdr! marker '())
                         (for-each (lambda (x) (display x) (display " "))
                                   next)
                         (set-cdr! marker next)))
                   (newline))
          (else (delegate base-object msg)))))))
```

Program 12.19   stack-maker

```
(define stack-maker
  (lambda ()
    (let ((c (circular-list-maker)))
      (lambda msg
        (case (1st msg)
          ((type) "stack")
          ((push!) (send c 'insert! (2nd msg)))
          ((pop!) (send c 'delete!))
          ((top) (send c 'head))
          ((print) (display "TOP: ") (send c 'print))
          ((insert! head delete! move!) (delegate base-object msg))
          (else (delegate c msg)))))))
```

In order to avoid this in the case of **print**, we use the trick of temporarily resetting the cdr pointer of **marker** to point to the empty list. Then the list is no longer circular, and we can use **for-each** without fear of looping indefinitely.

We are now ready to look at the definitions of stack and queue making use of a circular list. In implementing the stack, a circular list is used and the marker stays fixed. When the stack receives a **push!** message, it sends it to the circular list as an **insert!** message. Similarly, the **pop!** message is sent to the circular list as a **delete!** message. When the **print** message is received by the stack, the word **TOP:** is first printed, and then the message is sent to the circular list. The stack messages **size** and **empty?** are delegated to the circular list. The code for **stack-maker** using a circular list is in Program 12.19.

The **queue-maker** is similarly defined in terms of a circular list, but this time, the marker is moved each time an item is inserted, so that it points to the cell containing the new item. Again, most of the queue operations are delegated to the circular list. The code for **queue-maker** making use of a circular list is given in Program 12.20.

This is an elegant way of implementing both the **stack-maker** and the **queue-maker**. They take advantage of delegation by passing messages on to the circular list. The circular list was flexible enough because we were able to move the **marker** to keep track of certain cells. Notice that we have gained in efficiency by making use of the internal gauge in the circular list to keep the size of the stacks or queues. The circular list is, in general, a useful data structure.

Program 12.20   `queue-maker`

```
(define queue-maker
  (lambda ()
    (let ((c (circular-list-maker)))
      (lambda msg
        (case (1st msg)
          ((type) "queue")
          ((enqueue!) (send c 'insert! (2nd msg)) (send c 'move!))
          ((dequeue!) (send c 'delete!))
          ((front) (send c 'head))
          ((print) (display "FRONT: ") (send c 'print))
          ((insert! head delete! move!) (delegate base-object msg))
          (else (delegate c msg)))))))
```

Exercises

Exercise 12.15

Redefine the `stack-maker` and `queue-maker` procedures presented in Programs 12.19 and 12.20 so that, instead of the illegal method names being disabled, the legal method names are enabled.

Exercise 12.16

Draw the box-and-pointer diagrams for a stack implemented using a circular list. Start with the empty stack, push on the items a, b, c, and d, and then pop these four items. Show the box and pointer diagrams for the successive stages as the stack increases and decreases in size.

Exercise 12.17

Make the same sequence of box and pointer diagrams as in the previous exercise but this time for a queue.

Exercise 12.18

Redefine `circular-list-maker` in Program 12.18 keeping a local variable that is initialized to zero to keep the size of the circular list without using a gauge. Then do it without any local variables.

Exercise 12.19

When building a circular list, it is not necessary to build a circular structure. Instead, the method names, which rely on the circular structure, must be redefined. For example, if before, the cdr of **marker** was a cell **c**, then using a simple list, it would be necessary to test (**null? (cdr marker)**) and then return **c**. This approach has a cost because there is an additional local variable to maintain, which requires setting and testing. However, the benefit is that no structures are built that can unintentionally enter infinite loops. Redefine **circular-list-maker** without actually using an explicit circular structure.

Exercise 12.20
Add a method **reverse** to the **circular-list-maker** that reverses the circular list in such a way that the cdr pointer of each cons cell is changed to point to the previous cell in the list instead of the next cell. The diagram in Figure 12.21 shows a circular list containing four items before and after reversing. As in the diagram, be sure your method moves the marker.

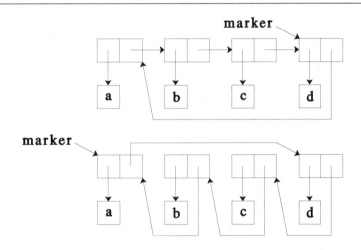

Figure 12.21   Reversing a circular list

12.6 Buckets and Hash Tables

In Chapter 11, we used a table to store the values computed by procedures by memoizing those procedures. The values were retrieved from the table by calling a procedure **lookup**. In this section, we construct objects that have the properties of tables. These objects are called *buckets*. We also present a second way of storing data using *hash tables*, which are vectors in which the entry for each index is a bucket. In this way, large amounts of data can be stored in relatively small vectors.

Buckets respond to two messages:

- **update!**, which adds (or alters) a bucket entry.
- **lookup**, which retrieves a bucket entry.

A *bucket* is a structure like a stack or queue whose internal representation can be thought of as a flat list. Unlike a stack or queue, the order in which things are entered into a bucket is unimportant, and a bucket can only get bigger. An entry in a bucket (much the same as in a table) consists of two parts: the *key* and its *associated value*. When we memoize the Fibonacci procedure, each table entry consists of the procedure's argument and the value of the procedure when called with that argument. In our bucket, the procedure's argument would be the key, and the value of the procedure for that argument would be the associated value.

When we update a bucket, if the key is present, then the value associated with the key is the argument to an updating procedure. The value returned by this invocation of the updating procedure determines the new value to be associated with this key. If the key is not present, then the new value to be associated with this key is determined by invoking an initializing procedure. The message **lookup** is like the procedure **lookup** introduced in the previous chapter for tables. In that use, we invoke (**lookup key table success fail**), and in the object-oriented view, we invoke (**send bucket 'lookup key success fail**). Thus if there is a value associated with **key**, that value is passed to **success**, and if **key** is not in the table, **fail** is invoked on zero arguments.

For **update!** messages there is some similarity with **lookup** because there are separate responses to the existence or nonexistence of the key in the table. The call structure for **update!** is (**send bucket 'update! key proc-if-present proc-if-absent**). Again a search of the bucket for the key occurs. If **key** exists with associated value, *val*, that value is replaced with the result of evaluating (**proc-if-present** *val*). If **key** does not exist, it is added with the associated value (**proc-if-absent key**). A typical session with a bucket is given as an example in Figure 12.22. Program 12.23 is an implementation of a **bucket-maker**.

Recall that we defined memoize in the previous chapter as a mechanism for improving the efficiency of any single-argument procedure **proc**. We can use the bucket mechanism to obtain another version of **memoize** (Program 12.24). The key will be the argument, n, and its associated value will be the value of (**proc n**).

```
[1]  (define b (bucket-maker))
[2]  (send b 'lookup 'a (lambda (x) x) (lambda () 'no))
no
[3]  (send b 'update! 'a (lambda (x) (add1 x)) (lambda (x) 0))
[4]  (send b 'lookup 'a (lambda (x) x) (lambda () 'no))
0
[5]  (send b 'update! 'a (lambda (x) (add1 x)) (lambda (x) 0))
[6]  (send b 'lookup 'a (lambda (x) x) (lambda () 'no))
1
[7]  (send b 'update! 'q (lambda (x) (+ 2 x)) (lambda (x) 1000))
[8]  (send b 'lookup 'q (lambda (x) x) (lambda () 'no))
1000
[9]  (send b 'update! 'q (lambda (x) (+ 2 x)) (lambda (x) 1000))
[10] (send b 'lookup 'q (lambda (x) x) (lambda () 'no))
1002
[11] (send b 'update! 'q
       (lambda (x)
         (send b 'lookup 'a (lambda (y) (- x y)) (lambda () 'no)))
       (lambda (y) 'no))
[12] (send b 'lookup 'q (lambda (x) x) (lambda () 'no))
1001
```

Figure 12.22   Using bucket operations

Exercise

Exercise 12.21
The two invocations of **send** in **memoize** can be simplified to one by adding
a new method name to **bucket-maker** (see Programs 12.23 and 12.24) that
combines the update and lookup into one operation and thus avoids one of the
two searches. Rewrite **bucket-maker** to run the definition of **memoize** below.

```
(define memoize
  (lambda (proc)
    (let ((bucket (bucket-maker)))
      (lambda (arg)
        (send bucket 'update!-lookup arg (lambda (val) val) proc)))))
```

Requiring no upper bound on the size of a bucket has its own cost. As
the bucket gets bigger, we discover that the search for updating and looking
information up in the bucket gets more and more expensive. Let us consider
another program that uses a bucket. Suppose we have a list of strings, like

Program 12.23 bucket-maker

```
(define bucket-maker
  (lambda ()
    (let ((table '()))
      (lambda msg
        (case (1st msg)
          ((type) "bucket")
          ((lookup)
           (let ((key (2nd msg)) (succ (3rd msg)) (fail (4th msg)))
             (lookup key table (lambda (pr) (succ (cdr pr))) fail)))
          ((update!)
           (for-effect-only
             (let ((key (2nd msg))
                   (updater (3rd msg))
                   (initializer (4th msg)))
               (lookup key table
                 (lambda (pr)
                   (set-cdr! pr (updater (cdr pr))))
                 (lambda ()
                   (let ((pr (cons key (initializer key))))
                     (set! table (cons pr table))))))))
          (else (delegate base-object msg)))))))
```

Program 12.24 memoize

```
(define memoize
  (lambda (proc)
    (let ((bucket (bucket-maker)))
      (lambda (arg)
        (send bucket 'update! arg (lambda (val) val) proc)
        (send bucket 'lookup arg
          (lambda (val) val) (lambda () #f))))))
```

the contents of a book. We would like to find the word count frequency of the articles *a*, *an*, and *the* and possibly some others. We could solve this as follows:

```
(define word-frequency
  (lambda (string-list)
    (let ((b (bucket-maker)))
      (for-each
        (lambda (s) (send b 'update! s add1 (lambda (s) 1)))
        string-list)
      b)))
```

This defines the procedure word-frequency, which, when passed a text (a list of strings), returns a bucket that has each of the different strings in the text as a key and the number of times that string appears in the text as its associated value. Now suppose that the variable string-list is bound to some text; for example, the text might start with ("four" "score" "and" "seven" "years" "ago" "our" "fathers" ...). By writing

```
(define word-frequency-bucket (word-frequency string-list))
```

we define a bucket, called word-frequency-bucket, that contains each of the different words in our text as keys and the frequency of that word as its associated value. To see how many times the three strings "a", "an", and "the" appear in the text, we write:

```
(map
  (lambda (s)
    (cons s (send word-frequency-bucket 'lookup s
            (lambda (v) v)
            (lambda () 0))))
  '("a" "an" "the"))
```

This returns a list of the form (("a" . 7) ("an" . 0) ("the" . 10)).

If we were maintaining a frequency count for a book with 1,000 different words, then the bucket would be a list of 1,000 items, and searching it would be expensive. We next show how to avoid this problem.

We have now seen two ways of handling the building of tables for such purposes as memoizing. The first method was to use lists or buckets, which has the disadvantage that when the table gets long, lookup becomes a costly operation. The other method was to use a large vector so that each entry can be stored with a unique index and can be accessed randomly. This has the disadvantage that the vector has a predetermined fixed length and can hold a limited number of entries. We are now ready to look at a surprisingly simple solution to avoid the long searches and to allow for an unlimited number of entries. We create a vector that holds one bucket per index. This way we can partition the pairs by placing individual keys and their associated values in a bucket as a function of what the key is.

A rather naive solution to the word frequency problem would be to associate a bucket with each letter. This would create 26 buckets, and if we were lucky, the average length of each bucket would be $1000/26$ (approximately 40). Then we could use the first or last letter of a string to determine which bucket to update. Of course, words in English being what they are, the z-bucket will not carry its load. The choice of function and the length of the vector vary with the nature of the data being stored. The function must take a key and replace it by some *nonnegative integer that can reference the vector*. This function is called a *hash function* because it hashes up the data and turns them into integers, which are then used to access the vector. The important point here is that we want the hash function to spread the data evenly in the buckets. For the Fibonacci numbers example, a reasonable hash function is the remainder with the size of the vector. Here is how to create hash tables.

Program 12.25   `hash-table-maker`

```
(define hash-table-maker
  (lambda (size hash-fn)
    (let ((v ((vector-generator (lambda (i) (bucket-maker))) size)))
      (lambda msg
        (case (1st msg)
          ((type) "hash table")
          (else
            (delegate (vector-ref v (hash-fn (2nd msg))) msg)))))))
```

An empty bucket is placed at each index of the vector, v. Then, using the key, an index is determined by applying the `hash-fn` to the key. The value at that index is a bucket that responds to the same messages as hash tables. By delegating to the bucket the original message, the same information is forwarded to the bucket. We now write the new definition of `memoize` using a hash table in Program 12.26. In order to write this new memoize we only need to supply arguments to `hash-table-maker`. Everything else remains unchanged. This version of `memoize` is restricted to numerical data since its associated hash function invokes remainder on its argument. The hash function can be as general as the problem for which it is being used demands.

Program 12.26 `memoize`

```
(define memoize
  (let ((hashf (lambda (x) (remainder x 1000))))
    (let ((h (hash-table-maker 1000 hashf)))
      (lambda (proc)
        (lambda (arg)
          (send h 'update! arg (lambda (v) v) proc)
          (send h 'lookup arg (lambda (v) v) (lambda () #f)))))))
```

Similarly we can rewrite `word-frequency` by including a hash table where we earlier had a bucket. For this, we need a way of converting the first letter of each string into an integer. The code that assigns to each keyboard character a unique integer (see Appendix A1) provides us with just the help we need. Scheme has a procedure `string-ref` that takes a string and an integer as arguments and returns the character in the string having that integer as its index. Scheme also has the procedure `char->integer`, which takes a character as its argument and returns the integer associated with that character. We shall study the character data type more fully in Chapter 15. We use these two procedures now to define the hash function for the procedure `word-frequency`:

```
(define word-frequency
  (let ((naive-hash-function
          (lambda (s)
            (remainder (char->integer (string-ref s 0)) 26))))
    (let ((h (hash-table-maker 26 naive-hash-function)))
      (lambda (string-list)
        (for-each
          (lambda (s) (send h 'update! s add1 (lambda (s) 1)))
          string-list)
        h))))
```

A popular hash function for strings is one that sums the `(char->integer (string-ref s i))` for i = 0 to `(sub1 (string-length s))` and finds the remainder with the length of the vector. The important aspect of the choice of hash function is that it must spread the data randomly into the buckets so that each bucket carries its load.

The advantage of hash tables is that when order is not important, a table can be stored in a vector so that retrieval and updating are far more efficient than in simple linear search. The disadvantage is that we rely on a hash function that cannot know in advance what the data will look like. To demonstrate this, consider the following definition of new-bucket-maker:

```
(define new-bucket-maker
  (lambda ()
    (hash-table-maker 1 (lambda (d) 0))))
```

This hash table is as inefficient as a bucket. We chose the vector too small, and we chose the hash function too naively. Of course, this would never be done. In practice, most systems discourage the user from worrying about the size of the hash table or the nature of the hash function.

Exercises

Exercise 12.22
Construct a list of strings from some paragraph in this section, and run word-frequency over that list. Determine how many of each of the articles *a*, *an*, and *the* were used.

Exercise 12.23
Using the list of strings from the previous exercise, introduce a hash function that uses a large prime number for the vector length and uses the *sum of integers corresponding to characters* hash function as described in this section.

Exercise 12.24
Include a message re-initialize! in the definition of bucket-maker and hash-table-maker. In both cases, this method returns the object to its initial state.

Exercise 12.25
Lists that can only grow can get expensive.

a. Include a remove! message in bucket-maker that removes the key and its associated value from a bucket. The operation guarantees that if b is a bucket, then the following expression is always false.

```
(begin
  (send b 'remove! key)
  (send b 'lookup key (lambda (v) #t) (lambda () #f)))
```

is always false.

b. Include a `remove!` message in `hash-table-maker` that removes the key
   and its associated value from the hash table. If b is a hash table, then the
   expression above is always false.

Exercise 12.26: `store!`

Define a procedure `store!` that takes a hash table (or bucket), a key, and a
value and is defined so that if b is a hash table (or bucket), then

```
(begin
  (store! b key value)
  (send b 'lookup key (lambda (v) (equal? value v)) (lambda () #f)))
```

is always true. Do this without adding any new messages to `hash-table-maker` (or `bucket-maker`).

Exercise 12.27

Include an `image` message in `bucket-maker` whose value is a list of the key-
value pairs. Design it so that in the event of a subsequent update to an existing
key, that update will not mutate the list previously returned by the `image`
message. If b is a bucket and `(send b 'lookup key number? (lambda ()
#f))` is true then

```
(let ((prs (send b 'image)))
  (send b 'update! key add1 (lambda (k) 0))
  (= (cdr (assoc key prs)) (cdr (assoc key (send b 'image)))))
```

is always false.

Exercise 12.28

Using the previous exercise, include an `image` message in `hash-table-maker`
whose value is a list of key-value pairs. Design it so that in the event of a
subsequent update to an existing key, that update will not mutate the list
previously returned by the image method. If b is a hash table and `(send
b 'lookup key number? (lambda () #f))` is true, then the equation of the
previous exercise holds. *Hint:* You may be tempted to use `append`, but here
is an example where if you defined `bucket-maker` correctly, you should be
able to use `append!`.

```
```

The next four problems are related. Work them in order and you will discover
an interesting generalization of delegation.

Exercise 12.29: `theater-maker`
Consider the definition of `theater-maker` below. When entering a theater,
there is usually a line to purchase tickets. Sometimes what is showing at the
theater attracts a massive audience. When that happens, the doors to the
theater may close while there is still a line to purchase tickets. By using a
gauge for modeling the flow of patrons into the loge and a ticket queue where
each patron waits, we can model these facets of a theater. What are the
advantages of using `delegate` in the else clause of `theater-maker`? What are
the disadvantages?

```
(define theater-maker
  (lambda (capacity)
    (let ((ticket-line (queue-maker))
          (vacancies (gauge-maker capacity add1 sub1)))
      (lambda msg
        (case (1st msg)
          ((type) "theater")
          ((enter!) (if (zero? (send vacancies 'show))
                        (display "doors closed")
                        (begin
                          (send ticket-line 'dequeue!)
                          (send vacancies 'down!))))
          ((leave!) (if (< (send vacancies 'show) capacity)
                        (send vacancies 'up!)
                        (error "leave!: The theater is empty.")))
          (else (delegate ticket-line msg)))))))
```

Exercise 12.30
In `theater-maker`, suppose we would like to know how many seats are vacant
for the next showing. We cannot find this out without introducing a message,
say `show`, in the definition of `theater-maker`. See the code below. Why must
we include the extra message?

```
(define theater-maker
  (lambda (capacity)
    (let ((ticket-line (queue-maker))
          (vacancies (gauge-maker capacity add1 sub1)))
      (lambda msg
        (case (1st msg)
          ((type) "theater")
```

```
((enter!) (if (zero? (send vacancies 'show))
               (display "doors closed")
               (begin
                 (send ticket-line 'dequeue!)
                 (send vacancies 'down!))))
((leave!) (if (< (send vacancies 'show) capacity)
               (send vacancies 'up!)
               (error "leave!: The theater is empty.")))
((show) (send vacancies 'show))
(else (delegate ticket-line msg)))))))
```

We have two active objects: ticket-line and vacancies. The default
line has (delegate ticket-line msg). This means that we do not have
(delegate vacancies msg). We are only allowing one default. With *double
delegation*, we can have two defaults. If the message is not applicable to the
first default, it tries the second. So far, we have only seen objects with single
delegation. In this exercise, we build objects with *multiple delegation*.

We introduce a binary function, combine, that, like compose, takes two
procedures (in this case, objects) as parameters and returns a procedure as a
value.

Program 12.27   combine

```
(define combine
  (lambda (f g)
    (lambda msg
      (let ((f-try (delegate f msg)))
        (if (eq? invalid-method-name-indicator f-try)
            (delegate g msg)
            f-try)))))
```

The returned procedure will delegate a message, in order, to the two objects
until it finds one that does not return invalid-method-name-indicator. If
f is not such an object, it invokes g. The procedure combine takes only two
arguments. Rewrite combine to take two or more arguments. Below we have
changed theater-maker to use combine so that the vacancies messages will
be delegated too. The result will be multiple delegation, which will delegate
show messages without the additional line in theater-maker.

```
(define theater-maker
  (lambda (capacity)
    (let ((ticket-line (queue-maker))
          (vacancies (gauge-maker capacity add1 sub1)))
      (lambda msg
        (case (1st msg)
          ((type) "theater")
          ((enter!) (if (zero? (send vacancies 'show))
                        (display "doors closed")
                        (begin
                          (send ticket-line 'dequeue!)
                          (send vacancies 'down!))))
          ((leave!) (if (< (send vacancies 'show) capacity)
                        (send vacancies 'up!)
                        (error "leave! The theater is empty.")))
          (else (delegate (combine ticket-line vacancies) msg)))))))
```

Exercise 12.31

The multiple delegation used with combine in the previous exercise is sometimes dangerous because method names are symbols. What would happen
if show were used instead of front as the message for looking at the first
element in a queue? Consider both expressions:

```
(delegate (combine ticket-line vacancies) msg)
```

and

```
(delegate (combine vacancies ticket-line) msg)
```

Exercise 12.32

In the interests of security, we would like to disable some operations from
delegation. For example, we would like to keep anyone from resetting the
gauge. This would correspond to yelling "fire," clearing the loge before the
showing, and then allowing just the current contents of the ticket line to enter
the loge. That would not be fair. The patrons who were already in the
loge would have paid without receiving any entertainment. Or perhaps an
update! message might be sent so that everyone might think the loge was
full. Such skullduggery is possible with the current configuration of theater-
maker. However, if we form a list of those "unfriendly" messages and disable
them, we can keep these theaters from allowing such nefarious acts. Below is
a partial solution where we have disabled reset! and update!. Rewrite the
definition of theater-maker below to include all of the messages that should
be disabled:

```
(define theater-maker
  (lambda (capacity)
    (let ((ticket-line (queue-maker))
          (vacancies (gauge-maker capacity add1 sub1)))
      (lambda msg
        (case (1st msg)
          ((type) "theater")
          ((enter!) (if (zero? (send vacancies 'show))
                        (display "doors closed")
                        (begin
                          (send ticket-line 'dequeue!)
                          (send vacancies 'down!))))
          ((leave!) (if (< (send vacancies 'show) capacity)
                        (send vacancies 'up!)
                        (error "leave!: The theater is empty.")))
          ((reset! update!) (delegate base-object msg))
          (else (delegate (combine ticket-line vacancies) msg)))))))
```

The next six problems are related. Work them in order, and you will discover some interesting generalizations of objects as we have defined them in this chapter.

Exercise 12.33
Consider a new definition of send.

Program 12.28   send

```
(define send
  (lambda args
    (let ((try (apply (car args) args)))
      (if (eq? invalid-method-name-indicator try)
          (let ((object (car args)) (message (cdr args)))
            (error "Bad method name:" (car message)
                   "sent to object of"
                   (object object 'type)
                   "type."))
          try))))
```

According to this definition, uses of send are the same as before, but each message includes the receiver of the message as the first element of the message. Here is an example that uses this send to build counter-maker:

```
(define counter-maker
  (lambda (init-value unary-proc)
    (let ((total (box-maker init-value)))
      (lambda message
        (let ((self (car message)) (msg (cdr message)))
          (case (1st msg)
            ((type) "counter")
            ((update!) (let ((result (unary-proc (send total 'show))))
                         (send total 'update! result)))
            ((swap!) (delegate base-object message))
            (else (delegate total message)))))))))
```

The variable **message** contains the receiver as its car and the original **msg** as its cdr. When we delegate, we use the whole **message**. Rewrite **box-maker** so that this definition of **counter-maker** works. Be sure to redefine **base-object**.

Exercise 12.34

Below is the definition of **cartesian-point-maker**:

```
(define cartesian-point-maker
  (lambda (x-coord y-coord)
    (lambda message
      (let ((self (car message)) (msg (cdr message)))
        (case (1st msg)
          ((type) "Cartesian point")
          ((distance) (sqrt (+ (square x-coord) (square y-coord))))
          ((closer?) (< (send self 'distance) (send (2nd msg) 'distance)))
          (else (delegate base-object message)))))))
```

Fill in the gaps in the experiment below:

```
[1] (define cp1 (cartesian-point-maker 3.0 4.0))
[2] (send cp1 'distance)
?_____
[3] (define cp2 (cartesian-point-maker 1.0 6.0))
[4] (send cp2 'distance)
?_____
[5] (send cp1 'closer? cp2)
?_____
[6] (send cp2 'closer? cp1)
?_____
```

Exercise 12.35

Using the definitions of the previous exercise, we add a new kind of point. In the Cartesian point, we found the distance to the origin as a straight line. In this definition, we determine the distance as the sum of two straight lines: the distance to the x-axis and the distance to the y-axis. This type of point is called a Manhattan point because it is reminiscent of distances traveled in cities. Below is the definition of `manhattan-point-maker`:

```
(define manhattan-point-maker
  (lambda (x-coord y-coord)
    (let ((p (cartesian-point-maker x-coord y-coord)))
      (lambda message
        (let ((self (car message)) (msg (cdr message)))
          (case (1st msg)
            ((type) "Manhattan point")
            ((distance) (+ x-coord y-coord))
            (else (delegate p message)))))))))
```

With this definition, we have refined `cartesian-point-maker` by determining the distance differently. The determination of which of two points is closer to the origin stays the same, but if the point is a Manhattan point, it determines its distance to the origin by summing instead of finding the square root of the sum of squares. Fill in the gaps in the experiment below:

```
[7] (define mp1 (manhattan-point-maker 6.0 1.0))
[8] (send mp1 'distance)
?_____
[9] (send cp2 'closer? mp1)
?_____
[10] (send mp1 'closer? cp2)
?_____
```

Exercise 12.36

Suppose that we always create points at the origin (0,0). Then we could add a method name `moveto!` that would take an x-coordinate and a y-coordinate as arguments. In addition, we want a list of the two current coordinates. Add the method names `current-coordinates` and `moveto!` to the definition of `cartesian-origin-maker` below. We have left the type as `"Cartesian point"` because it still is a point as one would find in the plane.

```
(define cartesian-origin-maker
  (lambda ()
    (let ((x-coord 0) (y-coord 0))
      (lambda message
        (let ((self (car message)) (msg (cdr message)))
          (case (car msg)
            ((type) "Cartesian point")
            ((distance) (sqrt (+ (square x-coord) (square y-coord))))
            ((closer?) (< (send self 'distance) (send (2nd msg) 'distance)))
            (else (delegate base-object message))))))))
```

Exercise 12.37

Using the definition of your solution to `cartesian-origin-maker` from the previous exercise, fill in the gaps in the experiment below.

```
[1] (define cp1 (cartesian-origin-maker))
[2] (send cp1 'distance)
?_____
[3] (send cp1 'current-coordinates)
?_____
[4] (send cp1 'moveto! 6.0 1.0)
?_____
[5] (send cp1 'distance)
?_____
[6] (send cp1 'current-coordinates)
?_____
```

Exercise 12.38

Fill in the rest of the definition of `manhattan-origin-maker` below, but do *not* use p. Test `closer?` on a Manhattan point and a Cartesian point that have both been moved to (6.0,1.0).

```
(define manhattan-origin-maker
  (lambda ()
    (let ((p (cartesian-origin-maker)))
      (lambda message
        (let ((self (car message)) (msg (cdr message)))
          (case (1st msg)
            ((type) "Manhattan point")
            ((distance) ?_____  )
            (else (delegate p message))))))))
```

13 Simulation: Objects in Action

13.1 Overview

One of the many uses of computers is in *simulation*, that is, in the modeling of real-world phenomena with the computer to study how varying the conditions (parameters) affects the behavior of the system. We generally select characteristics of the system to be modeled and define objects and actions that enable a computer program to mimic the real world. If the real-world behavior is adequately described in the computer program, the results of the program should predict what happens in the real-world situation. In many instances, the actual system we are studying is unwieldy and does not lend itself to experimentation. By using computer simulation, we can see the effects of parameter changes without tinkering with the actual system. Simulation is extensively used in decision making in government, business, and industry. We shall illustrate the use of object-oriented programming in a simulation of a gasoline station. We have selected this example because we can build a fairly realistic model for it with relatively few parameters. It also gives us an opportunity to use a number of the data structures introduced in Chapter 12, such as queues, boxes, counters, and accumulators.

13.2 Randomness

Simulation problems often deal with phenomena that involve uncertainty. A number of the variables that we use will have values that are generated randomly. We already used such randomly generated values when we generated lists of numbers to be sorted in Chapter 10. We say that simulations that make use of randomness to approximate the values of certain variables are using *Monte Carlo methods*. For our gas station simulation, we describe three different random number generators: uniform, exponential, and normal.

In our gas station simulation, the customers have a choice of full service or self-service. We estimate the percentage of the customers that choose self-service, say, 75%, so that 25% select full service. Then when a customer arrives, we must decide whether he wants self or full service. For lack of better information, we could toss two coins, and if both come up heads, we assume that he wants full service. We accomplish this coin-tossing ploy in the computer by generating a number that is equally likely to assume any integer value from 0 through 99. If that number is less than 75, we assume the customer wants self-service. The number that takes values in the range from 0 through 99 and is equally likely to assume any such value is an example of a uniformly distributed random variable. In general, a variable whose value is determined by chance (tossing a coin or a simulation of such an act) is called a *random variable*. If the values it takes on are all in some fixed interval and any value in that interval is equally likely to be assumed, we say the random variable has a *uniform distribution*. The procedure **random**, introduced in Chapter 10, generates a uniformly distributed "random" variable with a nonnegative integer value less than n when (**random** n) is called. To generate a decimal number between 0 and 1, excluding 0 but including 1, we can use the procedure **unif-rand-var-0-1** in Program 13.1.

Program 13.1   unif-rand-var-0-1

```
(define unif-rand-var-0-1
  (let ((big 1000000))
    (lambda ()
      (/ (+ 1 (random big)) big))))
```

In an actual gas station, we cannot always tell exactly when the next customer will arrive. The variable that tells us when the customers arrive is also a random variable. It is shown in probability theory that the time between the successive arrival of customers is a random variable with an *exponential distribution*.[1]   (See Program 13.2.) That is, the time between the arrival of successive customers can be taken to be $a \log \frac{1}{u}$ where a is the average time

---

[1] See, for example, Feller 1950, p. 218.

between arrivals and u is a uniformly distributed random number with values between 0 and 1, not including 0. We omitted the value 0 to be able to take the logarithm of the random number. We can then define a procedure called `arrival-time-generator`, which randomly generates the arrival time of the next customer, using the parameter `av-arr-time`, which is set when the program is initialized, and rounding the resulting time to be an integer with 1 minute as its smallest value.

Program 13.2 `exponential-random-variable`

```
(define exponential-random-variable
  (lambda (mean)
    (* mean (- (log (unif-rand-var-0-1))))))
```

Program 13.3 `arrival-time-generator`

```
(define arrival-time-generator
  (lambda (av-arr-time)
    (+ 1 (round (exponential-random-variable (- av-arr-time 1))))))
```

The number of gallons of gasoline that a customer buys is also a random variable. It seems reasonable to assume that the number of gallons of gasoline that a customer buys will cluster around some average value. Very few buy 1 or 2 gallons and very few buy large quantities above 25 gallons. It might be appropriate for us to assume that the average number of gallons that a customer buys is 12 gallons and that most buy between 8 and 16 gallons. This leads us to assume that if we draw a graph showing the number of gallons bought on the horizontal axis and the number of people who bought that many gallons on the vertical axis, we would get the well-known bell-shaped curve known as the *normal distribution*. This distribution has the property that its highest probability is at the mean (or average) value m, which we shall take as 12 gallons. There is also the standard deviation s, a number that indicates the fatness of the bell-shaped curve. About two-thirds of the purchases fall in an interval, which extends a distance s on each side of the mean m. In our case, we shall take the standard deviation to be 4 gallons, so that about two-thirds of the customers purchase between 8 and 16 gallons.

We have seen how to get a uniformly distributed pseudo-random variable between 0 and 1. Let us call this uniformly distributed random variable u, and let us generate 12 such random numbers: $u_1, u_2, \ldots, u_{12}$. We can then simulate a normally distributed random variable v with mean m and standard deviation s by using the formula[2]

$$m + s \sum_{i=1}^{12} (u_i - .5)$$

The Greek letter sigma, $\sum$, indicates that we form the sum of terms of the form $(u_i - .5)$ for the index i going from 1 to 12. Program 13.4 generates the normally distributed random variable. Program 13.5 generates the number of gallons of gasoline purchased.

Program 13.4   `normal-random-variable`

```
(define normal-random-variable
  (lambda (mean std-dev)
    (letrec ((compute (lambda (i)
                        (if (zero? i)
                            0
                            (+ (- (unif-rand-var-0-1) .5)
                               (compute (sub1 i)))))))
      (+ mean (* std-dev (compute 12))))))
```

Program 13.5   `gallons-generator`

```
(define gallons-generator
  (lambda ()
    (max 1 (round (normal-random-variable 12 4)))))
```

---

[2] We always use 12 uniform random variables to generate a normal random variable because it can be shown that the mean of *any* uniform random variables u on the interval 0 to 1 is .5, and its standard deviation is $1/\sqrt{12}$. By adding 12 independent uniform random variables, we get an approximation to a normal random variable with mean .5 and standard deviation 1. We subtract .5 in each term to get the mean to be 0 and multiply the resulting sum by s to get a standard deviation of s and add m to get a mean of m.

Exercises

Exercise 13.1
In the game of *odds and evens*, two coins are tossed. If the result of a toss is one head and one tail, we call it *odds*. Otherwise, we call it *evens*. Write a program to simulate this game for 1000 tosses and determine the number of *odds* and *evens* that occur.

Exercise 13.2
While riding in a car with a friend, he proposes a wager that involves keeping track of the last two digits of the license plates of passing cars. He bets you $10 that within the next twenty cars that pass, at least two passing cars will have the same two-digit number as the last two digits in their license plates. This may be any number from 00 to 99. Develop a program to simulate this game to determine whether you should take the bet. Perform the simulation 100 times and determine the amount of money you would have won or lost.

Exercise 13.3
The random number generator implemented in most computers generates what are known as pseudorandom numbers rather than true random numbers. Footnote 1 in Section 10.2.5 describes an algorithm for such a pseudorandom number generator. Here is a Scheme implementation of that algorithm:

```
(define random-maker
  (lambda (m a seed)
    (lambda (n)
      (let ((u (/ seed m)))
        (set! seed (modulo (* a seed) m))
        (floor (* n u)))))))


(define random-time (lambda () 1000))

(define random
  (random-maker (- (expt 2 31) 1) (expt 7 5) (random-time)))
```

If your implementation of Scheme has a procedure that gives you the time of day, it should be used instead of `random-time`. If not, our naive definition will suffice. Consider these two ways to test a random number generator.

a. Divide the range from 0 to 99 into k equal parts. Generate n random numbers in that range and count how many fall into each part. The fraction of those that fall in each part should be approximately the same and equal to $\frac{n}{k}$.

b. Count the number of upward runs (that is, sequential runs of random numbers in ascending order) of length k and the number of downward runs (that is, sequential runs of random numbers in descending order) of length k when a large number of random numbers is generated. For each value of k, the counts should be approximately the same.

Implement these two tests in Scheme, and run them using the random number generator defined above. If your implementation of Scheme has a random number generator, test it too. Interpret the results.

13.3 The Gas Station Simulation

Our simulation concerns a gasoline station that has two lanes leading to self-service pumps and two lanes leading to full-service pumps. This is not an uncommon configuration in small stations. To run the simulation, we specify the following initialization parameters:

- `close-time`: The closing time in hours assuming that the station opens when the clock reads 0 hours.
- `%-self-service`: The percentage of the customers who choose self-service.
- `av-arr-time`: The average time interval in minutes that passes between the arrival of customers. The customers arrive at random times, but the average time between arrivals is what is estimated here.
- `profit-self`: The profit that the station owner makes on each gallon of self-service gas sold.
- `profit-full`: The profit that the station owner makes on each gallon of full-service gas sold.
- `extra-time@self-pump`: The average time spent at the self-service pump in excess of the time actually pumping the gas (e.g., cleaning windows, paying for purchase, etc.).
- `extra-time@full-pump`: The average time spent at the full-service pump in excess of the time actually pumping gas (e.g., waiting for service, paying for purchase, etc.).
- `pump-rate`: The number of gallons of gasoline per minute that the pumps deliver.

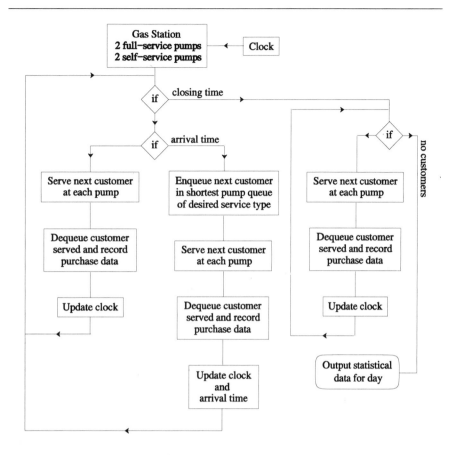

Figure 13.6   Flowchart for the gas station simulation

Figure 13.6 shows a *flowchart* or diagram of the gas station simulation. The box on the top shows the gas station with four pumps. Moving downward, we pass through various diamond-shaped boxes, which correspond to conditionals or branches. Each branch follows a customer through the wait in the pump queue until he or she is served and is dequeued and the purchase is recorded. At closing time, those customers still in line are served but no new ones are admitted. When all are served, the statistical data for the day are printed out.

To implement this gas station simulation, we use several types of objects, each made by an object maker. Figure 13.7 shows the various objects and the method names to which they respond. It also shows the lines of com-

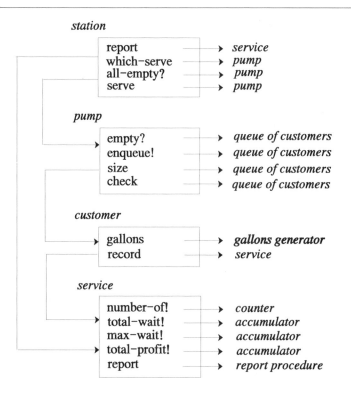

station

report	→	service
which–serve	→	pump
all–empty?	→	pump
serve	→	pump

pump

empty?	→	queue of customers
enqueue!	→	queue of customers
size	→	queue of customers
check	→	queue of customers

customer

| gallons | → | **gallons generator** |
| record | → | service |

service

number-of!	→	counter
total–wait!	→	accumulator
max–wait!	→	accumulator
total–profit!	→	accumulator
report	→	report procedure

Figure 13.7   Objects and messages used in the simulation

munication between the objects, that is, the objects that send messages to other objects. The gas station itself is an object named station created by station-maker (see Program 13.10). The object station responds, in ways that will be described later, to four messages: report, which-serve, all-empty?, and serve. Each pump in the gas station is an object created by the procedure pump-maker (see Program 13.11). The pump object, which manages its queue of customers who are waiting for service, responds to the four messages: empty?, (referring to its queue of customers), enqueue!, size, and check. The customers are objects created by the procedure customer-maker (see Program 13.12). Each customer responds to the messages: gallons and record. We also use objects created by the procedure service-maker (see Program 13.13). These objects, which are associated with each customer, know the type of service (self or full) and the profit per gallon and use that information to store information about the customer's purchase.

We use several other objects that are created by object makers defined in Chapter 12. For example, the object `clock`, which keeps time in minutes, is a counter that has initial value zero and update procedure `add1`. The object `arrival` is a box that stores the arrival time of the next customer. Each pump has a queue denoted by `q` and made by `queue-maker` in Chapter 12. The total amount of time a customer spends at the pump is kept by a box object called `timer`. Finally, for each type of service (self and full), we keep a record of the following four items: (1) A tally is kept of the total number of customers in a counter object called `number-of`. (2) The total waiting time for all customers is kept in an accumulator object called `total-wait`. (3) The maximum waiting time for all customers is kept in an accumulator object called `max-wait`. (4) The total profit is kept in an accumulator object called `total-profit`.

The values of the eight initialization parameters are passed to the procedure `simulation-setup&run`, defined in Program 13.8, which starts the simulation by invoking the procedure `simulation` with four arguments. The first operand passed to `simulation` invokes `station-maker`, which itself takes six arguments. The second and third operands passed to `station-maker` are the two services that set up the mechanism for recording the data we want to collect in our simulation. The rest of the code is clarified when we look at the definitions of the object makers given below. The second operand passed to `simulation` creates the `clock`.

The management of the gas station simulation is done by the procedure `simulation` that is invoked by `simulation-setup&run`. We see the progress of the customer through the station illustrated in the flowchart of Figure 13.6 reflected in the code for the procedure `simulation`, given in Program 13.9.

The value bound to the parameter `station` in the procedure `simulation` is an object created by the procedure `station-maker`, for which the code is given in Program 13.10. Looking at the code for `simulation`, we see that the box `arrival` stores the sum of the current clock time plus the time increment until the next customer arrives, which is generated by the `arrival-time-generator`. We enter `loop` and assume that it is not yet closing time and that it is the arrival time of the next customer. Then the `station` is passed the two-part message in which the first part is `which-serve` and the second part is a customer, created by invoking the procedure `customer-maker` (Program 13.12) with the two arguments, the arrival time stored in `arrival` and `clock`. From `station-maker` in Program 13.10, we see that the customer so created is enqueued to the pump with the shortest queue that gives the desired kind of service (full or self).

Next, `station` is sent the message `serve`. This causes each of the four

Program 13.8   `simulation-setup&run`

```
(define simulation-setup&run
  (lambda (close-time %-self-service av-arr-time
            profit-self profit-full
            extra-time@self-pump extra-time@full-pump pump-rate)
    (let ((self-service (service-maker "Self" profit-self))
          (full-service (service-maker "Full" profit-full)))
      (simulation
        (station-maker
          %-self-service
          self-service
          full-service
          extra-time@self-pump
          extra-time@full-pump
          pump-rate)
        (counter-maker 0 add1)
        av-arr-time
        (* 60 close-time)))))
```

pumps to check its queues. Looking at the code for `pump-maker`, we see that when `pump` is passed the message `check` and the queue q associated with that pump is not empty, the pump refers to its timer. Whenever a customer is finished and dequeued, the timer is reset to −1. Thus if the timer is found to store the value −1 when the message `check` is received, it updates the timer to store the total time the customer at the front of the queue spends at the pump. This total time includes both the actual pumping time and the average extra time at the pump (one of the initial parameters). From then on, each time `pump` receives the message `check`, the number stored in `timer` is reduced by one, until the value stored is zero. When that happens and `pump` is passed the message `check`, the customer has completed what had to be done at the pump, and that customer is dequeued.

The dequeued `customer` is then passed a two-part message. The first part is the method name `record`, and the second part is the variable `service`, which is bound to an object that is either `full-serv` or `self-serv` created by `service-maker` (Program 13.13) and passed into `pump-maker` when the object `pump` was created. The `service` stores in itself the kind of service (full or self) at that pump and the profit per gallon at that pump, and it keeps the following statistics:

1. a tally of the number of customers using that kind of service,

Program 13.9 simulation

```
(define simulation
  (lambda (station clock av-arr-time close-time)
    (let ((arrival
            (box-maker (+ (send clock 'show)
                          (arrival-time-generator av-arr-time)))))
      (letrec
        ((loop
           (lambda ()
             (if (= (send clock 'show) close-time)
                 (prepare-for-closing)
                 (begin
                   (if (= (send clock 'show) (send arrival 'show))
                       (begin
                         (send station 'which-serve
                           (customer-maker (send arrival 'show) clock))
                         (send station 'serve)
                         (send arrival 'update!
                           (+ (send clock 'show)
                              (arrival-time-generator av-arr-time)))
                         (send clock 'update!))
                       (begin
                         (send station 'serve)
                         (send clock 'update!)))
                   (loop)))))
         (prepare-for-closing
           (lambda ()
             (if (send station 'all-empty?)
                 (send station 'report)
                 (begin
                   (send station 'serve)
                   (send clock 'update!)
                   (prepare-for-closing))))))
        (loop)))))
```

2. the total waiting time of all customers who have passed through the queues for that kind of service,

3. the maximum waiting time for all such customers, and

4. the total profit so far at the pump for that kind of service.

```
(define station-maker
  (let ((check (lambda (p) (send p 'check)))
        (all-empty? (andmap-c (lambda (p) (send p 'empty?))))
        (shorter (lambda (p1 p2)
                    (if (< (send p1 'size) (send p2 'size)) p1 p2))))
    (lambda (%-self self-serv full-serv extra-time-self extra-time-full pump-rate)
      (let ((selfs (list (pump-maker extra-time-self pump-rate self-serv)
                         (pump-maker extra-time-self pump-rate self-serv)))
            (fulls (list (pump-maker extra-time-full pump-rate full-serv)
                         (pump-maker extra-time-full pump-rate full-serv))))
        (lambda msg
          (case (1st msg)
            ((type) "station")
            ((report) (send self-serv 'report) (send full-serv 'report))
            ((which-serve)
             (let ((pump (apply shorter (if (< (random 100) %-self)
                                            selfs
                                            fulls))))
               (send pump 'enqueue! (2nd msg))))
            ((all-empty?) (and (all-empty? selfs) (all-empty? fulls)))
            ((serve) (for-each check selfs) (for-each check fulls))
            (else (delegate base-object msg))))))))
```

When customer receives the method name record and the service object,
we see in the code for customer-maker in Program 13.12 that each of the
above statistics is updated with the information for the dequeued customer.
Then if the pump's queue is empty, its timer is reset to −1; otherwise it is
updated to show the total time at the pump for the customer who is now at
the front of the queue.

Returning again to the code for simulation, we have completed (send
station 'serve), so clock is updated and arrival is updated to show when
the next customer will arrive. When it is not the arrival time for a new
customer, we only pass the message serve to station and then update clock.

When clock shows that it is closing time, we enter the loop prepare-for-
closing. If at least one of the queues is not empty, those customers in the
queues are served as above, but no new customers are enqueued. Finally,
when all queues are empty, the message report is passed to station. In

Program 13.11   `pump-maker`

```
(define pump-maker
  (lambda (extra-time pump-rate service)
    (let ((q (queue-maker)))
      (let ((increment (lambda ()
                         (let ((gallons (send (send q 'front) 'gallons)))
                           (ceiling (+ extra-time (/ gallons pump-rate))))))
            (timer (box-maker -1)))
        (lambda msg
          (case (1st msg)
            ((type) "pump")
            ((check) (if (not (send q 'empty?))
                         (let ((c (send timer 'show)))
                           (cond
                             ((negative? c) (send timer 'update! (increment)))
                             ((zero? c) (let ((customer (send q 'front)))
                                          (send q 'dequeue!)
                                          (send customer 'record service)
                                          (if (send q 'empty?)
                                              (send timer 'reset!)
                                              (send timer 'update! (increment)))))
                             (else (send timer 'update!
                                         (sub1 (send timer 'show)))))))
            (else (delegate q msg))))))))
```

the code for `station-maker` (Program 13.10), we see that the message `report` is sent to both objects `self-serve` and `full-serv`. In `service-maker` (Program 13.13), the procedure `report` is invoked with the final values of the statistics stored when each customer was dequeued. The procedure `report`, defined in Program 13.14, displays this information. We shall run the simulation for various parameters and see how this information is displayed.

We have taken a quick walk through the gas station simulation to illustrate the use of objects in a somewhat longer program than others we have been studying. The program contains many interesting and subtle features that are worth studying in detail until they are fully understood. The time spent in coming to grips with each of the steps will contribute much to your development as a programmer.

Let us now run the simulation. We call `simulation-setup&run` with the following parameters:

Program 13.12 `customer-maker`

```
(define customer-maker
  (lambda (arrival-time clock)
    (let ((gallons-pumped (gallons-generator)))
      (lambda msg
        (case (1st msg)
          ((type) "customer")
          ((gallons) gallons-pumped)
          ((record) (let ((service (2nd msg))
                          (wait (- (send clock 'show) arrival-time)))
                      (send service 'number-of!)
                      (send service 'total-wait! wait)
                      (send service 'max-wait! wait)
                      (send service 'total-profit! gallons-pumped)))
          (else (delegate base-object msg)))))))
```

> close-time: 12 hours
> %-self-service: 75%
> av-arr-time: 4 min.
> profit-self: $0.10 per gallon
> profit-full: $0.10 per gallon
> extra-time@self-pump: 5 min.
> extra-time@full-pump: 8 min.
> pump-rate: 4 gallons per min.

We then have:

```
[1] (simulation-setup&run 12 75 4 .1 .1 5 8 4)
Self-Service:
   The number of customers is 111
   The average wait is 11
   The maximum wait is 20
   The total profit is 127.3
Full-Service:
   The number of customers is 37
   The average wait is 13
   The maximum wait is 21
   The total profit is 46.8
```

The program for our simulation does produce the information we want, but it does not have a user-friendly interface in the sense that the user must know what the parameters are and the order in which to put them when the

Program 13.13   service-maker

```
(define service-maker
  (lambda (full-or-self profit)
    (let ((number-of (counter-maker 0 add1))
          (total-wait (accumulator-maker 0 +))
          (max-wait (accumulator-maker 0 max))
          (total-profit (accumulator-maker 0 +)))
      (lambda msg
        (case (1st msg)
          ((type) "service")
          ((number-of!) (send number-of 'update!))
          ((total-wait!) (send total-wait 'update! (2nd msg)))
          ((max-wait!) (send max-wait 'update! (2nd msg)))
          ((total-profit!)
           (send total-profit 'update! (* profit (2nd msg))))
          ((report) (for-effect-only
                      (report full-or-self
                              (send number-of 'show)
                              (send total-wait 'show)
                              (send max-wait 'show)
                              (send total-profit 'show))))
          (else (delegate base-object msg)))))))
```

Program 13.14   report

```
(define report
  (lambda (full-or-self num-cust total-wait max-wait profit)
    (if (zero? num-cust)
        (writeln "   There were no " full-or-self "-Service customers.")
        (begin
          (writeln full-or-self "-Service:")
          (writeln "   The number of customers is " num-cust)
          (writeln "   The average wait is " (round (/ total-wait num-cust)))
          (writeln "   The maximum wait is " max-wait)
          (writeln "   The total profit is " profit)))))
```

procedure **simulation-setup&run** is called. There are so many parameters that it is hard to remember their order. Thus we design an interface to

Program 13.15   prompt-read

```
(define prompt-read
  (lambda (prompt)
    (display prompt)
    (display " ")
    (read)))
```

the program that will prompt the reader for the information needed to run the simulation. For that purpose, we use the procedure **prompt-read**, which prints its argument (the prompt) to the screen and waits for a response to be read from the keyboard. It then returns that response. The code for **prompt-read** is in Program 13.15. An example illustrating the use of **prompt-read** is

```
[2] (let ((hours
             (prompt-read
               "Enter the number of hours the station is open:")))
      (writeln "The station is open " hours " hours."))
Enter the number of hours the station is open: 12
The station is open 12 hours.
```

We build our user-friendly interface by first constructing a list of all of the prompts that we want to display. We name this list **station-prompts**:

```
(define station-prompts
  '("Enter the number of hours the station is open:"
    "Enter the percentage of self-service customers:"
    "Enter the average time in minutes between arrivals:"
    "Enter the profit per gallon from self-service customers:"
    "Enter the profit per gallon from full-service customers:"
    "Enter the extra time at the pump for self-service customers:"
    "Enter the extra time at the pump for full-service customers:"
    "Enter the delivery rate of the pumps in gallons per minute:"))
```

We next write a program, **gas-station-simulator**, with a loop in it that applies **prompt-read** to each prompt in the list and builds a list of the responses in the order in which they are entered. It then applies **simulation-setup&run** to the arguments in that list using the procedure **apply**. The code for **gas-station-simulator** is presented in Program 13.16

Simulation: Objects in Action

Program 13.16   gas-station-simulator

```scheme
(define gas-station-simulator
  (letrec
    ((loop (lambda (ls)
             (if (null? ls)
                 '()
                 (let ((v (prompt-read (car ls))))
                   (cons v (loop (cdr ls)))))))
     (lambda ()
       (apply simulation-setup&run (loop station-prompts)))))
```

```
[3] (gas-station-simulator)
Enter the number of hours the station is open: 12
Enter the percentage of self-service customers: 75
Enter the average time in minutes between arrivals: 4
Enter the profit per gallon from self-service customers: .10
Enter the profit per gallon from full-service customers: .10
Enter the extra time at the pump for self-service customers: 2
Enter the extra time at the pump for full-service customers: 4
Enter the delivery rate of the pumps in gallons per minute: 4
Self-Service:
    The number of customers is 110
    The average wait is 6
    The maximum wait is 12
    The total profit is 120.70
Full-Service:
    The number of customers is 35
    The average wait is 8
    The maximum wait is 10
    The total profit is 44.40
```

Figure 13.17   The simulation input and output

The result of invoking **gas-station-simulator** is given in Figure 13.17. The experiment records the data entered in a clearly readable form, as well as the output of the simulation.

We can now use this simulation to see what happens when certain parameters are changed. For example, if we keep all of the parameters fixed except the average arrival time, we can see what happens when the time between arrivals decreases. We kept the station open 12 hours, 75% of the customers selected

Average Arrival Time:	8	4	3	2	1
Self-Service:					
The number of customers is	60	110	131	192	274
The average wait is	6	6	7	9	84
The maximum wait is	9	12	14	20	169
The total profit is	70.00	123.10	160.40	232.20	334.90
Full-Service:					
The number of customers is	22	35	40	53	86
The average wait is	9	9	8	9	9
The maximum wait is	11	11	12	17	18
The total profit is	28.10	44.40	45.70	66.10	100.40

Table 13.18   Gas station simulation with varying average arrival time

self-service, the profit per gallon on self-service sales was $0.10 and for full-service sales was $0.10, the extra wait at the pump for self-service customers was 2 minutes and for full-service customers was 4 minutes, and the pumps delivered gasoline at the rate of 4 gallons per minute. The simulation was run with the average time in minutes between the arrival of successive customers taken to be 8, 4, 3, 2, and 1. The results are summarized in Table 13.18.

When the time between arrivals is large and long queues do not form at the pumps, it is faster to use self-service. As the queues get longer with more frequent arrivals, the smaller volume of full-service customers allows the attendants to keep the waiting time relatively short, whereas the self-service customers pile up and ultimately take hours to get out. Although a wait of more than an hour is generally considered intolerable, there were times during the oil crisis of 1978 when people did stay for hours in gas station queues which extended for blocks around the station. In normal times, the station would have to provide more lanes or lose the business, and a larger percentage of customers would opt for full service.

In this simulation, after the data were entered, the program printed out a summary of the day's business. It is possible to write simulations showing on the screen a picture of the cars entering and advancing through the queues, as well as the current values of the variables. There are many creative ways in which simulations can be written using the tools developed in this text.

Exercises

Exercise 13.4

Write a simulation of the following experiment. Two dice are thrown n times. A record is kept of how many times each possible sum comes up. Since each die is a cube with the numbers from 1 to 6 on its faces, the possible face sums are the integers from 2 to 12. The output should be a table with the face sum in the first column and the percentage of times that sum came up in the second column. Run the experiment with n taking the values 100, 200, 400, and 800. To record the results of each toss, use 11 counters (as defined in Section 12.2.3), one for each possible face sum, and increment the counter each time that sum appears. Compare your results with the theoretical percentages, which are 2.78%, 5.56%, 8.33%, 11.11%, 13.89%, 16.67%, 13.89%, 11.11%, 8.33%, 5.56%, and 2.78%. These are easily found by counting the number of ways a given face sum can be obtained, dividing by 36 (the total number of ways two dice can come up), and multiplying by 100. For example, a 7 can come up in six ways, so $\frac{6}{36} \times 100\% = 16.67\%$.

Exercise 13.5: Estimation of π

We can use simulation to compute the value of π. For this we use the fact that a circle of radius 1 has area equal to π. We shall play the following game. We throw a dart at a square board with sides of length 2 feet. The area of this board is 4 square feet (see Figure 13.19). We assume that the dart is equally likely to land at any point on the square. Thus the percentage of time it falls within the circle of radius 1 inscribed in the square should be approximately equal to the ratio of their areas. If we perform the experiment N times (N a large number) and if K of these throws fall inside the circle, then we would expect $\frac{K}{N}$ to approximate $\frac{\pi}{4}$, which is $\frac{\pi r^2}{(2r)^2}$. We would also expect that this approximation gets better as N increases. Let x and y be the coordinates of the point (x, y) on the square. Then x and y are both real numbers between -1 and 1. Write a program that takes as argument the number N of times the experiment is repeated; generates the values of x and y as uniformly distributed random variables, each in the interval between -1 and 1; and counts how many of them satisfy the condition that $x^2 + y^2 < 1$. The program should then use this information to estimate π. Run the experiment with $N = 100, 1000, 10000$, and 100000.

Exercise 13.6

The definition of `shorter` in `station-maker` does not handle stations with fewer than or more than two pumps of the same variety. Rewrite `shorter`

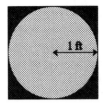

Figure 13.19 Monte Carlo method for estimating π

and any other procedures so that the simulation supports arbitrary numbers of pumps of these two varieties.

Exercise 13.7
Modify the gas station simulation to apply to a case where there are three lanes dedicated to self-service and only one lane dedicated to full service. Run the same input data as in the simulation runs given above and compare the results you get with the data in the tables.

Exercise 13.8
The gas station simulation does not generalize as simply as we might hope. For example, what if the station also wanted information on their diesel fuel? Diesel fuel has a different pump speed, but that would not be any cause to make significant changes in the program. You would need to make a small alteration to the argument list of **simulation-setup&run** and a few other minor changes. However, by adding diesel fuel, you would have to add much to **station-maker**. Make those changes, and test your program. Next, add corn fuel in a similar fashion. Go back to the program and build an object or apply abstraction principles so that if the station needs to support yet another kind of fuel, the task will be simple.

Exercise 13.9: **prompt-read**
Consider the definition of **prompt-read** below.

```
(define prompt-read
  (lambda items
    (for-each display items)
    (display " ")
    (read)))
```

Can this definition be used in place of Program 13.15? How is it better than Program 13.15?

Exercise 13.10

In Program 13.16, the `gas-station-simulator` prompts for the initial data, but it does not echo that data back to be sure that the correct data was entered. For example, when the response to the prompt "Enter the number of hours the station is open:" is 12, the echo printed on the screen could say "The station is open 12 hours." Rewrite the definition of `gas-station-simulator` so that it provides an appropriate echo for the response to each prompt.

Exercise 13.11

Add a report figure for the longest line that appeared at each pump.

Exercise 13.12

Modify `report` so that dollar figures are printed with two decimal places.

Exercise 13.13

Explain why the following definition of `gas-station-simulator` can not be used in place of Program 13.16:

```
(define gas-station-simulator
  (lambda ()
    (apply simulation-setup@run (map prompt-read station-prompts))))
```

Hint: See the discussion of evaluation order on Page 38.

Part 4

Extending the Language

Let us think back to the introduction to Part 1. The restaurant where you dine is a little café in Paris. Ordering may not be simple; you might not be able to read the menu; it is in French. If that were the case, however, you would probably be carrying with you a dictionary, which is analogous to our *syntax table*, for looking up all the unfamiliar words. Here's one from the menu: *Poulet rôti*. First you look up the meaning of *poulet*, and it is "chicken," and then you look up *rôti* and it is "baked." So you know that it is "baked chicken." The whole menu is full of such unfamiliar French words. However, with your dictionary, you can look up each word and translate the entire menu into your native language before placing your order. Derived special forms are like words in a foreign language. When you do not know what they mean, you look them up in a derived special forms dictionary. For example, let expressions can be translated into applications of lambda expressions. Applications and lambda expressions correspond to words in your native tongue.

Suppose that you do not have a dictionary but your Parisian waiter and you know a bit of German. You ask him what *poulet rôti* is, and he says that he does not know how to translate *poulet rôti* into your native tongue, but he can say it in German. He says "*Backhuhn*," and you translate it to "baked chicken." The French is translated into German, and the German is translated into something you understand. This also happens with derived special forms.

For example, let∗ expressions are first translated into let expressions, and then the let expressions are translated into familiar words: lambda expressions and applications. Chapter 14 presents two different mechanisms for inserting derived special forms into the syntax table. This allows us to extend our vocabulary of expression types. Delay expressions, introduced in this chapter, are then used in Chapter 15 to develop unbounded (or infinite) lists.

These lists are not really infinite, but there is no way to show they are not. Most of the *finite* list-processing procedures can be recast, with infinite lists replacing finite lists. In fact, by removing the tests for the empty list, the task is virtually complete. Working with infinite lists requires thinking about lists that never end. You have already seen circular lists, which also never end, but those lists always repeat their values. With infinite lists, different values can appear in every position. Consider an infinite list of the positive integers (1 2 3 ...). If such a list exists, its car would be 1, its cdr would be (2 3 ...), and consing 0 onto it would form the nonnegative integers. All that remains is to convince you that such a list does exist.

14   Declaring Special Forms

14.1   Overview

In Scheme, operators are applied to their operands by enclosing the operator followed by its operands in parentheses. The call structure for applying an operator to its operands is:

$$(operator\ operand\ \ldots)$$

When such an application is made, the operator and the operands are evaluated in an unspecified order,[1] and then the procedure (which is the value of the operator) is applied to the arguments (which are the values of the operands).

We have also encountered several special forms in which the subexpressions following the keyword are treated differently from the operands of a procedure. Examples of these are **and, begin, cond, case, define, if, lambda, let, let*, letrec, or** and **set!**, each with a syntax of its own. Some of these, like **let**, have been introduced to make it easier to read programs, for any program using **let** could be rewritten using an application of a **lambda** expression in place of each **let** expression. Such keywords are referred to as *derived keywords*. One of the convenient features of Scheme is that it is an extensible language that allows the user to add new special forms to make the language more convenient to use and to provide a mechanism to do tasks that procedures cannot perform. We shall study two mechanisms for making such additions in this chapter.

---

[1] Programs that rely on an order of evaluation are said to be ill formed. Since the order of evaluation is implementation dependent, such programs are not portable, and they can not, in general, be transferred from one implementation to another.

The action of taking an expression and rewriting it in terms of something we understand happens when we work with natural language. As we read a passage, we often look in a syntax table, a dictionary, and substitute the meaning of the word for the word itself. In Scheme, however, we restrict those items for which substitutions can be made (we also say "which can be transformed") to lists that begin with a keyword (these are the special forms). Before an expression can be evaluated, all special forms in the expression must be transformed into expressions that are "understood." To carry the metaphor a bit further, we cannot understand the complete thought conveyed by the author of a passage until we have transformed all terms into words we understand. In a sense, we cannot evaluate the author's passage without the appropriate substitutions taking place. Similarly, we cannot evaluate a Scheme expression until all the transformations have occurred. Each transformation brings the expression closer to one in which all terms are familiar. Thus, we do not evaluate an expression with a list that begins with a derived keyword. When all such lists have been transformed, it is time to evaluate the expression. Prior to evaluation there is a recursive program that removes all such lists.[2]

14.2 Declaring a Simple Special Form

In this book we have used several special forms without defining them as procedures. In fact, it is the nature of these forms that they cannot (or should not) be defined as procedures either because some of their *operands* are not to be evaluated or because the order of evaluation of their operands is not the same as in a procedure application. We use the terminology that we *define* procedures, but we *declare* special forms. The mechanism for declaring special forms will be explained in the course of making a specific extension to the syntax.

If we write

```
(define sm (+ 3 4))
```

[2] We shall not write that procedure here, since the way it is written is determined by what the system assumes it *knows*. For purposes of discussion, we assume the system knows define, if, lambda, quote, and set!. Other systems might know about a different set of special forms. For example, if might be described in terms of cond, thereby causing us to assume that the system knows cond. This freedom of choice gives implementors the flexibility they need for efficient implementation.

the expression (+ 3 4) is evaluated and its value is bound to the variable
sm. Suppose that we want to assign this expression to the variable **sm** but
postpone the evaluation of the expression (+ 3 4) until we actually need the
value of **sm**. One way of doing this is to encapsulate the expression (+ 3 4)
within the body of a lambda expression having no arguments. We could then
write

```
(define sm (lambda () (+ 3 4)))
```

The body of a lambda expression is not evaluated until that lambda expression is applied to its arguments, and since the thunk (lambda () (+ 3 4))
has no arguments, it is invoked by merely enclosing the lambda expression in
parentheses. Since the thunk in this case is bound to the variable **sm**, we can
invoke it by enclosing **sm** in parentheses, that is, by writing (sm). We are thus
able to postpone the evaluation of an expression until we need it by making it
into a thunk and binding a variable to that thunk. It would be nice to have a
procedure **freeze** that, when applied to an operand, has the effect of forming
a thunk that has that operand as its body. Suppose we write:

```
(define freeze
  (lambda (expr)
    (lambda () expr)))
```

Then we would write:

```
(define sm (freeze (+ 3 4)))
```

But when the define expression is evaluated, before being bound to **sm**, the
expression (freeze (+ 3 4)) is evaluated. Since **freeze** is a procedure,
its operand (+ 3 4) is evaluated. Thus we defeated the purpose for which
we wrote the procedure **freeze**, which was to postpone the evaluation of its
operand until **sm** is called. What happened is that (+ 3 4) is evaluated during
the definition of **sm** instead of when **sm** is called. Thus **freeze** cannot be a
procedure; it has to be the keyword of a special form if it is to accomplish
what we want.

To declare this special form with keyword **freeze**, we make use of a special
form with keyword **macro**.[3] We would like **freeze** to have the syntax (freeze
expr) and to transform into the thunk (lambda () *expr*) without evaluating

---

[3] At the time this book is being written, the Scheme community has not yet agreed upon a
standard way of declaring special forms. In this book, we use two methods that have been

the expression *expr*. We call the expression (freeze *expr*) the *macrocode*, and we want to transform the macrocode into the *macroexpansion*

$$\texttt{(lambda () } expr\texttt{)}$$

In general, a *macro* is a procedure that transforms macrocode into the corresponding macroexpansion.

When an expression is entered into the system, the first subexpression is checked to see if it is a keyword of some special form. If it is, then the macrocode (in our case, (freeze *expr*)) is replaced by the corresponding macroexpansion. Then at run time, the computer sees only the macroexpansion (lambda () *expr*) in the program as if we had written the macroexpansion into the program instead of the macrocode. Thus the subexpression *expr* of the special form (freeze *expr*) was not evaluated when the procedure (or thunk) was created by evaluating (lambda () *expr*).

How is the macroexpansion accomplished? We have to write a procedure that literally transforms the macrocode into the macroexpansion of that code. Let us call that procedure freeze-transformer; it takes the macrocode code as its argument and returns the code for the macroexpansion. In our case, the macroexpansion is a list containing the three items that make up a lambda expression: the symbol lambda, the empty list of arguments, and the body. Thus we can define freeze-transformer to be:

```
(define freeze-transformer
  (lambda (code)
    (make-lambda-expression '() (list (2nd code)))))
```

where make-lambda-expression is applied to the formal parameter(s) (in this case, it is the empty list) and a list of expressions (in this case, it is a list containing only one element). The second expression in the macrocode is *expr*. In our specific example, that is the list (+ 3 4). We define make-lambda-expression to be:

```
(define make-lambda-expression
  (lambda (parameters body-expressions)
    (cons 'lambda (cons parameters body-expressions))))
```

---

included in some implementations. These methods use special forms with keywords macro and extend-syntax. If these are not implemented in the version you are using, read the manual for your implementation to see how it declares special forms, and use that method instead. In general, until a standard is agreed upon, code including user-made special forms is not portable.

Declaring Special Forms

Now that we have defined the `freeze-transformer`, we can declare the special form with keyword `freeze` using the special form with keyword `macro` as follows:

```
(macro freeze freeze-transformer)
```

We can conceive of this process of declaring a special form as if `macro` places the keyword `freeze` in a global table we call the *syntax table*, along with its *transformer*, which is the procedure `freeze-transformer`. Thus each entry in the syntax table consists of a keyword and its associated transformer. When a program is entered and the symbol `freeze` is found in the first position of an expression, it looks it up in the syntax table, and if it finds it there, it passes the macrocode ((`freeze` *expr*) in this case) to the transformer. The transformer then returns the macroexpansion (in our example, (`lambda` () *expr*)). This macroexpansion is inserted into the program in place of the macrocode. It is customary to refer to the keyword `freeze` as a macro, though the macro actually is the whole macrocode. Following custom, we shall say "the macro `freeze`."

We can also unwrap the various helping procedures used in defining the procedure `freeze-transformer` to get a self-contained representation for the macro declaration. For example, we can replace

```
(make-lambda-expression '() (list (2nd code)))
```

by the body of its lambda expression with its parameters replaced by the arguments to which they are bound to get:

```
(define freeze-transformer
  (lambda (code)
    (cons 'lambda (cons '() (list (2nd code))))))
```

Finally, replacing `freeze-transformer` by its lambda expression gives us

Program 14.1   freeze

```
(macro freeze
  (lambda (code)
    (cons 'lambda (cons '() (list (2nd code))))))
```

as a self-contained form of the declaration of the macro **freeze**. Either the version using the helping procedures or this final self-contained version declares the macro **freeze**. You may use the version you find more convenient.

14.3 Macros

In general, the special form with keyword **macro** has the syntax

$$(\texttt{macro } name \ transformer)$$

where *name* is the keyword of the new special form being declared and *transformer* is a procedure of one argument that takes the macrocode and returns the macroexpansion. In our example above, **freeze** is the keyword, and

```
(lambda (code)
  (cons 'lambda (cons '() (list (2nd code)))))
```

is the transformer. Thus we summarize by recalling that when a program containing an expression starting with a keyword for a special form is entered, the system replaces the macrocode by the code returned when the macrocode is passed to the keyword's transformer. It is this expansion that is seen when the program is run.

The macro **freeze** can also be implemented to take several subexpressions; this would let us write, for example,

```
(freeze (writeln "Hello") "How are you?")
```

and would macro expand into

```
(lambda () (writeln "Hello") "How are you?")
```

In general, we would like **freeze** to have the syntax

$$(\texttt{freeze } expr_1 \ expr_2 \ \dots)$$

where the ellipsis (three dots) means that there is a finite number of expressions following the word **freeze** and that there is at least one such expression.[4]

---

[4] In general, the notation *thing* ... means zero or more occurrences of *thing*, whereas *thing_1* *thing_2* ... means one or more occurrences of *thing*.

This is a pattern for our macrocode but it cannot be used as the macrocode itself since it contains the ellipsis and the special form `macro` will not know what to do with it. Using a similar notation, we can say that a pattern for the macroexpansion is:

$$(\text{lambda } ()\ expr_1\ expr_2\ \ldots)$$

A convenient notation to indicate that the first pattern is to be expanded into the second pattern is:

$$(\text{freeze } expr_1\ expr_2\ \ldots) \equiv (\text{lambda } ()\ expr_1\ expr_2\ \ldots)$$

The symbol $\equiv$ can be read "macro expands to." We call a statement that has the macro pattern on the left and the expansion pattern on the right a *syntax table entry*.

In any actual case, the macrocode is a list that starts with the keyword `freeze` and always has at least one expression following it. If we represent this macrocode by the variable `code` again, then `(cdr code)` is just a list of the expressions that make up the body of the lambda expression into which the macrocode is expanded. The `freeze-transformer` procedure defined above can be modified so that it produces the right macroexpansion for this version of `freeze`:

```
(define freeze-transformer
  (lambda (code)
    (make-lambda-expression '() (cdr code))))
```

It would be convenient if Scheme were to have a way of taking the two sides of the syntax table entry and declare the special form for us. In essence, the system would be writing the transform procedure for us and using it to declare the macro. Such a special form, called `extend-syntax`,[5] was developed (see Kohlbecker, 1986). It has the following syntax:

---

[5] Here is a way to get `macro` if you have `extend-syntax` in your implementation of Scheme:

```
(extend-syntax (macro)
  ((macro name transformer)
   (let ((t transformer))
     (extend-syntax (name)
       (x ((with ((w 'with)) w) ((v (t 'x))) v))))))
```

See Dybvig, 1987, for a discussion of `extend-syntax`'s with clauses.

$$(\text{extend-syntax } (name \ldots) \; (macro\text{-}pattern \; expansion\text{-}pattern) \ldots)$$

where *macro-pattern* and *expansion-pattern* are the left and right sides, respectively, of the syntax table entry for the macro called *name*. Using **extend-syntax**, the declaration of the macro **freeze** becomes:

Program 14.2   freeze

```
(extend-syntax (freeze)
  ((freeze expr1 expr2 ...) (lambda () expr1 expr2 ...)))
```

Since no standard way of making special forms has been agreed upon, we shall demonstrate both ways of doing it—that is, using **macro** and **extend-syntax** in the rest of this chapter.

Along with the macro **freeze**, there is the procedure **thaw**, which invokes a frozen entity (a thunk) and returns its value. The procedure **thaw** is defined as follows:

Program 14.3   thaw

```
(define thaw
  (lambda (thunk)
    (thunk)))
```

To show how it is used, we define:

```
(define th (freeze (display "A random number is: ") (random 10)))

(thaw th) ⟹ A random number is: 7
(thaw th) ⟹ A random number is: 3
```

Each time the thunk is thawed, the expressions are reevaluated. Thus each time we thawed the thunk **th** in the example, another random number is computed and returned.

There are occasions when we want to postpone the evaluation of an expression but have it be evaluated only the first time it is called and thereafter not have to reevaluate the expression each time it is called again but rather return on each subsequent call the value already evaluated. This would be advantageous if the same long calculation is involved each time the procedure

Program 14.4 `make-promise`, `force`

```
(define make-promise "procedure")
(define force "procedure")

(let ((delayed-tag "delay") (value-tag "-->"))
  (set! make-promise (lambda (thunk) (cons delayed-tag thunk)))
  (set! force
    (lambda (arg)
      (if (and (pair? arg) (eq? (car arg) delayed-tag))
          (begin
            (set-car! arg value-tag)
            (set-cdr! arg (thaw (cdr arg)))))
      (cdr arg))))
```

is called and the result obtained is the same, in the absence of side effects. We propose to evaluate the postponed expression only the first time it is called and on subsequent calls to return the already computed value. We declare the special form `delay` to postpone the evaluation by creating a *promise*, and a corresponding procedure `force` to evaluate (or "force") the promise. When the promise is forced for the first time, the value of the postponed expression is computed and returned. Each succeeding time the promise is forced, the same value that was computed the first time is returned. Consider the following:

```
(define pr (delay (display "A random number is: ") (random 10)))
```

```
(force pr) ⟹ A random number is: 6
(force pr) ⟹ 6
(force pr) ⟹ 6
```

and it continues returning 6 each time it is forced from now on.

The syntax table entry for `delay` is

$$(\text{delay } expr_1 \; expr_2 \; \dots) \equiv (\text{make-promise } (\text{freeze } expr_1 \; expr_2 \; \dots))$$

where `make-promise` is a procedure that takes a thunk as its argument and returns a promise, which is a thunk tagged with `"delay"`. (See Program 14.4.) If `force`'s argument is a promise, force converts the promise into a *fulfillment*. A promise is converted into a fulfillment by tagging with `"-->"` the value obtained by thawing the promise's thunk. In any event, the value stored in the fulfillment is returned. Program 14.4 is written so as to protect the tags from accidental reassignment.

We can now proceed to declare the macro `delay`. It has the macrocode

$$\text{(delay } expr_1 \ expr_2 \ \ldots)$$

which macroexpands into

$$\text{(make-promise (freeze } expr_1 \ expr_2 \ \ldots))$$

As before, we cannot define `delay` to be a procedure because its arguments $expr_1 \ expr_2 \ \ldots$ would be evaluated too early. Using `extend-syntax`, we can declare `delay` by simply writing:

Program 14.5   delay

```
(extend-syntax (delay)
  ((delay expr1 expr2 ...) (make-promise (freeze expr1 expr2 ...))))
```

Or, by using `macro`, we get

Program 14.6   delay

```
(define delay-transformer
  (lambda (code)
    (list 'make-promise (cons 'freeze (cdr code)))))

(macro delay delay-transformer)
```

As we have seen, in a procedure call, Scheme first evaluates the operands (producing arguments) and the operator (producing a procedure) and then applies the procedure to the arguments. We say that the arguments are passed to the procedure "by value." In some languages, arguments are passed to procedures as if they were thunks, and they are not thawed until they are actually used in the procedure. Such arguments are said to be passed to the procedure "by name."[6] We can write programs in Scheme so that procedures

---

[6] In the presence of side effects, this is an oversimplification.

accept arguments that are thunks. These arguments are thawed when they are used in the body of the procedure, so that passing of arguments by name can be accomplished in Scheme. Similarly, it is possible to pass arguments to procedures as promises, which are not forced until they are needed in the body of the procedures. In such cases, the arguments are said to be passed "by need." In Chapter 15, we shall study streams, which use arguments passed by need.

We have been using the special form with keyword **let**, which has the syntax[7]

$$(\text{let } ((var \ val) \ \dots) \ expr_1 \ expr_2 \ \dots)$$

The syntax table entry for **let** is

$$(\text{let } ((var \ val) \ \dots) \ expr_1 \ expr_2 \ \dots)$$
$$\equiv$$
$$((\text{lambda } (var \ \dots) \ expr_1 \ expr_2 \ \dots) \ val \ \dots)$$

The declaration of **let** is now a simple matter when we use **extend-syntax** as in Program 14.7.

Program 14.7   let

```
(extend-syntax (let)
  ((let ((var val) ...) expr1 expr2 ...)
   ((lambda (var ...) expr1 expr2 ...) val ...)))
```

To declare **let** with **macro**, we have to build an application that consists of a list containing a lambda expression followed by its operands. For the lambda expression, we need its parameter list and its body expressions. If **code** represents the macrocode, then the list of parameters is built up by first taking the (**2nd code**) to get a list of pairs of *var*'s and *val*'s. We extract the list of *var*'s by taking the **1st** of each pair in the list using **map** as follows:

---

[7] When using user-declared macros that have the same keywords as special forms in Scheme, you might want to avoid collisions with the built-in forms. We suggest that you surround the keywords of those you declare with equal signs; e.g., =let= in place of **let**.

```
(define make-list-of-parameters
  (lambda (code)
    (map 1st (2nd code))))
```

Similarly, we can build the list of operands from the macrocode by taking the **2nd** of each pair. This leads to:

```
(define make-list-of-operands
  (lambda (code)
    (map 2nd (2nd code))))
```

A list of the items in the body of the lambda expression we are building is obtained by taking the cddr of the macrocode. Thus:

```
(define make-list-of-body-items
  (lambda (code)
    (cddr code)))
```

With these helping procedures, we can write the transform procedure and declare it as the macro for **let**.

Program 14.8   let

```
(define let-transformer
  (lambda (code)
    (cons (make-lambda-expression
            (make-list-of-parameters code)
            (make-list-of-body-items code))
          (make-list-of-operands code))))

(macro let let-transformer)
```

This is really only half of the declaration of the macro **let** since there is also the so-called *named* **let**, which has a different syntax. We shall return to the *named* **let** in the exercises, where we rely on the following discussion of **letrec**. The above version of the macro declaration of **let** using the special form with keyword **macro** clearly illustrates the advantage of using **extend-syntax** to declare a macro. Exercise 14.6 at the end of this section suggests some interesting modifications to **let** so that it displays appropriate messages when an expression with keyword **let** is entered with an incorrect syntax. For example, if we write (**let** ((a 3))), incorrect syntax should be signaled since a let expression must contain at least one subexpression following the binding pairs. If we use `macro` to declare our special forms, we must explicitly include tests in the definition of the transformer to determine if the syntax is correct. On the other hand, one of the great advantages of using `extend-syntax` is that it has built-in syntax checking, so we do not have to include our own tests for correct syntax. You may find it instructive to enter some let expressions with incorrect syntax in your implementation of Scheme and see the messages that are displayed.

We observed that in a let expression of the form

$$(\text{let } ((var\ val)\ \dots)\ expr_1\ expr_2\ \dots)$$

the expression $val\ \dots$ whose value will be bound to $var\ \dots$ cannot contain $var\ \dots$ recursively, for looking at the pattern for the macroexpansion,

$$((\text{lambda } (var\ \dots)\ expr_1\ expr_2\ \dots)\ val\ \dots)$$

we see that $val\ \dots$ is not in the scope of $var\ \dots$, so any instance of $var\ \dots$ in $val\ \dots$ refers to an outer scope. The special form `letrec` does allow for a recursive scope.

The macro `letrec` has the syntax table entry:

$$(\text{letrec } ((var\ val)\ \dots)\ expr_1\ expr_2\ \dots)$$
$$\equiv$$
$$(\text{let } ((var\ "any")\ \dots)\ (\text{begin } (\text{set! } var\ val)\ \dots)\ expr_1\ expr_2\ \dots)$$

In this expansion, if any one of the val's contains instances of any of the var's, that val is in the lexical scope of those var's in the let expression of the macroexpansion. This allows the use of recursion in var. Let us now write the macro for `letrec`. Again, it is a simple matter to do so using `extend-syntax`.

Program 14.9   `letrec`

```
(extend-syntax (letrec)
  ((letrec ((var val) ...) expr1 expr2 ...)
   (let ((var "any") ...)
     (set! var val) ...
     expr1 expr2 ...)))
```

Consider the definition of the procedure odd?, which is defined using a letrec expression:

```
(define odd?
  (letrec
    ((even? (lambda (n) (if (zero? n) #t (odd? (sub1 n)))))
     (odd? (lambda (n) (if (zero? n) #f (even? (sub1 n))))))
    odd?))
```

It macroexpands into the following let expression:

```
(define odd?
  (let ((even? "any")
        (odd? "any"))
    (begin
      (set! even? (lambda (n) (if (zero? n) #t (odd? (sub1 n)))))
      (set! odd? (lambda (n) (if (zero? n) #f (even? (sub1 n))))))
    odd?))
```

Let us next look at how to declare `letrec` using `macro`. We first consider how we construct the pairs of the form `(var "any")`, which are in the let expressions of the macroexpansion. After we get the `var`'s from the 2nd of the macrocode, we use `map` to give us the desired pairs of the form `(var "any")`. Similarly, we build the set! expressions, and finally, we build a list of expressions that complete the body of the let expression. This leads to the declaration of `letrec` using `macro` that is given in Program 14.10.

Program 14.10 `letrec`

```
(macro letrec
  (lambda (code)
    (cons 'let
      (cons (map (lambda (x) (list (1st x) "any")) (2nd code))
        (append
          (map (lambda (x) (cons 'set! x)) (2nd code))
          (cddr code))))))
```

Something you usually want to avoid is the creation of infinite loops. However, as an interesting demonstration of the use of `letrec`, we shall write a special form `cycle` that takes an arbitrary number of subexpressions and runs each subexpression in succession and then starts over again, repeating this loop indefinitely. The syntax table entry for `cycle` is

$$(\text{cycle } expr_1 \ expr_2 \ \ldots) \equiv (\text{cycle-proc } (\text{freeze } expr1 \ expr_2 \ \ldots))$$

Program 14.11   `cycle-proc`

```
(define cycle-proc
  (lambda (th)
    (letrec ((loop (lambda ()
                     (thaw th)
                     (loop))))
      (loop))))
```

where `cycle-proc` is defined in Program 14.11. In Chapter 17, we shall encounter several uses of `cycle-proc`.

The last special form that we discuss has keyword `or`. First why must `or` be a macro instead of a procedure? When we write $(or\ e_1\ e_2)$, the first subexpression e_1 is evaluated, and if it is true, then its value is returned. If e_1 is false, only then is e_2 evaluated. If `or` were a procedure, both subexpressions would be evaluated before they are passed to `or`. The fact that the second subexpression is not evaluated unless the first is false allows us to include the following expression in a program:

```
(or (zero? x) (> (/ 10 x) 2))
```

and be sure that division by zero does not occur because the second subexpression is not evaluated if `x` is zero. Thus we want `or` to be a macro that can take any number of subexpressions, including no subexpressions. If `or` is called with no subexpressions, it returns false. Having taken care of the case of no subexpressions, we consider the following syntax table entry for `or` with several subexpressions:

$$(or\ e_1\ e_2\ ...) \equiv (if\ e_1\ e_1\ (or\ e_2\ ...))$$

This works because `if` first evaluates e_1 and if it is true, it returns the value of e_1 in the consequent. If e_1 is false, it skips to the alternative and returns the "recursive" value obtained for the alternative. This looks like recursion, but we must remember that these `or` expressions are not being evaluated. Rather they are macrocode, which is being transformed into `if` expressions that are the macroexpansions. We have treated the case of $(or\ e)$, which should have the same value as e, because using the syntax table entry, $(or\ e)$ expands to $(if\ e\ e\ (or))$ and (or) expands to `#f`.

We could use the above macroexpansion for `or`, but it does not work efficiently since if e_1 is true, it must be evaluated a second time in the consequent.

If e_1 includes some side effects, these would be done twice instead of once, and that is generally incorrect. We can avoid this double evaluation by including a let expression in the macroexpansion:

$$(\text{or } e_1 \ e_2 \ \ldots) \equiv (\text{let } ((\text{val } e_1)) \ (\text{if val val } (\text{or } e_2 \ \ldots)))$$

Once again, if we declare the macro according to this expansion pattern, it will work the way we want *almost* all of the time. But an unwanted behavior, known as *capturing*, can occur, as the following example illustrates. Suppose the macro or has been declared according to the above pattern. We then use it in the following program:

```
(let ((val #t))
  (or #f val))
```

We expect this to return #t. However, when the program is entered, the or expression is expanded into

```
(let ((val #f))
  (if val val val))
```

and the value returned is #f because the last val has been *captured* within the scope of the nearest binding, and unfortunately the variable val was also used in the let expression in the declaration of the macro or. There are several ways of avoiding this capturing. We shall make use of the fact that when a frozen entity is thawed, it is evaluated in the environment that was in effect when the entity was frozen. We first define a procedure, called or-proc, which takes a list of thunks as its operand. Then to declare the macro or, we freeze the operands and pass them to the procedure or-proc. Here is the definition of or-proc:

Program 14.12   or-proc

```
(define or-proc
  (lambda (th-list)
    (cond
      ((null? th-list) #f)
      (else (let ((v (thaw (car th-list))))
              (if v v (or-proc (cdr th-list))))))))
```

In this version, the thunks are not evaluated until they are thawed, so only one of the thunks is evaluated at a time until a true value is obtained. The rest remain unevaluated.

With this definition of or-proc, the syntax table entry for the macro or becomes:

$$(\text{or } e \ \ldots) \equiv (\text{or-proc (list (freeze } e) \ \ldots))$$

How are the cases of zero expressions and one expression handled by this entry? Now or-transformer can be defined and or can be declared:

Program 14.13   or

```
(define or-transformer
  (lambda (code)
    (list 'or-proc
          (cons 'list
                (map (lambda (e) (list 'freeze e))
                     (cdr code))))))

(macro or or-transformer)
```

We can also use extend-syntax to declare the macro or based on the above syntax table entry. We have:

Program 14.14   or

```
(extend-syntax (or)
  ((or e ...) (or-proc (list (freeze e) ...))))
```

Several more special forms are developed in the exercises. The ability to write your own special forms in Scheme is a powerful tool that can be used to make programs more readable. Most important, it allows you to build your own textual abstractions. In the next chapter, we shall make use of the special form delay to develop the idea of streams or "infinite lists."

Exercises

Exercise 14.1
What is the output of

```
(freeze-transformer '(freeze (cons 'a '(b c))))
```

What is the output of

```
(let-transformer '(let ((a 5) (b 2)) (* a b)))
```

What general statement can you conclude from these examples concerning the output when a transform procedure is applied to the quoted macrocode? Some implementations of Scheme have a procedure called **expand**, which converts the quoted macrocode into its macroexpansion.

Exercise 14.2
Declare the letrec macro using **extend-syntax** without using **let** in its macroexpansion.

Exercise 14.3
Consider the declaration of the macro or, below. Does this declaration suffer the variable capturing that we were able to avoid using or-proc and a list of thunks?

```
(extend-syntax (or)
  ((or) #f)
  ((or e) e)
  ((or e1 e2 ...) (let ((val e1) (th (freeze (or e2 ...))))
                    (if val val (thaw th)))))
```

Exercise 14.4: and
Declare a macro with keyword **and**, which, like or, may take any number of subexpressions. If called with no subexpressions, it is true. If all of its subexpressions are true, it evaluates to the last one; otherwise it is false. Test your macro on:

```
(and)
(and #t)
(and #f)
(and #t #t #t)
(and #t #t #f)
```

Note that the capturing problem need not arise in declaring **and**.

Exercise 14.5
The let expression

```
(let ((x 3))
  (let ((x 10) (y x))
    y))
```

evaluates to 3 because the **x** in the binding pair (**y x**) must look up its value in an environment other than the local environment of the expression

```
(let ((x 10) (y x))
  y)
```

The value 3 is found since that let expression is nested within the let expression with binding pair (**x 3**). If we had wanted the **x** in (**y x**) to refer to the **x** in (**x 10**), we would have had to put the (**y x**) in another nested let expression, as follows:

```
(let ((x 3))
  (let ((x 10))
    (let ((y x))
      y)))        ⟹ 10
```

In general, in the let expression

$$(\text{let } ((var_1 \; val_1) \; (var_2 \; val_2) \; (var_3 \; val_3)) \; expr_1 \; expr_2 \; ...)$$

instances of var_1 in val_2 and instances of var_1 or var_2 in val_3 cannot refer to var_1 or var_2 in this let expression but must find their values in a nonlocal environment. However, if we were to write nested let expressions, such as

$$
\begin{array}{l}
(\text{let } ((var_1 \; val_1)) \\
\quad (\text{let } ((var_2 \; val_2)) \\
\quad\quad (\text{let } ((var_3 \; val_3)) \\
\quad\quad\quad expr_1 \; expr_2 \; ...)))
\end{array}
$$

then instances of var_1 in val_2 can refer to the var_1 in the first binding pair, and instances of var_1 or var_2 in val_3 can refer to the var_1 or var_2 of the preceding two binding pairs. We used the Scheme special form **let*** in Section 10.2.5. It has a syntax similar to that of **let** but behaves as though the successive binding pairs are in nested let expressions. In fact, if there is only one such binding pair, then **let*** is the same as **let**, so that

$$(\texttt{let* ((}var \ val \texttt{))} \ expr_1 \ expr_2 \ \ldots \texttt{)} \equiv (\texttt{let ((}var \ val \texttt{))} \ expr_1 \ expr_2 \ \ldots \texttt{)}$$

and if there is more than one such binding pair,

$$(\texttt{let* ((}var_1 \ val_1 \texttt{) (}var_2 \ val_2 \texttt{)} \ \ldots \texttt{)} \ expr_1 \ expr_2 \ \ldots \texttt{)}$$
$$\equiv$$
$$(\texttt{let ((}var_1 \ val_1 \texttt{)) (let* ((}var_2 \ val_2 \texttt{)} \ \ldots \texttt{)} \ expr_1 \ expr_2 \ \ldots \texttt{))}$$

Write `let*-transformer` or use `extend-syntax` to declare `let*`. Test it on the following:

```
(let* ((a 1) (b (+ a 2)) (c (* a b))) (+ a (- c b)))
```

Exercise 14.6
The procedure `let-transformer` is correct only if the user obeys `let`'s syntax. The special form `let` expects a list of $n + 2$ elements. The first must be the symbol `let`; the second must be a list of pairs where each pair is a list of two elements, in which the first element must be a symbol. The remaining $n > 0$ elements can be arbitrary expressions. Here are some incorrect examples:

```
(let ((x 3) (y 4)))
(let ((3 3) (y 4)) (* x y))
(let ((x 3) (y 4 5)) (* x y))
(let x 3 (* x y))
(let (("x" 3) (y 4)) (* "x" y))
```

Rewrite `let-transformer` so that reasonable error indications, such as those shown below, are given to the user of `let`. Test these examples by invoking `let-transformer` on the individual lists in question:

```
(let-transformer '(let ((x 3) (y 4)))) ⟹
    Error: illegal let expression: (let ((x 3) (y 4)))

(let-transformer '(let ((3 3) (y 4)) (* x y))) ⟹
    Error: illegal let expression: (let ((3 3) (y 4)) (* x y))

(let-transformer '(let ((x 3) (y 4 5)) (* x y))) ⟹
    Error: illegal let expression: (let ((x 3) (y 4 5)) (* x y))

(let-transformer '(let x 3 (* x y))) ⟹
    Error: illegal let expression: (let x 3 (* x y))

(let-transformer '(let (("x" 3) (y 4)) (* "x" y))) ⟹
    Error: illegal let expression: (let (("x" 3) (y 4)) (* "x" y))
```

Exercise 14.7

The error information from the previous exercise does not pinpoint exactly where the error occurred. Redesign the information displayed so that you can better determine where the error occurred.

Exercise 14.8: named `let`

The macro `let` declared above did not include the case of the named `let`. The *named*-`let` has the syntax table entry:

$$
\begin{array}{l}
\text{(let } name \text{ ((}var\ val\text{) } \ldots\text{)} \\
\quad expr_1\ expr_2\ \ldots\text{)} \\
\qquad \equiv \\
\text{((letrec} \\
\quad \text{((}name\ \text{(lambda (}var\ \ldots\text{)} \\
\qquad\qquad\qquad expr_1\ expr_2\ \ldots\text{)))} \\
\quad name\text{)} \\
\quad val\ \ldots\text{)}
\end{array}
$$

Define `let-transformer` or declare `let` using `extend-syntax` to include both cases, the ordinary `let` and the *named*-`let`. Do Exercise 5.7 using *named*-`let`.

Exercise 14.9: `cycle`

Define `cycle-transformer` or declare `cycle` using `extend-syntax`.

Exercise 14.10: `while`

The special form `while` is a control structure common to many programming languages. In `while`, an expression is evaluated repeatedly as long as a given condition is true. We can effect the behavior of a while expression as illustrated by the following program, which sums the numbers from 1 to 100:

```
(let ((n 100) (sum 0))
  (letrec ((loop (lambda ()
                   (if (positive? n)
                       (begin
                         (set! sum (+ sum n))
                         (set! n (sub1 n))
                         (loop))))))
    (loop)
    sum))
```

We would like to introduce the special form `while`, which allows us to write the above program as:

```
(let ((n 100) (sum 0))
  (while (positive? n)
         (set! sum (+ sum n))
         (set! n (sub1 n)))
  sum)
```

Thus **while** has the syntax table entry:

```
(while test expr₁ expr₂ ...)
              ≡
(letrec
  ((loop (lambda ()
            (if test (begin expr₁ expr₂ ... (loop)))))))
  (loop))
```

Define **while-transformer** or declare **while** using **extend-syntax**. You must take into account the variable capturing that is caused when the variable **loop** occurs free in *test* or *expr* ... in the macroexpansion. The syntax table entry for **while** must then be modified to be of the form

```
(while test expr₁ expr₂ ...)
              ≡
(while-proc (freeze test) (freeze expr₁ expr₂ ...))
```

where **while-proc** is defined in Program 11.8. Test **while** on the above program.

Exercise 14.11: repeat

The special form **repeat** takes two expressions. It executes the first expression. Then it executes the second expression. If that returns true, the expression terminates with an unspecified value. If not, it repeats in much the same way as **while** from the previous exercise. Define **repeat-transformer** or declare **repeat** using **extend-syntax** by including **while** in its macroexpansion. Then redo the exercise without using **while**. Finally, write an expression using **repeat** that models the test program of the previous exercise.

Exercise 14.12: for

Write a special form that models the behavior of for expressions. Such expressions have the following syntax:

$$(for\ var\ initial\ step\ test\ expr_1\ expr_2\ ...)$$

The for expression is used for modeling iteration. The variable *var* is initialized to *initial*. Then the *test* is evaluated to determine whether it should terminate. If *test* is true, it does terminate. If *test* is false, then *expr* ... is evaluated. Finally, *var* is reset to the evaluation of *step*, and the process repeats.

Define `for-transformer` or declare `for` using `extend-syntax` given the syntax table entry below.

```
(for var initial step test expr₁ expr₂ ...)
                        ≡
(let ((var initial))
  (let ((step-thunk (freeze step))
        (test-thunk (freeze test))
        (body-thunk (freeze expr₁ expr₂ ...)))
    (while (not (thaw test-thunk))
           (thaw body-thunk)
           (set! var (thaw step-thunk)))))
```

This solution is subtle because each of *step*, *test*, and *expr₁ expr₂* ... will be using *var*. For example, a typical use of for expressions is to add the elements of a vector:

```
(define vector-sum
  (lambda (v)
    (let ((n (vector-length v))
          (sum 0))
      (for i 0 (add1 i) (= i n) (set! sum (+ sum (vector-ref v i))))
      sum)))
```

Exercise 14.13: do
The special form `do` has the syntax table entry:

```
(do ((var initial step) ...)
    (test exit₁ exit₂ ...)
    expr₁ expr₂ ...)
                 ≡
((letrec
    ((loop (lambda (var ...)
             (cond
               (test exit₁ exit₂ ...)
               (else (begin expr₁ expr₂ ...)
                     (loop step ...)))))))
  loop)
 initial ...)
```

The variable `loop` must not be among *var* ... and it must not be free in *test*,

$exit_1$ $exit_2$ ..., $expr_1$ $expr_2$ ..., and *step* ... Redesign for's syntax table entry using do. (See the previous exercise.)

Exercise 14.14: `begin0`
Consider the following syntax table entry for `begin0`:

> `(begin0 `e`)` $\equiv$ e
> `(begin0 `e_1 e_2 e_3` ...)` $\equiv$ `(begin0-proc `e_1` (freeze `e_2 e_3` ...))`

`begin0` evaluates its subexpressions in order and returns the result of evaluating the first one. Define the procedure `begin0-proc`, which always takes exactly two arguments. Why is the syntax table entry

> `(begin0 `$expr_1$ $expr_2$` ...)` $\equiv$ `((lambda args (car args)) `$expr_1$ $expr_2$` ...)`

incorrect? (*Hint*: Read the specification carefully. What can we say about the order of evaluation of operands?) Test `begin0-proc` by defining `begin0-transformer` or declaring `begin0` using `extend-syntax`.

Exercise 14.15: `begin`
Define `begin-transformer` or declare `begin` using `extend-syntax` without using `freeze` or the implied `begin` associated with lambda expressions.

Exercise 14.16: `cond`
Consider cond expressions that are restricted to including at least one expression following each test in every clause and where the last clause must be an else clause. They can be transformed into nested if expressions using the following two-patterned syntax table entry:

$$\text{(cond (else } e_1 \ e_2 \ ...)) \equiv \text{(begin } e_1 \ e_2 \ ...)$$

$$\text{(cond (} \textit{test } e_1 \ e_2 \ ...) \text{ clauses ...)}$$
$$\equiv$$
$$\text{(if } \textit{test} \text{ (begin } e_1 \ e_2 \ ...) \text{ (cond clauses ...))}$$

Redefine `member-trace` and `factorial` below, using just the syntax table entry for cond expressions.

```
(define member-trace
  (lambda (item ls)
    (cond
      ((null? ls) (writeln "no") #f)
      ((equal? (car ls) item) (writeln "yes") #t)
      (else (writeln "maybe") (member-trace item (cdr ls))))))

(define factorial
  (lambda (n)
    (cond
      ((zero? n) 1)
      (else (* n (factorial (sub1 n)))))))
```

Exercise 14.17: cond

In order to declare the simplified **cond** with **extend-syntax**, the symbol **else** must be included in the first operand to **extend-syntax**. That is because **extend-syntax** has to be told what symbols it is supposed to be treating literally. In most cases, it is just the special form name, but for **cond** and **case**, it includes the symbol **else**. Fill in the rest of the declaration of **cond** below. (See the previous exercise.)

```
(extend-syntax (cond else)
  ((cond (else e1 e2 ...)) ?_____ )
  ((cond (test e1 e2 ...) clauses ...) ?_____ ))
```

Exercise 14.18: variable-case

Consider a variant of the case expression called **variable-case**. This expression is similar to **case**, except that instead of allowing its first operand to be any expression, it is limited to being a variable. Thus, using case we can write:

```
(case (remainder 35 10)
  ((2 4 6 8) (writeln "even") (remainder 35 10))
  ((1 3 5 7 9) (writeln "odd") (remainder 35 10))
  (else (writeln "zero") (remainder 35 10)))
```

but with **variable-case** we must write:

```
(let ((x (remainder 35 10)))
  (variable-case x
    ((2 4 6 8) (writeln "even") x)
    ((1 3 5 7 9) (writeln "odd") x)
    (else (writeln "zero") x)))
```

Complete the declaration of `variable-case` presented below, and then define `variable-case-transformer`. Explain why `keys` has been transformed into `(quote keys)`. *Hint*: Remember that `keys` will be a list.

```
(extend-syntax (variable-case else)
  ((variable-case var (else e1 e2 ...)) ?_____ )
  ((variable-case var (keys e1 e2 ...) clauses ...)
   (if (memv var (quote keys))
       (begin e1 e2 ...)
       (variable-case var clauses ...))))
```

Exercise 14.19

If we did not have `variable-case` from the previous exercise, then the case example above would require an additional evaluation of `(remainder 35 10)`. Instead, we can choose a variable, say `target`, that will always hold the value of the first operand of the most deeply nested case expression. Given this constraint, declare this variant of `case` using `extend-syntax`. *Hint*: If you use `variable-case`, you need only one rule for its syntax table entry, but remember to include `else` in the list of symbols to be taken literally. Test your program with the following case expression:

```
(case (remainder 35 10)
  ((2 4 6 8) (writeln "even") target)
  ((1 3 5 7 9) (writeln "odd") target)
  (else (writeln "zero") target))
```

Exercise 14.20: `object-maker`

In Chapter 12 we presented a set of object-oriented programs that had a particular pattern of use. For example, each object maker includes

```
(lambda msg (case (1st msg) ...))
```

Design a special form `object-maker` that abstracts this pattern of use. Are there other patterns of use with object makers that can be abstracted?

15   Using Streams

15.1 Overview

In this chapter, we discuss streams, a data structure that enables us to process infinite lists of items. We apply streams to handle input and output from files; in particular, we construct a rudimentary formatter. To do this, we include a brief introduction to the Scheme character data type.

15.2 Delayed Lists

In Chapter 14, we discussed the special form with keyword `delay`, which is used to postpone the evaluation of an expression until it is needed. Thus when we write (delay $expr_1$ $expr_2$ ...), a *promise* is returned, and the body $expr_1$ $expr_2$ ... is not evaluated. When this promise is *forced* using the procedure `force`, the body is evaluated, and the value is *remembered*. Thereafter, each time the promise is forced, it returns the remembered value instead of reevaluating its body. Thus, creating a promise has the effect of "memoizing" the body, as well as delaying its evaluation. We shall now see how we use this "lazy evaluation" to handle infinite lists.

Suppose that our work requires that we process a list of random numbers, but we are not sure how long the list has to be. We can choose a very large number and make a list that long, each member of the list being a random number, say, between 2 and 12, inclusively. Thus, the list can be generated by

```
(define random-2-to-12-list
  (lambda (n)
    (if (zero? n)
        '()
        (cons (+ 2 (random 11)) (random-2-to-12-list (sub1 n))))))
```

Then when (random-2-to-12-list 100) is called, a list of 100 random numbers is created. Suppose we now add the numbers from the beginning of the list until the first time the number 7 is reached, at which time the sum is printed along with the number of integers summed. The following program does this:

```
(define sum-until-first-7
  (letrec
    ((local-sum
       (lambda (rl sum count)
         (if (null? rl)
             (writeln
               "A seven was not found; sum = "
               sum " and count = " count)
             (let ((next (car rl)))
               (if (= next 7)
                   (writeln "sum = " sum " when count = " count)
                   (local-sum
                     (cdr rl)
                     (+ next sum)
                     (add1 count))))))))
    (lambda (rand-list)
      (local-sum rand-list 0 0))))
```

Here are some sample runs of this program:

```
[1] (sum-until-first-7 (random-2-to-12-list 100))
sum = 31 when count = 4
[2] (sum-until-first-7 (random-2-to-12-list 4))
A seven was not found; sum = 28 and count = 4
```

When we called (sum-until-first-7 (random-2-to-12-list 100)), a list of 100 random numbers was generated, and they were processed from the beginning of the list, adding the successive numbers until the first 7 was encountered, at which time the sum and count were printed. But a list of 100 random numbers was generated, and only 4 were used. Is there any way to create a list that has the property that the next random number will not be generated until we are ready to process it?

We have seen how to postpone the evaluation of an expression by delaying it. This will let us redefine the procedure that builds the random list so that each time cons is called, its second operand is delayed. We shall call a list built using such conses a *delayed list*. We illustrate this method of producing a delayed list by constructing `del-list` containing the two elements (fib 8) and (fib 9):

```
(define del-list
  (cons (fib 8)
        (delay (cons (fib 9)
                     (delay '())))))
```

In order to look at the first element of `del-list`, we take the car. Our goal now is to define operators on the data type delayed lists. The first of these is `delayed-list-car`, which is the same as car, since we do not delay the first argument to cons. Thus

```
(define delayed-list-car
  (lambda (x)
    (car x)))
```

Observe that this definition can be written more compactly:

Program 15.1   `delayed-list-car`

```
(define delayed-list-car car)
```

If we call (delayed-list-car del-list), 21 is returned. To get to the second element in `del-list`, we must first take the cdr of `del-list`, yielding a promise, and then force that promise. The result is another delayed list:

```
(cons (fib 9) (delay '()))
```

If we next apply `delayed-list-car` to this delayed list, 34 is returned. We often use the sequence of operations consisting of taking the cdr and then forcing the resulting promise. Thus, we define `delayed-list-cdr` to be that sequence of two operations:

```
(define delayed-list-cdr
  (lambda (x)
    (force (cdr x))))
```

or, more compactly,

Program 15.2 delayed-list-cdr

```
(define delayed-list-cdr (compose force cdr))
```

Then we can get the second element of del-list by calling:

```
(delayed-list-car (delayed-list-cdr del-list)) ⟹ 34
```

Because of the memoizing effect of delay, (fib 9) is evaluated the first time the above call is made, and the value 34 is stored. The next time the call is made, 34 is returned without reevaluating the (fib 9) in (cons (fib 9) (delay '())).

If we apply delayed-list-cdr to del-list and then apply delayed-list-cdr to that result, we get the list '(), which we call the-null-delayed-list. We test for the-null-delayed-list with the predicate delayed-list-null? defined as

```
(define delayed-list-null?
  (lambda (delayed-list)
    (null? delayed-list)))
```

We collect the definitions of the delayed list operators in Program 15.3.

Program 15.3 Basic definitions for delayed lists

```
(define the-null-delayed-list '())

(define delayed-list-null? null?)

(define delayed-list-car car)

(define delayed-list-cdr (compose force cdr))
```

In order to add a new object a to a delayed list b, we cons a onto (delay b) to get (cons a (delay b)). In the spirit of what we did in Program 15.3, we shall introduce delayed-list-cons to produce the above code, remembering that we want to delay the evaluation of the second operand b. If we were to define delayed-list-cons to be a procedure, then if we were to call (delayed-list-cons a b), the fact that procedure applications evaluate their operands before passing their values to the procedure defeats the purpose of the delay. Thus, we must declare delayed-list-cons as a special form using the following syntax table entry:

$$(\text{delayed-list-cons } \textit{expr } \textit{del-list}) \equiv (\text{cons } \textit{expr } (\text{delay } \textit{del-list}))$$

We can declare it with the techniques of Chapter 14.

With delayed-list-cons, we can rewrite the definition of del-list as

```
(define del-list
  (delayed-list-cons
    (fib 8)
    (delayed-list-cons
      (fib 9)
      the-null-delayed-list)))
```

so that building delayed lists looks analogous to building lists. We can also rewrite the definition of random-2-to-12-list using our new constructor delayed-list-cons to give us random-delayed-list:

Program 15.4   random-delayed-list

```
(define random-delayed-list
  (lambda (n)
    (if (zero? n)
        the-null-delayed-list
        (delayed-list-cons
          (+ 2 (random 11))
          (random-delayed-list (sub1 n))))))
```

We now rewrite the procedure sum-until-first-7 using delayed lists as follows:

```
(define sum-until-first-7
  (letrec
    ((local-sum
       (lambda (delayed-list sum count)
         (if (delayed-list-null? delayed-list)
             (writeln
               "A seven was not found; sum = "
               sum " and count = " count)
             (let ((next (delayed-list-car delayed-list)))
               (if (= next 7)
                   (writeln "sum = " sum " when count = " count)
                   (local-sum
                     (delayed-list-cdr delayed-list)
                     (+ next sum)
                     (add1 count)))))))))
    (lambda (rand-delayed-list)
      (local-sum rand-delayed-list 0 0))))
```

The output from this procedure has the same form as that of our previous version, but now a random number is computed only when it is used.

In order to see the elements of a delayed list, it is convenient to have a procedure delayed-list->list, which converts a delayed list delayed-list into a list of its elements:

```
(define delayed-list->list
  (lambda (delayed-list)
    (if (delayed-list-null? delayed-list)
        '()
        (cons (delayed-list-car delayed-list)
              (delayed-list->list (delayed-list-cdr delayed-list))))))
```

We can now use this to look at the elements in the delayed list (random-delayed-list 20):

```
[1] (delayed-list->list (random-delayed-list 20))
(7 5 11 3 7 5 8 10 5 8 8 2 2 12 9 7 12 4 5 6)
[2] (delayed-list->list (random-delayed-list 20))
(2 4 3 4 7 3 9 9 5 10 4 4 12 7 7 7 11 5 5 3)
[3] (define rdelayed-list20 (random-delayed-list 20))
[4] (delayed-list->list rdelayed-list20)
(7 5 11 3 7 5 8 10 5 8 8 2 2 12 9 7 12 4 5 6)
[5] (delayed-list->list rdelayed-list20)
(7 5 11 3 7 5 8 10 5 8 8 2 2 12 9 7 12 4 5 6)
```

Exercises

Exercise 15.1
Define the delayed list consisting of the first n even integers starting with 0.
Define the delayed list consisting of the first n odd integers starting with 1.

Exercise 15.2: `list->delayed-list`
Define a procedure `list->delayed-list` that takes a list as its argument and
returns the corresponding delayed list. This procedure is useful for testing the
delayed list data type at the prompt.

Exercise 15.3: `delayed-list-sum, delayed-list-product`
Define a procedure `delayed-list-sum` that adds the first k elements in a
delayed list whose elements are numbers. If the delayed list has fewer elements
than k, add them all. Do the same for `delayed-list-product`, and then use
procedural abstraction to define a procedure `delayed-list-accumulate` from
which these can be obtained by suitably choosing its arguments. If one of the
elements of the delayed list evaluates to 0, the value 0 should be returned for
the product without evaluating any additional elements of the delayed list.

Exercise 15.4
Delayed lists can be treated as an abstract data type with a few basic operators. Convince yourself that if the definitions of the five entities are given, all
of the remaining definitions in this section would still be defined:

- `the-null-delayed-list`,
- `delayed-list-null?`,
- `delayed-list-car`,
- `delayed-list-cdr`,
- `delayed-list-cons`.

One alternative way of defining these entities is based on the decision to delay
the car part as well as the cdr part of a cons cell. Thus, the syntax table entry
for `delayed-list-cons` becomes:

`(delayed-list-cons val del-list)` $\equiv$ `(cons (delay val) (delay del-list))`

How must the other four basic definitions of Program 15.3 be changed? Does
the behavior of any of the procedures defined in this section change using
these definitions of the five basic entities? Discuss the behavior of `del-list`

if these five definitions are used. In particular, discuss when (fib 8) and (fib 9) are evaluated. What other syntax table entries can you suggest for delayed-list-cons? How does each of them affect the other four basic entities?

15.3 Streams

In the delayed list rdelayed-list defined by

```
(define rdelayed-list (random-delayed-list 100))
```

(delayed-list-car rdelayed-list) is a random number. It really does not matter how long the delayed list is at this point, for no further calculation is done. When delayed-list-cdr is invoked, another delayed list is returned. Thus it is not necessary to indicate at any time how much of the delayed list still remains, and hence the variable n and the terminating condition may be omitted from the definition of random-delayed-list.

When the terminating condition is omitted in the definition of a delayed list, we get what appears to be a nonterminating list, or what we can call a *stream*. We have delayed-list-car, delayed-list-cdr, and delayed-list-cons that use delayed lists. We have now introduced streams as a new data type and, in order to be consistent about the data types, we limit their use to delayed lists and give them new names when they are used with streams. The new names are stream-car, stream-cdr, and stream-cons. The definitions of stream-car and stream-cdr are in Program 15.5. The syntax table entry for stream-cons is:[1]

$$(\text{stream-cons } expr \; stream) \equiv (\text{cons } expr \; (\text{delay } stream))$$

---

[1] Using techniques from Chapter 14, we can declare stream-cons with

```
(extend-syntax (stream-cons)
  ((stream-cons expr stream) (cons expr (delay stream))))
```

or with

```
(macro stream-cons
  (lambda (code)
    (if (not (= (length code) 3))
        (error "stream-cons: Wrong number of expressions" code)
        (list 'cons (2nd code) (list 'delay (3rd code)))))))
```

Program 15.5   `stream-car, stream-cdr`

```
(define stream-car car)

(define stream-cdr (compose force cdr))
```

Now we return to considering the elimination of the terminating condition from the definition of `random-delayed-list`. We get:

Program 15.6   `random-stream-generator`

```
(define random-stream-generator
  (lambda ()
    (stream-cons (+ 2 (random 11)) (random-stream-generator))))
```

and

Program 15.7   `random-stream`

```
(define random-stream (random-stream-generator))
```

This looks as though the code for `random-stream-generator` contains a nonterminating recursion and its invocation in `random-stream` (see Program 15.7) causes an infinite loop, but when `stream-cons` is expanded within `random-stream-generator`, it produces a stream whose cdr is not evaluated but instead is waiting to be forced. When `(stream-car random-stream)` is invoked, a random integer is returned. When `(stream-cdr random-stream)` is invoked, a stream is returned, waiting for the next `stream-car` call, carrying out the next recursive step. In general, a stream is defined recursively to be a cons cell whose car pointer refers to a value and whose cdr pointer refers to a delayed stream. Thus we may think of a stream as a nonterminating (or infinite) delayed list. The discussion in Exercise 15.4 also applies to the corresponding stream operations.

Another example of a stream is `the-null-stream`, all of whose elements are the same; that common value is `the-end-of-stream-tag`, which we define to be the string `"end of stream"`:

Program 15.8   `the-null-stream`

```
(define the-null-stream
  (stream-cons the-end-of-stream-tag the-null-stream))
```

Program 15.9   `list->stream`

```
(define list->stream
  (lambda (ls)
    (if (null? ls)
        the-null-stream
        (stream-cons (car ls) (list->stream (cdr ls))))))
```

Program 15.10   `end-of-stream?`

```
(define end-of-stream?
  (lambda (x)
    (eq? x the-end-of-stream-tag)))
```

```
(define the-end-of-stream-tag "end of stream")
```

We use `the-null-stream` (see Program 15.8) to define `list->stream`, which converts any list into a stream that contains the same elements and *terminates* with `the-null-stream`. See Program 15.9.

If `list->stream` is given a circular list, then the result is an infinite stream. For example,

```
(list->stream (let ((x (list 1 2 3))) (append! x x)))
```

A stream is called a *finite stream* if it has the property that from some element on it becomes `the-null-stream`. Any noncircular list that is converted into a stream is an example of a finite stream. We use the term *infinite stream* to refer to those streams that are not finite when such a distinction is called for.

The predicate `end-of-stream?` defined in Program 15.10 tests whether a given stream element is `the-end-of-stream-tag`. In Program 15.11, the predicate `stream-null?` uses `end-of-stream?` to determine whether its argument is `the-null-stream`.

Program 15.11   `stream-null?`

```
(define stream-null? (compose end-of-stream? stream-car))
```

To look at the first n elements of a stream strm, we use a procedure that builds a list out of those n elements. If strm is a finite stream, we show the list of its elements only up to where the-null-stream starts by passing stream->list any negative number as its second argument. We define the procedures stream->list and finite-stream->list as

Program 15.12   `stream->list, finite-stream->list`

```
(define stream->list
  (lambda (strm n)
    (if (or (zero? n) (stream-null? strm))
        '()
        (cons (stream-car strm)
              (stream->list (stream-cdr strm) (sub1 n))))))

(define finite-stream->list
  (lambda (finite-strm)
    (stream->list finite-strm -1)))
```

We can use stream->list to look at numbers generated by random-stream-generator:

```
[1] (stream->list (random-stream-generator) 25)
(7 5 5 4 6 4 5 11 2 11 11 7 5 11 11 8 9 3 5 10 4 12 7 7 10)
[2] (stream->list (random-stream-generator) 25)
(8 5 10 12 10 8 2 8 3 5 4 9 2 5 4 12 6 3 7 5 12 3 12 2 9)
[3] (stream->list random-stream 20)
(7 7 9 5 6 8 2 3 5 6 7 10 12 3 3 11 5 4 4 5)
[4] (stream->list random-stream 25)
(7 7 9 5 6 8 2 3 5 6 7 10 12 3 3 11 5 4 4 5 10 11 12 8 4)
```

We see that random-stream (Program 15.7) contains a fixed stream of random numbers, while calling (random-stream-generator) generates a different stream of numbers each time it is called.

Other streams can be defined using stream-cons. For example, the stream of positive integers can be defined as:

Program 15.13 `positive-integers`

```
(define positive-integers
  (letrec
    ((stream-builder
       (lambda (x)
         (stream-cons x (stream-builder (add1 x))))))
    (stream-builder 1)))
```

The stream of even positive integers can be defined as follows:

Program 15.14 `even-positive-integers`

```
(define even-positive-integers
  (letrec
    ((stream-builder
       (lambda (x)
         (stream-cons x (stream-builder (+ x 2))))))
    (stream-builder 2)))
```

Similarly, the stream of powers of 2 can be defined as:

Program 15.15 `powers-of-2`

```
(define powers-of-2
  (letrec
    ((stream-builder
       (lambda (x)
         (stream-cons x (stream-builder (* x 2))))))
    (stream-builder 1)))
```

The definitions of these three streams share common features that lead us to think about abstraction. We define a procedure **build-stream** that abstracts the structure of the definitions of these streams. The first place in which the three differ is in the initial value of the argument **x**. We call this initial value **seed**. The other place where they differ is in the procedure in the last line, which appears as the operand to the local procedure. This procedure is the

Program 15.16   build-stream

```
(define build-stream
  (lambda (seed proc)
    (letrec
      ((stream-builder
         (lambda (x)
            (stream-cons x (stream-builder (proc x))))))
      (stream-builder seed))))
```

rule for going from the current value of **x** to the next value of **x**. We call this transition procedure **proc**. Then the procedure **build-stream** is defined in Program 15.16. The three streams defined above can now be defined in terms of **build-stream**, as follows:

```
(define positive-integers
  (build-stream 1 add1))
```

```
(define even-positive-integers
  (build-stream 2 (lambda (x) (+ x 2))))
```

```
(define powers-of-2
  (build-stream 1 (lambda (x) (* x 2))))
```

and the stream of random numbers defined above can be defined using **build-stream** if the seed is **(+ 2 (random 11))** and the transition procedure is **(lambda (x) (+ 2 (random 11)))**. We have:

```
(define random-stream-generator
  (lambda ()
    (build-stream (+ 2 (random 11)) (lambda (x) (+ 2 (random 11))))))
```

With a slight modification of the above technique, we can define the stream of factorials. To do so, we define a local procedure **stream-builder** with two parameters. We have:

Program 15.17 `factorials`

```
(define factorials
  (letrec
    ((stream-builder
       (lambda (x n)
         (stream-cons x (stream-builder (* x n) (add1 n)))))))
    (stream-builder 1 1)))
```

Certain of the procedures that were defined in the previous section for delayed lists can be redefined for streams. For example, we can redefine the procedure `delayed-list-sum` of Exercise 15.3 to get the procedure `stream-sum`, which sums the first k terms of a stream of numbers. If a stream of numbers is a finite stream, then by putting in the appropriate test for `the-null-stream`, we can write `sum-finite-stream`, which sums all of the numbers in the stream preceding `the-null-stream`. If the stream is infinite, we *cannot* ask for the sum of all of the elements of the stream. Similarly, we *cannot* append one infinite stream onto another, since the first stream has no end. *Always be sure operations will terminate before applying them to infinite streams.*

From a given stream `strm`, we can build a new stream in which a given procedure `proc` is applied to each element of `strm`. The procedure `stream-map`, which builds this new stream, is defined by

Program 15.18 `stream-map`

```
(define stream-map
  (lambda (proc strm)
    (if (stream-null? strm)
        the-null-stream
        (stream-cons
          (proc (stream-car strm))
          (stream-map proc (stream-cdr strm)))))))
```

This enables us to define the infinite stream of odd positive integers as shown in Program 15.19.

Now let `strm1` and `strm2` be two infinite streams, and let a_n be the nth element of `strm1` and let b_n be the nth element of `strm2`. If `proc` is a procedure that takes two arguments such that (`proc` a_n b_n) is defined, a stream can be

Program 15.19 odd-positive-integers

```
(define odd-positive-integers
  (stream-map sub1 even-positive-integers))
```

built that has the element (proc a_n b_n) as its nth element. The procedure
that applies proc to the corresponding elements of the two infinite streams
to form the new stream is called stream-apply-to-both and is defined in
Program 15.20. This enables us to define stream-plus and stream-times
as the streams obtained by taking the element-wise sum and element-wise
product of two streams of numbers. (See Program 15.21.)

Program 15.20 stream-apply-to-both

```
(define stream-apply-to-both
  (lambda (proc)
    (letrec
      ((str-app
         (lambda (s1 s2)
           (stream-cons
             (proc (stream-car s1) (stream-car s2))
             (str-app (stream-cdr s1) (stream-cdr s2))))))
      str-app)))
```

Program 15.21 stream-plus, stream-times

```
(define stream-plus (stream-apply-to-both +))

(define stream-times (stream-apply-to-both *))
```

In Program 15.22, we define a procedure stream-filter-out that removes
from a stream all of those elements for which a given predicate test? is true.
This gives us another way of defining the stream of odd integers from the
stream of integers by writing:

```
(define odd-positive-integers
  ((stream-filter-out even?)
   positive-integers))
```

Program 15.22   `stream-filter-out`

```
(define stream-filter-out
  (lambda (test?)
    (letrec
      ((helper
         (lambda (strm)
           (let ((a (stream-car strm)))
             (if (test? a)
                 (helper (stream-cdr strm))
                 (stream-cons a (helper (stream-cdr strm)))))))))
      helper)))
```

We can give another interesting recursive definition of the stream of positive integers using `stream-map`:

Program 15.23   `positive-integers`

```
(define positive-integers
  (stream-cons 1 (stream-map add1 positive-integers)))
```

For if we add 1 to each of the elements in the stream of positive integers, we get a stream of integers from 2. Then stream-consing 1 onto this stream of integers starting from 2 gives us the stream of positive integers. We can also look at the definition from another point of view that says we first **stream-cons** 1 onto the stream, so the **stream-car** of **positive-integers** is 1. The **stream-cdr** of **positive-integers** is the stream obtained by adding 1 to each element of **positive-integers**, so its **stream-car** is 2. Continuing in this way, we see that this procedure recursively defines the stream of positive integers.

Another definition of the stream of factorials can be motivated by the observation that if the items in the list of factorials shown below are multiplied element-wise by the items in the list of positive integers, then we reproduce the list of factorials with the first element missing.

	1	1	2	6	24	120	720	...
	1	2	3	4	5	6	7	...
multiply								
	1	2	6	24	120	720	5040	...

The stream of factorials can then be defined recursively by:

Program 15.24 `factorials`

```
(define factorials
  (stream-cons 1 (stream-times factorials positive-integers)))
```

In a similar way, we can motivate the definition of the stream of Fibonacci numbers by observing that if the list of Fibonacci numbers shown below is added element-wise to the same list (without its leading 0) shifted one element to the left, the resulting list is again the list of Fibonacci numbers, this time without the first two numbers 0 and 1.

$$
\begin{array}{r}
0 \quad 1 \quad 1 \quad 2 \quad 3 \quad 5 \quad 8 \quad 13 \ldots \\
1 \quad 1 \quad 2 \quad 3 \quad 5 \quad 8 \quad 13 \quad 21 \ldots \\
\text{add} \hspace{6em} \\
1 \quad 2 \quad 3 \quad 5 \quad 8 \quad 13 \quad 21 \quad 34 \ldots
\end{array}
$$

The definition of the stream of Fibonacci numbers is then:

Program 15.25 `fibonacci-numbers`

```
(define fibonacci-numbers
  (stream-cons 0
    (stream-cons 1
      (stream-plus
        fibonacci-numbers
        (stream-cdr fibonacci-numbers)))))
```

A prime number is a number, other than 1, that has only 1 and itself as factors. Thus 2, 3, 5, 7, 11, and 13 are the first six primes. Eratosthenes, who lived in the third century B.C., devised a clever way of finding all of the primes up to some given number N. First, write a list of all of the integers from 2 up to N. Then, with 2 as the base, remove all multiples of the base that are greater than the base. Now take the first remaining number after the base (in this case, 3) and call it the base. Once again, remove all multiples of the base greater than the base. We continue this process, choosing as the new base the first remaining number that follows the preceding base, and then removing all multiples of the new base that are greater than the new base, until there are

```
(define divides-by
  (lambda (n)
    (lambda (k)
      (zero? (remainder k n)))))

(define sieve (compose stream-filter-out divides-by))

(define prime-numbers
  (letrec
    ((primes
        (lambda (s)
          (stream-cons
            (stream-car s)
            (primes ((sieve (stream-car s)) (stream-cdr s)))))))
      (primes (stream-cdr positive-integers)))))
```

no more numbers to take as the base. The remaining numbers are the primes
less than or equal to N. This method is called the Sieve of Eratosthenes. It is
used below to find all of the primes up to 20. Each successive list is the result
of removing multiples of the next base.

```
(2 3 4 5 6 7 8 9 10 11 12 13 14 15 16 17 18 19 20)
(2 3   5   7   9      11      13      15      17      19)
(2 3   5   7          11      13              17      19)
```

The last list contains all of the primes up to 20.

Each step of the sieve process is an application of a filter to the stream of
remaining integers that removes those numbers that are multiples of the base
and are greater than the base. Such a filter, which we call sieve, and the
stream prime-numbers are defined in Program 15.26.

In Program 15.27 we show another way of defining the stream of all prime
numbers that combines the ideas of Exercise 7.20 and the data recursion used
in Program 15.23. Instead of testing with all odd integers $\leq \sqrt{n}$, we now can
restrict our testing to the odd prime numbers $\leq \sqrt{n}$. Assuming we have the
stream odd-primes, we first define a divisibility test has-prime-divisor?
which returns #t if its operand, an odd number, has a prime divisor. Then
the stream prime-numbers is defined by stream-consing 2 onto the stream
of odd primes. The stream odd-primes is defined by stream-consing 3 onto
the stream of all primes from 5 on, which is generated by the procedure odd-

Program 15.27   has-prime-divisor?, prime-numbers

```
(define has-prime-divisor?
  (lambda (n)
    (let ((max-value (sqrt n)))
      (letrec
        ((try (lambda (primes)
                (and (<= (stream-car primes) max-value)
                     (or (zero? (remainder n (stream-car primes)))
                         (try
                           (stream-cdr primes)))))))
        (try odd-primes)))))

(define prime-numbers (stream-cons 2 odd-primes))

(define odd-primes (stream-cons 3 (odd-primes-builder 5)))

(define odd-primes-builder
  (lambda (n)
    (if (has-prime-divisor? n)
        (odd-primes-builder (+ n 2))
        (stream-cons n (odd-primes-builder (+ n 2))))))
```

primes-builder. The invocation (odd-primes-builder n) with n odd and
$>= 5$ generates the stream of those prime numbers $\geq$ n.

Exercises

Exercise 15.5:   integers-from, multiples-of, squares-of-integers
Define the procedure integers-from such that (integers-from m) is the
stream of all integers beginning with the integer m and increasing. For example, if $m = 6$, the stream will contain the integers 6, 7, 8, 9, ... Then define the
procedure multiples-of such that (multiples-of k) is a stream of integers
that starts with 0, whose elements are increasing and are multiples of the
positive integer k. Finally, define the stream of squares-of-integers whose
first few elements are 1, 4, 9, 16, 25, 36, ... Test your streams by printing a
list of the first 20 elements of each stream using stream->list.

Exercise 15.6: `all-integers`
Write the definition of `all-integers` (including both the positive and negative integers and 0). Your stream does not have to contain the integers in increasing order. For example, you can start with 0, then take 1, then -1, then 2, and then -2, etc.

Exercise 15.7: `stream-filter-in`
Define a procedure `stream-filter-in` that takes as arguments a predicate and a stream and returns a stream consisting of those elements of the original stream for which the predicate is true. Test your program by filtering the stream of positive integers using the predicate, which tests whether a number is an odd multiple of 3. Use `stream->list` to print the first 20 elements of the resulting stream: (3 9 15 21 ...).

Exercise 15.8: `stream-ref`
Write a procedure `stream-ref` that is the analogue of `list-ref`. Then use Programs 15.26 and 15.27 for the `prime-numbers` along with your procedure `stream-ref` to find the hundredth, three-hundredth, and seven-hundredth prime. Which of the two programs ran faster?

Exercise 15.9: `stream-member?`
Define a procedure `stream-member?` that takes three arguments: an item `a`, a stream `strm`, and a nonnegative integer `n`, which is true if `a` is one of the first `n` elements of the stream `strm`. If `strm` is a finite stream with length less than `n`, it tests whether `a` is an element of `strm`.

Exercise 15.10: `prime?`
Write the definition of a procedure `prime?` that tests whether a given positive integer is prime using `has-prime-divisor?` of Program 15.27. Test `prime?` on numbers such as 37, 35, 51, 57, and 100000007.

Exercise 15.11: `positive-rationals`
The positive rational numbers, which are ratios of two positive integers a/b, can be enumerated by listing them in order of increasing sums $a + b$, with those numbers having the same sum listed in order of increasing numerator a. Those fractions that are not in lowest terms are omitted from the enumeration. Thus the enumeration begins with 1/1, 1/2, 2/1, 1/3, 3/1,... Define a stream `positive-rationals` that contains all of the positive rational numbers with numerator and denominator having no common divisors

```
(1 1) (1 2) (1 3) (1 4) (1 5) ...
(2 1) (2 2) (2 3) (2 4) (2 5) ...
(3 1) (3 2) (3 3) (3 4) (3 5) ...
(4 1) (4 2) (4 3) (4 4) (4 5) ...
(1 5) (5 2) (5 3) (5 4) (5 5) ...
 ...   ...   ...   ...   ...  ...
```

Table 15.28   Table with constant sum diagonals

greater than 1. Represent the rational number a/b as a pair (list a b) and use the Scheme procedure gcd to test whether a/b is in lowest terms. Test your program by listing the first 20 elements of the stream.

Exercise 15.12: stream-cdr
The procedure stream-cdr should have been implemented without the "-->" tag. Modify the definitions of stream-cdr and force so that when a promise is fulfilled, just its value is stored. (See Programs 14.4 and 15.5.) Compare this version of the stream operators with those used earlier to evaluate the expression (begin (stream-ref positive-integers 20) positive-integers).

Exercise 15.13: diagonal
In Table 15.28, the ith diagonal (going up to the right) consists of all integer pairs in which the two integers have sum $i + 1$; that is:

$$(i\ 1)\ (i-1\ 2)\ (i-2\ 3)\ ...\ (2\ i-1)\ (1\ i)$$

Define a procedure diagonal that takes an integer, i, and returns a finite stream containing as its first i elements the ith diagonal, followed by the-null-stream. Test it with 4 and 5.

```
(finite-stream->list (diagonal 4)) ⟹ ((4 1) (3 2) (2 3) (1 4))
(finite-stream->list (diagonal 5)) ⟹ ((5 1) (4 2) (3 3) (2 4) (1 5))
```

Exercise 15.14: stream-append
Consider the incorrect code for stream-append given below:

```
(define stream-append
  (lambda (finite-stream stream)
    (cond
      ((stream-null? finite-stream) stream)
      (else (stream-cons
```

```
          (stream-car finite-stream)
          (stream-append (stream-cdr finite-stream) stream))))))
```

Next consider int-pairs-generator, which uses stream-append:

```
(define int-pairs-generator
  (lambda (i)
    (stream-append (diagonal i) (int-pairs-generator (add1 i)))))
```

Find out what happens when (int-pairs-generator 1) is evaluated. Explain.

Exercise 15.15
The problem with stream-append mentioned in the previous exercise can be corrected by treating stream-append as a syntactic extension with the following syntax table entry:

$$(\text{stream-append } \textit{finite-stream } \textit{stream})$$
$$\equiv$$
$$(\text{stream-append/delay } \textit{finite-stream } (\text{delay } \textit{stream}))$$

Declare stream-append and define stream-append/delay. Then complete the following experiment:

```
[1] (define int-pairs (int-pairs-generator 1))
[2] (define first-300-int-pairs (stream->list int-pairs 300))
[3] first-300-int-pairs
    ?_____
```

15.4 Using Character Data

In Section 15.5, we look at an application of streams to input and output. That will make use of a data type known as *characters*. These are the letters, numbers, and other symbols on the computer keyboard, as well as certain control characters such as newline and space. In this section, we see how this data type is handled in Scheme.

Since information is stored in the computer in the form of binary numbers, each letter in the alphabet is assigned an integer number. An example of such a system that is used in many computers is the ASCII character set, which assigns numbers to 128 symbols that can be entered on the computer keyboard. The ASCII codes are given in Table A1.1 in Appendix A. The characters on the computer keyboard are represented in Scheme by the character data type, and each character is entered with #\ preceding it. For example, the character representation of the letter "A" is #\A. There is a Scheme procedure char->integer that takes a character as its argument and returns an integer representation of that character. In this book, we assume that the integer representation of a character is the ASCII code for that character. For example:

```
(char->integer #\A) ⟹ 65
(char->integer #\B) ⟹ 66
(char->integer #\a) ⟹ 97
(char->integer #\b) ⟹ 98
(char->integer #\0) ⟹ 48
(char->integer #\1) ⟹ 49
```

Scheme also has the procedure integer->char, which is the inverse of char->integer; that is, if n is any number between 0 and 127, inclusive, then (integer->char n) returns the character corresponding to n, and we again use the ASCII code to determine that character. For example,

```
(integer->char 65) ⟹ #\A
```

Special Scheme characters are used to denote some of the control characters on the computer keyboard. For example, a blank space, which corresponds to pressing the space bar on the computer keyboard, is denoted by the character #\space, and a newline (or line feed) is denoted by the character #\newline. Some implementations of Scheme also contain the character #\return, which produces the control character corresponding to pressing the return or enter key on the computer keyboard.

There are also a number of predicates that are used to test the order of two characters by comparing the order of their ASCII codes: char=?, char<?, char>?, char<=?, and char>=?. We have:

```
(char<? #\C #\F) ⟹ #t
(char<? #\B #\A) ⟹ #f
(char<? #\A #\a) ⟹ #t
(char=? #\A (integer->char 65)) ⟹ #t
```

Sometimes it is desirable to ignore the case of a letter and consider upper- and lowercases of a given letter as the same. Then we would treat #\A and

#\a as if they were the same. In order to do this, there are case-insensitive predicates corresponding to the ones listed above: **char-ci=?**, **char-ci<?**, **char-ci<=?**, **char-ci>?**, and **char-ci>=?**. For example, (char-ci=? #\A #\a) has the value true. Two other procedures relevant to the case of characters are **char-upcase** and **char-downcase**. Both take a character as argument and return another character. The first leaves all characters unchanged except that it returns an uppercase character when its argument is a lowercase alphabetic character; the second returns a lowercase character when its argument is an uppercase alphabetic character. Along with these are the two predicates **char-upper-case?** and **char-lower-case?** which test the case of a letter:

```
(char-upcase #\a) ⟹ #\A
(char-downcase #\Z) ⟹ #\z
(char-upper-case? #\A) ⟹ #t
```

There are some string procedures that also make use of characters. For example, **string->list** is a procedure that takes a string and returns a list of characters that make up the string. Thus,

```
(string->list "Have fun.")
        ⟹ (#\H #\a #\v #\e #\space #\f #\u #\n #\.)
```

To go in the opposite direction, we have the procedure **list->string**, which collects together the items in a list of characters and produces a string.

Exercises

Exercise 15.16: **string->list**
We can think about a string as a vector composed of characters, but each vector operation has become a string operation. For example, for **vector** there is **string**, for **make-vector** there is **make-string**, for **vector-ref** there is **string-ref**, for **vector-set!** there is **string-set!**, and for **vector-length** there is **string-length**. Using only **string-ref** and **string-length** from this set of string-processing operations, write **string->list**, which takes a string (of characters) and returns a list (of characters).

Exercise 15.17: **list->string**
Using the discussion of the previous exercise, write **list->string**. Here is a start:

```
(define list->string
  (lambda (list-of-characters)
    (let ((len (length list-of-characters)))
      (let ((result-string (make-string len)))
        ...))))
```

Test your solution with the following examples:

```
[1] (define string-tester
      (lambda (strng)
        (let ((chars (string->list strng)))
          (let ((s (list->string chars)))
            (write (list s chars))
            (newline)))))
[2] (for-each string-tester '("abc" " " "uv xyz" ""))
```

Exercise 15.18: string
Define string, which, like list and vector, takes an arbitrary number of
arguments. In the case of string, all must be characters.

Exercise 15.19: string-append
Define string-append, which takes two strings and returns a string (see Exercise 9.6). string-append is the analog of append using strings instead of
lists. Define string-append using only list->string, string->list, and
append.

Exercise 15.20: lower
Define a procedure lower that takes a string and returns a new string where
all uppercase characters become lowercase. *Hint*: Use map and string->list.

Exercise 15.21: lower!
Define a procedure lower! that takes a string and side effects it so that all
uppercase characters in the string are replaced by lowercase characters.

Exercise 15.22: flipflop
Define a procedure flipflop that takes a string and returns a new string
where all uppercase characters become lowercase and all lowercase characters
become uppercase.

Exercise 15.23: `hash-function`

In Section 12.6, a `naive-hash-function` was used as a local procedure to assign an integer to a string. It assigned the ASCII code of the first character in the string, modulo some fixed number (26 was used in `naive-hash-function`). This method has the disadvantage that some letters are used more frequently than others to start words, so the buckets would not be filled uniformly. A better hash function is one that uses the sum of the ASCII codes of all the characters in the string modulo some fixed number m. This will tend to distribute the words more evenly through the m buckets. Define the procedure `hash-function`, which has as its parameter an integer `m` and returns another procedure, which, when passed a string, returns the sum of the ASCII codes of the first n characters in the string modulo `m` (that is, the remainder when the sum is divided by `m`). First, define `hash-function` so that it is case sensitive, and then redefine it with the name `hash-function-ci` so that it is case insensitive and treats all letters as if they were lowercase. Test your procedures on:

```
((hash-function 26) "Hello") ⟹ 6
((hash-function 26) "hello") ⟹ 12
((hash-function-ci 26) "Hello") ⟹ 12
((hash-function-ci 26) "hello") ⟹ 12
```

15.5 Files

In this section, we discuss reading from and writing to files. We shall also develop an application of streams when we develop a formatter that reads text from one file, reformats it, and writes it to another file. This will necessitate the reading and writing of characters.

You have probably been using files in your work to store the text of programs that you write in the editor and to store the output of your Scheme programs by using a transcript facility or by saving the contents of a window. It is also possible to have Scheme programs read directly from a file or write directly to a file. In all cases, the material entered using a read expression comes from an *input port*, and the material printed using a display or write expression is sent to an *output port*. In general, a port is associated with an input or output device. In our programs so far, the input port for the read expressions has been associated with the computer's keyboard, known as the *standard input*. Similarly, the output port for our display and write expressions has been associated with the computer's video display, known as the *standard output*. These are the default values if no other port is specified for the input or output.

It is also possible to make the input port be associated with a file from which we want to read items, or to make the output port be associated with a file to which we want to write items. To associate an input port with a file, we use the Scheme procedure `open-input-file`, which takes as an argument a string that contains the name of an existing file or the path to the file, and returns a port associated with that file. For example, the expression

`(open-input-file "input1.dat")`

returns an input port associated with the file named `"input1.dat"`. The port returned is capable of delivering characters from the file `"input1.dat"`. The procedure `read` takes a port as an optional argument, and if that argument is present, it reads from that port. For example, suppose that the file `"input1.dat"` contains the following:

```
This is "a test string."
((1 2) (3 4))
```

Then we assign the port that we defined above to the variable `port-in` and see how `read` successively reads each item:

```
[1] (define port-in (open-input-file "input1.dat"))
[2] (read port-in)
This
[3] (read port-in)
is
[4] (read port-in)
"a test string."
[5] (read port-in)
((1 2) (3 4))
[6] (read port-in)
some implementation-dependent end-of-file message
[7] (close-input-port port-in)
```

When the reading of the file is finished, we invoke `close-input-port`, which has the effect of closing the input port so that no further operations can be performed on it. Since many computer operating systems limit the number of ports that can be opened at the same time, it is good practice to close ports when they are no longer needed.

When the end of the file is reached, a special end-of-file object is encountered and is generally not treated as data. Thus Scheme provides a predicate `eof-object?` that tests whether the item read is the end-of-file object. For example, if the file `"input2.dat"` contains

```
100
150
200
250
```

then the following program

```
(let ((p (open-input-file "input2.dat")))
  (letrec
    ((add-items
       (lambda (sum)
         (let ((item (read p)))
           (cond
             ((eof-object? item)
              (close-input-port p)
              sum)
             (else (add-items (+ item sum)))))))))
    (add-items 0)))
```

returns the sum of the numbers in the file `"input2.dat"`, namely `700`.

In addition to the procedure **read**, which reads the next item, Scheme provides the procedure **read-char**, which reads the next character. Scheme writes that character using the `#\`-notation for characters. For example, the character A is written as `#\A`. If **read-char** is called with no argument, it reads the next character from *standard-input*. If it has one argument, that argument must be a port, and it reads the next character from that port. Thus if a file `"input3.dat"` contains

```
Testing 1 2 3
```

then the following program

```
(let ((p (open-input-file "input3.dat")))
  (letrec
    ((reader (lambda (ch)
               (if (eof-object? ch)
                   '()
                   (cons ch (reader (read-char p)))))))
    (let ((ans (reader (read-char p))))
      (close-input-port p)
      ans)))
```

returns the list

```
(#\T #\e #\s #\t #\i #\n #\g #\space #\1 #\space #\2 #\space #\3)
```

To write directly to a file, we must first associate an output port with that file. This is done with the procedure `open-output-file`, which takes as its argument a string that identifies the file to which the output should be sent. Thus, the expression

```
(open-output-file "output.dat")
```

returns a port associated with the file "output.dat". The port returned is capable of writing characters to the file "output.dat". If the file does not already exist, it creates the file "output.dat". If the file does exist, the behavior depends upon the particular implementation of Scheme you are using.[2]

We have used `write` and `display` as procedures of one argument. They printed their argument on *standard-output*, which has been the computer's video display. Both of these procedures accept a port as an optional second argument. When a port is present as its second argument, the procedure sends a printed representation of its first argument to that port. Similarly, `newline` can take a port as an optional argument. Here is an example:

```
(let ((port-out (open-output-file "output.dat")))
  (display "This is an output test." port-out)
  (newline port-out)
  (close-output-port port-out))
```

sends the sentence

```
                    This is an output test.
```

to the file "output.dat". As was the case with input ports, it is good practice to close the output port when one is finished. This is done with the procedure `close-output-port`, which takes a port as its argument. Had we used `write` instead of `display`, the sentence would have been printed in the file surrounded by double quotes.

---

[2] For example, PC-Scheme and MacScheme delete the file and create a new one with the same name, so that the previous contents of the file are destroyed. Some implementations of Scheme may signal an error if one tries to open an output file that already exists.

Program 15.29   `file-copier`

```
(define file-copier
  (lambda (infile outfile)
    (let ((p-in (open-input-file infile))
          (p-out (open-output-file outfile)))
      (letrec ((copier (lambda (ch)
                         (if (not (eof-object? ch))
                             (begin
                               (write-char ch p-out)
                               (copier (read-char p-in)))))))
        (copier (read-char p-in))
        (close-input-port p-in)
        (close-output-port p-out)))))
```

It is also possible to write individual characters to a file using the Scheme procedure `write-char`, which takes a character as its first argument and takes an output port as its optional second argument. If the second argument is not present, it sends the character to *standard-output*; otherwise it sends it to the port identified by the second argument. Program 15.29 copies the contents of the file identified by the string `infile` character by character into the file identified by the string `outfile`.

We close this section with an example of a program that reads the text stored in one file, reformats it to have some given line length, and prints it to another file. We are demonstrating this formatter to indicate how to treat input and output as streams, so we are making no effort to have it handle all possible grammatical constructions. It is a simplified formatter that illustrates the ideas we want to convey. We think of the input from the input file as a stream of characters that we process. We can define this stream by writing the procedure `file->stream` given in Program 15.30.

When `file->stream` is invoked, the first character is read from the input file and made the first element of the stream. No other characters are read until they are needed. We shall describe when reading happens in this process after we define `stream->file`. As long as the input port is open, characters are read from that port and the stream is built. When the object denoting the end of the file is encountered, the input port is closed and the **the-null-stream** is installed.

Our strategy is first to remove all of the newlines and returns in the stream of characters, for these are where the original line breaks were. We insert a space wherever we remove a newline or return, for otherwise there would be

Program 15.30   `file->stream`

```
(define file->stream
  (lambda (filename)
    (let ((port-in (open-input-file filename)))
      (letrec
        ((build-input-stream
           (lambda ()
             (let ((ch (read-char port-in)))
               (if (eof-object? ch)
                   (begin
                     (close-input-port port-in)
                     the-null-stream)
                   (stream-cons ch (build-input-stream)))))))
        (build-input-stream)))))
```

no space separating the last word on one line from the first word on the next line. In some cases, we may have put more than one space between words, so we next eliminate all excess spaces; that is, whenever there are more spaces than one between words, the extra ones are removed. Next we insert double spaces at the end of each sentence. Finally, we count the characters and insert a newline character so as to give us a line length not exceeding the desired amount given by `line-length` and then write the resulting stream to the desired output file. These operations are performed so that the output of one is the input of the next one. The procedure `formatter` applies these operations one after the other. The three arguments to `formatter` are a string giving the name of the input file, a string giving the name of the output file, and the desired `line-length` of the output. We first look at the definition of `formatter` in Program 15.31 and then proceed to the definitions of each of the operations that `formatter` composes.

The procedure that removes the newlines from the input stream is given in Program 15.32.

If there is more than one space between words, the excess is removed by the procedure `remove-extra-spaces` given in Program 15.33. This procedure uses the helping procedure `trim-spaces`, which removes all spaces from the beginning of the stream passed to it until the first character different from a space is encountered. (See Program 15.34.)

The procedure `insert-double-spaces` in Program 15.35 is used to guarantee that each sentence-ending punctuation is followed by double spaces. After we have inserted the two spaces we use `trim-spaces`, defined in Pro-

Program 15.31   `formatter`

```
(define formatter
  (lambda (input-file output-file line-length)
    (stream->file output-file
      (insert-newlines line-length
        (insert-double-spaces
          (remove-extra-spaces
            (remove-newlines
              (file->stream input-file))))))))
```

Program 15.32   `remove-newlines`

```
(define remove-newlines
  (lambda (str)
    (stream-map
      (lambda (ch)
        (case ch
          ((#\return #\newline) #\space)
          (else ch)))
      str)))
```

Program 15.33   `remove-extra-spaces`

```
(define remove-extra-spaces
  (lambda (str)
    (cond
      ((stream-null? str) str)
      ((char=? (stream-car str) #\space)
       (stream-cons #\space
         (remove-extra-spaces
           (trim-spaces (stream-cdr str)))))
      (else (stream-cons
              (stream-car str)
                (remove-extra-spaces (stream-cdr str)))))))
```

Program 15.34   trim-spaces

```
(define trim-spaces
  (lambda (str)
    (cond
      ((stream-null? str) str)
      ((char=? (stream-car str) #\space)
       (trim-spaces (stream-cdr str)))
      (else str))))
```

Program 15.35   insert-double-spaces

```
(define insert-double-spaces
  (lambda (str)
    (cond
      ((stream-null? str) str)
      ((end-of-sentence? (stream-car str))
       (stream-cons (stream-car str)
         (stream-cons #\space
           (stream-cons #\space
             (insert-double-spaces
               (trim-spaces (stream-cdr str)))))))
      (else (stream-cons (stream-car str)
              (insert-double-spaces (stream-cdr str)))))))
```

Program 15.36   end-of-sentence?

```
(define end-of-sentence?
  (lambda (ch)
    (or (char=? ch #\.) (char=? ch #\!) (char=? ch #\?))))
```

gram 15.34, to remove any that might be left. Although at most one space needs to be inserted because we know that for this problem, there is exactly one space following a sentence terminator, it is better to make the procedure do what its specification dictates and be more independent of its input. The helping procedure end-of-sentence? in Program 15.36 merely tests whether its argument is a period, an exclamation mark, or a question mark.

Program 15.37   `insert-newlines`

```
(define insert-newlines
  (lambda (line-length str)
    (letrec
      ((insert (lambda (str count)
                 (if (stream-null? str)
                     str
                     (let ((n (count-chars-to-next-space str)))
                       (if (and (< count line-length)
                                (<= (+ n count) line-length))
                           (stream-cons (stream-car str)
                             (insert (stream-cdr str) (add1 count)))
                           (stream-cons #\newline
                             (insert (trim-spaces str) 0))))))))
        (insert (trim-spaces str) 0))))
```

Program 15.38   `count-chars-to-next-space`

```
(define count-chars-to-next-space
  (lambda (strm)
    (letrec
      ((count-ahead
         (lambda (str count)
           (cond
             ((stream-null? str) count)
             ((char=? (stream-car str) #\space) count)
             (else (count-ahead (stream-cdr str) (add1 count)))))))
        (count-ahead strm 0))))
```

The last step before writing the reformatted stream to the output file is to reintroduce line breaks. The procedure `insert-newlines` given in Program 15.37 does this. Whenever a newline is inserted, we must remove any remaining spaces. This is accomplished by using `trim-spaces`.

Whenever a new word is encountered, the above procedure has to know how many characters it contains in order to know whether it fits on the same line or whether it should be the first word on the next line. This counting of the number of characters in the next word is done by the help procedure `count-chars-to-next-space`, defined in Program 15.38.

Program 15.39   `stream->file`

```
(define stream->file
  (lambda (filename stream)
    (let ((port-out (open-output-file filename)))
      (letrec ((write-stream
                 (lambda (str)
                   (if (not (stream-null? str))
                       (begin
                         (write-char (stream-car str) port-out)
                         (write-stream (stream-cdr str)))))))
        (write-stream stream)
        (close-output-port port-out)))))
```

The reformatted stream is printed to the output file by the procedure `stream->file`, defined in Program 15.39.

When processing small files, it does not matter whether we use streams or lists to handle the data. However, if the file is enormous, the advantages of streams are as follows. Although it appears as though each processing procedure such as `remove-extra-spaces` or `insert-newlines` is completed over the entire data before the next procedure is invoked, in reality, the demand for the `stream-car` in `stream->file` starts the process. That demand is propagated through `insert-newlines`, `insert-double-spaces`, `remove-extra-spaces`, `remove-newlines` all the way to `file->stream`. Then the procedure `file->stream` responds to the demand by actually reading the next character. That character is sent back to `remove-newlines`, which decides if it has enough information to send the next character to `remove-extra-spaces`, etc. Thus the demand is propagated down the procedures, and values are propagated up through the procedures. We see that only the minimal information is used at any one time.

This extended example illustrates the use of input and output to files and the use of streams in reading from and writing to a file and processing the information stored in the stream. There are many ways in which this formatter can be modified to take into account textual features that it now ignores. For example, the quotation mark that ends a sentence is usually after the period, and this program will insert spaces after the period. It also does not preserve blank lines that separate paragraphs or paragraph indentation. It makes an interesting exercise to add some of these features to the formatter.

Exercises

Exercise 15.24
A file contains a column of integers, one per line. Write a procedure that reads the integers in this file and produces another file that contains two columns: the first column containing the integers in the original file and the second containing the running sum of the integers in the first column. The number of integers in the original file is not specified. Place an appropriate header at the top of each column.

Exercise 15.25
A file contains a column of integers, one per line. Write a procedure that reads the integers in this file and produces two additional files that contain two columns: the first column of both files contains the integers in the original file and the second contains the running sum and running product, respectively, of the integers in the first column. The number of integers in the original file is not specified. Place an appropriate header at the top of each column.

Exercise 15.26
Write a program that will count the number of words in a file containing text. You may make reasonable assumptions about the nature of the text.

The next six problems are related. Work them in order and you will discover a more elegant way of writing **formatter**.

Exercise 15.27
Test **formatter** developed in this section.

Exercise 15.28
Test the procedure **formatter** defined below. In order to do this, you will need to curry **insert-newlines** and **stream->file**.

```
(define formatter
  (lambda (input-file output-file line-length)
    ((stream->file output-file)
     ((insert-newlines line-length)
      (insert-double-spaces
        (remove-extra-spaces
          (remove-newlines
            (file->stream input-file)))))))))
```

Exercise 15.29

Test the procedure formatter defined below. In order to do this, you will need to pass output-file and line-length first and then pass input-file to that result.

```
(define formatter
  (lambda (output-file line-length)
    (lambda (input-file)
      ((stream->file output-file)
       ((insert-newlines line-length)
        (insert-double-spaces
          (remove-extra-spaces
            (remove-newlines
              (file->stream input-file)))))))))
```

Exercise 15.30: apply-procedures, compose

Consider the definition of apply-procedures below.

```
(define apply-procedures
  (lambda (procedures)
    (if (null? procedures)
        (lambda (x) x)
        (compose
          (car procedures)
          (apply-procedures (cdr procedures)))))))
```

Test it on ((apply-procedures (list add1 add1 add1 add1)) 3). Next, define compose to take an unrestricted number of single-argument procedures so that (compose p1 ...pk) applied to argument is the same as ((apply-procedures (list p1 ...pk)) argument). Test compose with ((compose add1 add1 add1 add1) 3).

Exercise 15.31

Test the procedure formatter defined below, which uses compose from the previous exercise.

```
(define formatter
  (lambda (output-file line-length)
    (compose
      (stream->file output-file)
      (insert-newlines line-length)
      insert-double-spaces
      remove-extra-spaces
      remove-newlines
      file->stream)))
```

Exercise 15.32

In the definition of `formatter` from the previous exercise, we see that we merely pass any desired procedures as arguments to `compose`, and the invocations are taken care of automatically. Now we will consider different variations on the arguments to `compose`. Test the following:

a. ```
(compose
    (stream->file output-file)
    file->stream)
```

b. ```
(compose
    (stream->file output-file)
    remove-newlines
    file->stream)
```

c. ```
(compose
    (stream->file output-file)
    remove-extra-spaces
    remove-newlines
    file->stream)
```

d. ```
(compose
    (stream->file output-file)
    (insert-newlines line-length)
    remove-extra-spaces
    remove-newlines
    file->stream)
```

e. ```
(compose
    (stream->file output-file)
    (insert-newlines line-length)
    remove-newlines
    file->stream)
```
```

Part 5

Control

When we think about the dining-out procedure discussed in the introduction to Part 1, we can begin to understand the power of abstracting control. Imagine that there is a genie photographing us while we dine. Here is a photo of us just about to order. Do you see the waiter standing by our table? Now, here is one of us polishing off dessert. The genie saves these photographs. When a meal has been particularly good and we long to go back to that little café in Paris whose name we have long since forgotten, there is one way we can relive the experience. We may ask the genie to rub a magic liquid on a photograph. When that happens, we escape to the same café where we were long ago. We will have the same waiter and perhaps order the same food. Whether the waiter aged or not, or whether we are heavier, will depend on whether changes have occurred. If not, then we are the same. If so, then some aspects may be the same, like the café, but other aspects may have changed. Perhaps the genie rubbed the wrong photograph, and instead of rubbing the photograph to get us to the café, he rubbed the photograph of us paying the waiter. What a shame, thrust back to that delicious café and not reliving the meal. What happens after the meal is over? You have two choices. You can stay in Paris and enjoy the night life, as you did long ago, or you can ask the genie to rub another photograph. Each time one is rubbed, you are escaping to another point in your past but with possible changes.

A computer is like a genie. While computing, it takes a snapshot of where you are in the computation. However, rather than keep every photograph around, it keeps only the ones that you tell it are worth saving. The photographs correspond to what are called escape procedures, and invoking an escape procedure corresponds to rubbing the photograph. The point of Part 5 is to show you how to reason with the power of escape procedures.

16 Introduction to Continuations

16.1 Overview

Did you ever lie in bed early in the morning and think about what you were going to do that day? Your thinking probably led to something like this: "I've got to shower, then brush my teeth, eat breakfast, find my way to campus, and get to my first class. After I get to my first class, I'll think about what I have left to do for the rest of the day." You packaged *the rest of the day* into a single concept, relative to some point in the morning. You did not consciously figure out what you would do with the rest of the day; you formed an abstraction of the rest of the day. This notion can carry over to computations as well. In Scheme *the rest of the computation* relative to some point in an evaluation can also be packaged in the same way that we packaged *the rest of the day* in our real-world experiences. The rest of a computation is a *continuation*. This chapter is an introduction to the use of continuations in Scheme. It shows what they are, how they work, and when to use them.

When we learn to deal with continuations, we shall be able to do all sorts of interesting things. For example, we shall be able to exit with a result from within a deep recursion. In addition, we shall be able to design *break packages* and *coroutines*, new concepts introduced in this and the next chapter.

In order to understand continuations, two new concepts—*contexts* and *escape procedures*—must be acquired. The first concept formalizes the creation of a procedure with respect to a subexpression of an expression. The second characterizes a procedure that upon invocation does not return to the point of its invocation. A continuation is a context that has been made into an escape procedure. Such continuations are created by invocations of `call-with-current-continuation`.

We have already encountered an escape procedure, **error**. When **error** gets invoked, its context, a procedure that represents the rest of the computation, is abandoned. Consider the very simple expression:

```
(cons (if (zero? divisor)
          (error "/:" dividend "divided by zero")
          (/ dividend divisor))
      '(a b c))
```

The result of invoking this expression is either an invocation of **error** or a list of length four, whose first element is a number. If **error** were a conventional procedure, then when it returned, we would do the cons and get a list of length four, whose first element would not likely be a number. But we know that that is not what happens, so **error** is not a conventional procedure. We describe how to construct such escape procedures in Section 16.3, but for now we observe that if **error** gets invoked, no consing occurs. In the next section we develop contexts, procedures that describe what does *not* happen when such escape procedures get invoked.

16.2 Contexts

A *context* is a procedure of one variable, □. We use the symbol □, pronounced "hole," to distinguish contexts from other procedures. If e is a subexpression of E, then we use the terminology that "the procedure c is a context of e in E." In the absence of side effects, the procedure c applied to the value of e is the value of E.

Consider the following expression that evaluates to **47**:

```
(+ 3 (* 4 (+ 5 6)))
```

The expression is evaluated using the following scheme. First, add **5** and **6** and get **11**. Next multiply **11** by **4**, yielding **44**, and then increase that result by **3**. Now, what is the context of (+ 5 6) in that expression? We must find a procedure that, if passed the value **11**, will produce **47**. There are lots of such procedures, but we will find one by using a simple two-step technique. In the first step we replace e, that is, (+ 5 6), by □. In the second step, we form a procedure from the value of the result of the first step wrapped within (**lambda** (□) ...). The context of (+ 5 6) in

```
(+ 3 (* 4 (+ 5 6)))
```

Introduction to Continuations

is the procedure, which is the value of:

```
(lambda (□)
  (+ 3 (* 4 □)))
```

Then applying this context to **11** results in **47**.

Let's look at another example. What is the context of (* 3 4) in

```
(* (+ (* 3 4) 5) 2)
```

To form this context, we simply replace (* 3 4) by □ and then wrap what remains by (lambda (□) ...) leading to the procedure, which is the value of:

```
(lambda (□)
  (* (+ □ 5) 2))
```

Applying this context to **12** results in (* (+ 12 5) 2), which evaluates to **34**. But we can apply it to other values. Applying it to **3** yields **16**. What does applying it to **24** yield?

Let us next extend the mechanism for creating contexts. The second step remains the same, but the first step does more. Before, all we did in the first step was replace a subexpression by □. Now we extend the first step by evaluating the expression with the hole. When evaluation can no longer proceed because of the hole, we have finished the first step. Thus contexts are procedures created at the point in the computation where we can no longer compute because of the existence of □. The previous examples were correct because no evaluation was possible. To demonstrate this way to form contexts, consider the slightly more complicated expression:

```
(if (zero? 5)
    (+ 3 (* 4 (+ 5 6)))
    (* (+ (* 3 4) 5) 2))
```

In finding the context of (* 3 4), the result of the first step is what is left after evaluating

```
(if (zero? 5)
    (+ 3 (* 4 (+ 5 6)))
    (* (+ □ 5) 2))
```

(zero? 5) is false, so we choose the alternative of the if expression, which leads to (* (+ □ 5) 2). No more computation can take place. Thus, the procedure formed as a result of the second step is the value of

```
(lambda (□)
  (* (+ □ 5) 2))
```

Consider the context of (* 3 4) in:

```
(let ((n 1))
  (if (zero? n)
      (writeln (+ 3 (* 4 (+ 5 6))))
      (writeln (* (+ (* 3 4) 5) 2)))
  n)
```

The result of the first step is:

```
(begin
  (writeln (* (+ □ 5) 2))
  n)
```

The begin is needed because it is a sequence of expressions. We cannot do the addition because of the hole. We cannot do the multiplication because we cannot do the addition, we cannot do the displaying because we cannot do the multiplication, and we cannot return the value of n because we cannot determine the value of the expression that precedes it. In figuring out the value of expressions, we work from the inside and try to work outward. The procedure formed as the result of the second step is responsible for remembering the value of the free variable n. Thus we observe that contexts are procedures and must respect *free variables*. We do not need to worry about the let expression, and we do not need to worry about the if expression. Evaluation proceeds until the presence of □ makes it impossible to continue and then we do the second step that forms the context, which is the value of:

```
(lambda (□)
  (begin
    (writeln (* (+ □ 5) 2))
    n))
```

Applying it to 6 leads to (begin (writeln (* (+ 6 5) 2)) n), and with n bound to 1 the value displayed is 22 with the result 1. Applying it to 8, 26 is displayed.

The let expression is just a procedure invocation. We can reformulate the last example with a global procedure:

```
(define tester
  (lambda (n)
    (if (zero? n)
        (writeln (+ 3 (* 4 (+ 5 6))))
        (writeln (* (+ (* 3 4) 5) 2)))
    n))
```

Then we can determine the context of (* 3 4) in the expression (tester 1). Although (* 3 4) does not appear physically within (tester 1), we know that the computation will eventually get to that point, so the same context will be formed. If we were looking for the context within the expression (* 10 (tester 1)), then the context would be formed from the value of:

```
(lambda (□)
  (* 10 (begin
          (writeln (* (+ □ 5) 2))
          n)))
```

Let us apply these rules to a begin expression:

```
(begin
  (writeln 0)
  (let ((n 1))
    (if (zero? n)
        (writeln (+ 3 (* 4 (+ 5 6))))
        (writeln (* (+ (* 3 4) 5) 2)))
    n))
```

We are still forming the context of (* 3 4). At the first step, (* 3 4) is replaced by □ just prior to evaluation:

```
(begin
  (writeln 0)
  (let ((n 1))
    (if (zero? n)
        (writeln (+ 3 (* 4 (+ 5 6))))
        (writeln (* (+ □ 5) 2)))
    n))
```

First, a 0 is displayed. Then the context is determined as the procedure, which is the value of:

```
(lambda (□)
  (begin
    (writeln (* (+ □ 5) 2))
    n))
```

Invoking it with 9 causes the displaying of 28 and then returns 1.

A context might involve the use of set!. The example below is similar to the last one, except that within the scope of the let expression is an assignment to the local variable n. The context of (* 3 4) in

```
(begin
  (writeln 0)
  (let ((n 1))
    (if (zero? n)
        (writeln (+ 3 (* 4 (+ 5 6))))
        (writeln (* (+ (* 3 4) 5) 2)))
    (set! n (+ n 2))
    n))
```

is the value of

```
(lambda (□)
  (begin
    (writeln (* (+ □ 5) 2))
    (set! n (+ n 2))
    n))
```

The free variable n, initially 1, is taken from the let expression. Each time the context is invoked, the variable n is incremented to the next positive odd integer, and what gets subsequently returned is also increased. If <c> is this context, then the first invocation of <c> assigns 3 to n, and the second invocation assigns 5 to n. From the way in which n changes upon each invocation of <c>, it follows that contexts are *procedures* that may even maintain state.

In the next example, we look at the terminating condition of a recursive procedure invocation. Consider the definition of the procedure map-add1, which adds one to each element of a list, but instead of returning the empty list, it returns (23) as the result of the terminating condition:

```
(define map-add1
  (lambda (ls)
    (if (null? ls)
        (cons (+ 3 (* 4 5)) '())
        (let ((val (add1 (car ls))))
          (cons val (map-add1 (cdr ls)))))))
```

For example, (map-add1 '(1 3 5)) is (2 4 6 23). What is the context
of (* 4 5) in (cons 0 (map-add1 '(1 3 5)))? This is the same as "run
this until the existence of □ stops the computation, and what is left is the
context." We compute the expression looking for □:

```
(cons 0 (map-add1 '(1 3 5))) ⟹
(cons 0 (cons 2 (map-add1 (cdr '(1 3 5))))) ⟹
(cons 0 (cons 2 (map-add1 '(3 5)))) ⟹
(cons 0 (cons 2 (cons 4 (map-add1 '(5))))) ⟹
(cons 0 (cons 2 (cons 4 (cons 6 (map-add1 '()))))) ⟹
(cons 0 (cons 2 (cons 4 (cons 6 (cons (+ 3 □) '())))))
```

Because of the hole, no additional computation can be performed, so the
context is the procedure formed from

```
(lambda (□)
  (cons 0 (cons 2 (cons 4 (cons 6 (cons (+ 3 □) '()))))))
```

If we invoke this context on 5, we create the list (0 2 4 6 8), and if we
invoke it on 13, we get (0 2 4 6 16). What makes this a bit unusual is the
fact that the hole does not show up in the expression right away, and in this
case, it shows up just as the termination condition is considered.

   In the next example, we cannot initially find a place to insert □. However,
we know that □ will occur, so we can compute until it occurs and eventually
stops the computation. Consider the simple procedure sum+n, which adds n
to the sum of the numbers from 1 to n:

```
(define sum+n
  (lambda (n)
    (if (zero? n)
        0
        (+ (add1 n) (sum+n (sub1 n))))))
```

What is the context of (add1 n), just when n is 3, in (* 10 (sum+n 5))?
As in the previous example, we are looking for a context associated with

a recursive procedure invocation. However, this differs from the previous example by the additional detail used in its description. Stepping through the computation leads eventually to an occurrence of □:[1]

```
(* 10 (sum+n 5)) ⟹
(* 10 (if (zero? 5) 0 (+ (add1 5) (sum+n (sub1 5)))))) ⟹
(* 10 (+ 6 (sum+n 4))) ⟹
(* 10 (+ 6 (if (zero? 4) 0 (+ (add1 4) (sum+n (sub1 4)))))) ⟹
(* 10 (+ 6 (+ 5 (sum+n 3)))) ⟹
(* 10 (+ 6 (+ 5 (if (zero 3) 0 (+ □ (sum+n (sub1 3))))))) ⟹
(* 10 (+ 6 (+ 5 (+ □ (sum+n 2)))))
```

Thus, the context is the procedure formed from:

```
(lambda (□)
  (* 10 (+ 6 (+ 5 (+ □ (sum+n 2))))))
```

The final example uses the predicate of an if expression. Consider the context of (* 3 4) in (if (zero? (* 3 4)) 8 9). First, determining the expression prior to evaluation results in (if (zero? □) 8 9). There is no evaluation possible, so the context is the value of

```
(lambda (□)
  (if (zero? □) 8 9)).
```

When this context is applied, its value will be 8 or 9, depending on what value gets bound to □.

In order to understand continuations, you will need to have lots of experience forming contexts. The exercises below should give you enough practice.

Exercises

Exercise 16.1
What is the context of (cons 3 '()) in (cons 1 (cons 2 (cons 3 '()))))? What results when we apply this context to '(a b c), '(x y), and '(3)?

---

[1] The trace that follows assumes a left to right order of evaluation of the operands to +. The procedure map-add1 imposed a left to right order of evaluation of the operands to cons by using a let expression.

Exercise 16.2

For the following exercises assume these bindings: a is 1, b is 2, c is 3, d is 4, n is 5, x is 6, y is 7, and z is 8. Each answer will be in two parts. In the first part, describe the context of each expression; in the second part, determine the resultant values found by sequentially applying the context to each of 5, 6, and 7.

a. (+ a b) in (* c (+ a b)).

b. x in (+ x y).

c. y in (- x y).

d. x in (let ((a 4)) (+ a x)).

e. (* c (+ a b)) in (+ d (* c (+ a b))).

f. (zero? n) in (if (zero? n) a b).

g. x in (if x y z).

h. a in (let ((x 3)) (set! x (+ a x)) x).

Exercise 16.3

For each expression below, determine the context of (cons 3 '(4)) and the result of applying that context to (1 2 3).

a. (letrec ((f (lambda (n)
            (if (zero? n)
                (car (cons 3 '(4)))
                (* n (f (sub1 n)))))))
     (f 3))

b. (letrec ((f (lambda (n)
            (if (zero? n)
                (car (cons 3 '(4)))
                (* n (f (sub1 n)))))))
     (+ 1000 (f 3)))

16.3 Escape Procedures

We now introduce a new procedure type, called *escape* procedures. An escape procedure upon invocation yields a value but never passes that value to others. When an escape procedure is invoked, its result *is* the result of the entire computation. Anything awaiting the result is ignored. Let us assume the existence of a procedure, escape-*, which is an escape multiply:

```
(+ (escape-* 5 2) 3)
```

This expression evaluates to 10. The waiting + is abandoned. It is as if (* 5 2) were the entire expression.

At this point we do not have a mechanism for creating escape procedures such as escape-*. Let us further assume there is a procedure escaper that takes any procedure as an argument and returns a similarly defined escape procedure. Then with escaper we can define escape-*

```
(define escape-* (escaper *))
```

and

```
(+ ((escaper *) 5 2) 3)
```

evaluates to 10.

Consider the invocation:

```
(+ ((escaper
      (lambda (x)
        (- (* x 3) 7)))
    5)
   4)
```

Here the addition cannot happen, so this is the same as

```
((lambda (x)
   (- (* x 3) 7))
 5)
```

so the answer is 8. Consider the following expression with an escape subtraction procedure:

```
(+ ((escaper
      (lambda (x)
        ((escaper -) (* x 3) 7)))
    5)
   4)
```

This is also 8, because once (escaper -) is invoked, the result is determined, and + is abandoned. But consider what happens with the following escape multiplication procedure:

```
(+ ((escaper
        (lambda (x)
            ((escaper -) ((escaper *) x 3)
                          7)))
    5)
    4)
```

The invocation of (**escaper ***) results in 15. The (**escaper -**) is never invoked, so the subtraction never occurs. The following four expressions have the same value. Why?

1.
```
((lambda (x)
    (* x 3))
 5)
```
2.
```
(+ ((escaper
        (lambda (x)
            (- ((escaper *) x 3)
               7)))
    5)
    4)
```
3.
```
(+ ((lambda (x)
        ((escaper -) ((escaper *) x 3)
                      7))
    5)
    17)
```
4.
```
(+ ((lambda (x)
        (- ((escaper *) x 3)
           7))
    5)
    2000)
```

Does this fully characterize the behavior of escape procedures? Not quite. Consider the following:

```
(/ (+ ((escaper
           (lambda (x)
               (- (* x 3) 7)))
       5)
      4)
   2)
```

The awaiting addition is abandoned. Is the division, which awaits the addition, also abandoned? Yes. Since the division awaits the addition and since the addition has been abandoned by the escape invocation, the division has also been abandoned. This behavior can be characterized by an equation: if e is an escape procedure and f is any procedure, then (compose f e) = e. That is, (f (e expr)) is the same as (e expr) for all expressions expr. The context of (e expr) in (f (e expr)) is (lambda ($\Box$) (f $\Box$)), which is the same as f. Since the result of (f (e expr)) is the result of (e expr), we say that an escape invocation *abandons its context*. In our last example, the context of the escape invocation included the awaiting addition and the awaiting division. We discuss special escape procedures in the next section where we characterize call-with-current-continuation.

Exercises

Exercise 16.4
Evaluate each of the following:

a. ((escaper add1) ((escaper sub1) 0))

b. (let ((es-cons (escaper cons)))
     (es-cons 1 (es-cons 2 (es-cons 3 '()))))

Exercise 16.5
Using the definition of es-cons from the previous exercise, determine the context of (es-cons 3 '()) in (es-cons 1 (es-cons 2 (es-cons 3 '()))).

Exercise 16.6: reset
Consider the definition of reset:

```
(define reset
  (lambda ()
    ((escaper
       (lambda ()
         (writeln "reset invoked"))))))
```

Determine the value of (cons 1 (reset)).

Exercise 16.7
Let e be an escape procedure, and let f and g be any procedures. To what is (compose g (compose f e)) equivalent? Can this be generalized to an arbitrary number of procedure compositions?

Exercise 16.8
Let f be any procedure. When can f be replaced by (escaper f) and still produce the same value as f?

16.4 Continuations from Contexts and Escape Procedures

We are about to discuss `call-with-current-continuation` (or `call/cc`). If `call/cc` is not available on your Scheme, define it as follows:

Program 16.1   call/cc

```
(define call/cc call-with-current-continuation)
```

`call/cc` is a procedure of one argument; we call the argument a *receiver*. The receiver is a procedure of one argument. Its argument is called a *continuation*. The continuation is also a procedure of one argument. Regardless of how we form the continuation, (`call/cc receiver`) is the same as (`receiver continuation`). What is left is to understand how *continuation* is formed. To form *continuation*, we first form the context, *c*, of (`call/cc receiver`) in some expression *E*. We then invoke (`escaper c`), which forms *continuation*. We have now completely characterized `call/cc`. All we have left to do is see how our understanding of how to form continuations leads us to determine correctly the evaluation of expressions using `call/cc`.

Consider the following expression:

```
(+ 3 (* 4 (call/cc r)))
```

The context of (`call/cc r`) is the procedure, which is the value of

```
(lambda (□) (+ 3 (* 4 □)))
```

so our original expression means the same as:

```
(+ 3 (* 4 (r (escaper (lambda (□) (+ 3 (* 4 □))))))))
```

That is, after the *system* forms the context of (`call/cc r`), the *system* passes it as an escape procedure to `r`. Since this is now just a simple invocation, *all the rules for procedure invocation apply*. A little practice is helpful. Let us consider `r` to be the value of (`lambda (continuation) 6`). What is the value of the expression derived from the call/cc expression above?

```
(+ 3 (* 4 ((lambda (continuation) 6)
           (escaper (lambda (□) (+ 3 (* 4 □)))))))
```

The value of

```
((lambda (continuation) 6)
 (escaper (lambda (□) (+ 3 (* 4 □)))))
```

is 6; it does not use continuation, so the result is 27 (i.e., $3 + 4*6$). What about this one?

```
(+ 3 (* 4 ((lambda (continuation) (continuation 6))
           (escaper (lambda (□) (+ 3 (* 4 □)))))))
```

The explicit invocation of continuation on 6 leads to

```
((escaper (lambda (□) (+ 3 (* 4 □)))) 6)
```

and then the result is 27. Is this one any different?

```
(+ 3 (* 4 ((lambda (continuation) (+ 2 (continuation 6)))
           (escaper (lambda (□) (+ 3 (* 4 □)))))))
```

The explicit invocation of continuation on 6 leads to

```
((escaper (lambda (□) (+ 3 (* 4 □)))) 6)
```

and then the result is 27. Remember, an escape invocation abandons its context, so (lambda (□) (+ 3 (* 4 (+ 2 □)))) is abandoned. continuation has the value (escaper (lambda (□) ... □ ...)). Because the context of a call/cc invocation is turned into an escape procedure, we use the notation <*ep*> for procedures that get passed to r.

Scheme supports procedures as values, and since <*ep*> is a procedure, it is possible to invoke the same continuation more than once. In the next section there are three experiments with call/cc, and in the last experiment the same continuation is invoked twice. The countdown example of Chapter 17 shows what happens when the same continuation is invoked many times.

Exercises

Exercise 16.9
For each expression below, there are four parts. In Part a, determine the expression's value. In Part b, define r locally using let, and form the original application of (call/cc r), which leads to this expression. In Part c, define r globally, and in Part d, using the global r, form the original application of (call/cc r), which leads to this expression. The solution to problem [1] is given below:

```
[1] (- 3 (* 5 ((lambda (continuation) (continuation 5))
              (escaper (lambda (□) (- 3 (* 5 □)))))))

    a. -22

    b. (let ((r (lambda (continuation)
                  (continuation 5))))
         (- 3 (* 5 (call/cc r))))

    c. (define r
         (lambda (continuation)
           (continuation 5)))

    d. (- 3 (* 5 (call/cc r)))

[2] (- 3 (* 5 ((lambda (continuation) 5)
              (escaper (lambda (□) (- 3 (* 5 □)))))))

[3] (- 3 (* 5 ((lambda (continuation) (+ 1000 (continuation 5)))
              (escaper (lambda (□) (- 3 (* 5 □)))))))
```

Exercise 16.10
If r is

```
(lambda (continuation) (continuation body))
```

in (... (call/cc r) ...), why can r be rewritten as

```
(lambda (continuation) body)
```

Exercise 16.11

If `r` is

> `(escaper (lambda (continuation) (continuation` *body*`)))`

in `(... (call/cc r) ...)`, when can `r` be rewritten as

> `(lambda (continuation)` *body*`)`

16.5 Experimenting with call/cc

We next consider three simple experiments. Each experiment includes one use of a receiver (remember that a receiver is just a single-parameter procedure) without using `call/cc` and one that uses `call/cc`. The point of these experiments is to show the simple behavioral characteristics of `call/cc` expressions. Although the differences may seem minor in the first two experiments, their differences are important. In the last experiment, however, the differences demonstrate the unusual behavior of continuations. The receivers we use to demonstrate these properties are presented in Program 16.2.

Program 16.2   receiver-1, receiver-2, receiver-3

```
(define receiver-1
  (lambda (proc)
    (proc (list 1))))

(define receiver-2
  (lambda (proc)
    (proc (list (proc (list 2))))))

(define receiver-3
  (lambda (proc)
    (proc (list (proc (list 3 proc))))))
```

Each receiver consumes a procedure (possibly a continuation) that is invoked at least once. In `receiver-3`, not only is the procedure invoked at least once, but it is also used as an argument. We consider the behavior of each of these receivers using two global variables, `result` and `resultcc`, given

Program 16.3 `result, resultcc`

```
(define result "any value")

(define resultcc "any value")
```

Program 16.4 `writeln/return, answer-maker, call`

```
(define writeln/return
  (lambda (x)
    (writeln x)
    x))

(define answer-maker
  (lambda (x)
    (cons 'answer-is (writeln/return x))))

(define call
  (lambda (receiver)
    (receiver writeln/return)))
```

in Program 16.3, and three simple procedures, `writeln/return`, `answer-maker`, and `call`, given in Program 16.4. The procedure `writeln/return` displays and returns its argument. The procedure `answer-maker` is like `writeln/return`, but instead of returning its argument, it returns the consing of `answer-is` to its argument. Thus, `(receiver-1 answer-maker)` displays `(1)` and returns `(answer-is 1)`. The procedure `call` invokes its argument on `writeln/return`.

For reasons that are not yet clear but will be by the end of this section, we use `set!` to hold the results of each experiment. Recall that `receiver-1` is the value of

```
(lambda (proc)
  (proc (list 1)))
```

Experiment 1:

A.

```
[1] (set! result (answer-maker (call receiver-1)))
(1)
(1)
[2] result
(answer-is 1)
```

B.

```
[3] (set! resultcc (answer-maker (call/cc receiver-1)))
(1)
[4] resultcc
(answer-is 1)
```

These results are identical except that in Part A writeln/return is invoked in call so there is an additional (1). The continuation formed in Part B is the value of:

```
(escaper
  (lambda (□)
    (set! resultcc (answer-maker □))))
```

Then this continuation is invoked on (list 1), and since it is an escape procedure, that is all that happens. The procedure answer-maker is invoked on (list 1), causing (1) to appear, and its result, (answer-is 1), is assigned to resultcc. At [4] we verify that resultcc is indeed (answer-is 1).

For Experiment 2, recall that receiver-2 is the value of:

```
(lambda (proc)
  (proc (list (proc (list 2)))))
```

Experiment 2:

A.

```
[1] (set! result (answer-maker (call receiver-2)))
(2)
((2))
((2))
[2] result
(answer-is (2))
```

B.

```
[3] (set! resultcc (answer-maker (call/cc receiver-2)))
(2)
[4] resultcc
(answer-is 2)
```

In Part A the main difference is the extra set of parentheses around the value, which is the result passed to answer-maker. Both invocations of proc do a writeln/return. The first time is with (2) as its argument. When this returns, its argument is passed to list, resulting in ((2)). Now we are ready for the second invocation of writeln/return. It displays its argument ((2)) and returns it to answer-maker, which displays its argument by invoking writeln/return and returns the result (answer-is (2)). This is the value assigned to result. In Part B, why is there just one displaying of (2), and where did the extra set of parentheses go? Recall that the continuation built from the context of (call/cc receiver-2) is an escape procedure. Thus, once invoked, it abandons its context, the value of

```
(lambda (□)
  (set! resultcc (answer-maker (proc (list □)))))
```

The list invocation and the proc invocation waiting for the result of list are abandoned. The list invocation not occurring accounts for the missing set of parentheses, and the proc invocation not occurring accounts for why only one (2) is displayed. In Part B when proc, the continuation, is invoked, its argument is passed to the waiting answer-maker. The value (2) is displayed, and the result (answer-is 2) is sent to the waiting set!. The set! causes the value (answer-is 2) to be associated with resultcc. The result of the experiment is verified at [4].

We have come to our last experiment. This one is slightly trickier than the earlier ones. Because of this, we discuss all of Part A before we look at Part B. We recall that receiver-3 is the value of

```
(lambda (proc)
  (proc (list (proc (list 3 proc)))))
```

Experiment 3:[2]

---

[2] To denote the procedure that is the value of the variable procedure-name, we use the notation *<procedure-name>*.

A.

```
[1] (set! result (answer-maker (call receiver-3)))
(3 <writeln/return>)
((3 <writeln/return>))
((3 <writeln/return>))
[2] result
(answer-is (3 <writeln/return>))
[3] ((2nd (2nd result)) (list 1000))
(1000)
(1000)
[4] result
(answer-is (3 <writeln/return>))
```

The result of (call receiver-3) to be passed to answer-maker is

```
(<writeln/return>
  (list (<writeln/return>
          (list 3 <writeln/return>))))
```

First, the list (3 *<writeln/return>*) is passed to *<writeln/return>*. It dutifully displays its argument. Then a set of parentheses is wrapped around it, and that result, ((3 *<writeln/return>*)), is displayed and passed to **answer-maker**. The procedure **answer-maker** displays that list and passes (**answer-is** (3 *<writeln/return>*)) to the waiting **set!**. The **set!** does the appropriate assignment. At [2] the experiment is verified. At [3] the procedure *<writeln/return>* is extracted using (2nd (2nd result)). That procedure is then invoked on (1000). As expected *<writeln/return>* displays its argument (1000) and returns (1000). At [4] nothing has changed **result**. Although this is a contrived experiment, only simple procedures are used to do simple things. We are now ready to consider Part B.

B.

```
[5] (set! resultcc (answer-maker (call/cc receiver-3)))
(3 <ep>)
[6] resultcc
(answer-is 3 <ep>)
[7] ((3rd resultcc) (list 1000))
(1000)
[8] resultcc
(answer-is 1000)
```

The result of (call/cc receiver-3) to be passed to answer-maker is

```
(<ep>
   (list (<ep>
            (list 3 <ep>)))))
```

where *<ep>* is the continuation, which is the value of

```
(escaper
   (lambda (□)
      (set! resultcc (answer-maker □))))
```

but since *<ep>* is invoked, the outer `list`, *<ep>*, and `answer-maker` invocations are abandoned, as well as the `set!` expression. Therefore, the result of (`call/cc receiver-3`) is the result of invoking (*<ep>* (`list 3` *<ep>*)). The escape procedure *<ep>* is invoked giving the value (3 *<ep>*) as the value that is passed to `answer-maker`, which displays the list (3 *<ep>*). Next `answer-is` is consed to the front of (3 *<ep>*), which yields (`answer-is 3` *<ep>*). Then the `set!` is done, which changes the value of `resultcc`. At [6], we verify that what was expected has indeed occurred. We are about to execute the code at [7]. The expression (`3rd resultcc`) yields the escape procedure *<ep>* that was saved earlier. It is passed the list (1000). What is (*<ep>* (`list 1000`))? Recall that *<ep>* is an escape procedure that passes its argument to `answer-maker` and then assigns to `resultcc` the result of the `answer-maker` invocation. The procedure `answer-maker` displays its argument and then returns (`answer-is 1000`). The list (`answer-is 1000`) is for the waiting `set!` and so the `set!` happens again. This time `resultcc` gets the value (`answer-is 1000`), and the role of the escape procedure has ended. Was `resultcc` really changed? How do we find out? At [8], we check the value of `resultcc`. This time it has been changed to (`answer-is 1000`)! Although the `set!` was done back at [5], the escape procedure *<ep>* included doing everything again once it was invoked.

Exercises

Exercise 16.12
Rewrite `answer-maker` using `call`.

Exercise 16.13
Run the experiment with `exer-receiver`.

```
(define exer-receiver
   (lambda (proc)
      (list (proc (list 'exer proc)))))
```

Exercise 16.14

For each expression below, describe the binding that `continuation` gets, and give the value(s) of the expression. Each expression must be tested more than once. We include the solution for Part a.

a. (let ((r (lambda (continuation)
            (continuation 6))))
    (* (+ (call/cc r) 3) 8))

The value of (escaper (lambda (□) (* (+ □ 3) 8))), 72.

b. (let ((r (lambda (continuation)
            (+ 1000 (continuation 6)))))
    (* (+ (call/cc r) 3) 8))

c. (let ((r (lambda (continuation)
            (+ 1000 6))))
    (* (+ (call/cc r) 3) 8))

d. (let ((r (lambda (continuation)
            (if (zero? (random 2))
                (+ 1000 6)
                (continuation 6)))))
    (* (+ (call/cc r) 3) 8))

e. (let ((r (lambda (continuation)
            (if (zero? (random 2))
                (+ 1000 6)
                (continuation 6)))))
    (+ (* (+ (call/cc r) 3) 8)
       (* (+ (call/cc r) 3) 8)))

f. (let ((r (lambda (continuation)
            (continuation
              (if (zero? (continuation (random 2)))
                  (+ 1000 6)
                  6)))))
    (+ (* (+ (call/cc r) 3) 8)
       (* (+ (call/cc r) 3) 8)))

Exercise 16.15

Determine the outcome of Experiment 3 with [1] and [5] replaced by the expressions below.

    [1] (begin
          (set! result (answer-maker (call receiver-3)))
          'done)

```
[5] (begin
      (set! resultcc (answer-maker (call/cc receiver-3)))
      'done)
```

Exercise 16.16
We define a procedure **map-sub1** that takes a list of numbers and returns a
list with each element of the list decremented by one. In addition to doing
the work of **map-sub1**, it also sets the global variable **deep** to a continuation.

```
(define deep "any continuation")

(define map-sub1
  (lambda (ls)
    (if (null? ls)
        (let ((receiver (lambda (k)
                          (set! deep k)
                          '())))
          (call/cc receiver))
        (cons (sub1 (car ls)) (map-sub1 (cdr ls)))))))
```

Consider the following experiment:

```
[1] (cons 1000 (map-sub1 '()))
(1000)
[2] (cons 2000 (deep '(a b c)))
?_____
[3] (cons 1000 (map-sub1 '(0)))
(1000 -1)
[4] (cons 2000 (deep '(a b c)))
?_____
[5] (cons 1000 (map-sub1 '(1 0)))
(1000 0 -1)
[6] (cons 2000 (deep '(a b c)))
?_____
[7] (cons 1000 (map-sub1 '(5 4 3 2 1 0)))
(1000 4 3 2 1 0 -1)
[8] (cons 2000 (deep '(a b c)))
?_____
```

After each invocation of **map-sub1**, **deep** is reset. The first continuation
formed at [1] is:

```
(escaper
  (lambda (□)
    (cons 1000 □)))
```

At [3], the next continuation formed is:

```
(escaper
  (lambda (□)
    (cons 1000 (cons -1 □))))
```

The third continuation formed at [5] is:

```
(escaper
  (lambda (□)
    (cons 1000 (cons 0 (cons -1 □)))))
```

At [7], a fourth continuation is formed and bound to **deep**. Write an expression that characterizes that continuation, and then fill in the four blanks of the experiment.

16.6 Defining escaper

We now have all the tools we need to define **escaper**:

Program 16.5   **escaper**

```
(define *escape/thunk* "any continuation")

(define escaper
  (lambda (proc)
    (lambda (x)
      (*escape/thunk* (lambda () (proc x))))))
```

Although ***escape/thunk*** is defined as a global variable, it does not yet have the right value. To remedy this, one more experiment must be performed. For this experiment, a receiver is used to assign a value to ***escape/thunk***.

Program 16.6 `receiver-4`

```
(define receiver-4
  (lambda (continuation)
    (set! *escape/thunk* continuation)
    (*escape/thunk* (lambda () (writeln "escaper is defined")))))
```

We then have:

```
[1] ((call/cc receiver-4))
escaper is defined
[2] (*escape/thunk* (lambda () (add1 6)))
7
[3] (+ 5 (*escape/thunk* (lambda () (add1 6))))
7
```

At [1], the continuation (escaper (lambda (□) (□))) is formed by the system. It becomes the value of continuation and, in turn, the value of *escape/thunk*, indirectly changing the definition of escaper in Program 16.5. This escape procedure takes as its argument a procedure of zero arguments and immediately invokes it. Next *escape/thunk* is passed the procedure

```
(lambda () (writeln "escaper is defined"))
```

This escapes while binding □ to

```
(lambda () (writeln "escaper is defined"))
```

Finally,

```
((lambda () (writeln "escaper is defined")))
```

displays **escaper is defined**. At [2], invoking *escape/thunk* on

```
(lambda () (add1 6))
```

yields **7**; at [3], invoking it on

```
(lambda () (add1 6))
```

once again yields **7**. Because *escape/thunk* is an escape procedure, the context

```
(lambda (□) (+ 5 □))
```

is abandoned. Earlier we hypothesized **escaper**'s existence in order to explain the continuations formed from invocations of **call/cc**. Now we have defined **escaper** using **call/cc**, which *is* in Scheme. The procedure **call/cc** is not built with **escaper**, as we suggested earlier, but it behaves as though it were. On some systems, it may be necessary to determine the value of ***escape/thunk*** at the prompt by invoking ((**call/cc receiver-4**)).

Using ***escape/thunk*** we can redefine **escaper** so that it accepts procedures of any number of arguments:

Program 16.7   escaper

```
(define escaper
  (lambda (proc)
    (lambda args
      (*escape/thunk*
        (lambda ()
          (apply proc args)))))))
```

This definition of **escaper** can be used to test all the results and exercises of this chapter.

Exercises

Exercise 16.17
Assume the existence of **escaper** and then define ***escape/thunk*** with **escaper**. You may not use **call/cc**.

Exercise 16.18
Determine the value of (/ 5 (***escape/thunk*** (lambda () 0))).

Exercise 16.19: reset
Use **call/cc** to define a zero-argument procedure **reset** that upon invocation abandons its context and causes the string "reset invoked" to be displayed. In Chapter 7, when we defined **error**, we assumed the existence of **reset**. For example,

```
[1] (cons 1 (reset))
reset invoked
```

Exercise 16.20
Explain why (*escape/thunk* *escape/thunk*) causes an error.

Exercise 16.21
Determine the value of the following expressions:

```
[1] (let ((r (escaper
              (lambda (proc)
                (cons 'c (proc (cons 'd '())))))))
      (cons 'a (cons 'b (call/cc r))))

[2] (let ((r (escaper
              (lambda (proc)
                (cons 'c (cons 'd '()))))))
      (cons 'a (cons 'b (call/cc r))))
```

Exercise 16.22
Consider the procedure new-escaper below.

```
(define new-escaper "any procedure")
(let ((receiver (lambda (continuation)
                  (set! new-escaper
                    (lambda (proc)
                      (lambda args
                        (continuation
                          (lambda ()
                            (apply proc args))))))
                  (lambda () (writeln "new-escaper is defined")))))
  ((call/cc receiver)))  displays new-escaper is defined
```

Are new-escaper and escaper the same? Why is new-escaper *better* than escaper?

16.7 Escaping from Infinite Loops

Suppose we would like to separate some code into control and action. To be a bit more specific, consider a piece of program that we want to run forever:

```
(let ((r (random n)))
  (if (= r target)
      (begin (writeln count) (set! count 0))
      (set! count (+ count 1))))
```

Program 16.8 `how-many-till`

```
(define how-many-till
  (lambda (n target)
    (let ((count 0))
      (cycle-proc
        (lambda ()
          (let ((r (random n)))
            (if (= r target)
                (begin (writeln count) (set! count 0))
                (set! count (+ count 1)))))))))
```

Then using `cycle-proc` (see Program 14.11), which runs a zero-argument procedure forever, we can write Program 16.8. The procedure `how-many-till` continuously reports how many values are unequal to the target. If the number displayed is always the same, then we ought to question the randomness of the random number generator. Each time it displays a count, the counter is reset. The only way to stop this program is by some kind of keyboard interrupt mechanism. However, we can build into `how-many-till` an exit facility using `call/cc`. Instead of looping indefinitely, we exit whenever the sum of the counts is greater than some threshold. We need an additional local variable that maintains the sum. We invoke the procedure `how-many-till` with the threshold as an additional argument. This version of `how-many-till` is given in Program 16.9. If `exit-above-threshold` is ever invoked, then we come out of the invocation of (`how-many-till n target thresh`); otherwise we stay within `cycle-proc`. What is interesting about this example is that it is possible to exit an infinite loop without changing the definition of `cycle-proc`.

An example of the use of `how-many-till` is given in Program 16.10, where we can invoke (`random-data 10 20`).

The first continuation formed (by the `call/cc` in `how-many-till`) is the value of

Program 16.9   `how-many-till`

```
(define how-many-till
  (lambda (n target thresh)
    (let ((receiver
            (lambda (exit-above-threshold)
              (let ((count 0) (sum 0))
                (cycle-proc
                  (lambda ()
                    (if (= (random n) target)
                        (begin
                          (writeln "target " target
                                   " required " count " trials")
                          (set! sum (+ sum count))
                          (set! count 0)
                          (if (> sum thresh)
                              (exit-above-threshold sum)))
                        (set! count (+ count 1)))))))))
      (call/cc receiver)))))
```

Program 16.10   `random-data`

```
(define random-data
  (lambda (n thresh)
    (letrec ((loop (lambda (target)
                     (cond
                       ((negative? target) '())
                       (else (cons (how-many-till n target thresh)
                                   (loop (sub1 target))))))))
      (loop (sub1 n)))))
```

```
(escaper
  (lambda (□)
    (cons □ (loop (sub1 target)))))
```

where `loop` is as it is defined in **random-data** and target is 9.

Exercise 16.23
Explain why the test for termination within **random-data** is (**negative? target**).

16.8 Escaping from Flat Recursions

The **call/cc** operator gives the ability to escape from recursive computations while basically throwing out all the work that has stacked up. A simple example clarifies in what sense the mechanism avoids doing pending computations. We look at the problem of taking the product of a list of numbers and adding the number n to the product if the result is nonzero:

```
(product+ 5 ’(3 6 2 7)) ⟹ (+ 5 252) ⟹ 257
(product+ 7 ’(2 3 0 8)) ⟹ 0
```

Here is the solution in a functional style:

Program 16.11 product+

```
(define product+
  (lambda (n nums)
    (letrec
      ((product (lambda (nums)
                  (cond
                    ((null? nums) 1)
                    (else (* (car nums) (product (cdr nums)))))))))
      (let ((prod (product nums)))
        (if (zero? prod) 0 (+ n prod)))))))
```

This solution can be improved by adding a test to determine if one of the values in the list is zero. This stops the recursion upon encountering the first zero. This version is in Program 16.12. Consider the following subtle fact: *Finding a zero in the list does not stop the computation of* **product**. In fact, what happens is that if the first zero is in the *k*th position, then there are *k* − 1 multiplications using zero. This is because the context of the **product**

Program 16.12   product+

```
(define product+
  (lambda (n nums)
    (letrec
      ((product (lambda (nums)
                  (cond
                    ((null? nums) 1)
                    ((zero? (car nums)) 0)
                    (else (* (car nums) (product (cdr nums)))))))))
      (let ((prod (product nums)))
        (if (zero? prod) 0 (+ n prod)))))))
```

invocations includes $k - 1$ multiplications. When the zero is found, each of the $k - 1$ waiting multiplications must still be done.

Is it possible to exit the invocation of **product** so that the result causes no waiting multiplications to occur? A solution is in Program 16.13. Consider the invocation (+ 100 (product+ 10 '(2 3 4 0 6 7))). Since the list of numbers contains a 0, the continuation, which is the value of

```
(escaper
  (lambda (□)
    (+ 100 □)))
```

is invoked, and the result is 100. This follows because the continuation is being invoked on 0. If, however, no zero is found, then (product nums) terminates normally, and (+ n prod) is returned as the value of (receiver <ep>). Since prod cannot be zero, the result returned is (+ n prod). The let expression can be shortened to (+ n (product nums)). This version is in Program 16.14.

We see that finding a zero in the list produces a value to pass to the continuation formed from the invocation of (call/cc receiver) and finishes the computation of **product+**. Moreover, we observe the rather surprising fact that *if there is a zero in the list, then no multiplications occur regardless of where in the list that zero occurs.*

Program 16.13   product+

```
(define product+
  (lambda (n nums)
    (let ((receiver
            (lambda (exit-on-zero)
              (letrec
                ((product (lambda (nums)
                            (cond
                              ((null? nums) 1)
                              ((zero? (car nums)) (exit-on-zero 0))
                              (else (* (car nums)
                                       (product (cdr nums)))))))))
                (let ((prod (product nums)))
                  (if (zero? prod) 0 (+ n prod)))))))
      (call/cc receiver))))
```

Program 16.14   product+

```
(define product+
  (lambda (n nums)
    (let ((receiver
            (lambda (exit-on-zero)
              (letrec
                ((product (lambda (nums)
                            (cond
                              ((null? nums) 1)
                              ((zero? (car nums)) (exit-on-zero 0))
                              (else (* (car nums)
                                       (product (cdr nums)))))))))
                (+ n (product nums)))))
      (call/cc receiver))))
```

16.9 Escaping from Deep Recursions

Let us take a look at a slightly more complicated example. The problem is to
redefine product+ for a larger class of lists. Specifically, we allow deep lists
of numbers. Thus we can invoke

```
(product+ 5 '((1 2) (1 1 (3 1 1)) (((((1 1 0) 1) 4) 1) 1)))
```

Program 16.15   product+

```
(define product+
  (lambda (n nums)
    (let ((receiver
            (lambda (exit-on-zero)
              (letrec
                ((product
                   (lambda (nums)
                     (cond
                       ((null? nums) 1)
                       ((number? (car nums))
                        (cond
                          ((zero? (car nums)) (exit-on-zero 0))
                          (else (* (car nums)
                                   (product (cdr nums))))))
                       (else (* (product (car nums))
                                (product (cdr nums))))))))
                (+ n (product nums))))))
      (call/cc receiver))))
```

Program 16.16   *-and-count-maker

```
(define *-and-count-maker
  (lambda ()
    (let ((local-counter 0))
      (lambda (n1 n2)
        (set! local-counter (+ local-counter 1))
        (writeln "Number of multiplications = " local-counter)
        (* n1 n2)))))
```

which results in 0. However, if the 0 had been a 3, then the result would have
been 77. The new definition of **product+** is given in Program 16.15.

Some, but not all, multiplications are avoidable. By counting the number of
multiplications, we can discover how many can be avoided. This can be done
by invoking a special multiplication procedure ***-and-count-maker**, given in
Program 16.16, and then passing the result of its invocation as an argument
to **product+**. The procedure **product+** in a functional style would have once
again introduced all those multiplications by zero. (See Program 16.17.) Thus
we can invoke:

Program 16.17 product+

```
(define product+
  (lambda (n nums *-proc)
    (letrec
      ((product
         (lambda (nums)
           (cond
             ((null? nums) 1)
             ((number? (car nums))
              (cond
                ((zero? (car nums)) 0)
                (else (*-proc (car nums) (product (cdr nums))))))
             (else
               (let ((val (product (car nums))))
                 (cond
                   ((zero? val) 0)
                   (else (*-proc val (product (cdr nums)))))))))))
      (let ((prod (product nums)))
        (if (zero? prod) 0 (+ n prod))))))
```

```
(let ((counter (*-and-count-maker))
      (num-list '((1 2) (1 1 (3 1 1)) (((((1 1 0) 1) 4) 1) 1))))
  (product+ 5 num-list counter))
```

When product+ of Program 16.17 is used on the given tree, there are 12 multiplications, and when product+ of Program 16.15 is used there are fewer than 12 multiplications. There is, of course, a way to avoid all multiplications, but it involves walking through the entire list looking for 0's before starting the multiplication process. This makes the algorithm two-pass (it would require two passes through the list).

Exercises

Exercise 16.24
Run product+ of Program 16.14 with the *-proc argument over a list of numbers to verify the claim that no multiplications occur if the list contains a 0. Run product+ of Program 16.12 with the *-proc argument over the same list to compare with the first part of this exercise.

Exercise 16.25

Run product+ of Program 16.15 with the *-proc argument over the nested list of numbers given above. Run product+ of Program 16.17 with the *-proc argument over the same list to compare with the first part of this exercise.

Exercise 16.26

Rewrite product+ of Program 16.15 where n is always 0.

Exercise 16.27

Rewrite product+ of Programs 16.14 and 16.15 using a local variable to maintain the accumulating product. Can this be done without using call/cc?

17　Using Continuations

17.1　Overview

In this chapter we discover some unusual properties of continuations. We demonstrate how to build a *break* facility. This allows computations to halt and then restart an indefinite number of times. Each time the computation halts, the user will be able to interact with the system. In addition, we show how to build a *coroutine* system. In such systems, multiple procedures can interact with each other without actually returning control from within each process. Before we begin this development, we review the fundamental rules concerning `call/cc`.

17.2　Review of call/cc

1. `call/cc`'s argument is called a *receiver*.

2. A receiver's argument is called a *continuation*. It is an escape procedure <*ep*> of one argument formed from the context of the call/cc invocation.

3.¡A continuation's argument is passed to the context from which <*ep*> was formed by invoking <*ep*> on that value.

4. If the escape procedure <*ep*> is formed from the call/cc invocation and is then ignored, the following hold, where the use of ellipses surrounding an expression indicates that the expression may be embedded:

```
(let ((receiver (lambda (continuation) body)))
  ... (call/cc receiver) ...)
  =
(let ((receiver (lambda (continuation) body)))
  ... (receiver 'anything) ...)
  =
... body ...
```

and

```
  ...
  (let ((receiver (escaper (lambda (continuation) body))))
    ... (call/cc receiver) ...)
  ...
  =
  ...
  (let ((receiver (escaper (lambda (continuation) body))))
    ... (receiver 'anything) ...)
  ...
  = (receiver 'anything)
  = body
```

where the next to the last equality holds since receiver is an escape procedure, and the last equality holds since continuation is ignored.

5. In all circumstances the following hold:

```
(let ((receiver (lambda (continuation) (continuation body))))
  ... (call/cc receiver) ...)
  =
(let ((receiver (lambda (continuation) body)))
  ... (call/cc receiver) ...)
```

and

```
(let ((receiver (escaper (lambda (continuation) (continuation body)))))
  ... (call/cc receiver) ...)
  =
(let ((receiver (lambda (continuation) body)))
  ... (call/cc receiver) ...)
```

```
(define countdown
  (lambda (n)
    (writeln "This only appears once")
    (let ((pair (message "Exit" (attempt (message "Enter" n)))))
      (let ((v (1st pair))
            (returner (2nd pair)))
        (writeln "    The non-negative-number: " v)
        (if (positive? v)
            (returner (list (sub1 v) returner))
            (writeln "Blastoff"))))))
```

17.3 Making Loops with One Continuation

In the previous chapter we introduced continuations. We noted that continuations were escape procedures and could be the value returned by any procedure or could be stored in data structures; however, our examples (except for the third experiment and **escaper**) ignored that feature. Each example shared the property that once a receiver was exited, the continuation was useless. Each receiver's continuation was always invoked; it was never passed as an argument or considered as the value of any procedure invocation. This property led us to refer to the continuations with such names as **exit-above-threshold** and **exit-on-zero**, because each was invoked only once for each invocation of its associated receiver. Now we abandon this property so that a continuation survives beyond giving a value to its associated receiver's invocation.

Earlier we used a continuation to exit deep recursions with the various definitions of **product+**. However, we have not yet developed an interesting use of a continuation, other than ***escape/thunk***, that can be returned as a value and stored in a data structure. To illustrate such a continuation, we define a procedure **countdown** that counts a positive integer down until it reaches zero. This is a very simple loop. We use two different definitions of the auxiliary procedure **attempt**. The first does not create any continuations and does not perform a loop. The second does create a single continuation and with this continuation is able to perform a loop. The definition of **countdown** uses a trivial displaying procedure **message** for tracking the flow of the computation. The definitions are given in Programs 17.1, 17.2, and 17.3.

The value of **proc** is just the identity procedure we denote as *<proc>*. Here is what appears when (**countdown 3**) is invoked:

Program 17.2   message

```
(define message
  (lambda (direction value)
    (writeln "   " direction "ing attempt with value: " value)
    value))
```

Program 17.3   attempt

```
(define attempt
  (lambda (n)
    (let ((receiver (lambda (proc) (list n proc))))
      (receiver (lambda (x) x)))))
```

```
This only appears once
   Entering attempt with value: 3
   Exiting attempt with value: (3 <proc>)
     The non-negative-number: 3
(2 <proc>)
```

"**This only appears once**" appears once. The next event is an attempt to find the value of the expression (**message "Enter" 3**). This produces the message, "**Entering attempt with value: 3**" and **message** returns its second argument, 3. So now we attempt to find the value of the invocation (**attempt 3**). This invocation yields the list (3 *<proc>*) because once the list (**list n proc**) is constructed, **attempt** is exited. Next we attempt to find the value of the expression (**message "Exit" (3 *<proc>*)**). Once again the message is displayed, but this time it is an exiting message, "**Exiting attempt with value: (3 *<proc>*).**" The invocation's value is (3 *<proc>*). Now we bind **pair** to this list, take the pair apart, bind **v** to 3, and bind **returner** to *<proc>*. We display a message that acknowledges where we are and that we do indeed have the correct value. The message is, "**The non-negative number: 3.**" We then check to see if the number is positive. In this case it is. We invoke (**returner (list (sub1 v) returner)**). We form the list (2 *<proc>*) and hand this list to *<proc>*, which returns (2 *<proc>*). With the definition of **attempt** in Program 17.3, we did not create a loop nor did the result end with **Blastoff**.

We now redefine **attempt** (see Program 17.4) to create a continuation *<ep>* that we return in place of *<proc>*. In the discussion that follows, we explain

Program 17.4 `attempt`

```
(define attempt
  (lambda (n)
    (let ((receiver (lambda (proc) (list n proc))))
      (call/cc receiver))))
```

how that continuation is powerful enough to build a looping construct.

The result of (countdown 3) using attempt of Program 17.4 follows:

```
This only appears once
   Entering attempt with value: 3
   Exiting attempt with value: (3 <ep>)
    The non-negative-number: 3
   Exiting attempt with value: (2 <ep>)
    The non-negative-number: 2
   Exiting attempt with value: (1 <ep>)
    The non-negative-number: 1
   Exiting attempt with value: (0 <ep>)
    The non-negative-number: 0
Blastoff
```

"This only appears once" appears once. The next event is an attempt to find the value of the expression (message "Enter" 3). This produces the message, "Entering attempt with value: 3" and message returns its second argument, 3. So now we attempt to find the value of the invocation (attempt 3). This invocation yields the list (3 <ep>) because once the list (list n proc) is constructed, attempt is exited. Next we attempt to find the value of the expression (message "Exit" (3 <ep>)). Once again the message is displayed, but this time it is an exiting message, "Exiting attempt with value: (3 <ep>)." The invocation's value is (3 <ep>). Now we bind pair to this list, take the pair apart, bind v to 3, and bind returner to <ep>. We display a message that acknowledges where we are and that we do indeed have the correct value. The message is, "The non-negative number: 3." We then check to see if the number is positive. In this case it is. We invoke (returner (list (sub1 v) returner)). We form the list (2 <ep>) and hand this list to <ep>.

To this point, everything has been the same as in the analysis of attempt of Program 17.3. In fact, all we did to write the above paragraph was change instances of <proc> to <ep>. Now we are doing something new. Instead of invoking <proc>, we are invoking <ep>. The continuation <ep> is the value of

```
(escaper
  (lambda (□)
    (let ((pair (message "Exit" □)))
      (let ((v (1st pair))
            (returner (2nd pair)))
        (writeln "   The non-negative-number: " v)
        (if (positive? v)
            (returner (list (sub1 v) returner))
            (writeln "Blastoff"))))))
```

This continuation is formed as the result of the first and only invocation of
attempt. That is, the value passed as an argument to *<ep>* becomes the
second argument to **message** in the let expression that binds **pair**. The
next event is the displaying of the message, "Exiting attempt with value:
(2 *<ep>*)." To go a bit further, the value of this message invocation is (2
<ep>). We bind **pair** to this list, take the pair apart binding **v** to 2 and
binding **returner** to the same *<ep>*. Once again we display a message that
acknowledges where we are and that we do indeed have the correct value.
The message is, "The non-negative number: 2." We then check to see if
the number is still positive. In this case it is. We invoke

$$\text{(returner (list (sub1 v) returner))}$$

Clearly we are in a loop, with v replaced by (sub1 v). The loop terminates
when v is no longer positive. An important point is that call/cc is invoked
only once. Therefore, we know for certain that *<ep>* is always the same
continuation. The procedure **attempt** of Program 17.4 is invoked only once
and its body is never reentered. This follows because the sentence "Entering
attempt with value: *n*" appears only when *n* is 3.

Exercise

Exercise 17.1: cycle-proc
Rewrite cycle-proc using continuations instead of recursion as presented in
Program 14.11.

17.4 Experimenting with Multiple Continuations

In this section we consider an experiment where we use more than one continuation. Everything until now has worked with just one continuation. Now we shall use several continuations. To keep track of the full meaning of each continuation, we shall plug in values for variables that will not change. This frees us from having to remember their values for use later.

In this experiment we need a receiver and a testing procedure. The receiver returns <*ep*>, which it receives as an argument. There are several continuations formed in this one example, so it is easy to get confused.

Program 17.5   receiver

```
(define receiver
  (lambda (continuation)
    (continuation continuation)))
```

Program 17.6   tester

```
(define tester
  (lambda (continuation)
    (writeln "beginning")
    (call/cc continuation)
    (writeln "middle")
    (call/cc continuation)
    (writeln "end")))
```

Experiment:

```
[1] (tester (call/cc receiver))
beginning
beginning
middle
beginning
end
[2]
```

The first event is to form <*ep*>, which, if it ever gets an argument, passes that argument to **tester**. *<ep>* is the value of:

```
(escaper
  (lambda (□)
    (tester □)))
```

We can think of *<ep>* as (**escaper tester**). We invoke (**tester** *<ep>*).
Now **continuation** is bound to *<ep>*. We write **beginning**. We next invoke
(**call/cc** *<ep>*). This causes us to create *<epa>*. Before we figure out anything about what *<ep>* does with *<epa>*, we must understand what *<epa>*
does if it ever gets invoked. *<epa>* is the value of:

```
(escaper
  (lambda (□)
    □
    (writeln "middle")
    (call/cc <ep>)
    (writeln "end")))
```

The continuation *<epa>* ignores its argument, □, displays **middle**, then invokes (**call/cc** *<ep>*), and when that returns, it displays **end**. Now recall
that *<ep>* takes its argument and invokes (**escaper tester**) on its argument,
so **continuation** is bound to *<epa>*. We write **beginning**. We next invoke
(**call/cc** *<epa>*). This causes us to create *<epb>*. Before we figure out anything about what *<epa>* does with *<epb>*, we must understand what *<epb>*
does if it ever gets invoked. *<epb>* is the value of:

```
(escaper
  (lambda (□)
    □
    (writeln "middle")
    (call/cc <epa>)
    (writeln "end")))
```

The continuation *<epb>* ignores its argument, displays **middle**, then invokes
(**call/cc** *<epa>*), and when that returns, it displays **end**. Now recall that
<epa> takes its argument (ignores it) and displays **middle**, which we do now,
and then invokes (**call/cc** *<ep>*). Once again we form the new continuation
<epc>, which is the value of:

```
(escaper
  (lambda (□)
    □
    (writeln "end")))
```

This continuation ignores its argument and displays **end**, so now we invoke ((escaper tester) *<epc>*). First, we display **beginning**. Next we invoke (call/cc *<epc>*). This causes the creation of the new continuation *<epd>*, which is the value of:

```
(escaper
  (lambda (□)
    □
    (writeln "middle")
    (call/cc <epc>)
    (writeln "end")))
```

This continuation displays **middle**, invokes (call/cc *<epc>*), and when that returns, it displays **end**. What is (*<epc>* *<epd>*)? The continuation *<epc>* is an escape procedure that ignores its argument and displays **end**. So we ignore *<epd>*, after having gone to all the trouble of constructing it, and display **end**.

Exercises

Exercise 17.2
During the experiment, how many more continuations were formed than were invoked?

Exercise 17.3
Determine what this expression represents:

```
(let ((receiver (lambda (continuation)
                  (call/cc continuation))))
  (call/cc receiver))
```

What is (call/cc call/cc)?

17.5 Escaping from and Returning to Deep Recursions

In product+ of Section 16.9, we demonstrated how to escape from deep recursions. Sometimes we want to escape from deep recursions but jump right back in when we so desire. In this section, we present a use of continuations that allows such behavior. We leave the deep recursion, but we give ourselves the ability to get right back where we were at the time we left. We assume

Program 17.7 `flatten-number-list`

```
(define flatten-number-list
  (lambda (s)
    (cond
      ((null? s) '())
      ((number? s) (list (break s)))
      (else
        (let ((flatcar
                (flatten-number-list (car s))))
          (append flatcar
                  (flatten-number-list (cdr s)))))))))
```

Program 17.8 `break`

```
(define break
  (lambda (x)
    x))
```

Program 17.9 `break`

```
(define break
  (lambda (x)
    (let ((break-receiver
            (lambda (continuation)
              (continuation x))))
      (call/cc break-receiver))))
```

that the data for the example are the same as those of product+: a deep list of numbers. (See Section 16.9.)

Consider the definition of `flatten-number-list` in Program 17.7, where the first version of `break` is the identity procedure given in Program 17.8. Hence:

`(flatten-number-list '((1 2 3) ((4 5)) (6))) ⟹ (1 2 3 4 5 6)`

Another way to write `break`, which uses continuations but has the same meaning, is given in Program 17.9. This follows because we return as a value the argument to `break`. Since that value is x, we get the equivalent of (lambda

Program 17.10   break

```
(define get-back "any procedure")

(define break
  (lambda (x)
    (let ((break-receiver
            (lambda (continuation)
              (set! get-back (lambda () (continuation x)))
              (any-action x))))
      (call/cc break-receiver))))
```

Program 17.11   any-action

```
(define any-action
  (lambda (x)
    (writeln x)
    (get-back)))
```

Program 17.12   any-action

```
(define any-action
  (lambda (x)
    ((escaper (lambda () x)))
    (get-back)))
```

(x) x). But now we have access to continuation, and, moreover, we can characterize its behavior. Whenever break is invoked, we can think about the call as temporarily halting the computation; by invoking continuation on the same argument, we can continue the computation where it left off. We do not notice anything about the *pause* taking place because the continuation invocation happens immediately. But that is not required. For example, in Program 17.10, we display the value of the argument to break, using any-action, which is defined in Program 17.11. But since any-action is any action whatsoever, we may rewrite it as shown in Program 17.12 instead of explicitly writing the value of x.

Does the invocation of (get-back) in any-action of Program 17.12 ever happen? Because we are invoking an escape procedure prior to invoking

Program 17.13 break

```
(define get-back "any escape procedure")

(define break
  (lambda (x)
    (let ((break-receiver
            (lambda (continuation)
              (set! get-back continuation)
              (any-action x))))
      (call/cc break-receiver))))
```

(get-back), the answer is no. Is there a way to get back into the original computation? The answer is yes. Since get-back is bound globally, we can invoke it at the prompt. Below is an experiment using these tools.

```
[1] (flatten-number-list '((1 2) 3))
1
[2] (get-back)
2
[3] (get-back)
3
[4] (get-back)
(1 2 3)
```

The procedure **break** has a limitation. There is no control over what value is sent back. Unfortunately, that is determined by the definition of get-back. We can soften the definition by allowing get-back to accept an argument. Then get-back becomes

```
(lambda (v) (continuation v))
```

which is the same as continuation and gives us Program 17.13. We can still use any-action defined in Program 17.12 since the escaper invocation guarantees that (get-back) will never be invoked. Whenever get-back is invoked, it must be passed an argument.

Then the experiment could produce different results:

```
[1] (flatten-number-list '((1 2) 3))
1
[2] (get-back 4)
2
```

Program 17.14 any-action

```
(define break-argument "any value")

(define any-action
  (lambda (x)
    (set! break-argument x)
    ((escaper (lambda () x)))))
```

```
[3] (get-back 5)
3
[4] (get-back 6)
(4 5 6)
```

Why is the result (**4 5 6**) in this experiment, whereas it was (**1 2 3**) in the previous experiment? By returning the values **4**, **5**, and **6** to the **get-back** continuation, we are returning a different value each time. The computation was repeatedly suspended waiting for a value, which we supplied interactively at the prompt.

We might want to make public the value of the argument to **break**. We can do this in **any-action**, as shown in Program 17.14.

Finally, we note in Program 17.15 that **any-action** is not strictly necessary and can be included in the definition of **break-receiver**. The procedure **break** is an interesting program. It is very useful for interactive debugging. For example, by changing the argument to **break**, we can construct a mechanism for accessing and modifying part of the local state at the point of the invocation of **break**. This can be accomplished by passing to **break** procedures such as

$$\text{(lambda () x) or (lambda (v) (set! x v))}$$

In this case, if **x** is locally bound at the time of invocation of **break**, the list composed of these two procedures gives a lot of power to affect the internal state of a computation. Program 17.16 shows how **flatten-number-list** changes to support **break**. Whenever **break** occurs, **break-argument** gets bound to a two-element list and we define the extract and store procedures as shown in Programs 17.17 and 17.18.

This is just the tip of an iceberg. We are concerned only about one variable. This idea for debugging can be generalized to lists of arbitrarily many variables, but its utility diminishes as the number of variables increases. If

Program 17.15   break

```
(define get-back "any escape procedure")

(define break-argument "any value")

(define break
  (lambda (x)
    (let ((break-receiver
            (lambda (continuation)
              (set! get-back continuation)
              (set! break-argument x)
              ((escaper (lambda () x))))))
      (call/cc break-receiver))))
```

Program 17.16   flatten-number-list

```
(define flatten-number-list
  (lambda (s)
    (cond
      ((null? s) '())
      ((number? s) (list
                     (break
                       (list (lambda () s)
                             (lambda (v) (set! s v))))))
      (else
        (let ((flatcar
                (flatten-number-list (car s))))
          (append flatcar
                  (flatten-number-list (cdr s))))))))
```

Program 17.17   extract

```
(define extract
  (lambda ()
    ((1st break-argument))))
```

there are too many variables, it may be time to redesign the procedures. With break we have seen how there are many continuations coming from one pro-

Program 17.18 `store`

```
(define store
  (lambda (value)
    ((2nd break-argument) value)))
```

cedure invocation of **flatten-number-list**. Each of these continuations is eventually invoked after escaping to the prompt. The escape to the prompt is not very exciting. In the next section we allow far more interesting behavior to balance each continuation. Because the behavior of such uses of continuations is balanced, these continuations are called *co*routines.

Exercises

Exercise 17.4: `flatten-number-list`
Consider the new definition of **flatten-number-list** below. What changes are needed to make the sequence of invocations to **get-back** in the first experiment produce the same result? How about for the second experiment?

```
(define flatten-number-list
  (lambda (s)
    (letrec
      ((flatten
         (lambda (s)
           (cond
             ((null? s) '())
             ((number? s) (break (list s)))
             (else (let ((flatcar (flatten (car s))))
                     (append flatcar (flatten (cdr s)))))))))
      (flatten s))))
```

Exercise 17.5
Consider how we can repeat the results of the first experiment using **flatten-number-list** of Program 17.16. A condition imposed on this exercise is that no number may be input from [2] to the end of the experiment. *Hint*: Do not use **store**.

Exercise 17.6: `product+`
Consider **product+** below and define **break-on-zero**, which displays a **0** and escapes to the prompt. Each time it displays a **0**, resume the computation

as if the 0 had been a 1. This can be done by typing (get-back 1) at the prompt. If more than three zeros are found, then the result is "error: too many zeros." This is actually a form of exception handling where finding the 0 corresponds to an *exception* and finding the fourth 0 corresponds to an *error*. Experiment with different models of user interaction.

```
(define product+
  (lambda (n ls)
    (letrec ((product
               (lambda (ls)
                 (cond
                   ((null? ls) 1)
                   ((number? (car ls))
                    (* (if (zero? (car ls)) (break-on-zero) (car ls))
                       (product (cdr ls))))
                   (else (* (product (car ls))
                            (product (cdr ls))))))))
      (+ n (product ls)))))
```

Experiment with

```
(product+ 5 '((1 2) (3 4) (0 6) (7 0)))

(product+ 5 '((1 2) (0 3) (2 ((0 0 5) 0) 0)))
```

Exercise 17.7: break-var

A syntax table entry for break-var can be written so that:

$$(\text{break-var } \textit{var})$$
$$\equiv$$
$$(\text{break (list (lambda () } \textit{var}) \text{ (lambda (v) (set! } \textit{var } \text{v))))}$$

Test flatten-number-list of Program 17.16 using break-var.

Bonus: This works for all variable names except one. Why is the variable name, for which it does not work, a bad choice?

Exercise 17.8

Consider the following experiment:

```
[1] (flatten-number-list '((1 2) 3))
1
[2] (get-back 4)
2
[3] (flatten-number-list '((5 6 7) 8))
5
```

In this experiment, (**flatten-number-list** '((1 2) 3)) never gets a value. Why? Generalize **break** to maintain a list (as a stack) of **get-back** continuations so that no information is lost. Then continue the experiment to get these results.

```
[4] (get-back 7)
6
[5] (get-back 8)
7
[6] (get-back 9)
8
[7] (get-back 10)
(7 8 9 10)
[8] (get-back 5)
3
[9] (get-back 6)
(4 5 6)
```

Exercise 17.9

Consider the results of the experiment from the previous exercise. How would the results differ if the list of continuations were treated like a queue instead of a stack?

17.6 Coroutines: Continuations in Action

There are lots of ways to package control information. We next look at a famous problem along with a well-known control mechanism. The problem is Grune's problem, and the control mechanism is called coroutines. Before we look at Grune's problem, we consider a simplified version of the use of coroutines. It is sometimes legitimate to imagine that several procedures are running at the same time, sending information among themselves. In this model, only one procedure is running at any given time. When information is sent from an active procedure to a dormant procedure, the active procedure becomes dormant, and the dormant procedure, the one receiving the information, becomes the active one.

One of the best examples for thinking about coroutines comes from game playing. Imagine a typical board game with three players. Each player is modeled by a coroutine, so there are three coroutines. Let us name these coroutines A, B, and C. Let us further assume that A plays first, hands the dice to B, B then plays and hands the dice to C, and then C plays and hands the dice back to A, and so on. In translating this game into a computer program, the code for A indicates a transfer of control by *resuming* B, and it indicates a transfer of the dice by passing them as an operand with the *resume* operation. This is accomplished by including in the code for A an instance of (**resume B dice**). Similarly, the code for B includes (**resume C dice**), and the code for C includes (**resume A dice**). The act of resuming means that the coroutine stops processing, and the entity that is the first argument to **resume** continues processing where it left off.

The board game's control flow is very regular. A plays, then B plays, then C plays, then A plays, and so on. As a result, not enough of the generality of coroutines can be seen through a board game simulation. If each player determined randomly which opposing player was to play next, this would require much of the generality of coroutines. Rather than using random numbers we simply picked an unnatural ordering that is illustrated in Program 17.19. Remember that nothing is displayed in a writeln expression until *all* of its operands have a value. Now if we invoke (**A '***) we get the following output:

```
[1] (A '*)
This is A
                This is B
                                This is C
Came from C
Back in A
                                Came from A
                                Back in C
                Came from C
                Back in B
Came from B
```

Let us see what it takes to make these programs work. We need the procedure **coroutine-maker**, which takes a procedure as an argument. This argument is a procedure that obtains a meaning for **resume** and **v** when it is invoked. The variable **v** is of little concern. We focus on the variable **resume**. From these examples, we see that **resume** necessarily must look like a procedure of two arguments. When **resume** is invoked, it does not immediately return a value. In fact, it gives up control to whomever it is resuming and eventually gets an answer when someone else resumes it. (Since coroutines are first class, not only can they be passed as the required first argument to **resume**, but they can also be included in the second argument to **resume**.) Program 17.20 contains **coroutine-maker**.

The first thing that **coroutine-maker** does is create a local variable that will only hold continuations. Next, a procedure **update-continuation!** is

Program 17.19 Coroutines for a simple board game

```
(define A
  (let ((A-proc (lambda (resume v)
                  (writeln "This is A")
                  (writeln "Came from " (resume B "A"))
                  (writeln "Back in A")
                  (writeln "Came from " (resume C "A")))))
    (coroutine-maker A-proc)))

(define B
  (let ((B-proc (lambda (resume v)
                  (writeln (blanks 14) "This is B")
                  (writeln (blanks 14)
                           "Came from " (resume C "B"))
                  (writeln (blanks 14) "Back in B")
                  (writeln (blanks 14)
                           "Came from " (resume A "B")))))
    (coroutine-maker B-proc)))

(define C
  (let ((C-proc (lambda (resume v)
                  (writeln (blanks 28) "This is C")
                  (writeln (blanks 28)
                           "Came from " (resume A "C"))
                  (writeln (blanks 28) "Back in C")
                  (writeln (blanks 28)
                           "Came from " (resume B "C")))))
    (coroutine-maker C-proc)))
```

formed so that local side effects to **saved-continuation** can be done within other procedures. This is reminiscent of some of the techniques we presented in Chapter 12 when we showed how objects were built. The procedure **resumer**, having the properties of **resume** we discussed above, is next defined using **resume-maker**, whose code is given in Program 17.21. A boolean flag, **first-time**, is initially true. Then a procedure is returned. The first time this procedure is invoked, **(proc resumer value)** is evaluated. This is where the binding of **resume** and **v** in the programs above takes place. Subsequent invocations of this procedure invoke a continuation that was stored as a result of an earlier invocation of a **resume** to some other coroutine. Basically, the structure of **resumer** is

Program 17.20 `coroutine-maker`

```
(define coroutine-maker
  (lambda (proc)
    (let ((saved-continuation "any continuation"))
      (let ((update-continuation!
              (lambda (v)
                (set! saved-continuation v))))
        (let ((resumer (resume-maker update-continuation!))
              (first-time #t))
          (lambda (value)
            (if first-time
                (begin
                  (set! first-time #f)
                  (proc resumer value))
                (saved-continuation value)))))))))
```

Program 17.21 `resume-maker`

```
(define resume-maker
  (lambda (update-proc!)
    (lambda (next-coroutine value)
      (let ((receiver (lambda (continuation)
                        (update-proc! continuation)
                        (next-coroutine value))))
        (call/cc receiver)))))
```

```
(lambda (next-coroutine value)
  (let ((receiver (lambda (continuation)
                    (<update-continuation!> continuation)
                    (next-coroutine value))))
    (call/cc receiver)))
```

Thus far the code has not shown us where the continuations are being created. In `coroutine-maker`, this is done in the procedure formed by invoking `(resume-maker update-continuation!)`.

When `resumer` is invoked with a coroutine, say **B**, and a value, say **"V"**, a continuation is bound to `continuation`. That continuation is stored in the `saved-continuation` associated with the code of the invoker of `resumer`. For example, if the code (`resume B "V"`) is invoked from within **A**, then the updating takes place in the `saved-continuation` associated with coroutine **A**. When the updating is finished, the value `"V"` is sent to coroutine **B**. **B** then causes the invocation of the `saved-continuation`, which was stored as a result of an earlier invocation of its resumer.

Exercises

Exercise 17.10
To clarify the behavior of `coroutine-maker` and `resume-maker`, we used many variables. Very few are required. Furthermore, `resume-maker` itself is not necessary. Using this knowledge, rewrite `coroutine-maker` with as few variables as possible.

Exercise 17.11
Look at the results of the previous exercise. If there is a `first-time` flag, rewrite `coroutine-maker` so that it no longer requires such a variable.

Exercise 17.12
Study the definitions of `ping` and `pong` below:

```
(define ping
  (let ((ping-proc (lambda (resume v)
                     (display "ping-")
                     (resume pong 'ignored-ping))))
    (coroutine-maker ping-proc)))

(define pong
  (let ((pong-proc (lambda (resume v)
                     (display "pong")
                     (newline)
                     (resume ping 'ignored-pong))))
    (coroutine-maker pong-proc)))
```

What happens when we evaluate `(begin (ping '*) (pong '*))`?

17.7 Grune's Problem

Now we are ready to look at Grune's problem (Grune 1977). The problem is described as follows:

We have a process A that copies symbols from input to output in such a way that where the input has *aa*, the output will have *b* instead. And we have a similar process B that converts *bb* into *c*. Now we want to connect these processes in series by feeding the output of A into B. Input with *aab* yields *c*, as does *baa*.

If we line the processes up as:

$$\text{Input} \rightleftharpoons \text{A} \rightleftharpoons \text{B} \rightleftharpoons \text{Output}$$

we can think of the flow of requests emanating at Output. *Requests for values* flow from right to left and *values*, themselves, flow from left to right. This is reminiscent of streams. The coroutine Output requests of B to find a symbol for Output to display. The coroutine B requests of A to find a symbol for B to consider in its analysis of a "possible *c*." The coroutine A requests of Input to find a symbol for A to consider in its analysis of a "possible *b*." Having made these requests, control now lies within Input. It does a read by first prompting the user. It responds by resuming A with that symbol. It does this with the following code, (resume right (prompt-read "in> ")), where A is bound to right. A is now in control. If the symbol is an *a*, A cannot pass it along to B because the next symbol read might be an *a*. The only possible alternative for A is to give control back to Input. Once again Input prompts for the next symbol. This symbol is also sent to A. Now A has enough information to send something to B. Here are the conditions under which information flows to the right. In these rules, x and y are the symbols in question, q is not the same as x, where x is *a* (respectively, *b*) and y is *b* (respectively, *c*):

1. x x $\Longrightarrow$ send y to the right.
2. x q $\Longrightarrow$ send x to the right, saving q for the next request.
3. q $\Longrightarrow$ send q to the right.

The code segment for this characterization follows:

```
(let ((symbol-1 (resume left 'ok)))
  (if (eq? symbol-1 x)
      (let ((symbol-2 (resume left 'more)))
        (if (eq? symbol-2 x)
            (resume right y)
            (begin
              (resume right symbol-1)
              (resume right symbol-2))))
      (resume right symbol-1)))
```

Program 17.22 `reader`

```
(define reader
  (lambda (right)
    (let ((co-proc (lambda (resume v)
                     (cycle-proc
                       (lambda ()
                         (resume right (prompt-read "in> ")))))))
      (coroutine-maker co-proc))))
```

In order to replace *aa* by *b*, **x** is *a*, **y** is *b*, **left** is Input, and **right** is B; in order to replace *bb* by *c*, **x** is *b*, **y** is *c*, **left** is A, and **right** is Output. Here is a description of the code segment. Get a symbol from **left**. If that symbol differs from **x**, send it along to **right**. If not, get another symbol from **left**. If that symbol is the same as the first, send **y** to **right**. If it differs, send both symbols, one at a time, to **right**.

The action of **Output** is simple. It makes a request from its left neighbor (i.e., **B**). If it finds a symbol matching **end**, it invokes an escape procedure, and the computation halts. If not, it writes the symbol. The code segment for this **Output** action is:

```
(let ((symbol (resume left 'ok)))
  (if (eq? symbol 'end)
      (escape-on-end symbol)
      (writeln "out> " symbol)))
```

The action of **Input** sends to its right neighbor whatever it read after first displaying a prompt:

```
(resume right (prompt-read "in> "))
```

Given that these are the basic actions, it is a relatively simple task to make sure all free variables have the correct values and that each code segment is run as a nonterminating loop with **cycle-proc**. The three procedures for forming the coroutines are given in Programs 17.22, 17.23, and 17.24.

We still have the task of building the wires into the communication channels. We are now going to use **letrec** to create the mutually recursive coroutines **Input**, **A**, **B**, and **Output**. One might expect the following letrec expression to work:

Program 17.23 `writer`

```
(define writer
  (lambda (left escape-on-end)
    (let ((co-proc (lambda (resume v)
                     (cycle-proc
                       (lambda ()
                         (let ((symbol (resume left 'ok)))
                           (if (eq? symbol 'end)
                               (escape-on-end 'end)
                               (writeln "out> " symbol)))))))))
      (coroutine-maker co-proc))))
```

Program 17.24 `x->y`

```
(define x->y
  (lambda (x y left right)
    (let ((co-proc (lambda (resume v)
                     (cycle-proc
                       (lambda ()
                         (let ((symbol-1 (resume left 'ok)))
                           (if (eq? symbol-1 x)
                               (let ((symbol-2 (resume left 'more)))
                                 (if (eq? symbol-2 x)
                                     (resume right y)
                                     (begin
                                       (resume right symbol-1)
                                       (resume right symbol-2))))
                               (resume right symbol-1)))))))))
      (coroutine-maker co-proc))))
```

```
(letrec
  ((Input (reader A))
   (A (x->y 'a 'b Input B))
   (B (x->y 'b 'c A Output))
   (Output (writer B escape-grune)))
  (Output 'ok))
```

Each of Input, A, B, and Output is built by invoking the procedures reader, x->y, x->y, and writer, respectively. The procedures reader, x->y, and

Program 17.25   grune

```
(define grune
  (lambda ()
    (let ((grune-receiver
            (lambda (escape-grune)
              (letrec
                ((Input (reader (lambda (v) (A v))))
                 (A (x->y 'a 'b (lambda (v) (Input v)) (lambda (v) (B v))))
                 (B (x->y 'b 'c (lambda (v) (A v)) (lambda (v) (Output v))))
                 (Output (writer (lambda (v) (B v)) escape-grune)))
                (Output 'ok)))))
      (call/cc grune-receiver))))
```

writer have been carefully designed to avoid invoking any of their coroutine arguments: **Input**, **A**, **B**, and **Output**. Here is the problem. All of the procedures are being created at the same time as they are being passed as arguments. For example, to create **Input**, we need **A**, and to create **A**, we need **Input**. To solve this problem, we must *freeze* the coroutines that are arguments in the right-hand sides of definitions. This has the effect of postponing the evaluation of the variables that refer to the coroutines. Unfortunately, if we freeze these variables, we get the wrong arity; that is, coroutines take one argument, but frozen objects (i.e., thunks) take no arguments. The code that follows, however, works:

```
(letrec
  ((Input (reader (lambda (v) (A v))))
   (A (x->y 'a 'b (lambda (v) (Input v)) (lambda (v) (B v))))
   (B (x->y 'b 'c (lambda (v) (A v)) (lambda (v) (Output v))))
   (Output (writer (lambda (v) (B v)) escape-grune)))
  (Output 'ok))
```

Program 17.25 shows the final definition of **grune** with all the necessary uses of `(lambda (v) (--- v))`. In the exercises, we develop a more natural way to think about this unusual behavior.

Exercises

Exercise 17.13: `wrap`

Consider the special form `wrap`, which has the following syntax table entry:

$$(\text{wrap } proc) \equiv (\text{lambda args (apply } proc \text{ args)})$$

This works in all cases but one: when `args` is a free variable in the `proc` expression. Rewrite `wrap` using thunks to avoid this potential free variable capture.

Exercise 17.14

Using the results of the previous exercise, write the syntax table entry for `wrap` when `proc` is known to refer to a procedure of just one argument. This is the case for the coroutines used in `grune`. Is free variable capture still a problem?

Exercise 17.15

Using the results of the previous exercise, redefine `grune` using `wrap`.

Exercise 17.16: `safe-letrec`

Another way to implement `grune` is with a special form `safe-letrec`. This special form is like `letrec` except that each right-hand side variable is wrapped if it also appears as a left-hand side variable. Using the results of the previous exercise, create the syntax table entry for `safe-letrec` so that the following definition of `grune` works. (*Hint*: Use `let` to bind `proc` to `(wrap proc)` to avoid processing each right-hand side.)

```
(define grune
  (lambda ()
    (let ((grune-receiver (lambda (escape-grune)
                            (safe-letrec
                              ((Input (reader A))
                               (A (x->y 'a 'b Input B))
                               (B (x->y 'b 'c A Output))
                               (Output (writer B escape-grune)))
                              (Output 'ok)))))
      (call/cc grune-receiver))))
```

Exercise 17.17: `process-maker`

Sometimes processes are perceived as automatically being in an infinite loop. Use the following variation of `coroutine-maker`, called `process-maker`, and rewrite the solution to the Grune problem using processes.

```
(define process-maker
  (lambda (f)
    (let ((saved-continuation "any continuation"))
      (let ((update-continuation!
              (lambda (v)
                (set! saved-continuation v))))
        (let ((resumer (resume-maker update-continuation!))
              (first-time #t))
          (lambda (value)
            (if first-time
                (begin
                  (set! first-time #f)
                  (cycle-proc
                    (lambda ()
                      (f resumer value))))
                (saved-continuation value))))))))
```

Exercise 17.18

Using the results of the previous exercise, explain how `process-maker` differs from `coroutine-maker` by constructing an appropriate example.

Exercise 17.19

Redesign Towers of Hanoi using `coroutine-maker` so that each disk is a coroutine. Can `process-maker` be used?

Exercise 17.20

Redesign the solution of the Eight Queens problem using `coroutine-maker` so that each queen is a coroutine. Can `process-maker` be used?

Exercise 17.21

Implement Grune's problem using streams instead of coroutines.

Exercise 17.22

Extend **grune** to any number of x->y pairs. *Hint*: This can be accomplished by rewriting the procedure **grune** leaving everything else unchanged.

Exercise 17.23

Rework the previous exercise using streams.

We have not shown you all the interesting things you can think about with continuations, but we have tried to show you some of the ways that continuations can be used. Most of the time, you should be content to solve problems with conventional procedural techniques. Occasionally you will be tempted to use state changing operations like those we used when we worked with object-oriented programming. And even less frequently you will run across a need for continuations. This is your basic bag of tricks.

The existence of the computer has been incidental to the understanding of the concepts conveyed in this book. The computer's role has been much like that of a chemist's laboratory, used primarily for experimentation. What would happen if you added two parts hydrogen to one part oxygen? If you are curious about what happens when you compose two procedures, use the computer as your laboratory. What happens when you compose the procedure (lambda (x) (+ x 1)) with the procedure (lambda (x) (- x 1))? This book has been about ideas and how we can combine separate categories of ideas to create procedures that do our computing. Although some emphasis has been placed on how fast the computer determines the value of a computation, we have tried to approach the ideas in this book more in terms of capturing the essence of a computation. Subtle issues of efficiency can come much later. We have challenged you at every turn. Each piece of the computational puzzle fits together and is described in terms of simple ideas. Under our guidance, you have entered the universe of computer science. It was our goal to cause you to look forward to future explorations into this fascinating field.

PROBLEMS

Problems worthy
of attack
prove their worth
by hitting back.

Piet Hein, *Grooks*

A1   The ASCII Character Set

A1.1 The ASCII Table

Hex	0	1	2	3	4	5	6	7
0	NUL	DLE	SP	0	@	P	'	p
1	SOH	DC1	!	1	A	Q	a	q
2	STX	DC2	"	2	B	R	b	r
3	ETX	DC3	#	3	C	S	c	s
4	EOT	DC4	$	4	D	T	d	t
5	ENQ	NAK	%	5	E	U	e	u
6	ACK	SYN	&	6	F	V	f	v
7	BEL	ETB	'	7	G	W	g	w
8	BS	CAN	(	8	H	X	h	x
9	HT	EM	)	9	I	Y	i	y
A(10)	LF	SUB	*	:	J	Z	j	z
B(11)	VT	ESC	+	;	K	[	k	{
C(12)	FF	FS	,	<	L	\	l	|
D(13)	CR	GS	-	=	M	]	m	}
E(14)	SO	RS	.	>	N	^	n	~
F(15)	SI	US	/	?	O	_	o	DEL

A1.2 Abbreviations for Control Characters

NUL	null	DC1	device control 1
SOH	start of heading	DC2	device control 2
STX	start of text	DC3	device control 3
ETX	end of text	DC4	device control 4
EOT	end of transmission	NAK	negative acknowledge
ENQ	enquiry	SYN	synchronous idle
ACK	acknowledge	ETB	end of transmission block
BEL	bell	CAN	cancel
BS	backspace	EM	end of medium
HT	horizontal tabulation	SUB	substitute
LF	linefeed	ESC	escape
VT	vertical tabulation	FS	file separator
FF	form feed	GS	group separator
CR	carriage return	RS	record separator
SO	shift out	US	unit separator
SI	shift in	SP	space
DLE	data link escape	DEL	delete

A1.3 How to Use the ASCII Table

ASCII stands for the American Standard Code for Information Interchange. (Scheme now supports the broader International Character Code.) The number at the top of a column represents the first digit, and the number at the left of a row represents the second digit of the hexadecimal number that is used to represent the character in that row and column. Thus the hexadecimal code for the letter G, which is in the 4th column and 7th row, is 47. The hexadecimal code for the letter g is 67, and for M is 4D. To get the decimal representation for the ASCII code, multiply the number at the top of the column by 16 and add the number at the left of the row of the given character. Then G has decimal code $(4 \times 16) + 7 = 71$, and M has decimal code $(4 \times 16) + 13 = 77$. The first two columns contain the control characters that do not print. To enter those characters from the keyboard, we hold down the CONTROL key while pressing the key for the character located four columns to the right of the desired control character. For example, to enter BEL, we press <CTRL>G, and to enter ESC, we press <CTRL>[.

References

Abelson, Harold, and Gerald J.Sussman, with Julie Sussman. 1985. *Structure and Interpretation of Computer Programs*, Cambridge, MA: MIT Press and New York, NY: McGraw-Hill Book Company.

Bronowski, Jacob. 1978. *The Visionary Eye*. Cambridge, MA: MIT Press.

Church, Alonzo. 1941. *The Calculi of Lambda-conversion*, Annals of Math. Studies, No. 6. Princeton, NJ: Princeton Univ. Press.

Dybvig, R. Kent. 1987. *The Scheme Programming Language*. Englewood Cliffs, NJ: Prentice-Hall.

Eisenberg, Michael. 1988. *Programming in Scheme*. Redwood City, CA: Scientific Press.

Feller, William. 1950. *An Introduction to Probability Theory an its Applications*, Vol. 1. New York, NY: John Wiley and Sons.

Friedman, Daniel P., and Matthias Felleisen. 1988. *The Little LISPer,* Third Edition, Chicago, IL: SRA, and Trade Edition, Cambridge, MA: MIT Press.

Grune, Dick. 1977. A view of coroutines. In *ACM SIGPLAN Notices.* 12(7):75-81.

Hein, Piet. 1966. *Grooks*. Cambridge, MA: MIT Press.

Hofstadter, Douglas R. 1985. *Metamagical Themas: Questing for the Essence of Mind and Pattern*. New York, NY: Basic Books, Inc.

Kohlbecker, Eugene E. 1986. *Syntactic Extensions in the Programming Language Lisp*. Ph.D. Thesis, Indiana University, Bloomington, IN.

Marling, William. 1990. Maestro of Many Keyboards. In *Case Alumnus.* 67(8):2-7.

McCarthy, John. 1960. Recursive functions of symbolic expressions and their computation by machine. In *Communications of the ACM*, 3(4):184-195.

Minsky, Marvin L. 1967. *Computation: Finite and Infinite Machines*. Englewood Cliffs, NJ: Prentice-Hall.

Park, Stephen K., and Keith W. Miller. 1988. Random number generators: Good ones are hard to find. *Communications of the ACM.* 31(10):1192-1201.

Rees, Jonathan, and William Clinger, editors. 1986. The revised[3] report on the algorithmic language Scheme. In *ACM SIGPLAN Notices* 21(12):37-79.

Semantic Microsystems. 1987. *MacScheme+Toolsmith*[TM], *a LISP for the future.* Beaverton, OR: Semantic Microsystems.

Schönfinkel, Moses. 1924. On the building blocks of mathematical logic. In *From Frege to Gödel, A source book in mathematical logic, 1879-1931*. Edited by Jean van Heijenoort, Cambridge, MA: Harvard Univ. Press, 1977.

Smith, Jerry D. 1988. *An Introduction to Scheme*. New York, NY: Prentice-Hall.

Steele, Guy Lewis, Jr., and Gerald Jay Sussman. 1978. The revised report on Scheme, a dialect of Lisp. Memo 452, MIT Artificial Intelligence Laboratory.

Sussman, Gerald Jay, and Guy Lewis Steele Jr. 1975. *Scheme: an Interpreter for Extended Lambda Calculus*. Memo 349, MIT Artificial Intelligence Laboratory.

Texas Instruments. 1988. *PC Scheme, User's Guide & Language Reference Manual*. Redwood City, CA: The Scientific Press.

Index